Lectures & Essays

LECTURES AND ESSAYS

OF

WILLIAM ROBERTSON SMITH

AGENTS

America . The Macmillan Company
64 & 66 Fifth Avenue, New York

Australasia The Oxford University Press
205 Flinders Lane, Melbourne

Canada The Macmillan Company of Canada, Ltd
St Martin's House, 70 Bond Street, Toronto

India Macmillan & Company, Ltd
Macmillan Building, Bombay
309 Bow Bazaar Street, Calcutta

PROFESSOR WILLIAM ROBERTSON SMITH

From a Posthumous Portrait by Sir George Reid, R.S.A., now in the Free Church College, Aberdeen.

LECTURES & ESSAYS
OF WILLIAM
ROBERTSON SMITH

EDITED BY

JOHN SUTHERLAND BLACK

AND

GEORGE CHRYSTAL

LONDON
ADAM AND CHARLES BLACK
MCMXII

PREFACE

THE present volume contains a selection from the writings of Professor Robertson Smith which are either wholly unpublished or have not yet been collected in book-form. It has not been found possible within the compass even of a large volume to give more than a strictly limited selection from the manuscript material in the hands of the editors, and much that in their opinion is of considerable interest and value must be withheld, at any rate for the present.

Their main purpose in compiling this volume has been to provide a supplement to Professor Smith's *Life* and to furnish a series of illustrative documents possessing an intrinsic interest of their own, but also valuable as throwing light on the development of his mind and of his attitude towards the theological controversies and the scientific inquiries which were the chief concern of his life.

The Scientific Papers which form the first group now reprinted belong to the period before Professor Smith was definitely settled in his theological career, or at any rate before he was finally embarked on the series of critical inquiries which led to the celebrated heresy case. In their capacity as biographers the editors consider these papers worthy of reproduction as illustrating the remarkable acuteness and vivacity of Professor Smith's mental powers as a very young man. They were received with marked favour by Lord Kelvin, Professor Tait, and other eminent men of science with whom he was then associated, and the editors are permitted to print an estimate which has been kindly furnished by the present Sadleirian Professor of Pure Mathematics at Cambridge who was Smith's colleague and friend during his Cambridge period.   Professor Hobson writes —

"The three papers entitled 'Theory of Geometric Reasoning,' 'Hegel and the Metaphysics of the Fluxional Calculus,' and 'Dr. Stirling, Hegel, and the Mathematicians' are of a controversial character, and relate to the Philosophy of Mathematics.   The incisive vigour with which they are written, and the acuteness of the dialectic therein displayed, are characteristic of Robertson Smith. At the present time their interest is, however, mainly biographical and historical.   Much of the criticism of Hegel's views relating to the Infinitesimal Calculus is no doubt valid, but it is clothed in a form which implies ideas of the foundations of Analysis which are not in accord with the conceptions of mathematicians at the present time.   Robertson Smith's criticism of Mill's ideas about the nature of geometric reasoning are made from the point of view of a disciple of Kant in relation to the space-problem.   The study of the foundations of Geometry, to which a vast amount of attention has been given since the time of the publication of this criticism, has resulted in revelations which make the ideas of Kant in this regard no longer tenable, at least without very considerable modification.   The paper 'On the Flow of Electricity in Conducting Surfaces' is not controversial, and thus comes under a different category.   It contains detailed work which amounted to a distinct contribution to the development of the subject of which it treats at the time it was published, and was regularly consulted by

students for years afterwards. It shows that Robertson
Smith possessed powers which would have enabled him
to produce further useful contributions to Mathematical
and Physical Science, had he not turned away from these
branches to quite other domains."

The editors have to express their cordial thanks to
Mr D. B. Mair, ex-Fellow of Christ's College, Cambridge,
who was kind enough to read the proofs of this part of
the book, and to undertake the necessary corrections.

Of the Theological Essays and Lectures composing the
next three sections it is enough to say generally that they
have been selected with a view to exhibiting the evolution
of Professor Smith's opinions on Biblical questions, the
ever-widening range of his scholarship, and the painstaking
and cautious character of his teaching. The undergraduate
papers of the second section show the effects of his first
contact with the German theological genius in Rothe, the
first-fruits of the influence of Ritschl, and an approximation to his final views of the results reached by the School
of Kuenen The Aberdeen Lectures in Sections III. and IV.
give a series of characteristic samples of the educational
work he was able to do for Theology and for the Church
before his ecclesiastical career was cut short

The controversies which centre round the topics
treated in these papers have to some extent lost the
freshness which they had in Smith's time ; new points of
detail have arisen, and with the advance of scholarship
new internal evidence has been accumulated. But the
fundamental positions in Biblical criticism are almost as
keenly debated as ever, and the spirit of the conflicting
tendencies in criticism is practically the same as it was in
the days of the Aberdeen Heresy. The reprint, therefore,
of a selection from Smith's earlier critical writings, which
in the opinion of those competent to judge are models of

their kind, will, the editors hope, be of more than an antiquarian or even a purely biographical interest.

The task of making the selection from Professor Smith's later writings which is presented in the last two sections was comparatively simple. The two reviews of Wellhausen and Renan respectively were chosen by the editors as good examples of the great mass of occasional writing to which Professor Smith gave so much of his time, and in which so much of his best work was done. No representative collection of his papers would be complete which did not include the paper on Animal Worship, which was one of his most original contributions to knowledge, and the desirability of reprints of the Letters from the Hejâz, which at the time of their publication received the highest commendation from the most eminent Orientalists of the day was equally obvious.

The difficulty of presenting a correct and scholarly version of these letters was considerable, and the editors are deeply indebted to the invaluable help of Mr. Stanley A. Cook, ex-Fellow and Lecturer, Gonville and Caius College, Cambridge, to whom they wish to express their obligation Mr. Cook kindly agreed to read the proofs, and to deal with the necessary alterations of detail. The editors are permitted to quote the following observations by Mr. Cook on the text of this section as it is now presented .

" Professor Smith unfortunately left no marked copy of the letters, and the task of seeing that they were reprinted in a satisfactory manner was one of some difficulty. They were written at intervals and for popular publication, and contained various not altogether scientific spellings ; these it did not seem necessary to change. But there were some inconsistencies of transliteration and several obvious misprints, and these have been corrected. The dialect spoken in the Nejd has certain peculiarities of its own, and to adjust the spellings to the ordinary written forms would have been a step which Professor Smith himself clearly did not propose. Where the forms are in virtual agreement with those in other sources (*e g.* Lane, Doughty, Jaussen) they have been left. In some cases, however, the misprints were unintelligible, and it was necessary to resort to emendation. I have to express my indebtedness to Professor A. A Bevan for some valuable corrections, but am myself responsible for any obvious errors that still remain uncorrected."

Mr. Cook's assistance was not limited to Section V , and the editors are grateful to him for helpful advice and suggestions on points of Oriental scholarship arising throughout the volume.

J S. B.
G. W. Ch.

April 24, 1912

CONTENTS

I

SCIENTIFIC PAPERS (1869–1873)

II

EARLY THEOLOGICAL ESSAYS (1868–1870)

III

EARLY ABERDEEN LECTURES (1870–1874)

IV

LATER ABERDEEN LECTURES (1874–1877)

V

ARABIAN STUDIES (1880–1881)

VI

REVIEWS OF BOOKS

I

SCIENTIFIC PAPERS

(1869–1873)

I

THEORY OF GEOMETRICAL REASONING

Mr Mill's Theory of Geometrical Reasoning Mathematically Tested [1]

AN amusing and instructive example of the way in which logicians are accustomed to dogmatise upon the theory of sciences that they do not understand is afforded by Mr. Mill's explanation of the nature of geometrical reasoning.

Those who remember that Mr. Mill assures Dr. Whewell that he has conscientiously studied geometry (*Logic*, 7th ed 1. 270), will probably find some difficulty in believing that the demonstration of Euc. I. 5, which Mr Mill offers as an illustration of the justice of his theory of geometrical reasoning, depends on the axiom, that triangles, having two sides equal each to each, are equal in all respects. Such, nevertheless, is the case, and when one sees this absurdity pass unmodified from edition to edition of Mr. Mill's *Logic*, and when even Mansel, Mr. Mill's watchful enemy, tells us that " against the form of the geometrical syllogism, as exhibited by Mr. Mill, the logician will have no objections to allege " (Mansel's Aldrich, 3rd ed., p. 255), one cannot but think that logic would make more progress if logicians would give a little more attention to the processes they profess to explain.

[1] Communicated by Professor Tait to the Royal Society of Edinburgh on February 1, 1869, and published in its *Proceedings*, vol vi pp 477-483.

It may perhaps be worth while to show how Mr Mill was led into this extraordinary mistake. We shall find that Mr. Mill chooses rather to sacrifice geometry to his philosophy, than to modify his philosophy in accordance with the facts of geometry.

Mr Mill holds that all general knowledge is derived from experience, meaning by experience the comparison of at least two distinct experimental facts In other words, all knowledge is ultimately gained by induction from a *series* of observed facts That any general truth can be got at intuitively, by merely looking at one case, Mr. Mill emphatically denies. The fact that two straight lines cannot enclose a space is not self-evident as soon as we know what straight lines are [*i.e.* can mentally construct such lines]; but is got at only by experiments on " real " or " imaginary " lines (*Logic*, 1 pp 259, 262). Now it is certain that, in the demonstrations of Euclid, we are satisfied of the truth of the general proposition enunciated, as soon as we have read the proof for the special figure laid down. There is no need for an induction from the comparison of several figures Since then one figure is as good as half a dozen, Mr Mill is forced to the conclusion that the figure is no essential part of the proof, or that " by dropping the use of diagrams, and substituting, in the demonstrations, general phrases for the letters of the alphabet, we might prove the general theorem directly " from " the axioms and definitions in their general form " (p. 213).

We may just mention, in passing, that this view, combined with the doctrine that the definitions of geometry are purely hypothetical, leads Mr. Mill to the curious opinion that we might make any number of imaginary sciences as complicated as geometry, by applying real axioms to imaginary definitions. We mention this merely to illustrate Mr. Mill's position—our present business is to see how these views of geometry work in practice.

Mr. Mill's example, as we have said, is Euclid I 5, which he undertakes to deduce from the original deductive foundations. We have first (p. 241) some preliminary remarks, which afford a remarkably happy instance of the way in which Mr. Mill is accustomed to keep himself safe from all opponents, by alternately supporting each of two contrary views of a subject. ." First," says he, speaking of the angles ABE, CBE; ACD, BCD, " it could be perceived intuitively that their differences were

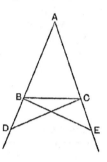

the angles at the base " If this intuition is really a step in the proof, then since intuition is just actual looking at the figure, what becomes of the doctrine that the figure is not essential, or of the still more fundamental doctrine, that no general truth can flow from a single intuition ? [1] In this, however, Mr. Mill only falls foul of himself. A more serious matter is, that when he sets about his regular demonstration, he falls foul of the truths of geometry.

Having shown that AD = AE, Mr. Mill proceeds thus :— " Both these pairs of straight lines " [AC, AB   AD, AE] " have the property of equality ; which is a mark that, if applied to each other, they will coincide. Coinciding altogether means coinciding in every part, and of course at their extremities, D, E, and B, C." Now, " straight lines, having their extremities coincident, coincide. BE and CD have been brought within this formula by the preceding induction ; they will, therefore, coincide " ['] If Mr. Mill generalises this conclusion, I think he will

---

[1] This is no mere slip on Mr. Mill's part. To show that the angles at the base are the differences of the angles in question, without appealing to the figure, we must have a new axiom [proved, of course, by induction !], viz that if a side of a triangle be produced to any point, the line joining that point with the opposite angle falls wholly without the triangle

find it to be that two triangles, having two sides of each equal, are equal in all respects ; and from this theorem he may at once conclude, by his own fourth formula [" angles having their sides coincident, coincide "], that angles contained by equal straight lines are equal ! It is clear that Mr. Mill did not see that the point is to show that, *the triangles ABE, ACD, remaining rigid,* AB may be applied to AC, and AE to AD at the same time. But this can only be brought out by figuring to oneself AB moved round to coincide with AC, and then the triangle ABE rotated about AB through two right angles ; and this process was not competent to Mr. Mill, whose theory bound him to prove the equality of the triangles by pure syllogism from the two formulas, " equal straight lines, being applied to one another, coincide," and " straight lines, having their extremities coincident, coincide "

But Mr. Mill may say, " I have only to add, that equal angles applied to one another coincide."

Very well, you have then three syllogisms .—

| Equal straight lines coincide if applied ; AC, AB, are equal. | Equal straight lines coincide if applied , AD, AE, are equal. |

Equal angles coincide if applied ;
CAD, BAE, are equal.

Logically these three syllogisms can give only three independent conclusions :—

AC, AB coincide if applied. | AD, AE coincide if applied.

The angles CAD, BAE coincide if applied —

but by no means the ONE conclusion that the rigid figure ABE, ACD coincide if applied. If Mr. Mill still contends that there is no need for intuition here, let him substitute for the words " equal straight lines," " equal arcs of great circles " The premises of his syllogisms are still all right ; but, owing to circumstances that must be *seen* to be understood, the spherical triangles cannot be made to coincide.

There are only two courses open to Mr. Mill—either to confess that the attempt to square geometry with a preconceived theory has forced him into a grossly erroneous demonstration, or to invent a new formula, viz. that if in two plane figures any number of consecutive sides and angles taken one by one may be made to coincide, they may also be made to coincide as rigidly connected wholes But, then, Mr. Mill must maintain that the man who reads Euc. I. 4 for the first time does not at once conclude the general truth of this formula from the one figure before him, but either brings the formula with him to the proof as a result of previous induction, or requires to pause in the proof, and satisfy himself of the truth of the formula by a comparison of a series of figures.

It is easily shown, by the same species of analysis as we have adopted here, that wherever a real step is made in geometry we must either use the figure or introduce a new general axiom [not of course in mere converses, as Euc. I. 19, I. 25]. All geometrical construction is in the last resort a means of making clear to the eye complicated relations of figures.

Now, if we can at once and with certainty conclude from the one case figured in the diagram to the general case—if, that is, axioms are proved not by induction, but by intuition, and are necessarily true—there is no difficulty about geometrical reasoning ; but if each new axiom is gained by a new induction (and that, on Mr. Mill's showing, an "*inductio per enumerationem simplicem*"), we get a difficulty which Mr. Mill curiously enables us to state in his own words (I. p. 301)—"If it were necessary," in adding a second step to an argument, "to assume some other axiom, the argument would no doubt be weakened." But, says Mr. Mill, it is the same axiom which is repeated at each step. If this were not so, "the deductions of pure mathematics could hardly fail to be among the most uncertain of argumentative

processes, since they are the longest." If now we do
call in new axioms whenever we construct an essentially
new figure, must not Mr. Mill admit, on his own showing,
that every advance in geometry involves an advance in
uncertainty ; that the geometry of the circle is less
certain than that of the straight line, solid geometry
than plane, conic sections than Euclid, etc ? Surely
this is a *reductio ad absurdum* of the whole theory

The principles of geometry involved in the question
are so important that we may profitably separate them
from Mr. Mill's blunders in a special case.

I. The proofs of geometry are clearly not inductive.
There is no mental comparison of various figures needed
during the proof The inductions involved (if any)
must have been previously formed

II. The proofs then must be reduced either to actual
perception (intuition), or to deduction from axioms.
But since the proof is general, the former assumption
involves the reality of general intuition, *i e.* of a general
judgment from a single perception.

III The theory of intuition is sufficient, but is disputed in two interests ·—

(α) In the interest of syllogism, which claims to give
indefinitely extensive conclusions from limited premises
[but many, as Whewell, hold that these premises are
intuitive axioms].

(β) In the interests of empiricism, which makes all
arguments be ultimately from particulars to particulars.

Mr. Mill combines the two objections.

Now we have seen that if objection (α) falls (*i.e* if
the premises of geometry are not reducible to a limited
number of axioms from which everything follows analytically), the security of geometric reasoning can be
established only if each premise has apodictic certainty
To overthrow Mill's whole theory, it is therefore enough
to show the fallacy of the limited-number-of-axioms
hypothesis. On this we observe .—

1st, The axioms are more numerous than Mr. Mill thinks, for his proof of Euc. I. 5 is lost for want of more axioms.

2nd, The indefinite extension of geometry depends on the power of indefinitely extended construction [but where there is construction there is intuition—nay, mental intuition is mental construction] Now here our opponents may suppose [A] that the general conclusion really flows from the particular construction, which, in the language of logic, supplies the middle term. But since the construction is particular, we should thus be involved in the fallacy of the undistributed middle. Again, [B] it may be said that the construction is only the sensible representation of a general axiom. But as the construction is new and indispensable, the general axiom must be so also. Therefore, if geometry is proved from axioms, these axioms must be unlimited in number

3rd, Obviously it is not by logic that we can satisfactorily determine how far geometry contains synthetic elements peculiar to itself. We have, however, in analytical geometry a ready criterion how far geometry can be developed without the addition of new geometrical considerations

Now we find that we cannot begin analytical geometry from the mere axioms and definitions. We must by synthetic geometry, by actual seeing, learn the qualities of lines and angles before we can begin to use analysis. Then, given so many synthetic propositions, we can deduce others by algebra ; but only by a use of actual intuition, *first*, in translating the geometrical enunciation into algebraic formulæ ; and, *second*, in translating the algebraic result (if that result is not merely quantitative) into its geometric meaning. The answer to a proposition in analytical geometry is simply a rule to guide us in actually constructing, by a new use of our eyes or imagination, the new lines which we must have to interpret the result. Analysis does not enable us to dispense with

synthetic constructions, but simply serves to guide us
in these constructions, and so to dispense more or less
completely with the tact required to find out the geometrical solution.   This is true in every case, but most
obviously in the investigation of new curves.   The
tracing of curves, from their equations, is a process in
which no man can succeed by mere rule without the
use of his eyes   Suppose asymptotes, cusps, concavity,
everything else found, the union of these features in *one*
curve will remain a synthetic process

Still more remarkable is the use made in analysis
of imaginary quantities.   To the logician an imaginary
quantity is nonsense, but geometrically it has a real
interpretation.   The geometrical power gained by a new
method like quaternions is radically distinct from that
gained by the solution of a new differential equation.
The latter is a triumph of algebra, the former is a triumph
of synthetic geometry—the discovery of a whole class of
new guides to construction.

[A brief discussion followed, in the course of which
Professor Tait remarked that an excellent and interesting instance of the incapacity of metaphysicians to
understand even the most elementary mathematical
demonstrations, had been of late revived under the
auspices of Dr. J. H. Stirling.   His name, with those of
Berkeley and Hegel, formed a sufficient warrant for
calling attention to the point

It is where Newton, seeking the fluxion of a product,
as ab, writes it in a form equivalent to

$$\frac{1}{dt} \left[(a + \tfrac{1}{2}\,\dot{a}dt)\,(b + \tfrac{1}{2}\dot{b}dt) - (a - \tfrac{1}{2}\dot{a}dt)\,(b - \tfrac{1}{2}\dot{b}dt) \right]$$

which gives, at once, the correct value

$$a\dot{b} + b\dot{a}.$$

Now Berkeley, Hegel, Stirling, and others have all in
turn censured this process as a mere trick (or in terms

somewhat similar) and say, in effect, that it is essentially erroneous. The fact, however, is that, as in far greater matters, Newton here shows his profound knowledge of the question in hand ; and adopts, without any parade, a method which gives the result *true to the second order of small quantities.* The metaphysicians cannot see this, and Dr Stirling speaks with enthusiastic admiration of the clear-sightedness and profundity of Hegel in detecting this blunder, and for it " harpooning " Newton !

What Newton seeks is the rate of increase of a quantity at a particular instant. Instead of measuring it by the rate of increase *after* that instant (as the metaphysicians would require) he measures it by observing, as it were, for equal intervals of time *before and after* the instant in question.

Any one who is not a metaphysician can see at once the superior accuracy of Newton's method, by applying both methods to the case of a rapidly varying velocity ; such as that of a falling stone, or of a railway train near a station.

In reference to what Professor Tait had said, Mr. Sang remarked that the line of argument attributed to Newton had been used by John Napier before Newton's birth Napier's definition of a logarithm runs thus (Descriptio, lib. i cap. i def 6), (Constructio, 23, 25) that if two points move synchronously along two lines, the one with a uniform velocity (arithmeticè), the other (geometricè) with a velocity proportional to its distance from a fixed point, the distance passed over by the first point is the logarithm of the distance of the second from the fixed point. In order to compare this variable velocity at any instant with the constant velocity, he takes a small interval of time preceding, and another succeeding the given instant, shows that the true velocity is included between the two velocities thus obtained, and (28, 31) takes the arithmetical mean as better than either, and as true (*inter terminos*).

It may be added, that Napier devotes several sections of his Constructio to the discussion of the doctrine of limits (*de accuratione*) , that his logarithms were denounced by the metaphysicians of his day as founded on the false system of approximation, but that, fortunately for the progress of exact science, their objections were unheeded.

Sir W Thomson said that the metaphysicians, wishing to find the speed of a vessel at 12 o'clock from an hour's run, would choose the hour from 12 to 1 , whereas Napier, Newton, and the rest of the world would take it from 11.30 to 12 30.]

II

HEGEL AND THE METAPHYSICS OF THE FLUXIONAL CALCULUS [1]

IT is now many years since Dr. Whewell drew the attention of the Cambridge Philosophical Society to the courageous, if somewhat Quixotic, attempts of Hegel to cast discredit on Newton's law of gravitation, and on the mathematical demonstrations of Kepler's laws given in the *Principia* At the time when Whewell wrote, it would probably have been difficult to find in Britain any one ready to maintain the cause of Hegel in this matter, or even to hint that the astounding arguments of the Naturphilosophie flowed from any deeper source than self-complacent ignorance.

The present state of matters is different. The philosophy of Hegel is now for the first time beginning to have a direct and powerful influence on British speculation. Men are beginning to study Hegel ; and an author whose works confessedly demand the labour of years, if they are to be fully understood, can hardly be studied at all except by devoted disciples. A man whose determination to master Hegel's philosophy survives the repelling impression which the obscurity and arrogance of the philosopher are sure to produce at first, is very likely to be carried away by the calm assumption of omniscience which runs through Hegel's writings. It is not, therefore,

[1] Communicated by Professor Tait to the Royal Society of Edinburgh on May 17, 1869, and published in its *Transactions*, vol. xxv pt. ii. pp 491-511

surprising that Dr. Stirling extends his admiration to Hegel's physical positions , and if he does not venture to say that Hegel's proof of Kepler's laws is right, at least feels sure that it would repay the attention of mathematicians.

It would not, perhaps, be impossible to rob Dr. Stirling of even this sorry consolation , but there is less occasion for retracing any part of the ground gone over by Whewell, in so much as *The Secret of Hegel* calls attention to another point, in which Hegel criticises Newton, and in which Dr. Stirling has no hesitation in pronouncing Hegel's findings " perfectly safe from assault," and Newton guilty of an obvious mathematical blunder.

Such a statement, proceeding from the most powerful of our living metaphysicians, and recently reiterated in the newspaper press, as a sort of challenge to mathematicians, seems to call for some remark from a mathematical point of view   It is true that a confirmed Hegelian is not likely to be influenced by any reasoning that we can offer   " The judgment of a pure mathematician," we are told, " has really been so peculiarly trained that, perhaps, any such will never prove decisive as regards any Hegelian element "   We are told, too, that Hegel's " most important note " on the mathematical infinite " has remained hitherto absolutely sealed," for C Frantz, who does take up the subject " as in opposition to, is to be assumed ignorant of, the views of Hegel, which plainly, so far as they go, are inexpugnable " (!)

Now I do not profess to be able to treat this question from the standpoint of Hegel's own philosophy.   I have no desire to criticise Hegel's doctrine of the Infinite, in so far as it forms an integral part of his system.   But the note to which Dr. Stirling calls attention is itself a critical note, in which Hegel proposes " to consider in detail the most remarkable attempts to justify the use of the mathematical notion of the Infinite, and get rid of the difficulties by which the method feels itself burdened " (Hegel's

Werke, iii. 286).[1] What Hegel seeks to show is, " that
the mathematical Infinite is at the bottom the true
Infinite " (p. 283) ; imperfectly conceived, however, by
the mathematicians, who have therefore never been able
to put the higher calculus on a basis thoroughly free from
confusion, or even error. Thus, not to speak of Fermat,
Leibnitz, Euler, and others, whose views Hegel takes up
more or less fully, we are told that Newton himself,
although his fundamental thought was quite in harmony
with Hegel's views, was not so far master of his own
thought as to be able fairly to deduce the practical rules
of his method. In the actual application of the new
instrument, Newton clung " to the formal and superficial
principle of omission because of relative smallness." He
thus fell into real errors , and even so fundamental a
problem as the determination of the fluxion of a product
was solved in a manner analytically unsound. Now
these, I maintain, are assertions that can fairly be
examined by one who does not profess to have mastered
Hegel's system. They even afford a fair test whether
that system is really so complete in all its parts, and so
light-giving in its applications, as we are told to believe.
If Newton is really confused and in error, it must be
possible to make this clear by an argument based on
Newton's own principles   For if to the mathematician
Newton's method is perfectly clear and self-contained,
and if its errors can only be observed from an entirely
different point of view, we have not one truth, but two
truths, mutually destructive. And this surely Dr Stirling
will not assert.

It is possible, however, to go further than this. To
the subject of the calculus Hegel devotes two notes. The
first of these alone is taken up by Dr. Stirling. And in
this note Hegel adds to the destructive criticism of which

[1] Here and elsewhere I adopt, as far as possible, the language of
Dr. Stirling's own translations from Hegel, which may be viewed as
authoritative

we have been speaking only a very general account of the principles on which he would base the calculus. These general principles are, as Hegel says, "abstract" (we would rather say vague), "and therefore in themselves also easy" (p. 327). The real difficulty lies "in the concrete side," in the deduction from these generalities of the practical rules of the method. To this subject Hegel devotes his second note, professing to point out a purely analytical method whereby, without any application of the doctrine of limits, everything necessary for practice can be deduced. If we can demonstrate that the analytical method is radically unsound, producing results mathematically false, it will surely be vain to appeal in defence to any "deficiency in the judgment of a pure mathematician."

The plan that suggests itself is therefore the following ·—*First*, to consider the real character of Newton's method, and to show what may, I think, be made quite clear to an unprejudiced mind, that that great man really did know what he was doing; and, in the *second* place, to show that Hegel having refused to be instructed by Newton's real knowledge, but having acutely enough caught sight of something like the ghost of an idea, which he could not for want of solid knowledge really make his own, was first ensnared by the plausible but fallacious method of Lagrange, and then, in attempting to improve that method, lost any glimpse of the truth that he had before, and was swamped in hopeless absurdity.

The ingenuity of a great deal that Hegel has said on this subject I do not wish to dispute   No doubt he,

> " with as delicate a hand,
> Could twist as tough a rope of sand "

as any man that ever lived.   But the question is, after all, one of plain truth and error ; and however much we may admire the chivalry with which Hegel rushes into an unequal encounter with so gigantic an antagonist as Newton, it will never do to

" Coin a formal lie on't
To make the knight o'ercome the giant "

We must begin, then, by examining the principles on
which Newton based his doctrine of Fluxions. In doing
this, it is not necessary to inquire how far Newton's own
views varied during his life. Hegel knows Newton's
method from the *Principia* only, and a quotation from the
second Lemma of the Second Book (*Werke*, iii. 305) shows
that it was the current text of the *Principia* (that of the
second edition) which he had before him. In fact, Hegel's
acquaintance with Newton's writings was clearly of the
most superficial character, embracing apparently little
if anything beyond the section on Prime and Ultimate
Ratios, and the Lemma just referred to. These facts
make all merely bibliographical inquiries superfluous in
dealing with Hegel's objections. I may refer, however,
to a paper by Professor de Morgan, in the *Philosophical
Magazine* for 1852, on the " Early History of Infinitesimals
in England," in which it is shown " that Newton never
varied in his meaning of $\dot{x}$ " ; or, in other words, that
Newton "held to the conception of the velocity or fluxion,"
although he at first " used the infinitely small increment "
(only of the first order, however), " as a means of determining it." What follows will, I hope, serve to show that
these facts imply that Newton had all along a firm grasp
of the principle of his method, and that his frequent
employment of abbreviated practical processes was really
based on a consciousness of the strength of his method,
according to the general principle of mathematicians,
who never hesitate to apply the boldest symbolical
methods in detail, when they feel confident of the starting-
point in the use of these symbols. This, in fact, is a point
that metaphysicians have never properly attended to.
One is disposed to cap Dr. Stirling's wish that some great
analyst would study Hegel, by expressing a hope that
some metaphysician of real ability may pay sufficient
attention to what are technically called the " Symbolical

2

Methods " of mathematics, to enable him to appreciate
Boole's profound preface to his treatise on " Differential
Equations." This exercise would at least make it clear
that metaphysical criticism on mathematics is still—I
speak without any desire to be disrespectful—in the circle-
squaring stage, *i.e.* still treats as the real questions for
discussion points that mathematicians have long seen to
be merely special cases of general principles, and therefore
to be no longer possessed of independent interest.

To return from this digression Newton saw that there
were two ways in which quantities might be conceived as
generated The first of these is that which the usual
processes of arithmetic have made familiar to everybody,
viz. the addition of discrete units. The theory of numbers
thus viewed is contained in the arithmetic of integers,
to which may be added the doctrine of arithmetical
fractions as an extension of the method reached by
supposing the unit itself to change in value Newton
was especially attentive to the importance of the doctrine
of decimal fractions, in which the change of unit is so
regulated as to give the greatest possible increase of power
that the *arithmetical* conception of quantity admits of ;
and the opening pages of his *Geometria Analytica* are
expressly directed to show that these advantages may be
made available in literal as well as in numerical calculations. [See also the treatise *De Analysi per Equationes
Numero Terminorum Infinitas.*]

Newton saw, however, that arithmetic in its most
perfect form could give full mastery over quantity, only
on the supposition that quantity, as it comes before us in
the universe, is always produced by the synthesis of
ultimate units, or, in other words, of indivisibles. And
this, says Newton, is contrary to what Euclid has proved
concerning incommensurables in the tenth book of the
Elements (*Princ.* lib. i. sec. i. schol.).

Instead, therefore, of endeavouring to eke out this
view of quantity by arbitrary assumptions, Newton

resolved to turn to Nature herself, and inquire how quantity is really generated in the objective universe. " Lineae," he writes, " describuntur ac describendo generantur non per appositiones partium sed per motum continuum punctorum ; superficies per motum linearum ; solida per motum superficierum ; anguli per rotationem laterum ; tempora per fluxum continuum et sic in caeteris. *Hae Geneses in rerum natura locum vere habent et in motu corporum quotidie cernuntur."* (*Introd. ad Quad. Curv.*)

In a word, Newton's fundamental position is, that the arithmetical conception of quantity is not that with which Nature herself presents us, and is not, therefore, universally applicable.   On the other hand, every quantity that has objective reality [*i.e* is an object of real intuition] is generated by continuous motion, with definite (constant or variable) velocity within definite limits of time.   The metaphysical nature of time and motion Newton has nothing to do with.   It is enough for him that mathematical time, conceived as an independent variable flowing uniformly, is clearly the *true* time made known to us in nature (*Principia* ; Schol. to the Defs.), and that the existence of a definite velocity at each point of a motion is in like manner an undoubted physical fact.

By means of these profound yet simple considerations, Newton is at once able to revolutionise the whole theory of quantity, and to substitute for the relation of unit and sum that of velocity and quantity generated, or, in Newton's own language, of fluxion and fluent.   It must be remembered that we have said nothing of *space*, so that fluent is not limited to extensive quantity, while velocity, or as we should rather say *rate*, has a correspondingly wide application.   Thus, any fluxion may itself be treated as a fluent quantity, and its fluxion sought, the only independent variable being time, which is thus a fluent which has no variable fluxion.

This conception of time, as the one absolute and independent variable, is undoubtedly one of the most splendid and fruitful in the history of human thought, and well deserves the attention of metaphysicians.   Only let it be said that no criticism of Newton's *time*, which starts from the arithmetical view of quantity, and urges the old objections about infinite divisibility, and so forth, is competent ; for the arithmetical theory is a product of abstract reflection, and so stands on a lower platform than the pure objective notion of Newton

There is no difficulty in comprehending the mathematical power which the conception of fluxions at once puts in Newton's hands, if we remember that it is not in any sense an extension of the theory of numbers that he is seeking.   It is true that the calculus has revolutionised algebra as well as geometry , but it has done so by transforming algebra from the abstract science of numbers to a *physical* science—the science of pure time.   In Newton's own mind, however, this conception was probably not explicitly present.   What he did see was, that all difficulties in geometry (and to Newton, as to the old geometers, geometrical magnitude is the type and exponent of all magnitude whatsoever, when viewed with respect to its generation) are reducible to the general form .— " Given the fluent as a function of time to determine the fluxion and *vice versa* "

The one class of problems that can be thoroughly treated without explicit reference to a generation by flux, is that which has for its geometrical type systems of straight lines , and thus geometers were tempted to introduce the fiction of indivisibles, in order to reduce higher problems to this type.

But these higher problems are not simply complicated cases of the rectilineal type ; on the contrary, that type is produced by one of the two essentially distinct elements (generated and generating quantity), which usually appear side by side, ceasing to be explicitly manifest.

Take, for example, Newton's own instance at the beginning of the " De Quadratura."   Suppose the abscissa

AB of a curve to flow uniformly, in which case it may be
taken as the graphic representation of the independent
variable, *i.e.* of time, while the ordinate BC is of course
a function of the abscissa.
Then Newton shows that the
reason why the determination
of the tangent at C is a difficult problem is that the ratio
of the ordinate BC to the
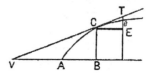
sub-tangent VB is the graphical representation of the
fluxion of the ordinate. In fact, the *meaning* of the
tangent is, that it is the direction in which the curve is
flowing at the point C ; and all attempts to give it another
explanation without reference to motion simply ignore
the real gist of the problem, and of course end in difficulties
that can be escaped only by violent assumptions   It is
only in the straight line where the fluxion of the ordinate
is constant, or the tangent sinks into the curve, that the
conception of *rate* can be dispensed with

Before we go farther, it is proper to remark that in
criticising Newton, Hegel coolly ignores the whole foundation of the doctrine of fluxions as here developed   " The
thought," says he (*Werke*, iii. 302 ; Stirling, ii. 354),
" cannot be more correctly determined than Newton has
given it ; that is, the conceptions of movement and
velocity (whence fluxion) being withdrawn as burdening
the thought with inessential forms and interfering with
due abstraction "—*i.e.* because Hegel thought that the
calculus should be based, after the manner of Lagrange,
on purely analytical considerations, it never enters his
head that if Newton thought otherwise there might be
some deeper ground for this course than a want of insight
into his own method   On the contrary, Hegel comments
in the most edifying manner on the " early still naïve
period of the calculus " in which " mathematicians sought
to express, in words and propositions, results of the newly
invented calculus, and to present them in geometrical

delineations," assigning to the " definitions and propositions so presented a real sense *per se*," in which sense they
were " applied in proof of the main positions concerned."
If there is any meaning at all in these statements, which
are the gist of a somewhat lengthy discussion (*Werke*, iii.
324 ; Stirling, ii. 375), that meaning must be that Newton
and others first differentiated a function, then sought a
geometrical construction to suit, and finally invented a
physical proposition to correspond.   Purely analytical
considerations without any physical basis were held,
Hegel thinks, to furnish in this way physical laws   In
support of this view, Hegel triumphantly refers to " the
Newtonian proof of his fundamental proposition in the
theory of gravitation compared with Schubert's *Astronomy*,
where it is admitted that .   in the point, which is the
nerve of the proof, the truth is not as Newton assumes
it " [!]   And so upheld by the dictum of this forgotten
astronomer, Hegel goes on to inveigh against the mere
jugglery by which Newton, already knowing Kepler's
results, avails himself of the " mist of the infinitely little "
to bring out apparent mathematical proofs of these
results.   One does not know whether the singular perver-
sity of this accusation against Newton's moral character,
or the incredible ignorance of the argument by which it is
supported, is most to be wondered at ; for, not only do
the reasonings of the *Principia* rest throughout on the
experimental laws of motion on which Newton's first
proposition is expressly based, but the proof itself depends
not on the interpretation of an analytical process, but on
the essentially physical or, more definitely, kinematical
considerations above developed.   Nay, so little is it the
case that the " mist of the infinitely little " is needed to
give a show of plausibility to Newton's process, that the
whole gist of the proof lies in the one conception of quantity
generated at a definite though variable rate, and that
thus, without any change in the spirit of the proof, by
simply introducing explicitly a theorem about moments

of velocity which the demonstration in the *Principia* implies, the law of equal areas can be deduced without even that apparent use of the infinitely little which, as Newton himself warns his readers, is always merely apparent (Thomson and Tait's *Natural Philosophy*, § 234). In one word, Newton's proofs are always physical throughout, and really belong to the essence of the thing to be proved ; while Hegel first shuts his eyes to the real import of the fluxional method, insisting that it must be made purely analytical, and then rails at Newton for using the method to do work for which, if it had been purely algebraic, it would not have been fit.   A Hegelian calculus, as we shall see, would certainly have been of little service to physics ; but the doctrine of fluxions is itself a part of physics, and absolutely indispensable in some form or other to the right understanding of physical problems.

We have still, however, to see how it is that Newton's system comes to have anything at all to do with the infinitely little which, as he himself says (*Introd. ad Quad. Curv.* § 11), it is the peculiar merit of that system to render unessential.   The reason is simply, as we are told in the scholium at the end of the first section of the *Principia*, that he was anxious to provide for ease of conception, and also to introduce all legitimate abbreviations in his arguments.   When Newton is called upon to justify his method, he always refers to the simple fact that a velocity definite, yet never for the shortest space of time uniform, is a notion really furnished by nature, and that the true measure of that velocity is to be got by allowing the motion at any point to become uniform for a unit of time.   But if one wishes, as Hegel would say, to substitute for this *notion* a convenient " Vorstellung " to assist the imagination, Newton is ready, by means of the doctrine of prime and ultimate ratios, to point out a way in which we may avail ourselves of the method of indivisibles, always remembering that this method shall have merely a symbolic value, and so must be used with caution.

If two quantities have the same fluxion at any moment, they begin at that moment to increase at the same rate. It does not follow from this that the two quantities shall receive equal increments in any space of time however small, unless during that time the rates of flow remain constant. But Newton shows that in a very large class of cases, which he takes up one by one in the first section of the *Principia*, not only may we, by taking the time of flow small enough, make the difference of the increments generated in that time as small as we please, but if we enlarge both increments on the same scale up to any given size, we may make the differences of the increased increments as small as we please, while the time of flow has still a definite value. Since, then, the ratio of the increments is always nearer to unity the less the time of flow, and may be brought as near to unity as we please by taking the time short enough, but still finite, the ratio must ultimately be unity—*i e* that quantity which, varying according to a definite rule, always represents at any given time the ratio of the increments, may still be constructed when the time is made zero, and is now equal to unity, or is equal to the ratio at which the increments *start*, which Newton calls their prime or ultimate ratio

The practical application of this reasoning is, of course, that in virtue of it, we may in certain cases with strict accuracy treat the increments of two variables (of a curve, for example, and its tangent) as equal, if, before closing our reasoning, we proceed to *take the limit*. Thus, if any one finds that it assists his imagination to deal with magnitudes as if they were composed of indivisibles, instead of confining himself to fluxions, Newton provides in the method of prime ratios a criterion by which the applicability of the process may be judged The details by which it is shown in the *Principia*, that the limit of the ratio of the increments is equal to the ratio of the fluxions whenever the fluents may be geometrically represented as curves of continuous curvature, involve no new principle in geometry. Everything is as plainly and undeniably reduced to ordinary geometrical intuition as anything in Euclid, when we once bring with us the fundamental kinematical ideas of velocity and acceleration. It is obvious, moreover, that to Newton the fraction $\frac{0}{0}$, as above explained, means simply the ratio of the rates at which two quantities are flowing at the moment at which they pass together through the point from which we have agreed to reckon their magnitude backwards and forwards Except where such rates can be assigned possessing a definite ratio, Newton does not pretend to recognise $\frac{0}{0}$ as a mathematical reality

This outline of Newton's principles is, of course, very meagre. It will probably, however, suffice to enable us to estimate the real value of Hegel's criticisms.

Hegel highly approves of Newton's statements of what he means by prime and ultimate ratios, viz. that he always deals not with indivisible, but with vanishing divisibles. This is very satisfactory so far, but the next paragraph makes one doubt whether Hegel knew what he was approving.

" Newton," we are told, " only explained what he means by his terms, without showing that such a notion has internal truth." [1]

This is an accusation constantly recurring in various forms. Its source is, of course, that determination which we have already noticed in Hegel to pay no regard to considerations of velocity and motion. Now it is quite true that Newton does not condescend to offer any explanation of his " notion " to the man who has failed to familiarise himself by actual intuition with the nature of velocity, and acceleration, and the genesis of quantities

[1] Dr. Stirling (ii 355) seems to have read " Nach dem damaligen Stande der wissenschaftlichen Methode wurde *nun* erklärt " In the collected edition of the *Werke*, iii 303, I read " wurde *nur* erklärt," which seems to give a more intelligible sense

by flux.   But these notions are just as truly capable of being constructed by pure intuition as those of ordinary geometry, and so Newton's definitions enjoy fully the advantage which Kant ascribes to mathematical definitions in general.   They cannot err, because they simply unfold a construction by means of which the notion is actually produced.

If Hegel, however, shut his eyes to Newton's notion, he has got one of his own, which he is sure is just what Newton wanted.   I do not intend to attempt to take up anything but the concrete applications of this notion , but perhaps it may be well to give here part of Hegel's abstract statement of what he conceives to be the mathematical infinite.   " Das unendliche Quantum . . . ist nicht mehr irgend ein endliches Quantum, nicht eine Grossebestimmtheit die ein Daseyn als Quantum hatte, sondern es ist einfach, und daher nur als Moment ; es ist eine Grossebestimmtheit in qualitativer Form ; seine Unendlichkeit ist als eine qualitative Bestimmtheit zu seyn " (iii. 289 , Stirling, ii. 341).   Now, says Hegel, this is clearly what Newton needs.   His vanishing magnitudes have ceased to exist as quanta, and exist only as sides of a relation ; but further, the relation itself, in so far as it is a quantum, vanishes.   " The limit of a quantitative relation is that in which it both is and is not, or, more accurately, that in which the quantum has disappeared, and there remains the relation only as qualitative relation of quantity."   This sentence must mean that in the equation

$$\text{Lt} \frac{\delta y}{\delta x} = \frac{\dot{y}}{\dot{x}}$$

the left-hand side vanishes as quantum in the same sense in which δx and δy vanish, or, as Hegel often puts it, $\frac{dy}{dx}$ is " infinite," just as truly as δy and δx.   Now, we are told again and again that the " infinity " of the δx and δy

does not lie in their being infinitely small, but in their having ceased to be any determinate magnitude, and only representing the qualitative principle of a magnitude. To this statement Newton would probably not have objected, as his whole use of infinitely small quantities is, as we have seen, merely to help the imagination, and scientific strictness is given to his method from another side. But certainly he would never have dreamed of admitting that $\frac{\dot{y}}{\dot{x}}$ is also indeterminate; for both numerator and denominator of this fraction are in their nature definite quantities. That the fraction can be expressed as $\frac{0}{0}$ is to Newton by no means the essential point. On the contrary, he argues distinctly that $\frac{0}{0}$ must have a definite value, just because this is the form in which certain processes present to us a quantity which, from kinematical grounds, we know to be definite. To Hegel, however, the fascinating element is just this $\frac{0}{0}$, which for his ends would be quite spoiled by being evaluated. That would reduce it to a mere quantum, but, in the meantime, it is "a qualitative relation of quantity," which is a far finer thing. Not unnaturally, however, Hegel has now to ask himself, what is to be the practical use of this $\mathrm{Lt}\frac{\delta y}{\delta x}$, which certainly "expresses a certain value which lies in the function of variable magnitude." In asking this question, he still supposes himself to be criticising Newton and the mathematicians, and accordingly proceeds, with much severity of manner, to knock down the indeterminate $\frac{dy}{dx}$ which he has just set up (p. 318). To apply the conception of limit in the concrete we must determine the limit. This is done by Taylor's theorem, from which if $y=f(x)$ we get

$$\frac{\delta y}{\delta x} = p + q\, \delta x + \text{etc.,}$$

and then letting δx and δy vanish Lt $\frac{\delta y}{\delta x} = p$,—not as it should have been $= \frac{0}{0}$. This, of course, is sadly inconsistent ; for instead of our fine qualitative determination, here is a stubborn quantum turning up. Now, says Hegel, the mathematicians try to get over this by saying that p is not really $= \frac{0}{0}$, but is only a definite value, to which $\frac{0}{0}$ comes as near as you please. Of course, if this is so, it is as evident as anything can be that the difference between p and $\frac{0}{0}$ is not a quantitative one. But, adds the philosopher, naively enough, that doesn't help one over $\frac{dy}{dx} = \frac{0}{0}$ Suppose now that we were to say $\frac{dy}{dx}$ really $= p$ (a definite quantity), as, in fact, mathematicians *do* say, then it is obvious that δx couldn't have been $= 0$ Or if, finally, it is conceded that $\frac{\delta y}{\delta x} = 0$ (which Hegel seems to think most likely, since δy and δx vanish together), then what can p be ?

Now, can any one say that the man who devised this argument knew what he was doing ? When did any mathematician suppose that after evaluation $\frac{0}{0}$ is indeterminate ? Or had Hegel never read Newton's first lemma, with its " fiunt ultimo aequales " ? Or, again, if Hegel allows that there is no quantitative difference between p and $\frac{0}{0}$, why does he assume a qualitative one ? Or, above all, why try to explain Newton's doctrine without ever deigning more than a contemptuous glance at the one central point of the whole ? Hegel boasts that half an hour would suffice to learn the calculus. Certainly he might have employed a good many hours in unlearning his false conceptions of it.

Hegel has next something to say about the way in which mathematicians have developed the details of the calculus. Since none of them had a clear notion of the matter in hand, their proofs, we are told, are very weak   They always fall back into methods merely approximate, subjecting infinitely small quantities to the laws of finite quanta, and yet rejecting them as relatively unimportant, in despite of these laws.   Of course, adds Hegel, we need not look for the rigour of demonstration of the old geometry, for the analysis of the infinite is of a nature essentially higher than that geometry.   However, mathematicians have sought this rigour, and they have all failed —Of course, it would be easy for any one to point out numerous mathematicians who have failed ; but let us simply ask whether Newton has done so.   Hegel unhesitatingly affirms that he has, and Dr. Stirling is jubilant at the discovery.

The error is supposed to lie in the deduction in *Prin.* II. Lem. 2, of the fluxion of a product.   The statement of Newton is as follows   If A B be two quantities increasing continuously, and their moments or rates of change a and b, the moment or change of the rectangle A.B is $aB + bA$.   By moment Newton does not mean the increment actually received in any time, however short, but the nascent principle of the fluent quantity—a notion, of course, made clear by the previous discussion of prime and ultimate ratios   The moments, in fact, are any quantities proportional to the rates at which A and B are flowing—the products of the fluxions of A and B by an arbitrary increment of time.   If moments, then, are called increments, the meaning is increments which would be received if the rate of flow remained constant, and the ratio of two moments is simply the ratio of the fluxions, and therefore equal to the limit of the ratio of the actual increments, while it is quite independent of the magnitude of the separate moments. Now, says Newton, when A and B are diminished by half their moments, the rectangle is $AB - \frac{1}{2}aB - \frac{1}{2}bA + \frac{1}{4}ab$; and when A and B are increased by half their moments, it is $AB + \frac{1}{2}aB + \frac{1}{2}bA + \frac{1}{4}ab$; and so to the increments a and b in the sides corresponds an increment $aB + bA$ in the rectangle This demonstration is certainly very curt, and intended only for those who have mastered Newton's fundamental notions, and may therefore be saved the tedium of a long *reductio ad absurdum*. More at length, the proof would be of this kind. The fluxion of the rectangle must, since the flow is continuous, be a definite quantity, depending only on the magnitudes and fluxions of the sides at each moment Thus the fluxion of AB will be unchanged, if we suppose that from the values $A - \frac{1}{2}a$, $B - \frac{1}{2}b$ the sides flow with uniform velocity, equal to $\dot{A}$ and $\dot{B}$, until they attain the values $A + \frac{1}{2}a$, $B + \frac{1}{2}b$ In this case the increments a and b will represent exactly upon the same scale the fluxions $\dot{A}$ and $\dot{B}$ Meantime, the rectangle has been flowing with a constantly increasing velocity, which at the moment when the value AB was reached, was the velocity Newton is seeking to determine. The whole increment of the rectangle is $aB + bA$, which therefore represents the average velocity of the rectangle on the same scale as a, b represent the uniform velocities of the sides. Clearly the average velocity with which the increment is described is greater than the velocity at the beginning of the motion, and less than that at the end, and therefore, since the velocity is continuous, is strictly the velocity at some intermediate point. But this point can be none other than that at which the rectangle $= AB$, for were it any other point, we could take a and b small enough to throw this point out, and there would still be another point at which the fluxion of the rectangle must $= aB + bA$. But this is contrary to the intuitive fact that the velocity is continuously increasing. To the mathematician, however, this roundabout process is unnecessary. He sees at once that if the average velocity is independent of the duration of flow, and depends solely on a certain point being included within the flow considered, the velocity at that point must be strictly the average velocity, for *in the limit* the two coincide.

Now, Hegel, of course, did not see this, because he would not admit the kinematical reality of fluxions He, therefore, supposes that Newton wants to find the *differential* of AB—a way of stating the problem which Newton would have rejected as misleading. The differential can be nothing else than $(A + dA)(B + dB) - AB$. But Newton writes instead of this $(A + \frac{1}{2}dA)(B + \frac{1}{2}dB) - (B - \frac{1}{2}dA)(B - \frac{1}{2}dB)$, thereby making an error in so elementary a process as the multiplication of two binomials ! But where is Hegel's justification for saying that what Newton is seeking is $(A + dA)(B + dB) - AB$? Newton says nothing about differentials at all , his *a* is, as we have seen, not the infinitely small increment of A, but an arbitrary multiple of the fluxion of A, which need not be infinitely small. Newton's $\dfrac{aB + bA}{a}$ is, if you please,

$$= \text{Lt} \frac{(A + dA)(B + dB) - AB}{dA} ;$$

but even this, which is very different from what Hegel writes, is simply a different, by no means a more fundamental, view of the problem than Newton's

Dr. Stirling tells us that Hegel's expression *is* what Newton *says his* is, " *the excess of the increase by a whole dA and dB.*" But what Newton says is only that when the sides are increased from $A - \frac{1}{2}a$ and $B - \frac{1}{2}b$, through increments *a* and *b* the rectangle increases by $aB + bA$. That this is true surely cannot be denied In fact $(A + a)(B + b) - AB$ would have represented not the velocity at value AB, but the average velocity of the rectangle during the interval between values AB and

$(A + a)(B + b)$, and therefore the real velocity at a point between these limits which Newton was not wanting. We know, in fact, that it would have been the velocity when the sides are $= A + \dfrac{a}{2}$ and $B + \dfrac{b}{2}$. Instead, therefore, of Newton rejecting a quantity on the ground of relative smallness, we find that Hegel has gratuitously introduced such a quantity.

Of course, the Hegelian will reply to all this, that our method is "rendered impure by the concrete adjunct of motion." And here, of course, we can say nothing, except that the fluxional calculus is essentially kinematical, and that to construct it apart from motion is as likely a task as to make a geometry without lines. To make bricks without straw is a light task compared with that which Hegel has set himself.

Happily unconscious of these difficulties, Hegel goes on to moralise with much satisfaction upon Newton's melancholy self-deception, in palming on himself such a proof.

After this specimen of Hegel's analytical subtilty, it is perhaps sufficient to confront the assertion which immediately follows (*Werke*, iii. 313 ; Stirling, ii 364), that Newton, in finding fluxions by the method of expansions, uses a process analogous to his method of solving approximately numerical equations, constantly "neglecting what is relatively unimportant," with the explicit words of the *De Quadratura* (Introd. § 5)—"Errores quam minimi in rebus mathematicis non sunt contemnendi." The terms omitted are, of course, always terms which we know to become not relatively but absolutely zero in proceeding to the limit. The motive for using such expressions as "minuatur quantitas o in infinitum," instead of simply saying, let $o = $ zero, is merely to show that o becomes zero not by a discontinuous process, as subtraction, but by a continuous flow. Nay, cries Hegel, for in the 3rd Problem of Book ii. of the *Principia*, Newton fell into an error, by "throwing out, as Lagrange has shown, the very term which—for the problem in hand—was wanted. Newton had erred from adhering to the formal and superficial principle of omission from relative smallness." This error, by the way, is only in the first edition of the *Principia*, which Hegel, one may safely affirm, had never seen. The whole statement here is taken from Lagrange, and applies much better to Lagrange's analytical way of putting Newton's argument than to that argument in its geometrical form.

Newton, in fact, investigating the law of resistance, that a body under gravity may describe a given path, seeks a geometrical expression for the *moment* of the sagitta—a small quantity of the third order. It is clear, therefore, that no such expression can be exact unless account is taken of every small quantity of an order not higher than the third in the geometrical construction involved, for such quantities will not vanish in the limit, or are not "relatively small," in a mathematical sense. The principle of the problem, then, presents no difficulty on Newton's method; and the true account of the error is, that by a mere slip in the details of a complicated process, Newton failed to see that he was omitting a term (or better, a line) *not* small relatively to the moment of the sagitta. Hegel, however, conceives that so far as this goes Newton was all right. The error, according to him, lies in neglecting a term which, though "relatively small," "possessed the qualitative value sought." "In mechanic, a particular import is attached to the terms of the series in which the function of a motion is developed, so that the first term, or the first function, relates to the moment of velocity, the second to the accelerating force, and the third to the resistance of forces." The terms are thus to be regarded as "qualitative moments of a whole of the notion", and, of course, in a problem about resistances Newton needed the third term. Now here we have, *firstly*, a laxness in the use of terms so gross as to make

3

it hardly possible to criticise our author fairly. Luckily, we can see that Hegel is leaning entirely on Lagrange, and that " the series in which the function of a motion is developed must therefore mean the series which expresses space in ascending powers of time And this enables us to ask, *secondly*, What reason Hegel has for supposing that it is in this series that we are to find the basis for a truly philosophical view of kinetics ? It was Hegel's misfortune to live at a time when, among other fruits of the "Aufklärung," Lagrange's "formal and superficial " method of treating physics was in great repute , and surely it was a cruel fate that the great enemy of the "Aufklarung " should, through a defective mathematical education, be made a willing captive to a mathematical " Aufklarung," which has, from its intrinsic weakness, fallen as fast as it rose. In details, it is true, Hegel is keen enough in detecting the unsatisfactory character of Lagrange's standpoint (see, for example, a note at this very point) ; but that the whole method was artificial he could not see, not for want of mental power, but because, having never studied the subject, he knew nothing whatever about it—had not even mastered its technicalities Then, again, if it is true that successive differential co-efficients have a qualitative difference, how can that be brought out except in virtue of the relations established in mathematics between quantity and quality, relations which are not reached by pure analysis, but only in Newton's way, *i e* by intuition ? And would not these relations be violated, and all mathematics rendered absurd, if the term that is qualitatively important *could* be quantitatively negligible ? And, last of all, let me challenge Hegel to bring forward any proof on his own principles, that the third term relates to the resistance of forces ; or for that matter, to show that this statement has any real meaning whatever.

But most men, I imagine, have now had enough of Hegel's criticisms—criticisms which simply show that the

" half-hour " which he had devoted to the calculus had not sufficed to give him any just idea of that great method It is certainly much to be regretted that so able a man did not study mathematics thoroughly, for such a course might have proved useful to the theory of mathematics, and could not have failed to be profitable to himself.   As it is, he has only given us criticisms such as we have seen, and an attempt to which we now proceed to establish the calculus on a new and very inadequate basis.

The point which we have always found Hegel urging is, that mathematical functions, when they become quantitatively indefinite or " infinite," may still have a real qualitative value   Passing over the fact that this is not the technical sense of infinite in mathematics, we may grant that there is a kind of meaning, however vague, that may be attached to the view.   Thus an incommensurable is infinite in the Hegelian sense, not because it can be expressed arithmetically only by an infinite series, but because it is essentially *not* a sum of units, but, as Hegel vaguely says, a " relation "   For relation we should say *function*, and then we should be able to read in Hegel's words some meaning like this.   Algebraic and geometrical functions are qualitatively different from mere arithmetical functions.   They imply an entirely different way of looking at quantity, expressing, in fact, *steps* in time or space (or in kinematics, both in time and space).   So, again, the differential coefficient which takes the form $\frac{0}{0}$ ceases to be intelligible on the mere arithmetical view, but gives us a real result of a different quality, when we understand it as equivalent to a proposition about the rates of the vanishing quantities.   But then Hegel does not seem to have seen that $\frac{0}{0}$ has a real *quantitative* value, expressing accurately a definite quantity of a different quality.   And further, there was in Hegel a rigid determination *not* to see the real qualitative difference between the continuous quantity of the higher analysis and of actual nature, and the discrete quantity of arithmetical abstraction.[1] He thus fell into the delusion, that a writer like Lagrange who, from the extreme nominalistic stand-point of the eighteenth century, seeks to make analysis a merely formal instrument, in no way expressing the essence of things, and who, for example, boasts that in his *Mécanique Analytique* one will find no such unnecessary incumbrances as figures—Hegel, I say, imagined that such a writer had really reached a higher generality than Newton, when he had only reached an untenable extremity of one-sided abstraction, and hence, without a moment's hesitation, resolved that by simply treating the successive differential coefficients as the successive derived functions obtained by expanding y in terms of x, we shall be quit " of the formal categories of the infinite, and of infinite approximation, and of the equally empty category of continuous magnitude " (iii 320)

The differential calculus, then, is a special branch of mathematics which has to deal (by purely arithmetical methods) with qualitative forms of quantity, *i e.*, says Hegel, with relations of powers. A power, it should be said, means with Hegel a quantity raised to a higher power than the first, and the link between the clauses of the foregoing sentence is as follows. " In the equation $\frac{y}{x} = a$ the relation of y to x is an ordinary quantity, and $\frac{y}{x}$ a common fraction, just like $\frac{a}{b}$, so that the function is only formally one of variable magnitudes. On the contrary, if $\frac{y^2}{x} = p$, $\frac{y}{x}$ has no determinate quotient, and, in fact, x has no ratio to y, but only to y^2. Now the relation

---

[1] Hegel absolutely identifies *analysis* with arithmetical process— " Auf analytische d i. ganz arithmetische Weise " (iii 328)   Had Hegel ever studied the treatment of incommensurables in ordinary algebra? If algebra is " ganz arithmetisch," the whole doctrine of indices is false

of a magnitude to a power is not a quantum, but qualitative." It is needless to say that the man who could
make " no constant ratio " identical with " no ratio,"
and who did not see that $\sqrt{px}$ has a definite value for each
value of x, or who did not see that p is a quantum, though
not of the same dimensions as y^2 (which probably was
what confused Hegel), is hardly fit to construct a new
theory of the calculus   But let us pass on.

The subject matter of the calculus is then, we are to
believe, equations in which one variable appears as a
function of a second, one of these at least occurring in a
power higher than the first.   In such a case the variation
of the variables is qualitatively determined, *and therefore*
continuous.   It would be vain to ask *why* ; but since we
are told that in the equation $s = ct$ there is no scope for
differentiation, $\frac{s}{t}$ not being qualitative, we may at least
conclude that Hegel does not regard uniform motion as
continuous !

So far as the principle goes it is quite sufficient, continues
Hegel, to consider the equation $y = x^n$, the advance to
more complicated functions is quite mechanical.   Now
both y and x are really numbers, and so may be expressed
as sums. (This, of course, is a very bold assumption, as
Hegel says nothing of the possible case of incommensurables.)   The simple and yet comprehensive way of representing x as a sum is to write it as binomial.   Now expand
x^n as a binomial function, and we have a series of terms
which are " wholly functions of the potentiation and
the power."   The differential calculus seeks the relation
between these terms and the original components of x.
As we are not concerned with the sum, but merely with
the relation of the terms of the expansion, it would be best
simply to expand $(x + 1)^n$, and to define the particular
" Potenzenbestimmung " got by considering the second
term of this series as the first derived potence-function
of y.   In short, the true mathematical commencement in

this part of analysis is no more than the discovery of the functions determined by the expansion of a power.

We see at once that this is simply an excessively clumsy adaptation of the method of Lagrange, which is based on the proposition that $f(x + i)$ can always be expanded in a series of ascending integral powers of i, and then defines the successive fluxions (or derived functions) of fx with reference to the series   Hegel adds to Lagrange nothing but confusion, and a degree of vagueness which is quite pitiable ; and, of course, his method has the same fundamental fallacy as that of Lagrange, in so much as $f(x + i)$ cannot always be expanded as Lagrange proposes, or, what comes to the same thing, the details of the calculus cannot be deduced by processes purely arithmetical from the definition (for it is no more) $\frac{dx^n}{dx} = nx^{n-1}$. I do not, therefore, think it needful to go into details on this part of Hegel's method. The really important point is the use to be made of these magical " Potenzenbestimmungen," which, according to Hegel, depends on the discovery of concrete relations which can be referred to these abstract analytical forms. Hegel proceeds as follows —

There is always a fall of one dimension in passing to the first derived function. Hence the calculus is useful in cases where we have a similar fall in the powers. We are also to remember that, by differentiating an *equation*, we get not an equation, but a *relation*. Whenever, then, we wish to investigate relations connected with any equation, but of a lower dimension, we have room for the calculus. A case in point is the investigation of the relations between the tangent, subtangent, and ordinate, for example, in a curve of the second degree. These relations are linear, while the equation contains squares. They depend, therefore, on the first derived function (pp. 341, 342, 344).

That such a statement is mere guesswork is clear, if we observe that by a linear relation Hegel means indifferently the ratio of two straight lines, or a ratio involving only first powers of x and y Or, again, since the value of the radius of curvature is also on Hegel's principles linear, why does it involve the *second* derived function ? Let us, however, follow our philosopher further. "Suppose we have $2ax - x^2 = y^2$, and take the derived function, we get a ratio $a - x : y$,—a linear ratio representing the proportion of two lines.   The real point is to show that these two lines are the ordinate and subtangent."   This is very plausible, no doubt ; but let us try a cubic equation, say $2ax - x^2 = y^3$.   Now the resulting ratio, to put it in Hegel's way, is $2(a - x)$ $3y^2$.   Is this a linear ratio ? Yet it still represents the ratio of the ordinate and subtangent.   Clearly Hegel does not know that when x and y become definite co-ordinates of a point on the curve, the ratio $\dfrac{y}{a - x}$ ceases to be a linear function of variables in any proper sense, and is simply a determinate fraction. This mistake augurs ill for the validity of Hegel's proof, that the two lines, whose ratio is the ratio of the derived functions, are really ordinate and subtangent.   But he has Lagrange luckily to help him, who, he says, has entered on the truly scientific way   We get, therefore, a wordy and loose description, which would be utterly unintelligible to any one who did not know the thing before, of the way in which Lagrange proves that the line $q = fx - xf'x + pf'x$ lies nearer to the curve $y = fx$ in the neighbourhood of the point (x, y) than any other straight line through that point.   Hegel's confusion is not diminished by the fact, that Lagrange deduces this proposition from a general theorem about the contact of curves, and originally writes the straight line as $q = Fp$. This piece of tactics so puzzles the philosopher that, after all his invective against the differentiation of linear functions, he allows Lagrange, without rebuke, to write $f'x = F'x$.

In other respects, however, we have great improvements on Lagrange. It is absurd to write $q = a + bp$ [1] as the equation of the line to be compared with the tangent, $q = pb$ being quite general   That the line $q = bp$ would not necessarily pass through the given point of the curve at all is, of course, a trifling consideration !

A still greater improvement regards the process by which Lagrange shows that we can always find a point (with abscissa $x + i$), at which $q = fx - xf'x + pf'x$ shall be nearer the curve than any other assigned straight line. At this point Hegel begins to dread (not unjustly) that the conception of limit, or rather " das beruchtigte Increment," is to be employed. However " this apparently only relative smallness contains absolutely nothing empirical, $i\,e.$ dependent on the quantum as such ; it is qualitatively determined through the nature of the formula, when the difference of the moment on which the magnitude to be compared depends, is a difference of powers   Since this difference depends on i and i^2, and i, as a proper fraction, is necessarily greater than i^2, it is really not in place to say anything about taking i of any size we please, and any such statement is quite superfluous " (p. 347)   One word in explanation of these. Lagrange takes an abscissa $(x + i)$, and gets

$$f(x + i) = f(x) + if'(x) + \frac{i^2}{2}f''(x + j),$$

and

$$F(x + i) = F(x) + iF'(x) + \frac{i^2}{2}F''(x + j),$$

or for the straight line given above,

$$= fx + if'x.$$

Thus the difference of the ordinates of the curve and straight line with abscissa $x + i$ is $\dfrac{i^2}{2}f''(x + j)$ For any other straight line the difference may be written mi. Now, the ratio of these increments is $i\dfrac{f''(x + j)}{2m}$, which

[1] Hegel uses $p = aq + b$, but I keep Lagrange's own letters throughout.

may always be made less than unity by taking $i < \dfrac{2m}{f''(x+j)}$.

Hegel, however, asserts that $\dfrac{i^2}{2} f''(x+j) < mi$, whenever i is a proper fraction, which is an obvious analytical absurdity, and, in fact, is equivalent to saying that it is impossible to draw a chord to a curve, the difference of the abscissæ of whose points of section is less than unity, since for the chord through (x, y) cutting the curve again at $(x + i)$, $mi = 0$. In the face of this absurdity, it is scarcely necessary to add, that Hegel having resolved to simplify matters, as we saw, by getting his derived functions from the expansion of $(x + i)^n$, has no right even to form for every curve the expansions on which Lagrange's proof depends.

I shall, in passing from the subject of geometry, merely enunciate a simple deduction from Hegel's result in an intelligible form. " At any point of a curve there are an infinite number of tangents, which may be got by uniting that point with any other point on the curve whose abscissa is not different by a quantity greater than unity." I present this proposition, which is *entirely* due to Hegel, and in the development of which my share has been " purely mechanical," for the admiration of all Hegelians whatsoever.

Hegel's account of the application of the calculus to mechanic is much briefer, and presents less interest after what Whewell has written on a connected point. I cull only one or two illustrative points. For the purposes of the calculus, Hegel classes motion as uniform, uniformly accelerated, and motion returning into itself, alternately uniformly accelerated and retarded. Variable acceleration, which in the form of harmonic motion is by far the most common in nature, is quite ignored.

Again, criticising the assertion that $\dfrac{ds}{dt}$ represents the velocity at any point of a course, he tells us that it is

" schiefe Metaphysık " to speak of the velocity at the end of a part of tıme. " Thıs end must still be a part of tıme ; if it were not, there would be rest, and no motion ; velocity can be measured only by the space passed through in a definite tıme " (p. 352). An appeal to Attwood's machine would probably be too empırical for our philosopher, but the law of energy might surely convınce Hegel of the realıty of a variable velocıty dependent on potentıal energy lost or gained. It is clear, at least, that Hegel lacked the first elements of physical notıons, and these were not lıkely to be supplied by the method of Lagrange to which he adheres, begınnıng with $s = ft$, and deducıng every other consideratıon by differentiation.

The following criticism on a remark of Lagrange ıs splendıd " We find," says Lagrange, "the motıon represented by $s = at^2$ in the actual fall of bodies. The next simplest motıon would be $s = ct^3$, but nature shows no such motıon, and we do not know what c could mean " (The ground of thıs ıs, of course, to be found ın the law of the conservatıon of energy.) " If so, we have at least a motıon whose equatıon is $s^3 = at^2$,—Kepler's law of planetary motıon ; and here the ınvestigation of the first derived function $\frac{2at}{3s^2}$, etc., the direct treatment of this equation by differentiatıon, the development of the laws of that absolute movement from this starting-poınt, must certainly be a most interestıng task, ın which analysis would appear ın the brıghtest splendour " [!]. That t and s in Kepler's law are not varıables, but constants determıned for each planet ; that the equatıon has no analogy whatsoever with the equatıon of motıon ; that its differentiatıon would be meanıngless unless space were filled with planets ; and that then ıt would have nothing to do with " the determinations of that absolute motion," are considerations that never entered Hegel's head.

It ıs rather hard that, from a metaphysıcal standpoint, a man ıs still allowed to wrıte about thıngs he has not studied ; and more than this, that men so able as Dr. Stirling should be found imploring great mathematicians to come and read such utter nonsense as naturally results from the attempt.   Certainly Hegel's fame is not likely to rise higher the more his notes on the calculus are studied ; for these notes show quite clearly—*first*, substantial ignorance of the subject in hand, bolstered up by some hasty glances at the " literature of the subject " , *secondly*, great disingenuousness in criticising Newton, without having ever given his views a careful study , *thirdly*, almost incredible confusion of mind, in so far as he seems to have thought that he knew his own meaning when he really had no meaning at all ; and *lastly*, to add nothing more, such a degree of self-complacent arrogance as led him to fancy the results of his " half-hour " more valuable than the fruit of the whole life of men like Newton.

This paper has already grown to such a length that it seems better to say nothing of Hegel's remarks on integration in the closing pages of his second note on the calculus, or of the third note, in which he treats " some other forms connected with the qualitative determination of quantity." The subject, in fact, has a purely adventitious interest, and no one will care to linger longer over such a mass of confusion, both as to language and thought, than is absolutely necessary in self-defence.   And the preceding pages may perhaps suffice to show that he who would exchange Newton's clear ideas, based on nature's own showings, and alike removed from shallow empiricism and self-conceited dogmatism, for the vague pomposities of a Hegel, exchanges

$$\chi\rho\acute{\upsilon}\sigma\epsilon\alpha\ \chi\alpha\lambda\kappa\epsilon\acute{\iota}\omega\nu,\ \acute{\epsilon}\kappa\alpha\tau\acute{o}\mu\beta o\iota'\ \acute{\epsilon}\nu\nu\epsilon\alpha\beta o\acute{\iota}\omega\nu.$$

III

ON THE FLOW OF ELECTRICITY IN
CONDUCTING SURFACES [1]

THE conditions of a steady flow of electricity in a conducting surface are completely determined, if we know either the nature of the electrical distribution throughout the surface, or the direction and intensity of the flow at every point. On the first of these ways of considering the question, the problem is solved if we can express the potential v at any point as a function of the co-ordinates, and the nature of the distribution will be indicated to the eye by forming the equipotential curves

$$v = \text{const.} \qquad . \qquad . \qquad . \qquad (1)$$

From the second point of view, we should endeavour to determine the lines of flow by equations of the form

$$u = \text{const.} \qquad . \qquad . \qquad (2).$$

The curves determined by equations (1) and (2) are obviously orthogonal, and since

$$\frac{d^2v}{dx^2} + \frac{d^2v}{dy^2} = 0,$$

we know, by a theorem of Lamé and Stokes,[2] that

$$\frac{d^2u}{dx^2} + \frac{d^2u}{dy^2} = 0.$$

Kirchhoff, in the year 1845, took up the problem for plane

[1] Communicated by Professor Tait to the Royal Society of Edinburgh on February 21, 1870, and published in its *Proceedings*, vol vii pp. 79-99
[2] See Thomson and Tait's *Natural Philosophy*, 1 542

surfaces [1] in the first of the two ways we have indicated. By an application of Ohm's law he expressed analytically the conditions to be satisfied by v. When the electricity enters and issues by a number of individual points, he found (apparently by trial) that an integral of the form $\Sigma(a \log r)$, where $r_1 \, r_2$ etc are the distances of the point (x, y) from the successive points of entrance and issue, satisfies these conditions when the plate is infinite. For a finite plate it is necessary that the boundary of the plate should be orthogonal to the curves

$$\Sigma(a \log r) = \text{const.} \qquad . \qquad (3).$$

He was thus led to form the orthogonal curves, whose equation he gives in the form

$$\Sigma(a \, [r, \mathrm{R}]) = \text{const.} \qquad . \qquad (4),$$

where $[r, \mathrm{R}]$ is the angle between r and a fixed line R. These equations he applies to the case of a circular plate, completely determining the curves when there is one exit and one entrance point in the circumference, and showing that in any case a proper number of subsidiary points would make the equipotential lines determined by (3), cut the circumference at right angles. Kirchhoff's paper is throughout properly busied with the function v, and the stream lines are only dealt with incidentally. There is no attempt to give a physical meaning to the equation (4)

In 1846 Thomson drew attention to the orthogonal systems (3) and (4), as an example of Lamé's theorem.[2] He showed that the rings and brushes of biaxal crystals are a special case of these curves They correspond, in fact, as we shall see, to the equipotential lines and lines of flow in an infinite plate with two equal sources of electricity

Maxwell, in 1856, suggested the application to problems

---

[1] Poggendorff's *Annalen*, Bd. lxiv.
[2] *Camb and Dub Math Journ* vol 1 p 124

of electric currents of his beautiful theory of the motion of
an immaterial incompressible fluid in a resisting medium,
but does not appear to have developed the suggestion.[1]

The object of this paper is to show that, by regarding,
in accordance with Maxwell's suggestion, every point of
exit or issue as a source or sink, spreading or absorbing
electricity, independently of all other sources, Kirchhoff's
general equations may be deduced by easy geometrical
processes, and extended to certain cases of flow in curved
surfaces. We shall, by this method, be naturally led to
look mainly at the function u, which in the analytical
investigation is subordinated to v. The equation $u = 0$
will receive an obvious physical interpretation, and we
shall then proceed to consider in detail the nature of the
flow in certain special cases apparently not yet examined.

If a source P, in an infinite uniformly resisting plate,
steadily give forth a quantity of electricity E per unit of
time, the flow per second over the whole circumference of
all circles with P as centre is equal   Hence the rate of
flow at each point of the circumference of such a circle is
inversely as the radius and $= \dfrac{E}{2\pi r}$. The potential due to P
satisfies the equation

$$\frac{dv}{dr} = -\frac{E}{2\pi r}$$

or,

$$v = C - \frac{E}{2\pi} \log r.$$

The potential due to any number of sources P_1 P_2 etc.,
and sinks P_1' P_2' etc., all of equal power, is got by simple
superposition. If E be equal for all points,

$$v = C - \Sigma\frac{E}{2\pi} \log r + \Sigma\frac{E}{2\pi} \log r',$$

where r corresponds to a source, and r' to a sink. Hence
the equipotential lines are

$$\frac{r_1\, r_2\, r_3 \cdots}{r_1'\, r_2'\, r_3'} = C \qquad . \qquad . \qquad . \qquad (5).$$

---

[1] *Cambridge Phil. Trans* vol. x

The equation of the lines of flow follows at once from the equation of continuity. Across any element ds of a stream line subtending angles $d\theta_1$ $d\theta_2$ etc. at the sources, and $d\theta_1'$ $d\theta_2'$ etc. at sinks, no fluid must flow. But the quantity of fluid per second reaching ds from P_n is $\dfrac{d\theta_n}{2\pi}$ E.

The quantity withdrawn by P'_n is $\dfrac{d\theta'_n}{2\pi}$ E. Hence the differential equation of the stream line is

$$\Sigma d\theta - \Sigma d\theta' = 0.$$

Integrating, $\Sigma\theta - \Sigma\theta' = \text{const.}$

where θ and θ' are the angles between radii vectores and any fixed lines. If we agree to reckon θ in opposite directions for sources and sinks, the equation becomes

$$\Sigma\theta = a \qquad . \qquad . \qquad . \qquad (6).$$

The following are elementary consequences of this equation .—

(a) When we have one source P and one equal sink P', the stream line through any point Q has for its equation

$$\Sigma\theta = QPP' + QP'P = \frac{\pi}{2} - PQP' = a.$$

Hence the locus of Q is a circle through P and P', which is Kirchhoff's case. The orthogonals are circles whose centres (R) lie in PP' produced, and whose radii $= \sqrt{PR\,P'R}$.

(b) If we have two equal sources and no sinks, or what is the same thing, sinks at an infinite distance, the stream lines are rectangular hyperbolas. For in this case,

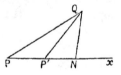

$QPN + QP'N = a = QNx$ if we make $P'QN = QPN$. Also QN touches the circle through PP'Q, therefore

$$QN^2 = NP'.NP$$

—the equation of a rectangular hyperbola through P and P', whose centre is the middle point of PP', and which is referred to conjugate diameters inclined at angle a.   The orthogonal system in this case consists of the lemniscates $rr' = c$.   One of the hyperbolas consists of the straight line PP', and the line equidistant from P and P'.   Dividing the plate along the latter line, we have the case of one source in a plate bounded in one direction by an infinite straight line, but otherwise unlimited or bounded by a lemniscate of infinite conductivity, having P and its image due to the boundary line for poles

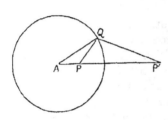

(c) To find the image of any point in a circular boundary, *i.e.* to find the source which in combination with a source at the centre of the circle, and an equal sink at any other point, will make the circle a stream line.

Let A be the centre of the circle, and P the given sink. In AP take P', so that $AP.AP' = AQ^2$.   Then PAQ and QAP' are similar triangles, and $QPA = AQP'$.

Therefore $QAP + QP'A + QPA = 2\pi$, or (6) is satisfied for any point in the circle by assuming at P' a sink $= P$.

(d) Hence if there be within a circle m sources and n sinks, we must assume the same number of sources and sinks without the circle, and $n - m$ sources at the centre.

(e) The straight line equidistant from two equal sources of the same sign is clearly a stream line for these points. Hence the image of any point in a straight line is an equal point, which is its optical image.

I have constructed the equation

$$\Sigma\theta = a$$

on the assumption that all the sources are equal, because the degree of the stream line is equal to the number of equal sources (positive and negative) to which the system can be reduced   For if h, k be the co-ordinates of P, the equation becomes

$$\Sigma \pm \tan^{-1} \frac{y-k}{x-h} = C, \qquad . \qquad . \qquad (7).$$

If $\left(\frac{y-k}{h-x}\right)_m$ denote the sum of all the combinations of expressions $\pm \frac{y-k}{x-h}$, taken m at a time, we may write this

$$1 - C\left(\frac{y-k}{x-h}\right)_1 - \left(\frac{y-k}{x-h}\right)_2 + C\left(\frac{y-k}{x-h}\right)_3 + \left(\frac{y-k}{x-h}\right)_4 - \&c. = 0 \quad (8),$$

an equation of the nth degree if there be in all n sources.

The degree of the equipotential lines is also $= n$ if there be an equal number of sources and sinks   In general, if there be m sources of one sign, and $n - m$ of another, and $m > n - m$, $2m$ is the degree of the equipotential lines.   This is one of many features which make it more convenient to work with stream lines.

It is obvious from equation (8), that every stream line must pass through all the sources.   Thus, the circle in case (c), which passes through no source, is not a complete stream line, the other branch being the straight line APP′, which passes through all the sources.   Distinct stream lines can intersect only at a source, for at no other point can $\Sigma\theta$ be indeterminate.   Where two branches of the same stream line intersect the velocity is necessarily zero, changing sign in passing through the point.   The physical meaning of a branch is that two streams impinge, and are thrown off with an abrupt change of direction.

The same result is easily found from the analytical condition for a singular point $\frac{du}{dx} = \frac{du}{dy} = 0$.

For $-\frac{du}{dx} = \frac{dv}{dy} =$ velocity parallel to axis of y,

$\frac{du}{dy} = \frac{dv}{dx} =$ velocity parallel to axis of x,

or directly by differentiation

4

$$\left. \begin{aligned} \frac{du}{dx} &= \Sigma\left(\mp\frac{y-k}{r^2}\right) \\ \frac{du}{dy} &= \Sigma\left(\pm\frac{x-k}{r^2}\right) \end{aligned} \right\} \qquad . \qquad . \qquad (9).$$

The nature of the intersection of the branches of a stream line at a multiple point is easily determined.

At an m-point, the angles at which the branches cut the axis of x are the roots of the equation—

$$\left(\frac{d}{dx} + \tan\phi\,\frac{d}{dy}\right)^m u = 0 \qquad . \qquad . \qquad (10).$$

Where, since $\quad \dfrac{d^2u}{dx^2} = -\dfrac{d^2u}{dy^2}$

$$\frac{d^m u}{dx^m} = -\frac{d^m u}{dx^{m-2}dy^2} = \frac{d^m u}{dx^{m-4}dy^4}\ \&c.,$$

$$\frac{d^m u}{dx^{m-1}dy} = -\frac{d^m u}{dx^{m-3}dy^3}\ \&c$$

Whence (10) becomes

$$\frac{d^m u}{dx^m}\left(1 - \frac{m\,.\,m-1}{1\ 2}\tan^2\phi + \&c.\right) +$$

$$\frac{d^m u}{dx^{m-1}dy}\left(m\tan\phi - \frac{m\,.\,m-1\,.\,m-2}{1\,.\,2\,.\,3}\tan^3\phi + \&c.\right) = 0.$$

We can choose the axes so that $\dfrac{d^m u}{dx^m} = 0$, and reduce the equation to

$$m\tan\phi - \frac{m\,.\,m-1\,.\,m-2}{1\,.\,2\,.\,3}\tan^3\phi + \ .\ = 0 \quad (11),$$

or

$$\tan m\phi = 0 \quad . \qquad . \qquad (12),$$

$\phi = \dfrac{l\pi}{m}$, where l is any integer from 1 to m.

Thus the branches make equal angles with each other. This proposition depends solely on the relation $\nabla u = 0$.

It is therefore true, also, for the equipotential lines, as is otherwise obvious.[1]

The general nature of the stream lines will be different, according as the number of sinks is or is not equal to the number of sources.   In the former case, $\Sigma(\theta) = 0$ is satisfied at all points infinitely distant, the radii being all parallel, and the positive and negative angles equal in number. Hence one stream line has the straight line at infinity as a branch, or intersects the straight line at infinity at right angles, and therefore has an asymptote.   This stream line will, in general, be of the $n - 1^{\text{th}}$ degree.   In some cases it may be of a lower degree ; as, for example, when the conic at infinity is its other branch.   A case of this sort will be given below.   The other stream lines of the system cannot meet the line at infinity, and cannot have asymptotes.   However far they run out, they must therefore loop and return.

When there are more sources than sinks, $\Sigma\theta$ becomes indeterminate at an infinite distance, as might have been anticipated from the fact, that in this case there is a constant flow of electricity outwards, implying a sink at an infinite distance.   The line at infinity is not in this case a stream line, and will be cut by all the stream lines, which do not loop except at finite distances, and have all asymptotes.

The asymptotes, in this case, may be easily constructed by the aid of equations (6) and (8).

At the infinitely distant point of contact the velocities due to all sources are in the same direction, or the asymptote must be parallel to the radii.

If there are m sources and $n - m$ sinks, the stream line whose asymptote makes an angle a with the initial line is obviously

---

[1] I have since found that this result has been already proved for plane curves by Professor Rankine and Professor Stokes (*Proc R S.*, 1867), and for spherical harmonics by Sir W. Thomson and Professor Tait, in their treatise on Natural Philosophy.

$$\Sigma\theta = (2m - n)a = \tan^{-1} C . \quad . \quad (13).$$

This equation has $2m - n$ roots

$$a_1, \quad a_1 + \frac{\pi}{2m - n}, \quad a_1 + \frac{2\pi}{2m - n}, \text{ &c.}$$

So that each stream line has $2m - n$ asymptotes equally inclined to one another.

Transforming to rectangular co-ordinates, and choosing the asymptote as axis of x, (8) reduces to

$$\left(\frac{y - k}{x - h}\right)_1 - \left(\frac{y - k}{x - h}\right)_3 + \quad . \quad . \quad = 0$$

When $y = 0$, x has two roots $= \infty$ if

$$\Sigma(\pm k) = 0 \quad . \quad . \quad (14).$$

Hence the asymptote is such that the algebraic sum of the perpendiculars from the sources diminished by the sum of the perpendiculars from the sinks is zero. It is obvious without analysis that this condition is necessary, that the velocity perpendicular to the asymptote, at its point of contact with the curve, may be absolute zero. If sinks weigh upward, all lines passing through the centre of gravity of the system are asymptotes, and $2m - n$ of these lines, equally inclined to each other, belong to one stream line   The system must have a centre of gravity, for by pairing sources and sinks we produce couples which will always give a single resultant when compounded with the weights of the extra sources.

A complete system has no centre of gravity, but (14) is satisfied for all lines perpendicular to the axis of the resultant couple   If the axis of the couple formed by pairing a source and sink at distance ρ_m makes an angle ψ_m with the axis of the resultant couple,

$$\Sigma(\rho \sin \psi) = 0 . \quad . \quad . \quad (15),$$

an equation with only one root to determine the direction of the asymptote. In this case the asymptote meets the curve in a double point, and has contact of the third order, or x has three roots $=\infty$.

The condition for this is obviously—

$$\Sigma \left(\pm kh \right) = 0 . \qquad . \qquad (16),$$

which since $\Sigma \left(\pm k \right) = 0$, does not depend on the point of the asymptote from which h is reckoned.

If (15) is satisfied identically, the asymptote meets the curve in a triple point. Two of the branches belong to the line at infinity, and the finite branch sinks to the $n-2$ degree.

In this case not only $\Sigma \left(\pm k \right) = 0$, but $\Sigma \left(\pm h \right) = 0$. Hence (16) no longer gives a fixed point on the asymptote, but only fixes its direction   A further analytical condition is easily found, but is unnecessary. For in this case the centre of gravity of the sources coincides with the centre of gravity of the sinks. The stream lines due to the sources alone would have the same sets of asymptotes as those due to sinks. One of these sets is necessarily asymptotic in the complete system, which has always one line with real asymptotes   The set will consist of $\frac{n}{2}$ rays, all passing through the common centre of gravity of the sources and sinks, and equally inclined to one another.

Rectilineal Branches are asymptotes coinciding with their curves.

Hence, in an incomplete system, all straight lines pass through the centre of gravity of the system, and belong to one stream line, unless the centre of gravity be a source. In any case they are equally inclined to one another, for if not branches of one stream line, they would be so for the system got by removing the source at their intersection.

In a complete system there can be only one rectilineal stream line, unless sinks and sources have a common centre of gravity   In the latter case, there can be at most $\frac{n}{2}$

straight lines, forming equally inclined rays through that point.

The condition for a rectilineal branch is in general that the sources must be either on the line or be two by two, each other's images on the line   For if not, remove all the sources on the line and all pairs of sources which are each other's images in the line. Next, remove all sources on one side of the line by placing equal sources of opposite sign at the place of their images. The straight line is still a stream line, and on one side of it there are no sources, and therefore constant potential, which is absurd. Similarly it can be shown that a circle is a possible stream line only when the sources are on the curve or image each other. From this it follows that no finite number of sources can give parallel rectilineal streams or non-intersecting circular streams.

A similar investigation applies to equipotential lines. The image of a point in a rectilineal equipotential line is the same in position as the image in a stream line, but of opposite sign.   No source can lie on an equipotential line. Hence, to show that for right equipotential line the points must image two by two, we have only to remove all sources on one side of the line, placing equal sources of the same sign at their images   The line is still equipotential, therefore we may suppose it charged to constant potential, and all sources removed.   Hence all stream lines become rectilineal, which is absurd.   Similarly if a circle is equipotential, the sources must balance about it two by two, i.e. must be in a straight line with its centre, at distances to which the radius is mean proportional—otherwise we can find a system reducible to a single point at the centre of the circle, and in which all stream lines are rectilineal Hence, no incomplete system can have a rectilineal or circular potential line.

Points of Inflexion occur at all points on the locus—

$$\frac{d^2u}{dx^2} + 2\frac{d^2u}{dxdy}\frac{dy}{dx} + \frac{d^2u}{dy^2}\left|\frac{dy}{dx}\right|^2 = 0 \quad . \quad (17)$$

Remembering that

$$\frac{d^2u}{dx^2} = -\frac{d^2u}{dy^2} = \Sigma\left(\pm\frac{\sin 2\theta}{r^2}\right),$$

$$\frac{d^2u}{dxdy} = \Sigma\left(\mp\frac{\cos 2\theta}{r^2}\right),$$

we can readily bring (17) into the form—

$$\Sigma\left(\frac{\sin 2\theta}{r^2}\right)\Sigma\left(\frac{\cos(\theta+\theta')}{rr'}\right) - \Sigma\left(\frac{\cos 2\theta}{r^2}\right)\Sigma\left(\frac{\sin(\theta+\theta')}{rr'}\right) = 0,$$

or,

$$\Sigma\frac{\sin(2\theta-\theta'-\theta'')}{r^2r'r''} = 0 \qquad . \qquad (18).$$

In this last expression θ' and θ'' may assume the value θ.

The radius of curvature may be similarly expressed, but such expressions can hardly have a practical application

The cases of practical interest are mainly those where the number of sources is small. We have already examined the cases of two sources of the same or opposite signs We will now proceed to consider the cases that arise when there are three or four sources.

Three Sources.—In general the curves will be cubic passing through the three sources, and having asymptotes determined as above. The direction of flow at any point of the field may be found by observing that if ϕ be the angle between the tangent and a radius vector,

$$\Sigma\pm\frac{\sin\phi}{r} = 0.$$

It will sometimes be possible to find the direction of flow geometrically by the following obvious theorem.

If a circle be described touching a stream line at any point, and cutting off from the radii vectores of that point, fractions of their lengths, μ μ' etc , where μ is negative if the point of intersection is in the radius vector produced, and also negative if the radius vector is drawn from a sink, then—

$$\Sigma(\mu) = 0.$$

When the number of sources is large this theorem is

not in general convenient, but it is often applicable where there are only three points.

The lines of flow can, however, be readily described with any degree of accuracy when there is one sink, by describing segments of circles with constant difference of angle through the sink and one source, and drawing through the other source straight lines with the same difference of angle. The stream lines will be diagonals of the quadrilaterals into which the field is thus divided. The process may be extended to the case of two sources and two sinks by taking the intersections of two sets of circles.

When there are two sources and one sink, the singular points may be found by an easy geometrical method. Let A, B, be sources, C the sink, and P a point of zero velocity. The resultant velocity due to A and C is in the tangent to the circle PAC, and also—since P is a singular point—in the line PB. Therefore—

$$BPC = PAC.$$

Similarly

$$APC = PBC.$$

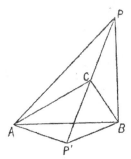

Hence PCA, BCP are similar triangles, and there are two points of zero flow, P and P′, lying in the line bisecting the angle C, and such that PC is a mean proportional to BC and AC. The directions of the orthogonal branches at P bisect the angle APB and its supplement.

For the initial line is a tangent at the singular points if

$$\frac{d^2u}{dx^2} = \Sigma\left(\frac{\pm \sin 2\theta}{r^2}\right) = 0 \quad . \quad . \quad (19).$$

Let now $APC = a$, $BPC = \dfrac{C}{2} - a = \beta$, and assume the bisector of APB as initial line. Then

$$\sin\frac{C}{2}\left(\frac{1}{PA^2}-\frac{1}{PB^2}\right)+\frac{\sin\overline{\alpha-\beta}}{PC^2}=\Sigma\frac{\sin 2\theta}{r^2},$$

which since

$$\left.\begin{array}{l}\dfrac{1}{PA^2}=\dfrac{1}{PC^2}\cdot\dfrac{\sin^2\beta}{\sin^2\dfrac{C}{2}}\\[3ex]\dfrac{1}{PB^2}=\dfrac{1}{PC^2}\cdot\dfrac{\sin^2\alpha}{\sin^2\dfrac{C}{2}}\end{array}\right\}$$

becomes

$$\sin^2\beta-\sin^2\alpha+\sin\overline{\alpha-\beta}\,.\,\sin\overline{\alpha+\beta}=0,$$

which satisfies (19).

The chief interest lies in the cases where the cubic breaks up into a straight line and a conic. This takes place for one stream line of the system when all the sources lie on a straight line, or when they form an isosceles triangle with points of the same sign at the base. The cases are—

1. *Two Sources and a Sink*—The conic is always a *circle* with the sink as centre. If the sink lies in the line of the sources produced, the radius of the circle is a mean proportional to the distances of the sink from the sources. If the sink lie between the sources, the circle is impossible. If the sink is the vertex of an isosceles triangle, the circle passes through both sources, and all asymptotes meet in the point of zero flow furthest from the sources. If the sink is half way between the sources, there are two straight lines and a real and impossible circle.

2. *Three Sources of the same Sign.*—Every stream line has three asymptotes, meeting in the centre of gravity, and inclined at angles of $\dfrac{\pi}{3}$. If one of these asymptotes becomes a branch, the other branch is a hyperbola, with centre of gravity as centre, and axes in ratio of $\sqrt{3}$ to 1. If the points form an isosceles triangle, the hyperbola passes through the extremities of the base If the triangle is equilateral, the hyperbola coincides with its asymptotes.

If the vertical angle is less than $\frac{\pi}{3}$, the rectilineal branch
is the transverse axis , if greater than $\frac{\pi}{3}$, it is the conjugate.
If the points are all in a line, the vertices of the hyperbola
lie on that line, and are the points of zero flow, which are
easily found   If one point is half way between the other
two, we have two rectilineal branches and two hyperbolas,
the conjugate axis of the one being equal to the transverse
axis of the other.   The hyperbolas are, therefore, confocal.

Four Points —Complete System.

Singular Points.—If A and B are sources, C and D
sinks, there is a singular point at P, if the circles APC,
BPD, and also APD, BPC touch at P. Hence, there are
no real singular points if the sides of the quadrilateral
ACBD intersect, unless all the points be on a circle,
which in this case contains all the singular points

Straight Lines —The one stream line which has as
asymptote is of the third degree   If a straight line is one
factor, the other factor is a conic, which is always a circle.
For if A, C are the images of B, D respectively in the
straight line, a circle can be drawn through them, which
is obviously the branch sought   But if A, B lie without
the line, and C, D on it, a circle through A, B having its
centre O in CD produced, so that OA is a mean proportional between OC and OD is the circle required.   If
ABCD are all on a straight line, the other branch is
manifestly a circle with centre on the line

Conics.—The parabola is an impossible conic for any
finite number of points   For the parabola has two
asymptotes meeting at infinity   Hence the centre of
gravity of an incomplete system, or of the sinks and
sources separately in a complete system, must be at an
infinite distance, which is absurd   The conics are therefore central.

The *hyperbola*, which has two asymptotes, is only

possible when the cubic reduces to a conic This demands that the centre of gravity of sinks and sources shall coincide, *i.e.* that AB, CD are diagonals of a parallelogram The asymptotes must meet at right angles, and the hyperbola is equilateral It is obvious, indeed, that in this case the sources and sinks give separately sets of concentric rectangular hyperbolas, of which the one passing through the four points belongs to both sets, and is the only asymptotic curve of the complete system.

In this case the equipotential lines are lemniscates Let the origin be the centre of the system, $2a$ and $2b$ the diagonals of the parallelogram, α and β their angles with the initial line   At any point P

$$AP^2 . BP^2 + \lambda CP^2 . DP^2 = 0.$$

That is,

$$r^4 + a^4 - 2a^2 r^2 \cos 2\overline{\theta - \alpha} + \lambda (r^4 + b^4 - 2b^2 r^2 \cos 2\overline{\theta - \beta}) = 0$$
$$(1 + \lambda)(r^4 + a^4) - 2r^2 \cos 2\theta (a^2 \cos 2\alpha + \lambda b^2 \cos 2\beta)$$
$$+ 2r^2 \sin 2\theta (a^2 \sin 2\alpha + \lambda b^2 \sin 2\beta) = 0.$$

When $\qquad \lambda = -\dfrac{a^2 \sin 2\alpha}{b^2 \sin 2\beta},\qquad$ the curve becomes

$$(b^2 \sin 2\beta - a^2 \sin 2\alpha)(r^4 + a^4) - 2a^2 b^2 r^2 \sin 2(\beta - \alpha) \cos 2\theta = 0,$$

a lemniscate, with foci on the initial line, and centre at the origin

If the parallelogram is a rectangle $a = b$, and the curve is

$$r^4 - 2a^2 r^2 \frac{\cos \overline{\beta - \alpha}}{\cos \overline{\beta + \alpha}} \cos 2\theta + a^4 = 0.$$

It is easily shown that the stream lines orthogonal to these are lemniscates with the same centre, passing through the four points, one of which becomes a circle when the parallelogram is rectangular.

The ellipse appears to be an impossible conic for four points, for conics occur in pairs orthogonal to each other The orthogonal of the ellipse must be a confocal hyperbola, which is impossible, the only hyperbola being that discussed above.   Orthogonal circles, however, are possible, and fall under two classes, according as all the points are on one circle, or two on each.

If A B C D lie on a circle, that circle is obviously a stream line. Let BA.DC produced meet in O. Then OA OB = OC.OD, and the circle, with centre O and radius $\sqrt{\overline{OA.OB}}$ is the other branch of the stream line. If O lies within the circle ABCD, the second circle becomes impossible. If CA.BD produced meet R and CB.AD in S, R and S are centres of equipotential circles, only one of which is real, unless the second stream circle is imaginary. We may take as an example the case of a rectangle, points of the same sign lying on the same diagonal. Let the circle through the four points be (2a and 2b being the sides of the rectangle)

$$x^2 + y^2 - a^2 - b^2 = 0.$$

The other branch is the imaginary circle

$$x^2 + y^2 + a^2 + b^2 = 0 ;$$

and we know that another stream line is the hyperbola

$$y^2 - x^2 - a^2 + b^2 = 0$$

Hence the stream lines are

$$(x^2 + y^2)^2 - (a^2 + b^2)^2 + \lambda(y^2 - x^2 - a^2 + b^2) = 0,$$

lemniscates as above.

The equipotential circles degenerate into the straight lines

$$x = 0 \ \text{and} \ y = 0.$$

If O be the point in CD produced which is equidistant from A and B, and OC.OD = OA² = OB², the circle with O as centre passing through A,B is a line of flow.

The circle having its centre P in AB produced, and passing through CD, is obviously orthogonal ; and since PA.PB = PC² = PD² is also a line of flow. In this case both circles are necessarily real.

It is clearly impossible that the same system should

have two pairs of circular stream lines of either of the classes we have analysed. Nor can two complete pairs of different classes occur, since otherwise two stream lines would intersect. But three real and an imaginary circle are possible, if A B C D lie on a circle, and at the same time obey the condition for a pair of circles of the second class, that is, if AB produced pass through the pole of CD with respect to the circle ABCD. The three circles are manifestly orthogonal, and their radical centre is centre of the fourth (imaginary) circle.

If the circle through ABCD is

$$S = x^2 + y^2 - a^2 = 0,$$

the lines AB, CD respectively

$$u = hx + ky - a^2 = 0$$
$$v = h'x + k'y - a^2 = 0,$$

we have

$$hh' + kk' - a^2 = 0,$$

and the second and third circles become

$$S - 2u = 0$$
$$S - 2v = 0.$$

The fourth or imaginary circle is

$$S - 2w = 0,$$

where

$$w = \frac{a^2(k' - k)x}{hk' - kh'} + \frac{a^2(h - h')y}{hk' - kh'} - a^2,$$

$w = 0$ representing the polar of the intersection of AB, CD.

Thus the equation to the stream lines may be written

$$(S - 2u)(S - 2v) + \lambda S(S - 2w) = 0,$$

or,

$$(1 + \lambda)S^2 - 2(u + v + \lambda w)S + 4uv = 0,$$

which degenerates into a cubic when $\lambda = -1$.

The equations may, in general, be simplified by a proper choice of co-ordinates.

Take, for example, the case when $S - 2u$, $S - 2v$ are equal circles.

Then $$h^2 + k^2 = h'^2 + k'^2,$$

and by proper choice of axes,

$$h = -h'$$
$$k = \ \ k'$$
$$k^2 - h^2 = a^2$$

Hence,

$$w = \frac{a^2 y}{k} - a^2.$$

The lines become

$$(1 + \lambda)S^2 - 2\left(2ky - 2a^2 + \frac{\lambda a^2 y}{k} - \lambda a^2\right)S + 4(ky - a^2)^2 - 4h^2 x^2 = 0.$$

If the three circles are equal, we have further,

$$h^2 + k^2 = 2a^2$$

$$h = \frac{a}{\sqrt{2}}$$

$$k = \frac{\sqrt{3}a}{\sqrt{2}}$$

Accurate drawings of this case, and of the lemniscates in the case of a rectangular parallelogram, have been prepared, to accompany this paper, by Messrs. Meik and Brebner, in the Physical Laboratory of the University. The dotted lines in these diagrams show the lines of flow when the signs of a source and sink are transposed [1]

Verifications have been sought by determining equipotential lines experimentally, and superposing them upon drawings of the stream lines. The experiments were executed by students in the Physical Laboratory. The process employed was essentially that of Kirchhoff, but the use of Thomson's galvanometers has made it much more rapid, as well as more delicate.

Spherical Surfaces.—To extend the method above used to spherical surfaces, we must take as starting-point, not a single source, but a source and sink at the extremi-

[1] That a greater variety of curves might be given, without overcrowding the figure, the two sides of one of the diagrams have been made unsymmetrical, some of the curves being given (in half) on the one side, others on the other.

ties of a diameter. For brevity, we shall speak only
of the source, assuming the existence of a corresponding
sink.

When there is one source, the stream lines are mani-

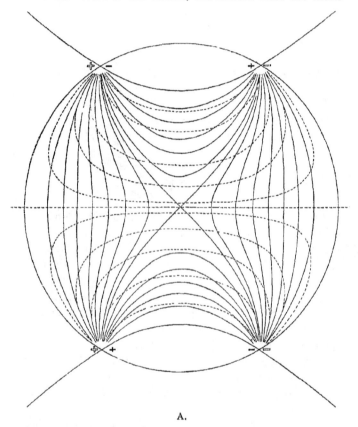

A.

Lines of flow when the sources form a rectangular parallelogram,
whose diagonals make an angle of $\frac{\pi}{3}$ The unbroken lines are lines of
flow when sources of the same sign are diagonally opposite   One line
sinks to a circle, another to a rectangular hyperbola, the rest are
lemniscates   When a source and sink are transposed, the circle is still
part of a stream whose other branch is a straight line, but the lemniscates pass over into the dotted curves.

festly great circles through it, and the equipotential lines small circles, of which it is the pole.

If the radius of the sphere is a, the circumference of the small circle, whose angular radius is θ, is $2\pi a \sin \theta$. Hence if u be the potential,

$$\frac{du}{d\theta} \propto \frac{1}{\sin \theta}$$

$$u \propto \frac{1}{2} \log \frac{1 - \cos \theta}{1 + \cos \theta}$$

For any number of sources the potential will be

$$\frac{1}{2}\left(\Sigma \pm \log \frac{1 - \cos \theta}{1 + \cos \theta}\right),$$

and the equation of the equipotential lines,

$$\frac{1 - \cos \theta_1}{1 + \cos \theta_1} \cdot \frac{1 - \cos \theta_2}{1 + \cos \theta_2} = C \frac{1 - \cos \theta'_1}{1 + \cos \theta'_1} \cdot \frac{1 - \cos \theta'_2}{1 + \cos \theta'_2} \cdots,$$

the accented angles belonging to sinks.

For the lines of flow we have, precisely as in a plane, $\Sigma(\pm \phi) = c$, where ϕ is the angle between the great circle through a source and a point on the line, and a fixed great circle through the source.

Let us take, as an example, the case of one source and one sink. Let the co-ordinates of these points be $h, k, 0$; $h, -k, 0$, and those of any point on an equipotential line, x, y, z.

We have for the equation of this line,

$$\frac{1 - \cos \theta}{1 + \cos \theta} + \lambda \frac{1 - \cos \theta'}{1 + \cos \theta'} = 0,$$

where

$$\cos \theta = \frac{hx + ky}{a^2}, \quad \cos \theta' = \frac{hx - ky}{a^2}.$$

Hence the projections of the equipotential lines on the plane of xy have as equation,

$$(a^2 - hx - ky)(a^2 + hx - ky) + \lambda(a^2 - hx + ky)(a^2 + hx + ky) = 0,$$

or—

$$a^4 + k^2y^2 - h^2x^2 - 2\frac{1 - \lambda}{1 + \lambda} a^2 ky = 0$$

—a series of similar hyperbolas, whose centres lie on the axis of y, whose axes are parallel to the co-ordinate axes, and inversely proportional to the co-ordinates of the

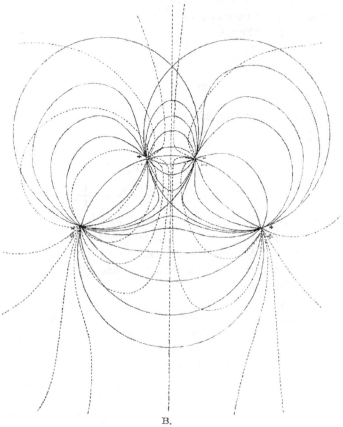

B.

Case of two sources and two sinks giving three equal stream circles with two points of zero flow. When a source and sink are transposed, the lower circle is still a line of flow. The other lines assume the dotted form.

source, and which all cut the axis of x at points distant $\pm \dfrac{a^2}{h}$ from the origin. Obviously one of the lines is

5

the great circle perpendicular to the line joining the sources.

For the stream lines we have in this case,

$$\phi - \phi' = c,$$

observing that

$$\tan \phi = \frac{az}{xk - hy}$$

$$\tan \phi' = \frac{-az}{xk + hy}.$$

This equation becomes

$$k^2x^2 - h^2y^2 - a^2z^2 + \lambda xz = 0,$$

a cone which intersects the tangent plane to the sphere at the extremity of the axis of x, in a series of similar ellipses, having their centres on the intersection of the plane with the plane of xz, and passing through the points a, $\pm \frac{ak}{h}$, 0   Two of the stream lines are manifestly great circles, whose equations are $x = 0$ and $z = 0$

If we divide the sphere along the former of these circles, we cut off the subsidiary source and sink, and get the case of a hemisphere, in which the source and sink are equidistant from the pole. A curious hemispherical case is got by dividing the sphere along the equipotential hemisphere. In this case we have two sources of the same sign within the hemisphere, one being the subsidiary source of the removed sink. But in order that the distribution may remain unchanged, we must have the potential maintained constant at the edge of the hemisphere   This may be effected by making the base a conductor with a sink at its centre, or, indeed, by placing the sink at the vertex of any conducting surface of revolution which joins the hemisphere   From these hemisphere cases, obvious cases of half and quarter hemispheres follow

IV

NOTE ON PROFESSOR BAIN'S THEORY OF EUCLID I. 4[1]

IN a paper communicated to this Society last session I pointed out that the proof of Euc. I 5, given by Mr. Mill, is unsound; endeavouring, at the same time, to show that this is no mere accident, but that it is impossible to give a mathematically correct analysis of the processes of Synthetic Geometry on any theory that holds figures to be merely illustrative, and does not admit that intuition in the Kantian sense—*i.e.* actual looking at a single engraved or imaginary figure—may be a necessary and sufficient step in a demonstration perfectly general   I now venture to draw the attention of the Society to the confirmation which I conceive that this argument derives from the way in which Euc. I 4 is treated by Professor Bain in his recent *Logic*—a book which, on the whole, is based on Mr. Mill's principles, and which is mainly original in an attempt, which I cannot regard as felicitous, to bring these principles into closer contact with the special sciences, especially with Physics and Mathematics

It will be remembered that Mr. Mill, undertaking to demonstrate Euc. I. 5 from first principles, has to supply, in the course of his proof, a demonstration of Euc. I 4, and it is in the attempt to give to this process the form of

[1] Communicated by Professor Tait to the Royal Society of Edinburgh on June 6, 1870, and published in its *Proceedings*, vol vii pp 176-179

syllogistic inference from Euclid's axioms that he errs. Professor Bain does not attempt to defend the blunder of his predecessor. He admits that Euclid's proof cannot be reduced to a chain of syllogisms. But, instead of surrendering Mr. Mill's theory of mathematical reasoning, he concludes that Euclid has not demonstrated his proposition—that the superposition which he enjoins is only an experiment, and that " if his readers had not made actual experiments of the kind indicated, they could not be convinced by the reasoning in the demonstration." [1]

Now I believe, and in my former paper expressly pointed out, that the position that Euc. I. 4 is really an inductive truth, and that the usual demonstration is not in itself convincing, is the only ground that remains to Mr Mill and his adherents   So far, then, I am confirmed by Professor Bain . it remains only to show that this new position is mathematically as untenable as that from which Mr. Mill has been dislodged.   If Professor Bain grants that the proof of Euc I 4 is not by syllogism from axioms—if, again, mathematically it is plain that there is none the less a real proof, not merely an induction—we shall have gone far to establish the validity of proof by intuition.

Professor Bain tells us that Euclid, while professedly going through a process of pure deduction, requires us to conceive an experimental proof.   There is surely an ambiguity here.   Does Mr. Bain mean that Euclid merely calls to our mind former concrete experiments with triangles of card-board or paper, for these alone are actual and concrete to our author ?   Does Euclid's " experiment " agree with the descriptions of experiments in books of Physics, save only in this, that we have all made Euclid's experiment before ?   Clearly not.   In picturing to myself an experimental proof in the usual sense, I imagine mentally, or with the help of a diagram, certain arrangements, and then I am told to imagine a certain

[1] *Logic*, vol. ii. p. 217.

result following—or rather, I am told to believe this result, for to picture it is quite superfluous and often impossible. Euclid, on the other hand, tells me to superpose ideally the point A on C, the line AB on CD, and so forth, and then I do not require to be told that the coincidence of the whole triangles follows   I have no choice to imagine coincidence or non-coincidence   I see that it follows, and that quite apart from previous experiment

Professor Bain allows the possibility of ideal experiments on mathematical forms [1]   I presume, therefore, that he will not deny that the intelligent reader of our proposition does, as he reads, make a valid experiment in favour of the proposition   But if this be so, where is the deception in Euclid's proof, and what is the necessity of supplementing that proof by further " ideal " or " actual experiments " ?   The course of Euclid's argument shows that the two triangles are not only equal, but equal in virtue of the way in which they have been constructed, viz. the equality of the two sides and the included angle. The fact that the proof is not syllogistic does not make it any the less a case of that parity of reasoning which Professor Bain, in another connection, admits to be not induction but demonstration.[2]

Our author draws a broad line between the fourth proposition, with its " appeal to experiment or trial in the concrete," and the mass of geometrical proofs in which the figure is referred to for verification only, " the effect of every construction and every step of reasoning being judged of by actual inspection "   But if the inspection follows the construction, what is the construction itself ? A construction is not proved by syllogism from axioms It is necessarily drawn, and in the drawing (mental or other) looked at.   Every construction involves a figure and an intuition, which, while it looks at the individual figure, sees in it the general truth.[3]   Mr. Bain grants that

---

[1] *Logic*, vol 1 p 225   [2] *Ibid* vol 11 p. 5
[3] *Cf* Kant, *Kritik der reinen Vernunft*, p 478, Ed Hartenstein, 1867.

of such consequences as that the diagonal of a parallelogram divides it into two triangles, Euclid offers no other
proof than an appeal to the eye.[1] In fact, no other proof
can be offered. Yet surely it will not be asserted that this
too is an induction. In one word, if no proposition is fairly
demonstrated where it is essential to look at the figure,
there is no sound demonstration in synthetic geometry

Finally, Professor Bain himself seems not quite satisfied
as to the inductive nature of Euc. I. 4   " The proof,"
he says, " rests solely on definitions," and hence " the
proposition cannot be real—the subject and predicate
must be identical " Surely an identical proposition is
not an induction ! And surely, too, the proof rests not
on definitions merely, but on definitions and the use of the
figure ! But I do not think that Professor Bain means
to speak here in strict logical terms, for he straightway
adds in explanation, " The proposition must, in fact, be
a mere equivalent of the notions of line, angle, surface,
equality—a fact apparent in the operation of understanding these notions. It is implicated in the experience
requisite for mastering the indefinable elements of
geometry, and should be rested purely on the basis of
experience." We should have known better what this
sentence means, if the author had adopted here the
distinction between synthetic and analytic judgments.
He cannot mean that a truth that is an induction, and
rests on experience, is an analytic judgment, that it can
be reached by a purely formal dividing and compounding
of the definitions of terms. Such a proposition could be
shown to be true without any figure or any experiment.
Yet the proposition is, we are told, involved in the
notions , we cannot know what lines, angles, etc., are
without knowing this too. If this means anything, it
means that Euc. I. 4 is a synthetic judgment *a priori* ;
and that, after all, Kant and the mathematicians are
right, and Mr. Mill and the empirical logicians wrong.

[1] *Logic*, vol. ii. p 218

DR. STIRLING, HEGEL, AND THE MATHEMATICIANS

(From the *Fortnightly Review*, April 1873)

THE names which head this paper will suggest to those who are interested in metaphysical and scientific discussion a controversy which has never been quite extinct since Dr. Whewell attacked Hegel's statements on the law of gravitation, and which from time to time has burst into somewhat lurid flame. The controversy as opened by Dr. Whewell dealt with questions of physics. But in the year 1865, Dr Stirling, in the second volume of *The Secret of Hegel*, enlarged the field of discussion by translating Hegel's note on the precise nature of the notion of the mathematical Infinite, in which the philosopher joins issue with the mathematicians, particularly with Newton, on certain alleged imperfections in their treatment of the fluxional calculus. To his translation Dr. Stirling subjoins remarks laudatory of Hegel, and emphasising those defects in the mathematical doctrine on which Hegel animadverts. Such imperfections are—

" Quanta by very definition no longer Quanta, yet treated as Quanta ;—omission *because of* insignificance, but omission obligatory and indispensable *in spite of* insignificance, proof necessary from elsewhere, yet pretensions above any elsewhere ; great results of the operation, but the operation itself granted incorrect , an incorrect operation, but absolutely correct results." (*Secret*, ii 380)

Dr. Stirling further refers to striking and instructive

" observations in regard to the show of mathematical
proof " (put forth by mathematicians) " in matters
known from experience alone," takes delight in the
felicitous home-thrusts delivered to Newton and others
(p. 381), and above all, finds that in a criticism of the
process by which the second lemma of the second book of
the *Principia* determines the fluxion of a product, " Hegel
has succeeded in striking his harpoon into that vast
whale—Newton " (p. 363). These utterances were virtually a challenge to mathematicians, and the challenge
became express and personal when Dr Stirling, anim-
adverting in the *Edinburgh Evening Courant* on allusions
to Hegel made by Professor Tait in a University lecture,
called that gentleman's attention to the " harpoon "
passage just cited, and asked him " whether or not even
in his opinion Hegel is right and Newton wrong ? "
This challenge appeared December 21, 1868   On
February 1, 1869, Professor Tait and Sir William Thomson
found opportunity to allude to the matter in a discussion
in the Royal Society of Edinburgh, and without entering
into detail, showed by concrete examples of varying
velocity, such as are offered by railway trains and steam-
boats, that Newton's process was that which was naturally
suggested by his physical conception of a fluxion, and
that Hegel's criticism was based on an unnatural (and
therefore incorrect) view of the problem.   It seemed,
however, to be desirable to take up the matter more fully ,
and on May 17 Professor Tait laid before the Society a
paper on " Hegel and the Metaphysics of the Fluxional
Calculus," written by me.   The publication of this paper
elicited a newspaper controversy between Dr. Stirling and
myself, in which neither party gave way on any point ,
and then the discussion slumbered for three years, to be
again awakened by the publication of Dr. Stirling's recent
book [1]   Of this book about forty pages are devoted to

[1] *Lectures on the Philosophy of Law   Together with Whewell and
Hegel, and Hegel and Mr W. R Smith, a Vindication in a Physico-
Mathematical Regard* (1873)

the vindication of Hegel in the mathematical reference,
partly criticising my paper, partly giving new statements
of Hegel's doctrines on this head

Were the controversy thus reopened, one merely
personal between Dr Stirling and myself, it would be
unfair to claim for it the interest of the literary public
But the little history which I have just given will suffice
to show that the cause of which I appear as advocate is,
in fact, the cause of mathematics, and particularly of
Newtonian mathematics, impugned by the head, in our
country, of a great metaphysical school. And while I
alone am responsible for the way in which the cause is
conducted, the interests at stake are not merely those of
my own literary reputation—though that certainly must
suffer a severe shock if Dr. Stirling's strictures are just—
but essentially the interests of mathematical science, and
especially of that physico-mathematical school which is
the heir of Newton's methods and ideas   So much Dr.
Stirling evidently feels when he " laments the compromise
I have brought upon important interests " (p 105), and
when he associates with my paper " the rabid nonsense,
not only in English, but even in French, that our mathematicians have written against him " (p. 139)   The last
allusion must necessarily be obscure to the public ; but
those who have followed the controversy in its earlier
stage will judge that the reference is to a translation in a
French journal of the remarks of Professor Tait and Sir
William Thomson, already referred to as forming part of
the *Proceedings* of the Royal Society of Edinburgh   Let
me observe, in passing, that the words of these leaders of
science were confined strictly to the mathematical point
involved in Newton's process.   Dr Stirling, I imagine,
is the only man in Europe who would care to apply to such
a statement of such men the words " rabid nonsense."

But while Dr. Stirling is correct in assuming that I did
not step forth in this controversy without the conviction
that I have the mathematicians on my side, he has fallen

into serious errors of fact as to the malign influence which
he supposes me to have exercised over the opinions of the
leaders of physical science in Scotland.   It is asserted at
p 127 that a supposed mistake in my paper (which I shall
presently show to be no mistake) " misled " these gentlemen into their statements before the Royal Society of
Edinburgh—statements we have seen made months before
my paper was written, and nearly a year before it was
published [1]

Let us pass, however, to take up on their own merits
the questions in dispute.   The dispute, it has been seen,
turned in the first instance on a single point—on the
correctness of the process by which Newton derives the
fluxion of a product.   But, as every mathematician knows,
this point is so cardinal that any flaw in the deduction
necessarily vitiates the whole processes of the fluxional
calculus.   When Hegel, therefore, in this connection speaks
of an operation performed by Newton which, though
elementary, is nevertheless incorrect ; when he talks of
the pressing necessity which could bring a Newton to palm
on himself the deception of such a proof, he, in fact, teaches
that the whole proof of the algebraic relation between
fluent and fluxion is deceptive and unsound   Dr. Stirling
does not seem to see this ; but I think it may be possible
to convince him of so much on Hegel's own showing.
" The whole method of the calculus," says Hegel at the
commencement of his second mathematical note,[2] " is
settled in the proposition that $dx^n = nx^{n-1}dx$ . . . the
derivation of the following forms—*of the differential of a*

[1] Still more extraordinary is the liberty which Dr. Stirling has
allowed himself in suspecting my influence in certain utterances of
Professor Tait with regard to Leibnitz—a suspicion utterly ungrounded,
and which can have occurred only as the development of a fixed idea, by
which Dr. Stirling has come to conceive of me as the evil genius of
Scottish physicists.

[2] *Werke* (Ed 1841), vol. iii p. 316   The paging of this edition differs
from that of the edition quoted by Dr. Stirling and formerly by myself.
Passages cited from the book now before me will be found about eleven
pages further on in the other edition.

product, of an exponential magnitude, and so on, flows mechanically therefrom." That is, the method of the calculus is settled (*absolvirt*) when the fluxion of x^n is known. And Dr. Stirling must see that if I know the fluxion of xy, I have only to put $y = x$ to get the fluxion of x^2, from which, by an ordinary mathematical induction, I can again rise to x^3, x^4, and finally to x^n, so putting myself in possession of the whole method Thus surely the vital nature of the deduction of the fluxion of the product xy is abundantly manifest, and if Newton deceived himself in this matter the whole structure of his calculus is built on delusion. For Newton certainly imagined that his method rested on a system of strict mathematical deduction, in which " the very smallest errors are not to be neglected " (*Introd. ad quadraturam curvarum*), and the keystone of this system of deduction is just the fluxion of a product.

Will it then be believed that under these circumstances Dr. Stirling flatly denies that Hegel in this matter accuses Newton of any error whatever ? The only errors of Newton to which Hegel has made any allusion are, we are told, two quite different mistakes, made known to the philosopher by Lagrange and Schubert respectively. For in the matter of the fluxion of the product, *Hegel admits the result to be right, and objects only " to the formal expedient in justification of it,"* that is, to the mathematical proof of the result (p. 109). Is not Dr. Stirling aware that the gravest charge of error that can be brought against a mathematician is by universal consent just this, that he has brought out a true result by expedients formally incorrect ? Were Dr Stirling a man of less moral earnestness, one would be tempted to see in such an argument a mere play of conscious sophistry But manifestly in this case the apparent jest is put forth in bitter earnest. It is even made matter of grievous accusation against me that I have " enormously misrepresented " Hegel, " confounding logical unsatisfactoriness with mathematical inaccuracy," when I venture to state that the German philosopher represents Newton as having fallen into " real errors," and as having determined the unlucky fluxion before us "in a manner analytically unsound." The expressions " real errors," " analytically unsound," are quoted from my Royal Society paper, and the second expression is recurred to by Dr. Stirling on p 127, as a clear proof that I have misunderstood·Hegel   The latter " knows the result to be analytically *sound* , he only objects to an apparent arithmetical " (more correctly *algebraical*, since the operation is performed on letters, not on numbers) "stratagem in deduction of it." At first sight this sentence appears meaningless, for every arithmetical or algebraic operation falls as species under the genus *Analysis* , and so the objectionable arithmetical (algebraical) stratagem involves of necessity analytical unsoundness   But Dr Stirling, as we learn at page 124, has a meaning of his own for the word *analysis*, which shall indicate what concerns the higher calculus, as opposed to what is merely arithmetical.   Dr. Stirling seems to have concluded that I must necessarily take the word in this sense because I had taken objection to Hegel for identifying analytical with arithmetical process.   In fact my objection was directed against the identification of the genus with the species   This would have been obvious to any one familiar with mathematical language , and it is simply the lack of such familiarity that has led Dr. Stirling to say that I have " utterly failed to see what Hegel meant, whether arithmetically or analytically." [1]

The sum of our argument then is this · Hegel admits the correctness of Newton's result, in the sense of admitting that the fluxion which Newton gives is that which, applied in concrete problems—say of geometry—gives correct results   But he denies that Newton has got the

[1] I am thus not called upon to go into the lesson on the etymological sense of the word " analytical " which Dr Stirling reads me at p 124 But a very moderate knowledge of Greek would have shown that the word cannot possibly mean " dissoluble."

fluxion by a process analytically, technically, algebraically, formally correct. To Dr. Stirling, this seems a small matter, a matter of logic rather than of mathematics, a matter not amounting to real error. But to Newton, and to all Newtonians, the charge is of the gravest order ; for they know that with the deduction of this fluxion the whole calculus, in its concrete applications as well as in its theory, must fall, and that Newton's grand scheme of subduing the unconquered realms of geometry by a method rivalling the logical precision of the ancients, must be reckoned as a vain chimæra. But they know, too, that Newton's plan is no chimæra, that his method does possess every particle of the precision of the ancient method of exhaustions, and therefore they regard with contempt, rather than with anger, the attempt of Hegel to subvert the insubvertible. And, strange to say, *they have Dr Stirling on their side.* For it is now admitted that the expedient which in *The Secret of Hegel*, and in letter after letter in the *Courant*, was declared utterly indefensible, is, as a matter of fact, " unimpeachable, and in its simplicity and efficiency does the usual honour to Newton's extraordinary penetration and unrivalled resource " (p. 129).

In admitting for himself and Hegel a " misleading " on this point, Dr. Stirling is careful to observe that his admission " is wholly unavailable in excuse of Mr Smith, who has utterly failed to see what Hegel meant, whether arithmetically or analytically " But perhaps the recollection of former persistency for so many years in one error, may dispose a man so candid as Dr. Stirling to contemplate the possibility of his having misrepresented me as well as Newton. He may possibly be aided in this contemplation by the statements of the present paper ; and he may even be inclined to admit that the fact that I and the other mathematicians, whose utterances are characterised as " rabid nonsense," have always upheld the view which Dr. Stirling now admits to be right, creates an appreciable

presumption in favour of the hypothesis that we have
some understanding of the matter in hand.   But instead
of dwelling on these purely personal, and therefore indifferent, matters let me signalise the important consequences for this whole controversy of the admission so
gracefully made by Dr. Stirling.   In one word—if Newton
is right in this matter it appears, on Dr. Stirling's and
Hegel's own showing, that the whole theory of the calculus,
which can be deduced from this one determination by the
very processes which Hegel himself calls mechanical (as
quoted above, p. 3), is " really unimpeachable," is free
from the paradoxes enumerated in *The Secret of Hegel*
(above, p. 1), and, in brief, is a reasoned system of mathematical truth which gives no ground whatever for Hegel's
assertion " that there is a contradiction in the very
method on which, as a science, it rests " (Hegel, iii. 274 ;
Secret, ii. 339).   And with this result the mathematicians
may very well rest satisfied, and, while heartily inviting
metaphysicians to study so invaluable a branch of science,
and to find, if they can, its place in the whole of human
thought, they are quite entitled to use their own freedom
in deciding whether they shall concern themselves further
with the lucubrations of a philosopher who, as Dr. Stirling
himself suggests (p. 129), did not give himself the trouble
to examine Newton's investigations at first hand.

But while this position is very legitimate to mathematicians as a class, I, personally, am bound to go further,
having undertaken in my former paper not merely to
vindicate Newton, but to inquire into the positive mathematical worth of the remarks which Hegel offers in order
to clear up in his own way that obscurity which he finds
spread over the statements of mathematicians on the
theory of the calculus   Now there are, of course, unwise
mathematicians, as there are unwise metaphysicians.   It
was, therefore, quite possible for Hegel to find utterances
about the calculus in which an acute, even though mathematically unpractised, eye could detect obvious absurdity

But on the whole the result to which my investigation led me was, that the darkness experienced by Hegel was due to his imperfect training, not to any defect in the mathematical theory, notably at least not in Newton's theory. And I found that in this darkness Hegel was so unlucky as to stumble upon the method of Lagrange, and to accept it as relatively best as his guide.   This method he proposes to bring " into its due abstraction " (cf Stirling, p 134), but, while still darkly labouring at his task, is clumsy enough to make modifications on the method, which not only changes its mathematical character and analytical accuracy, but really (though, of course, unconsciously) amount to the suggestion of what I have ironically called " a Hegelian calculus." On these results Dr. Stirling joins issue with me, and, curiously overlooking the obvious irony of my statements, assumes that I imagine that Hegel *intended* to suggest new mathematical processes. I am assured, therefore, that I have simply deluded myself, and that Hegel never made a mathematical suggestion in his life. I shall show in due time that he made more than one such suggestion ; but of course I shall not deny that he did so in ignorance, out of sheer incompetence to distinguish between metaphysical and mathematical modification of the statements of Lagrange. And thus Hegel points to his own disciples the lesson that no one has a right to speak on the principles of a science which he has not mastered in its essential detail.

My work, then, falls very clearly into two parts. Hegel and Dr Stirling detect in the calculus an obscurity, manifesting itself to their eyes in the logical inconsistency of processes correct in result , and they claim a light thrown on the method by the introduction of the "Notion" which suggests that the operation shall be made " to depend not on the quantity but on the quality required " (Stirling, p. 129)   To this I object, *first*, that the supposed obscurity and logical inconsistency are to be found in the mind of Hegel, not in the processes of Newton ; and *second*, that be the Notion what it may, we need not look for light from it on this matter, since it has lighted its great master himself—into a mathematical ditch.

Now the first of my two points seems really to be proved when we find Hegel vitally wrong in so essential a matter as the fluxion of a product. Dr. Stirling, however, is too little of a mathematician to be able to distinguish between vital and venial error in such a subject, and finds that " on the whole Hegel made himself very sufficiently acquainted with whatever he was minded to talk upon." If this means only, as regards the case before us, that Hegel had glanced through a number of mathematical books, new and old, I have nothing to object, but if it is claimed that he understood what he read, I can only say that he thoroughly miscomprehended Newton and Lagrange, and that he never learned what mathematicians mean by a *Limit*, by *Continuity*, and by *Evaluation*. I offered in my former paper a few of the many proofs of these assertions, which are heaped up *a misura di carboni* in Hegel's writings. The proofs were given by me as far as possible in the precise and unambiguous language and formulæ of mathematics, and I am the less called upon to repeat these technical arguments, that it is perfectly evident that Dr. Stirling was unable to follow my symbolic statements But as this inability has not modified the fierceness of assertion with which he condemns all this portion of my work as absolute misapprehension, I may be permitted to offer some examples of the way in which he has thought it fair to cut knots that he cannot untie.

My first example shall be one in which Dr Stirling rests his case on a charge of garbling Hegel's words. In my paper of 1869 I wrote as follows :—

" Purely analytical considerations without any physical basis were held, Hegel thinks, to furnish in this way physical laws. In support of this view, Hegel triumphantly refers to ' the Newtonian proof of his fundamental proposition in the theory of gravitation, compared with Schubert's *Astronomy*, where it is admitted that . . . in

the point, which is the nerve of the proof, the truth is not
as Newton assumes it ' (!) And so, upheld by the dictum
of this forgotten astronomer, Hegel goes on to inveigh
against the mere jugglery by which Newton, already
knowing Kepler's results, avails himself of the ' mist of the
infinitely little,' to bring out apparent mathematical
proof of these results.''

I naturally add that this judgment not only indicates
incredible ignorance of the reasonings of the *Principia*,
but casts a most unfair slur on Newton's honesty. Now,
Dr. Stirling does not pretend to say that there is any real
error in Newton's reasonings. But he urges (p 112) that
Hegel had been told, if not by Newton, yet certainly by
others, that these proofs amount to a supersession of
Kepler's discovery ; and that the philosopher's protest
is directed simply against this idea   The answer to this
apology is that Hegel was told no such thing by any one
able to read the *Principia* ; for, in fact, Kepler's discovery
is the express experimental basis of the Newtonian theory
And it is plain from the reference to Schubert that Hegel
is objecting, not to some sense put by others on Newton's
work, but to that work itself viewed as mathematical
reasoning.[1] Hegel, therefore, cannot be defended unless
it can be shown that I have misstated the force of his
reference to Schubert. This Dr. Stirling accomplishes as
follows .—

" Hegel has to allude to an astronomer, Schubert, who
shall have ' admitted that in the point which is the nerve
of the proof, it is not *exactly* so situated as Newton
assumes.' Mr Smith's manner of stating this is as follows.
. . . That one sees is categorical, and to accomplish this
categorical effect, Mr Smith made a break in his quotation,
and omitted the italicised ' not *exactly* ' Yet one might
not be very wide of the truth if one said, that very

---

[1] In dealing with Whewell on this same subject of Kepler and
Newton, Dr Stirling observes, " that what Hegel means by proof is
Hegel's own metaphysics " (p. 97)   But this observation cannot apply
here , for the defect of proof, which Hegel has heard of from an astronomer, must be mathematical, not metaphysical.

italicising of 'exactly' is precisely the 'nerve' of the quotation." (Pages 108, 109.)

This is a grave charge. Yet, strange to say, it is my translation that is right, and Dr. Stirling's that is wrong ; for what Hegel says is, " dass es sich nicht *genau* so, d.i., in dem Punkte, welcher der Nerv des Beweises ist, sich nicht so verhalte, wie Newton annimmt." And still more strangely, Dr. Stirling himself translates the passage correctly in *The Secret of Hegel*, ii. 377, " admitted that the truth is not *exactly* so, *i.e.* that in the point which is the nerve of the proof the truth is not as Newton assumes it." I simply transcribed Dr. Stirling's own words , and, if I omitted the words " not *exactly* so," I gave Hegel's own explanation of their meaning.

This is not the only case where philological inexactitude has prevented Dr. Stirling from doing justice to my arguments.

In the case of a falling body, the space described is proportional to the square of the time during which the body has been falling. Lagrange, stating this fact, remarks that Nature does not present any case in which the distance passed through is proportional to the cube of the time. On this Hegel, always full of Kepler's laws, says that we have at least a motion for which the cube of the distance is proportional to the square of the time, and begs the mathematicians to apply their calculus to the differential of this motion. This remark of Hegel is equivalent to a proof of absolute mathematical incompetency. Kepler's law does not mean that the cube of the distance traversed by the planet is proportional to the square of the time during which it has been moving , but simply that each planet goes round the sun in a time the square of which is proportioned to the cube of its mean distance from the sun The proposal to differentiate the formula expressing this fact shows that Hegel did not know what sort of quantities are really capable of differentiation. Now, Dr. Stirling's own knowledge on this matter is plainly on a level with Hegel's, for, without admitting or denying the justice of my comments on so ludicrous an error, he simply shrinks behind the ægis of Lagrange He repeats Hegel's citation from Lagrange, and the philosopher's own remark, in one continuous quotation, and adds . " What part Lagrange has in this must be determined by others Hegel certainly begins by quoting Lagrange." Now, I will not urge that Dr. Stirling was bound to consult Lagrange's book for himself , but it was his duty to observe that Hegel carefully distinguishes, by the use of indirect speech, between Lagrange's statement and his own comment. To ignore this implies either serious philological inaccuracy, or a conscious imitation of the tactics of the ostrich when overtaken by her pursuers.[1]

Perhaps the most absolute proof of Hegel's incompetency to criticise the doctrine of the calculus, as set forth by mathematicians, is to be found in the fact that he never learned to understand such fundamental notions as *limit*, *variable*, and *continuous quantity* This fact was brought out in my paper with the aid of a certain array of mathematical symbols which I cannot reproduce here. But as it is precisely this part of my work which has been most vigorously impugned by Dr. Stirling, I shall leave my symbols to fight their own battle, which they are very well

[1] These are not the only cases in which Dr. Stirling's translation is defective. Thus, in the passage cited at p 120, there is no contrast between generative and generated magnitudes, but only between generated and vanishing magnitudes Again, at p. 112, a variation from the text of Hegel, which I ventured to point out, is defended as a necessary emendation against " the air of correctness to the contrary due to—Mr Smith's judicious collocation of passages." This sneer is uncalled for, as I simply pointed out a fact, in justification of a trifling divergence from the translation given in the *Secret* But I have no hesitation in saying that Dr. Stirling's emendation is based on absolute misapprehension of Hegel's meaning, which is not that " Newton *now* proceeds to explain what is to be understood by such and such an expression," but that it was the custom of the time merely to explain the way in which terms are to be understood. Dr. Stirling's rendering does violence to the context, and demands, not simply the change of *nur* to *nun*, but of *wurde erklärt* to *wird erklärt*

able to do, and will endeavour to give fresh proof of my assertions in a more popular form [1]

I begin with the conceptions of *variation* and *continuity*, conceptions which in the calculus occur associated, in the notion of *continuous variation* A variable quantity is one which can take various values. A quantity continuously variable, which is the only kind of quantity that admits of differentiation, is one which between certain limits can have any value you please, which, in fact, runs on between these limits, not by leaps, but by a continuous flow. Time, for example, is such a quantity ; for since the birth of Christ it has run through every possible value between o and 1872 years But the time which a planet takes to go round the sun is not continuously variable , for you cannot find a planet to fit any periodic time you may please

---

[1] One or two remarks may be allowed by way of note on certain criticisms directly affecting the use of symbols At the foot of p 113, Dr Stirling seems to take an objection *in limine* against the translation of " perfectly general " Hegelian language into symbols which Hegel had not before him He might as well object to translation from German into English Again, to my statement, that a differential coefficient, or, what is the same thing, the ratio of the fluxion of y to the fluxion of x, is a fraction with definite numerator and denominator, it is replied that Newton himself cannot have regarded mere symbols as possessing " definite values " (p. 114) Here perhaps Dr. Stirling and I are at cross purposes from attaching different senses to the word *definite*, which I do not use as equivalent to *constant* But questions of language apart, the matter is clear What I assert, and what of course is a mathematical truism, is that the differential coefficient of y with respect to x is no more indeterminate, no less fully quantitative than x and y themselves This Hegel denies, when he says (iii 292) that on proceeding to the limit the ratio $\frac{dy}{dx}$ vanishes " insofern es ein Quantum wäre " This is what I mean when I speak of Hegel as setting up an indeterminate $\frac{dy}{dx}$. Dr Stirling, not observing that the " nerve " of this expression lies in the word *indeterminate*, allows himself (p 125) to be sarcastic on me for " seeing Hegel ' set up ' $\frac{dy}{dx}$ " Again, this false conception of $\frac{dy}{dx}$ vanishing, *quatenus* Quantum, leads Hegel to find certain insoluble logical difficulties in the mathematical use of a binomial expansion to determine the actual value of $\frac{dy}{dx}$. This I have called " knocking down the indeterminate $\frac{dy}{dx}$ which he has just set up " Dr Stirling calls these words " incredibly inapposite " (p 130) But if a philosopher insists on holding a quantity to vanish when it does not do so, and then, a few pages later, expatiates on the contradictions arising from his own conceptions, he surely *is* knocking down what he set up.

to name   If Hegel had mastered this distinction, he could
not have made that unlucky suggestion about differentiating Kepler's law of periodic times.   Nevertheless, Dr.
Stirling holds that the great merit of Hegel in this department is just the stress he lays on the qualitative difference
between continuous and discrete quantity, and he cannot conceal his amazement that I should have asserted
the opposite (p 124).   Obviously there is some mis-
understanding here as regards the meaning of words.   In
fact, the idea which Dr. Stirling attaches to continuity is
not that of quantity running through a continuous series
of values, but that of quantity hanging together ; of a
connected space, for example, as contrasted with a series
of unconnected lines.   That is, continuity is not to his
mind associated with the idea of variability, but with the
idea of squares and cubes, in which we pass from relatively
discrete lines to continuous area, and from relatively
discrete planes to continuous solids.   It is with transitions
of this sort that Hegel and Dr. Stirling conceive the
calculus to be interested   We have not yet reached a
point where we can ask what value pertains to this way of
looking at the matter   But as Dr. Stirling and his master
are clearly quite unconscious that they have here diverged
in language as well as in thought from the mathematicians,
it is quite plain that they have not apprehended the
meaning which the latter attach to continuous variation

As to the *limit*, I can be more brief   Mathematical
tyros almost invariably stumble at this notion, and Hegel
is no exception to the rule when he speaks of the calculus,
in contrast to the method of indivisibles, as beginning with
" *limits* between which the independently determinate
thing (das Fursichbestimmte) lies, and at which it aims as
its goal " (iii. 353)   No more absolute misapprehension
is possible.   A mathematical limit is not the boundary
within which something lies, but the actual value of a
quantity under certain extreme circumstances   For
example, the line joining the points in which two circles

intersect becomes *in the limit* a common tangent—*i.e.*
the tangent is the substitute for the chord, when the
circles come to touch instead of to cut.   But evidently
the tangent is in no sense a boundary within which the
chords lie, nor is any implication of inexactness or approximation to be found in the expression.   I may observe that
the application to the calculus of the idea of a limit is not
to be accomplished in a satisfactory way, except in connection with the idea of *rate*, which Hegel is quite absolute
in refusing to admit.   This is the source of all the supposed
logical difficulties which he finds to encompass the method
of limits, but which really attach to his own refusal to
conceive of quantity as generated by flux.

Now, to Dr. Stirling this refusal is one of Hegel's chief
virtues   To call on the philosopher, as I have done, to
look at quantity in the Newtonian way, is to introduce
" contradictory commixture of the dross and slag of the
Vorstellung with the metal of the *Begriff*," is to " muddle
and puddle the notion—the quality—that that Newton
himself declares independent of quantity—by mixed
expressions *through* which the due abstraction only *shows*
but to an eye that is educated."   Or again, Hegel says the
same thing as I, reporting Newton, say, only he says it in
due abstraction, " in the language of the Begriff."   Now
if this were only true, one would be very glad to have it so
If Hegel had understood Newton's notion as Newton
himself states it, and then had freed it from unnecessary
dross, we could have nothing but admiration for his
philosophic skill.   But what I object to Hegel is, that he
applied his powers of abstraction to Newton's *language*
before he understood its meaning, and so cut himself off
from all intelligent contact with Newtonian processes, and
fell into the absurd errors which have been sufficiently
exposed.   In fact, here as elsewhere, Hegel and Dr.
Stirling have simply been indulging in that metaphysical
pride which goes before a fall.   Had they first learned the
calculus as Newton teaches it, and condescended to use for

a time the humble but perfectly truthful *Vorstellungen*
of the fluxional method, they might have spoken with
authority, and found willing hearers. But when Dr.
Stirling, disclaiming for himself " all pretensions to the
position even of a student " in mathematics, takes it upon
him to separate the dross from the pure gold of a Newton,
the incongruity between the humility of the disclaimer
and the arrogance of the enterprise is manifest to every
reader.   And of course we find accordingly that Dr.
Stirling is not even able to reproduce the despised *Vorstellung* with accuracy. He tells us that Newton himself
declares the *quality* independent of the *quantity* (p. 113).
Newton does no such thing.   He tells us that a " square
is a quantum , but it may be conceived as increasing or
decreasing, and if it be so conceived, there can be conceived also to lie in it a principle that, whether there be
increase or decrease, is always the same—infinite, then,
non-quantitative, qualitative only " (p. 121).   Newton
would have held up his hands in horror at such a caricature
of his view, and would have told his critic that, to say
nothing of other points, one great use of the moment was
to show, *by changes in itself*, whether the quantity of which
it is the moment is increasing, diminishing, or stationary
Again, Dr. Stirling obviously misunderstands the sense
in which Newton says that Nature shows us the generation
of quantity by flow.   " Who ever saw lines flowing into
planes, planes into solids, or sides rotating into angles ?
And yet who has not seen sand and salt . . . and a
pocketful of marbles ? " (p. 110).   Well, no one has ever
seen sides rotating into angles ; and Dr. Stirling would
not have imagined that Newton had said this, had he not
been hampered by his queer conception of mathematical
continuity, by which the continuum must always arise
out of the discrete—the angle out of something that is not
angle.   What Newton says is that when Nature presents
us with the process of *measuring out* quantity, the operation is not performed by successive applications of foot-

rule, but by continuous motion. The astronomer, for
example, has to deal with the eccentric angle of the
earth's orbit. Is it according to Nature to say that for
every minute of time some two seconds of arc are clapped
on to this angle ? Does not Nature compel him to say
that the sides of the angle are opening out continuously,
and that so the angle grows ? So blind is the critic to this
sense that, in quoting from my paper Newton's statements
on the point, he breaks his quotation in order to omit the
decisive sentence which I had carefully italicised. *Hae
Geneses in rerum natura locum vere habent et in motu
corporum quotidie cernuntur.* And now, in passing from
this head, I will simply ask Dr. Stirling whether he believes
in a geometry without intuition, whether the necessity for
intuition may not extend to the geometry of motion as well
as the geometry of rest, and whether, therefore, it may not
be the case that in this matter the notion is inseparable
from the intuition ? A presumption at least that this is
the case flows from the fact which I now pass on to
establish, that Hegel's own abstract notion breaks down
mathematically in the completest way   This, it will be
remembered, is the second and last part of the work
before me

In *The Secret of Hegel*, only the *first* of Hegel's mathematical notes were reproduced. But as the philosopher
himself considers the real difficulty of the calculus to lie
in its *application*, my paper extended to the *second* note,
and showed that it is just in the application that Hegel's
notion fails.   Dr. Stirling now suggests that it is best
to begin with the *third* note, which deals mainly with
Cavalleri's method of indivisibles.   There is something to
be said in favour of this suggestion   Cavalleri's method,
in its more elementary examples, is easier than the general
theory of Newton, and on the whole Hegel has understood
the mathematical work involved pretty well   He does
not, however, follow with intelligence anything that is not
extremely elementary, and still very remote from that

general doctrine of fluxions which is the proper subject of the present controversy, and he again (iii. 356; cf Stirling, p 117) talks absolute nonsense about Kepler's laws The advantage to be drawn from the study of this note is a clearer grasp of that Hegelian view of the relation of the continuum to the discrete, which I have already signalised, and to which I need not now return But before passing on to the controversy proper, I may observe that Dr. Stirling certainly does not understand Cavalleri. Thus, he says that there is present in a parallelogram "a single regula, a single proportion, which is determinative of it," and which "is wholly qualitative," "is the spiritual soul, as it were, of the actual parallelogram." This mystical conception of the regula runs through several pages, and gives a fine Hegelian colour to Cavalleri's work. And obviously the regula is supposed to be at bottom one with the Newtonian moment, of which we have found a similar account (cf. p. 126) But what is the regula ? Simply as its name denotes, a rule or ruler, a perfectly arbitrary straight line, set down in order that other lines may be drawn parallel to it Give me a parallelogram, and any line anywhere in the plane of the parallelogram may be taken as the regula, the ruler by which lines important for the investigation shall be drawn. The regula is just as much the spiritual soul of the parallelo-gram as the carving-knife is the soul of a leg of mutton. Dr. Stirling, then, has not understood Cavalleri, and I suspect, though here I speak with diffidence, that he has not understood what Hegel says of Cavalleri , for though the German philosopher is unmathematically vague in what he says of regula, he does not seem to give any countenance to the error of his expositor.

Although thus, as regards Cavalleri and the mathe-matical side of Hegel's third note, Dr. Stirling is talking quite beside the question, we are told that the gist of what Hegel says in this note is pretty well " the gist, at the same time, of all that he has to say in the mathematical reference generally " Hegel, namely, teaches us to regard " the mathematical infinite, whether as in series or as in the fiction of infinitesimals," as a mere disguise by which it is attempted to conceal the necessary incommensurability of quantities differing in quality (pp. 118, 119) Right lines, for example, are not curves, and so when we attempt to rectify a curve—*i.e.* to treat it as if it were homogeneous with the straight line—incommensurability arises (p 115). Hence the mathematical obscurity of the calculus, the necessity for introducing infinite series to fill up the practical rift between the pieces. It would probably be vain to object that the mathematical doctrine of the incommensurable is by no means connected with the doctrine of infinitesimals in the way here supposed—that no mathematician ever used an infinitesimal to express or elude incommensurability But in view of the distinct assertion that the rectification of a curve always gives rise to infinite series or their equivalents, I will state that the perimeter of the cardioid is four times the length of the straight line which divides the curve symmetrically It appears, therefore, that the " gist " of Hegel's mathematical remarks involves a proposition mathematically untrue , and the inconsistency with fact here brought out, of course vitiates the subsequent argument, that the algebraic exponent of difference of quality is the occurrence of squares or higher powers in the variables, and that therefore the presence of powers higher than the first is the essential character of such variability as invites fluxional treatment. All this only shows that Hegel and his expositor, instead of learning the science on which they desire to theorise, have made a few superficial and inaccurate abstractions from half-digested facts, and have covered the nakedness of their scientific induction with the ample and impenetrable mantle of the Notion.

Instead of dwelling on this point, I shall bring the whole matter to a final issue by taking up the *application* of this Hegelian notion. We have seen, in dealing with the criticism of Newton, that Hegel finds invincible logical obstacles to all attempts to give a mathematical proof of the relation of fluxion to fluent. The fluxion, he says, is simply one term of a mathematical expansion—the term, namely, in which a certain qualitative meaning lies. It is vain to attempt to isolate this term from the other terms of the series by regarding the latter as relatively insignificant in quantity ; you should simply define such a term of the expansion as the fluxion, and then show, in concrete problems of geometry, that this term has a geometric (and so qualitative) meaning. Any other way of dealing with the matter, and therefore all ways previous to Lagrange, involve certain inadmissible logical assumptions, and so give but a simulation of proof, where there is really only the observation of the fact, that the calculus, regarded as a rule of art, gives (methodically and more easily) results which the ancient geometry had proved synthetically These strictures are developed in a passage translated by Dr Stirling (p. 134, *sq.*) with special reference to Barrow, but it is certain that Hegel regarded them as not wholly inapplicable to Newton. It is really incredible that Dr. Stirling should not see that the whole state of the case as here set down is quite changed, when we find that Newton, contrary to Hegel's belief, had actually succeeded in proving the deduction of the fluxion without any objectionable use of the infinitely small. For in this case the supposed " simulation " had disappeared from the calculus long before Lagrange was born, and there is no particle of ground for bestowing on the French analyst the credit of " striking into the scientific path proper." Therefore I have said, and now repeat, that Hegel stumbled on Lagrange's method *in the dark*, through sheer ignorance of what Newton had already achieved.

But, again, Hegel pursues Lagrange's method in darkness, or rather, proposing to pursue it, diverges from it into absurdity. What the mathematician and the metaphysician have in common is to make the formation of the

fluxions matter of mere definition, and thereafter to seek
for them a geometrical or other practical meaning.   To
this end, Lagrange proves (but in a way not convincing)
that it is always possible to expand $f(x + i)$ in ascending
powers of i, and defines the coefficients of the expansion
as derived functions (fluxions) of $f x$.   Hegel, to simplify
matters, expands, not $f(x + i)$, but $f(x + 1)$, *i.e.* takes *unity*
as the increment of x In view of this change, his process
becomes what I have formerly called " an excessively
clumsy adaptation of the method of Lagrange."   Yet
Dr. Stirling without comparing, without even professing
to compare, Hegel with Lagrange, " sees no reason for
assuming Hegel not to have correctly described what he
had simply before him " (viz. Lagrange's method), and
finds that in using the word *adaptation* I have " mis-
apprehended what it is all about " and " fooled myself
into a formal wrangling against a mathematical ratiocina-
tion that nowhere exists "   That is, Hegel shall make the
mathematical change from i, which is sense, to 1, which is
nonsense, and the mathematician who checks him shall
be " fooling himself " [1]

The next step is to find the use of the fluxions after we
have derived them, and this Hegel does, still in dependence
on Lagrange, for the special problem of the tangents of
curves   As Lagrange in this problem uses from the very
first $x + i$, and not Hegel's useless $x + 1$, there is something
touching in the *naïveté* with which Hegel here throws himself into the arms of his friend   But soon his natural
independence of spirit revives, and, having signalised
himself by proposing to throw away a constant in one of
Lagrange's equations, by which the meaning of the equation is utterly changed, he is emboldened to tamper again
with the i, to which he seemed for a moment to have

---

[1] In re-reading my paper, I observe with regret that on p 507, l 10,
i has been printed instead of 1   This erratum obscures the magnitude of Hegel's divergence from Lagrange, but should have been at once
observed by any one who had his eye on the quite explicit statements
of Hegel (iii pp 326, 327) to which I refer

resigned himself   Lagrange cannot prove his point unless he is allowed to make i as small as he pleases   Hegel, afraid of the " notorious increment," will have it that this demand is quite " out of place," and only allows it to become a proper fraction.   No doubt in all this the philosopher is not conscious of spoiling Lagrange's mathematics, to which, as I have said, he returns from time to time with affecting confidence and confusion.   But the error is not the less for that , and the last touch about i involves, as my former paper showed, certain very diverting geometrical absurdities

Through all this Dr. Stirling remains grimly resolute not to consult Lagrange—whose analysis, in fact, is rather difficult to read—and sternly determined to "see no reason for assuming Hegel not to have correctly described what he simply had before him."

II

EARLY THEOLOGICAL ESSAYS

(1868–1870)

I

PROPHECY AND PERSONALITY

A FRAGMENT

*   *   *   *

WHILE it is true that history and prophecy alike are in all their parts the work of God, it is equally true that both in all their parts are products of human personality. Some, perhaps, who agreed to our previous leading principle may object to this statement as evacuating prophecy of its properly supernatural character But such an objection is baseless , history as well as prophecy is supernatural, and if we recognise in miracles not mere occasional outbreaks of divine power, but the continuous manifestation of God in history terminating in the great permanent miracle of the incarnation, we shall not fear to dishonour prophecy by placing it side by side with history. And just as history, in spite of the supernatural factor that has always been present in it, and still is present in the working of the divine Spirit in believers,— as history is notwithstanding in all its parts the product of human personality , so it is with prophecy also. The prophet in becoming a prophet never for one instant ceased to be a man. Not one element of his personality was destroyed or suspended ; the prophetic inspiration added something, but took away nothing of the feelings and thoughts and desires that built up his previous life. It is not enough to say that the prophet is not a mere

lyre struck by the plectrum of the Spirit ; to admit that
the revelation was not only *through* the prophet but *to* the
prophet, and so had to be intelligently apprehended by
him before it could be given forth to others—this is not
enough unless we carefully observe how much of real
personal activity such an intelligent apprehension involves.   For many who claim to have risen above a mere
mechanical theory of prophecy yet seem to think that
what the Spirit presented to the prophet was a ready-
made thought or a complete visionary picture of a purely
objective kind which he was then able to lay hold of,
embody in words, and utter.

Now this view seems to me not so much false as
meaningless.   For whatever difference of view exists as
to the objective *per se* (Noumenon or *Ding-an-sich*), there
is no difference of opinion among competent psychologists
as to the fact that what appears to us as objective is
really a product of personal activity acting on certain
subjective elements, that the objective is never apprehended except through the subjective.   If, for example,
a picture stands before me, I do not perceive the colour,
figure, etc., as noumenon, I receive from the picture only a
series of subjective impressions which an exercise of my
own personality builds up into the picture I *really* see
And since all that I really get from without is a series of
impressions which an act of mental activity combines
into a whole, the only guarantee that this whole—the
picture as seen by me—will not contain certain other
elements˙(that the recollection of colours and forms
previously seen, for example, will not mingle with the
sensations I am now receiving, and modify my apprehension of the picture), are the superior vividness of the
sensation over the recollection, and the power I have of
correcting my false impression by constantly renewed contemplation of the object.   These guarantees are clearly
not perfect, and in fact no two men ever carry away the
same image of an object.   On the contrary, if the painter

being omniscient knew exactly what recollections were
running through my mind, he might—though no doubt
the skill required would be infinite—so arrange his
colours that the impression they produced *plus* what my
own mind added would give me exactly the image he
desired.

To apply this to the case of Revelation.   The objective
nature of the vision seems to have been postulated as a
security for the infallibility of the Revelation   But if
nothing can be apprehended as objective in the first
instance, since the vision must anyhow be first broken
down into subjective feelings and built up again by the
person affected before he can apprehend it,—this being
so, it is clear that no absolute security can be given that
the prophet will not add elements of his own.   The
amount of such addition might be indefinitely reduced by
a great vividness of the vision, or by the lengthened
presence thereof, to the eye of the prophet ; but no
complete freedom from admixture would be possible unless
all the prophet's previous recollections were for the time
cancelled, *i.e.* unless he lost his self-consciousness, which
we know he never did.   After all, this would not matter
practically if all revelation were, like that on Sinai, an
actual vivid spectacle before the eye of sense and real
words directed to the bodily ear, but no one will maintain
that the objectivity of the prophetic revelation was of
the nature of material externality to the body.   On the
contrary, we have reason to suppose that the outward
senses were generally closed and the vision seen, or
words heard, presented within.   And in this case all talk
of an objective vision is absurd   When the external
senses are closed to the world without, nothing can remain
but certain subjective feelings succeeding and mingling
with one another, from which objective images or objective thoughts are produced by the pure activity of
the mind.   Now suppose that some of these feelings are
directly excited by the action of the Spirit, yet if self-

consciousness be not annihilated, others will mix with
these which are purely natural, and the thoughts or
pictures that the mind of the prophet produces—and
produces, observe, *wholly* by its own activity—must
contain a mixture of these two elements   We are thus
forced to the conclusion that, since the prophetic consciousness was continuous with the ordinary consciousness, the supernatural revelation was not independent of
the previous thoughts of the prophet but only supplemented these thoughts so as to bring forth a new and
perfect revelation.   The result of the whole process is
an image, visible or audible, if the process of mental
combination be carried on unconsciously ; a thought, if
the operation of the mind be conscious.   In the first
case the whole process falls under the ordinary laws of
mental association, and may be regarded as fully explained
by psychologists.   The process by which certain successions of feelings are interpreted into certain images,
sounds, etc , has in every one become by long habit
quite instinctive, requiring no conscious exertion of the
mind   Here the Divine action must, I think, be confined
to the production of certain of the ultimate subjective
elements thus to be combined.   These elements would
be connected with the organs of sight or hearing according
as the object was to produce a vision or an internal
voice , and as there is little doubt that such feelings are
invariably connected with excitation of the nerves of
sense, we may reasonably suppose that the point at which
the natural explanation fails us and the supernatural
must come in, is when we have traced back the prophetic
visions to an excitation of the nerves not explicable on
natural causes and not subject to any natural limitation
But the capacity of the nerves themselves to conduct
certain definite excitations only will limit the range of
the feelings thus miraculously excited, to which may be
added the further limitation that only a feeling previously
experienced can form part of a visionary image that owes

its formation to the laws of association. These restrictions might be interesting in regard to such visions as
contain theophanies, but otherwise are of little importance. They do not seem to prevent almost any tableau
of a visionary kind being presented to the prophet, provided only that tableau were of such a kind as to incorporate the feelings which the continued natural action
of the mind would engender, and which would correspond
to the material excitations propagated by the cerebrum
through the nerve circles. Every mental operation has
for its counterpart a bodily phenomenon. Mental reproduction is thus connected with the spontaneity of
the cerebrum propagating currents outwards through
the nerves of sense By the dynamical principle of the
" superposition of small motions " these undulations
would produce their own effect in spite of the superadded
supernatural excitation.

But this spontaneity of the cerebrum may flow out in
many different channels, and the supernatural stimulation
will serve in great measure to draw the spontaneous flow
into its own channel, if no strong emotion is present.
But strong emotion or a strong bias of character in any
direction has also a coercing power over the spontaneity,
strongly forcing it into a special course. The course of
these natural movements would more or less readily be
assimilated to those of the supernatural very much in
proportion to the harmony between the vision produced
and the general emotional and intellectual character of
the prophet. Now the prophets seem to have been
generally men of strong character, whose minds could
not readily have been forced out of their current course.
But at the same time that course was almost always, I
believe, the course that the revelation followed. The
strong productiveness of the prophet's mind became a
most important factor in the production of the divine
visions even where the prophet's personality was properly
not involved ; and these visions were generally built out

of the various elements familiar to the mind of the seer.
In the case of men possessed, like all prophets, of a
strong historic sense we must expect that the events of
contemporary history would play an important part in
moulding the visions.

These remarks apply not only to visions proper, in
which, perhaps, the poetic sensibility of the prophet would
be most important, but also to such divine communications as took the form of an internal voice   Here, however, the matter becomes more complicated, for while
the uncontrolled play of the associative powers generally
produces visible images, the internal voice is the form in
which voluntary thinking is generally carried on   For
the present voluntary thought must be excluded ; we
are dealing only with the case, parallel to vision, when
the divine word arose unbidden in the prophet's breast,
and appeared to come from without. In dreams and
even in reveries such cases occur. The course of thought
is determined by the associative powers and kept in a
more or less rational channel not by the will but by
some cause—generally emotive—that retains the mental
currents in a definite course.[1]

On the current supposition that the whole prophecy
was supernaturally announced, it seems impossible that
the naturally generated currents should have failed to
interfere with the divine word, and so the prophet could
not have given a true prophecy. But clearly there was
no double process, a divine word and a running accompaniment of suggested human reverie. Nor was the
human thought suppressed , on the contrary, so much
stimulus was given as kept the associations in the right
course and produced precisely the required effect, without
suspending any natural law. This clearly was only
possible where the prophet's mind was in natural harmony

[1] This is clearly brought out by Iessen (*Psychologie*, p 710), who,
however, hardly reaches the general principle, for which see Bain's
Senses and Intellect (esp pp. 570, 599).

with the revelation. Perhaps the want of this harmony and the necessity of crushing down conflicting currents by a more violent action on the nerves may explain the physical and mental prostration that we read of in the cases of Saul and Balaam.

These considerations tend to show that wherever the prophet was deeply absorbed in the history of his time, all the revelations presented to his mind would be deeply coloured thereby   The deep insight into the hearts of men and the moral bearings of events with which the prophets were gifted must have produced a habitual disposition to view everything in its bearings on the moral necessities of the age. And so, even in the involuntary associations we are treating of, no long train of thought could fail to incorporate some very direct reference to the ethical position of the time. This quite coincides with one half of the principle laid down in the first part of our inquiry, viz. that prophecy could omit no important moral development of the prophet's period   More delicate is the question whether any new moral development of history, which represented quite a new turn in the contest of good and evil, and was not merely the bringing into prominence of something lying latent, could be brought into prophecy

Such an element could not be manifested in a vision proper, but only in the word of the Lord explaining the vision. We have seen that it would be presumptuous to limit the range of the pictorial part of the revelation.   If we admit the supernatural, no reason can be given why infinitely various combinations and successions of images might not rise up in the prophet's mind   But the vision without an accompanying word would give very little real information for two reasons ·

1. The coexistent and the successive can never be clearly separated in a vision. In actual life the distant in space and the distant in time are distinguished by the fact that the former is brought near by muscular exertion

(at least by moving the eyes), while the second approaches independently of bodily movement In the panoramic vision this difference vanishes, and everything rises in a sort of vague succession without even a clear measure of time.

2. The vision *per se* gives only external circumstances which, uninterpreted, would be void of prophetic significance.

Thus if a new moral development be laid open to the prophet, this must happen through the prophetic word. Moreover, the question is not whether it is physically possible that the prophet should be lifted out of his own age to consider the new necessities of a future time, but whether this is morally possible. Now the possibility of really new developments of evil in the world depends on the fact that evil is not an impersonal leaven propagating itself among men, but is disseminated by the active personal thought and energy of evil spirits. So the new element of evil is really a new evil thought, and as this cannot be objectively presented to the prophet, he would have to think it out for himself We have not yet come to speak of the conscious thought of the prophet , but that only makes matters worse. If the prophet could anticipate a new development of evil, this would be by virtue of a Satanic thought coming to him, built up in his mind by precisely the same inspiration that produced the Divine word. There would be a very great moral difficulty in supposing this. But, moreover, there is a great, though not perhaps insuperable psychological difficulty The emotion which filled the whole mind of the prophet was faith in God, a full sympathy with the Divine activity in Redemption. The grand idea that filled the prophet's mind and formed the substratum of all revelation, conditioning all the mental processes by which the details of prophecy were filled in, was that which for the Hebrews was summed up in the word Jehovah. There can be no doubt that this feeling was greatly intensified during the prophetic inspiration which always crushed down all mere personal imperfect feelings which separate man from full harmony with God.   There can be no doubt that the symbolism of Isa. vi. points to this.   In a mind so elevated every mental association would have its direction determined accordingly.   The difficulty that prevented depraved men from becoming prophets of divine truth would still more thoroughly prevent the prophetic inspiration from running along the course of a new development of evil.   I do not think this resistance could be overcome without a mental struggle violent enough to raise the prophet from the state of reverie to a state of conscious thought.

Before passing to this perhaps more interesting part of prophecy, where the prophet was conscious of mental effort in producing his prophecies, we may sum up briefly the results already obtained

The apparent objectivity of any revelation does not prove that it was given objectively to the prophet, but only that his *involuntary* mental energy built it up from subjective elements   These latter are partly supernatural, but also of necessity partly natural, the supernatural part being so adjusted that the result, be it dream or vision, is exactly the desired revelation   But this revelation is built up from its subjective elements by a natural process of association determined in its direction, partly by the material it is working on, but in great measure by the habitual character of the prophet and his emotional state at the time.   In this respect the prophetic vision and Divine word do not differ from an ordinary dream or reverie , for these too depend *in part* only on recollections present to the mind and impressions transmitted by the not wholly dormant senses, and receive their whole colouring and character from the character and emotions of the mind in which they are produced.   It does not therefore appear that the revelations thus presented could ever free themselves from the

limitations of those historical circumstances in which the
prophet was so deeply immersed, and least of all in such
a way as to incorporate a new development of evil, to
think out a new Satanic thought

I must add, with some hesitation, a doubt whether *any*
of the highest forms of revelation, any essentially *new*
thought, not a mere combination of old principles, could
occur where the personality of the prophet was not consciously at work   The laws of association are only capable
of rearranging representative notions (Vorstellungen)
already familiar to the mind.   An entirely new element
supernaturally presented, could find no place in a whole
produced without conscious effort according to these laws,
but could only be apprehended by an effort of personality.   Mere predictions of new *events* might be thus
given, for a new *event* does not imply a new *thought*   So
far then as prophecy means merely the applying of old
principles to new events, this quasi-objective or impersonal
prophecy might suffice ; but where a new thought had
to be reached, some *new* principle deduced from the
general law of Jehovah's working among men and revealing a new part of the redemptive work—here, I imagine,
the prophet must have felt that he was thinking out quite
a new thought   In the case of Moses, to whom God spake
face to face, this effort would be just like the effort we
use to follow a new thought spoken or written by another
But to other prophets God spoke *behîdôth*, an expression
that can hardly mean " in enigmas," but rather points to
the more general fact that the divine revelation was not
given fully and directly, but so that thought was necessary
to apprehend it and bring it into an articulate form
We must not suppose that *hîdah* is like a cypher which
only needs translation   The Hebrew enigma does not
contain the thought that is expressed in the answer, but
only hints at it and affords a direction for the thoughts
of the person to whom it is proposed   Analogously,
though not identically, the prophetic revelation, when it

did not come purely in dream or vision, called for a
conscious effort of inventive thought to elaborate it. The
matter from which the new thought is to be elaborated
is, as Rothe points out,[1] certain ideas and representative notions ("Begriffe" and "Vorstellungen") already
present to the prophet's mind. These, however, may be
either natural or embrace images presented in supernatural vision—for, as we have already seen, a perfectly
new image presented in such a vision will at once call
for an exercise of personal thought. Upon the matter
thus presented the prophet's mind must now act to supply
the formal element of the thought which is what is properly new. The method must be a teleological reasoning
bringing the matter into subordination to the general
principle of God's redemptive work. But no mere
natural deduction could suffice for this ; and here comes
in the feature that distinguishes prophecy from other
forms of the supernatural. No mere material supernatural modification of the nerves can serve here. The
power of producing a new thought depends on man's
spiritual nature, and the only means by which this faculty
can be raised to correspond with the necessities of prophecy
is by a direct action of the Spirit of God on the spirit of
man   What this action is we cannot tell , it lies in a
region even the *natural* features of which have baffled
human science. All that we know is that the formal
part of thought is that in which the human and therefore
the Divine Spirit come into play—in that unexplained
process by which general and abstract truth is extracted
from concrete notions. But this perhaps suffices to show
how far this mysterious process can affect the relation of
prophecy to history. So far as the resulting truth is
abstract and general, it will rise above all the conditions
of a special time ; but, so far as a concrete element
remains, that concrete element will not be a new one
but what was already present. So the relation of pro-

[1] As quoted by Tholuck, *Die Propheten, u.s.w.*, p 45

phecy to history will still depend on the result of the more concrete processes already analysed, and can only be modified in so far as the new thought lies out of relation to time and circumstance altogether.

In general, then, prophecy has two factors : the one abstract and formal, viz the grand idea of יהוה, of a divine immanence in history swaying all things to a perfect end, the other concrete and relative, containing all conditions of time, place, and so on.   The former is the same for all time , the latter must always attach itself to the concrete and conditioned in the prophet's own life, that is, to his own place in history   The synthesis of these two factors will produce a prophecy that goes directly from the concrete basis—the history of the prophet's age—to the final solution.   The events that link these together may be revealed with any degree of fulness, but of course in subordination to the [*explicit MS.*]

II

CHRISTIANITY AND THE SUPERNATURAL

IT is a common observation that all theology is running into apologetics. It might be difficult to say how far an analysis of the theological activity of our age and country would justify this statement; but the currency of the saying proves at least that apologetics is the branch of theology which bulks most largely in the minds of men at large.

We live in an age which is not much interested in strict theology. The mass of the laity and not a small proportion of the clergy do not view a strong interest in practical Christianity as at all inconsistent with small regard for Christian science or even with scepticism as to the possibility of such science.

But to this apathy as to theological questions there is one marked exception. Almost every one feels a keen interest in some branch of apologetics. No one seems to grudge learning, ability, or labour bestowed in the defence of Christianity against unbelievers. We do not seem much interested in the internal development of Christian science. We either acquiesce in the traditional solution of nice theological questions, or regard the solution of the questions either way as unimportant; but the outposts as it were of theology—all points that touch on science, history, criticism, and, in so far, on philosophy—are guarded with restless jealousy.

At first sight the statement that theology is running

into apologetics seems intelligible enough ; but the thing is not so clear when one begins to look at it   The word apologetical seems to point rather to a peculiar treatment than to a peculiar class of theological problems.   Do we mean then that theology is ceasing to be constructive and must henceforth stand on the defensive only ?   If so, what are we called upon to defend ?   A theology already completely and scientifically constructed ?   Surely not , for when a scientific system is complete, it ceases to demand apologetical treatment.   Or are we called on to admit that theological science has not attained, never can attain, constructive completeness ?   Then it will be no longer the results of theology that we are required to defend, but something prior to theology   What we shall have to defend is not our Christian knowledge but our Christian belief.

As a matter of fact there seems no doubt that those who view the increasing importance of apologetics as natural and inevitable must hold this view.   They not only reject the *intelligo ut credam* of Abelard for the *credo ut intelligam* of Anselm, but they deny that any advance in the *intelligam* can modify the necessity or limit the sphere of the *credo*.   All positive theology starts not from axioms but from postulates to be believed, not to be proved.

It is with these postulates then that apologetics will have to do—not to demonstrate them but to show that it is not unreasonable that we should believe them ; nay, that reason itself calls for this belief.   But still there is a difficulty here.   I can understand a man saying that our belief in the postulates of Christianity rests on purely subjective grounds—that we can enter into no argument whatever on the subject—but this position abolishes apologetics.   I can understand also that a man should refuse to accept this view, and say that he can give as good a reason for this belief as for any other belief he holds ; but in this case, too, why the name apologetics ?

I believe many things that cannot be demonstrated—the great facts of history, for example ; but the moral evidence by which I support this belief is as little apologetical, is as fully constructive, as the demonstrative evidence of geometry.

How is it then that in supporting our belief in Christianity we must be always rebutting objections, and can never say : Here is a complete and reasoned exposition of the grounds of my belief which no new facts and no new arguments can ever shake ?

There is an ambiguity about the word belief. A man is said to believe a thing when he cannot prove it, but has got something towards a proof. The object of belief is in this case really a hypothesis which suits certain facts so much better than any other hypothesis that I feel bound to accept it till further facts turn up *pro*, or *con*. There is a strong tendency to class our belief in Christianity under this head—a good instance of which may be found in Butler's *Analogy*.

But, if so, whence the moral warmth that mingles with our discussion of Christianity ? Why are we eagerly apologetic in behalf of a hypothesis ? What interest can we have to maintain this hypothesis more than any other which will suit the facts equally well ? I am sure no Christian would feel that a hypothetical Christianity was worth having. And the reason is plain. For the essence of personal Christianity lies in love to a personal Saviour. That such a Saviour really lives and really loves me must be more than a hypothesis if I am really to love Him.

In the other sense of the word I believe that which I receive as truth from a person whose veracity I trust. It is not possible, as many would do, to reduce this kind of belief under the previous head. This is not the place for a philosophic discussion ; but I do not think that sound philosophy will deny that the relations of person to person are the deepest and truest in human life, and must lie at the foundation of all explanations of human knowledge and belief. The sifting of the masses of evidence where the character of the witness is not accessible does fall under the rules of mere probability ; but no one can deny that it is possible for one human soul to penetrate into another with such full appreciation and sympathy as to render faith in that other something far deeper than a mere balancing of probabilities.

Clearly it is a faith of this sort that must lie at the bottom of Christianity. A faith in mere probable evidence may be good ground for calling a man acute or stupid, but can never be a subject for moral blame or approbation   But my faith in a fellow-man is a subject on which I am not only allowed but bound to show warmth of feeling   If a man doubts the veracity of my friend, whose pure and guileless character he has had every means of learning, I am bound to resent the insult. A truth that I believe on a friend's testimony becomes morally sacred to me   Here and here only do we find the type of the feeling with which every Christian regards divine truth.

A belief in certain truths resolving itself ultimately into a belief in a person may of course have various degrees   I may so far understand and believe in a man without that thorough interpretation of character above described   All certainty in history may be referred to this.   History that merely balances probabilities is never certain ; but where we have a historian in whose works we may so far read his character, we have a basis for higher certainty.   In estimating the evidence of an event, each man must learn for himself to enter into the historian's mind.   The argument can never be reduced to mere calculation.   And yet we do not find that the standard of historical truth is necessarily vague or doubtful, and therefore we must conclude that one man can really be known by others even if we have only his writings or actions before us, and never met him face to face.

We come then to this conclusion. So far as our belief in the postulates of Christianity is based on mere phenomenal probabilities, it contains no moral element, and does not justify an apologetic. So far as it resolves itself into a belief in a person or persons there is a moral element involved ; but we should not despair of gaining an objective criterion of the truth of our beliefs. There is no reason why here, as elsewhere, men should not come at length to a consistent judgment as to how far this personal faith is justifiable Whatever, on the other hand, lies beyond the limits of those personal relations on which Christianity rests is not a subject for apologetic treatment but for impartial criticism.

It is not difficult to see the practical bearing of these somewhat abstract arguments. What makes our Christianity precious to us is that it is essentially a real fellowship between God and man mediated through Jesus Christ as our Redeemer from sin. It is a personal relation to Christ and to God in Christ that we seek in Christianity, and it is the reality of this relationship that we are concerned to maintain with all the energy we may against all who deny it.

Here for the first time we come in proper contact with the subject indicated in the title of this essay.

For such a fellowship with God as Christianity contemplates is necessarily supernatural To say that no such fellowship naturally subsists between God and man is no more than to say that mankind is sunk in sin and misery—a fact that lies patent to all observation and in no sense is a specifically Christian doctrine. But what Christianity does assert is that there is no remedy for misery where there is no redemption from sin, and the hope that Christianity holds out for the world is the hope of entering into new and deeper personal relations with God. The universe of man is not and never can be self-contained. God must come down into the world and appear working among men, loving man and loved

8

by man before a truly harmonious universe of persons can be constituted.

Personal fellowship is ever based on personal action and reaction, and so must it be in Christianity. The Christian consciousness of God as our God rests on His historical manifestation of Himself to man,—rests, in a word, on a supernatural history. There is more in history than a record of human passions and activities, of human love and hatred, ambition, heroism, or crime. Nor must we think that we explain history, if behind these human forces we see the unconscious workings of an all-pervading world-spirit moulding man's career with benignant but inexorable fatality. It is the personal working of God on man consciously exerted and consciously responded to that gives history its life and hope. All men's lives indeed are unconsciously moulded by an all-pervading divine providence ; but this could never have sufficed to redeem the world. Man must know that God is dealing with him in person and must willingly submit himself to the divine influence. This it is that constitutes Christianity supernatural. Our Christian faith that God in Christ Jesus has made Himself personally known to us, has entered into personal relations with us, is then in one word our faith in a supernatural self-manifestation of God ; and the apologetic in which we seek to justify our Christian faith must have for its central point this idea of the supernatural.

Thus in the widest sense all apologetic turns about the personality of God as speculatively true and historically manifested. The strong dislike to this doctrine, taking the double form of deism or pantheism, which runs through modern speculation, is what really forces us into apologetics. If men were as ready *a priori* to admit a divine personality working in history as to refer the facts of history to human persons as cause, there would be no difficulty in justifying our Christian faith. Not the remoteness or imperfect evidence of the supernatural history that culminated in the resurrection of Christ, but an *a priori* refusal to acknowledge such a history as reconcilable with the philosophic idea of God, is what we have to contend against in apologetics. It is a notorious fact that the school that attacks the historic truth of Christianity takes for its presupposition the impossibility of the supernatural—does not for a moment profess to be able to carry out its destructive criticism without this presupposition With such a school Christianity can proclaim no truce. Such theories we can never consent to view as matter for friendly discussion. Our Christian loyalty is tampered with when we are invited to embrace a Christianity that leaves no room for personal intercourse between God and man. All this of course will seem to all of us obvious enough The danger rather is that we may think that our argument has carried us further than it really has done. We must remember that, while postulating the supernatural as the characteristic of Christianity, our definition of the supernatural is still in the most abstract form. We have seen no cause to deny the name of Christian to any one who believes that through the mediatorship of Christ man has entered into true personal relation with God—who sees in history God dealing personally with man. How this personal dealing is to be more nearly defined, how we are to conceive God's self-manifestation as carried out, is still an open question, and a question, so far as appears, for free and friendly discussion within the pale of a common Christianity, *not* for apologetic handling And this, be it observed, is a most weighty point in the present state of theological opinion. I may be allowed in illustration to quote a few words from the writings of Bunsen, which will show that this much-misrepresented man stands fully on the side we have recognised as Christian. " It is," says Bunsen, " a thoughtless delusion or a bitter mockery when men are now arising who would make themselves or us believe that " on the mythical theory of

the gospel history a common Christianity can still endure.
" If the gospel of John is not the historical testimony of
an eye-witness, but a myth, there is no historical Christ ;
and without an historical Christ all the common faith of
Christians is a phantom—all Christian confession, mockery
or delusion, and Christian worship a juggle " In these
words, I repeat, Bunsen thoroughly sets himself on our
side. He appears as a friend, not as a foe. And yet
Bunsen refused to believe in the possibility of miracles—
he refused to believe that God's personal dealings with
men could interfere with the fixed laws of nature Nor
does Bunsen stand alone in this. The opposition to
miracles, so strong in Schleiermacher, to whom Christianity
owes so much, still prevails among many whom we dare
not call enemies of our faith I believe indeed that this
tendency is growing less strong in Germany. I believe,
and I hope in this essay to do something to show, that a
belief in miracles is the necessary development of the
conception of the supernatural above laid down. But I
do urge that with such examples before us we must give
serious and earnest thought, lest in drawing the line
between the friends and foes of our faith we shut ourselves out from fellow-feeling with men who are themselves fighting on behalf of God.

    There is none of us, I suppose, who has not felt puzzled
on this point. We are constantly forced to recognise
true Christian feeling in men who seem, from the standpoint of our Scottish orthodoxy, to reject most precious
and fundamental truth. We rather feel than know that
amidst differences that seem vital we and they are yet
really at one But it is most dangerous to leave the
decision in these cases to subjective feeling. We are
imperatively called on to find an objective—I do not say
a doctrinal—criterion between Christian and *pseudo-*
Christian thought.

    That our current apologetic possesses such a criterion
I cannot but deny It is a fact that is pressing itself

on all thoughtful men that there is much Christian
thought which we may perhaps sympathise with in
spite of our theological position, but which our theology
refuses to have anything to do with And this, I suppose,
more than anything else, is what is leading educated men
to doubt and disparage all theological truth , to give
very little confidence to a Christian teaching that dares
not offer recognition to men that only a bigot can call
infidels.

No one can say that our apologetical theology stands
on firm ground while these things are so. It is weak,
and because weak unjust, and because unjust tends
continually to repel from Christianity all who are not
drawn to the truth by a moral necessity strong enough
to overpower their sense of this weakness and injustice.

It is absurd to attempt to compensate for this narrow-
ness of scientific view by cultivating a sentimental breadth
of sympathy. It is not unreasoning sympathy but
thoughtful recognition, combined if you will with dissent,
that is called for. In a word, we must reconsider the
whole treatment of the premises of Christianity. Such a
reconstruction the Germans have long seen to be necessary,
and have in no small measure succeeded in effecting. I
do not therefore speak on my own authority simply, but
seek to lay before you what in a land more favourable
to theological progress is regarded as an established
fact, when I say that the guiding conception in this reconstruction must be the notion of the supernatural above
laid down

The leading thought of our present apologetics is
very different. The older orthodoxy held that the
foundation of our Christianity is " a knowledge of the
religious object communicated to men from without in
the form of doctrine." In the words of our Confession
" The light of nature is not sufficient to give the knowledge of God and of His will, which is necessary to salvation , therefore it pleased the Lord to reveal Himself

and declare His will unto His Church." Divine revelation, then, is a communication of truth from God to man. Only by apprehending this truth is salvation possible, and so, in the words of Rothe, " All religious interests in Christianity seemed finally to converge in the necessity of experiencing with certainty where the religious doctrine promulgated among men by divine revelation is deposited in trustworthy fashion."

Such an authoritative statement of saving truth the Protestant churches could seek in Scripture only, and hence the belief in the authority and infallibility of the Bible was necessarily conceived as the indispensable foundation of all other religious convictions. Till this belief is established, no Christianity seemed possible, and so an apologetic was called for which should treat of the possibility, necessity, and criteria of a supernatural communication of truth, and should maintain that these criteria are found in Christianity, and that the truth itself is contained in an infallible book. Only when these results are reached can we on this theory feel that we have our feet on firm ground, and all who cannot go thus far with us must be viewed as consciously or unconsciously sapping the very foundations of Christianity.

This is not the place to dwell in detail on the formidable difficulties and unending toils to which such an apologetic is exposed. The point on which we have to dwell is the position here assigned to the supernatural in Christianity. The supernatural appears on the traditional theory primarily as a supernatural communication of truth. Christianity is necessarily supernatural, because the truth needed for salvation cannot be reached by the natural intellect It is not to some positive principle in man's nature but to a weakness and deficiency of our faculties that the supernatural in Christianity is due. We must put this proposition side by side with the doctrine that the weakness of human reason is one part of the corruption brought in by sin. Our Protestant

theology justly includes under regeneration the illumination and strengthening of the reason; so that the
Christian advances more and more in rational comprehension of saving truth.   And so while the truths of the
Bible are, in the language of Dogmatic, *supra rationem
empiricam*, we cannot think them as also *supra rationem
absolutam*   And thus the significance of the supernatural
is only relative and temporary.   A supernatural communication of truth from God to man—a supernatural
inspiration to secure an infallible record of this truth—
these are necessary only while man's redemption is
imperfect, and must fall away when all that is partial and
transitory is abolished.

It is this way of looking at things, making as it
does the supernatural a merely accidental feature in
Christianity, which has rendered us so jealous of speculative theology.   Every attempt at a rational demonstration of Christian doctrines is viewed as an attempt
to diminish the value of the Bible—for the Bible is held
valuable only as communicating to us supernaturally
what natural reason cannot attain to.   A complete
speculative theology, we imagine, would supersede the
Bible just as many have supposed that a body of doctrine
drawn from Scripture—say the Shorter Catechism—
might supply the place of the Bible.

The supernatural features in Christianity, however,
cannot be all brought under the heads of prophecy and
inspiration.   What is the significance which on the
current theory attaches to *miracles*?   This is the point
wherein the most obvious deficiencies appear.   Clearly
the importance of miracles must be secondary only.
Miracles must somehow be subsidiary to the revelation
of truth   The accidental character which attached to
the supernatural communication of truth still more
clearly belongs to miracles as the supernatural attestation
of divine truth.   The miracles of the Old and New
Testament have no value in themselves, but serve to

attest that the miracle-worker is a divinely commissioned ambassador of God.   Miracles, in short, are, in common with prediction, the criteria of revelation.

Thus viewed, miracles have merely an apologetic function.   And yet it may be questioned whether they have not given far more trouble than assistance to apologetic theology.   We propose to use the miracles recorded in Scripture as one link in the proof of the paramount authority of Scripture ; but we are confronted with the objection that a book relating such occurrences cannot possibly be trustworthy   And as this argument is generally based by recent objectors on the moral, not on the metaphysical, difficulties of a belief in miracle, we can meet the objection fairly only by showing that miracles have more than a mere adventitious importance in Christianity.

That this is really the case is obvious from a glance at the greatest of all miracles—the incarnation and resurrection of our Lord.   These are not events of a mere apologetic value, they are the central facts of Christianity.   And these events are only the culminating point of a long miraculous history.   The miracles of Scripture are not isolated facts but a connected chain running onwards from the fall, and so interwoven with the history of redemption, that that history evacuated of miracles would be absolutely meaningless.   Now the current apologetic teaches us only that the scheme of redemption required to be supernaturally made known and attested to men,—it takes no account of the fact that redemption was miraculously worked out among men. And hence arises the vast disadvantage that while the idea of the supernatural must always remain the key of our Christian position, which we must defend at all hazards, that idea has on the current view no intrinsic value to correspond to its strategic importance.   The fate of the whole citadel depends on a single outwork.

Let us look a little more closely at the neglected fact

that the work of redemption is itself supernatural. The saving truth by believing which men are to become Christians has the form of history. I am not to be saved by believing some eternal truths about God. I must believe that my salvation is rendered possible only by the work of Christ which took place historically and among men The old dogmatic does lay stress on this point, maintaining in the doctrine of the atonement that our salvation is rendered possible only by a divine trans-action. But the neglected point is that we have not here a divine transaction supernaturally made known to man, but a transaction that is at once human and divine — a transaction supernaturally worked out in human history in the person of the Godman And here we return to the conception of the supernatural developed in the first part of this essay, viz. the conception of a personal intercourse between God and man, and see that thus viewed the supernatural is the very centre of Christianity. But from this point of view we can no longer hold that Christian piety is primarily a belief in Christian doctrine. For then our Christianity would be quite different from the Christianity of the apostles. To the companions of Christ the history of redemption was not presented as something external to be believed : it was a matter of fact in which they were personally engaged. " That which we have heard, which we have seen with our eyes, which we have looked upon, and our hands have handled of the word of life " This it is that the apostles testify to. The essence of their Christianity was their actual fellowship with their Master, and the new life of which in this fellowship they were conscious. And so must it be still. For the fellowship of men with God in Christ, which was realised in the life of our Lord on earth, can be no passing gleam in the world's history. " The history of Jesus," says Hofmann, " which issues in resurrection and glorification, in His state of exaltation, cannot remain without an activity of the Exalted one, in virtue whereof we actually become what this issue of the history promises. Whoever then holds the historical for the essence of Christian teaching is convinced thereby that the Christianity which has its origin in such a history is no mere doctrine."

" Whoever," adds Hofmann, " recognises the fact of regeneration as the beginning of a new life of joyous peace with God and free love to God affirms hereby that Christianity is an essentially new relation between God and man, and so a matter of fact which only bears witness to itself in the word of Christian doctrine—not a human doctrine of divine things which has merely some kind of influence in determining and shaping an already present relation between God and man." So soon as we come to view personal Christianity not as belief in a bygone history but as participation in a present history, when we see that Christians are not mere passive recipients of the benefits of a transaction in which they take no part, but that the conscious moral agency of man is one factor throughout all the history of redemption, the whole course of our apologetic is changed. We can no longer sever the work of redemption from the communication of the knowledge of that work to men, and demand of apologetic as a preliminary to all theological inquiry a complete theory of this latter point For the work of redemption, like all other facts of history, made itself known to men by being actually worked out among them. And so God's activity in revelation is not something added to, but one form of His activity as Redeemer. It would be absurd to say that we cannot be assured that Christ's redeeming work ever took place till we have proved that the Bible is an infallible record of that work ; for it is only through the Christian miracles, i.e through the phenomena of Christ's supernatural work, that the way is cleared for the doctrine of inspiration.

The traditional dogmatic draws only a formal distinction between revelation and Bible, and often inter-

changes these conceptions. From the modern standpoint such a course would entail inextricable confusion.
The Bible is not revelation but the record of divine
revelation—the record of those historical facts in which
God has revealed himself to man. That God really has
so revealed Himself to man—not that we possess an
inspired record of this revelation—is the point on which
Christianity stands or falls. Of course on this view we
can no longer speak of revelation as a revelation of
truths. The knowledge given in revelation is not the
knowledge of facts but the knowledge of a Person. What
God reveals is simply HIMSELF—His own character and
His disposition towards men Thus the death of our
Lord is not a fact of revelation The apostles believed
it on the evidence of their senses ; we believe it on their
testimony accredited to us by their known character.
But in this historical fact God revealed Himself as the
God who so loved the world, that He gave His only begotten Son, that whosoever believeth in Him should not
perish, but have everlasting life.

It cannot be too strongly urged that our Christian
faith is no mere subjective feeling—no mere self-consciousness, but essentially consciousness of God. " Is
it correct," asks Dorner, " that we first come to a knowledge of God and Christ by syllogism from the fact of our
being redeemed and enlightened ? Much rather we are
led by the Son to the Father through the Holy Ghost, who
illuminates us with His gifts To the religious process
which culminates in the atonement belongs not only an
act of God but consciousness of God and Christ. In
faith and to faith the eye of the understanding is opened,
and God is revealed to this eye—namely, God in Christ."
The immediate object of faith is thus no act of God, no
truth about God, but God Himself

Such a faith, in which we feel ourselves brought into
personal knowledge of and fellowship with God, becomes
possible only in virtue of the work of redemption, for

sin brought in a real alienation between God and man. As the objective effects of sin run through the whole human universe, the work of redemption is also a many-sided work. This is not the place to attempt an analysis of the various forms in which God's redemptive activity presents itself, but this at least must be common to all these forms—that they set before us an action of God upon human personality. Not an organic but a personal redemption of the world is what Christianity teaches. Man is not saved without his own personality, much less in spite of his personality, but in and through his personality. This is the reason why the work of redemption is a gradually progressive work. A personal redemption cannot be effected at a blow by external forces; for personality cannot be shaped from without, but must be developed from within by its own self-determining power. And so the redemptive agencies must be brought down among men and work historically upon men age after age, gradually moulding the whole universe through no magical force from without, but by the moral influence of the presence in history of a divine personality "The Christian religion," says Rothe, "is characteristically distinguished from all other religions as the essentially moral religion and accordingly as morally, *i.e.* personally, mediated. In virtue of this, Christianity is the truly human, the truly spiritual, in every sense the true religion, and so the diametrical antithesis of the heathenish or magical religions; for in the sphere of the spiritual the magical is just that which is not personally or morally mediated."

This canon, which virtually coincides with the conception of the supernatural in Christianity developed above, enables us to work out more fully the nature of the Christian revelation; and on this point I shall follow somewhat closely the ideas laid down in the epoch-making work of Rothe   That I should do so is indeed inevitable, for it was from Rothe that my first clear insight into

the subject was gained. I do not, however, profess to
expound the views of Rothe further than they have
recommended themselves to me as true ; so that while
I think it right to express my obligations to this author,
no one but myself is responsible for the details of my
argument.

If Christian faith is rendered possible only by the
work of redemption, and if this faith is essentially consciousness of God, it follows that no true consciousness
of God is possible to sinful man except through the work
of redemption. Revelation then is that form of God's
redemptive activity whereby man's consciousness of
God is purified and strengthened, and so man is enabled
rightly to apprehend God. And here I must repeat, at
the risk of being tedious, that the knowledge communicated *directly* by revelation is from this very conception
of revelation knowledge of God only. " Indirectly indeed," as Rothe beautifully expresses it, " revelation
diffuses its light over everything else, over the whole
world. For by making the sun of the true idea of God
rise in our firmament it sheds over the whole world the
brightness of day in which we perceive all things quite
otherwise than in the dim twilight in which we wander
without revelation " There is surely no obscurity here ;
no knowledge of phenomena will save man—it is a
personal acquaintance with God that is required. And
so soon as this is given all other knowledge receives its
proper significance—the whole world appears no longer
a dismal and insoluble problem, " for God who commanded the light to shine out of darkness hath shined in
our hearts to give the light of the knowledge of the
glory of God in the face of Jesus Christ."

How then is this knowledge of God imparted to men ?
Clearly not by a mere mechanical process—not by a sheer
exertion of omnipotence infusing certain conceptions into
men's minds. God must so act on man that man may
come to know Him just as he comes to know any other

person by an exertion of his own mental powers.   Thus
the first step in revelation must come to man from
without.   God must manifest himself to man in external
events of such a kind that man is constrained to see
God in these events just as I see a person in his actions

All the phenomena of nature are of course a manifestation of God ; but this manifestation cannot suffice
for the purpose in hand.   A true consciousness of God
must embrace a right conception of God's moral and
personal character, and must therefore be based on an
historical manifestation of God.   We must learn that
God is ready to enter into deeper relations with man
than those of nature.   We must know God as coming
nearer to man than nature brings him.   God must enter
as an actor into human history so that even the eye
dimmed by sin cannot fail to recognise His presence
The essential point here is, of course, that revelation is
no mere organic process, no mere evolution of energies
naturally existent in the world, but a new and specifically
divine history let down into human history.   Now it is
not of course impossible for a man to maintain that this
is possible without any disturbance of the laws of nature.
At all events we cannot directly characterise such a
statement as unchristian   In fact, it is not uncommon
to find orthodox writers speaking of miracles as products
of a higher law of nature, which is in fact to concede all
that men like Bunsen would ask.   Only, of course, the
orthodox writer, believing in the infallibility of Scripture,
would say that all the miracles of the Bible must be
instances of this ; while Bunsen would allow himself
to apply a detail criticism to many of the recorded
miracles.

At the same time, I think that a clearer consideration
of what is involved in revelation as above determined
will show that no mere adjustment of the laws of nature
will serve the purpose of a divine revelation.   For any
such adjustment whereby God manifests Himself in a very

peculiar providence, is not essentially different from the ordinary revelation of God in nature, which on the fundamental Christian antithesis of sin and grace has shown itself to us to be quite insufficient, revealing only what we may call the natural, not the personal, side of God.

We may conceive the natural providence of God as so adjusted that mankind once possessing a true consciousness of God would always see Him as personally active in the world ; but what revelation has to supply is precisely the want of such a consciousness. The process by which we find God in nature is always more or less a ratiocinative one ; so that in this way the knowledge of God as our Redeemer would be a deduction from our experience of the benefits of redemption. But this, as our whole argument shows and an appeal to the Christian consciousness will confirm, is a precise reversal of the true state of the matter. The first step in redemption is revelation, if the first step in salvation is personal faith. The divine revelation must be primarily an immediate manifestation of God ; a manifestation of God in events that are at once seen to form no part of the chain of nature but to be directly personal and explicable *only* as acts of God. If any step whatever must be intercalated in tracing the manifestation up to God the sinful intellect can still stop short with this natural explanation, and has no new necessity laid upon it of ascending to a higher cause In a word, God's supernatural manifestation of Himself in redemption is miraculous,—breaking through the natural course of the universe. We do not in saying this deny the reality and necessity of a natural manifestation of God ; but we say that such a manifestation is valuable only as subsidiary to a miraculous and immediate manifestation.

Deny this and it is still possible to maintain that in Christianity man enters into personal fellowship with God, but the realising of this fellowship appears no

longer as the first step in salvation, but as the crowning
point of an organic process. The growing belief in
God's moral kingdom on earth follows instead of preceding the successive development of that kingdom ,
and so Christianity, though thoroughly personal in its
issue, is not thoroughly personal at each stage of its
growth. And so, as is notably the case with Bunsen, the
history of redemption ceases to be the history of the
establishment of God's kingdom on earth and becomes
the history of the progress of faith in that kingdom.
But a theory which thus destroys the immediacy of
faith, making it the gradual product of an historical process not the immediate outgoing of man's personality to
God, is obviously not a theory which satisfies the facts
of Christian consciousness or can be reconciled with the
substantial identity of saving faith in all dispensations

Without dwelling on the essential importance of
miracles here developed, or the inconsistency of the
theories that attempt to get rid of miracles while yet
holding Christian ground, let us look at the necessity
that God's miraculous self-manifestation should consist
not of isolated acts but of a continuous history As a
witness to doctrine isolated miracles might suffice , but
as a display of God's character a continuous action of
God in history is needful. There must be a plan in the
divine miracles as there would be in the activity of a
human actor in history. Not one act but a whole life is
needed fully to declare a character. And then this
supernatural activity of God is not merely something
superadded to natural history, but enters into natural
history, gradually moulding it in conformity with God's
redemptive purpose. Each manifestation of God is more
than a meteor flashing through the sphere of man's
spiritual vision ; it " remains henceforth, like the sun in
the firmament, a shining fact in human consciousness "
And so each manifestation prepared mankind for a new
and higher display of God's character, until at length in

the fulness of time God Himself became man and in the person of our blessed Lord the supernatural was permanently and inseparably incorporated in human history. In the incarnation God's self-manifestation was absolutely complete, and that in no mere external manner, but in the perfect union of the divine and human natures.

Beyond this point it was not necessary that the series of miraculous occurrences should be continued. No more perfect manifestation of God was possible—the remainder of the world's history has for its task the full recognition by all mankind of this perfect revelation of the divine character.

And this consideration leads us to see that in the divine manifestation revelation has not yet reached its goal It is not enough that God manifest Himself to men unless this manifestation be rightly understood And here it will be convenient to separate the recognition of divine manifestation by us who are not brought face to face with it from the right understanding thereof by those who were themselves actors or onlookers in supernatural events. That all who stood in the latter position did not rightly comprehend the divine manifestation is a familiar fact. Nay, it is obvious that no fallen man can naturally comprehend even the clearest display of God's character. Our consciousness is not only weakened, but distorted by sin. And it is not enough that we should be forced to recognise a superhuman agency in the history of redemption—we must so recognise God as to love Him. To effect such a recognition of God no strength of external impression could suffice; it was needful that God as He showed Himself to men should also by the inner operation of His spirit enlighten man's consciousness rightly to apprehend His self-manifestation. It is clear that this influence falls under the regenerating work of the Spirit. It is not an imparting of knowledge, it is a renovation of the human consciousness whereby

9

man is enabled to see God in manifestation. Clearly such an inspiration without a manifestation would be meaningless and void of all power to save mankind. To say that a spiritual renewal of man's consciousness of God is possible except as attaching to and dependent on a supernatural activity of God in history, is equivalent to saying that regeneration is not dependent on an objective redemptive work. And this is to sink back into the Socinian doctrine which makes our Lord only an inspired teacher.

In revelation then we must distinguish and yet regard as inseparable two sides. The outer and objective side is manifestation, the inner and subjective inspiration. The manifestation becoming part of history must necessarily have men as its organs. In all the miracles of Scripture human agencies are more or less directly engaged. It is among these agents then that we must specially look for inspiration. If the manifestation remained unintelligible to these it could never enter into human history at all. Only by being rightly, though not necessarily exhaustively, comprehended by those who are in actual contact with it does the supernatural event become a permanent force in the world ; for all redemptive activities must flow through personal channels. And so side by side with the stream of miracle we have a stream of inspired prophecy. The development of this side of revelation would demand an essay for itself, and it is the more necessary that I should pass over this topic because I have had on a former occasion an opportunity of directing the attention of the Society to the manner in which prophecy and history are interwoven—so that each new step in redemptive history is in prophecy truly interpreted under the inspiration of God's Spirit, and so interpreted becomes at once a power to shape history and a key whereby the prophet is enabled more and more fully to unriddle God's eternal purpose in history. Especially important is it to understand that prophecy does not merely follow history, but strictly rather precedes history. For, though every new step in prophecy is dependent on a divine manifestation, that manifestation is not properly absorbed into human history till interpreted in prophecy. This consideration might, I think, be profitably worked out in reference to the peculiar nature of revelation in the pre-Mosaic dispensations.

It need hardly be said that the conception of inspiration just developed is by no means identical with the ecclesiastical notion of inspiration. Nor does this inspiration necessarily present itself as exclusive of that generally received. For even writers like Dr. Bannerman are forced to distinguish revelation and inspiration, and all that we have yet said falls (so far as our theory can at all fall under the forms of one so diverse) under the former of these heads.

So long, however, as revelation is treated as a revelation of doctrines, the infallible communication of truth may be distinguished, but cannot be separated, from a provision for the infallible transmission of the truth. That prophets or apostles were miraculously enabled to communicate divine truths to men would be quite a valueless fact to us did we not know that these saving truths have been authentically handed down to us. The process of revelation is itself incomplete till the fleeting word is fixed in the abiding letter, for only then does the truth gain complete objectivity even for the prophet himself.

On our view the state of things is quite different. The true objectivity of the revelation is secured in the divine manifestation, while inspiration brings this objective datum into real union with man's consciousness. This done, the revelation is already a power in the world; an historical fact not to be got rid of. So far as the generation which was in contact with the divine manifestation is concerned no further supernatural step is necessary to give the revelation its full force. But the

divine manifestation is to remain a permanent power in
history. It is not enough that the saving influences
flowing from the Person of our Lord should be transmitted from generation to generation so that to us the
Church would fill the room of the divine manifestation.
It is necessary that every generation should be able to
stand directly under the influence of the historical
manifestation of Christ. Now this is only possible
through an historical tradition, fixed in writing, during
the very course of the revelation itself. Without such an
original record both of the manifestation and inspiration—
a record breathing the fresh life of the age from which it
flows—it would be impossible for us to have such a
lively vision of the events of revelation as to feel ourselves
to be under the personal influence of the divine manifestation. Apart from this no knowledge of religious
truths can save us. We must have such a record of
revelation as may serve as the medium to bring us into
personal contact with Christ. That the events of revelation can be brought before us in a perfectly real and
lively form only by a record at first-hand—a record
whose author was himself an actor in the history he
records and whose narrative thus becomes itself a part
of the history—is obvious. The great point is not the
superior accuracy of a contemporary record, but its
superior personality. In the record of an actor the
events of history live again. A subsequent historian
may by the help of criticism produce a much more
accurate narrative, but never a narrative possessing the
same living power. The authors of Scripture are in great
part the men who were directly in contact with the
divine manifestation, and in whom themselves one part
of revelation—that which we have called inspiration—
took place. These men then are of necessity the
authentic expositors of revelation. If they did not
understand it rightly revelation fell dead upon the world.
And thus arises at once—without any inquiry into the

infallibility of Scripture, without any theory of inspiration *in actu scribendi*—the complete proof of the normative authority of the Bible.

The doctrine of Holy Scripture, if developed from this point of view, cannot be placed as the foundation of all Christian belief The belief in the normative authority of Scripture is here developed not from grounds of pure reason, but on grounds of faith—on the assumption that Christianity is really supernatural and possesses a real revelation. But indeed I do not believe that any man ever believed in Christ because he believed in the authority of Scripture; our belief in the authority of Scripture much rather is derived from a belief in Christ. It is the testimony of the Holy Spirit to which our Protestant theology ultimately refers the authority of Scripture. And what can this mean but that Scripture is the medium through which we come face to face with the divine revelation in Christ, and being thus brought under the living influence of the Person are by the Holy Spirit enabled rightly to apprehend Him as so presented to us, and so of course to recognise the medium whereby alone we can approach the historical Christ as really divine?

That this view of the function of the Bible is far more true to Christian experience than that which seeks in Scripture primarily a body of infallible truth seems undeniable. " I confidently appeal," says Rothe, " to the testimony of all really thoughtful readers of the Bible, whose own experience will witness to them that that which so peculiarly edifies them in their intercourse with the Bible is far less the instructions and admonitions that they draw from it than the purifying and quickening influences of a holy world ruled by supernatural powers ; yea, of the immediate nearness of God and Heaven itself into which they find themselves raised as soon as they cross the threshold of the wondrous book."

On these grounds we would wholly exclude the doctrine of the infallible inspiration of Scripture from the sphere of apologetics and relegate it to dogmatic theology. The true place for the doctrine of Holy Scripture is indeed already indicated in Protestant dogmatic. In our Catechisms, for example, Scripture is mentioned not only as the starting-point of the whole system, but in the discussion of the means of grace. Now we would refer the subject altogether to this latter sphere, to which alone it properly belongs, and choose as the basis of our Christianity not the record of revelation, but the historical facts of revelation themselves. Not on the Bible as an infallible book, but on the historic manifestation of God in Christ must our faith rest. And when this is understood we shall no longer be constantly uneasy at the progress of criticism in Scripture. We shall not hesitate to test the doctrine of inspiration like every other doctrine of Christianity with all impartiality and calmness and by all additional light that science or criticism can cast upon it

No criticism can take from us our personal fellowship with God in Christ—no criticism can withdraw from the Bible its living power as the medium wherein we are brought face to face with Christ; for a personal faith lies too deep to be touched by criticism. All historical certainty rests ultimately on personal belief, and no attack on the Gospel history can have such a personal weight as is at all comparable to the Christian's conviction of the reality of the historical Christ. And if this be so, criticism may aid us in gaining more and more clear knowledge, but cannot destroy personal faith We may or may not be able to satisfy ourselves of the infallibility of Scripture, but we can never doubt that Scripture gives all that is required to attain a true image of our Lord. And if this function of Scripture does not involve infallibility (and it cannot so far as we have seen be declared at once that it does), the criticism, scientific or historic, that lays bare this fact will have done us the good service of removing a false impression which,

as false, could not fail to be most injurious to the full
understanding and even a stumbling-block in the way
of a true belief of Christianity. We are not bound to
welcome a science that bases itself on antichristian assumption ; but we must ever welcome the freest criticism
that rests on impartial weighing of facts, and an apologetic which cannot take up once for all a position which
no such criticism can approach transcends its just limits
and confesses its own weakness. The root of a true
apologetic must be in the immediate certainty of Christian
faith wherein we feel ourselves supernaturally brought
into fellowship with a divine personality ; and the
scientific development of our apologetic must take the
form of a speculative theology in which the subjective
consciousness of redemption is objectively evolved into
a harmonious theory of the universe as reconciled to God
in Christ. It is the business of Christianity to conquer
the whole universe to itself and not least the universe of
thought.

" Attacks on our Christian faith," says an eminent
thinker, " can come only from the region of thought
that is not yet thoroughly incorporated in and appropriated by Christianity. The more thoroughly the yet
hostile territories are conquered for Christianity and the
Christian view of the universe, the more secure is our
faith from these attacks." But such conquests can be
gained only by free thought in the spirit of Christianity,
not by urging men to build their faith on a completed
system of infallible doctrine. How thoroughly this conviction has worked for good in the recent theology of
Germany, and how little the interests of living Christianity
have to fear from the adoption of these convictions in our
own land, may perhaps be best illustrated by a brief but
weighty quotation from one of the most truly Christian
of modern theologians. " So long," says Dorner, " as
we suppose that faith in inspiration and the divine
authority of Holy Scripture is the first step in Christian

piety, so long we must fall into distress and terror, when [those doctrines seem to be impugned]."

The secret of the equanimity of our newer theology, even in the dangers of critical operations, lies precisely in the clear knowledge that faith in the inspiration of the ecclesiastical canon is not the condition, not the necessary first step, in coming to faith in Christ—that with such a faith in Scripture Christian faith is not yet given or even grounded. We draw our conviction of the authority of Scripture from the authority of Christ ; after His redemptive power and worth has been made certain to us in faith, Scripture and the Word of God are never given to separate us from Christ or to fill the place of Him and His Spirit. Were communion with the Bible to fill for us the place of communion with Christ, we should treat the Bible with superstition and be guilty of sin against Christ who is Lord and Master of the Scripture, and not less against Scripture which seeks only to be His minister to lead us up to Christ and to keep us close to Him.

III

THE WORK OF A THEOLOGICAL SOCIETY

GENTLEMEN,—On the first evening of a new session, when we find ourselves gathered again in the old familiar room to renew our fellowship for another winter, it is natural that we should wish to set clearly before us the work which as a Society we are met together to do. And it is all the more necessary that we should be able to give a distinct utterance on this point, because we see among us to-night not a few who are not yet of our number, but whom we must hope to interest for the work of our Society if that work is to be carried on with vigour and success.

Clearly it is not enough to have recourse to the official definition of our Society as a Theological Society meeting to discuss subjects connected with theology; for a common interest in theology is by no means a sufficient guarantee for the degree of unity of standpoint, method and aim, without which friendly discussion is impracticable. And that our discussion must be friendly discussion lies in the very conception of an organised society. Were we in principle divided against ourselves our house could not stand. The floor of a Theological Society must not be the arena for the contest of opposing parties, each striving to pull down what the other has built up; all the members must feel that they are labouring at the same work and that in that work the labour of each finds a fitting place.

This mutual recognition of one another's services implies more than the consciousness of a common aim, for we may be compelled to regard efforts made from a false starting-point and by an unfitting method as only prejudicial to the aim they are meant to further. The best intentions do not constitute a man a fellow-worker unless we see some fruit of his work which we can recognise as valuable. It is true that unity of aim may form a basis for mutual respect, and therefore in a sense for friendly discussion in spite of fundamental differences as to the way in which the aim is sought. But in this case the friendliness is personal and the discussion in itself is still polemical; for the object of the discussion is not mutual instruction by a dialectical process, but the destruction of the whole position of the one or of the other disputant The friendliness in fact is merely personal, the discussion itself is of the nature of war.

But from a Society like ours hostile discussion must be excluded. The opposition of opinions must be dialectical, not polemical; that is, we must recognise that different views are maintained not from opposing interests, but only because unequal stress is laid by various speakers on different parts of those determining principles which all admit to have real weight.

And so it will be found that the subjects discussed by us have always been more or less of a concrete nature, and so soon as an abstract and ultimate difference of principles appears in the course of a discussion we all feel that the progress of the debate is cut short at that point. The debate is profitable only so long as each side feels that the other is bringing out in a clearer light some point which is really weighty, which really is a moment in the solution of the question, although perhaps in this case pushed too far. And the advantage to be reaped from such debate is far less change of opinion on concrete points of detail than a clearer grasp of the principles which must regulate us all in the formation of our theological views.

For in fact, although our opinions on specific points can never be really firm and satisfactory until they are evolved from definite principles, it is always in the consideration of secondary questions that we first reach a clear view of these principles ; and to be able to lay down the guiding notions according to which the system of our theological beliefs is constructed and by which our theological researches are directed is by no means an early or an easy acquisition. Principles which are to form the basis for the activity of a whole life cannot be given from without ; they must grow up within us and gradually unfold themselves before us as the explicit development of that which is already implicitly a necessary part of our life. Nor is the value of that dialectic in which we are here practised merely educational. Not our progress in theology alone, but the advancement of theology itself is subject to the conditions just described. The difficulties of theology, though it is in points of detail —in exegesis, perhaps, or in the details of some minor point of doctrine—that they first come to be felt, are really difficulties as to principle, and are to be solved only by determining more justly than has hitherto been done the real order and true balance of the fundamental notions of the whole science. A progress thus conditioned by constant successive reflections between the concrete question and the general principle is necessarily of a dialectic character.

From these considerations, I think, it is manifest that our Society has acted rightly in always refusing to formulate the unity of spirit and aim which is necessary to our success. Were all first principles fixed, not discussion, but deduction would remain, were some principles fixed and others left undetermined we should render our discussions one-sided and lose that free play of dialectic which is gained by bringing all the principles involved to bear freely on one another.

To dwell on the real opposition between the dialectical and deductive methods of advancing a science would, of course, be out of place here. It will, I suppose, be readily admitted that the distinction here drawn between the dialectical and deductive methods is a real one, that an orderly deductive argument proceeding from conceded premises may admit of refutation or vindication, but hardly in the proper sense of discussion, and that true discussion is found where the inquiry starts not from explicit principles, but from a consciousness which is not yet fully given as scientific knowledge, and from which general principles and special applications may be evolved side by side. But when it is further maintained that theology necessarily advances by discussion, whether that discussion be between a man and himself as he allows now this, now that, moment of the fundamental consciousness to assert itself, or whether the different parts be maintained by different persons who all share that consciousness, but on whom the various moments thereof act with unequal force : when this is maintained one can hardly expect to meet with general concurrence. For practically there is a very considerable part of theology which not a few regard as quite exempt from any discussion save that polemical discussion which we have carefully excluded from our consideration We were recently told, for example, by a man of great mark in our Church, that the function of a Professor of Dogmatic Theology is simply the elucidation and vindication of the system of doctrines already deduced from Scripture and embodied in our Confession of Faith and other orthodox confessions We are to believe that systematic theology has passed entirely and conclusively from the dialectic to the deductive stage ; the dogma of the Reformed Churches admits only of such discussion as may serve to vindicate it from attack.

But if systematic theology is really in this state it is vain to speak of theology as a science advancing dialectically. We cannot even say that the other parts of theology are dialectical; for it is the characteristic of a dialectical progress that all parts advance together, and no one part can be perfect before the others. But, in fact, we have seen reason to assert that the organism of theology is such that no one part can be mastered till the whole is known. We have been able to appeal to experience as establishing the fact that a serious consideration of any vexed theological question invariably drives us to ask for clearer principles, and surely till these are supplied systematic theology is not complete and not impeccable. I may in illustration refer to a familiar instance. So soon as we pass from the merely grammatical to the *real* interpretation of Old Testament prophecy, we find a series of difficulties arise which may ultimately be shown to depend in great measure on the true theory of the Hebrew theocracy; and that again is a problem which goes far beyond the sphere of exegesis and can only be resolved from the general principles of God's historical dealings with man. And this is clearly a question for systematic theology, but one which the orthodox dogmatic has no means of solving. If now our dogmatic is not a loose collection of doctrines, but an organic unity, the existence of such a defect necessarily implies a positive faultiness in the system. But, indeed, the same thing will appear without going beyond the limits of systematic theology itself. " The orthodox Confessions of the Reformed Churches," which embody, we are told, the true system of dogmatic theology, are themselves not absolutely alone. Even if we assume an entire unity between the Calvinistic Confessions—an assumption that will hardly be made out—what are we to say to the articles of the Lutheran Church? Are we justified in excluding these articles from the number of the orthodox confessions wherever they disagree with us? True, the Lutherans and Calvinists are in principle at one. The differences are minor differences; but these minor differences, running as they do through the whole system of theology, are not mere slips on the one side or on the other in a process of logical "deduction from Holy Scripture rightly interpreted." Slips of that kind may be made by individuals, but not surely by all theologians of one Church and no theologian of another. The cause of the theological differences of Churches must be looked for in the character of the Churches themselves; in the fact that the same Reformation principles are not grasped quite in the same way by Lutherans and Calvinists, that the tendency is for the two Churches to lay stress on different sides of the same truth; that in short, there is between the two branches of reformed theology that dialectical opposition which is not inconsistent with fundamental unity, and which, for that very reason, can never be got over by the refutation of the one party, but only by the advance to a higher position, which, while it adopts the individual conclusions now of this, now of that party, not seldom it may be of neither, will differ from eclecticism by satisfying and reducing to harmony the divergent tendencies of both Churches.

It is absurd to think that such a position can be honestly aimed at unless we are prepared to allow that there may be in our present theology not only defect, but error, that even leading ideas may have a relative rather than an absolute validity, and that those requirements of the Christian consciousness which they supply approximately may be fully supplied partly by a new arrangement, partly by real modifications of our main theological principles.

The source of that confidence in the absolute truth of the confessional dogmatic, which has in some measure come to play the same part in the Reformed Churches as the belief in the infallibility of the Church does in the Romish Communion, is very aptly indicated in the expression quoted above—"System of doctrines fairly and honestly deduced from the Holy Scriptures rightly interpreted " It would be calumnious to suppose that it is as for human compositions that Protestants are so jealous for their symbolical books. The confessions are reverenced as containing plain deductions from the teaching of inspired writ or, in the words of a recent Moderator of our General Assembly, because we are satisfied that our standards " are but an echo in human language of the infallible Word." Now so long as the confessional theology is viewed in this light we must receive with suspicion and dislike every suggestion that the historical circumstances and religious character of the several branches of the Protestant Church have influenced more than the mere externals of the orthodox theology; that something more than Scripture and the rules of logic went to the formation of the Reformed Confessions. For this *something more* must have had a purely negative and injurious effect, serving only to make the " echo of the infallible Word " imperfect and incorrect or to make the path of theological deduction swerve from the true line of logical accuracy. It is not strange that the Church should indignantly refuse to admit that any influence, wholly and purely perverting and therefore unchristian and sinful, permeates her whole official teaching, for that would be to admit that the theology of the Church can be corrected only by a hostile hand,—only through the pangs and dangers of another Reformation.

It is clear that we are here brought face to face with a very serious dilemma. So long as we hold fast the theory that the true ideal of Protestant dogmatic is a mere echo of the infallible Word in human language, we must either despair of the Reformation theology or shut our eyes to obvious historical facts which forbid us to suppose that only accidental causes have operated to prevent the realisation of that ideal in the confessional theology. If it is impossible for us to rest in either of these alternatives we must venture to open up the question of the true relation of theology to Scripture.

At this point, however, we encounter a somewhat per-
plexing degree of haziness in the current theological
opinions The old theologians were on this as on most
points very explicit. They held that every fundamental
dogma was so clearly propounded in some place of
Scripture that only guilty negligence or perversion could
miss the truth And accordingly they are accustomed
to deny that theology is properly a science. " For
every science," says Owen in his *Theologumena*, " is the
effect of, and is, therefore, regulated by the activity of, the
intellect with regard to its special object ; but theology
which is nothing else than the revelation of the divine
mind and will, the *purum putum Dei verbum*, necessarily goes before every conception of our mind concerning
its proper object and is the infallible rule of all our knowledge " (pp. 36, 37, 38) " Scriptura," says Owen expressly, " est nostra theologia." So far as a theological
statement or confessional book aims at being more than
a mere compend of statements each of which rests immediately on divine revelation, it passes beyond the
bounds of theology.

This position of Owen, though it rests on the false
conception of revelation as a supernatural communication of doctrines and on the false identification of
Scripture and revelation which were current in his day,
is manifestly clear and consistent The conservative theology of our day on the other hand, though not free from the
influence of the fundamental errors of the older view, has
felt itself constrained to make very considerable modifications on that view which by no means tend to clearness.

No one now feels able to assert with Owen that the
doctrinal statements of Scripture yield in clearness to
no science. On the contrary, it is admitted—I quote
from Dr Cunningham—" that there is not one of the
peculiar doctrines of the Christian system which is set
forth in Scripture with such an amount of explicitness
as it was abstractly possible to have given to the state-

ment of it " (*Hist. Th.* ii. 231). And hence we no longer
treat our symbols as a compendious statement of those
saving truths which the Church rejoices to have found
clearly laid down in Scripture and which she feels herself
bound to re-echo with all her might, not because she can
make them clearer or plainer than she found them in
Scripture, but because it is her duty and privilege as a
Church to profess to the praise and glory of God her faith
in the way of Salvation which He has provided. The
confession is to us no longer the spontaneous utterance
of the faith of the Church, offered for subscription only
because no one who sincerely accepts Scripture could for
a moment hesitate to endorse its doctrines, but a theological formula claiming an independent theological value
as a statement of doctrine, and devised as a more crucial
test of theological views than the words of Scripture afford.

I do not think it can be questioned that the current
theory of the necessity of confessions as the legal standard
of theological orthodoxy does imply that as a statement of
doctrine the symbols of our Church are better and more
distinct than Scripture. And it seems equally plain
that this can be reconciled with the paramount authority
which, as Protestants, we must ascribe to the Bible only
by admitting a difference of kind between the Bible and
the confession, *i.e.*, since there can be no question that
the contents of the confession are dogma, by denying
that Scripture comes to us in the first instance at least
as a book of doctrines. But this is just the point which
the orthodox theology of our days seems unable either
to concede or to deny ; and it is this half-heartedness
that exposes us to the insinuations of those without that
we really set our orthodox theology above the Bible.

The compromise which is often attempted lies, as stated
by Dr. Cunningham, in the observation " that Scripture
was constructed upon the principle of testing our candour
and love of truth ; that the peculiar doctrines of the
Christian system are set forth in Scripture with a force

10

of evidence amply sufficient to satisfy every candid man, so that the resistance of these doctrines proves a hatred of the truth." The reasonableness of trying men in this method is maintained by an appeal to the general principles of God's moral government. That is, those who after Butler adopt this line of argument still go on the view that Scripture is essentially a revelation of doctrines necessary to salvation, so that eternal blessedness follows from the acceptance of these doctrines. And then it is argued that man would be no longer dealt with as a moral being, if the acceptance of saving doctrine was forced upon him from without by the doctrines being so framed that no sane man could reject them. But as it would be absurd to suppose that this moral element was to be gained only by an imperfection and want of clearness in the book whose aim was just to reveal the doctrines necessary to salvation, the explanation is compelled, on the other hand, to speak as if not the ready-made doctrines but their materials lay in Scripture, or, as Cunningham puts it, " God has given us sufficient evidence of what He requires us to believe."

And in this case either the act of faith ceases to be in immediate contact with Scripture (which is unprotestant), or else it is no longer the doctrine that is the object of saving faith but only the materials from which the doctrine is educed and which are directly presented to us in Scripture. And further these materials cannot be themselves fragments of doctrines which are merely placed side by side in our Confessions, for the fragments of doctrines are still doctrines, and so the whole round of objections just urged would begin anew The compromise, in short, is self-contradictory, and yields on examination no escape from the conclusion that doctrine is not the object of saving faith, and that the communication of doctrine is not the object of Scripture.

And hence dogmatic theology is not an echo of Scripture, nay, since like can only be deduced from like,

our theological systems are not simply *deductions* from
Scripture, or, to come back to our first line of thought,
they are the product of an activity of the human mind
which is not merely *formal*, not mere classification of
immediately revealed data, but the development, in a
dialectical process, into more and more definite scientific
form, of a religious consciousness which must always find
its canon in Scripture, but which none the less has a life
and growth of its own specifically determined, now in
this direction, now in that, by historical circumstances
and individual or national character, so that the true and
harmonious growth of theology as a whole is only attain-
able through the dialectical action and reaction of many
one-sided growths of the theological consciousness of
various individuals or Churches.

Now in all this investigation we have remained, as it
were, outside of the real nature of theology and have
busied ourselves only with its method. And, in fact, our
results have been mainly negative. We have not seen
what the real principle of theological progress is, except
in so far as it has appeared that theology does not advance
by deduction from axioms which lie outside of the theologian, and therefore, if it be a science at all, can only
advance by the evolution of a consciousness lying *within*
him. And therefore our results, though they certainly
go to justify our position here as a Society for the *discussion* of theology—for *real* discussion in which each
man is called upon to give free play to his own individuality—do not give us any light as to the positive principles
of theological progress, the common consciousness con-
trolling and moulding the various individualities, the
objective canon by which that consciousness is to be
measured. It is from the consideration of these points
that we can gain positive guidance in our theological
work, whether in this Society or by ourselves ; and therefore I propose to devote the remainder of this paper to
some remarks—not exactly in systematical form—which

may help to show what are the real principles of theological progress as they have been manifested in the history of the Church, and must be grasped by us and manifested in us if we are to do real service to theology.

It is not altogether accidental that our negative results have preceded this positive investigation   For the line of thought which brought us face to face with the problem of the relation of theology to Scripture and convinced us that theology is no mere deduction from Scripture is a line of thought in the main historical   We saw that the transition from the position of Owen to that of Cunningham takes place through the influence of the philosophy of the eighteenth century as exhibited in Butler.   And the conclusion that theology must ultimately rest on an inner consciousness, not on purely objective data, represents the stage of thought which essentially characterises our own century and belongs to the rebellion against the formalism both of the old rationalism and the old supernaturalism which marks the religious tendencies of the present day.   Now this new current of thought which surrounds us all and from which we cannot, even though we would, entirely separate ourselves, has a positive as well as a negative side ;   but historically viewed it was the negative side that appeared first.   Thus the first-fruits of the new movement in German theology appeared to be wholly destructive.   The overthrow of the old rationalism seemed to be bought too dear by the fall of the old supernaturalism and by the rise of a school which attacked Scripture in a way of which the rationalists had never dreamed.   Even Schleiermacher appeared to observers in this country to be a baneful power in theology   But soon the so-called reaction followed, and we began to assert that Germany was returning to the old theology ;   whereas, in fact, the properly reactionary movement was very narrow indeed, and the real restorers of a believing theology were disciples of the new school, followers mainly of Schleiermacher, in whom the positive side of

the new movement was beginning to assert itself. While
we still talk of a probable return of the Continental schools
to the conservative theology, the men who are the real
hope of Germany are conscious that as impassable though
not as wide a gulf exists between the new theology and
the old supernaturalism as between the new theology and
the old rationalism.

We are at this moment surrounded by indications that
the movement which has passed over Germany is about
to pass, *mutatis mutandis*, over us. And with us as in
Germany, it is the negative side of the movement which
has come first. There is an uneasy feeling abroad that
the current theology has not rightly defined its relation
to Scripture and its relation to human thought. It is
not, of course, to be supposed that this movement touches
theology only ; something analogous, no doubt, must run
through the whole religious life. But, speaking generally,
the practical side of our Church is so far in advance of the
theoretical that within the Church at least it is mainly
the confessional theology that men are dissatisfied with.
There is a pretty widely diffused impression, not so much
that individual doctrines of the Church are false as that
the whole method and system of theology is artificial,
insecure, and hampering to the legitimate freedom of the
individual ; and it would be quite a mistake to suppose
that this sort of feeling is to be found only among
irreligious men. It must be granted, indeed, that the
mass of earnest church-members are still satisfied with
the confessional theology, the power of which they
have actually experienced, but there is a growing feeling
that that theology does not *fully* supply the needs of the
Church and the individual.

Now the answer which is too often given to this feeling
is simply a challenge to lay down definite points in which
the confessional theology is in error, *i.e.* to show that in
certain cases the *opposite* of the confessional teaching is
laid down in Scripture. This answer ignores the difficulty,

which is not whether the doctrine of the Church is relatively true as against the opposite heresy, but whether it is absolutely and scientifically reliable, and whether the whole system of the confession is a mere reproduction of express Scripture doctrine. Very often, however, those who are unable thoroughly to rest in the old dogmatic are not able exactly to point out the real source of their uneasiness, and are quite ready to grasp at the suggestion that the true remedy is a more careful exegesis of Scripture which is expected to result either in a clear proof or in a clear refutation of the puzzling points. But when the round of exegesis has been gone through the old questions always return unsolved. Everything goes well so long as we stick to grammatical exegesis ; but after all the result is not dogma, and when we come to build up our dogmatic system the proof-texts are no more decisive than before. And the consequence is that men who are by no means unbelievers practically give up theology altogether, resolving that exegesis is the beginning and end of theological science. And this again is a mere transition point ; for if exegesis is not to do service for theology it comes to be asked in what sense exegesis is profitable to the Christian life. Is the spiritual life of the religious subject ministered to by an exact exegesis better than by the simple study of perspicuous passages ? It is easy to see that through questions of this sort the whole question of the nature, functions, and authority of Scripture may be opened up and that in a way which leaves little hope of a satisfactory solution. And, in fact, we see that the inspiration of Scripture is precisely one of the points around which the greatest amount of offensive and defensive activity is at present gathered.

These hints may serve to indicate how vain it is to try to meet the new currents of thought from the old point of view in which the attitude of the theologising subject is one of mere receptivity over against Scripture. The constant appeal to Scripture proof in the sense of the old dogmatic, combined with an apologetic activity in justification of the conception of Scripture on which this system of proof rests, cannot yet dispose of doubts which are based on the perception of the real inadequacy of very much in the present attitude of the conservative theology. And thus the only way to escape the wave of violent unbelief which has already swept over the German Churches is frankly to recognise the need of progress in our theological conceptions, not to suppress the new currents of thought as wholly dangerous, but to urge the positive side of a movement which if discouraged by the Church can express itself only in doubt and negation. And this we are justified in doing if it is really the case that it is no unchristian motive but simply a fair consideration of undeniable facts that compels us to refuse to regard theology as a system of deductions from fixed axioms or a mere compend of Scripture statement, and calls for a recognition of a positive activity of the theologising subject dialectically evolving the contents of an internal consciousness.

Every view of this kind is liable to be accused at first sight of being rationalistic. For we have been accustomed to accept the contrast of reason and revelation as quite ultimate. There are two kinds of theology according to the common teaching, consisting respectively of doctrines revealed by God or doctrines devised by human reason, and so soon as we speak of a theological consciousness we commit ourselves to the latter kind. Happily the answer to this *prima facie* objection is not difficult. The hostility of Rationalism to Revelation is only a part of the wider enmity between Pelagianism and Free Grace. It is only where Revelation is recognised as a part of God's redemptive work that Rationalism has ever refused to acknowledge it. The Socinians themselves are quite ready to submit themselves to Scripture if Scripture is accepted as a book of doctrines only, and not as a means of grace. Rationalism, in short, is Pelagianism of the

intellect, the assertion of man's natural ability to know the
things of the Spirit of God quite apart from the question
whether it is by Revelation or not that these spiritual
things are first set before man's reason   The true antithesis to Rationalism is the position which the Reformation theology justly urges, that there can be no true theology
where there is no true Christian life, that no knowledge
of revelation will make a man a theologian without the
regenerating influence of the Holy Spirit.   " Theologia,"
says Amesius, "est doctrina Deo vivendi."   " Theologicae
vitae natura est vivere Deo."   " And this life," adds
Amesius, " is the spiritual act of the whole man by which
he lays hold of God , and therefore it is the will or heart
that is the proper seat of theology."

It is obviously quite in the spirit, almost in the very
words, of these statements of Amesius that the recent
theology speaks of the Christian consciousness of fellowship with God through Christ Jesus our Redeemer,
as the necessary foundation of theology, or says in
the words of Neander, " Pectus est quod theologum
facit "

The older theologians failed, however, to carry this
view in its full force all through the system of theology.
So long as revelation was treated not as a revelation of
God's person but as a communication of doctrine, so long
as doctrine was regarded as even in a secondary sense the
object of faith, the great principle which was always
acknowledged at starting could hardly fail to get im-
prisoned under the rubrics *De Analogia Fidei* or *De
Fundamentalibus*.   For if there are certain theses which
are of such a kind that, to speak with Turretin, to believe
in them necessarily brings salvation, while to be ignorant
of them is damnable, to doubt dangerous, to deny them
impious, the postulate of theological life naturally resolved
itself into the postulation of these theses as the rule or
analogy by which all doctrines must be tried.

Yet this apparently obvious step is in reality dangerous,

even fatal, to a living theology. For even with regard to
the fundamentals of Christianity there is a wide difference
between an intellectual assent and an experimental conviction. Granted that no true Christian could fail to
subscribe the " fundamentalia," it was not made out that
a theology that held the doctrines was necessarily a
" theologia regeneratorum." And then theology might
be quite orthodox and yet stand in no necessary relation
to the Christian life ; thus the living faith of the Reformers
passed over into the lifeless orthodoxy from which the
rationalism of the eighteenth century arose. In fact,
it was already rationalism to assert that intellectual
assent to certain fundamentals secured the existence of
the true Habitus Theologicus, without which divine truth
could not be understood.

The merely formal conception of the analogy of faith
was surrounded also by theoretical difficulties. What is
the criterion of a fundamental doctrine ? How can we
know that a doctrine is necessary for salvation except
from the actual experience of the saved ?

In the main, with some attempts to reach a firmer
basis, the criterion of a fundamental doctrine was sought
in an express declaration of Scripture. But then the
" dogma de S.S. theopneustῷ, sola et perfecta fidei
regula," is in turn one of the fundamentals, and necessarily
that fundamental on which all the others rest. And does
not this position involve a vicious circle ? In what sense
is it possible that the authority and inspiration of Scripture can be proved at once from its own words ? When
the question reaches this stage the original religious significance of the Analogy of Faith is lost altogether, and the
real basis of theology becomes (as we find it, for example,
in the manual of Hodge) an apologetical inquiry into the
evidences of Christianity with the view of bringing out
the doctrine of inspiration in isolation from all other
doctrines as the absolute prius in the system of Christian
theology, capable of being demonstrated by evidence

convincing even to those who have not experienced the power of Christianity.

It must be admitted that the decline into this way of looking at theology is from one point of view so easy and natural that we need not be surprised that many men conceive that in upholding it they are true to the principles of the Reformation.   And yet it is an historical fact that this way of thought first sprang up in an age which had ceased to be absorbed in the great problem of the Reformation—the problem of realising experimentally in the individual consciousness and in all the functions of social and Church life no less than in the schools what true Christianity is   Nor, indeed, could it be otherwise. So long as the Church of the Reformation was rejoicing in the discovery that forgiveness of sins and all the privileges which Christ bought for His Church are not to be applied to men in a magical manner by a privileged caste which alone can say whether the application is effectual, but that fellowship with God in Christ is a living personal fellowship of which we can be as fully assured as of fellowship with our fellow-men; so long as it was understood that the consciousness of this fellowship with God is no mere subjective feeling but the consciousness of a life far more true than the natural life which no man dreams of doubting—a life which is not bounded by the circuit of my own subjectivity, but in which I am linked together with all my fellow-believers with the whole Church and its glorious Head—a life which is hid with Christ in God, but which is not so hid that it does not manifest itself even now as a real life in, though not of the world, absorbing into itself my whole earthly life, so long as all this was felt, it was impossible for the Church to turn away from the assurance of its calling in Christ which it bore within itself and base the scientific exposition of its position as a Church—and to be such an exposition is the aim of Protestant theology—on mere grounds of natural reason and probability.

The Church is not redeemed by its theology, it theologises because it is redeemed. Theology has done its work when it has given scientific expression to all that is bound up in the consciousness of redemption and the life that flows therefrom. And therefore the theology of a living Church must not start from the mere outward form and vehicle of Christianity, be that form never so divine, but from the true substance of Christianity which the Church knows that she has already grasped. In this spirit it is that the Reformers with one accord, and nowhere more clearly than in our own Confession, assert that it is only the inward work of the Holy Spirit bearing witness with the Word in our hearts that is the true evidence of the infallible truth and divine authority of Scripture. The authority of the Church, or a mere natural contemplation of its incomparable excellences, may serve to make us bow before a mystery that we cannot comprehend; but so long as God's revelation stands only over against us—even though it stand before us as evidently divine— we have not even won a starting-point from which to develop the confession of our faith. The testimony of the Church begins with the inward work of the Holy Spirit—with a Christianity realised in the heart.

From this standpoint it was simply impossible for theology to start from an apologetical estimate of the outer evidences of Christianity. Apologetic speaks to those that are without the Church and serves to make the opponents of Christ inexcusable, to reduce them to silence before a phenomenon that they cannot fathom. But theology speaks to the Church, to those to whom Christianity is no mere phenomenon but a part, the only valuable part, of life. To suppose that the Church has to be nurtured on Christian evidences is to suppose that she has forgotten her own identity. And, therefore, it was a melancholy day for Christendom when the Reformation Church ceased to vindicate its rights as a Church by striving more and more fully to realise its calling in Christ, and began to justify itself to itself much more than to the world without by constantly reiterating the evidences of Christianity. For what clearer proof could be given that the Church had forgotten itself, had come to look upon Christianity as only a doctrine, not a life, or as a body of past history, not as the kernel of all history, and so as something quite external to be accepted on the authority of the miraculousness of its form, not to be fed on and assimilated in virtue of the divineness of its substance ?

It is no accident that the age of the supremacy of " The Christian Evidences " is also the age of moderatism in which the truest spiritual life, the deepest Christian thought, is forced to be unchurchly, and therefore too often sinks into sectarianism and heterodoxy.

But not only is the apologetic way of starting in theology perverse and unchurchly—it is also inconsistent with itself. For to show that Christianity bears in its outer form previous to any realisation of its substance infallible marks of divine authority is only possible when it is agreed what manner of marks these must be. On this point, it is clear, no appeal to natural reason can suffice. The Deist of the old type saw the sure marks of deception in the very miracles which to his opponent proved Christianity to be from God. In short, the Christian even in his so-called natural theology reasons from a conception of God—a consciousness of the relation of God to man which is not merely natural—because not shared by honest antagonists,—which is in a word specifically Christian, though not supporting itself by an appeal to the authority of Scripture. The sure proof that natural theology is not the scientific basis of revealed theology lies in the fact, which the history of the Deistic controversy made abundantly plain, that natural theology, as a knowledge of God true as far as it goes, is, apart from Christianity, an absolute fiction.

If now it appears that even the doctrines which were

supposed natural, and which the written word always presupposes, are consequences, not presuppositions, of true Christian faith, it follows that Christianity is in the first instance so absolutely a thing of the heart that it has to construct for itself even the very elements of a knowledge of God. The subjective consciousness of union with God in Christ is absolutely the first thing in true Christianity, and it is from this consciousness outwards that the Christian develops for himself a true notion of God and a true notion of man. All doctrine even of revelation that had previously been presented to a man's mind from the outside has to be made over again from the inside as soon as the Holy Spirit has begun true faith in the soul.

Thus the rejection of natural theology in the sense of the old theology bears with it the characteristic principle of the new theology that subjective religion necessarily precedes true religious knowledge. That is, theology is no longer the sum of those doctrines by believing which we are united to God in faith and which, from the witness of the Holy Spirit to this their saving power, are received as indubitably true; but the doctrines of theology are the product of faith, the knowledge of the subject and object of faith which are evolved by dialectical necessity from the assurance of the primitive act itself.

It may perhaps be granted that there is force in the argument which repels the accusation of rationalism so often brought against the new theology. But then, some will say, you fall back into the no less dangerous extreme of mysticism, giving an unbounded play to an unrestrained subjectivity. The analogy just mentioned will readily suggest the true answer here. A consciousness originally subjective in character is not, therefore, purely subjective in origin. And so the Christian consciousness does not arise in man from within. Faith is wrought in the believer only by the Holy Spirit making known Christ unto us. It is a real objective revelation which operating in our hearts produces a consciousness in the first instance indeed subjective, but capable of being developed into true knowledge of the revealing God.

It is, indeed, true that this explanation would be inadequate on the old idea of revelation as a body of truth received on the testimony not of a human witness but of God , for truth received on testimony is either not understood at all or at once grasped in its full objectivity. But the truth that has a saving power is truth experienced It is an experimental knowledge of God Himself in Christ, an experimental knowledge of sin and salvation, that must be the content of Christian theology.

A mere dictation from on high of truths about God and man would be revelation in a heathen, not in a Christian sense.

The true idea of revelation is such an activity of God among and towards men as shall enable man to apprehend God in His holiness, justice, and redemptive love, just by the same kind of experience as enables us to know our fellow-men. It is the record of such a revelation that lies before us in Holy Scripture. For there we read how God from the earliest time dealt personally with mankind in a supernatural history culminating in the incarnation, death, and resurrection of our Lord, and how, from age to age, the Church of God was able to lay hold on the divine person thus manifested, by faith unto salvation. Christ Himself appears in this history as the full manifestation of God. He is the *Word of God*, *i.e.* revelation is a *word* not in the sense of a truth dictated by God but as the living expression of the inmost heart of the speaker.

Let us look for a moment at the way in which the historical personality of Christ influenced those that were brought face to face with Him. We know from the Gospel history, especially from that Gospel which is the direct record of an apostle's experience, that the bond which knit the faithful disciples to their Master was not in the first instance a distinct conception of the Godhead im-

manent in Him. The surrender of their whole heart to
Christ was the condition, not the fruit, of a correct Christology. Even the Resurrection left much that was vague
in the Apostles' theology, and perhaps the full development of the Christology of John was only attained towards the end of a long life of devoted service to a risen
Saviour. And yet the actual historic personality of the
Saviour did not vary, but was as truly divine when John
first saw Him as after the Ascension. Not mainly the
addition of new facts, of new phenomena, in the life of
our Lord, but a growth in the regenerated personality of
the disciple, explains the growth of John's theology. The
first effect of contact with Christ was the production of
faith and love, and then it required only the continued
presence of the same contact with the Saviour to develop
a true knowledge of Him with whom the life of the apostle
was now inseparably bound up. And so the historical
Christ was ever the foundation and rule of John's Christology, though only the inner life of union with Christ
supplied the power to pierce through the phenomena and
know what this wondrous person really is.

The growth of the Christian personality cannot be
essentially different for an apostle and for the Christian
in our own day. And this essential identity must clearly
extend itself to the growth of that necessary knowledge
whereby the new man comes to understand his own new
life. With us, too, the first thing must be that we are
brought through the word read and preached into contact with the historical realities of Christianity. We can
no longer see Christ with our bodily eyes, but to us, as
Luther delighted to say, "the written word is the $\sigma \grave{\alpha} \rho \xi$
$X \rho \iota \sigma \tau o \hat{\upsilon}$, the outward vehicle which manifests the person
of the God-man." But this mere outer contact with the
phenomenal Christ has no saving power Nor can we
by natural reason construe for ourselves the true living
person set before us in the word Only the Spirit working
faith in us can carry us beyond the form and bring us

into living union with the substance. Our first apprehension of a living Christ lies in the first spark of love for
Him who first loved us. And then, when this bond of
inner sympathy unites us to the person of Christ, the true
living substance shines effulgent through all the form, but
not at first in clear lineaments. Only by a gradual
growth, by constant experimental intercourse with the
historical person of Christ, *i.e.* by comparing every point
in the gospel history with our own personal necessities,
does our faith develop into knowledge. And even so
this knowledge is as yet empirical, in crude practical
form not grasped with scientific exactness. Side by side
with Christian experience, and acting on the data it
furnishes, must go an exercise of real hard thought before
our knowledge takes scientific shape and is really worthy
to be called theology.

In this process Scripture is not, as it was in the old
dogmatic, the sole instrument of theology. Much rather
the instrument of our theology is the whole compass of
the regenerated mental powers. But Scripture is still the
sole foundation and rule of theology, for in Scripture only is
the object of that faith which we desire to comprehend
laid down in an authoritative form, *i.e* as it presented
itself historically and was apprehended by men enlightened
by God's Spirit to grasp it truly. And, therefore, we are
called upon to construe the object of faith to ourselves,
as it appears in Scripture, to see the true depth of meaning
lying in the history If our intelligible Christ differs
from the Christ of history, if the salvation we receive
differs from the salvation which Christ bestowed on those
who were eye-witnesses of His saving work, then we
may be sure either that we have argued falsely from our
faith, or that our faith itself is false, having its source within
ourselves and not in a true operation of God which can
never be out of harmony with His working in days gone by.

The truth of all this is not really affected by the fact
that no theologian goes through this process in its ideal

simplicity. So far, our theology is always presented ready-made for our acceptance, not constructed by ourselves at first hand. Even Scripture contains not only normal Christian experience, but in some measure developed theology But all this only simplifies, does not dispense with, the necessity of re-thinking a theology which is actually to become part of our personality. The thing has still to be thought out by every man for himself, though not thought out without guidance from those who have gone before.

The mutual support and assistance which men can thus render one another in thinking out their Christianity into an intelligible form is just one case of the general doctrine of the Church as an organism in which no part can be developed save in and through the development of the whole. And thus we pass from the theology of the individual to the theology of the Church. The theology of the individual is always a one-sided imperfect development of that common faith which binds the whole Church to Christ. But all these imperfect developments supplement each other. And because the individual is united not only to Christ but to his fellow-believers, every growth of one member reacts on the others and makes it easier for them to grow in that direction. And thus in each age arises a unity in the theology of the whole Church—a theology which is not strictly the explanation of any one-sided individual development, but which is the explanation of the faith of the Church as one whole And as this theology of the Church is a part of the life of the Church it reacts on all other departments of life, so that the next generation of the Church grows easily and naturally into the ideas which the fathers elaborated with much toil Thus room is given for a further development of theology according to the new experiences of the new generation, so that wherever the Church is really strong in faith and living union with its Head, theology advances to an ever fuller and fuller comprehension of the ideal relation between Christ and the Church made perfect.

In all this Scripture can never wax old.   To Scripture we must ever turn to realise the true historic Christ until the Risen and Ascended One returns to His people.   But all *theology* must advance, if it were only because the Christ of the gospels so far transcends the theology of any age that to cling to an unchangeable dogma is really to cease to look to Him whom we must ever seek to comprehend more fully, to love more singly, to follow more devotedly.

Finally, to apply all this in one word to our own case ·—

Three things, I suppose, will make our theological work harmonious and profitable

1. That we take Christ as the A and Ω of our theology : the foundation of our theology, the historical Christ manifested in the gospel ; and the goal of our theology, Christ coming again in glory as the Head of a spotless Church.

2 That we seek to think and reason, not in our own strength, but by the Holy Spirit strengthening us to see Christ as He is.

3. That we patiently and laboriously avail ourselves of our historical position as inheritors of the theological fund which the Church has already gained, not yielding our freedom to man's judgment, yet not forgetting that we are but parts of a great whole, and that true advance is possible only by diligently developing those results which God's providence has already given to the Church.

And now may the Father of our Lord Jesus Christ, of whom all fatherhood in heaven and on earth is named, grant us according to the riches of His glory to be strengthened with might by the Spirit in the inner man, that Christ may dwell in our hearts by faith, that we, being rooted and grounded in love, may be able to comprehend with all saints what is the length and breadth and depth and height, and to know the love of Christ which passeth knowledge that we may be filled with all the fulness of God.

IV

ON THE QUESTION OF PROPHECY IN
THE CRITICAL SCHOOLS OF THE CONTINENT

(From " The British Quarterly Review," April 1870)

THE works whose title head this article [1] are too divergent in character and purpose to allow us to think of completely discussing them in a single paper. We propose to make use of them only in their bearing on a single subject—the present state of the question of prophecy in the Continental critical schools ; and we have chosen these books partly because they are among the most recent that deal with the subject of prophecy, and partly because they seem to us to be typical in their character, marking out leading lines of thought among the very various conceptions of prophecy which prevail in Continental theology at the present day. In saying this, we do not, of course, mean that these books are of equal or even similar intrinsic value. In Ewald's great work, despite the waywardness and arbitrary self-reliance which so often disfigure his criticism, we everywhere recognise a man of original and creative power, who never fails to put great questions in a fresh and instructive light. In Kuenen, again, we are most impressed by the cold pellucidity of thought which

[1] [They were four in number, viz : the second edition of Ewald's *Prophets* (1867-68) , the second part of Kuenen's *Historical and Critical Inquiry* (1863) ; the first part of Kuenen's *Religion of Israel* (1869) , and the first part of Gustav Baur's *History of Old Testament Prophecy* (1861).]

lays bare to himself and others the real principles and unavoidable problems of a purely naturalistic criticism ; while in Gustav Baur, with less genius than Ewald, and less acuteness than Kuenen, we find most fully the qualities, happily by no means rare among German critics, which seem to us to give most hope for the future— an honest painstaking spirit of inquiry which, though heartily devoted to the critical method, has reached, and is not afraid to speak out, the conviction that *that* is not a true criticism which refuses to find in the Old Testament the special hand of a revealing God.

In the choice of these typical writers, we confine ourselves to disciples of the critical school—men who approach the questions of prophecy from the historical, not from the theological side. We do not think that this is the only line of inquiry that can be fruitful ; we are persuaded, indeed, that the want of a clear theological position has greatly limited the real value of the work of men like Ewald, and we see in the labours of such theologians as Hofmann and Delitzsch, to mention two names only, very much which has merited the lasting gratitude of every Old Testament student. But in their starting-point, at least, the historical and theological methods are so different, even where they lead ultimately to the same result, that it is impossible to speak of both in the limits of a single article ; and in our country the critical method seems most to call for exposition, especially in view of the unscrupulous pertinacity with which the enemies of Christianity in England are accustomed to claim every critic as a witness on their side.

The fundamental principle of the higher criticism lies in the conception of the organic unity of all history We must not see in history only a medley of petty dramas involving no higher springs of action than the passions and interests of individuals. History is not a stage-play, but the life and life-work of mankind continually unfolding in one great plan. And hence we have no true history where we cannot pierce through the outer shell of tradition into the life of a past age, mirrored in the living record of men who were themselves eye-witnesses and actors in the scenes they describe.   Not mere facts, but the inner kernel of true life, is what the critical student delights to find in every genuine monument of antiquity ; and the existence of such a kernel is to him the last criterion of historical authenticity.   A tradition that violates the continuity of historical evolution and stands in no necessary relation to the conditions of the preceding and following age must be untrue ; and, above all, an ancient writing which is no frigid product of the school, but is instinct with true life, must be the product of that age which contained the conditions of the life it unconsciously reflects.

It is clear that this theory of history contains much that is true. That a unity of plan runs through all history, all must hold who in any sense believe in Providence.   But just as the name of Providence may be used to express the most diverse theories of God's working in the world, the word *organic*, applied to the providential development of history, may cover the widest differences of thought ; for to one thinker the organic development of history will mean the unbroken sweep of natural law without one breath of the creative Spirit from on high, while to a higher school of thought the one purpose of history is the purpose of everlasting love, worked out, in, and through human personality, by a personal redeeming God.   Now, the sphere in which all differences on this point appear in clearest relief is that part of history of which the Bible is the most authentic monument.   For the problems of Israel's history are essentially religious problems   Rightly to conceive the progress of religious faith, thought, and life in the people of Israel, until the theocratic development received its absolute conclusion in the life of Him who gathered all the rays of splendour that flash through the Old Testament into the effulgent focus of His transcendent personality, and in the course of this task to inweave the Bible record with the history of which it is itself a part—such is the critical problem of the theocratic history.

Of all the monuments of Israel's history, the most precious by far to the critical student are the Old Testament prophecies, witnessing as they do to the inner life of the noblest and truest Israelites, representing at once the purest religious conceptions and the deepest national feelings that these ages could show These are qualities to which no disciple of the higher criticism can remain insensible The time is gone when the sources of the prophetic inspiration could be sought in an artificial æsthetical culture, in political intrigue, above all, in pious fraud.   The starting-point in all critical study of prophecy lies in the acknowledgment that the prophetic writings are the true key to the marvellous religious development, which is, in fact, the kernel of all Israel's history.   And with this awakened sense of the historical value of prophecy has come the universal conviction that such writings cannot be forgeries.   It may be fair to ask whether they belong in all instances to the prophets whose names they now bear ; but that they really are the writings of prophets, unquestionable witnesses to the true life of the age that produced them, no one doubts.   In truth, the tendency of the critical school is rather to overvalue the historical importance of these monuments at the expense of books properly historical.   The dislike for the miraculous which the long predominance of rationalistic philosophy has almost engrained into German thought, has often produced, even in critics like Ewald—who, we hope to show, are by no means naturalistic at heart—an unwarranted mistrust for many Old Testament narratives, and has encouraged the formation of arbitrary historical theories for which scattered hints in the prophets form almost the only basis.   Yet it would be unfair to dwell only on this side of the case.   It is certain that much of the Old Testament history is not contemporary ; and the truest history must always bear witness not only to the age of which it speaks, but to the age in which it was written, in a way that often makes it hard to read the inner life that underlies the historical fact, save by the aid of contemporary records. It can hardly, in truth, be doubted that, if we desire to gain the clearest insight into the religious history of Israel, our true starting-point must be the period of the earliest extant prophetic writings.

If we put out of account the Book of Joel, the date of which is still disputed, the age to which we are thus referred is the eighth century before Christ, the age of Amos and Hosea, of Isaiah and Micah This period is known to historians as the Assyrian period of Israel's history. But the early years of the century are not yet impressed with the destroying stamp of the monarchs of Nineveh. The century opens on a period of prosperity both in Judah and in Ephraim. Jeroboam II had restored the ancient frontier of his realm ; Judah flourished under the vigorous sceptre of Uzziah. In one of these prosperous years there appeared at the great sanctuary at Bethel, at which the whole northern kingdom was met for solemn festival, a prophet from Judah, Amos, a herdsman of Tekoa. With unsparing words he laid bare the inner disorders of the realm, that combination of the rudest violence with effeminate luxury so characteristic of the breaking up of society in an oriental kingdom. But it was not with the eye of a statesman that Amos viewed these corruptions. They were fatal because they were the fruit of a national rebellion against Jahveh,[1] the God

---

[1] Since Delitzsch in the second edition of his *Psalmen* renounced the pronunciation Jahavah, Continental scholars may be said to be agreed in regarding Jahveh as the true punctuation of the " ineffable " Name. The example of Delitzsch was at once followed by his disciples, *e g* by Köhler, of Bonn (now of Erlangen), who in his habilitation thesis of the year before had defended Delitzsch's earlier view. When men like the lamented Hupfeld write Jhvh, they do so only to confine themselves to what MSS. authorise—not because they doubt that Jahveh or Jahaveh is the true pronunciation By adopting a pronunciation

of Israel   The corrupt and sensual service of Bethel and
of Gilgal—half Jahveh-worship, half Canaanitish idolatry—
was the root as well as the symbol of the sickness of the
land   " Thus saith Jahveh, Seek me, and live ! "   Stroke
after stroke from the hand of Jahveh had fallen upon the
people, and yet they refused to turn to Him.   And now
the judgment must be final · " The high places of Isaac
shall be wasted, and the sanctuaries of Israel destroyed.
  .   And Israel shall go forth as a captive from his land " [1]
Nor does the prophet content himself with vague fore-
bodings of woe.   His keen vision detects the instrument
of Jahveh's wrath in the distant Assyrians—as yet so
unfamiliar to his hearers that he describes them with
precision, without once mentioning their names.[2]

This sketch of the prophecy of Amos enables us to
illustrate the kind of questions of detail which divide the
critical school.   That Amos prophesied the fall of Israel
by the Assyrians, and the overthrow of Jeroboam's house
at a time of undisturbed prosperity, all are agreed.   Not
less unanimous, on the other hand, is the resolution to
find the true centre of the prophecy not in this prediction,
but in the religious and ethical ideas drawn from a profoundly spiritual Theism which constrain the prophet to
look for an inevitable judgment.   But the question
remains, how far the definite colouring of this judgment
passes beyond the limits of the impressions which present
facts would naturally make on an able and reflecting mind
That is, in the present case, How far had the westward
development of the Assyrian empire extended itself when
Amos wrote ?   Ewald, whom we have mainly followed
above, judges from Amos vi. 2, that even Ctesiphon
on the Tigris had not yet fallen before Assyria   Accordingly he places Amos in the first half of Jeroboam's reign,
when Israel was still the first of the nations (chap vi. 1)

---

which, though little current amongst us, is heard in all the lecture-rooms
of Germany, we shall, moreover, avoid the awkwardness of writing the
name differently in extracts from our authors and in the text itself

[1] Amos vii 9-11   [2] Ewald, *Propheten*, 1 11 ṣ

knowing no neighbour of equal strength.[1] Kuenen, again, draws from the same passage (we cannot but think at the expense of the context) the conclusion that Ctesiphon had already fallen,[2] and so that it was not more than natural that the prophet should see in the Assyrians the nation designed to fulfil the judgment which he firmly expected. On this view Amos is brought down to the latter half of Jeroboam's reign, when Assyria, as appears from Hosea, was already much nearer the thoughts of the Israelites. It is easy to see the divergent tendencies of these views. Ewald is ready to ascribe to the prophet a spiritual insight into the course of Jahveh's purpose which no man could attain by mere natural reasoning. They are the thoughts of Jahveh, not thoughts of his own, that the prophet thinks ; and so he is able to apprehend new combinations in history before they begin to arise. Kuenen, on the other hand, would have everything explained by the psychology of ordinary life. He ascribes to the prophet no really new creative thought, as will appear more clearly when we trace the way in which he accounts for the rise of a spiritual conception of the God of Israel. If we hold fast the clue which this instance affords, we shall soon see how wide the difference is between two men who on the surface may seem closely allied, and whom, in fact, Kuenen declares to hold the same principles of prophetic criticism [3]

The predictions of Amos received a speedy fulfilment. The death of Jeroboam was the signal for an outburst of anarchy which overthrew the house of Jehu, and dissolved every band of political and social union. A struggle conducted with barbarous ferocity placed in the hands of Menahem a sceptre so feeble that only foreign aid could ensure his position. And so for the first time the Assyrians became the arbiters of Israel's fortunes, a position from which they never again retired.[4] The remaining history

---

[1] *Propheten*, 1. 152   [2] *Onderzoek*, 11 334
[3] *Ibid*, 11 25.   [4] 2 Kings xv 8-20

of the kingdom of Ephraim is tumultuous and confused. Again and again the throne is gained and lost by violence. A truly national policy never appears. Pekah alone felt himself strong enough in combination with Syria, the old enemy of Israel, to attack the kingdom of Judah. But this attempt at a bolder policy only served to drive Judah, too, into the hands of Assyria.[1] The fall of Damascus brought the outposts of the king of Nineveh close to the land of Canaan, which seemed now no more than the " bridge of battle " between the rival empires of the Nile and the Tigris. Pent up between two such monarchies, the most daring politician could not hope for the independence either of Judah or of Ephraim. The only importance of the land lay in the strength of the almost impregnable mountain fastnesses which Egyptians and Assyrians alike were eager to secure. The utmost that the Hebrew princes could hope for was to maintain a partial independence by holding these fortresses in the interests of one or the other powers   Thus all political life, at least in the northern kingdom, resolved itself into a struggle between an Egyptian and an Assyrian party, whose every step was guided from without, and whose alternate victories were marked by more than one bloody revolution. At length King Hoshea threw himself with decision into the cause of Egypt. Then came the final heroic struggle with Nineveh. The last energies of the people were concentrated in the defence of Samaria, and the fall of the city marks the disappearance of the ten tribes from history

If the last years of the kingdom of Ephraim showed us nothing more than the passionate death-struggle of a long-forgotten monarchy, we might claim for this narrative a tragic interest, but hardly a place among the great events of the world's history. But, side by side with the political parties that we have sketched, there existed in Israel a third party, which stood so far apart from both the others,

---

[1] 2 Kings xvi. , Isa. vii.

and which was guided by principles so remarkable as to
possess an undying interest for the student of history.
This party—to borrow the language of Kuenen—

" was as averse to alliance with the stranger as to subjection under his yoke. A citizen of the kingdom of
Ephraim, Hosea the son of Beeri, condemns the league
both with Asshur and with Egypt.   Ephraim and Judah,
he writes, were sick , the former had sought help from
Assyria, but ' they cannot cure you, and cannot heal your
wound.'   To call now on Assyria, now on Egypt, is folly.
' Ephraim is like a silly dove, without understanding.'
To make a league with Assyria, to send balsam to Egypt
is ' to herd the wind, to pursue the east wind '; it is of
one piece with the fact that ' they multiply lies and
violence all day long.'   The time is coming when the nation
itself shall confess, ' Asshur cannot save us, we will not
ride upon war-horses,' the time when bow and sword
shall be broken and war cease from the earth.' . . .
' Strange as this policy may seem to us, at first sight,'
adds Kuenen, ' it is quite explicable when we view it in
connection with the religious convictions of which it is
the counterpart.   When the men whose words we have
quoted condemn alliance with the stranger, reliance on
chariots and horses—in one word, trust in man, and in
man's strength, it is because they wish Israel to rely on
Jahveh, and on him alone." [1]

In truth, the political attitude of Hosea and his
fellow-prophets, however remarkable, is not the side from
which their characteristic standpoint may be best comprehended.   Their policy, if such a word is applicable, was
mainly negative.   At an earlier time, we know, there had
been prophets in Israel who habitually directed great
affairs of state—who had more than once made and
unmade kings. The prophets of the eighth century had
no such ambition.   In the northern kingdom their political
influence was almost inappreciable ; for, in these days of
violence, a political party could exist only by the sword.
But, even had they been able to influence the heads of the
people, it is certain that they had no policy to propose.

[1] *Godsdienst*, p. 40

Amos, we saw, had ceased, even during the brilliant
administration of the house of Jehu, to believe that any
policy could save a nation that had departed so far from
Jahveh and His law.   And now the dimmest eyes could
see that the days of the nation were numbered   When
Hosea calls upon the people to turn from schemes of
Egyptian alliance or Assyrian vassalage, he does not
dream that the result will be present deliverance.   He
calls not for the correction of a political error, but for the
forsaking of political sin   The worldly policy of the rulers
is of one piece with the moral corruption that pervades the
whole people.   " The people," he says, " fear not Jahveh,
and what can a king do for them ? " [1]   The calf worship,
the Baal worship, the impurity, the deceit and violence
that filled the land, called for a judgment that could not
fail

> The trumpet to thy lips !
> He swoops like an eagle on the House of Jahveh,
> Because they have transgressed my covenant,
> Trespassed against my law
> Israel hath cast off the gracious One,
> The foe pursue him ! [2]

The prophet is conscious indeed that he is called to
proclaim truths which, if listened to, would save the
people.   Could they be brought to trust in Jahveh, and
obey Him, He would save them ; but so little does he look
for such an issue that he feels that the prophetic spirit
too must stumble and fall in the general ruin.   But with
all this, there is in Hosea another side, which we may
characterise in the words of Ewald :—

" If Hosea had resigned himself to these painful feelings
alone, he might have been a poet, but could never have
been a prophet.   As a prophet of Jahveh, he can indeed
forebode the necessity of the fall of the present form of
the kingdom, but must not overlook the eternal truths and
hopes that lie beyond ; and to these, in the last instance,
he must expressly point, as the only light which dissipates
the darkness of the present and the nearest future. . . .

---

[1] Hosea x 3   [2] Ibid viii 1 seq

To Hosea the corner-stone of the truth of all hopes is just this : Jahveh, whose love long since created and formed the people, cannot for ever forsake his own work ; his love must complete what it has designed, the salvation of the people, which, just because it has from the first experienced this love, must at length remember its origin, and turn again to the true source of love and salvation ; and just when the more powerful human foreboding is ready to utter the final sentence of eternal extinction—just then it springs back confounded, and itself extinguished before the higher Divine presentiment which, at the decisive moment, presses forward with overpowering force " [1]

In this unshaken confidence in Israel's future all the prophets are agreed. But by none, perhaps, is the love of Jahveh for His people delineated so profoundly and tenderly as by Hosea—himself a man of the tenderest affections, chastened and deepened by the calamities of his people. The history of mankind contains no more touching instance of faith than the way in which Hosea closes a book that again and again foretells the captivity, by introducing the converted people addressing Jahveh in words of submission and thanksgiving.[2] So striking a union of faith that no mishap could shake, with an insight that never failed to read the fatal signs of the times, marks off the prophets as clearly from ordinary religious enthusiasts as from ordinary moral teachers.

In the kingdom of the ten tribes, as Hosea himself foresaw, even the prophetic word must be swept away helpless in the general ruin, finding no response in the hearts of the people. But in Judah it was otherwise. There, too, the people had sunk, under Ahaz, into deep religious and social corruption. The heathenism into which that fantastical king threw himself from the first, was accompanied by a rapid growth of luxury and sensuality, and by a general decay of the vigorous theocratic system by which alone the small and isolated kingdom could maintain its position among its neighbours.

[1] *Propheten*, i. 179.   [2] Hosea xiv 3.

Soon the foreign wars of the king were marked by continual reverses, which only drove the court to seek deliverance in still wilder superstitions, and at last in the horrid
worship of Moloch—the fruit of that lowest grade of
religious feeling which knows no sentiment but terror.
But meantime the true national and spiritual life of
Israel gathered round the prophets of Jahveh. Two of
these prophets, Isaiah and Micah, we know from their
extant writings. In external circumstances no two
men could be more unlike. Isaiah was a man of noble
family and high culture, moving in courtly circles and
versed in all the political movements of the day. Micah,
a simple unpolished countryman, knew only so much
of the state of the nation as a keen, uneducated sense
could read in the affairs of his own province. Yet so
thoroughly did the prophetic fire penetrate and assimilate
the whole natural life, that, amidst considerable differences
of detail, these men represent at bottom precisely the
same religious and political standpoint. Let us pause for
a moment at this point. The critical study of prophecy
has by no means borne out the view that, in points of
detail, especially in predictive details, the prophets are
fully at one   But, precisely, these discrepancies bring out
in stronger relief the substantial unity of the prophetic
spirit. The unity did not lie in a system of dogmas. The
prophets were familiar indeed with the old theocratic
legislation and the writings of their own predecessors,
but their attitude towards both was perfectly free. They
knew that Jahveh was guiding His people to a higher
standpoint, in which even prophecy itself must fall away
It was not by a system of externals, but by participation
in the spirit of Jahveh, that the prophets felt themselves
bound together. Nor was a man a prophet merely in
virtue of his earnest faith in the God of Israel. The
prophet felt the hand of Jahveh upon him, impelling him
in a course that he could not have chosen for himself ;
and, in this course, his individuality was not obliterated,

but absorbed and swayed by the one Spirit of all prophecy.
He speaks and thinks, not his own thoughts, but the
thoughts of Jahveh, the living God, whose eternal purpose
flows in ever-varying form, but ever in substantial unity,
through all the history of his people   The man who,
amid the tumult of the ungodly within, the impotent
raging of the heathen without, can hear the voice of
Jahveh pealing through history, he is of necessity a
prophet

> The lion hath roared, who will not fear ?
> The Lord Jahveh hath spoken, who can but prophesy ? [1]

We return to the work of Isaiah.   Very early in life
he began to proclaim the judgment of Jahveh against his
countrymen, in tones not unlike those of the prophets of
Ephraim.   But while in the northern kingdom no judgment could suffice that was not—as regarded the present
order of things—final, in Judah there were still elements
of hope.   A remnant shall yet return , Jahveh will still
give help to them that call upon Him ; these are the
corner-stones of hope on which Isaiah's life-work was
built.[2]   But the hope is only in Jahveh, only in return to
him.   Not by chariots and by horsemen—" By returning
and resting shall ye be saved, in being still and trusting is
your strength." [3]

It was not long ere these principles were put to the test.
The united armies of Syria and Ephraim seemed ready to
crush the enfeebled kingdom.   Ahaz and all his court
were filled with panic, and saw no hope except in the
oppressive protection of Assyria.   Isaiah alone remained
calm, and confidently foretold the speedy desolation of
the hostile lands.   But let Ahaz beware of seeking this
deliverance at the hands of man. " If ye will not *believe*,
ye shall not endure." [4]   And when the king did refuse
belief, and persisted in his Assyrian policy, the prophet
boldly maintained that such a course would indeed end

---

[1] Amos iii 8.   [2] Ewald, *Propheten*, i 274.
[3] Isa. xxx. 15.   [4] *Ibid* vii 9.

in the overthrow of his enemies, but also in the no less
certain humiliation of his own land before the Assyrians,
who would pour over Judah like the Euphrates in flood.
Yet the faithlessness of Ahaz cannot change the issue of
God's care for His own.   Suddenly, as he describes these
calamities, the prophet turns against the invading heathen:

> Arm yourselves—and be undone ,
> Arm yourselves—and be undone ,
> Devise a counsel, and it shall be broken ,
> Speak a word, and it shall not stand,
> For with us is God [1]

And so Isaiah rises again to a bright vision of hope, when
the throne of David shall no longer be held by a renegade
like Ahaz ; but when the whole people, reconciled to
Jahveh, and joyful in the light of His countenance, shall
flourish under the unending government of a great and
perfect Davidic king, in whose days even the heathen
nations shall forsake their idols and join themselves to
Jahveh, God of Israel.

In this scheme, which grew up in Isaiah's mind at an
early stage of his prophetic activity, there was much that
could not be verified in his own lifetime.   There never
lived a true prophet whose hopes and aspirations were
bounded by the circle of his own circumstances.   True
prophecy is always ideal, seeking to grasp not the immediate future, but the eternal and unchanging principles
which Jahveh, the living God, is ever working out more
fully among His people   The critical study of prophecy
has done no greater service than to point out how small
a fraction of the prophetic writings is strictly predictive.
Not detailed events lying in the future, but broad religious
principles, are the ground on which the prophets are at
home.   But then these principles are grasped with such
firmness, with so *concrete* a hold, that they never remain
floating, as it were, in the air, but are always applied with
confidence to the special needs and special circumstances
of the theocracy.   And so it was with Isaiah.   Part, at

[1] Isa viii. 9.

least, of his general scheme did come to be tested in the most crucial way during his own lifetime.

The Assyrians came as he had foretold, overthrew the enemies of Judah, but pressed their allies scarcely less hardly.   Meantime, the words of the prophet and his compeers had not fallen dead upon the land.   A vigorous reaction was at hand, which should unite in one cause the patriotism and the faith of the kingdom.   Hezekiah, the son of Ahaz, threw all his heart into the cause of the prophets.   A great religious reformation ensued, and, as always was the case in Judah, there sprung up at the same time a powerful revival of patriotic feeling.   The king and his nobles were eager to throw off the yoke of the Assyrian, whose armies were no longer at their gates, and whose superior force they hoped to counterbalance by an Egyptian alliance.   There was much in this plan that might naturally attract the prophet, who, beyond doubt, had entered with lively interest into the religious reformation, and who was now an acknowledged power in the nation   Yet Isaiah steadily set his face against the Egyptian alliance.   Deliverance must come from God Himself.

> The Egyptians are men and not God,
> Their horses flesh and not spirit ,
> Jahveh stretches out His hand,
> And the helper stumbles and the holpen falls ,
> All of them perish together.[1]

It is very obvious that this policy of Isaiah was in fact the prudent course.   We can hardly doubt that, but for the persistence with which he exposed and combated the plans of the Egyptian party, Jerusalem would have shared the fate of Samaria.   But it is not in this light that the prophet's course can be appreciated aright.   He feared Assyria as little as he trusted Egypt ; he knew only that so long as Nineveh was executing God's judgment on the nations, no alliance could contend against it, but that Jahveh Himself would give deliverance from a power that

[1] Isa. xxxi 3.

went beyond his commission And therefore, as Senna-cherib's host rose to deeds of ever wilder violence, as the yoke was tightened around the neck of Jerusalem and human help seemed more distant, Isaiah's spirit rose. He stirred up the king and people to some share of his own confidence, persuaded them to reject an offer of alliance from Tirhakah, king of Ethiopia,[1] and to collect their strength within the fortresses in patient expectation of a God-sent deliverance. And now Sennacherib lay at the gates, deliberately preparing to sweep Judah from the face of the earth, and so remove the last barrier that lay between him and Egypt, and secure an impregnable posi-tion in which to await the assault of Tirhakah. The strength but not the faith of the nation was exhausted, but Jahveh fought for His people. A terrible pestilence ravaged the host of the Assyrians, and the panic-stricken remnant sought their own land in the wildest confusion.

We cannot better characterise this great blow, from which Assyria never recovered, than in the words of Ewald —

"In the evolution of these great events, Jerusalem had been the last knot round which all turned, but also the strong rock on which the arrogance of the Assyrian was broken ; and further, the fire that burned between Assyrian and Jew was no mere war of subjugation, but had at last risen to the height of a purely religious con-flict.[2] If, then, the victory here remained on the side of Jerusalem, it is no less true that Faith in the might of the spiritual God, whom the Jews worshipped, had gained a visible victory, as glorious as we can well conceive. It was one of those rare days when the truth, which is not to be grasped with hands, and which is so slow to find deep entrance among men, once more forced itself, with over-whelming certainty on the people. . . . The long and weary straits that went before, the hard temptation, the swift surprising deliverance, the compression of everything into Faith in the true Helper, makes this time parallel to the first foundation of the theocracy. And hence its

---

[1] Isa xviii   [2] On *both* sides   See Isa xxxvi 18 *sqq.*

influence on the future was extraordinary, and the history of the kingdom of Judah stands here at its third turning-point." [1]

In our sketch of these events we have inserted no trait on which the latest historians are not agreed. If Hitzig does not enter so warmly as Ewald into the spirit of the narrative, he concedes as completely the extraordinary effects of Isaiah's prophetic faith and prophetic word ; and Kuenen admits fully the unwavering confidence, based on religious faith, with which Isaiah foretold the wondrous deliverance.[2]   Even the distinctest prediction of the trial and deliverance (chap. xxix. 1-8) to which Bleek [3] appeals, as perhaps the most striking proof of the real predictive gifts of the prophets, he unhesitatingly places before the event ; but with these general admissions he seeks by one or two touches to give the whole narrative a far less striking colour than it possesses in the German histories.   Without venturing direct affirmation, he hints that the account of the final disaster is vague and incomplete, suggests that Isaiah was really encouraging the people to endurance, in the hope that Tirhakah's army would divert Sennacherib from the siege—an attitude not very consistent with the answer made by the prophet to the Ethiopian ambassadors, nor, indeed, psychologically reconcilable with the whole tone of his utterances—and insinuates that to no small extent the deliverance was the natural consequence of this policy.   It is clear, however, that these ingenuous suggestions derive their whole force from the hypothesis, nowhere directly stated, but in the *Godsdienst* plainly hinted at, that it was really a campaign with Tirhakah that broke the Assyrian force.   Unluckily the accounts preserved by Herodotus, in which the defeat of Sennacherib is associated with the field-mouse—a recognised symbol of pestilence— by no means favour this view.[4]

[1] *Geschichte* (ed. 2), III. 636
[2] *Onderzoek*, II. 92, 96. *Godsdienst*, 39.   [3] *Einl. ins A.T*, 437.
[4] Cf. Hitzig, *Geschichte Israels*, p. 125 (1869).

It is not necessary for our present purpose to trace farther in historical order the phenomena of Hebrew prophecy as recorded in the contemporary sources. To sketch even in outline the activity of the various prophets and the special character of their teaching, would require a volume, and would often involve much difficult discussion. It would be impossible to avoid intricate questions as to date and authorship depending frequently on purely technical arguments. Even to analyse Isaiah's works with accuracy is a task which critics have not yet accomplished with unanimity. We are able, indeed, to form a very distinct conception of his figure from prophecies of quite unambiguous date A large part of the book of Isaiah fits together with the historical records of the time into a picture of such obvious genuineness that no critic doubts the authenticity of these utterances But, side by side with these, the book contains many prophecies not less genuine and vigorous, not less obviously inspired by a religious feeling that was in full *rapport* with contemporary life, which yet find no historical basis in the known life of the prophet. This is a phenomenon which the critic cannot pass over In Hosea, in Amos, in Micah, in the other parts of Isaiah's own writings, we find every word not only instinct with Divine eternal truth that stretches far into the future, as its roots run far back into the past, but instinct also with fresh human life, with the daily experience of the prophet and his hearers. The prophets prophesied into the future, but not directly to the future. Their duties lay with their own age, and only by viewing them as they move amidst their contemporaries does the critic learn to love and to admire them. A prophecy, then, coming to us in the name of Isaiah, but having no roots in Isaiah's age, is to the historical student either an inexplicable phenomenon, or a phenomenon misplaced. Certainly, he is called upon to admit that another inquirer approaching the problem from a theological standpoint, taking the prophet on the Divine side, may be able to explain what he cannot understand.   But, meanwhile, we cannot deny him the right to test the phenomenon in his own fashion, to transpose the unintelligible utterance into a different historical setting, to ask whether, so transposed, it may not become doubly resplendent with the twofold brilliancy of an eternal Divine thought and a manifest historical propriety.   The principle on which the modern criticism herein acts is carefully to be distinguished from the old rationalistic absurdity of bringing down all prophecy *post eventum* : not the aim to which the prophet tends, but the starting-point from which he advances, affords to the historical inquirer the basis of his critical activity.   Take, for example, the second half of Isaiah, the grand trilogy that describes the restoration from the captivity in Babylon. It is not the prediction of the return that makes these chapters be placed by all critics in the later years of the captivity itself, for a prediction as precise was certainly uttered by Jeremiah ;   it is not the conception of a captivity of Babel that is viewed as impossible to Isaiah, for Micah we know anticipated such an event ;   it is not even the mention of Cyrus by name that is urged, for those who are puzzled by that fact could much more readily suggest an interpolation.   But the author of these chapters speaks everywhere to the exiled people ; he speaks to them face to face, with the pathos, the hope, the indignation of one who shared their sufferings and beheld their sins .   he speaks to them in conceptions fitted to an age when Jerusalem stood no longer, and the Davidic House had ceased to reign .   he has dropped, for example, the notion of a Davidic Messiah, and gives a still deeper and more wondrous picture of salvation through the suffering and death of the Servant of Jahveh, followed up by a glorious triumphal appearance of the Covenant God in person, filling His land and illumining His people with eternal radiance :   in one word, if Isaiah wrote these chapters he lived two lives—not a natural and a prophetic life, but two prophets' lives, one in his own day, and one in the far future. And if this be the real state of the case, Isaiah will be to the critic, for all practical purposes, two men , the whole historical significance of these chapters must still be transferred from the age of Hezekiah to the age of Labynetus.[1]

But, instead of pursuing these intricate questions, our present purpose calls us rather to consider the way in which critics of divergent tendencies have sought to explain the phenomena of Hebrew prophecy that are undisputed by the most sceptical inquirer. We have learned to regard the prophets as the leaders of the religious life of Israel, rising above the people, as men who bear within them a higher ground of trust in God, a deeper insight into His purpose, than falls to the lot of their fellow-countrymen. A prophet like Isaiah maintains, we can hardly fail to see, a kingly attitude. Nor was it the mere accident of success that enabled him to assume this position. The northern prophets, whose career was lighted up by no gleam of present hope, who were never privileged to take part in a national success, speak with no less undoubted authority. That the people whose sins they denounced, and whose speedy fall they proclaimed, hated and persecuted them, is not singular. But the persecutors were never able to proceed against the prophets as impostors, or as mere turbulent revolutionaries. The name in which they spoke, the life that witnessed to their words, inspired respect and even awe among their bitterest enemies The explanation of this fact is not far to seek. It lies not in the person of the prophet himself, for no historical fact can be clearer than

---

[1] The way in which believing critics, men who acknowledge not only the supernatural but the miraculous, deal with questions of date and authorship, is most instructively exemplified in Kamphausen's *Lied Mosis* The arguments employed in that work are not the less interesting because the learned author is an admiring disciple of a man who left a strong personal mark on all his hearers—we refer to the late lamented Rothe.

that the prophets were men of the most varied character and capacity. It lies simply in this that what they spoke, they spoke as the word of Jahveh, the God of Israel—a name which the rebellious people might often forget, but never dared to repudiate. We are not entitled to assume that when the prophets and the people spoke of Jahveh they had before their minds equally lofty or equally ethical ideas ; but it is obvious, as Kuenen puts it, that

"The whole preaching of the prophets would be unintelligible if we may not assume that their fundamental positions were generally conceded. The freedom with which they stand forth in the name of Jahveh, rebuking, approving, announcing punishment and reward, is an enigma if they did not stand, with their hearers, on the common ground of faith in the wholly peculiar relation of Jahveh to Israel."[1]

In a word, the historical circumstances of the eighth century leave no doubt that in that age Jahveh was fully acknowledged as the ancestral God of Israel—a God whose authority over His people was so supreme that His servants and ambassadors stood high above the ministers of all other gods. This conclusion may seem, perhaps, too obvious to demand formal statement, yet the consequences that flow from it are of the weightiest. It is not by a slow, insensible process that one among many gods can reach such a pre-eminence. A polytheistic nation has often gradually chosen out one god for special veneration ; but here we have one God so elevated above the rest that the men who, in His name, denounced all other gods as helpless idols were acknowledged by the idolaters themselves to be speaking with a name and a power that they dared not gainsay. Not an inward devotion of heart to the peculiar tenets of Jahvism, which much rather were impatiently borne and gladly cast aside, but the feeling that, by infallible signs, Jahveh had shown Himself a true God must have lain at the root of this reverence.

[1] *Godsdienst*, 77.

And such a demonstration of the might of Jahveh the history supplies in the deliverance from Egypt through Moses. Of this deliverance the prophets always speak as the creation of the people. They appeal to the Exodus, the wilderness journey, the law-giving, the establishment in Canaan, as undoubted proofs that Jahveh alone is the God of Israel, and the people silently admit the argument. Nor can the modern criticism refuse to add its assent. If the faith in Jahveh did not arise in the days of Moses, no subsequent crisis in the history can suffice to explain its origin. The growth of a purely fantastic myth about the Exodus is infinitely more inexplicable than the truth of the event.[1] That Moses really lived, that he led the people out of Egypt in the name of Jahveh, that he impressed upon his countrymen an imperishable conviction that to his God they stood in a peculiar indissoluble relation,—in short, in a covenant union which called on their side for a moral service, and, on the other hand, assured them of the all-powerful support of the Rock of Israel, is no longer questioned ; and the universal acquiescence in this result is due, not to the study of the Pentateuch, in which Kuenen, for example, acknowledges only the substance of the Decalogue as properly Mosaic, but to the critical study of the prophecy of the eighth century. This result, however, carries us but a little way A prophet is more than a worshipper of Jahveh asserting the ancestral religion against modern corruptions, for his authority is no less marked over the true worshippers of the God of Israel. We have seen that the prophet explained his words to himself as the words of Jahveh. So broadly, as Kuenen has observed, does the seer " distinguish between the inspiration of Jahveh and his own conceptions that there sometimes arises in him a struggle between his personal wishes and views and the thoughts of Jahveh, to which he yields only perforce." [2] How

---

[1] See this fully granted by Kuenen (*Godsdienst*, p 121)

[2] *Onderzoek*, ii. 32.

are we to construe to ourselves these remarkable facts ?

We know that the prophetic revelations were often associated with visions. May we assume that these ecstatic or half-conscious states were to the prophet the stamp of a Divine communication ? In opposition to the Montanists, the early church answered this question in the negative. Quite recently a view, closely allied to that of the Montanists, was revived by Hengstenberg, and has left no inconsiderable mark on the conservative theology of Germany. But with the critical school the theory has found little favour, least of all with those critics whose decided supernaturalism brings them nearest to the theological convictions of its author. By far the nearest approach to Hengstenberg is to be found in the stress which Kuenen lays upon the prophetic ecstasy. It is, indeed, clear that the theory of vision leaves the historical influence of the prophets quite unexplained. That they did not speak to the people in a state of ecstasy is certain Their prophecies bear on every page the stamp of a vigorous, healthy, waking life. Their influence lay not in their words only, but in the force of their whole personality which everywhere shines through their utterances. " The true prophet," to speak with Ewald, " never utters the word of Jahveh that has come to him until it has become within him quite clear and certain, a part, as it were, of his inmost life and thought." The theory of ecstasy is an attempt to divide the prophet from the prophetic word, while in truth the peculiar power of men like Amos and Isaiah lay just in the thoroughness with which the word of Jahveh filled and elevated the natural personality of the speaker This argument assumes slightly different phases according as the ecstasy is conceived as supernatural or natural. If, as we believe, God really dealt with Israel in an extraordinary way, entering personally into the history of the people, it is plain that this supernatural activity must have been so directed as to enter

into organic unity with the human life of Israel. There
are not in the Old Testament two histories, a Divine and
a human, but *one* history, in which the Divine agency
never quenches human personality. In the word of
Jahveh, spoken by the prophets, this fusion of the Divine
and human is already complete. The supernatural word
penetrates and quickens, but never suppresses the personality of the prophet. Sometimes, as we have just seen,
there arises a contest between the prophet's own desires
and the thoughts of Jahveh. But the end of this contest
is always that the prophet is not only silenced, but
convinced. Now, a supernatural thought that reaches the
prophet in a state of ecstasy has not these qualities. The
dualism of the Divine and human is not yet overcome,
and hence the Divine word has no power to enter directly
as a living factor into history. The theory of ecstasy,
therefore, explains nothing, unless we interpose between
the reception and the utterance of the revelation a living
personal power whereby the prophet makes the Divine
word his own. We must seek the true mark of the
prophet in something higher than passive ecstasy—in the
personal sympathy between himself and Jahveh, by virtue
of which the God-sent thought approves itself to him
inwardly, and not by mere external authority. In this
conclusion lies the key to the position of the believing
school of critics History deals with persons, not with
things The historical interest of prophecy does not
lie in tracing a sharp line of separation between the Divine
and human, but in realizing the personal union of these
two factors in the evolution of Israel's history. And so
the prophet presents himself to the critical inquirer, less in
the light of one who is the passive subject of supernatural
influence, than as a man whose life and thoughts are
determined by personal fellowship with Jahveh and by
intelligent insight into his purpose. No doubt what is
personal always rests on a background of the non-personal,
a background of merely physical elements which are

initially passive under the creative hand of God ; but to deal with these elements is not the function of historical inquiry. The limit of personal life is the limit of critical investigation. By what creative and inexplicable power God first wrought in the spirit of the prophet that sympathy with His own character which is the true characteristic of the prophetic life is a question for the theologian, not for the historian.

That this way of looking at prophecy is really applicable and fruitful, will, we hope, be clear even from the very scanty examples which we have given of the sort of phenomena that fall to be explained. Perhaps, however, the clearest illustration of the peculiar attitude of the prophets to Jahveh is to be drawn from the way in which they themselves describe their first call to their life work What Ewald says on this point is both instructive and characteristic .—

"No man can be a true prophet of Jahveh till he has first cast his glance into the full majesty and holiness of Jahveh Himself, and there has gained such an inner appreciation of the true eternal life that it now lives on, firmly grounded within him as *his* new life. The incipient prophet must, once for all, become unalterably sure of the true relation of the world and Jahveh ; gazing in a clear image on the whole lofty and holy essence of Jahveh, and feeling himself borne on by Him alone . . . he must have entered wholly, with all his inner powers of work and deed, into the Divine thoughts, and be so fettered by them for ever, that in this constraint he has found the truest force and freedom ; such is the first condition, the true beginning of all prophetic activity, the holy consecration and inner calling, without which no man becomes a true prophet. . . . When such a prophet undertook a written book he placed at its head, with just perception, the description of the holy moment when he first recognised Jahveh in His true majesty, and felt himself consecrated, strengthened, called by Him." [1]

---

[1] *Propheten*, 1. 22, referring to Isa. vi , Jer. i., Ez. i. 52. The attitude of Kuenen towards these narratives is, as usual, much less sympathetic. Yet he recognises the narrative of Isa vi as recording an actual experi-

What Ewald says on this topic could not be said in
the same sense by all members of the critical school , for
it is manifest that Ewald writes as a believer in prophecy.
He is persuaded that the prophets really did enjoy a
peculiar communion with their God which sharply distinguished them from their fellow-men, and bestowed upon
them the power of penetrating into eternal truths hid
from their contemporaries.   And these eternal truths
are not bare abstract generalisations about God.   The
prophet is essentially a *seer*.   His insight into the purpose
of Jahveh takes the form of a spiritual intuition, a clear,
ideal picture of past, present, and future history.   The
natural man stands in the midst of a vast and complicated
scene, filled with groups of actors moving to and fro without
unity of order and purpose.   Of these actors he is himself
one, but he understands his own destiny as little as that of
others, hurried along as he is by momentary impulses and
necessities.   But the prophet has gained the key to this
complex drama.   He has seen the Invisible One who
rules all by His irresistible will.   He has submitted himself
to that will, and now his own path opens up plainly before
him.   But he sees more than this   He sees one plan in
all the movements of history.   He does not, indeed,
perceive in full detail how the drama must be carried on ;
but his hold of the plot is so firm, and his comprehension
of the present situation so just, that scene after scene
opens before him in visionary outline leading on to the
great final issue when the purpose of Jahveh shall be fully
accomplished.   Thus when Ewald speaks of prophecy
as in the main intuition, rather than pure thought, he is
not thinking of vision in the sense of ecstatic mental
phenomena.   The conscious thought of the prophet must
take the form of a shifting series of pictures, all developed
out of the divinely illumined picture of the present which

---

ence of the prophet, which was decisive in forming his career   In Jer 1
he recognises a groundwork of fact freely embellished , in Ezekiel's
vision, hardly even so much as this (*Onderzoek*, ii 50, 173 *seq.* 262 *seq*).

he is enabled to form by his sympathy with the mind of
Jahveh.   This seeing, in truth, is not peculiar to the
prophet.   No man can really understand past or present
history unless he has it *vividly* before him.   The real
peculiarity lies in the way in which the prophetic image is
gained by " an effort of the gazing spirit starting from a
definite truth, to represent with more distinctness the
conformation of the future, and to break through the veil
of the unseen." [1]   The starting-point in this construction
is always the relation of the present to the Divinely-
appointed end.   And herein lies, according to Ewald, the
practical superiority of prophecy over mere moral teaching ; for in pointing the way in which the difficulties of
the present must, according to God's purpose, be resolved,
the prophet points out at the same time the principles of
action which he and his hearers, in following God's will,
are not only bound, but encouraged to make their own.

To Ewald, then, the reality of prophecy is an historical
fact.   The prophets really were what they claimed to
be—privileged ambassadors of God   And the proof that
they were so lies not in the supernatural process by which
they received the Divine message, not in the fulfilment of
individual predictions, but in their work as a whole
That work was true work.   It proved itself by its operation in history to be what it professed to be, no mere
natural efflux of the past history and past development of
the people, but a new and living power, the utterance of a
new life, which, because it is a new life, can spring only
from the infinite source of all life.   Just at this point of
Ewald's conception there is indeed a certain indistinctness,
which makes it difficult to put his position into words
without saying either too much or too little.   The *new
life* of which Ewald speaks so decidedly has its origin
above the sphere of history.   But instead of acknowledg-
ing the limits of his sphere, and admitting that history
itself has its beginning in the creative Spirit of God, the

[1] Ewald, *Propheten*, 1 29

historian is often tempted to shade off the boundaries of
history with a deepening haze, losing himself in vague
generalities about the relation of the Divine and human
spirit, couched in terms that might easily be taken to
imply that the mere natural development of man's faculties
brings with it all that gift of fellowship with God which is
the end of history.   Thus Ewald himself has been claimed
as a champion of the opinion that there was no specific
difference between Hebrew and heathen prophecy.   In
spite of some expressions that might seem to support it,
we do not hesitate to deny the justice of the allegation.
Ewald holds, indeed, with all Protestants, that man, as
created, has the capacity for fellowship with God.   But
this capacity is but a germ which lies dead till a Divine
agency calls it into life.   All through history this quickening agency works, calling men into a new life of fellowship
with God.   Thus there lies in every man the possibility
of becoming a prophet—as, indeed, the prophets themselves look forward to a time when all men shall see as
fully into the mind of Jahveh as the greatest prophet of
an imperfect dispensation.   But the realization of this
possibility is limited to a few.   Ewald does not hesitate
to speak of the spiritual religion of Israel as standing in
direct antithesis to heathenism as *the true religion*.   In
the very striking declaration of his faith which stands at
the head of the second edition of the *Propheten*, he speaks
of the Bible, and the Bible alone, as the mirror in which
we can read all the conditions and stages of the perfect,
true religion, which is necessary for all future generations
of men.[1]   He has the keenest perception of the historical
significance of Judaism and of Christianity.   But the one
question which is not historical—wherein namely the
specific agency of God lies, which so singles out individual
men and an individual nation to do so special a work in
the world—he never seems to have set before him.   The
question, of course, is a theological one.   On the answer

[1] *Propheten*, III 14

to it depends the whole conception of Divine grace.   The historian is not bound to give the answer, but he ought to see that such a question does exist.

There is, however, another class of critics, of which Kuenen is our chosen representative, who with no small gain in clearness do face this question.   They say distinctly that no discriminating Divine grace exists.   God works everywhere, and everywhere in the same sense. All religion is true, and no religion is perfect.   All men are in true communion with God, but no man is in full communion with Him.   Thus to Kuenen " the prophecy of Israel is a product of the religious disposition of the nation as it developed itself under the guidance of its fortunes and the continuous influence of God's Spirit.   The prophets are *geniuses* or *heroes* in the ethico-religious field, produced by Israel in the same sense as every nation produces its great men.   They differ from other Semitic prophets in degree, not in kind.   The difference corresponds to the high superiority of the Israelitish religion, and like the latter must be explained by the providential co-operation of national spirit and national history." [1]   The mention of Providence and of the Spirit of God must not mislead us, and has not misled Kuenen as to the true nature of the problem which Hebrew history on such a view presents. The influence of God's Spirit is not on this theory something over and above national disposition and history. These alone must give the full explanation of the phenomena of prophecy, though we must at the same time believe that God's hand was in all.   Ewald could appeal to a new life which marked off the prophets, and enabled them to see truths which no heathen saw, but the elements of religious life which are postulated in Kuenen's construction must be simply those which are common to all men.   Everything over and above this is the product of natural development, and hence the question between the positive and negative criticism resolves itself into a

---

[1] *Onderzoek*, ii. 27

plain question of historical fact   Is the prophetical
consciousness the highest fruit of a development common
to the whole people, and reacting on the nation only as the
explicitly stated will always draw out what is only implicitly present ?   Or is the work of the prophets of a
higher kind—really as well as in expression in advance of
their age, and leading it on to higher and new life ?

The prophets themselves would have accepted this
way of stating the question   All that distinguished
Israel from other nations it has, according to their view,
received at the hand of prophets   " By a prophet," says
Hosea, " Jahveh brought Israel out of Egypt, and by a
prophet he was watched over." [1]   From Kuenen's standpoint such a notion is inconceivable. Moses, he expressly
says, was not a prophet. In truth, prophecy, as a
phenomenon peculiar to the nation of Israel, must, on the
negative theory, only appear after the national character
had reached a very considerable development.   To carry
out this view involves a double task.   The earliest prophets
whose writings we know appear, as we have seen, not only
as men who did a remarkable work in their age, but as
members of an order to which the people looked for
remarkable work   It is necessary, then, for Kuenen not
merely to explain the extraordinary career of individual
prophets, but to explain the no less singular position of
the prophetic order as a whole.   These two tasks separate
pretty widely, insomuch as he does not recognise that all
prophets of the eighth century who really had a right to
claim the name were of the type of Hosea or Isaiah   In
short, it was not by performances analogous to those of
the great spiritual prophets that the prophetic order
gained, according to Kuenen, its recognised position.
To Ewald all prophecy is spiritual, but to Kuenen the
spiritual prophecy of the eighth century is a new development of a religious phenomenon which originally rested
on a purely physical basis. That basis he finds not

[1] Hosea xii 14 (I·v 1 3)

unclearly indicated in the Hebrew word the most general designation of the prophets. In opposition to most scholars,[1] who regard this word as an active participle, denoting one who speaks forth, or interprets, a word entrusted to him, Kuenen gives to the passive sense of a man inspired by the Divinity.[2]

"*What* Divinity remains undetermined. We hear in the Old Testament not only of prophets of Jahveh, but of prophets of Baal and Ashera. The person who is seized and breathed into by the Godhead falls into ecstasy; either into so strong a transport that he wholly loses his self-possession, utters sounds without clear consciousness, and even resembles a madman, or, it may be, simply into an excited condition, in which he expresses with emphasis and enthusiasm the testimony of the Godhead in his inner man." [3]

It is because history shows no trace that Moses ever was subject to this species of frenzy that Kuenen denies to him the name of prophet.

The psychological phenomena which, according to this view, are the physical bases of prophecy, are unquestionably associated with a sickly state. The arguments which forbade us to find in a supernatural ecstasy the true essence of prophecy, apply to such a state with double force. It is hard to believe that the life of Isaiah, in whom Kuenen himself recognises a religious hero—a life everywhere inspired by the noblest and clearest spiritual impulses—can have anything in common with mental disease. It is, in fact, not quite plain how far Kuenen supposes the ecstatic state to have characterised the later prophets. In the very latest prophets—as, for example, in Ezekiel—he is disposed to ascribe almost everything to sober thought. But in general a greater or less measure of ecstasy appears to him the only assumption that

[1] Ewald, *Propheten*, i 7 ; Baur, *Gesch* 381 ; Fleischer in Delitzsch's *Genesis*, p. 634 *seq* , may suffice as examples.

[2] *Onderzoek*, ii. 3. Compare the long note to chap. iii of the *Godsdienst*

[3] *Godsdienst*, 187 *seq*.

accounts for the prophet's firm conviction that he speaks, not his own words, but the words of Jahveh. It was the belief of the age that Jahveh did exercise an immediate influence in nature. Hence mental phenomena really natural could honestly be ascribed to Him by men unable to trace their origin. It naturally followed that visions and dreams were viewed as desirable, and this very desire operated to make them more common. Yet, on the other hand, Kuenen seems to allow that with the greatest prophets visions were not very frequent The operation of a single ecstasy occurring at a decisive moment of life, might produce upon the prophet the impression of a consecration to Jahveh which would give him confidence to speak as His messenger during all his future life. But how was it possible that a whole class of men could come to be characterised by ecstasy? How could such a phenomenon attain such a measure of organization as to become identified with a peculiar function in society? The origin of prophecy, answers Kuenen, falls in the days of Samuel.[1] Before his time the " seers " of Israel were little different from vulgar sooth-sayers The prophetic ecstasy was associated, not with Jahvism, but with Canaanite nature-worship, to which indeed, in the period of the Judges, the Hebrews had no formed aversion; but towards the end of that period a more hostile attitude sprung up between the Hebrew invaders and the old population In the religious sphere this hostility appears in the rise of the Nazarites, of whom Samson is the type, and whose simple and austere life betokens a reaction against the sensual worship of the Canaanites. Such a reaction was not without its historical justification; for though, according to Kuenen, Jahveh was to Moses still a nature-god, of whom fire and light were the essence, and

---

[1] The less negative criticism, on the other hand, makes Samuel the founder, not of prophecy, but of the prophetic order " Before Samuel," says the latest writer on this point, " prophecy had no special determinate form, no enduring position among the powers of the state " (Schultze, *Alttestamentliche Theologie*, 1 p. 151 , Frankfurt, 1869)

not merely the symbol, it is yet plain that the relation of Israel to this God, was conceived by him in such a sense as to give a strong impulse to national monotheism.

Of the monotheistic party, Samuel became the leader. By his national and religious zeal, the danger of an absorption of Jahvism in the Canaanite religions was for ever set aside ; but this success was accomplished, not by following in the steps of the Nazarites, but by the assimilation of a Canaanite element. In the prophetic ecstasy, Samuel saw an instrument worthy of adoption by his party. He enlisted this peculiar enthusiasm in the service of Jahveh, and he did so with enormous effect. A school of prophets was formed at Ramah, in which, by the use of music and by a sort of psychical infection, the ecstatic state was rendered chronic. But in this school Samuel ruled all.

" The enthusiasm which, left to itself, might easily have led to all manner of excesses, was confined within definite bounds, and made serviceable to the maintenance of Jahvism. The seer accustomed to practical efforts, the statesman whose eye was opened to the great necessities of his nation, laid his hand, as it were, on the awakened enthusiasm, and forced it to co-operate towards the mark at which he aimed." [1]

From this time prophecy and the prophetic schools had an acknowledged place in Israel ; but towards the age of Amos they had lost much of their vigour and influence. Their original enthusiasm had worked itself out and gave place to artificial stimulation. Then it was that a new kind of prophecy arose, not formed in the prophetic schools, but drawing its inspiration "from the same source from which these societies had originally sprung, from the enthusiasm that appeared among the people without artificial stimulation, as the fruit of their religion." Prophets like Amos and his successors appeared as ambassadors of Jahveh, without special preparation, just because they heard within them His call to the prophetic life.

[1] *Godsdienst*, p 192.

We cannot here criticise in detail the historical assumptions of this ingenious theory; but it is important to
consider what species of religious feeling is consistent with
such a kind of prophecy. If we seek a historical parallel
for Kuenen's Samuel, we can hardly fail to think of
Loyola. The " exercitia " of the Jesuits are the modern
counterpart of the disciplined enthusiasm of Kuenen's
scheme. Was it, in truth, a religious spirit of this kind
that did such marvels in Israel ?   The theory, indeed, has
not one particle of plausibility without the assumption
that we have no records of the earlier prophecy which
have not been strongly coloured by the more advanced
religious views of a later age. And even if we allow the
theorist, on the strength of this assumption, to evacuate
whole centuries of Old Testament history of almost all
their moral earnestness, the exigencies of the negative
school are not half met. Can we evolve the life-work of
the newer prophets from the categories of natural religious
feeling, physical enthusiasm, national temperament,
historical circumstances ? To gain even a show of
plausibility for such an attempt, the critic is forced
everywhere to look away from the noble spirituality, the
lofty comprehensiveness of view, which he cannot deny
to the prophets, and seek by a petty pragmatism to bring
out into exaggerated prominence the limitations of their
natural and religious convictions. Not even in so great
a crisis as the fall of Sennacherib, can he afford to look
at the grand and instructive side of the history. Everywhere his eye is directed to discover some inexactness
in the fulfilment of a prediction, some natural method by
which the fulfilment might have been foreseen or brought
about, forgetful how completely the facts forbid us to
identify the foresight of a prophet with the calculations of
a man of the world, and how often we are able not only
to say that certain predictions were made and fulfilled,
but in some measure to lay bare the Divine process by
which the prophet came to make them.

But the justice of Kuenen's views may be tested on other ground than these points of detail. The great question is, after all, to explain the origin in Israel of the spiritual conceptions of the prophets. Let us briefly sketch Kuenen's theory on this point.

Moses, as we have already seen, is not conceived as the upholder of a spiritual Jahvism. The children of Israel, in the times of Egyptian servitude, were, according to Kuenen, polytheists of no high type. Of their many gods one was an object of special veneration, a consuming fire-god, nearly allied to the Canaanitish Moloch, who bore the name of El Shaddai—the " mighty " or " violent god." Moses, a man of strong religious and national spirit, shared the faith of his brethren in an intenser form. The contest between Israel and Egypt seemed to him a war between the native gods of the oppressors and the majestic Fire God of his own people. He felt himself entrusted by El Shaddai with a mission to deliver his people. Associated with this mission was the introduction of the name Jahveh, by which Moses sought to express a new and higher conception of the God, probably his life-going power. The course of history could not fail to strengthen the religious convictions of the leader of Israel. The God who had delivered Israel was too great a God to suffer any rival. Let Israel worship Him, and Him alone! Thus viewed, the monotheism of Moses is neither absolute nor spiritual. Yet one important step towards the separation between God and nature Moses must be conceived as having taken. He brought Jahvism into union with moral ideas.

" The enduring merit of Moses was, not that he introduced into Israel certain religious forms and services, but that he established among his people a moral worship of Jahveh. ' I will be to you a God, and ye shall be to me a people ' · so speaks Jahveh, by the mouth of Moses, to the tribes of Israel. The union between Jahveh and his folk sealed by the deliverance from bondage, is secured by this, that the ark, the dwelling of Jahveh,[1] accompanies the Israelites during the wandering, and afterwards is set up in their midst. . . . But, on the other hand, the people must remain true to the conditions of the covenant with Jahveh. The chief of these conditions are moral. Jahveh is distinguished from other gods by deserving to be served, not only by offerings and feasts, but, in the first place, by the following of the moral commands, which make up the main contents of ' the ten words ' " [2]

But was this great step a fruit of natural development ? Yes, according to our author   The Israelites indeed were, before Moses, in a very low stage of development   But Moses was educated as an Egyptian, and in Egypt ethics were developed in connection with religion to no inconsiderable extent. The revulsion of feeling which Moses undoubtedly experienced against Egyptian religion might not extend to this sphere   On the religion of his own fathers he engrafted the moral ideas of the Egyptian priests. There is surely something violent in this hypothesis. If, as Kuenen is persuaded, Moses borrowed absolutely nothing from the religion of Egypt, could he have looked on Egyptian moral teaching in a more favourable light ? Or again, if he valued the ethics of the Egyptian priests so highly, could he ever have become such an enemy of their gods ? And yet we are to believe that the monotheism of Moses was based on his persuasion that Jahveh had covered these gods with the shame of a crushing defeat ! Once more, why did the Egyptian ethics remain without advance while the same teaching, brought over to a much less cultivated nation, bore fruits so remarkable ?

So far is Kuenen from ascribing to Moses a truly creative influence, that he tells us that " what distinguished Moses from his people remained the personal property of himself and a few kindred spirits , the popular way of thought assimilated only so much as was reconcilable with

[1] According to Kuenen, Jahveh was thought by Moses really to dwell between the Cherubim.

[2] *Godsdienst*, p 289.

itself." Most Israelites probably remained blind to the
real difference between the Jahveh of Moses and their old
god. They still continued to worship other gods, though
they never quite lost hold of the idea of a peculiar moral
covenant between Israel and Jahveh. We have seen how
Kuenen connects Samuel with a revival of Mosaic ideas.
From the time of this revival, we are told, Jahvism grew
steadily but slowly. But Jahveh was not yet a spiritual
God. The steer-worship of Jeroboam, though a retro-
gression from Solomon's temple-worship, was not inconsistent with the conceptions of Jahveh that prevailed
even among the prophets   The continual struggle of the
true prophets against the idolatrous Jahveh worship of
Bethel and Dan, depicted in the Book of Kings, is rejected
by our author as a fable. Jehu, he urges, could not have
upheld the steer-worship against the wishes of the prophets,
who raised him to the throne. In one word, the prophets
of the tenth century had not yet reached that spiritual
view of God which Ewald, Hitzig, and the whole weight of
German critics ascribe without hesitation to Moses and
himself. Towards the end of the tenth century, Ahab
ascended the northern throne, and influenced by his
Tyrian queen, though he did not forswear Jahvism,
favoured and endowed the worship of Baal. The prophets
of Jahveh were jealous of the innovation, and did not
hesitate to express their displeasure in a way that transformed the naturally liberal Ahab into a persecutor.
The struggle lasted for many years, till Jehu, the champion
of Jahvism, overthrew the dynasty of Ahab and extinguished the worship of Baal. But the contest had left
deep marks on the national faith. Jahvism had gained
in the bloody struggle a deeper and more spiritual character. How great must that God be than to forsake
whom it was better to die ! Not by calm arguments, but
by passionately earnest thought, the persecuted Jahvists
learned to contrast their God with all other gods in a way
they had never done before. And then, when at length

Baal was overthrown, there was no return of national prosperity ; Jahveh had delivered his people into the hand of Hazael, not because He was weak, but because He was angry—angry that even for a time His people had thought of other gods.   Now, the moral attributes of Jahveh already furnished a basis for a deep distinction between Him and other gods.   And so earnest worshippers began more and more to lay weight on this side of his character, and dropped the natural basis of the old religion, in order to realize more fully the deep separation between the God of Israel and all heathen gods.

It was not in the prophetic schools that these new ideas rose.   The movement went on in the heart of the nation, especially among the simple nomadic families from whom, for example, Amos sprung.   And thus it was that the great thoughts were ripened which burst forth in the new prophecy of the eighth century.

For this theory, Kuenen does not claim to have historical proof.   He gives it as the only plausible method of explaining the advance in religious conceptions between the tenth and eighth centuries.   We cannot regard it as a happy theory.   Everywhere it reverses the order of cause and effect.   It is true that only spiritual views of God could agree with a faith shaken neither by persecution nor by national misfortune.   But surely, these views must have been already present to the men who suffered so much, not for leave to worship Jahveh, but to escape tolerating Baal beside Him.   And when Baal fell, and misfortune, not prosperity, followed, could aught but spiritual faith have resisted the argument that the wrath of Baal was stronger than the favour of Jahveh ?

We do not care to develop these objections.   The whole theory, ingenious as it is, bears with it not only its own condemnation, but the condemnation of the principle on which it rests.   That is not a true historical criticism which does not acknowledge in history a higher element than the merely natural.

It is from a criticism that has learned this lesson, that can approach the weighty problems of prophecy from the human side without ignoring the hand of God, that we look for real fruit.   Already, indeed, the results of such a criticism extend through the whole field of prophecy, and are ignored by no school of theologians.[1]   Readers of last year's Bampton Lectures cannot have failed to observe how great an influence recent inquiry into the Old Testament from the human side has exerted on a theologian so little disposed as Dr. Payne Smith to do homage to the spirit of criticism, or to yield to the temptations by which even believing Continental thought is so readily beset.

The way in which the fundamental ideas, which are now the common property of the more positive criticism, are grasped and developed by believing inquiry, may be best illustrated by a few brief extracts from the third of our typical books—Gustav Baur's careful and learned *History of Old Testament Prophecy*, unhappily still unfinished —

" The peculiar interest of the Old Testament prophecies is due, purely, to their connection with the greatest fact in the world-history, the appearance of Christianity, and to the question, Have they found their fulfilment in Christianity or not ? . . . The religion of Israel stands to Christianity in the relation of its nearest positive preparation, and as the true sense of a riddle cannot be understood till its answer is known, so the full understanding of Old Testament prophecy is only possible from the Christian standpoint. . . . We are willing that our standpoint should be called theological, if it is only conceded that,

---

[1] Our limits forbid us to dwell on detailed results of critical investigation.   Many questions of Prophecy are so difficult, whether approached · critically or theologically, that we must thankfully accept the smallest additional insight into them   But almost all these questions have gained something from critical treatment   We may refer in particular to the subject of prediction, which critics have sometimes treated rather lightly, but which has again begun to receive the attention it deserves.   The Essays of Bertheau, in the *Jahrbucher fur Deutsche Theologie* (1859–60), in which a most interesting attempt is made to define the conditional element in prediction, while the results of this inquiry are applied to the long - vexed chiliastic problems, deserve special mention.

without so much of the theological attitude, a thorough
historical understanding of the Old Testament is impossible,
while, on the other hand, we gladly admit that a theological conception is good for nothing which violates the
fact and laws of history.   From this side, too, the understanding of prophecy has suffered much, especially at the
hands of the restored traditional exposition, which in
the Protestant Church, at least, has no right to claim the
name of Churchly.   If Revelation is really Revelation,
not unintelligible dead communication, if the faith that
grasps it is to be a living faith, the human spirit must
be prepared for its reception ; and such a preparation
must obey the law of continuity   .   To seek the New
Testament fulfilment in the Old Testament preparation,
or to seek in the New Testament the fulfilment of every
single hope that grew up on the always limited Old Testament ground, is to rob oneself of the possibility of gaining
a true insight into the wondrous course of Revelation."

From this point, prophecy appears to Baur as the " hope
and ever more and more distinct conception of the most
perfect religious relation, which developed itself out of the
consciousness of the insufficiency of the Old Testament
standpoint."   But this development is no merely natural
one, but due to a new principle of life implanted by
revelation in the natural God-consciousness through the
medium of a pre-eminent personality.   Thus Abraham is
to Baur the first recipient of the Divine revelation that is
peculiar to Israel.   But this one creative impulse was not
enough.   In Egypt, Israel must undergo a second birth,
not by mere natural development, but again through the
creative force of the personality of Moses.   With Moses
appeared the Covenant and the Law, and from the Law
prophecy in the strict sense grew.   Left to mere nature,
the Divine principles laid down in the Law must soon have
died out.   But the prophets, who themselves were pene-
trated with the truths of the Law, continually stirred up
the religious life of their countrymen by reassertion of the
principle of the Old Testament religion.   In the discharge
of this task, they learned to know the imperfection as well
as the divineness of the Law, and so were led ever more

and more clearly to look forward to a yet future salvation in which all these imperfections should be supplied.

With this outline of Baur's position we may appropriately close, for it shows more clearly than any comment of ours could do the attitude in which, on the whole, not one writer only, but the great mass of believing critics, stand toward the question of Old Testament prophecy. And may we not say that such an attitude, if still far from thoroughly consistent and complete, at least holds forth the hope of no mean advance in the study of a part of human history which, in deep and enduring interest, is second only to the history of the earthly life of Him to whom all prophecy points.

III

EARLY ABERDEEN LECTURES

(1870–1874)

I

WHAT HISTORY TEACHES US TO SEEK IN
THE BIBLE

AT a time when one school of theologians is loudly calling
upon us to study Scripture in subordination to the
teachings, and in accordance with the methods, of the
Old Catholic Church, while another school, no less eagerly,
proclaims that he only can understand the Bible who
wholly abandons every theological standpoint, it will, I
think, be not amiss that we should begin our winter work
by endeavouring to gain a clear idea of the way in which
the great principles of the Reformation, which must guide
all *our* studies, bear upon the sciences that aim at a just
interpretation and appreciation of Scripture Let us
try to understand how the defective hermeneutic and the
unhistorical exegesis of the pre-Reformation Church were
bound up with defects not less glaring in the Old Catholic
representation of the first principles of Christianity ;
and how, on the other hand, the truer conception of the
essential nature of the Christian faith, to which the
Reformation awoke, contained within it, at least implicitly, the necessary principles of all true Criticism and
Exegesis.

Every one is familiar with the fact that the Reformation vindicated for Scripture the place of the highest,
the only theological authority, over-against the traditions
of men and the decrees of the Church. At first sight this
principle appears to possess a purely negative character.

It seems even, viewed as a distinctive principle, to be subordinate in importance, and to contain no very pointed antithesis, to the doctrine of the Roman Church. For in general, the recognised teachers of the Church admitted the supremacy of Scripture. " Our faith," says Thomas, " rests on the revelation made to the Prophets and Apostles who wrote the canonical books, not on such revelations as may have been made to other teachers " (*Summa*, i. 1).

It was not till the Council of Trent that the Roman Church expressed the full co-ordination with Holy Scripture of *traditiones sine scripto*. Accordingly, the early Protestants were not conscious of being on this head in antagonism to the voice of the Church. The Augustan Confession and the Smalcald Articles contain no discussion of the authority of Scripture ; and when, among the abuses to be removed, human traditions are enumerated, these are not spoken of as authorities formally set up against the Bible, but are condemned on their material side as burdening consciences and pointing out false ways of coming to peace with God.[1] Not till the days of the Epigoni did the Lutheran Church feel it necessary to lay down at the head of the Formula Concordiæ the position that Scripture is " the only rule and standard by which all dogmas and all teachers must be valued and judged " (A.D. 1580). In the Reformed Churches the need of an express symbolical statement as to the place of Scripture was sooner felt. So early as 1536 the Helvetica prior declares that " canonic Scripture, the word of God, the most perfect and ancient of all philosophies, alone contains perfectly all piety, and the whole rule of life " ;[2] and the subsequent Confessions of France, Holland, Scotland, etc., follow this example. But in the Helvetic Confession, as in the Lutheran

[1] Conf. Aug , p. 1, Art. xv. ; Artt Smalc. p. 3, Art. xv.

[2] Art 1.—Scriptura Canonica, verbum Dei, omnium perfectissima et antiquissima philosophia, pietatem omnem, omnem vitæ rationem, sola perfecte continet.—Niemeyer, pp. 105, 115.

standards, the antithesis lies not between Scripture and Tradition, as mere formal authorities, but between Scripture as revealing God's goodwill to us, in Christ Jesus, to be received by faith alone (Art. 5), and human Traditions that lead us away from God and true faith. That it was from this material side that the Swiss, no less than the Saxon, churches first contemplated the antithesis of Scripture and Tradition, we see clearly from the Zurich articles of 1523, where value, independent of the Church, and pre-eminent over all other doctrine, is assigned, not to Scripture, but to the Evangelium, whose sum is " that our Lord Christ Jesus, very Son of God, has revealed to us the will of the Heavenly Father, and with his innocence has redeemed us from death, and reconciled us to God." [1]

You see then that the motive of the Reformers, in all their symbolical utterances as to Scripture, was not the theological motive of a desire to lay down more sharply the nature of the authority to which Christian teaching appeals, but the religious motive of a determination to assert the divinely revealed way of salvation against the corruptions and additions of men.   I do not suppose that the Roman Church would have objected to an attempt to define more exactly the relative authority of Scripture and Tradition.   That question indeed was not new, and, so long as men continued to be convinced that Scripture and Ecclesiastical Tradition taught the same doctrines, could not be regarded as dangerous   The theologians of the Church, though practically their method of reasoning put the Bible into a very secondary place, had no suspicion that they were dealing unfairly with it.   It is most instructive to observe how Luther, in his earliest polemical writings, appeals to Scripture with the fullest confidence that in so doing he is following a line of argu-

---

[1] Artt. 1, 2, cf. Zwingli, *Uslegen und Grund der Artikel.*—(*Werke*, ed. 1828, i 175 *sqq*)

14

ment which no one can challenge.[1] The new and deeper conception of the Gospel, which he had drawn from Scripture, could not possibly be heresy. And on this ground the earliest antagonists of the Reformation were content in great measure to take their stand. They conceived themselves able to meet Scripture with Scripture. But now it became manifest that the two parties had very different conceptions of Scripture proof. To Luther, the Scripture, as a whole, was clear, transparent, one consistent unity. His opponents treated it as a collection of fragments. If Luther had a text on his side, they had a text on theirs The whole question, so far as the appeal to Scripture went, reduced itself to a balancing of texts or interpretations, in which everything seemed involved in an uncertain flux, unless the interpretations were backed up by the authority of the Fathers and the Church And so we find Luther urging, on the one hand, the eternal consistency and unchangeableness of God's Word, and on the other complaining bitterly of the way in which his opponents read God's Word, dealing with it, as he says of Tetzel, "like a sow with a bag of oats," *i.e.* grubbing in it blindly and unintelligently, seeking only what may serve their own profane uses.[2]

Soon, indeed, the superior freedom and power of Luther's use of Scripture became manifest even to his opponents All, he complains, who wrote against him were afraid of Scripture, knowing well their own ignorance of it, and therefore using every manœuvre to reach a position in which they should not be compelled to attack him with Scripture proofs, or receive the blows which he, armed with Scripture, aimed at them.[3] The

[1] So, for example, in the *Protestation* at the end of the Wittenberg Theses, the " Freiheit des Sermons vom Ablass," etc

[2] " Freiheit des Sermons," etc (*Werke*, ed Irmischer, vol. 27, p. 13) Cf. the answer to Emser (xii in Irmischer, vol 27), especially " v. d bleiernen Degen Emsers," p. 243.

[3] Compare the similar complaints of Zwingli —*Werke*, 1. 77.

natural issue of these tactics was the decree of Trent, which, for the first time, formally denied to the Bible supremacy over Tradition

It is plain, then, that the divergence of view as to the authority of Scripture, which gradually became more distinct as the contest between Rome and the Reformation went on, really springs from the fact that the Reformers had got a new way of looking at the Bible, a way that enabled them to find in Scripture a living and powerful Gospel, enunciated with a clearness and fulness of which their opponents had no idea ; and that made the Bible in their hands a weapon that could be wielded for defence or attack with a readiness and effect that were new to the Church and to Theology. If Scripture has a higher place in the Reformed than in the Roman Church, it is because the Reformation has learned to wield it better, because it for the first time showed how the bow of Ulysses must be bent.

But in order thoroughly to comprehend what we owe to the Reformation in this sphere, we must look back to the way in which the Bible was handled in the earlier ages of the Church.

In the last generation no point of theology has been discussed with keener interest than the nature and origin of the Old Catholic Church. Whatever these discussions have left unexplained, it can no longer be questioned that the Old Catholic Christianity deviated from the first from the apostolic model.

It has been shown that the main source of this decadence lay in the incapacity of the Gentile Christians to understand the Old Testament ideas on which the teaching of Christ and His Apostles was built [1]   The Old Catholic Church was concerned on the one hand to maintain against the Gnostics that the Old Testament is a Divine revelation, and therefore canonic for the Christian Church, and on the other hand to assert against the Jews the

[1] See Ritschl, *Die Entstehung der Altkatholischen Kirche* (ed 2).

superiority of the Christian standpoint, as that to which the whole Old Testament pointed, the rights of the Christian Church as the true Israel of God.   But a true historical sense of the organic connection between the Old and New Testaments was altogether lacking.   The Apostles had lived under the Old Testament.   Their own experience witnessed to them the nature of the new things brought in by Christianity.   If not in the shape of an explicit historical theory, yet in the form of deep personal experience, they did understand how the New Testament was rooted in the Old, and grew out of it by a process of true development.   The early post-apostolic teachers had no such experience, and did not feel the need of supplying its lack by a historical study of the Old Testament.   They approached the Old Testament (which you must remember was, until the formation of the New Testament Canon, Scripture in an exclusive sense) with no further guide than the general principle that Christ and Christian truth was everywhere the true substance of what they read.   Reading mainly with a view to practical edification and purposes of exhortation, they were content to believe that they had understood a passage so soon as they could in any way detect in it a meaning that bore on Christian truth or Christian life. What the Scriptures had taught to the men of the old covenant it was not necessary to ask , God's meaning at least is unchangeable, and that meaning is revealed in Christ.[1]   That in the Old Testament, for pædagogic ends, the eternal truth was wrapped up in obscure forms, seemed a matter of no special interest to Christians ; their business was only to pierce through the letter to the spirit that lay within, and which was precisely the same as the spiritual truth of the New Testament, both in the intention of the inspiring Spirit and in the apprehension of the inspired writer.   You see that this theory is intelligible only on the supposition that the essence of

[1] Cf. Justin. *Dial. c. Tryph.* cap. 90, 92, etc.

Christianity lies in a series of formulæ expressing eternal abstract truths or unchanging principles of morality, which before the time of Christ were obscurely revealed, but which He, in His quality of the great Prophet and Lawgiver of His people, set forth clearly. No room was left for a recognition of the fact that salvation is made possible to man not merely by a revelation of Divine truth, but by an exertion of Divine power—by a historical work of redemption : that the Old Testament dispensation prepared the way for Christ, not by the enunciation of theoretical dogmas, but by the actual manifestation in a long miraculous history of a special redemptive activity , and that Christ Himself was incarnate, died, and rose again, not merely to announce Divine truths, but to complete the Divine work begun in the former dispensation. It was impossible to ignore the meaning of the Old Testament history, and yet to understand the historical position and work of Christ, or to appreciate the historical ground on which the Apostles stand in their delineations of Christianity. The life and work of Christ, even the resurrection, to which in Paul's teaching justifying faith stands in so direct a relation, sink into the background, and the Saviour appears simply (I quote from Origen, *Prin.* 4, 156) as ὁ εἰσηγητὴς τῶν κατὰ χριστιανισμὸν σωτηρίων δογμάτων—*dogmas* which, consisting partly of truths to be believed, and partly of a law to be obeyed, become saving to us if we give an intellectual assent to the *regula fidei*, and submit our lives to the new Law of Christ. In a word, the Church was speedily cut off from all historical appreciation of Revelation and Redemption, became unable to grasp in their fulness the deepest teachings of the Gospel, and was thrown back on an unhistorical intellectualism, that found its expression in a neonomian theology and an allegorical exegesis.

The allegorical exegesis was not the invention of the Old Catholic Church. It had already been applied to the Old Testament by the Hellenistic Jews, in their efforts to force into harmony the abstract speculations of the Greek philosophers and the living concrete truths of Jehovah's personal dealings with His people It was, indeed, the only system of exegesis which was in natural harmony with the spirit of Hellenic philosophy, which always moved by preference in a region apart from the wants of common humanity, and inevitably tended to a one-sided exaltation of the eternal, unchangeable, unhistorical νοῖς [1] The Christian Church was urged towards the same exegesis by many causes : the desire to draw from every verse of Scripture a direct practical application to Christian duty—the perception that in Old Testament prophecy much is really symbolical—the necessity of finding an answer to the Jewish objection that many prophecies were in no proper sense fulfilled in Christ But after all, the real reason why men failed rightly to understand the *record* of redemption, was because they had no true comprehension of the *work* of redemption. The theological conception of Christianity as a new law did justice neither to the Christian consciousness of personal union to Christ nor to the historical facts of Christ's work. It was impossible to interpret Scripture rightly so long as men sought in it for what it did not contain,—for a system of abstract intellectual truth instead of a Divine history of God's workings among mankind, and in men's hearts, to set up on earth the kingdom of heaven. Meantime the theological authority of Scripture was fully acknowledged as supreme.[2] The words of the Old Testament writers, equally with those of the incarnate Saviour, are the words and doctrine of Christ, from which alone the faithful gain the wisdom

---

[1] We need only call to mind the interpretation of an ode of Simonides, given by Socrates in the *Protagoras*, c. 26 *sqq* , to see how thoroughly prone the Greek culture was to spiritualizing exegesis

[2] Origen, *Prin* iv 156 Rue, κοιναὶ ἔννοιαι and ἐνάργεια τῶν βλεπομένων are not sufficient. Therefore προσπαραλαμβάνομεν μαρτύρια τῶν πεπιστευμένων ἡμῖν εἶναι θείων γραφῶν

that incites to a good and blessed life.[1] It is only to the
ignorant that the supernaturalness of the thoughts [τὸ
ὑπὲρ ἄνθρωπον τῶν νοημάτων] does not manifest itself in
every letter.[2] These and similar utterances ascribe to
Scripture not less, but more than its due ; for they give
to an intellectual assent to the doctrines of Scripture
the power to mould man's life without any direct personal
relation to Christ. More or less unambiguously they
make Scripture not an avenue to approach to Christ,
but in and by itself a Divine phenomenon magically
endued in every letter with saving treasures of wisdom
and knowledge. But this high perfection belongs to
Holy Writ, not in its obvious sense,[3] but in virtue of the
higher unhistorical sense. Now the heretics also professed to find in Scripture spiritual mysteries favouring
their system. Nor could it be said that their way of
exegesis was radically worse than much of the interpretation practised in the Church. Both parties alike
were seeking in Scripture a kind of truth that it is not
meant to teach, and so neither could be convinced of
error by arguments strictly hermeneutical. But if it
was vain to suppose that a criticism of methods could
distinguish the true sense of Scripture from the false,
there must at least be a standard to try results   And
therefore (again to quote Origen), " cum multi sint qui
se putant sentire quae Christi sunt, et nonnulli eorum
diversa a prioribus sentiant, servetur vero ecclesiastica
praedicatio per successionis ordinem ab apostolis
tradita et usque ad praesens in ecclesia permanens   illa
sola credenda est veritas quae in nullo ab ecclesiastica
et apostolica discordat traditione." Accordingly, when

---

[1] Or *Prin* 1 47 Rue

[2] Or. *ut supra*, 162

[3] " Formae enim," says Origen (*Prin* 1 4, 8), " sunt haec quae
descripta sunt sacramentorum quorundam, et divinarum rerum
imagines   De quo totius ecclesiae una sententia est, esse quidem
omnem legem (=Scripture from context) spiritualem : non tamen
ea quae spirat lex esse omnibus nota, nisi his solis quibus gratia Spiritus
S in verbis sapientiae ac scientiae condonatur."

Origen lays down in the fourth book of the περὶ Ἀρχῶν the laws of interpretation which, in their essential points, became normative for the whole ancient Church, he sets forth as the starting-point of his whole theory the three positions : that Scripture is Divinely inspired ; that interpretation must follow the ecclesiastical canon ; and that in Holy Scripture certain mystic dispensations are made manifest (p. 166 Rue). On these bases Origen erects his famous distinction of a triple sense in Scripture, —the flesh or literal sense, the soul or moral sense, the spirit or intelligible and heavenly sense. Everywhere the principal aim of the Spirit had reference to the " ineffable mysteries of matters concerning mankind " [ἀπόρρητα μυστήρια τῶν κατὰ τοὺς ἀνθρώπους πραγμάτων]. This sense alone was continuous through Scripture, and so carried out that a teachable mind throwing itself into the depths of the intelligible sense could fathom all the higher truths [δόγματα] of the Divine counsel (172). True, it is a special mark of God's power and wisdom, that in many parts of Scripture these spiritual truths are wrapped up in " a not unprofitable " shell of history, capable of benefiting many of weaker capacity (173) ; but, allegorizing after Hermas (169), Origen speaks of those who understand this sense only as orphans who cannot call God their Father, widows not yet worthy of the Bridegroom. Nay, often the literal sense is impossible, absurd, immoral, and this designedly even in the New Testament, lest cleaving to the letter alone men should remain at a distance from the δόγματα, and learn nothing worthy of God (173).

On the whole, as I have said, these principles of Origen became normal for the Church, and their influence was scarcely diminished by the condemnation afterwards pronounced on the peculiarly bold system of Christian philosophy which Origen himself evolved by their aid How far they were accepted in the Western Church, even in the school which in its conception of Christianity

departed most widely from the intellectualism of the
Greek fathers, and anticipated most fully much of the
Reformation theology, may be readily judged by reference
to Augustin's hermeneutical treatise *de Fide Christiana*.
Augustin, like Origen, appeals to the *regula fidei* as the
highest criterion of interpretation, as containing the
compass of the *res* which the *signa* in the Scriptures
must unfold. Under the *signa*, again, he includes not
words only as logical signs, but the *literal* sense of a
passage whenever it does not enounce a spiritual truth
(cf. i. 2, iii. 5, etc.). On the other hand, Augustin gives to
Scripture a more practical character than Origen, insomuch as the heavenly things with which it is busied are
conceived not as mere philosophemes, but as *res qua
fruendum est*, that is God Himself, whom we are enabled
to enjoy if we hold fast the Christian precepts of faith,
hope, and love (i 39). Thus the end of the law and
of all Scripture (i. 35) is the love of God, whom it is our
end to enjoy, and of the fellow-men who can enjoy
Him along with us. And manifestly this end is often
served by the literal sense So we are not always to
look for an allegorical interpretation, but only to remember that "whatever has no proper bearing on the
rule of life or the verity of faith, must be recognised as
figurative."

It is easy to see that in these rules a much deeper
Christianity than that of Origen is struggling more than
half unconsciously with the radical defects of view
common to the whole ancient Church. Christianity is
still a law—the law of faith, hope, and love. The
historical sense is valuable not as history of Redemption,
but as inculcating the Christian law. For manifestly
there can be no true recognition of the historic in Scripture,
where it is held that almost every narrative of the Old
Testament has a figurative as well as a literal meaning,
that the same truths may be expressed indifferently in
letter or figure, nay, that the truth figuratively conveyed

is more telling (ii 6), because " facile investigata plerum-
que vilescunt," and " nemo ambigit per similitudinem
libentius quaeque cognosci." And lastly, it is manifest
that on Augustin's principles the richness of Scripture is
entirely lost. Wherever any ambiguity occurs, recourse
is at once to be had to the *praescriptum fideli*. It is only
in the second instance that an appeal is made to the
original language or other such helps (iii. 3) In tropical
passages interpretation is a sheer system of guessing
which of the truths comprised in the rule of faith can be
got out of the words (iii. 24). Perhaps several good
senses are possible If so, the inspired author (who
was always spiritually illuminated (iii. 39), though his
first readers might not get beyond the letter) probably
saw both senses, and certainly the Holy Spirit foresaw
both. Can anything be more fatal to a true appreciation
of Scripture than this artificial confinement of every
thought it contains within the narrow compass of a crude
theological system, a truly Procrustean bed, of which
not even the earliest thoughts of the Old Testament
must fall short, and which the ideal completeness of the
New Testament must not transcend ? Yet, amidst all
these false notions, the purely rational part of Augustin's
hermeneutics is, on the whole, admirable. He fully
apprehends that the function of the interpreter is simply
the reproduction of the thoughts of the writer. The
error lies far deeper than the formal principles of exegesis
It lies in a conception of the essentials of Christianity,
a theory of the things that inspired men *must* wish to
speak about, that is utterly discordant with facts.

The great interpreter of the Western Church, through
all the middle ages, was Augustin's contemporary,
Jerome. As inferior to the former in original power,
as superior to him in learning, Jerome exhibits in his
exegesis a closer adherence to the methods of Origen. All
Scripture, he grants, shines even in the bark, but it is
sweeter in the pith, " fulget etiam in cortice, sed dulcius

in medulla est," *i.e* in the spiritual sense, which not only
in Moses, but in the Evangelists and Apostles, is covered
with a veil.[1] In an important letter to Paulinus (ii. 2)
in which he gives a general sketch of Scripture, he dwells
with delight on the Apocalypse, which has as many
mysteries as words. Nay, even this praise, he adds,
falls short of the merit of a book in which every vocable
conceals manifold meanings. Of the historical books
he speaks half apologetically. Thus the Acts seems
only a bare history of the infancy of the Church , though
no doubt Luke, the admirable physician, has concealed
in every word some medicine for the languishing soul.
As if, forsooth, next to the Gospel history, anything
could be more profitable to the soul than the plain literal
history of the first days of the Church ! For the rest,
the allegorical interpretation is carried out by Jerome
with greater formality, but with more timidity than by
the boldly self-conscious Origen. It was from him,
perhaps, that the mediæval Church derived its scheme
of four senses, Literal, Ethical, Dogmatic or Allegorical,
and Anagogic.[2] But in carrying out this scheme he is
oppressed by a feeling of insecurity, a dread of falling into
forced interpretations[3] If a prophet like David must
pray that his eyes may be opened before he can see the
wonderful things of God's law, " quâ nos putas parvulos
et paene lactantes inscitiae nocte circumdari !" There
is something more than modesty in these expressions of
infantile weakness face to face with God's Word, which
are only too closely copied through all the middle ages.[4]
They imply a real sense that the current methods gave

[1] Ad Paulinum ii. 14 of *Ep. Sel.*, Paris, 1639.
[2] Clemens Al had already hinted at this. Cf. Reuss, *Gesch. d N T*
sect. 510   In the west Reuss finds it first in Eucherius. But Jerome on
Amos iv. (T. vi p 270, ed. Veron., 1736), already distinguishes the Allegoric and Anagogic sense, though he maintains the division into three
senses by uniting the Literal and Ethical
[3] E g Comm on Micah ii. T. vi. p. 459.
[4] Cf Diestel, *Gesch. des A T.* p 157, sect. 20.

no true insight into the spirit of Scripture, which, in
Jerome, led to an increasing dependence not only on the
ecclesiastical faith, but on the exegetical labours of his
predecessors, and which soon bore fruit in the entire
subjection of all interpretation, not simply to the general
rule of faith, but to every detail of an authoritative
exegetical tradition.   In this last step the subordination
under human teaching of the still nominally supreme
authority of Scripture was really completed.   Nor was it
possible, without a complete upturning of all established
foundations, to vindicate for the Word its true place.
⌈On purely exegetical ground some advance was made
during the middle ages, especially since Nicolaus de Lyra.
Hebrew began to be studied   More attention was paid
to the literal sense as the foundation of higher meanings.
But a radical improvement was impossible except in
connection with a religious reformation, which should
convince men that the real essence of Christianity lay
in something deeper than mere instruction in supernatural
things, that Christian faith was not simply a function of
the intellect, assenting to higher truths than those of
reason.⌋ And these were convictions which the School
Theology never reached, even in the person of those
doctors who most closely followed Augustin, and thus
come nearer to the Reformation, and have least in
common with the post-Tridentine forms of Roman
doctrine

Thus Thomas begins his *Summa* with the consideration
that salvation becomes possible by the existence, in
addition to philosophic science, of a doctrine *per revela-
tionem de iis quae hominis captum excedunt et nonnullis
etiam aliis quae humana ratione investigari possunt*, a
doctrine argumentative indeed in its conclusions, but
resting in its principles on the authority of Scripture,
and so to be received by faith.   Faith, then, and reason
stand opposed.   They are two methods of reaching
truth : even the *same* truth, for, as Thomas elsewhere

says, that we may gain a knowledge of God more speedily
and firmly, we are to believe, not only things supernatural,
but also things that may be investigated by the light
of nature   Manifestly a faith directed indifferently to
supernatural or natural truth must be essentially intellectual.   In short, *fides est cum assensu cogitare*, faith is
thought accompanied by assent free from vacillation,
and in matters where *sight* is excluded.   Thomas seeks,
indeed, to bring faith into connection also with the will,
partly in so far as assent is an act of will, and partly by
the famous distinction of *fides informis*, or faith without
charity, which is no virtue, and *fides formata*, "faith
working by love," which turns to the divine Good (which,
as Augustin had already taught, is the essence of the
higher truths which the believer apprehends), and sees
in that Good its highest end.   But valuable as this
distinction is as giving a practical escape from mere
intellectualism, it has no firm basis in the theory.   After
all, *caritas non per se pertinet ad fidem*.   The sterile *fides
informis* is at bottom the same "habit" as the living
fides formata.   The possession of either delivers from the
crowning sin of infidelity   both are supernatural gifts,
the *merum Dei donum*, lifting a man above his nature ;
and both are wholly lost by the heretic who departs even
from one article of the *Symbolum fidei* put forth by the
Supreme Pontiff with the authority of the universal
Church over which he presides.   How thoroughly do
these determinations ignore, almost exclude, a personal
relation to the believer to Christ !   How entirely do they
tend to make Christian faith a dead thing, having only
a secondary relation to God's Word, and resting primarily
on merely human authority !   For in truth only an
implicit belief is required in what Scripture teaches,
while explicit faith has for its object the ecclesiastical
articuli fidei.   With all this it squares well that the
"intelligible" truths of Scripture are represented as
difficult to understand.   Our rude minds can rise to

intelligible only through sensible truth. Metaphor is, therefore, necessary and useful, and though all truths are somewhere given in the literal sense, the main use of Scripture lies in those figures through which the ray of Divine revelation elevates us *ad cognitionem intelligibilium*. It is plain, indeed, that this argument is not satisfactory to Thomas's own mind. He devises or collects many subsidiary reasons for the allegorical form of Scripture. But it was not possible to him to suppose that the literal sense is everywhere that which is truly profitable and truly fitted to awake and nourish faith, so long as faith was conceived as an intellectual assent to the *prima veritas*, not as *personal trust on God in Christ*

A personal trust on God in Christ! In these words lies the key-note of the great Reformation It was from this conception of faith, not merely adopted as a theologumenon, but realised as that by which the believer must live, that the Reformers drew all their strength, and not least the strength to wield the Bible as it had never been wielded before. Let us look at this point a little more closely. All must have observed in how great a measure the history of the beginnings of the Reformation is just the story of the inner religious life of one man, who, agonized by a deep sense of sin, finding no rest in the habits and feelings prescribed by the traditional ascetic, at length gained peace when he was able to feel for himself through personal experience, through the witness of the Holy Spirit in his heart, the meaning of Paul's great doctrine of justifying faith. In Luther's personal experience of sin and grace, an experience that had gone through all its stages long before he entered into any antagonism to the Roman Church, lay implicitly all that was new in the Reformation, while, in the explicit development that ended in the great division of the Church, Luther and his followers were rather borne on in spite of themselves by the self-asserting power of the truth already quick within them, than busied in spontaneously working out new principles.

It is plain that this quite singular phenomenon does not find its explanation in the vitality of Luther's own Christianity, or the impulse he gave to vital Christianity in others. The mediæval Church has never been without vital Christianity Experience of sin and experience of grace were no new things Again and again religious movements the most genuine, often springing from the influence of the intense religious experience of one individual, had proved to the Church before the Reformation, as similar movements have proved to the Roman Church since the Reformation, sources not of division but of strength. Nay, was not Augustin, the greatest doctor of the Western Church, as deeply versed as Luther in the antithesis of sin and grace ? But in the old Church the notion of grace is bound up, above all, with the doctrine of the sacraments ; in the Reformation it is bound up with the notion of justifying faith. Of course I do not mean by this that the old Church saw no connection between grace and faith, that Luther would allow none between grace and the sacraments. But while the one said, The sacrament gives me grace *ex opere operato*, because I receive the sign, the other said, The sacrament is a vehicle of grace only in so far as by faith I pass beyond the sign and lay hold of God's promise signified Now I do not wish to go into the theological niceties of this difference, nor to ask how far the *whole* old Church would have gone against Luther's position What I have just said represents sufficiently the attitude of the two parties as you will find it expressed, *e.g.*, in Luther's book on the Babylonian Captivity of the Church ; and the meaning of the difference is very plain. To the mediæval Church *grace* is a magical thing ; to Luther it is a moral, a personal thing. The Reformers are separated from their fore-goers not by a mere difference of theological opinion, but by a growth of the religious con-

sciousness. I cannot better explain what this means than
by an illustration drawn from man's natural life.   The
life of an infant is the same as the life of a grown man.
Not the mere animal processes only, but the functions
of the mind follow the same law in both ; yet it is only
gradually that the child begins to comprehend its life,
to grasp the meaning of its own personality, and of the
relation in which it stands to other persons ; and so the
child's life is in a great but ever decreasing degree a
magical life, surrounded by wonders, supported and
guided by outward rules and signs, the reasons and meaning of which it cannot understand.   Every one has
observed how formal children are, how necessary for them
it is always to do the same thing in the same way.   This
is but one of many marks of an incapacity to separate the
sign from the thing signified, of inability to grasp the
personal kernel of life directly, of a need of bodily things
to typify all personal relations.   But step by step the
child becomes a man, and at length a time comes when
all these signs and forms have lost their magic and their
power,—when the symbol is known to be only a symbol,
and through the now transparent organism of the outward life the full-grown personality looks face to face
into the spiritual world around, and there alone finds its
true interests and its worthy aims.   Just so it is in the
history of the Church. ⌐The Christian life is in all ages
the same life—a life worth living only in so far as it is a
life of personal relation to God in Christ.⌐ But this life
is not in all believers or in all ages equally self-conscious.
Although in Christ's incarnation, life, and death, God's
self-manifestation was perfect and freed from type, it
did not follow that all Christians could look face to face
at once on the glory that shone in the Saviour's countenance.   The incarnate Word was the absolutely full
and clear revelation of the Divine will, of the Divine
essence.   But every word has an outer as well as an
inner side, an expression as well as a meaning.   The

real meaning of every true heart-spoken word is just the
opening up of the heart of him who speaks it ; and only
he understands the word aright who pierces through
the expression and sees in the word this and this alone.
To possess such an understanding is the mark of a full-
grown man.   Where the meaning is confounded with the
mere outer impersonal expression, there we may be well
assured the understanding is that of a child ; and there,
too, the word must be rested on, not with a full self-
conscious personal trust in the speaker, but, in so far at
least, with a reliance on the magical power of the symbol.
So it was in the old Church.   Whether in the intellectualism that viewed the λόγος merely in correlation to
the *rational* faculty, or in the sacramentalism that
supplemented the defects of the former conception by
ascribing a magical power to the " natural body of
Christ," [1] the Christian consciousness of the middle ages
fell far short of grasping the personality of God's Word.
It was still the consciousness of the child, who does not
fully understand either his own life or the life of those
around.   But with the Reformation begins a great
awaking into new self-conscious personal life.   Luther
saw that the Word of God, in which he had learned to
live, and in which the Church too must live, was not an
outward letter, but a deep personal thing.   " Neither
in heaven nor on earth hath the soul any other thing in
which to live pious, free, and Christian, save the holy
gospel; the word of God preached of Christ, as He Himself
says, I am the Life and the Resurrection, whoso believeth
on me liveth for ever."   " As the word is, so the soul
becomes thereby ; even as iron becomes red and glowing
like fire, by union with the fire."—And then " not only
does Faith give so much that the soul becomes like the
Divine Word, full of all grace, free and blessed, but it
unites the soul to Christ as a bride to her bridegroom." [2]

[1] Luth Sermon v. d. Sacrament, 20th head.
[2] Freiheit eines Christenmenschen, Th 1.

15

" Let us open our eyes," says Luther at another time,
" and learn to look at the word more than the sign, at the
faith more than the work." You see, then, how Luther
conceives of Christianity : on the one side God pouring
out his whole heart, revealing the inmost treasures of his
righteousness and love in Christ the incarnate Word ;
on the other side, the believing soul looking straight
through all works and all symbols to Christ Himself, and
united to Him by faith in the closest personal union.

Such was the blessed consciousness to which the
Reformation awoke—the consciousness of direct fellowship between the believer and God incarnate in Christ—
not an impersonal *unio mystica* such as the middle ages
sighed for, but such a personal union as there is between
loving human souls, mediated by the twofold stream of
God's personal Word coming down to man, and man's
personal faith going up to God.[1]

Now we see at once that in this new conception of the
correlation of word and faith is given implicitly an entire
new theory of revelation   The pre-Reformation definition
of the inner word is, to speak with Thomas,[2] " intellectum
prout est in intelligente," while, by the outer word,
" hoc significamus quod interius in intellectu compre-
hendimus." And so, as we have already seen, Christ
was conceived above all things as a Teacher, and revelation
as the imparting of speculative truth. But to the
Reformers the Word of God is the direct personal message
of God's *love* to me ,[3] not doctrine but promise, not the
display of God's thoughts, but of His loving purpose, in a
word, of Himself as my God.   " The Word of God," says

---

[1] Very notable in this connection is an argument of Zwingli's in the
Sermon " Von klarheit und gewusse des worts Gottes." The image of
God in man must be something much more special than the possession
of intellect, will, and memory , it must lie mainly in a regard to God
and to His Word.   The great mark of our creation in the likeness of God
is the desire that all men have after fellowship with God (*Werke*, 1 pp 58,
60)   The whole development of the thought is well worth attention

[2] *Compendium Theologiae*, cap. 37

[3] Freiheit eines Christenm., 6th head of Pt. I

Zwingli,[1] " is God Himself ", or, as Calvin [2] puts it,
" He not only teaches His elect to look to God, sed SE
quoque exhibet in quem respiciant." [3]

[1] *Werke,* 1 70

[2] *Institutio,* Lib 1 cap. 6 , cf Lib. iii. cap. 2, esp sect 6 . " Verbum
ipsum, utcunque ad nos deferatur, instar speculi esse dicimus in quo
Deum intueatur fides "

[3] It is, I think, correct to say that the whole of God's redemptive
activity, all His saving manifestation of Himself, falls for the Reformers
under the head of God's *word,* just as His creative activity, His natural
self-manifestations, are spoken of as His *works.*   Thus to Luther work,
word, heart, form an ascending scale   Speech, he says in his Preface
to the German Psalter, is the mightiest and noblest activity of man,
especially such speech as shows how the heart stands   " I would much
rather hear a saint speak than see his works."   A beast can do, only a
man can speak.   Thus word as opposed to work is personal as opposed
to impersonal activity.   This way of looking at the word was kept
always before the Reformers, by the great stress they laid on the conception of Christ as the living Word   From this point of view, it is not
surprising that faith in Christ the incarnate Word, faith in Christ's work,
and faith in the Gospel word, are so readily used as synonymous in the
Reformation theology   It is in great measure this identification, combined with such unguarded statements as could not be wanting among
men whose intuition of spiritual truths greatly outran the power of
giving them dogmatical precision, that has led some writers—and even
such a man as Rothe—to say that the Reformation Church viewed
Revelation simply as a supernatural communication of doctrine (Rothe,
Zur Dogmatik, p 56)   Certainly this view of Revelation did enter the
Protestant dogmatic, in proportion as the religious spirit of the Reformation declined, and men sank back into the superficial conception of *the
word* as a mere sign of impersonal truth   But this was a decline from
the true principles of the Reformation, and one that never obscured
altogether the truer insight that found its expression in the doctrine of
the Word and of Faith.   We must remember that the philosophical and
psychological treatment of the subject of personality, which alone can
furnish the basis for a complete dogmatical separation between the
deeper and shallower conceptions of Word of God and Revelation, is
even now a new thing   A certain measure of confusion was thus inevitable , but while one school of theology (culminating curiously
enough in Turretin, whose skill in exposition has brought him into undue
favour in Scotland) drifted through this confusion into the error which
Rothe condemns, another and deeper school, of which Ames is one of
the best representatives, always held fast the personal character of
Faith and of Revelation   It is instructive to observe how the want of a
sharp distinction between Religion and Theology leads Ames—not to conceive of Christianity as a mere scientific doctrine, but conversely to rescue
the personal character of Revelation by the position : " Primum et pro-
prium Theologiae subjectum esse voluntatem."—*Medulla Theologica,* 1 9

And now how does all this tell on the point from which we started, the bearing, namely, of the Reformation on the right understanding of Scripture ?

That Scripture was God's Word all were agreed. The mediæval Church, understanding by God's Word an intellectual revelation, looked in Scripture for *that* alone, and where no intellectual mysteries appeared, saw only, as Luther complains, bare dead histories, " which had simply taken place, and concerned men no more." Not so the Reformers. If God's Word is the opening up of what is in God's heart, the declaration of the eternal love in which alone man can rest, the story of God's dealings with the believers of bygone days can never become a dead history. " Let no pious Christian," says Luther in the Preface to his German Bible, " stumble at the simple Word and Story that meet him so often in Scripture Nay, let him not doubt that, plain as they may seem, they are the very Words, Works, Judgments, and History of God's high Majesty, Might, and Wisdom." Or again, in his exposition of Genesis, he shows that the Bible history is a sacred history, because God's Word gleams forth in it. All history shows the great works of God , but the great pre-eminence of the Bible history is that in it *God speaks* Israel's history is precious to us, because it tells of the relations in which the people stood to God · but above all stands Abraham's history, " because it is filled so full of God's Word, with which all that befell him is adorned and made fair, and because God everywhere goes before him with His Word, promising, commanding, comforting, warning, that we may verily see that Abraham was God's special trusty friend. Let us mirror ourselves, then, on this holy father Abraham, who walks not in gold and velvet, but girded, crowned, and clothed with Divine light, that is, with God's Word."

We shall hardly be wrong, in the face of these and similar utterances, in saying that Scripture is precious to Luther, because it shows to us the actual realization

among men of that personal fellowship with God through
word and faith which alone can satisfy *our* souls, and so
assures us that the life of faith in Christ, which is the
grand ideal of the Reformation, is no vain phantom,
but a real fellowship with a self-revealing God. The
Bible, to use Luther's own phrase, is the garment of
Christ.[1] We do not lay hold of Christ by grasping His
garment, we have not fellowship with Christ by a mere
head-knowledge of the Gospel history; but Christ is
wrapped up in the historic record, and it is only within
this garment that faith can find Him.

It is certainly true that this historical conception of
the Bible was by no means defined with theoretical
clearness, or grasped with perfect firmness, by the Reformation theology;[2] but just as the principle of personal
faith is the foundation of all the fresh life of the Reformation, so the principle of a historical treatment of Scripture
is at bottom, though far less clearly apprehended, the
principle of the whole Reformation exegesis. I venture
to say, that from this one principle flows all that is new
and true in the Protestant interpretation of the Bible;
that the understanding of Scripture has advanced or
gone back in the Evangelical Churches just in proportion
as this principle, in connection with the great principle
of justifying faith, has been held fast or overlooked, and
that we, too, if we are really in earnest with our study of
the Bible, if we desire to deal truly with Scripture and
our Protestant freedom, must regulate all our exegesis
and all our criticism by the great principle that we are
to seek in the Bible, not a body of abstract religious
truth, but the living personal history of God's gracious
dealings with men from age to age, till at length in

[1] On Ps. xxii 19 (18), in his " Operationes in duas Psalmorum
Decades "
[2] Compare on this point an instructive Essay by Diestel, " Die kirch-
liche Anschauung des A T ," in the *Jahrbb f. D Theol*, 1869, p 232
sqq   Professor Diestel shows how *two* views of the Old Testament soon
branched off in the Protestant Churches.

Christ's historical work the face of the Eternal is fully
revealed, and we by faith can enter into the fullest and
freest fellowship with an incarnate God.

With what power this principle bears on all those
parts of Scripture which, through the long ages before
the Reformation, were almost wholly sealed to the
Church, what a flood of fresh light it casts even on the
plainest parts of the Sacred Record, how it fills with fresh
and ever - varying interest the narratives that to the
ancient Church afforded only a dreary monotonous
round of allegory, how it enables the reader to enter
everywhere into a personal fellowship with the saints
and the church of bygone days, and, if God's Spirit go
with the reading, into fellowship also with the great
Revealer Himself—these are things that can only be
learned by such a study of the Bible in its details, as we
must begin together in our meetings here, and carry out
each for himself in the prayerful labours of a whole life.
At this time it is only possible briefly to indicate a few of
the directions in which the new principle became fruitful
at the time of the Reformation, and may still be fruitful
to us.

I. Firstly, then, the new conception of Scripture gave
a death-blow to the *allegorical* way of interpretation, the
theory of a fourfold sense, which by its half-contemptuous
" *litera gesta docet* " made the history a dead history,
useless in teaching faith.[1] " There is," says Luther,
" one single, simple sense " : and this is the principle of
the whole Reformation ; for, however far the overstrained
typology of some Protestant schools may re-open an
entrance for what is really sheer allegorical exposition,
the principle of allegory is effectually condemned by the
symbolical definition of all Protestant Churches, that the
interpretation of Scripture must be drawn from Scripture
itself, *i.e.* as Bullinger explains in the *Helvetica Posterior*,
from the genius of the original language, the due con-

[1] Cf Luther on Ps. xxii *ut supra*.

sideration of the circumstances, with comparison of like
and unlike passages.[1]

II. The last of these postulates of a true interpretation
raises the question of the relation of exegesis to the
analogy of faith, which forms a long and perplexed
chapter in the history of the decadence, as well as the
growth, of Protestant theology.   But it is to be observed
that the Reformers everywhere place Scripture *above* the
Ecclesiastic Canon, in virtue of its own innate perspicuity
to every one that approaches it in the spirit of faith.
And so to the Reformers and their truest followers the
analogy of faith means not a dead rule of dogma, but
the living sympathy of a renewed soul living in fellowship with Christ, with the historic record of God's ever-
consistent working towards the establishment of His
kingdom upon earth.   Just as it requires a historic sense
to understand profane history, it requires a spiritual
sense to understand sacred history.

III. If the perspicuity of Scripture rests on the one
side on the illumination given by the Spirit to the faithful
reader, it is no less grounded on the other side on the
historicity of Scripture.   God's dealings with His people
were always personal   What His prophets and apostles
spoke, they spoke because by the Spirit they understood,
and would have others to understand, how God was
dealing with men.   And if we possess the same spirit, we,
too, shall understand the Word so soon as we place ourselves in the historical position of the first hearers   Hence
the Reformers emphasise the fact that the Old Testament
prophets (who, more than any other Scripture writers,
have been supposed to talk things unintelligible to their
first hearers) did in Israel precisely the work that ministers
of the Gospel must do now in ministering by special
application of the principles of law and grace to the ever-

[1] Niemeyer, p 469 —The *circumstantiae* are, I presume, mainly the
verbal context , but the principle implies that the historical circumstances be also considered.

varying needs of the people.[1] And so Luther writes in his Preface to Isaiah, that if we will understand prophecy we must study the contemporary history, and learn how things stood in the land ; how men's minds were bent, what designs of war or peace they had in hand, and, above all, their attitude to God, the prophet, and religion.[2]

IV. It is mainly to the comprehensive genius of Calvin that we owe the further development of these principles in the conception of the exegetico-historical problem in its totality. What Calvin set before him as the goal of Biblical studies, was the gathering up into one whole of all God's dealings with men from the fall to the Resurrection of Christ, the history of true religion, the adoption and education, from age to age, of the Church, in a continuous scheme of gradual advance. It is true that in that age the means for justly carrying out so great a conception were still lacking. The very idea of an historical evolution was but imperfectly understood. There were many tendencies, both in the age and in Calvin's own character, that prevented him from doing so much justice to the difference as to the unity of successive dispensations But not only did the example point out a course on which, after long neglect, the newer theology, armed with richer apparatus, must enter with fresh ardour ; the very idea of such a scheme gave to Calvin an elevation of view, a freedom of judgment, a superiority to prejudices that the mere student of details could hardly break through, which have justly elevated him to the rank of the greatest of uninspired expositors, and have left to his followers an ever precious example of believing courage in dealing with the Scriptures.

V. It is impossible to pass from this topic without in

---

[1] Cf Calvin, Praefatio in Esaiam

[2] Yet side by side with this goes another line of thought " Der Prophezeien Art und Natur ist, dass sie ehe erfullet denn verstanden sind," says Luther, at one time The two views are not irreconcilable.

one word pointing out that a necessary consequence of this way of treating the Bible is the honest practice of a higher criticism   The higher criticism does not mean negative criticism.   It means the fair and honest looking at the Bible as a historical record, and the effort everywhere to reach the real meaning and historical setting, not of individual *passages* of the Scripture, but of the Scripture Records as a whole ; and to do this we must apply the same principle that the Reformation applied to detail Exegesis.   We must let the Bible speak for itself   Our notions of the origin, the purpose, the character of the Scripture books must be drawn, not from vain traditions, but from a historical study of the books themselves.   This process can be dangerous to faith only when it is begun without faith—when we forget that the Bible history is no profane history, but the story of God's saving self-manifestation.

VI. And, finally, one word on the bearing of the Reformation principle on the use of Scripture for edification.   In the Bible history, as the Reformers conceived it, we hear two voices—the voice of God speaking love to man, and the voice of the renewed man answering in faith to God   " The Scripture," says Jurieu, " is almost nothing else than a tissue of prayers and thanksgiving " ; [1] and this loving communion of God and man is no dead bygone thing, but a thing in which we may share.   " God is not the God of the dead, but of the living, for all live unto Him."   And so when we draw near in faith to the Bible, we feel ourselves entering into a higher, holier world —" not to the mount that might be touched, and that burned with fire, nor unto blackness, and darkness, and tempest ; but unto mount Sion, and to the city of the living God, the heavenly Jerusalem, and to an

[1] " L'Écriture n'est presque autre chose que cela, qu'un tissu de prières et d'actions de grâces "—(*Jugement sur les Méthodes*, etc , Rott 1688, p. 84)   Luther's views on the answer of man to God, as expressed in Scripture, are beautifully developed in the Preface to the German Psalter.

innumerable company of angels, to the general assembly and church of the first-born which are written in heaven, and to God the Judge of all, and to the spirits of just men made perfect, and to Jesus the mediator of the new covenant, and to the blood of sprinkling, that speaketh better things than Abel . . . Wherefore, we receiving a kingdom that cannot be moved, let us have grace, whereby we may serve God acceptably with reverence and godly fear . for our God is a consuming fire "

II

EXTRACTS FROM EARLY LECTURES

1. *The Nazirate; date of P.* (June 19, 1870)

THE history of the Nazirate is, so far as our records go, very brief. All leading critics assign the law Num. vi. 1-21 to the so-called *Grundschrift*, Book of Origins—Book of the Elohist—which, though not the earliest written document entering into the Pentateuch, is regarded by those who reject Mosaic authorship as the first complete chronicle of the early history of Israel. This book is generally assigned to the time of Saul, or David's early years, and is viewed by all sober critics as a very weighty authority. Thus, apart from all questions of Mosaic authorship, inspiration, etc., it would generally be allowed that our record is correct in supposing the Nazirate to reach back to Moses (Ew. *Alt.* 117, with some hesitation ; cf *Gesch.* ii. 560 ; Knobel, *Kr. d. Pent.* p. 522, 593). The law, indeed, as we have it seems to be rather the regulation of an older institution.

2 *Beginnings of Prophetic Literature* (Jan. 1871).

There is no trace of prophets writing down their oracles till long after the epoch of Samuel. In truth, that prophets like Elijah and Samuel, who were essentially men of deeds rather than words, should have committed their prophecies to writing is in itself improbable. On the other hand, the prophetic schools seem to have early developed a literary activity in connection with the history of Israel. Inasmuch as the general diffusion of history in an age when few can read must mainly take place by ballads, it is natural (with Kuenen, *Godsd*. i. 208) to find a connection between the historical labours of the prophetic societies and the musical studies already described. The Psalter still contains many historico-religious ballads. In I Chron xxix. 29, we read that the acts (דברי) of David were written in the history (על דברי) of Samuel the seer, and in the history of Nathan the prophet, and in the history of Gad the seer. In this statement we cannot see evidence of books written by Samuel, etc., as the sense of *dibre S* must be " history of Samuel," parallel to the preceding *dibre D*.

But doubtless the records referred to, and which treated the history of the nation in connection with the work of distinguished prophets, were written in the Schools of the Prophets, and are referred to by the chronicler as old and authentic accounts. Moreover, the point of view from which the history is treated in the Books of Samuel and other parts of the Old Testament leaves no doubt that the history as we possess it is in great measure compiled from the labours of prophets or their disciples In 2 Chron. ix. 29, the " Acts of Nathan," mentioned above, are associated with two other prophetic books, " the prophecy (נבואת) of Ahijah the Shilonite," and " the visions of Iddo the seer concerning Jeroboam." Whether these books, which by their titles appear to have contained not only historical matter but written oracles, had for authors the prophets themselves, or were also collected by disciples, is uncertain. Perhaps the fact that they are now lost may so far favour the latter supposition, and show that they had not the authority of exact reproductions of the prophets' words. At all events the properly prophetic literature is of a later date, and naturally took its rise in the Southern School of Prophecy, which, as we have seen, separated itself from

the older and more impetuous Prophecy of the northern
kingdom in a way that made written prophecy much
more suitable to its purposes.

With regard to the motives that might lead a prophet
to commit his speeches to writing, "Nothing," says
Ewald (*Proph.* i 48), " is more instructive than what
Isaiah tells us in his own case. When his contemporaries
refused to comprehend and believe great truth which he
had repeatedly preached, then especially the prophetic
spirit which had led him to speak summoned him also to
write, that by this means he might work for his own time,
and lay down in an everlasting memorial for ages what
he felt to be as true as his own life (viii. 1, 16; xxx. 8).
Or, if a prophet had already laboured long and experienced
much, and now looked back on his whole past activity,
he might think it well to perpetuate the weightiest of his
speeches and deeds in writing as an enduring monument
for the instruction of far and near, of present and future
ages. Thus we read in Jer. xxxvi., that in the fourth
year of Joiakim, Baruch wrote to Jeremiah's dictation a
roll containing all the words which God had spoken to
him since his first call under Josiah—that is, through a
period of more than twenty years. Of course, such a
collection could not reproduce verbally all the prophet's
inspired speeches, but would gather together in a condensed form all that was most memorable, and present
these materials in a form shaped by the prophet's own
free judgment." Ewald further points out that such
passages as Is. viii. 1; xxx. 8, indicate that besides actual
prophetic books the prophets were accustomed to express
leading thoughts in short proverbial forms upon tablets
exposed to public view. This appears to have been done
in presence of witnesses (viii. 2; xxx. 8, אִתָּם with them
(witnesses), and in a large bold character (בְּחֶרֶט אֱנוֹשׁ),
so as to be easily read (cf. Hab. ii 2). An age in which
this was an effective way of appealing to the people at
large was manifestly one in which education was widely

diffused. Long before this time, therefore, there must have been in Israel all the conditions of literary activity, and sufficient motives to induce the prophets to write their oracles at large. Accordingly, Joel iii. 5 appears to contain a quotation from an earlier prophet. Similarly Isaiah ii 2, 4, and Micah iv 1, 4, quote the same passage from a predecessor, who may perhaps have been Joel himself. But whatever relics of early written prophecies may thus have been preserved, prophetic authorship in a strict sense begins for us in the book of Joel

(For further information on the literary activity of Prophets, see Ewald, *Pro.* i. 47)

3. *Authorship of* Isa xiii 2–xiv. 23.—*Prophecy of the Fall of Babel* (1871).

v. 1. What weight belongs to this title must appear below Meantime, I quote only Delitzsch . " If this ' burden of Babel ' lay before us entirely by itself, and without Isaiah's name attached to it, we would never venture to ascribe it to that prophet . . Here, at a time when the Assyrian empire was still standing, the fall of the Chaldean is without any connecting link foretold."

4. *Date of Zech.* ix.-xi (March 1871)

Besides Hosea and Amos we possess in the judgment of most critics an important prophecy referring to the decay of the N. Kingdom in Zech. ix -xi.

Doubts whether Zechariah is the real author of these chapters began very early. In 1653 Mede concluded from Mt. xxvii. 9, that Jeremiah is the true author of the whole section Zech. ix.-xiv. It was an Englishman also, Newcome, 1785, who first separated ix.-xi. from xii -xiv., and placed the composition of the former chapters before the fall of the kingdom of Ephraim. Of late this view has been supported by the whole strength of the critical school, and though opposed by Hengstenberg, Havernick,

Keil, Köhler, etc., is supported by arguments so strong that, *e g.* Pressel, a man not attached to the critical school, has lately given his assent to it. In this defection we may, probably, see the signs of a final abandonment of the traditional view on all hands

Were we discussing the Book of Zechariah as a whole, we should begin by calling attention to the great difference of style and manner between ch ix.-xi. and the preceding part of the book. Such differences are enumerated in the Commentaries and Introductions (*pro* Hitz. Kno ; *con ·* Bleek, Hävern), and are best felt by reading the two texts side by side Our plan confines us to a constructive plan. Laying aside the traditional view altogether for the present, let us examine this prophecy just as we examined that of Joel. If there we clearly were able to assign a date, it is surely not presumptuous to expect to find a similar task possible here ; especially as the prophecy is most rich with concrete historical colouring.

The outline is as follows ·—

ix. 1. The threatening word of Jahveh — the God whose eyes view the heathen and the tribes of Israel alike—sweeps like a storm through Syria and alights upon Damascus. Thence it passes to Hamath, and on to the rich cities of Phoenicia, smiting them with destruction. Still flying southward it lights upon the Philistines, and destroys the pride and independence of their cities, but at the same time drives them from their idols and unites them to Judah on the same terms as the Jebusites (whom Solomon made tributary). Meantime, God who has now looked down from heaven and seen what is done on earth, encamps over His house that it may no longer suffer from hostile incursions and oppression. And now (*v.* 9), amidst joyous shouts, the Messiah comes riding upon an ass, not escorted by chariots and horses and all the panoply of war, but upheld by His righteousness and so ever victorious. For before this peaceful king the hostile armaments that oppress Ephraim and Jerusalem shall fall—the kingdom shall regain its ancient limits, and the sovereign of Zion shall enjoin peace on all nations Yea, the memory of the blood-sealed covenant moves God to deliver the captive Israelites, and even now His heralds proclaim a double recompense for all their woes. In God's hand Judah and Ephraim are like bow and spear to strike down their oppressors—of whom the sons of Javan are expressed by name, who in Joel also appear as masters whose yoke is specially grievous.   Jahveh appears in a storm-cloud shielding His own, the lightnings are His arrows and the thunders His trumpets His people rush forth with irresistible fury against their enemies and, the victory finally secured, enjoy peace and plenty in their land (ix. 13).

Chap. x begins a new strain —

Such are the blessings God gives , but now it seems the people are apter to trust in teraphim, wizards, and dreams, than to pray to Him for help.   And so they are like a flock wandering without a shepherd, or rather the wrath of Jahveh has smitten the shepherds and the he-goats (*i e* the violent, insolent nobles . Ez. xxxiv.) ; but His flock, the house of Judah, He visits and strengthens and organises into an invincible host before which the riders on horses shall be ashamed.   He gives salvation to Ephraim and Judah, helping them as if He had never thrust them from Him, and these scattered children return at His call.   True ! this restoration is not the first thing First, they must in chastisement be sown among the Gentiles.   But even in captivity they take root and increase, and at length remembering God are brought back, a great multitude, from Assyria and from Egypt to occupy Gilead and Lebanon, and even there not to find room.   And while they walk joyously in God's name, the Nile and the Euphrates are smitten and the might of Egypt and Asshur pass away (x. 11, 12).

But to these bright hopes there is a counterfoil.   In

x 9 the prophet has already indicated that a period of suffering and captivity lies between the present state of sin and the future state of salvation. And this dark side, especially the dark present, is the subject of ch. xi. In *vv* 1-3 the destruction of the nation is figured, apparently with reference to the storm of chap. ix , under the image of a fire devouring the cedars of Lebanon and the oaks of Bashan, wasting the pastures and the thickets of the Jordan. This short burst of lyric lamentation serves to introduce the subsequent verses in which the fate of the people is handled in connection with the history of his own work among them. Jahveh sent him to feed the sheep of the shambles, *i.e.* the nation of Israel bought and sold by cruel and treacherous rulers who care not though the people perish if they themselves are enriched.

For Jahveh has no more pity on His people ; but sends civil strife among them and discord between people and king, so that the land is wasted and no help is found. Yet amidst these sad circumstances the prophet assumes the task of shepherd, armed with two staves, the staff of God's protecting (kindness) grace for His people and the staff of (harmony) union between Judah and Ephraim. Three of the false shepherds fall before the prophet in one month ; but his soul is wearied with his thankless charge, and the nation loathes his wholesome constraint. So he resolves to leave them to their fate, breaks the staff of grace (נעם not just = חסד) and sets free against the people the foreign nations whom Jahveh had till now restrained. Nor was this an empty symbol. Its fulfilment followed straightway, and the few who still hearkened to his word recognised hereby the divine mission of the seer. But still no such repentance follows as to lead him to draw back from his demission of the shepherd's office. That that demission may be formal and with mutual consent—that he may not, as Jonah or Elijah did, flee from his work—he demands of his flock such hire as they may think his due. His reward is the price of the meanest

16

slave—a price that he is commanded to cast into the treasury of the temple, for a prophet does not serve to enrich himself, and it is God, not man, whom they reward so meanly. Then he breaks his second staff, and Ephraim and Judah are allies no longer And now the prophet must symbolise the foolish and worthless shepherd that rules over the nation which rejects God's care, a shepherd who has no care for the weak and suffering, but who feasts on the flesh of the fatlings and breaks the hoofs of the sheep by driving them on stony roads (not like Jahveh's מָעְגְּלֵי צֶדֶק). The prophecy closes with a denunciation of wrath against this wicked ruler A sword upon his arm and upon his right hand, his arm shall be dried up and his right eye wholly extinguished.

A single glance shows that in this prophecy it is absolutely impossible to separate between the question of authorship and date and the exegesis of the passage. If we are to follow an historical interpretation at all— that is, if we are to suppose that here, as elsewhere, the prophet is speaking primarily to his own contemporaries and from the circumstances of his own time—or indeed, if we are to interpret literally at all, the idea of authorship by Zechariah is out of the question.

a. This appears clearly from *individual* traits (a) Ephraim and Judah or Israel (or Joseph) and Judah appear as distinct throughout. Certainly an allusion to this distinction is not impossible in a prophet writing after the captivity. Zechariah (viii. 13) writes . " As ye have been a curse among the nations, O house of Judah and house of Israel, so will I save you." (Zech ii. 2, Mal ii. 11 quoted by Hävernick are irrelevant here.) And Ezekiel (xxxvii 15 *sq.*) prophesies the restoration of Ephraim and Judah and their reunion into one kingdom. And so in our passage, though the use of the two names is much more extended, it may fairly be said that where a restoration of Judah and Joseph is mentioned (Ezek. x 6), there is no instance against Zechariah as author. But quite different is the prophecy of the breaking of concord between Judah and Ephraim. That cannot apply to the διασπορά, and so is interpreted by Hengstenberg and Keil of the divisions in Judæa between Christ's time and the fall of Jerusalem, by Hofmann (II. 2, p. 608) of the division between Christian and unbelieving Jews. In either case not historico-literal but symbolical allegorising interpretation.[1]

β. In ch ix. God's judgment lights on Damascus, Phœnicia, Philistia. All the states seem to be brought in as independent and as hostile to Israel. In Philistia especially there is still a king and the old aristocratic pride in pure blood which is to be brought down when a bastard population occupies Ashdod. It is answered that these nations still remained and were hostile to Israel after the Exile, and that the king who is destroyed from Gaza may be a Persian vassal. But if the king is a vassal his fall is not a proper expression for the transference of the sovereignty to the people of Israel , and this is what our prophet expects (ix 7). If in this case the post-exile authorship rhymes badly with literal interpretation the inconsistency is admitted in regard to Egypt and Asshur (lower, esp. ch. x.). These, it is admitted (Keil, *Introd.* § 103, 4 ; *cf.* Hengstenberg, *Integrity*, E.T 307), are mentioned merely as types and representatives of the enemies of the Kingdom of God. That is, the concrete colouring is here also not drawn literally from present history but allegorisingly from the past. (But *cf.* Ps. lxxxiii., where most critics make אשור non-historical.)

γ. The teraphim and false prophets of x. 2 are precisely analogous to the similar institutions mentioned in Hosea III. After the Exile there were certainly false prophets

---

[1] According to Hengstenberg, *Christol.* E T , 422, this is the literal fulfilment also of the obviously *distinct* step in the prophecy (ch xi. 6) where for the rest the king is Caesar (cf. מלכם אות אוה Hos xi 5)   But to Keil הארץ is the land outside Israel—the earth and king distributive like א ע.

(Neh vi. 10 *sqq.*). There was even a certain mixture with
idolatrous nations (Ezra ix). But there is no polemic in
the post-exile prophets or in Ezra and Nehemiah against
idolatry, and such a national idolatry as is here depicted
seems inconceivable at this epoch. Here, too, Hengstenberg allegorises " This is nothing more than Zechariah's
usual (?) mode of depicting the one main idea. The
people are led away by deceivers who draw them away
from the source of all truth, the revealed will of God."

δ. Most complete is the departure from the historical interpretation in ch. xi. Here the symbolical actions do not
in any sense represent, according to Hengstenberg, Keil,
etc., the prophet's own activity, but in general Jahveh's
dealings with His people The three herdsmen are the
civil authorities, the priests and prophets deposed from
their office during our Lord's ministry on earth (Hgstbg.
ch. iv. 28 *sqq.*), or the rulers of the three world monarchies
(Keil). The "month" remains a stumbling-block, and
Keil can only suggest that ten days are given for the
destruction of each shepherd. What follows is referred
directly to the rejection of Christ by the Jewish people
and the calamities following Finally, the foolish shepherd
who follows the rejection is, to Hengstenberg, collectively
the bad rulers of the Jewish nation, to Keil the master of
the world-power. This is not the place for a full discussion
of these interpretations ; but every one sees that by thus
shutting out the prophet's own person and age, and
finding a direct instead of a typical Messianic interpretation, the commentators just quoted lose themselves in the
usual confusing alternation between the Kingdom of
God in the universal sense and the literal nation of
Israel Part of the prophecy applies to the one, part to
the other. This in the by-going. But what must be
admitted from the instances just adduced is, that if the
concrete colouring of the picture is to be interpreted
historically—that is, according to the analogy of prophecy
in general—the prophet must have stood before the exile.

If Zechariah is the author, the concrete colouring is allegorical and symbolical.

Now this conclusion may not seem to carry us far in our present enquiry. But it is very important as regards the general theory of Old Testament criticism as regards the prophetical writings. It is often maintained that the only ground for disputing traditional authorship is rationalism—*i.e.* a desire to dispute the divine illumination of the prophet. But the present discussion shows us that this is not true, unless all literal interpretation is rationalism and allegorical exegesis is alone evangelical. And how little this is the case, we have already seen in discussing the book of Joel. Let us suppose that our prophecy had come to us in a separate form like the book of Joel without date   No one would have seen in it traces of composition after the Exile   Such traces are, indeed, sought by Hengstenberg and others (see a condensed list in Koehler's article in Herzog, xviii. 358), but rather weigh on the other side (are either futile or self-destructive). The mention of Greece (ix. 13) may be explained by Joel iv. 6, 7 ; or if this be denied, is it easier to explain it in connection with Zechariah's time ?   Ch. ix. 8 is said to imply a previous destruction of the temple. Really the oppressor in this verse is not a sovereign like the Great King, levying regular tribute, but a passing conqueror, making a raid in the land and again withdrawing.   This suits the first times of the Assyrian invasions or such a plundering of Jerusalem as we found indicated in Joel iv. 6, 7 ; (*cf.* 2 Chron. xxi. 17-18). Again (Hävern. 424) the time of the exile is said to appear in ix. 12, 10, 6, as already present. But the first passage has an exact parallel in Joel iv. (*cf.* Is. xi. 15-16 ; Micah vii. 12), while with the second we must connect the next verse in which the " sowing among the nations " appears as future—*i e.* just as in Amos and Hosea, etc., chastisement must precede deliverance.

Quite different, as we have seen, are the indications of

authorship before the exile. Of these we have enumerated only some of the more pointed which indicate in
general a date before the exile.   But if we gather the
various details up into one, we get (always assuming at
present the literal interpretation) a much more definite
result.   Asshur has already entered, but has not left the
stage of history. Nay, the judgment on Syria is still
future (ix. 1).   Jerusalem has probably not yet suffered
from Assyria at all, else that power would appear in
ch. ix. 1-6.   The threats of captivity (ch. x) to be
followed by deliverance agree with and probably presuppose Amos   The references to teraphim suit the age
of Hosea (ch. iii.)   Once more, the returning captives
in ch x. 10 occupy not the whole land but Gilead and
Lebanon, of which the former was greatly desolated so
early as the Syrian wars and the latter never occupied
fully   Parallel is Micah vii. 14, where the prophet prays
that the flock dwelling solitary in the wood of Carmel
may repossess Bashan and Gilead.   According to all this,
the prophet would be later than Amos, and a younger
contemporary of Hosea, an older contemporary of Isaiah
But as the bright side of his prophecy lies in the future,
the dark side which is present is most instructive here.
Now, if in ch. ix. the prophet appears as specially
interested in the Southern Kingdom, of which indeed he
may be supposed a citizen (from the general tone, the
personal אלהינו ix. 7, and the fact that retiring from
his office he goes to the *temple*), yet in ch. xi. he is
chiefly concerned with Ephraim. This is shown by the
introductory verses which threaten ruin to Lebanon,
Jordan, and Bashan.   In Ephraim, then, are sought the
slaughter-sheep. Here it is that the prophet ministers
with so little acceptance amidst evil rulers, anarchy,
civil war, then attacks from without, and finally broken
friendship between Israel and Judah. All this is found
in the period following Jeroboam's death, and exactly
in the order here mentioned—first internal tumult, then

Phul whose bargain with Menahem suits the buying and
selling of the flock (xi. 5), then under Pekah the quarrel
with Judah.   Still more definite is the destroying of three
shepherds by the prophet—*i.e* in accordance with God's
Word—in one month   Is it an accident that Shallum,
the murderer of Zechariah himself, fell in a month before
Menahem? (2 Kings xv. 13).   And though few will agree
with Ewald that the Hebrew text (2 Kings xv. 10) still
shows the name of a third usurper, it is nothing strange
that a third claimant to sovereignty should have appeared
at the same time.   Finally, the prophet's withdrawal
from his office seems to be in close connection with the
rise of the foolish shepherd, in whom it is easy to recognise
Pekah, the ruthless violent Gileadite.   That the whole
narrative of the prophet's pastoral work is to be taken as
a narrative more or less symbolically expressed, seems
plain from its standing in the perfect while the predictions
are given in the imperfect.   And such a point as the
immediate sequence of invasion on the breaking of the
staff and the acceptance of this by the believing sheep
as a proof of divine mission, is absolutely unintelligible
except on the historical interpretation.

    If, then, we had no external motive for going to a
time after the exile, we could find a natural historical
setting for our prophecy.   Should we by doing so lose
anything of the religious meaning ?   Surely not.   We
should still retain the great Messianic passage in ch. ix.,
we should have all through, as might easily be shown, a
precise analogy to prophecies of Hosea, Amos, Isaiah,
etc.   It can only be questioned if we do not lose the
reference to Christ in ch. xi.   Surely not.   If the prophecy
be taken as having its first application to Christ we get
rather into greater difficulties.   Thus the price was not
given to our Lord but to Judas.   It was Judas that
threw it into the House of the Lord.   Our Lord did not
refuse to feed the theocracy in a way just corresponding
to this.   Again, the same person who first bears the two

staves afterwards takes up the instruments symbolic of an evil shepherd.   If the reference is primarily to him, why is all this so ?   But the difficulty vanishes if the prophet's action is typical of Christ's ; for every type must not only have some things in common with, but some things diverse from, the antitype.   And thus, too, we get over the confusion above remarked between the true Kingdom of God and the fleshly Israel.   In the days of our Lord these fell apart.   But in the prophet's day the two were really bound up together, so that the whole prophecy is from his historical standpoint one and consistent.

And now there comes the question : Shall we cast all these harmonious internal evidences to the winds to save the tradition of authorship ?   Surely not, if we are to hold the Protestant principle that the Bible is to be interpreted by itself and not by tradition.   A tradition that overturns the whole natural exegesis must have strong proofs, indeed, to lead us to adopt it.   But, in fact, we have no distinct external evidence.   We have only the juxtaposition with Zechariah—unaccompanied by any such formal title as heads each of the prophecies that form Zech. i -viii.   We have not even the assurance that when the prophetic books were first collected this work was held to be Zechariah's, or that anything but its position made such an opinion prevail.   And, finally, there is at least one plausible theory that might explain how this state of things arose.   In Isaiah viii. 2 there appears in association with the prophet Isaiah a certain Zekharjahu, son of Jeberekhiahu.   Now the post-exile prophet who in Ezra is called the son of Iddo appears in the heading of his prophecy as son of Berekhja, son of Iddo.   Berekhiah and Berekhiahu are the same name. The older Zechariah from his association with Isaiah may have been a prophet, and if there were two prophets sons of Berechiah the juxtaposition of their oracles ceases to be surprising.   But this is, of course, only a conjecture

as to how the case might have arisen, and stands on quite
a different footing from the real arguments for dating
ix.-xi. from the 8th century. And it is characteristic
of the way in which certain critics are unable to distinguish conjecture from proof that Kuenen, without
hesitation, in his *Godsdienst* assumes this conjectural
identification of the author of the chapter as historical
fact.

5. *The Book of the Covenant* (Oct. 11, 1872).

Every discussion of the Covenant made at Sinai must
start from Exodus xix -xxiv., the so-called *Book of the
Covenant.* The name ספר הברית is in these chapters
themselves given to that first sketch of the Mosaic constitution, given from Sinai, to the observance of which
the people formally pledged themselves. And the same
name is rightly enough extended to the whole section
which simply contains these laws with the needful
historical elucidations. The six chapters of the Book
of the Covenant stand out in distinct relief from the
surrounding parts of the Pentateuch, and competent
critics of all schools are pretty much at one as regarding
them as forming the oldest part of the Pentateuch, the
basis of all subsequent legislation.

6. *The History of the Ark* (Dec. 13, 1872).

You may probably be inclined to think that before
saying anything of the history of the ark, one should go
on to the description of the *tabernacle* in which the ark
was preserved. A few years ago this would have been
the natural course to follow. But in recent times the
historicity of the Tabernacle, as described in the book of
Exodus, has been exposed to severe assaults, which do
not touch the historicity of the ark. In fact, the most
negative critics of the present day admit that the ark,
and of course a tent for its protection, were carried about

by the Israelites in the wilderness.[1]   But the same critics
who gladly admit this very often maintain that the whole
description of the Mosaic tabernacle is a fancy-piece in
imitation of the arrangements of Solomon's temple
This view, after various sporadic utterances on the part
of other critics, was set forth with much zeal and ingenuity by Graf in several publications, of which the
most accessible is his book—*Die geschichtlichen Bucher
des A.T.* (Leipzig, 1866)   The same view is warmly
supported, among other living critics, by Noldeke,
Untersuchungen zur Kritik des A.T., 1869, p. 12, and
by Kuenen, *Godsdienst van Israel*, 1869-70, ii. 75, etc.
Now, I have endeavoured throughout these lectures to
build upon ground which is historically undisputed, so
that you may see how much of the character of the Old
Testament dispensation stands on a basis that cannot
be shaken.   I have endeavoured to give the lesson of
institutions which every one admits to have existed,
though every one, of course, does not recognise in them
the same spiritual religion.   This is the case with the ark
itself.   There are critics who are bold enough to overlook
altogether the witness that the ark with its tables of the
law bears to the moral and spiritual character of the
religion of Moses and to assume against the whole history
that the *ark* must originally, like the arks of heathen
nations, have contained something in the shape of teraphim or a holy image.[2]   These are theories to which one
is not bound to give any consideration.   They are utterly
devoid of anything like testimony in their favour, and
are wholly suggested by an *a priori* belief that all religion was at first unspiritual.   But when real historical
difficulties are brought forward such as seem to exist

----

[1] So among others Kuenen , see his article in *Theol Tijdschrift*, 1872,
p 660   Almost a solitary exception is Hupfeld , see his (posthumous)
views on the subject communicated by Riehm, *Stud u Krit* , 1871,
p 422
[2] So Kuenen (as probable) *Godsdienst*, i 232 , similarly Nöldeke,
p 51

with regard to the tabernacle (and thus also with regard to certain points as to the Levitic priesthood which you remember I reserved for later treatment), we are bound to give these difficulties' careful consideration and proceed step by step from the clear to the obscure. In accordance with this principle, it will, I think, be best to speak first of the history of the ark, which in every sense carries much more important issues than that of the tabernacle while, at the same time, it is much clearer. The history of the ark is, in fact, the history of the idea of God's permanent revealing residence in Israel, that of the tabernacle touches only secondary points dependent on this residence   And the theological ideas taught by the tabernacle are after all taught with certainty by the temple in a way that no one disputes.

To the preceding extracts, with their careful references to the latest literature on the subjects to which they relate, may be added a seventh, which, though it does not occur in a class lecture, may be taken as illustrative of the character of Professor Smith's teaching on questions of criticism at this early period. It is from the notice of the latest issues of the *Theologisch Tijdschrift*, which he contributed to the *British and Foreign Evangelical Review* in July 1871.

7. *The Leiden School of Theology* (July 1871).

The organ of the " Leiden " or " modern " School of Dutch Theology enters on its fifth year without diminution in the scientific activity and zeal which claim our respect, but also without modification of the extremely rationalistic principles which separate it from our sympathy. In every page of the *Tijdschrift* we feel ourselves face to face with men to whom theology is a matter not of the Church, but of the School ; and Christianity itself not the principle of a new life, but an affair of religious philosophy. A theology that springs from such principles is, of course, uncompromisingly

radical   But the real merit of the school is just that its
radicalism is openly avowed. There is no pretence of
absolute impartiality in the discussion of theological
topics   The criticism, in particular, of the biblical
records, to which a great part of the strength of the
school is directed, has for its avowed end the explanation
of the religious ideas and progress of the Old and New
Testament, in accordance with a theory of the philosophy of religion that refuses to see a difference in kind
between Christianity and the other religions of the world.
We are not disposed to find fault with this departure
from the standpoint of absolute impartiality which is so
often urged as the necessary quality of a critic. We,
too, are of opinion that the " objectivity " which science
calls for is not really perilled, though we approach individual problems with strong convictions as to what
Christianity is in itself and must be to us. But for this
very reason we decline to believe that we and the men
of the *Theologisch Tijdschrift* are really fellow-workers on
one scientific edifice. It is absurd to ask for scientific
fellowship where there are radically opposite aims. We
are antagonists, but we, at least, can afford to be
honourable antagonists, believing that our opponents
are honestly seeking the truth ; that, like all truth-seekers,
they must in some measure be truth-finders ; and that
our theology can only gain in firmness of foundation and
accuracy of construction by being confronted with a
bold and consistent development of opposing principles.

III

THE FULFILMENT OF PROPHECY

I. General Statement as to the Problem

EVERY attentive reader of the Old Testament has observed that the Hebrew prophets not only always find the starting-point of their admonitions, threats, and promises in the covenant relations already subsisting between Jahveh and His people, but that their predictions as to the future glory of God's kingdom are all cast in the mould of the Theocracy under which they themselves lived. It is certain that the prophets were alive to the imperfection of the Old Testament dispensation ; that they longed for a more direct and personal relation between God and His people than that which was maintained by the theocratic ordinances, that they looked for a time when a new covenant should be established, according to which the Law of Jahveh should be written on the hearts of the people, when all should know Jahveh, when He should forgive their guilt and remember their sins no more. But while these features in their hopes clearly separate the views of the prophets from the crass material expectation of *Judaistic* thought, the fact remains, that whenever any degree of definite colouring is given to the prophetic images of the Messianic times, that colouring is drawn from the theocratic institutions   In the writings of the prophets all these institutions are idealised, spiritualised— but not in such a way as to deprive them of their characteristic shape and substance. The most notable example of this is, of course, the idea of the מָשִׁיחַ. The Messiah of the prophets and the psalms is the ideal Davidic King, and he appears as swaying a visible monarchy over the Jews and the dependent nations (Amos ix 11, 12). His throne is obviously conceived as set up on Mount Sion (Is. xi., cf. Is. ii. 2 sqq.). The nations bring tribute to him (Ps. lxxii.). He goes out to battle, and the Lord at his right hand smites hostile kings before him (Ps. xlv., cx.), although from another point of view he appears as the Prince of Peace. In short, his features are those of David or Solomon, cleansed from all stain of imperfection, elevated into ideal majesty and illuminated by the unchanging light of God's presence We are so accustomed to apply one by one the prophetic lineaments of the Messiah to the person of Christ, that we seldom ask ourselves what picture of the Messiah as a whole the Old Testament saints were able to put together from the scattered hints of prophecy. No doubt the fragmentary character of the old revelation which the New Testament so distinctly recognises ($\pi o \lambda u \mu \epsilon \rho \hat{\omega} s$), left much to be filled up by every one according to his own spiritual insight, or (it might be) his own carnal fancy ; but the slowness of the apostles to adjust their preconceived notion to the reality revealed in Christ Jesus, surely shows something more than a merely personal dulness of heart. It proves that the whole dispensation in which they had been brought up was so framed, that the idea of the Messiah necessarily appeared in it in a shape by no means obviously coincident with the historical figure of Christ. It is not a sufficient, taken alone it is not even an accurate, representation of our Saviour to view Him as the idealised David. But it is true that all that a second David could have done for Israel, Christianity has done, and continues to do, in a higher and wider sense. Our Lord Himself, if we may judge from the scanty specimens of His exegesis of the Old Testament which the evangelists have preserved

(Matt. xxii. 31, 32, 42 *sqq*), was accustomed to vindicate His spiritual understanding of the older revelation, not by mere citation of texts, but by a process of dialectic   The same way of handling the Scriptures is yet more apparent in the apostolic writings.[1]   Manifestly, the application of such a method implies that it does not everywhere lie on the surface that the New Testament gives the fulfilment of the former dispensation, but that it is only when encumbrances are cleared away, the earthly shell rubbed off, a more comprehensive view gained by the occupation of a higher standpoint, that the necessary harmony of the two dispensations is fully vindicated.

These considerations with regard to the fulfilment of prophecies so central as those that point to the person and work of Christ, may serve to suggest to us caution in considering other portions of the prophetic conception of the future of Israel.   If even the figure of the Messiah as delineated in the Old Testament bears traces of the limitation of the dispensation,—if while its essential features are manifestly fulfilled in Christ the whole setting of these features must be conceived, in conformity with the New Testament, as very different from that which was suggested to the Old Testament saints from the forms under which they had been brought to realise God's kingdom,—if, I say, all this is manifestly true with regard to a matter so central, we shall do well to be prepared to find the same characters even more markedly impressed on other parts of prophecy.   We must be prepared to distinguish throughout the Old Testament between the spiritual truth that can, and must, find its fulfilment in a

---

[1] *Cf* Gass, s v "Erfulling " in Schenkel's *Bibel-Lexicon*   The proof of fulfilment could be given either (1) by direct citation of the original passages from the Old Testament, or (2) rather in a historical way by delineation of the new gospel principle of faith as a providential development out of the preceding religious dispensation with which it is so closely and inwardly connected , (1) prevails in Gospels, but even there citation stands, not for its own sake, but as proof of an inner harmony of plan, while (2) prevails in the Epistles in the notions of οἰκονομία τοῦ πληρώματος τῶν καιρῶν, μυστήριον, πρόθεσις, etc

spiritual dispensation, and the merely local and temporary setting in which that truth presented itself to the men of the Old Covenant.

Now, the general truth of this position is, and always has been, in some sense admitted by the great body of Christian theologians. The theory of extreme literalism, which forbids the application of any dialectic whatever to the prophetic books, which allows no distinction between essence and form, no development in the Old Testament theology except by simple addition—which insists that every word of every prediction either has been, or will be, fulfilled exactly as it is written—which expects that the earth shall still see Ezekiel's temple with its sacrifices, and which regards a literal Feast of Tabernacles as an element in the Millennium, has never succeeded in gaining a place in the theology of the Church. Its natural home is in the bosom of sectarianism, for it can only subsist in connection with a thoroughly perverse view of the administration and ends of the economy of grace. The man, for example, who expects a literal Ezekiel's temple is in this dilemma. *Either* he supposes that the existence of such a temple in the latter days, and the offering of sacrifices therein, is an essential element in the glorification of God's people, and so, in direct opposition to the New Testament writings, places himself on the standpoint of the Pharisaic Christians who withstood Paul—*or*, conscious that such a view would be unchristian, he must suppose that the temple shall belong to the restored but unconverted Jews—in which case the interpretation is untrue to the whole purpose of prophecy and to the manifest design of Ezekiel himself, which is to describe the times of the restored theocracy. But it is unnecessary to dwell on this school of thought, or rather on these unthinking fancies which have their origin partly in an unhistorical, unbiblical theory of inspiration, partly in a perverse and superstitious curiosity, and partly in impatience at the real difficulties that beset the attempt to do justice at once to the limita-

tions and the transcendence of the Old Testament religion.
(If we set these extreme views on one side, there still
remains a wide range of view as to the fulfilment of
prophecy among theologians, not of sects, but of the
Church.)   At the other extreme from this view stands the
so-called purely historical or historico-psychological interpretation of prophecy, which finds the explanation of
every oracle solely in the historical position and natural
mental experience of the prophet, and which, agreeing
with the opposite extreme school in rejecting all fulfilments
not strictly literal, maintains that many prophecies have
never in any sense been, and never will be, fulfilled,
inasmuch as prophecy on the whole does not rest on
God-given revelation, but is solely the fruit of natural
hopes and desires

These extreme views I only mention to set them on one
side.   As theories neither of them can satisfy the theologian who desires to reach a view with regard to prophecy
which shall form an organic member in the system of the
theology of the Church   On some points of detail, indeed,
he may approach either the one or the other view   We
may expect, as some do, a literal fulfilment of many
prophecies which have already received what is called a
partial fulfilment in the New Testament dispensation.
Yet in principle we differ from the extreme literalists
so long as we do admit a distinction between the spirit
and the outer form and limitations of prophecy as of every
other feature of an imperfect dispensation.   Or, again,
we may hold (*e.g* Fairbairn) that there is in certain
prophecies a conditional element, so that for certain
reasons they are not to be fulfilled.   Yet in this position
we do not join hands with the negative school so long as
we recognise the difference in kind between God-given
revelation and human hopes, and, if we say that such a
prophecy is not to be fulfilled, do so on grounds based on
the recognition of the Divine economy in the Old Covenant.
Well, setting aside these extreme views (our coincidences

17

with which can at most lie in certain details), we shall yet
find a wide divergence of theories as to the fulfilment of
prophecy awaiting our consideration. The great problem
which, as we have already seen, comes before us for
solution is this :—

The hopes and predictions of the Old Testament
prophets with regard to the consummation of God's
gracious and righteous purpose are always moulded by
the forms of the theocratic constitution under which they
themselves stood They present, in fact, an idealised
image of the theocracy as it was theoretically laid down in
the law, and, practically at least, aimed at from age to age
by believing Israelites. Rising above the mere letter of
the special Mosaic ordinances, the prophets always regard
as the great feature of the Messianic age the realisation of
the spirit of the theocratic constitution. But while they
certainly seem to expect that, in the latter days, many
limitations shall disappear and must assume new forms,
it is yet plain that whenever they seek to give distinct
form and body to their Messianic hopes, the forms that
offer themselves to them are at bottom those of the
theocracy which they themselves knew. They idealise
and elevate these forms, but they do not change them.
The categories of prophet, priest, and king, the holy land,
Mount Sion, the temple, and the visibly luminous glory
of Jahveh therein—all these still form the basis of the new
theocracy as they did of the old. Even the covenant
blessings retain their earthly shape. Victory over enemies,
long life, plenty in the midst of a land restored to bound-
less fertility and beauty—such are the blessings which
appear as the necessary counterpart of the sense of God's
favour and forgiveness, the indwelling of His Spirit, the
renovation of the heart in conformity with His law. The
prophets, in short, never think that they can do more
honour to the spiritual things of their religion by cutting
them off from the earthly forms of the theocracy. Rather
these earthly forms are themselves to be idealised by

becoming full of spiritual meaning.   For there is not in
the Old Testament one particle of Manichæism.   Jahveh's
sovereignty over the earth is so absolutely supreme that
the shifting phases of material creation are essentially
an expression of His good pleasure or wrath towards men.
If at present the temporal experiences of God's people,
at least of individuals, cannot entirely be explained by
this principle—and that this is, indeed, the case the Book
of Job shows—yet this darkening of the essential trans-
parency of the earthly organisation by which Jahveh is
constantly acting on men is temporary only.   In the
Messianic age there shall be full harmony between heaven
and earth.   The regenerated theocracy is also blessed
with earthly glory—and (for here is the critical point) on
the whole with just such earthly glory as in a lower degree
has already been attained at every time when the nation
walked mindfully of its covenant relations.   The glorious
times of David's kingdom are the type of the glories of the
Messianic days.

   Now, then, given so much as to the prophetic hopes as
matter of general agreement, to what extent can we assume
that the theocratic forms and principles which to the
prophets appeared eternal really are so ?   How far is the
constitution of Christ's kingdom identical with, and how
far merely analogous to, the constitution of David's
kingdom ?   In how far have the elements of the Old
Testament theocracy found their realisation in New
Testament times, or in how far may we still expect to see
them realised ?   Or, on the other hand, in what measure
is the New Testament dispensation not merely an elevation—an idealisation—of the Old Testament, but something really and qualitatively new, which the Old Testament only shadowed forth without presenting essential
identity or even such an identity that the one can flow
from the other by mere regular growth ?

   This is the real problem of the interpretation of Old
Testament prophecy , but it is also the really critical

problem for the whole significance of the Old Testament
in the Christian Church. What are the new things brought
in by Christ, and in what relation do they stand to the
things of the Old Dispensation ?

I propose to examine some of the more current views
on this head ; but before beginning to do so, I premise
one or two general remarks.

1. The question now before us is not a mere question
of exegesis. The problem of exegesis is to determine by
means of the written word the precise mind of the writer,
or the precise meaning which he desired his words to
convey. And it is manifestly one thing to ask how the
prophet conceived, and how he sought to make his hearers
conceive of the future glory, and quite another thing to
ask how far the highest conception possible under an
imperfect dispensation can be precisely reproduced in
Christ. We must look at this point more closely , for
much confusion has arisen from neglect of it. In fact,
the precise question of exegesis with regard to prophecy
is often not very sharply conceived. In dealing with
inspired writings, a certain ambiguity appears to attach
to the expressions " mind of the writer," " meaning
which he desired to convey." For who is in this case the
writer ? Is it the mind of the prophet, or the mind of
the Spirit that is meant ? Did perhaps the Spirit mean
more than the prophet himself understood ? And, again,
was there precisely one meaning to be conveyed ? Might
not the words have various senses addressed to different
ages, so that to us the meaning may be deeper than
to the prophet's first hearers ? These are quite usual
suppositions. And they seem to give to the exegetical
question of prophecy such a breadth that it must come
to take in the whole question which we are now discussing.
For the Spirit, it is said, must have meant the prophecy
in the sense of its final fulfilment, and we, as Christians,
may by fair exegesis bring more out of the passage than
was designed to be conveyed to the first hearers or even

to be understood by the prophet himself   This you all
know is quite a common course of argument, but a course,
I venture to say, so essentially confused as to give no hope
of good fruit.

For, in the first place, the distinction between the
mind of the Spirit and the mind of the prophet as it is
here conceived has no biblical ground.   In the passage,
1 Peter i. 10-12, which is usually quoted in its support,
there is no distinction between the comprehension of the
prophet and the intention of the revealing Spirit, but only
(as Calvin long ago pointed out) between the " privatum
desiderium " and the " publica functio " of the prophet
himself   The revelation vouchsafed to them, and which
bare witness to the sufferings appointed for Christ and
the glory to follow, was incomplete and limited—especially
it was limited in so far as related to the indication of the
time of consummation.   The prophets knew only that the
evangelic truths which were the substance of their ministry
were to be realised in a future time, and so that the fruit
of their labours should be reaped by those who followed
after them.   Thus they knew that their work and word
was not in vain, even though in their own generation
it seemed fruitless , yet this consciousness could not
suppress the natural longing with which they strained
their eyes to gain a clearer view of the time of fulfilment.
And this circumstance the apostle uses to impress on his
readers a sense of their privileges.   " Salutis huius pretium
inde commendat, quod in eam toto studio intenti fuerunt
prophetae " (Calvin)

Thus understood, Peter gives no support to the idea
that the prophets did not understand all that was revealed
through them, or to the supposition that their words can
have a sense for us that they had not for themselves.
The reason why we, more than they themselves, reap
the fruit of their ministry, is simply because we have
entered into possession of those good things which they
saw afar off.

When this supposed biblical support has been removed from the opinion now under consideration, we shall have no difficulty in showing its thorough untenableness   If the prophet were a mere mechanical organ of the Spirit, exegesis would, of course, have nothing at all to do with his personality.   The human element would disappear from the Old Testament.   The exegesis of prophecy would have nothing in common with the principles of the interpretation of human writings because the psychological basis of all hermeneutic could have no application where the Divine Spirit is conceived as the immediate author. In general I presume the absurdities of extreme literalism are based on a fallacy at this point.   The human side of prophecy is ignored in favour of an overstrained doctrine of inspiration, and yet the canon of human hermeneutic which bids us always adopt the natural sense unless a figure is manifestly designed, is without scruple applied to utterances from which all human character has been withdrawn   If the divine revelation destroyed the human personality of the speakers, are we entitled to assume that it respected the principles of human expression ?   Far more consistent, though not less fanatical, is the theory that, since divine revelation is a thing absolutely *sui generis*, it must also have its own canon of interpretation.

If, on the other hand, the prophet's personality is not suppressed in the production of his prophecies, if he remained self-conscious, and if his own mind was at work in expressing the truth to which by divine revelation he . had attained, it is impossible to speak of the Spirit as the author of the prophecy in any strict sense.   Nor are the Spirit and the prophet joint authors, so that something comes from God and something is added by man.   Such an hypothesis is both religiously inadequate and critically untenable   Every prophecy of the Old Testament has a beautiful unity of plan.   There is nothing of patchwork about the prophetic utterances   They flow, as the

Germans say, from a single mould. We must therefore
regard the prophet alone as the true author of his writings
The operation of the revealing Spirit lies in a higher
sphere.   Whether the prophet records a vision vouchsafed
to him, or, as is oftener the case, works out a line of
thought to which he has been enabled to rise by spiritual
illumination, every link of the argument must be
thoroughly his own. The whole is shaped in his own
mind before it is committed to paper. And so he is the
real author of the whole, and what exegesis has to do is
just to determine what the thoughts were which the
prophet was expressing.   Nor, again, will it do to say that
the prophet had more than one sense in view,—a lower
sense for his contemporaries or for weaker men, a higher
sense for the spiritual or for a future dispensation.   This
is the essential position of the exploded allegorical exegesis.
It stumbles against the plain fact that a single line of
thought can have but a single meaning.   If two meanings
are covered by one expression, they can be so only by
virtue of a clever artifice by which two lines of thought
in place of receiving their natural twofold expression are
forced under a single verbal formula.   No one will suppose
that the prophets consciously engaged in such a process
of cryptography.   The parallels would be in Bacon's
" Omnia per omina," or in such verses as " Aio te Aeacida,
etc."   The theory of a double sense is always held on the
supposition that the two senses are so connected that the
one grows in a manner out of the other, that naturally,
and not by mere artifice, more lies in the prophet's words
than he directly expressed.

Now if we put this thought in its most general form,
we see that it is just an attempt to formulate the fact that
the fulfilment in Christ belongs to a higher sphere than the
view of the prophets themselves.   But the formula of a
double sense is inaccurate, in so far as it attempts to reduce
to a question of mere exegesis what is really based on the
difference of dispensations, and seeks by the hypothesis

of a twofold interpretation to get over the limitations of the old Covenant.

2. What the real nature of the question is becomes clearer when we put the Prophecy and the Typic of the Old Testament side by side. On this important point I give at this stage only a hint. When we say that Old Testament kings and priests were types of Christ, that Old Testament institutions were types of heavenly things, we mean this—that what Christ does for His people the king or priest really, though in a lower way, did for the Old Testament nation—that all these institutions played in a measure the same part in the preservation of a people for God's glory in the Old Testament, as Christianity and New Testament institutions play in the New Testament dispensation   Then it was the earthly kingdom of God , now it is the spiritual.   But the functions necessary for the maintenance of even an earthly theocracy must have much not only analogous, but really common, to the functions of the spiritual kingdom of God ; and this is what we mean when we constitute between the two the relation of type and antitype   Now surely the same thing will apply to prophecy too   The prophetic hopes rise above the mere historical type and stretch on towards the spiritual fulfilment.   But how far do they succeed in doing this ?   Do they not in many parts of their descriptions of things to come remain limited to the mere typical sphere ? so that, just as the Old Testament institutions have disappeared in the New Testament things which contain all their true spiritual meaning without the earthly husk ; so in some parts of prophecy the fulfilment, while a real fulfilment of the spiritual idea of the prophecy, may not carry out that idea in the form which was limited by the prophet's Old Testament standpoint

3. Once more, and again in a single word, let me indicate that it is only in this way that the idea of successive fulfilments of prophecy can receive an intelligible form and a firm basis.   The prophets are accustomed

to view the latter-day glory in connection with repentance on the part of the people from present sin, and with deliverance from present calamity. The whole course of history possesses to the prophets' eyes the unity of a God-given plan. Every turn in the history of the chosen people exemplifies the eternal principles of righteousness and grace by which the immovable kingdom of God is finally to be built up—and therefore the prophets are always able to rise from the consideration of God's dealings with their contemporaries to the ideal manifestation of the same divine principles of government in the consummation of all things. But really between the empirical exemplification and the ideal consummation there lies a long interval. During all this time God's principles of rule and of redemption are the same, and from time to time they appear with increasing clearness, affording ever fresh illustrations or fulfilments of the prophetic ideas. But always the actual historical forms in which these ideas are realised take new shapes, and, when the final consummation comes, and with it that absolute triumph of God's kingdom which constitutes the full fulfilment of the prophecy, it will no doubt come in a way that has never entered into the heart of man. And so you see that, as God's purpose gradually unfolds in human history, the hopes of the prophets may again and again receive partial fulfilments besides the great final fulfilment   But neither the final nor the partial fulfilments will exactly fit into the setting which the prophet drew from his own surroundings

Now these remarks I only throw out as hints of the kind of result that we may expect to find in conformity with the twofold truth of the unity of purpose and the variety of dispensation in God's dealings with men. Such general hints do not solve the difficult question of prophecy ; they only show us how to attack it. The real point that must be solved is how far circumstances of the new dispensation render the hopes of that preceding invalid , where the line is to be drawn between the

changing form and the permanent substance of prophecy ;
and, further, what are the principles on which the changes
of form depend.   This is a question so vexed and on the
whole so difficult that I can only propose to approach it
tentatively in the consideration of some of the current
views.

II. APPLICATION OF PRECEDING STATEMENT TO NEWMAN'S
    THEORY OF PROPHECY, CHURCH AND KINGDOM OF
    GOD, ETC.

The point dwelt on in last lecture, as to the connection
that necessarily subsists between any theory of the
fulfilment of prophecy and the views of the theoriser as
to the relation between the old and new dispensation as
wholes, has not always been clearly borne in mind.   I
propose to-day to call your attention to a theory advocated in J. H (now Father) Newman's *Sermons on Subjects
of the Day* which puts in a very strong light the truth that,
as a matter of fact, the two things of which I speak always
must go together.   Sermons XIV and XV. of Mr.
Newman's volume are, in short, at once a theory of
prophetic interpretation and a deduction from this theory
of a doctrine as to the relation of the Jewish Theocracy
and the Christian Church, which coincides with the
position maintained by the English High Church party
A glance at the way in which a question which is often
thought to be merely curious is thus brought to bear on
one of the most vital practical questions of our time can
hardly fail to be instructive ; besides which we shall find
it impossible to come to a distinct judgment on Mr.
Newman's views except by developing principles that
possess an independent value quite beyond their application in this special case.

" When the power and splendour of the family of David
were failing, and darkness was falling on the Church, and
religious men were fighting against dismay and distrust,
then the Prophets foretold that the kingdom of the saints

should one time be restored ; and that, though its glories were then setting, a morrow would come in due course, and that a morrow without an evening. Has this promise yet been fulfilled or no ? and if fulfilled, in what sense fulfilled ? Many persons think it has not yet been fulfilled at all, and is to be fulfilled in some future dispensation or millennium ; and many think that it has indeed been fulfilled, yet not literally, but spiritually and figuratively ; or, in other words, that the promised reign of Christ upon earth has been nothing more than the influence of the Gospel over the souls of men, the triumphs of Divine Grace, the privileges enjoyed by faith, and the conversion of the elect.

" On the contrary, I would say that the prophecies in question have in their substance been fulfilled literally, and in the present Dispensation ; and, if so, we need no figurative and no future fulfilment. Not that there may not be both a figurative and a future accomplishment besides ; but these will be over and above, if they take place, and do not interfere with the direct meaning of the sacred text and its literal fulfilment " [1]

Such is Mr. Newman's general position—a literal fulfilment in the present dispensation of the Old Testament hopes of theocratic glory. In the promises thus to be fulfilled are to be enumerated, not only such spiritual promises as the giving of a new Covenant and a law written on the heart, but such as the following . " David shall never want a man to sit upon the throne of the house of Israel, neither shall the priests the Levites want a man before Me to offer burnt offerings . . . continually "—or, " Jerusalem shall be called the city of truth and the mountain of the Lord of Hosts the holy mountain," and so on. Particularly among the things literally fulfilled fall " a conquest, a kingdom, a body politic, a ritual, a law." It is urged that, according to the words of James at the Council of Jerusalem, the restoration of the fallen tabernacle of David was in course of fulfilment in the apostolic times in the conversion of the Gentiles. And the fulfilment thus spoken of as present will also be

[1] J H Newman, *Sermons bearing on Subjects of the Day*, pp 180-181, ed 1869

recognised as literal, if we remember " that there *has* been, in matter of fact, in Christian times a visible church, a temporal kingdom, a succession of rulers such as the prophecies do describe " By this view, moreover, we shall not only indicate the literal truth of the prophetic oracles, but do strict justice to the strong language in which Moses inculcates the eternal obligation of the theocratic law.   In a word, temporal as well as spiritual greatness, visible dominion as well as secret influence, were under the Law promised to the Church in the future, and according to the promise has already come to pass in gospel times   In thus ascribing to the Church the character of a visible theocracy, Mr. Newman of course takes the usual standpoint of his school, according to which Christ's church " is a temporal power, and necessarily interferes in the concerns of this world " (p 252) by means of the outward organisation of governors which she has in common with other temporal powers

So far as this argument goes, it is not, you see, precisely self-supporting   It is rather assumed as otherwise manifest, that the Church of Christ is a temporal power , and then this result is in part applied in proof of, and in part itself confirmed by, the theory that prophecy is literally fulfilled.   This arrangement of the argument— not unsuitable for the ends of a sermon—is none the less scientifically unfortunate, and in the present case it serves, I think, to conceal the very fallacy so dangerous in the interpretation of prophecy.   For while it is assumed that the temporal power of the Church can be deduced from Old Testament prophecy by a simple application of the exegetical canon, that the most literal interpretation is always to be preferred, we shall find on viewing the matter a little more narrowly, that a great deal more than a mere formally exegetical canon is assumed   In short, while Mr Newman supposes himself to be discussing a question purely exegetical, and thence deducing a view as to the relation of the two covenants, this apparently

sound argument moves in a vicious circle in so much as
the *quasi*-exegetical canon involves a lemma from the
High Church Theology   To understand this, let us
observe that Mr Newman is by no means to be identified
with the extreme literalists who are also of necessity
extreme futurists   Jerusalem is to him not the capital of
Judæa, but the Church of Christ, Israel not the bodily
descendants of Abraham, but the Chosen people, just as
David in the prophecies means Christ.

In short, the literal fulfilment of a prophecy does not
imply the literal acceptation of every word of the prophecy   And this position is justified by the very obvious
remark " that the use of figures in a composition is not
enough to make it figurative as a whole.   We constantly
use figures of speech when we speak , yet who will say on
that account that the main drift of our conversation is not
to be taken literally ?"   This, our author continues, will
apply to the language of the prophets.   On the one hand
they use such figures as were natural to their poetic style,
and speak figuratively, with an allusion to the times
before the fall, of the lion lying down with the lamb and
the like.   Figures of this kind, however, are less frequent,
while, on the other hand, the language of the prophets
shows certain standing figures, such as David, Israel,
Jerusalem, which in truth are not so much figures as
proper names that have a figurative origin, or words
which, having first had a confined sense, come as language
proceeds to have a wide one

Something, I think, might be said in criticism of both
classes of figures which Mr. Newman here regards as not
sufficient to make the tenor of prophecy as a whole
allegorical.   But for the sake of simplicity, I will quite
pass over the so-called poetical figures, and look only at
those to which he himself gives most weight,—the standing expressions, " Jerusalem," " David," and the like.

And here I observe (1) that even of the three names,
David, Jerusalem, Israel, Mr. Newman does not give

such an account as shall put them exactly on the same
footing   The name of David for Christ is a proper name
with a figurative origin ; Christ is called David just as
Simon is called Peter   The name, therefore, is based
on a *resemblance* to David   On the other hand the use
of the name Israel for the chosen people is not based on
a mere resemblance   It is an extension of the name of
the chosen people in one age to cover the elect in all ages
So when Jerusalem is taken " for the body politic of the
chosen people in which the power lies, and from which
the action proceeds," we have, on Mr. Newman's views, not
a mere analogy, but a certain substantial identity between
the new and old Jerusalem, in a sense not stated as applicable to the relation of David to Christ. To produce
uniformity here, and to give any support to the argument
that Israel means the chosen people because the Christian
Church is the continuation of the Jewish, we must formulate in the same way the relation of Christ to David, and
say that Christ's kingdom is the continuation of David's
And I presume that Mr. Newman, though he does not
adopt, would not disapprove of this way of putting the
matter by which alone his view becomes consistent.
And so the figurative element comes to be just this, that
the names of the temporary sovereign of the theocracy,
of the temporary seat of the government of the Church,
and of the temporary possessors of the privileges accorded
to God's chosen people, are used in a universal and non-
temporary sense

(2) Now certainly if this were the whole extent of the
difference between the Old Testament prophecy and the
New Testament fulfilment, we might be justified in
regarding the fulfilment as literal. If it could be shown
that under other names merely the Christian Church
is—as Mr. Newman says—a great empire comprising
all that a great empire ordinarily exhibits—extended
dominion not only over its immediate subjects, but over
the kings of other kingdoms — aggression and advance

—warfare against enemies, acts of judgment on the proud, acts of triumph over the defeated—high imperial majesty towards the suppliant, and so on—if, I say, the Christian Church really does manifest all these attributes just in the literal sense in which they are meant by the prophets, and does so as the continuation of the Jewish theocracy, then I think we may fairly admit that Mr. Newman has justified his assertion of a present literal fulfilment of prophecy in spite of the figurative character of the mere names, and the poetical character of some descriptions in the Old Testament. But, on the other hand, Newman's theory is not proved unless it can be shown (*a*) that the Christian Church is a theocracy, (*b*) that the Church is in substance (names and poetic ornament apart) just such a theocracy as the prophets describe. Now both of these positions I deny ; and I maintain further that unless Mr. Newman had approached the subject with the *a priori* conviction that the Church is a theocracy, he would never have dreamed of asserting on purely exegetical grounds that it is literally such a theocracy as the prophets looked for. In looking at this matter more closely, let us begin with the latter point.

What is meant by a literal fulfilment ? I do not think the expression is a very happy one , but its meaning must be a fulfilment which in all fulness corresponds with the principle and details of the prophecy as these appear by a process of literal exegesis ; *i.e* a literal fulfilment is an exact fulfilment of the prophecy literally interpreted. In comparing the fulfilment with the prophecy we may, as already said, be allowed to make deduction of names that are *mere* names, and of manifest poetic figures , but if in any farther point the fulfilment falls short of the prophecy, it can no longer be proved to be the true fulfilment by *mere* exegesis, but some theological principle as to the proper relation between prophecy and fulfilment must be applied   Now I conceive that there is in the Old Testament prophecies very much that is neither matter of mere words nor matter of poetical diction, which even Mr. Newman cannot suppose fulfilled in the Christian Church.

Let us for the moment concede to our author the right to choose for comparison with the prophecies the Mediæval Church at the time when it was most fully persuaded that it was its function to realise the theocracy of the prophets, and when accordingly its rulers consciously gave it, as far as possible, the shape of a visible empire over the kings of the earth. Did the Church even in that day appear as in literal agreement with the images of prophecy in anything beyond the most vague generalities ? Can we suppose that any prophet would have realised in that Church the literal reproduction of his image of the theocracy ?

True, there were certain points of agreement He looked for a visible sovereignty of God's people, and here was an asserted sovereignty of the Church over the kings of the earth. He looked perhaps for the continuance of the priestly office and functions, here we have priests offering the Sacrifice of the Mass. He looked for a sovereignty of God's law in the theocracy ; the Church professes to rule by the new law of the gospel which is the continuation of the old. Let us concede farther that the prophet would so far fall in with the spirit of the Catholic Church as not to pierce through the hollowness of these pretensions, and declare that all this was but the parody of a theocracy ; he yet could not see in the then state of the Church a literal glorification of the theocracy The Kingdom of the Church if on the whole it had the upper hand over the kingdoms of the earth, yet found in them no willing subjects. There was no permanent visible security of the unending dominion of God's people

And at the time when the subjection of the powers of earth to the Western Church was most complete the Church itself was a divided Kingdom Once more, the dominion of the Church was so far from universal that in some parts of the earth it was continually falling back before the infidel powers. All these features are utterly inconsistent with the hopes of the prophets. Say what you will of the poetic colouring of their oracles, it is yet absurd to say that the continuance of a visible body politic of God's people, and of literal priests, was the real substance of their prophecies, but that the universality and final irrevocable victory of the theocracy were mere accidents. Surely it is fair to say that the real essence of the prophetic hopes lay not in the features which they simply transplanted from their own times to the latter days, but in the points in which the latter days were to be superior—in the more visible presence of God to His people—in the renewed hearts of the people themselves—in the overcoming in a regenerate earth of the blight of the fall—in the complete and willing subjection of the *whole* earth to the Messianic Kingdom. In short, the mere continuance of a visible God-Kingdom holding its own with varying success amidst or even over the kingdoms of the earth is no fulfilment of the prophets' hopes. That was a state of things actually present to them—not the object of their hopes, but the basis from which their hopes rose. Only in so far as the theocracy was spiritualised, strengthened, widened, so far as God came nearer to man, and man became liker God, and then the whole earth bore testimony to this reconciliation of the creature and the creator, could they acknowledge a literal or any true fulfilment of their hopes.

And surely, tried by this test, the Church has at no time approved itself such a theocracy as has already entered into visible possession of the latter-day glory to which the prophets looked.

How then could Newman think that he saw in the Church a literal fulfilment of Prophecy ? Simply because from his High Church standpoint the greatest glory of the Church is to be a theocracy—because what with the

18

prophets was the starting-point—the existence of a God-Kingdom on earth is with him the culminating point , because all his notions of the excellency of Christianity culminate in the visible Church, and in that Church in the shape of an imperial power.   In short, the Mediæval idea of the Church, an idea undoubtedly grand, and well calculated to occupy men's minds, really stands before him when he approaches prophecy, and everywhere he sees as the centre of prophecy the very image which he has himself brought with him to its study.

Now the very fact that to us it seems so obvious that the Christian Church never has taken the shape of a visible realisation of the prophetic latter-day theocracy, while to our opponent it is equally obvious that it has done so, makes it plain that we stand on ground so different that we can hardly argue about the fulfilment of prophecy in detail until we have adjusted our mutual relations on a more general question.   Are we and the High Church party at one on the question if the Church is, or is yet designed to be, a visible Theocracy at all ?   I think we are not.   The question is not merely one of present or future fulfilment.   It is not merely one of literal or figurative fulfilment.   While our antagonist holds that above all things the Church is a theocracy, an imperial power in, though not of, the world—we, I think, must hold that such a power the Church neither is now, nor ever shall be. I do not expect that you will all be prepared to give your assent to this proposition without further explanation. You will perhaps be inclined to say that I am running into the opposite extreme from our High Church antagonists ; but I beg at least that you will suspend judgment till I explain more fully what I mean.

The High Church position is (as we know) that the Church is essentially a Kingdom, that it is in the form of a Kingdom that it becomes visible, and that the present constitution of that Kingdom in the hands of a visible hierarchy is essentially the form of the final glory predicted by the prophets ; so that even now the Church as a theocracy exercises legitimate sway over the kingdoms of the earth.

We know, too, how this theory was carried out in the mediæval Church.   If the Church is now a visible imperial power among the nations, she must not only have a visible hierarchy of rulers, but some palpable sign to distinguish her subjects.   This sign was sought in the Sacraments. The use of the Sacraments constituted a man a member of the Theocracy ; just as birth in a certain land or some other outward sign made him member of a world-kingdom. True Church membership implied possession of an inward grace, but this grace was conveyed by the Sacrament *ex opere operato*.   The Reformers rose against this view. They denied the power of the mere external sacrament to convey grace *ex opere operato*.   To be a member of the Church implies, they said, direct personal union to the Head of the Church   Hence the sign of membership in Christ's body is not an outward visible mark like the sign of union to an earthly kingdom.   It is an invisible bond that binds together the mystic body of Christ ; and the Church so constituted—the Church invisible—is an object of *faith*, not of *sight*.   Yet the Church is not wholly invisible.   What is not an object of sight is only the one point—the bond uniting each of those who are true Church members to Christ.   But there are certain functions that pertain to the Church, and by the existence of which we have to recognise the real presence of the Church. Wherever the word of God is truly preached and the sacraments purely administered, there we must recognise a sign of the presence of the Church—only we cannot judge what individuals among the hearers of the word and partakers of the sacrament are true members of Christ. And again, the open visible functions of worship which the Church is called to perform—the administration of word and sacrament—can only be carried out by a visible organisation.   And hence arises the right and the necessity of an orderly Church-government chosen out of those who, by participation in the outward functions of the Church, profess adherence to Christ, and in the judgment of charity are to be regarded by us who cannot try hearts as really members of Christ. Now, I say that the Church so conceived is in no sense a visible theocracy. For Protestant Church government has for its aim solely the administration of the word and sacraments, and the discipline in its hand is purely spiritual for the maintenance of the purity of the word and preventing of profanation of sacraments. This is a function which in no sense conveys authority over the kingdoms of the world, while on the other hand, being itself purely spiritual, it can tolerate no control from these kingdoms. Moreover, a government which can only admit to, and exclude from, outward privileges, which has no list of the true members of Christ's body, and no right to admit to, or exclude from, the privileges of union to Him, cannot even with regard to the Church itself be an imperial government, but is simply ministerial. The Church, then, as organised is not and cannot be a theocracy, in so much as its rulers have not the kind of power without which a kingdom proper cannot exist. And if the Church of Christ as visible and organised is not a kingdom, then the theocratic prophecies neither now are, nor ever can be, fulfilled in the glorification of the visible Church.

And this argument, I conceive, touches some others than Christians of the Roman Catholic or English High Church. For we ourselves sometimes hear it asserted that the proper fulfilment of the prophecies of homage to be done by the kings of the earth to the renewed theocracy must lie in gifts offered by governments for the support of the organisation of the visible Church. But if the visible Church is not the theocracy, and if its organisation is not the imperial organisation of Christ's Kingdom, this argument must fall to the ground. But surely, you may urge, the invisible Church is the true Kingdom of Christ, the theocracy to which all are bound to do homage, and this homage can become visible only as done to the visible Church. Hence, the final glorification of the theocracy must become manifest just in the exaltation of the visible Church.

But what do we mean by the final glorification of God's Kingdom ? Is it not, according to the prophets and according to the teaching of our Lord Himself, the visible dominion of Christ and Christ's Kingdom over all the earth ? And can this find its expression in honour and homage done to the visible Church ? Surely not For the organisation of the visible Church to which alone such homage could be paid is essentially ministerial, and so has no right to accept sovereignty over the world. No doubt every advance of Christ's Kingdom will bring increased respect for the visible organisation of the Church; but this one result is not the full expression of the advance of the theocracy.

And if this is so, it is at least an incorrect expression to call the invisible Church the Kingdom of Christ. No doubt the same persons make up the body of Christ and the Kingdom of Christ, but they do so under different categories. The old sound Reformed doctrine is that there are not two churches, a visible and an invisible, but one Church—visible in respect to its organisation for the administration of the word and sacraments, invisible in respect to the criterion of individual faith in Christ. Hence, the only organisation of the Church *qua* Church is the organisation of visible Church government for the per- formance of purely spiritual actions   And so my actions as a member of the Church, and under the organisa- tion thereof, are purely spiritual actions—the worship of God and the bearing witness among men to his grace by special acts of cultus. But as a member of Christ's Kingdom my functions are not purely spiritual. That Kingdom is to subdue all the earth, and so every action has a relation to it. My discharge of my daily calling on

earth falls under the cognisance of the Church only in so
far as it is, or is not, outwardly inconsistent with my
public profession and participation in the cultus of the
Church.   But my whole life falls under the Law of God's
Kingdom, by which I am bound in every action to aim at
the advance of Christ's cause.   In the discharge of this
calling I am not answerable to man, but directly to the
King who, by His providence, has given me a special
calling to a post in His Kingdom and a work to do therein
The organisation of God's Kingdom is not then an outward
Church organisation, but a hidden organisation of God's
providence by which every man's calling in Christ is so
ordered that each, while doing his own work for Christ,
is doing a harmonious part of the great work that shall
yet fill the whole earth.   So long as Christ Himself is in
heaven, the Kingdom that is leavening the earth is essentially invisible save to the eye of faith.   True, the outward
effects of Christianity are seen, but the system, the
harmonious organisation in which some have a higher,
some a lower place, is unrevealed till the day when the
fire shall try every man's work, and when, all being burnt
up that is not of Christ's Kingdom, the city of God shall
stand forth in its full proportions.

And now let us ask how all this applies to the fulfilment of prophecy.   We may, I think, safely maintain
three positions.

(1) There is a continuity between the Old Testament
and the New Testament Kingdom of God.   The earthly
fabric of the Old theocracy did not perish till its spiritual
forces had been implanted in the invisible Kingdom of
Christ

(2) Hence, though we cannot say that the theocratic
prophecies have found a fulfilment in the Christian Church,
they have already found a fulfilment in Christ.

(3) And yet the full historical fulfilment of the theocratic prophecies has not yet come.   For the New Testament no less than the Old looks to a future glory, to a

time when at Christ's second coming the empire of God's Kingdom over the world shall become visible to all.

A word or two on each of these positions :—

(1) We are told by Mr. Newman that the theocratic prophecies are fulfilled in Christ because the Christian Church is a theocracy, a visible temporal power. Not very dissimilar in principle is the opposite extreme position which maintains that no fulfilment can be regarded as real which does not apply to the literal people of Israel For both of these views alike maintain that continuity of political existence is the necessary criterion of the identity of the people of the promise and the people of the fulfilment.[1] Now, I admit that the prophets do always represent continuity of political existence as the normal condition of the theocracy, so that suspension of this existence is to them always associated with a state of exile. I do not think that any prophet fully, or even approximately, conceived that the first grand step towards the final realisation of the kingdom of God would consist in the substitution of an invisible for a visible Kingdom, of a hidden leaven for an external conquering power None of them had fully comprehended that the Kingdom of God cometh not with outward show But then the question arises . Does this constant assumption on the part of the prophets that on the whole the earthly theocracy reaches on—continuously or broken by captivities—into the latter days belong to what was revealed to them, or is it simply the natural filling-up of what was left dark by the circumstances actually present to them ? It is expressly taught in the New Testament that the prophetic revelations were *partial*. No prophet had a full image of the time to come. So far, then as the contrary was not clearly taught him, he must more or less see the divine revelation against a background of present theocratic circumstances. And this was the more necessary

---

[1] Is not the interpretion of "till Shiloh come" mediæval, having no significance except on this theory of continuous political existence ?

because it is a special peculiarity of prophecy that the
time of fulfilment is always vague   The teaching of the
prophets takes this shape   These things God will bring
about , but the first step must be the people's repentance.
And when that might be they did not know   It might be,
often they seem to have hoped that it would, be soon.
Thus Joel seems to see the glory of the latter days in
direct connection with the great national repentance he
himself had witnessed.   And if this was so, the background
of the theocracies would always be of necessity drawn
from those present circumstances, which as the prophets
hoped and prayed would really be the very vestibule of
the latter-day glory.   We must, then, always aim at
distinguishing this mere background from the spiritual
hopes and promises that rose from it.

I do not say that it is easy to do this in detail   But
in general it is plain that to the prophets the real kernel
of the theocracy which was the true centre of their
promises lay in the *spiritual* things of God's Kingdom
To the prophets, even as to the New Testament, the great
hinges of the whole development of God's Kingdom are
sin and grace   Would they not always be ready to admit
that that is the true theocracy which fights against sin
most manfully, and which contains the strongest forces for
the subjugation of the world to God ?   It may be that
they always associated the victory of God's Kingdom
over sin with the victory of Israel over the Gentiles, that
the continual gracious presence of God with redeemed
man could be conceived by them only in a form derived
from Jahveh's glory enthroned on the Cherubim, and so on.
But if the spiritual things of their prophecies are accomplished in Christ in a fuller sense without these accessories,
would they not themselves have rejoiced to acknowledge
that in Him the true fulfilment of their oracles is
found ?

The true theocracy is found wherever those forces are
found, organised by the hand of God Himself and obeying

His kingly word, which are strong enough and pure enough to subdue all things under Him.

(2) Now, I need not say that all these forces are summed up in the one person of Christ, and that by His Spirit they vivify every member of His body. Whoever has the spirit of Christ is a member of the true theocracy ; for he is equipped with strength from God to do a work for Him in the world. That all will admit. But where, you ask, is the theocracy as a whole ? To the existence of a state belong not only citizens, but organisation. Now we have seen that the present organisation of the theocracy is not the organ of the visible Church. That is the organisation of public worship and Christian ordinances, the organisation by which a public and purely religious testimony to God's grace is kept up ; but it is not the organisation by which the world is subdued under Christ And the proof of it is that just in proportion as the Church has striven to bring all the Christian work for Christ under her outward organisation, the real work of bringing in those that are without has always declined

Shall we then say that there are at present members prepared for a future theocracy ; but that now the Kingdom of God is suspended—that the chosen people is, as it were, in exile ? Far from it Rather the Kingdom of God, though its organism is now invisible even as the King is invisible, is as truly and really existent among men as Christ is truly with us always even to the end of the world. Already in His sojourn among men, Christ could say to the Pharisees that the Kingdom of heaven was in their midst. And is not this much more true now ? The Kingdom of God organised by His invisible providence, preserved in oneness of plan and development by the operation in all its citizens of the one Spirit of Christ, is now upon earth and in our midst in a sense so far raised above the highest point ever reached by the Old Testament prophecies that even now we must acknowledge a true fulfilment of the prophetic hopes. And if we will

have the proof of this, we must not turn our eyes to the
mere outward organisation of the Church—we must not
even be content to behold the really great work which all
can see that Christianity has already wrought on earth ;
we must look up with the eye of faith to those heavenly
places where Christ our king, sitting at the right hand of
God, rules His kingdom with a wisdom and an omnipotence
far different from aught that appertained to the noblest
princes of the house of David.   Now here again an objection may be made.   The theocracy of which we are
speaking, we may be told, is visible only to the eye of
faith ; but the old Hebrew theocracy, and similarly the
Messianic theocracy of the prophets, was seen by the eye
of sense.   Between two such quantities there is no
compatibility.   To say that the one is the fulfilment of
the other must be, after all, mere spiritualising.   At first
sight, perhaps, such an objection is plausible ; but let
us ask . was the theocracy *as a theocracy* visible to the
Israelite by the eye of sense or by the eye of faith ?   Was
not the Kingdom of Israel to the unspiritual man a mere
earthly kingdom ?   That God was the true King of His
people, that His providence was everywhere the special
support of the nation, was then, as now, a doctrine of
faith ?   True, the Old Testament dispensation was a
dispensation of miracles.   But in this respect it differs
from the Christian dispensation only in this,—that while
in the Old Testament the element of miracle runs through
the whole history, the miracles of the New Testament
were requisite only at the founding of the dispensation.
And in truth, the reason why the faith of the Old Testament people needed to be maintained by constantly
recurring miracles, was just because in those days the
God-Kingdom was so much more easily lost sight of—
so much more easily confused with the world-kingdom
than it is now ; because to us the one great miracle of the
resurrection of Christ contains within itself all that could
be shown to us by a whole dispensation of miracles.   It is

not then true that Christ's Kingdom would be more real
if it possessed the outward form of a world-kingdom
It is not true that it was essentially easier to believe in
God's Kingdom when it took the form of an earthly
power.   Rather the necessity of such a theocracy as that
of the earthly Israel is a mark of the inferiority of a
dispensation in which spiritual truth had not yet shaken
itself free from limitations that disappeared in Christ.
And so the Kingdom of Christ *is* the fulfilment of the
Old Testament Theocracy, because it contains all that
made of it a *God-Kingdom*, though it has shaken itself free
from the forms of a *world-kingdom*.   And this change the
prophets themselves, in some degree at least, anticipate
when they prophesy that in the Messianic age God's law
shall be written on men's hearts.   For this is a mark
that the forms of a world-kingdom, in which the law
is always something external administered by a visible
executive, shall in the future theocracy be broken through.

(3) And yet Christianity, as we now see it, is not yet
the actual, though it is the potential, fulfilment of the
prophet's hopes.   In Christ the Kingdom of God is
equipped with all the world-subduing powers which the
old theocracy did not possess.   The victory is already
sure, but it is not already complete.   This is a distinction
not foreign to the Old Testament prophecy.   First the
spiritual renewal of Israel gathered around the Messiah—
then the victorious advance against the world-powers—
such is always the Old Testament conception.   And such,
too, is the teaching of Christ.   We are still saved by hope—
by a hope not yet seen.   We are still looking for the day
when the Kingdom of the world shall become the Kingdom
of our Lord and of His Christ (Rev. xi 5),—nay more,
for the day " when the creation itself shall be delivered
from the bondage of corruption into the liberty of the
glory of the children of God."   And in the New Testament, as in the Old, it is everywhere clear that when the
victory of God's Kingdom is thus complete, it shall be

visibly complete, and shall be testified not only by the
regeneration of man, but by the restoration of the harmony
of the whole creation.   This, I say, is clear without any
ignoring of the principle already laid down that we must
not confuse the mere setting of prophecy with the substance of the predictions themselves   For the *visible*
glory of God on Zion, the visible signs of his reconciliation
with His people in the New Earth, are *not* modelled on
anything that was part of the prophets' own circumstances.
The ever openly visible glory of God above His people
had no parallel since Sinai, the regeneration of the earth
had no parallel save in Eden   These were new things—
things essential in every way to the whole conception of
the full Theocratic Glory.   And these very things are
ensured to us in the New Testament, not merely by the
word of the whole New Testament, but by the cardinal
New Testament fact, by the resurrection of our Lord in a
glorified body which is at once the pledge of that physical
regeneration which Paul calls the liberation of the creature,
the " redemption of our bodies," and the actual constitution of that indissoluble bond between heaven and earth,
which ensures to the glorified theocracy the unending
bodily presence of its King

IV

THE PLACE OF THE OLD TESTAMENT IN
RELIGIOUS INSTRUCTION

IT is only in comparatively recent times that the question of this paper has come into prominence in our country. The Scottish Reformers, like the other Protestant Churches, were content to " believe and confesse the Scriptures of God sufficient to instruct and maik the man of God perfect " [Confession of 1560] without drawing any distinction between the use of the two Testaments , nay, affirming that by the " Evangell " they understood " nott onlie the Scripturis of the New Testament, but also of the Auld, the Law, Prophettis, and Histories, in quhilk Christ Jesus is no less conteaned in figure than we have him now expressed in veritie " [1st Book of Discipline]. These utterances indicate the principle of the diligent use of the Old Testament, for which Scotland has ever since been noted. Our Scottish love for the Old Testament does not proceed from adherence to a legal or Judaising standpoint, but from the belief that, in the Old Testament as in the New, Christ and the truths of His gospel are set forth with Divine authority. Nor can we say that this is a vain belief, if we remember that it is of the Old Testament (the New Testament Canon being not yet formed) that Paul affirms that it is able to make us wise unto salvation through faith which is in Christ Jesus—if we remember how deeply our Lord Himself had drunk of the Spirit of the Old Testament, how closely His words attached themselves to its teaching, how He found foreshadowed in the Books of the Old Covenant everything which in His own person and history is " now expressed in verity." At bottom, then, we must still hold fast the old Reformation position, that the Old Testament, like the New, is able to make us wise unto salvation, comes to us, not with transient human authority, but with eternal Divine power, and so must always occupy, in religious instruction, a place side by side with the New

A large question, however, remains. Though the Old Testament, like the New, is the record of a Divine Revelation, they belong to different stages of Revelation The Old Testament leads up to Christ, but the New Testament shows us Christ. What the Old Testament left incomplete, the New Testament fills up. The one plan of salvation unfolded itself gradually, and only the New Testament gives the plan in its full development. How are these facts to bear on our practical use of the record of the growing and of the completed Revelation ? This is a question which the Reformers, and still more, their successors, never fully answered, indeed, never fully set before them They were more interested in the unity than in the differences of the two dispensations. Justly laying stress on the fact that Christ is to be found in the Old Testament, they were often tempted to find Him there in the same way, and with the same clearness as in the New. And so in spite of the better example of Calvin and other great divines, a tendency arose to ignore the historical character of Revelation, the gradual development of God's saving purpose from age to age. That use of the Old Testament came to be thought soundest which extracted from it the greatest amount of specifically New Testament doctrine. And doctrine being thus thrust into one-sided prominence, the Old Testament History came to be valued only as an illustration of doctrine It was forgotten that without saving history there could be no saving doctrine, because without a work of redemption actually realised there could be no doctrine of redemption.

The erroneous way of thought which I have just characterised is still common enough amongst us, and we have all seen how it works in the use of the Old Testament for instruction. It issues either (1) in arbitrary spiritualising, or (2) in dry and shallow moralising. (1) The first of these ways of using the Old Testament is probably less common in the school than in the pulpit, and can never again reach the predominance accorded to it by some pre-Reformation Romish theologians, who value the Old Testament history only in so far as an allegorical reference to New Testament truth can be extracted from it. Yet the warning is not unnecessary, that the disposition everywhere to find types and figures is one of the most ensnaring tendencies with which we can approach the Bible , for there is no surer method of eliminating from the Scripture narratives that endless variety of human interest which is a chief source of their charm and power, and reducing them to limp and colourless uniformity. Take, for example, the story of Abraham offering Isaac. Can anything show more powerfully, not only to the understanding, but to the heart, the nature of the faith with which we are to cling to God, through all apparent hardness in His dealings with us, than this narrative taken literally ? But if instead of trying to bring ourselves, or those we teach, under the direct influence of Abraham's faith on the one side, and the issue that justified that faith on the other, we proceed to spiritualise, and seek in Isaac a type of Christ, instantly the rich direct personal lesson is gone, and we are brought back, in a roundabout way, to the doctrine of the Atonement in general. Of course there are *real* types in the Old Testament, but in them the typical lesson rises naturally out of the literal lesson, and shares its direct concrete personal character. Such types alone can

profitably be used for instruction. But when we are
always hunting for artificial types, it may be fairly asked
whether there is any profit in using the Old Testament
in order to get, by a round-about process, doctrines which
could be got in quite the same shape, and much more
directly, from the New Testament, or even from the
Catechism. (2) More common is the fault of artificial
abstract moralising. Let me illustrate this by an extract
or two from a Sabbath school syllabus, in which side by
side with the lessons from Old Testament history stand
associated " Doctrines to be proved." The following are
consecutive pairs ·—Joseph's brethren accused. Honesty
is the best policy   Joseph makes himself known to his
brethren—Brethren should love one another   Joseph
meets Jacob—Parents to be honoured. Jacob blesses
Joseph—The death of a believer is happy. Jacob's
burial--Sin brought death   The way of teaching which
such a scheme suggests, and to which in many hands it
certainly leads, is this :—to cut up the history into little
sections, in each section to find a doctrine or moral
precept illustrated, and to regard this precept as the
chief " lesson " of the passage. As a matter of course the
lesson must often be far-fetched. For the Old Testament
was not compiled as a series of short lessons, but as a
narrative of the continuous history of God's dealings
with His people. Thus the story of Joseph's brethren
was never meant to teach that honesty is the best policy ,
it is narrated because it was necessary to show, in detail,
how God's providence brought Israel into Egypt   If we
concentrate our attention on the doctrines to be gathered
from little atoms of the history—doctrines of a kind so
general that they find hundreds of illustrations, not only
in the Bible, but in everyday life—we throw into the
background that which is the real peculiarity of Bible
history—viz that it is the history of salvation. It is
only by laying stress on this last character, only by
showing how in the Bible the invisible and eternal things

of God's Kingdom became visible to the faith of the men
of the old covenant, that we can hope to impress on those
we teach the continual sense of a Kingdom of Christ,
into which we are brought by His redeeming work, and
to which we must consecrate all our lives.   We do not
need the history of Joseph to teach us that parents are
to be honoured and brethren loved ;   conscience teaches
that.   We do not need Jacob's burial to add another to
the many proofs that sin brings death, for indeed it
proves no such thing.   But we do need these narratives
as links in the long unbroken proof, which is a proof
only because it is unbroken, that God's Kingdom, His
kingdom of grace ruleth over all.   When this unity of
the Old Testament is thrown aside, and fragments of
history tortured till they yield fragments of doctrine
and morals, it is not strange that many should ask, what
is the profit of teaching the Old Testament to children
at all ?

Having thus glanced at the false methods which
bring into discredit the use of the Old Testament for
instruction, insisted on by our ancestors, let us now see
how the evangelical principles, handed down to us from
the Reformation, point out a sounder method of viewing
the Books of the Old Covenant.   What the Evangelical
Churches seek is a personal message of love from God in
Christ, to which we can return a personal answer of
faith.   Such a personal message cannot come as dry abstract doctrine   A word of salvation, on which we can
rest, must be a practically convincing declaration of God's
love ;   a declaration convincing, because made on the
analogy of the way in which men show love to one
another ;   made, that is, by words joined to deeds, by
God drawing nigh to men in history, and really proving
Himself a redeeming and gracious God.   Such a God He
showed Himself to Israel at the Exodus, and through the
long course of Old Testament history, in which He continually watched over His people, bearing with their

19

hard heart and dull ears, gradually showing them more
and more of His will, His perfections, His glorious decree,
and so leading on to the full manifestation of His saving
purpose in Christ Jesus. In the life, death, and resurrection of our Lord, God's saving self-manifestation
is absolutely complete. The sum and substance of
personal Christianity is just to come under the influence
of Christ's person as His Apostles did, giving up our
whole lives to Him, as one who shows Himself to us as
the ever-living, all-powerful, and all-loving Son of God,
by whom God reconciles the world to Himself Such a
Christianity cannot be taught, for no third party can
teach me to love and trust even the most lovely character. Saving faith is a thing directly between me and
God, and faith in Christ can be inspired only by God's Spirit,
by the Spirit of Christ What a third person, what
religious instruction can effect is to display and impress
on the mind of the pupil, as vividly as possible, a lively
image of God's self-manifestation, to present the Sacred
History, which is the ground of all faith, in such a way
that the child shall, from his earliest years, be accustomed
to give to God and to Christ a real place in his daily life,
a place as real as he gives to his father or his brother.
If we look at the three first Gospels, we see that this
was just the character of our Lord's own teaching The
Kingdom of Heaven — that kingdom, which, though
unseen, is really in our midst, and to which our true and
eternal interests belong, of which we must learn to feel
ourselves members, giving our allegiance to Him as the
King—such is the constant burden of His teaching to
which He seeks to give reality by every variety of statement and illustration But whence does this doctrine
of the kingdom come ? From the Old Testament !
Everywhere He assumes that there are certain ideas as
to the nature of the kingdom which do not now, for the
first time, need to be stated and proved. His miracles
proved the authority of Christ, as of Him by whom the

kingdom should be realised ; but the Old Testament
History had already shown that God had resolved to set
up a kingdom, and choose out a people upon earth.   And
this being so, the life teaching and saving work of Christ
can never be fully understood, except as the climax of
the Old Testament History.

In a word, the history of the Old Testament dispensation must be taught—

1. As the history of the preparation for Christ, without which much of His teaching cannot be understood.

2 As the visible illustration and proof of many things
· which, though involved in Christ's work, did not in His
life on earth receive detailed manifestation.   In the New
Testament, the King is manifested, but the kingdom, the
actual providential scheme by which the earth is being
conquered for and by Christ, is hidden and known by
faith only.   But in the Old Testament the kingdom, not
in its highest spiritual form, but cased in earthly forms,
became really manifest.   Thus there are many truths
about the kingdom, especially about the final victory of
the kingdom, of which the Old Testament alone gives us
clear illustrations by which to explain in our teaching the
spiritual things of the New Testament.   For example,
the power to overthrow His enemies by angelic help,
which Jesus claims, but did not use, is the same power
which was manifested in the fall of Sennacherib's host.

But, indeed, it is not needful to enlarge on the enormous
value of the Old Testament in every attempt to make
the spiritual, heavenly world appear *real* to those we
teach.   To children, reality is very much limited to
things that can be seen and handled.   Ideas—abstract
doctrines—are not suited for them.   They cannot be
expected to look much—it is not well they should look
much—at a life beyond the grave.   But they can and
should learn to recognise the supernatural, the saving
love and providential guidance of God in the present life
Now this is just the strong point of the Old Testament.

The Old Testament believers had but vague views of future life, but little apprehension of abstract doctrines. But they had the most intense, child-like faith in God's ever-present hand that can be conceived. In the whole Old Testament history, God appears as in no other history, as direct chief actor, ever near to His people; and so that history is indispensable for the religious teaching of the young

This sense of God's immediate presence to all our lives, which inspires the whole of the Old Testament, appears in various shapes. In the history, we have the actual proof of God's redeeming providence. To give this proof full weight, the narrative must be taught continuously and vividly, not made a text for abstract doctrine, but just allowed to impress its own lesson, on the principle that what God was in Old Testament times that He is now. Then, again, we have the Psalms —those inimitable answers of the believing heart to God. The Psalms are best explained by the history which shows the circumstances in which the prayers and praises they contain arose, and so at once gives their application to our case. Moreover, they are an indispensable companion to the history, for side by side with God's message to us, they show us how we shall answer to God. With the Psalms, as with the histories, nothing is more to be avoided than a fragmentary treatment. Let children begin with short Psalms, or with Psalms like cxix., where each verse is independent, and then, as they grow older, let them learn to enjoy the beautiful unity of thought in longer Psalms. The Prophetical and Didactic Books are only in part suitable for elementary instruction. The Proverbs, indeed, as the maxims of a wisdom resting on the fear of God, have an obvious and easy use. Books like Job and the Preacher will be admired for their poetry before they are understood in their argument. Parts of the prophets are easily understood, especially in the New Testament development of the truths they suggest.   But for children, the main thing is to learn to understand the prophets as men, and their work in Israel.   The details of their books are but little understood, even by adults who have access only to the English Version.   But one thing is to be avoided above all—the fantastic eschatology, or anticipations of the future history of the world, in which some take delight, but which inevitably result in hopeless confusion and perversion of the clearest principles of Biblical study.

V

ON THE VALUE OF CRITICAL STUDY OF THE PSALMS FOR THEIR PRACTICAL EXPOSITION

THE most interesting way of discussing the questions connected with the separate poetical books of the Old Testament would be to give a history of Hebrew poetry. Such a history would begin with the ancient fragments preserved in the Pentateuch—then pass on to the grand song of Deborah, and perhaps some other fragments of the age of the judges, and thereafter introduce us to Samuel, who appears in the Old Testament history as the reviver not only of prophecy, but of religious song among his people. These considerations would carry us on to the age of David, who, according to the whole testimony of the Old Testament, is the father of psalmody proper, then to the reign of Solomon, whose name is as indissolubly connected with the Gnomic Literature of the Hebrews, and so forth

At least one attempt—that of E. Meier—has been made to write in this way the history of the Old Testament poetic literature But however interesting the attempt may be, there are good reasons for our declining to imitate it.   There is so much uncertainty as to the dates of the various Hebrew poems, and so much discussion even as to the age of such as bear the name of known authors, that we should at every step have to deal largely in conjecture

and assumption, or pause to take up the most abstruse
critical questions in a way not very profitable for our
present purpose.   Thus, for example, such poems as the
Blessings of Jacob and Moses have been subjects of so
much discussion that we could make no use of them
without entering on the question of their genuineness.
Again, the dates of the Book of Job and of some parts of
Proverbs are still unsettled   The Song of Solomon is
still so far a mystery that critics are not agreed whether
it is a drama or a collection of lyrics.   And, finally, the
Psalms themselves, which are in many respects the most
important productions of all, are in part unprovided with
titles, in part titled in a manner so doubtful as to give
us little help.   We are not then, at present, in a state
to attempt the construction of a really trustworthy
history of Hebrew poetry ;   though after proceeding a
certain length with such critical enquiries as seem
absolutely unavoidable, we may be able to reconstruct
with some certainty certain chapters in that history.
But in the first instance at least we must be content to
take up the books one by one, and to go as far into the
criticism of them as seems needful in preparation for the
proper study of their contents.   In particular I wish to go
somewhat fully into the questions connected with the
Psalter, a book which for the Christian minister is perhaps
the most important in the Old Testament, and which
cannot be used with full profit even for devotional purposes
without considerable scientific preparation, both in the
way of historical criticism and in the line of Biblical
Theology.
    The Psalter is, as you know, the inspired hymn-book
of the Old Testament, containing a collection of songs of
prayer and praise, didactic pieces and the like, for use in
the service of the temple and in private devotion.   These
songs are of the most various age and character, and
reflect the religious convictions, hopes, prayers, and joys
of faithful Israelites under the most diverse circumstances.

There are no human feelings so catholic and unchanging in their character as those of true and deep personal religion developed, as the religion of the Psalms was, in contact with and under the guidance of God's special Revelation to His own   The Psalter, as was to be expected from its character as a Theocratic poetry—a poetry of God's Kingdom and Church—is quite free from all that one-sided individualism and fanaticism by which many later hymns, however deeply they may express a real personal conviction, are rendered unfit to express the experience of the Church and of God's people at all times. The Psalms are in the fullest sense hymns of the Old Testament Church, sung that is by men whose sense of personal relation to God was always based on and rooted in their sense of God's redeeming relation to Israel   No doubt there must have arisen in Israel hymns of another kind, reflecting a disturbed, one-sided, impure religious consciousness—in a word, uninspired. That such poems have found no place in the Old Testament Canon is doubtless the fruit of a similar providence to that which guided the New Testament Church to the rejection of the Apocryphal Gospels.   In neither case must the separation between Canonical and Uncanonical be ascribed to a judicious exercise of historical criticism — as if books and psalms were rejected which could not prove themselves to be the work of men recognised as inspired. Such considerations had at most a secondary part to play in the selection, which was guided rather by the fact that the same Spirit of God which breathes in the sacred writings is the Spirit that providentially rules the Church and that lives in every believer. The forming of the Canon was a gradual thing, and before the collection of Psalms was closed every one of them would have been tested by its fitness to express the prayers and praises of God's people for many years, or even for many generations. And this testing process was rendered still more sifting by two things. (1) The whole or the greater part of the

time during which the collection was growing was an age
of prophecy. And though we cannot show, and must not
assume, any formal collection by the hands of prophets,
yet at least the individual psalms would be subjected,
again and again, to be tried by that gift of διάκρισις
πνευμάτων which, as Paul teaches us, is closely associated
with prophecy (1 Cor. xii. 10). And again (2) just as in
New Testament times, a special sifting was no doubt the
fruit of the persecutions and distress of the people, particularly in the exile, not only the people themselves but their
literature would be smelted in the furnace of affliction.
Where it was possible to rescue so little from the destruction of the nation and all its accumulated treasures,
mental as well as material, that would, of course, be
saved which had planted itself most deeply in the hearts
of the true worshippers of Jahveh. Thus, then, while
much that was valuable in the ancient poetry of Israel was
no doubt lost before the close of the Canon, we have at
least received in the Book of Psalms a collection of the
noblest kind, embracing the most precious utterances of
the faith of the Old Testament, each one of which had by
long use and trial become the common property of the Old
Testament Church, which recognised in them a fitting
expression of her own faith, hopes, and prayers. And
again, whatever differences there are between the Church
of the Old and the New Testament, it is at least certain
that it is the same Spirit which gave life to both, and that
the Psalms in which our Lord found His own spiritual
experiences as Head and Saviour of the Church so fully
mirrored, must remain a no less necessary and sufficient
picture of true spiritual life for the Church, which is His
body, and for every believer who claims to be His follower.
And so, if we simply take the Psalms as they stand without enquiring at all into their origin, their authors, or the
occasions on which they were written,—if we simply take
them as utterances of a spiritual life far deeper and purer
than we have attained to, but yet similar in kind to those

we should aim at, if we take them as an inspired expression
of the faith and hopes which we ourselves must seek to
realise—if, that is, we read the Psalms in the light of our
own Christian life and strive, God helping us, to realise
more and more of the Spirit of the Psalms, in this way
without any scientific preparation, we may read the
Psalter aright and profitably, if only we are by grace
partakers of the same Spirit as wrought in the Psalmists.
And whatever may be said of the incompleteness of the
religious life of the men of the Old Covenant, and of a
supposed incompatibility between the more enlightened
Christian consciousness and some veins of thought that
run in the Psalms, I conceive it has yet to be proved that
any simple Christian ever suffered in his spiritual life by
unreservedly drinking in the streams of spiritual experience
that flow through these hymns.   But while I confess that
to me it seems an idea too absurd to need refutation that
the Psalms require, as so many seem to think, a sort of
remodelling, Christianising, even—to the mind of some—
an expurgation before they can be safely taken into the
mouths of simple Christians—while such an idea seems to
me to savour of Romanism, and to be nothing less than a
denial of the great Protestant principle that every part of
Scripture is precious to the meanest Christian who reads
with the help of God's Spirit—while this is so, it must be
held that to understand the Psalter *fully*, to get from it all,
or nearly all, its proper richness of meaning, we must arm
ourselves with all the apparatus of a scientific criticism,
and prepare, as I have already said, to face and answer
not a few difficult questions both historical and theological.
And in particular there is no book to which more fully
than to the Psalter the great truth applies, that while
every one who is taught of the Spirit is able to learn from
the Bible, not every one is fit to teach from it—no, not
every one even who has, what nowadays is often thought
to be sufficient, a familiarity with Bible language and a
certain readiness of speech.   In a word, while no man is

fit to be a teacher from Scripture who does not study the Bible devotionally, no man is fit to teach whose study is merely devotional, or devotional and rhetorical.   On this point there is current so much practical confusion of mind, and the temptations to neglect strict scientific study in premature pursuit of a practical readiness in preaching to which you are exposed during your divinity studies are so many, that you will allow me to point out with reference to the Psalter the grounds for insisting that you should all habituate yourselves to the practice of a strict scientifical and critical examination of Scripture as the necessary groundwork for all really profitable teaching.

That which commends the Psalter to us as an authoritative book is, of course, its inspiration.   But what is it that this inspiration guarantees ?   You will perhaps reply *infallibility*   But that is still a very vague term in its application to a book like the Psalter, in which the communication of matter of fact or religious doctrine is quite subordinate to the expression of religious feeling. On the other hand, it appears from what we have already said that the test at least of the Canonical quality of the Psalter which practically guided the formation of the collection, which commended it to the Old Testament Church and commends it with the authority of Christ Himself to the Church of the New Testament, is its fitness to serve at all times as a model and perfect image of the Spirit of true devotion.   The Psalms, that is, are the utterances of men who had learned by the Spirit rightly to understand God's redeeming voice to them, and rightly to return answer thereunto.   And because God's voice in revelation brings in all ages—though not always with equal clearness—the same message of love and grace, so in all ages the right answer of faith must breathe the same spirit and be based on the same model, and the Christian can never be wrong in expressing his devotional feelings in the language of the Psalms.

But when we begin to teach from the Psalms the case

is different. In teaching from the pulpit—and to this kind of teaching I confine myself—the object of the speaker is to stimulate and guide devotional feeling in his hearers, in whom as professing Christians he must in the judgment of charity assume a certain measure of grace, a certain degree of capacity to discern spiritual things, but who as sinful and imperfect men fall far short of such a normal spirit of devotion as breathes in the Bible.

Now this comparative dullness and imperfection in the spiritual life must, in so far as the true notion of Christian life is that of fellowship and converse with God through Christ, have two sides—a dullness to hear what God says to us, and an unreadiness or want of faith to make right answer to Him. How then can the Word of God taught be made instrumental in remedying these two defects? The principle of such a use of the word seems to be this— Whatever God speaks to *me* He speaks to me, not as an individual, but as a member of His Church, as one of His own elect. And thus, while on the one hand I have no right to seek for myself with the mystics a private revelation in which others have no share, I have the much nobler right of taking to myself every manifestation of God's love and grace made to any part of His Church in any age. And so, on the other hand, to answer God's message aright is not to make some private answer for myself alone, but to take up with full personal appropriation the one great answer of faith and hope, of praise and prayer, which goes up in all ages from the Church Universal Now, in both respects the Bible has normative authority. It contains the true message of God to His Church, the true answer of the Church to God, not in the way of bare abstract statement, but in a living picture, of which one side is the gradual development of God's plan of redemption, while the other side shows us from age to age the faith and answer of the Church To get into fellowship and sympathy with these two sides of the Bible is, therefore, the true way to the elevation of our

spiritual life on both its sides.   Now sympathy involves,
firstly, community of spirit.   Where that is wanting, no
preaching can edify.   The preacher, as we have already
said, can hope to build up his hearers only in so far as he
has a right to assume the presence of God's Spirit in the
visible Church, *i.e.* wherever the Word and Sacraments
are, there God's Spirit blesses the means.   But there is
another thing necessary to sympathy, viz. *recognised
similarity of position.*   Why, for example, does the
reading of the Decalogue often fail to move us, even
though there be in our hearts the germs of a true love to
God's Law ?   It is because we come to the Decalogue
without having passed through the Red Sea and marched
through the Wilderness ;   because we are not standing
beneath Mt. Sinai while the thunder rolls above us and the
lightnings flash in our eyes.   And so the minister who
would preach effectively from the Decalogue must seek
so to set before his hearers the essential oneness of what we
have experienced of God's mercy, with that experience
which prepared the Israelites for Sinai.   He must do this,
not in the fashion of the Jesuit preachers by simply
catching the outward aspects of the scene and impressing
these on the imaginations of his hearers, but by going
deeper into the heart of the matter, and bringing out by
careful critical and theological study the real oneness
of the spiritual meaning of the law then and now.   He
must (1) reconstruct for himself by painstaking historical
study the position of the Israelites, and then (2) by theological knowledge and by the help of his own Christian
experience and insight, he must lay hold of and draw out
of the historical situation the true and unchangeable
spiritual meaning which we are still called upon to enter
into, showing how the Israelites, though they had come
through external manifestations of God's purpose towards
them more startling than we have known, yet at bottom
stood in no other spiritual relation to the law than we do.
Thus opening up to his hearers their essential similarity in

position to the men of the Old Covenant, the preacher does his part to awake such a sympathy with the spiritual meaning of his text as is the really edifying thing in the reading and preaching of the Word. He helps his hearers to feel God's message not merely as a general message to man, but as a very special message addressing itself directly to distinct needs and capacities in the first hearers which are still needs and capacities of ours   Every Word of God is plain, direct, and powerful in its true historical setting. It is the restoration of this historical setting which is the real task that lies at the basis of interpretation, and therefore also of practical application.

Now the Psalms do not so much give us the Word of God to man in its direct form, as the true answer of faith in which, of course, the promise on which faith rests is taken up, and so expressed from the side of the believer. But here also the truth comes in, that these models of the believer's true attitude to God's Word will not work upon us to the purifying and strengthening of our Christian life, except in proportion as we add to the prime requisite of the beginnings at least of grace in our own soul, an appreciation of those points in which the experiences that called forth these expressions of Old Testament faith are our experiences also.   No doubt this requisite is some- times attained through the heart alone without careful study or analysis. The uneducated believer will learn to understand the Psalms in this way—He takes up his Psalter under the influence of a particular phase of devotional feeling. He finds that feeling expressed and developed in a much fuller way in some Psalm, and so at one and the same time his own spiritual life is nourished and strengthened, and the Psalm becomes for ever clear to him in such a way that it may afterwards serve to evoke the feeling which at first it had only strengthened.   But this method can never apply to public teaching from the Psalms.   The preacher must so handle the Psalm as to make it speak even to those who are not specially pre-

disposed to hear its lesson, even to those who may be
backsliding and averse to its teachings. Nor will it do
for him simply to dwell on such sides of religious truth
as find a special echo in the present circumstances of his
own spiritual life. For then his teaching would be quite
as much the teaching of his own imperfect, even abnormal,
experiences as the teaching of the pure Word of God.
The only thing that he would really contribute to his
hearers over and above what each of them could read for
himself would be illustrations drawn from his own inner
life ; his preaching might be experimental, but it would
be morbidly, pathologically, experimental. If he were an
honest man it would be often impossible for him to enter
the pulpit at all ; and all idea of being able from week to
week to feed his flock with a word not his own but the
Word of God Himself must be given up. Now what is the
alternative for this false style of teaching ? Manifestly
to draw the experimental side of preaching from the normal
experience laid down in the Bible—to let the Psalmists
speak for themselves. And surely they speak more
clearly, truly, powerfully than you can speak. If they
are not clear to us now, it is because we have not been
their companions in the experiences of which they sing—
and what they say will become clear to us if we recognise
the outward circumstances in which they stood, the
character of the revelation that supported them, the
nature of the temptations by which they were encompassed,
the sins that they were fighting, and the like. And all
this is matter of strict scientific enquiry. No doubt it
needs spiritual insight too. But when we set to study the
Psalms in this way, with the head as well as with the
heart, we shall be immeasurably freer from the risk of
putting our own word in the place of God's, immeasurably
more likely to preach the Psalmist's experience instead
of our own. And, then, there is another thing. The
Psalmists were neither perfect men nor did they stand
under a perfect revelation. As the spiritual gifts they

enjoyed did not interfere with the law that all sanctification is gradual, so neither did they violate the law that
all revelation is gradual   And so we are always apt to
go wrong if we begin to draw inferences from the Psalms
without clearly keeping in view the amount of light that
the writers possessed.   But in public teaching one must
draw inferences.   It is impossible, even were it desirable,
to remain wholly in the region of subjective devotional
feeling.   And the moment one begins to argue, to generalise, to theologise, every step must be guarded by the
closest scientific study.   It will never do to be content to
deal with proof-texts at haphazard, just as we can draw
them from so varied a collection as our Psalms.   The
subjective fitness of each utterance in the Psalter can form
the basis for an objective theological inference only when
the relations of the utterance, not only to the textual
context but to the whole position of the singer, are clearly
laid down.   And so it comes about that the Psalms,
though the plainest of all books for purposes of simple
devotion, demand in those who would use them for
teaching a patient labour, a clearness of judgment, an
exactness of analysis of the very highest kind.   Every
individual Psalm, which for the most part is found standing as an isolated fragment, must be again built into its
place in the historical and theological development of the
old Covenant, into its place in the spiritual life of the
singer, before we can exhaust its meaning.   It is, of course,
not often possible, and not often necessary, to give exact
place and date of authorship ; but at least we must
always aim at a historical exposition to the extent of
reconstructing in as full detail as may be the kind of
circumstances and experience from which the Psalm
sprang, and the general state of the Church's growth at
the time.   The precise degree of exactness with which
these desiderata can be satisfied cannot, of course, appear
even approximately till we have made some way in
discussing the various questions of introduction to which

we are now to proceed—the formation of the collection—
the value of the inscriptions, and so forth.   But I believe
that the more carefully the Psalms are studied the more
fully shall we be impressed that the historical interpretation of the Psalms is both possible and necessary in a much
higher degree than is admitted by some even of those
commentators who have done best service in the sphere
of grammatical exegesis.   No doubt when a writer like
Hupfeld maintains that we can only hope on the one
hand to distinguish by general marks of style, older from
younger, original from imitative pieces, and on the other
hand, historically to separate Psalms that presuppose
the independence of the nation from Psalms of the Exile
or the Return, he is actuated by a not altogether unjust
opposition to the blind dependence on the traditional
superscriptions which marks one class of commentators,
and to the bold subjection of all probabilities to preconceived hypothesis which governs expositors like Olshausen
and even in great measure Hitzig.   But that the reaction
against these extremes has led Hupfeld himself into a
not less false position, is manifest in the details of his
exegesis which often lacks precision, in spite of his grammatical exactness, on account of his obstinate determination to *generalise* statements and expressions that have
plainly a single specific reference.   And even at this stage
you will readily see that that is not a safe principle of
exegesis which leads to the assertion " that though David
cannot be without his share in the Psalter, it is not
possible to identify a single Psalm as certainly his,"—as if
David's life were so common a one, or the stamp it impressed on his poetry could be so obscure, that none of his
extant Psalms should bear indisputable traces of their
author.

But it is premature to go farther into this question just
now.   We must return to it when we have made some
progress in a critical analysis of the Psalter as it now
stands.

20

IV

LATER ABERDEEN LECTURES

(1874-1877)

I

THE PLACE OF THEOLOGY IN THE WORK
AND GROWTH OF THE CHURCH

THE study of theology may be looked at from several
distinct points of view. It is manifest, in the first
place, that a study which enters so deeply into the region
of personal life is capable not only of being loved and
cultivated, but of being hated and proscribed. This is a
character which in great measure distinguishes all the
sciences that deal with man from those that are concerned with nature. But the prerogative of appealing
to the heart as well as to the intellect belongs in peculiar
measure to the topics with which theology concerns
itself. No problems are so radical in their influence on
the whole scheme of human life as those that handle
the existence, the nature, the revelation of God ; and so
the very right of theology to exist and to discuss these
things becomes, in a pre-eminent degree, subject of fierce
controversy. But even the enemies of theology are
divided into several distinct camps There are those
who regard all theology as jugglery, because they hold
all religion to be superstition Religion is conceived
as a morbid condition, affecting certain stages of human
development ; and the study of its phenomena forms part
of the science of social pathology. A more modern school
of thinkers detects the unhistorical complexion of this
view, observing that religion has exerted an unquestionable influence in carrying forward the moral and social

development of our race.   An active and useful factor in
history cannot be a mere disease of humanity ; but it is
imagined that the truly beneficent forces of which religion
has hitherto been the vehicle have been clothed in a
false idealism, and unnecessarily engrafted on transcendental theories as to the relation of man to God.   It is
held that a better social philosophy would enable us to
find on earth all those ethical motives and all those
springs of bliss which the imagination of early ages
placed in heaven.   And this new religion of humanity
has no need for a theology, because it finds no place for
a God.   The religion of humanity is as yet in a somewhat undeveloped state, and its adherents are, for the
most part, either unable or unwilling to lay down with
logical precision the features that distinguish it from
Christianity.   But when we hear it asserted that religion
is a necessary and an excellent thing, while theology, on
the contrary, is useless or noxious, we may in general
assume that we have to deal with a man who, more or
less consciously, derives his views from the school in
question.   A religion without theology means, for the
most part, a religion without God.   It can mean nothing
else in the mouth of any man who does not possess that
mystical habit of mind which conceives of communion
with God as a state of the soul too purely passive to
become an object of intellectual cognition, too purely
individual to be the basis of a general doctrine.   And
this extreme form of mysticism is at present so rare and
so uninfluential that it cannot be credited with any
share in establishing the currency of the formula which
contrasts religion with theology.   That formula has a
clear meaning only for the man who has satisfied himself
that the really valuable elements of religion are quite
separable from all belief in God, or in any other transcendental fact.   It is a formula, therefore, which is so
far from being the self-evident foundation of a new
religious liberalism, that it possesses no value for any man

who has not got at it as the last result of an elaborate
criticism of all religious ideas, who has not satisfied himself, by a strictly philosophical inquiry, that the transcendental convictions of Christianity are not the true
mainsprings of Christian life, but simply an illogical
projection into the superhuman sphere of notions, which
have always had their reality and power only in immanent relations of a region purely human.   When the
assertion that theology perishes but religion remains
passes from mouth to mouth, among men who have no
pretensions to have even looked at these difficult problems
of the philosophy of religion, who, being either destitute
of all habits of exact thought or occupied only with purely
physical science, do not possess the most elementary
qualifications for the researches which alone can give
their words a meaning,—in the mouths of such men
the formula in question is nothing more than a cant
phrase, which decently veils pretentious ignorance, or
nothing less than a disguise of affected sentiment cast
over the nakedness of shamefaced atheism.

Thus if we set aside, on the one hand, the objections
drawn from a mysticism too exaggerated to deserve
serious refutation, and, on the other hand, those derived
from that old - fashioned atheism which, in its plain-
spoken contempt for all religion, can so easily be proved
unhistorical that even its friends are glad to disguise it
in scraps of new-fashioned philosophy,—if we set both
these classes of objections aside, it appears that the
only serious attack which can be made on theology as a
whole must proceed from a system of the philosophy of
religion not less elaborate in construction than Christian
theology itself.   The right of theology to exist can no
longer be disputed *in limine*.   The contest must now be
between the developed systems of the philosophy of
Christianity and the philosophy of the religion of
humanity.   Each of these systems must base its argument, not merely on speculative considerations, but on

the closest study of the whole history of religion, especially of the religion of Christ   The battle with unbelief which in last century was fought on broad general grounds and with arguments addressed to the general intelligence, is now resolving itself into a series of detailed contests, intelligible for the most part only to men specially trained, and extending over every theological discipline. True, this new phase in the contest between Christianity and infidelity has not yet been adequately realised by either side.   Nor can a time ever come when those cruder forms of unbelief, which have their strength in passion and prejudice, shall cease to advance the old objections and call forth the old replies.   But ever since the publication of Strauss's first *Life of Jesus*, the new conditions of the battle have been growing more and more visible. The more sober and cultivated opponents of our faith have ceased to regard theological studies as unworthy of their attention.   Theology, it is admitted, can be overthrown only by theologians.   Unlike those superstitions that vanish at once before the light of superior truth, Christianity can be subverted only by the most refined process of criticism operating against the detailed developments of Christian belief   This new wager of battle has not been refused by the defending camp.   The critical study of Christianity has been taken up both by friend and foe, with an energy which indicates considerable revival of interest in exact theological research ; and the conception of theology as a science, which in this country had very much dropped out of sight, is again impressed upon men's minds.

At first sight, the stimulus which has thus been given to theological inquiry seems very valuable.   But before we give ourselves up to the unreserved self-congratulation which we hear around us, it is well that we should ask whether it is a wholesome thing that all theological interest is at present so exclusively supported by apologetical and polemical motives.   We should ask whether such a theology is likely to be really fruitful, and whether such interest is likely to be really lasting. Both these questions, I apprehend, must be answered in the negative. Discussions which have for their object the defence or overthrow of Christianity as a whole may, indeed, attach themselves to the detailed problems of theology, but cannot possibly devote to questions of detail the loving interest by which alone the sciences advance. Such discussions, therefore, can hardly be very fruitful. Nor can they continue to inspire a wide and deep interest. For the apologetic problems are becoming yearly more intricate, so that, in an increasing degree, they either cease to interest all but a very few, or attract the attention of the many only when set forth in a superficial and inaccurate manner. The fact is, that no religion which contains within it such elements of power as still reside in Christianity, can be annihilated by a process of critical dissection Both assailants and defenders will at last weary of this endless conflict of detail. The battle, which can never cease, will assume a new form. It is probable enough that instead of a mere war of opinion we may have to face attacks of a more practical kind. But at all events, the preparedness of the Church to meet a new onset can bear a very remote relation to the completeness with which an apologetic adapted to the present system of attack has been organised. The merely propugnacular part of theology has very transitory value. A theology capable of doing permanent service must not allow itself to be shaped with reference to the present attitude of unbelief. It must not, in the first instance, look at unbelief at all, but must be framed in accordance with a large and just view of the service which systematic Christian knowledge is able to do in promoting the internal growth and the natural work of the Church herself.

The point of this argument may perhaps become more clear if put in another way. Apologetic theology, though .

practical in its bearing on those who are without the
Church, has, for those who are within the Church, either
no value at all, or a value purely speculative. The most
finished apologetic which can be conceived would, in
fact, be a complete theoretic delineation of the relations
of the different parts of the Christian system, and a
complete critical philosophy of the history of our religion.
But as apologetic is entirely directed to persons who
have no sympathy with the practical tasks that lie before
the Church, the theoretic disciplines in question would,
in the hands of the apologist, be necessarily framed in
quite an abstract manner. And, therefore, when all the
unbelievers were convinced, a new and higher theological
task would arise ; it would be necessary to recast the
abstract theory of Christianity, and construct a practical
theology for the guidance of the Church in the positive
task of attaining the ideal set before her by her Lord.
But of course a perfect apologetic can never be constructed
by an imperfect Church. It is the actual imperfection
of the existent state of the Church, much more than the
theoretic imperfection of our present theology, which is
the source of unbelief ; and it is not possible to give a
perfect theory of an imperfect organism. Thus not only
the highest, but the most immediately practical task of
theology, is to guide the internal growth and activity of
the Church. Those who allow themselves to be carried
away from this aim by the apparent urgency of danger
from without, and who, therefore, according to the
fashion of the present day, direct their whole energies,
as theologians, to apologetical tasks, misapprehend the
real needs of the Church and the real sources of the
weakness and the strength of Christianity, which is
always invincible from without, except when weakened
by corruption and divisions within

It appears, then, when the thing is looked at more
closely, that the extreme and one-sided development of
apologetic in the recent theological literature of our

country is by no means an unambiguous sign of a healthy
interest in theology. On the contrary, this is rather
to be regarded as one of many signs that we are lament-
ably deficient in theological interest of the right kind,
that we have very little sense of the real services which
theology ought to perform for the Church and kingdom
of Christ. When we observe that our whole theological
literature, even when not apologetical in subject, is
impregnated with an apologetic flavour ; that the most
popular commentaries, the most current works on doctrine, do little or nothing to carry theology forward to
new results, and direct all their energy to the refutation
of attacks from without, we are constrained to ask,
whether the Church itself is likely to be aggressive if her
theology is purely defensive. But, in fact, the mass of
men seem to think that, for all purposes except the
refutation of new objections, our theology is already
quite perfect enough. It is not felt that one main
reason why the Church falls short of her true ideal is
that the ideal has not yet been accurately conceived in
thought.

But, in truth, where the need for a growing theology is
not felt, the theological results which the Church has
already reached are sure to be very inadequately mastered
by individuals, and very imperfectly applied to the
details of Church work. When the Church as a whole
is quite content with the theology which she already
possesses, individual ministers and students will very
readily be content with the amount of theology which
they already possess If all our ministers were fully
impressed with the conviction that a thorough discharge
of their ministry is only possible if they bring to bear on
the details of their work the most developed theological
grasp of the meaning of the Church and the Church's
work as a whole, we should no longer have to complain
of a stationary theology. But, in the meantime, the
general indifference to the growth of theology finds

its counterpart in individual indifference to theological acquisition and thought. If nothing new is brought out except in the way of sermons, books of practical religion, and apologetic, it is only natural that our ministers and students in great measure confine their reading to these less profitable topics, and that their pastoral efficiency is correspondingly impaired. Finally, this indifference to theology is not confined to the ministry. It is widely spread among the members of the Church, and takes shape in depreciation of the value of a regularly trained ministry, and in an inclination to believe that personal earnestness, some natural eloquence, and a fair measure of familiarity with the easier parts of the Bible, and perhaps with the Shorter Catechism, are all that can reasonably be thought necessary to fit a man for the office of a teacher in the Church.

Against all these delusions we possess, humanly speaking, only one strong practical barrier—the institution of the divinity hall for the systematic training of our ministers. When we part for the session, after spending five months together in practical protest against tendencies which surround us on every side, and which sometimes threaten to exert an evil influence on our own minds, it is fit that we should endeavour to carry with us a clear conception of the purpose and value of the methodical studies on which we have been engaged. I propose, therefore, to spend the rest of this lecture in an attempt to develop, in a constructive manner, the subject which in my remarks up to this point I have approached indirectly, and in the way of criticism of current habits of thought.

Christianity is a new life. The Christian takes his place in a society where his life is guided by new motives, and supplied with strength arising from his new relation to God. Every point in this new situation implies knowledge of a quite definite kind. The believer's relation to God is not of the nature of a physical union, which can be realised in him without his knowing what

kind of relation it is. The new motives that stir him
have power only in proportion as they are intelligently
grasped. He is not mechanically grafted into Christ,
but becomes a member of the mystical body only in
conscious submission to the Head.   And the new strength
of grace by which he lives is not given magically by
physical infusion but morally to those that seek it by
prayer, and therefore with a real knowledge both of their
need and of the way in which it must be supplied.   In
short, whatever of real living power there is in Christianity
is *moral*, and deals with man as a conscious, intelligent
personality, who is in no sense fulfilling the ends for which
God placed him on the earth, if he is not fulfilling them
in the free play of understanding and of will.   A moral
growth such as Christianity sets before us means that
every step in advance is deliberately taken in pursuit of
a moral ideal already grasped in thought.   It is, indeed,
a law of such growth that the ideal unfolds itself more
and more perfectly as we come nearer to it, just as the
towers and spires of a fair city display themselves with
increasing clearness of detail to the pilgrim who approaches
its gates.   But the very first step of true advance towards
the goal implies a true, though it may be only a general,
knowledge of the ideal pursued.   No kind of moral
action, be it Christian or not, is an affair of pure subjectivity.   All morality implies purpose, and all purpose
is conditioned by antecedent knowledge of the thing
proposed.   If we refuse to apply this law to the Christian
life, we degrade religion to a mere material thing, and
place it on one line with the functions of bodily growth.
For every part of life that goes on working, whether it is
understood or not, is physical, not moral.   And so the
theorist who proposes as possible a life in God which is
not based on a knowledge of God, is really depicting
Deity in the manner of pantheistic materialism, as a
subtle principle of physical influence, which a man sucks
in as he does the breeze and the sunshine.

This extreme antithesis to the position that all real Christian life rests on true Christian knowledge, is characteristic of pronounced unbelief, with which in this part of our discussion we are no longer concerned. But even within the Christian Church, the pantheistic notion of God has always influenced a certain class of minds, and shows itself in that tendency to conceive spiritual and moral facts on the analogy of physical processes, which is technically called mysticism The mystical schools incline to make Christianity an affair of feeling and instinct rather than of knowledge and will ; though, of course, where this tendency is limited by positive Christian motives, it results not in absolute denial, but only in certain modifications of the moral character of our religion. The palmy days of mysticism fall in the Middle Ages, and in these ages, it must be remembered, even the Catholic Church exempted a most weighty part of the spiritual energies of Christianity from the laws of moral action The doctrine of the *opus operatum* in the sacraments unquestionably reduces certain features of the spiritual life to the level of a physical process, and this doctrine alone makes it possible for the Church of Rome to regard with complacency a degree of ignorance on the part of the laity, which is quite inconsistent with truly moral growth.

But in Protestantism, at least, it should be otherwise. When the Reformers taught that the means of grace are effective only in so far as they bring the *Word* of God into contact with personal faith, they distinctly asserted that all true religious life is morally nourished. For the Word of God meant to the Reformers the direct personal message of God's love in Christ ; so that saving faith is neither a mere intellectual persuasion, nor a mere subjective habit of mind, but the intelligent and moral outgoing of the personality and will towards a personal revelation of God. Hence the intense zeal with which early Protestantism threw itself on the study of the

Bible, no longer seeking therein, with the Middle Ages, a body of intelligible truths not directly in contact with the practical Christian life, but that living voice of God Himself, which, heard and joyously received into the heart, becomes the direct principle of all spiritual growth.

This principle is formulated in our Larger Catechism, in the proposition that Christ communicates to His Church the benefits of His mediation by means of His ordinances, the word, sacraments, and prayer. With this must be taken the doctrine—which historically was the very starting-point of the Reformation—that the effectual factor in the sacraments is not the outward sign, but the word of promise signified. Thus the proposition is, that all participation in the benefits purchased by Christ is to be gained in converse with God, in hearkening continually to His Word, and in making thereto the answer of prayer and thanksgiving. All Christian life becomes a thing of the understanding and of the will. Each step towards Christian perfection is possible only in the form of conscious submission of the will to a promise or precept of God, definitely grasped by the mind. The operation of the Holy Spirit in the calling and sanctification of the believer does not substitute a new and incomprehensible process for this plain rule of moral growth, but only makes that growth possible by enlightening the understanding and renewing the will.

Every endeavour to set forth the importance of theology to the Church must necessarily rest on a clear apprehension of the importance of Christian knowledge for the individual religious life And I have thought it the more necessary to recall to you the characteristic attitude of Protestantism on this point, because, where theology is undervalued by persons standing within the Protestant Churches, it will very often be found that behind this there lies a wrong conception of the whole nature of Christian faith and life. Instead of the Christian life being conceived as a conscious converse with

God, by the aid of the ordinary means of grace, an inclination will be found to imagine that the highest religious experiences dispense with these means altogether. In extreme cases, of course, this tendency leads to claims of special inspiration. But it is not in its extremest forms that the tendency does most harm, for then its falseness is easily seen. More generally what is put in the place of the objective converse of faith with God is some kind of subjective emotion or persuasion. Faith, instead of going outwards towards God in Christ, is turned inward upon itself. It is supposed that a man is saved by believing that he is saved, by gaining, through some kind of empirical experience, a conviction that he has passed from death to life Of course such a faith is not belief in God, but in something internal to oneself, and therefore has no necessary relation to any true knowledge of God, and gives no starting-point for a theology. But the people who hold these views still use the name of justification by faith, and so often imagine that they are sound Protestants. In reality they are a kind of Protestant mystics, greatly inferior to the old mystics in richness of æsthetic fancy and warmth of religious feeling ; and when they become sufficiently conscious of their own position to separate themselves from the Church, they form these monotonous sects, whose one spiritual weapon is the ever repeated question, " Have you believed ? " and whose theology consists wholly of abusive polemic and millenarian dreams.

It is plain, from what has already been said, that the tendency to depreciate theology which marks a leaning towards these views must be met in the first place by emphasising the true Protestant view of faith, and of its relation to the Word of God. It must not, however, be supposed that when due stress is laid on these points everything is done which is necessary to vindicate for theology its proper place. Indeed, at this part of the argument an error is frequently committed, which,

though precisely opposite in character to that of the
sects just characterised, is very nearly as fatal to a true
understanding of the nature and business of theology.
It is often said or implied that because all true Christianity involves definite knowledge of God and His Word
of Revelation, there is, therefore, no real difference between
religion and theology.   The specific Christian knowledge
which every believer possesses is called his theology, and
is hastily identified with the theology of the Church in
general   It is not, of course, pretended that every believer
is necessarily master of all theology, but it is held that
the knowledge indispensable to faith is, so far as it goes,
theological.

Now it is to be observed that the only kind of knowledge which it is necessary for every Christian to possess
is knowledge which stands in direct contact with faith and
practice.   It is not necessary that the knowledge in
question be systematised, logically formulated, put into
any scientific shape.   It is not even necessary that he
who has it shall be able to enounce it with precision in
words, if it is always at hand to him when he wishes to
act on it   In all practical ways of life there is a great
deal of knowledge requisite which is perfectly definite,
but which the practical man never learns to put into
words   He has acquired his knowledge by practice.
And so when any practical question arises he *knows* the
right thing to do, though perhaps he could not explain
so as to make another know it   An extreme instance of
the kind, which illustrates what I mean in the simplest
form, is the power of hitting a mark with a stone.   This
involves a real and accurate intellectual judgment of
the object, its distance, and so forth.   Implicitly, this
judgment contains applications of a number of laws of
anatomy, optics, dynamics, but not one of these laws is
present as a law to the mind of the actor.   The same
thing obviously holds good with regard to moral action.
Take the personal converse of a little child with its

father. This converse, which is one of faith, love, and obedience, is guided by a real knowledge of the father's love and the father's wishes. But the child could not describe its father's character, or tell you how it reads his meaning in his face The knowledge is a real knowledge, serving as a foundation for true moral action, but it cannot be expressed in propositions.

It is certain that similar considerations apply to the case of Christianity. The early Christians had no formulated doctrine of the person of Christ, and no theory of the atonement. But in a practical way they knew that Christ was a Divine Person, for they worshipped Him ; and they knew that He had reconciled them with God, for they walked in the joyful consciousness of reconciliation. The Mediæval Church had no doctrine of justification by faith, yet certainly in all ages the Church is justified by faith

Now, how does this bear on the position, that the specific Christian knowledge of the believer is always made up of theological propositions—differing only in extent and not in kind from a complete theological system ? We have seen that true Christian knowledge is often unsystematic, even inarticulate, presenting itself to the mind of the believer not in the form of propositions, but only as a sound practical judgment in each special act of Christian life. To reconcile this fact with the notion that all faith implies a measure of theological knowledge, one of two things must be done. Either it must be urged that, however inarticulate much of the believer's knowledge is, there must always be some part of it, embracing essentials, which is clearly formulated , or, on the other hand, it must be maintained that clear formulation, logical arrangement, systematic structure, are not essential to theology at all. In general, I believe those who uphold the position which we are at present examining are disposed to combine these arguments. But both arguments are inadequate, and both tend to establish a practical depreciation of theology.

Look first at the assertion, that every believer must at least have a definitely formulated knowledge about essentials, which is his theology. This argument is pertinent to establish the identity of theology with practical Christian knowledge, only on the assumption that it is the formulated part of his knowledge on which the Christian acts, the rest being really a superfluity. And this is obviously untrue, for the very doctrines which we rightly consider pre-eminently practical were not formulated till a comparatively late date in the history of the Church. And without any appeal to history, it is enough to point to the fact that genuine practical insight often keeps the simplest believer in the right path, on questions the theological discussion of which is full of subtleties. Here, obviously, we have action based not on elementary formulated knowledge, but on deep inarticulate knowledge elaborated in practice. The argument, then, is powerless for the end proposed to it.   But it is very powerful in leading people to undervalue theology.   For when an eminent degree of practical Christian wisdom and goodness is found in a man whose explicit knowledge is scanty, this argument prevents people from seeing that between these two things there lies a great development of unformulated knowledge. The importance of theology is supposed to be magnified by ignoring inarticulate knowledge altogether, and the result is, of course, that we have people saying on every hand, " What is the good of an elaborate theology when a man who is so little a theologian as A or B is so excellent and so useful a man ? "   This is an objection which can only be answered by showing that the supposed useless elaborations of theology are just explicit statements of the very truths which, in an inarticulate form, in the shape of practical tact and insight, lie at the root of untheological wisdom.

I pass now to the second way of defending the notion that all true religious knowledge is theology. Theology is often taken in a loose sense, and permitted to include all manner of unsystematic illogical odds and ends of Christian thought and knowledge. A book of sermons, for example, or a volume of practical meditations, is taken to be a contribution to theology. In this loose sense of the word, at least, every Christian, it is maintained, has a theology.

But this is also a thoroughly false position. Loose, unshaped knowledge, never leads to clear and decided action. If a practical man can only tell in a rude, general way the rules on which he works, you may be sure that he does not think of these rules at all in the actual process of his toil. The loose, vague rule is only an awkward attempt to express in words some piece of knowledge of which he has a practical grasp, perfectly firm and definite. In fact, vague and inaccurate theological generalisations are only a hindrance to Christian life. All generalised knowledge, which is not scientifically precise in its expression, contains some element of positive error, and applied in practice may very readily prove misleading. It will be found that the simple Christian argues safely only when, by direct personal sympathy with the personal Word of God, he takes it home to his own special case without any generalisation whatever. He does this with the perfectly definite knowledge that the word is spoken by God to *him* ; but this personal appropriation of a personal message of love is surely not by any straining of words to be called theology.

Let me, in a word, sum up this part of our argument. Personal Christianity is not a play of subjectivities, but moral converse with God practically dominating the life. Such converse is necessarily intelligent there is no faith without knowledge. But the essential quality of the knowledge is its personal and practical character. The believer must be able to say, I know that God speaks *thus* to *me* , that He gives me such a hope in my present trouble, such a command as to present duty. But this personal knowledge is not, for the most part, reached by making a special application of a general truth : it is got at by sympathetic appropriation of the concrete and personal utterances of God's Word. It is a mistake to call such knowledge theology. For however the notion of theology is stretched, it always must, to a certain extent, imply a knowledge which can be put into words, and so imparted to a man who has not shared the experience of him who imparts it. And of such knowledge a most experienced Christian may have very little, and that little very loose and inaccurate. And if it is supposed that this theology is really what his faith feeds on and his life is guided by, we must draw the inaccurate and dangerous inference, that a most rudimentary theology is practically quite as serviceable as the completest system of truth.

But, says one, if theology is not that by which individual Christians live ; if, on the contrary, the great majority of Christians have theological notions so defective that any attempt to live by them exclusively would do more harm than good, what is the use of theology at all ? And the answer to this question is, that the use of theology is to direct the administration of the Church.

So long as Christianity is looked upon as a purely individual thing, a converse of me by myself, and of you by yourself, with God in Christ, it is really not possible to make out for theology a sphere of genuine practical importance   For strictly individual religion, that growth in knowledge and spiritual wisdom which is got by pure practice without generalisation or system, seems adequate enough. But the moment we begin to contemplate Christianity as a social thing, as organised into a Church, we reach a point where inarticulate knowledge of divine truth breaks down.

Let us consider what sort of Christian society it is
possible to form, on the hypothesis that every member
has just that knowledge which is directly given in his
own personal religious experiences. Every society is
bound together by a common aim and common principles.
This society must be bound together by its common
Christianity. But the Christianity of each man presents
itself to him, on the hypothesis, only in the form of
strictly individual religious experiences and frames of
thought, so that the only bond of Christian union possible
is similarity of experience in details, identity of individual
frames and habits of mind. The society which arises
when men come together on this ground is a society of
the like - minded, all busy with their common religious
experiences. The principle of union goes no farther
than the similarity of experience. Two men, whose
Christian lives have run different courses, are, in proportion to the extent of this difference, debarred from
Christian fellowship We all recognise the description of
such a society. It is not the Church, but the conventicle,
the *ecclesiola in ecclesia*, the fellowship of separatists and
sectarians. It is a society which can never be catholic,
never a spiritual might, never permanent ; never catholic,
for its breadth of comprehension is limited by purely
individual accidents of Christian experience ; never a
spiritual might, for the attraction of homogeneous individuals means the repulsion of the heterogeneous ,
never permanent, for if it does not split up in the first
generation by the development of different types in the
farther experience of those who started from a common
point, it must at least fall to pieces in the next generation,
from the certainty that the children will not be like the
parents.

It appears, then, that the assertion that mere personal,
inarticulate knowledge serves all the necessities of
Christian growth, is necessarily bound up with another
assertion,—namely, that the whole growth of Christianity

on earth is simply the sum of the independent growths
of individuals; that Christian fellowship is not an
essential factor in Christian life, but merely an orna-
mental addition to that life,—a pleasure which the
believer enjoys when he falls in with men of like religious
tastes, not a Christian duty towards men even of unlike
tastes.   But all Christianity which has any pretence to
be catholic, not sectarian, proceeds on very different
principles, remembering that, according to the New
Testament, it is the Church as an organic unity that is
the object of God's electing love and of Christ's redeeming work, and that each member of the mystical
body of Christ grows up towards Him who is the Head
only in sympathy with the growth of the whole body.
On this view Christian fellowship is an essential thing;
and like all the essentials of Christianity it is a thing
which cannot be left to be secured by unconscious
agencies.   It is true that every believer is *ipso facto* a
member of the organic body of Christ.   But this membership is a moral, not a physical fact, and thus it is a supreme
Christian duty to give practical and conscious realisation
to the truth that growing union to Christ means fellowship in the united growth of all them that are His   The
Church, therefore, is a Divine ordinance, in which men of
all possible types of religion, and in every stage of spiritual
growth, are to come together on the broad ground of
professed faith in Christ and obedience to Him, and
unite in such common activities as shall give fit expression
to their unity and conduce to common edification.

There can be no difficulty in deciding the nature of
the common exercises in which the Church of Christ
expresses its conscious catholicity and seeks common
edification.   The fellowship of the Church is oneness in
fellowship with God in Christ; the growth of the Church
is increasing nearness to God of the life of the whole
society.   Thus the proper activity for which the Church
is visibly organised is just to sist itself before God in

visible oneness of faith, thanksgiving and prayer. Wherever the fellowship of believers is able to lay hold of the Gospel promise with common faith, to raise to God the voice of common thanksgiving, to unite with one mind in common confession and joint petitions , there the unity of all believers in Christ receives a fitting practical utterance, and the whole Church is edified together.

At first sight this appears a very simple thing, so simple that it may seem impossible that it should fail to be realised wherever there is true Christianity at all. But a glance at the present divided state of Christendom is enough to show that this is not so, and that the attainment of an object, apparently so easy, really requires Christian wisdom and Christian knowledge of no ordinary kind. However simple the elements of Christianity may be, their simplicity is that of a living germ, not of a mechanical complex, and they are, therefore, capable of development into an endless variety of distinct types of life and feeling. And because of the continued presence of sin and imperfection in the Church, not one of these types will be a pure type. All will err, both by unequal development of certain Christian motives to the neglect of others, and by the admixture of motives which are not Christian at all   Nor does this divergence between brethren in Christ end in the establishment of personal types not perfectly sympathetic. Personal differences become embodied in formulated opinions and definite courses of action, and so the unity of all believers is confronted with the sharp antagonism of parties

On the sectarian theory, at which we have already glanced, this state of things is accepted as inevitable. No attempt is made to give practical expression to the catholicity of the Church. The like-minded simply come together, and remain together as long as they can. The unlike-minded are suffered to depart, and, in the stricter forms of sectarianism, are even supposed to have no share in Christ. An opposite extreme characterises the

Broad Church It is observed that the divergent tendencies of Christians become fixed in the antagonism of parties only when allowed to take shape in explicit doctrines and courses of action It is suggested, therefore, that the catholicity of the Church may be secured by avoiding all such explicitness. Let it be understood that constructive theology, which has so long placed barriers between the Churches, has a purely speculative and individual interest. The bond of Christian love should be sufficient to secure unity among Christians, whatever their individual type may be This theory is so vague in all points that it is difficult to criticise it But it is obvious that no society can be organised simply on mutual love. Organised fellowship implies common interests, a common aim, some function in which the whole society visibly combines. In a word, the Church is not the fellowship of Christian love—which requires no unity of organisation—but the fellowship of Christian worship. The common worship of many individuals must be the expression in intelligible form of their common relation of faith towards God. We have already seen that all personal faith implies personal knowledge. The intelligent expression of faith, therefore, implies explicit and formulated knowledge Put face to face with this argument the Broad Church breaks at once into two camps. The one camp gives up the conception of the Church as the fellowship of worship, and proposes to have a national church simply as an instrument of national culture, a view essentially Socinian The other camp proposes either to omit everything from worship with which some may differ, or aims at a spirit of Christian charity which shall enable a man to be edified even by expressions of a faith which is not his own. On the first alternative, the Church must perish from inanition , on the second, worship becomes a mere sentimental enjoyment, and is no longer a real approach to God through Christ. But both the Sectarians and the Broad Church forget that church - fellowship has a moulding and up-building power on those who take part in it, that all believers are led by the one spirit of Christ, and that the unity of faith is stronger than the diversity of personal experience. It is not the shallowest and most jejune apprehension of Christianity which forms the basis for a worship truly Catholic. A full and all-sided development of Christian motives cannot fail to appeal to all true faith, if its fulness is not that of individual fancy, but of generalisation from the normal data of the Bible. Wheresoever the mind of Christ is set forth, there faith will be awakened and instructed. Men of diverse experience will not, indeed, lay hold with equal fulness and readiness on every aspect of Christian truth ; but a truth really Christian, when set forth in a devotional shape, will at length draw forth the sympathy of every child of God.

These considerations, I think, make it clear enough what the real problem of Church administration is, and in what direction its solution must be sought. The object to be attained is the practical expression of the catholic faith of the Church in acts of worship, in which the fellowship of believers unites to the praise of the glory of God in Christ. The faith that utters itself in such acts is necessarily articulate, otherwise there could be no conscious fellowship. If the articulate utterance of faith expresses only the personal experience of an individual, the like-minded alone are edified , if it avoids everything that is definite, no one is edified at all   But the extremes of sectarianism and the Broad Church may both be avoided if we observe that there is such a thing as a normal Christian faith, which is, in fact, the faith of the Church made perfect, and which has the power to draw all believers to it ; that whenever this normal faith is intellectually apprehended in all its bearings, and practically applied to the administration of every function of the Church, the Church has attained to catholicity, and that on this external unity cannot fail to follow. Thus the unity of the Church is not impracticable as the sectarians suppose—nor is it to be attained by compromise and mutual toleration on the principles of the Broad Church. Catholicity must be produced by the internal growth of the individual communions which actually exist, before it can be manifested in the disappearance of Church parties in an outward unity. The catholicity of an ecclesiastical communion means nothing else than that all its functions are so adjusted that in them every truly Christian impulse of the believing heart towards God finds utterance, and that every side of the gospel message is fully set forth to faith. And failures in catholicity are of two kinds : (1) failures lying in the direction of sectarianism—the admission into the constitution and worship of the Church of elements of local and temporary value, distinctive principles—political, national, or personal—which go beyond normal Christianity ; and (2) failures lying in the direction of the Broad Church, that is, the omission to make prominent genuine Christian motives which are capable of social expression. The Church is now imperfect and divided, because there is no communion which is free from defects in both these directions ; but every communion deserves the name of catholic only in proportion as it sets before it as the ideal aim of all Church administration to attain more and more fully to the expression in every social function of a full-grown, all-sided, and normal faith.

Thus the progress of the Church depends on the presence of two things—*first*, a vigorous theology, diligently engaged in bringing into clearer light all sides of Christian truth, giving to each Christian motive and belief its due prominence and right place in a comprehensive system, and placing in the light of this knowledge the present attainments of the Church. And with this must be conjoined in the *second* place a wise administra-

tion, by which every gain of insight into the ideal to
which the Church has to attain is duly applied in
government, discipline, and worship, so that the new
insight, which is in truth nothing more than the explicit
development of something involved in all true faith,
may now be consciously presented to the whole community, and find an answer in the hearts of all.

To recapitulate . The functions of the Church as the
society of public worship are imperfect, unless discharged
in a way corresponding to the ideal unity of the fellowship
of the Redeemed   Thus all Church worship must aim at
catholicity, and genuine catholicity is the principle that
must guide the whole government and administration of
the Church   But catholicity does not mean toleration
and compromise.   It means the gathering up of all aspects
of truly Christian converse with God into a unity of
devotional expression in which every believer can join.
This is an ideal remote from the present state of the
Churches   But it is an ideal that must at length be
realised.   For it is certain that a normal expression of
Christian faith has the power of appealing to every
believer, and of doing so, not in virtue of any abstractness
and hazy generality, but just in proportion to the fulness
with which it takes up everything that lies in the whole
compass of Christian truth   Such a normal statement of
Christian faith, rich in all Christian knowledge, but freed
from everything of human idiosyncrasy, is what every
communion that claims to be a branch of the Church
Catholic must seek to attain by theological research, and
to apply to the constant improvement of the practical
administration of Church functions.   A Church which
ceases to theologise ceases in the same moment to grow,
while conversely, from the constant action and reaction
that connect knowledge and practice in all moral
organisms, a Church whose life grows dull will also cease
to theologise aright.

And now let me, in conclusion, draw some practical

deductions as to the value of theology as a preparation for office in the Church.

When we say that every living Church must have a living theology we do not, in accordance with our argument, imply that every Church member must be familiar with the theology of the communion to which he belongs. On the contrary, our argument has been that a Church becomes capable of attracting and edifying *every* true Christian, whatever his stage of knowledge and growth may be, just in proportion as every act of public worship and every ecclesiastical function rests on full and normal theological attainments. Public worship is not a theological exercise in which men meet on the basis of common scientific knowledge , it is an exercise of common faith, in which the gospel message is personally set forth and received with personal affection and obedience. Thus no theology is required in order that a man may with edification join in the worship of the Church. Theology is the affair of him who conducts that worship, the system of knowledge by which he is enabled to lead the service, not as a man calling on the like - minded to sympathise with his own personal experience, but as one who, out of the riches of an all-sided grasp of the fulness of the gospel, can bring forth words of promise and admonition, words of thanksgiving and prayer, suited to every Christian need, and yet free from all individualism. And what is true of the central function of public worship, is true of every Church act. There is, indeed, no act of government or discipline in which Church rulers can deal with imperial authority, indifferent to the necessity of carrying with them the mind of the whole Church. But it is not necessary that each Church member should have the knowledge requisite to judge for himself from the first on all questions of administration. It is Church rulers that must use their special knowledge to solve each practical question ; but the question is not solved till the decision upon it is put into a form which, expressing the mind of Christ Himself, and so appealing directly even to uneducated faith, does carry with it the hearty sympathy of the faith of the whole Church.

Thus our principle assumes the practical shape that no Church act, whether of policy, discipline, or worship, can be rightly conducted except on the basis of a sound theology, and with such an application of theological principles as shall appeal to personal faith. The application of this rule demands a combination in the government of the Church of theological attainments with practical tact and sympathy with the untheological Christian, which is very fitly acknowledged in our Presbyterian system of Church Courts. But it is to be observed that Presbyterianism distinctly provides what there is now some inclination to forget, that no exercise of Church power shall take place, and no ordinance be administered, except under the presidency or with the active participation of men theologically trained. That is, the Presbyterian theory is strictly in accordance with the result of our argument, and is violated when a man who has not been duly recognised as adequately instructed in the theology of the Church takes upon him any such independent and individual piece of administration as the conducting of an ordinary diet of worship. The equality of the elder with the minister in acts of rule does not, in the sense of Presbyterianism, imply indifference to the position that every Church act must be theologically directed, but is the practical expression of the principle that theological knowledge is not rightly applied to practical questions, when it is not so applied as to carry the conviction of God-fearing and right-minded men who are not theologians.

Thus every candidate for the ministry who contemplates a sphere of life in which he shall be called to administer Church ordinances, to supply general principles of Christian knowledge for the whole internal administration of a congregation, and at the same time to take an

active part among the technically instructed members
of the higher courts, is looking forward to a life-work for
which the first and most indispensable qualification is a
sound and thorough knowledge of theology.   A minister
who is not a theologian may be a useful man in his parish
in the way in which an influential private Christian or a
good ruling elder is useful, but it is wholly impossible that
he can do well that work for which the Church places him
in ministerial office

The failure will be most striking and inevitable in the
pulpit, though perhaps it is just in the pulpit that such
men most readily imagine themselves strong.   Many, it is
to be feared, go forward to the ministry with the conviction that the necessary conditions of effective pulpit
work are not at all theological, but consist merely in
personal earnestness, combined with certain powers of
vigorous expression and a measure of literary culture.
It is thought that a congregation must be interested by
good expression and literary grace, in order that so they
may be edified by sympathy with the expression of the
minister's faith.   And so plausible does this view appear
to many that it is more than hinted that the ideal
divinity hall would be half a prayer-meeting and half a
school of rhetoric and style   But, in truth, rhetorical or
literary culture has just the same value to a minister as
to any other public man.   Purely literary interest is
wholly out of place in the pulpit, when it ceases to stand in
direct subordination to the devotional aim of the service.
It is no merit in a sermon that it is attractive to those who
have not come together with the single motive of common
edification in joint worship.   But the man who, when his
words are stripped of literary varnish, has nothing to offer
for the people's edification but sympathy with his own
faith, is not fit to be a minister.   It is the Bible which is
the true manual of a catholic religious life ; and the Bible,
not interpreted by that personal experience which only
culls stray flowers from its pages, but set forth through

diligent study in that many-sided fulness by which it supplies the Church's every need. That is no scriptural and no catholic knowledge in which the normal religious experience of the Old and New Testament is applied to the worship of the congregation only through the non-normal vehicle of uninspired experience. A man who handles God's Word thus may sometimes, if his piety is deep and his personality strong, become a great influence. He may even be instrumental in saving souls ; but, on the whole, his ministerial work will weaken the Church. Working always under the guidance of his own partial and impure religious life, he will carry with him the like-minded, and will fail to edify others. All men whose minds are not of a peculiar type will cease to be edified. The all-sided growth of the congregation, which depends mainly on the right and profitable administration of gospel ordinances, will sustain a grievous check. The few like-minded who retain some semblance of congregational vigour will grow more and more narrow and one-sided, being nourished, not on the sincere milk of the Word, but on so much thereof as the minister can himself assimilate ; and the usual marks of a sectarian develop-ment will appear in the alienation of the children of the congregation, whose places are taken by deserters from other churches. Of all the temptations to which the student of theology is exposed, there is none more insidious, and none more dangerous, than the temptation to excuse want of diligence in study by concentration on the qualification of personal piety. There is no path of Christian duty in which a man can walk unless he walks also near to God ; but, for this very reason, no advance in Christian life is in itself a qualification for one sphere of usefulness more than for another. Nay, a high degree of spirituality cannot be maintained by any man except in the discharge of duties for which he is properly qualified. The man, therefore, who seeks the office of the ministry in reliance on his personal piety and earnestness of purpose, will not only be deceived in his hopes of usefulness, but grievously perils his spiritual life. Personal piety is no call to the ministry, unless it is also a call to full and zealous preparation for the ministry.

If the central function of presidence in Gospel ordinances is entrusted by our Presbyterian system only to men theologically trained, the minister is associated in all other parts of his congregational work with untrained elders. But the minister who is supported by the Church in order that he may give his whole time to functions which the elders discharge voluntarily, manifestly lies under special responsibility in these duties also. In all congregational matters the minister is justly expected to take a leading part, not only in the amount of work he does, but in the way he does it. Yet it is absurd to expect that in natural talent, in Christian experience, in good sense and tact, the minister shall excel all his elders. Even that pre-eminence which comes of greater practice is not possessed by a young minister who is called to preside in a court of old and experienced men. What the Church reckons on in placing a young unpractised man in such a position is simply his theological training, his acquaintance with large views of truth, large principles of administration, deduced from the careful study of the Bible and the history of the Church. The minister who is really thus equipped will not fail to take the right place in his congregation, and to win corresponding respect ; for all men feel that he has a claim to preside in practical matters who is able to throw on them the light of general principles. But the minister who is not a theologian is nowhere weaker than in his own session or in the midst of his congregation. He has no principles of knowledge which can give him a wide grasp of administrative questions. He maintains, therefore, only that influence which is due to his purely personal qualities, or which he can assert by clerical pretentiousness—by claiming for his office, as an office, the respect which is due to the

22

right performance of its functions.   He becomes a leader
only to those weaker than himself, and the best office-
bearers, who should be his greatest helpers, either wholly
overshadow him or become objects of jealousy and centres
of party feeling.   There is no such source of congregational
divisions as an ignorant ministry.

It is hardly necessary to remark that the theology
which our argument contemplates as the proper preparation for congregational work does not mean such a
congeries of private speculations as some men pride
themselves upon. A theology useful for practical work
consists mainly (1) of Biblical knowledge, and (2) of a
grasp, both dogmatical and historical, of that system
based on the Bible which is embodied not only in the
constitution, but in the consciousness of the Church.
The man who is not prepared to discharge his functions
in the sense of the Church has no right to stand in the
ministry ; the pretension to subordinate the worship of a
congregation to personal conclusions of speculative
theology is in spirit sectarian, and must always be resisted by Church-government. An appreciative mastery
of the Church's present theology, with a recognition of its
positive value for practical work, is the true basis of
ministerial usefulness, and in congregational matters will
seldom fail to supply adequate guidance even to a man
destitute of theological originality. But the future of
our Church depends on the solution of problems not
purely congregational.

Every attentive student of the past history of Scottish
Presbyterianism, and especially of the last few years, must
admit that the larger problems that lie before a Church
which aims at visible catholicity, are not yet even
theoretically solved—that they remain problems partly
because our higher Church courts are not sufficiently
skilled in the practical application of our present theological ideas, but partly also because these ideas themselves
are on many points too unclear and defective to serve

present needs. The history of late events has shown that even those branches of the Scottish Church which have freed themselves from the hampering tutelage of the State still fall short, not only in knowledge of one another, but in clear comprehension of their own principles.

The fusion of separate communions has proved impossible, mainly because of the lack of true unity in our own Church ; because with much brotherliness of spirit, and much common zeal for the advancement of Christ's cause, there is not that clear oneness of Church consciousness which it is the object of a growing theology to supply. The problem of advance in visible catholicity remains unsolved, partly because a sound doctrinal and historical appreciation of the present theology of the Church in its relation to present needs is not diffused throughout the ministry, or even among leaders in our ecclesiastical courts, and partly because theology has not yet spoken any decisive and convincing word on the questions of the day ; because during two hundred years of Church life there has been hardly any marked advance in the Church's systematic knowledge.

It is plain that the supply of these two defects must go hand in hand. Only by diffusing through the whole ministry a higher ideal of theological attainments, a greater aptitude for theological reasoning, a fuller understanding of the historical personality of the Church, can we ensure that those men shall come to the front who are able to deal with practical questions in a way truly catholic , and that when the right solution of a problem is set forth, its adequacy shall be generally realised.

Unquestionably this is the first step to the removal of present evils. No novel speculations, no new theological lights, can save a Church which has not learned thoroughly to understand and appreciate her present constitution. But withal it must be remembered that the theological consciousness of the Church requires not only to be awakened, but to be guided forward to higher conceptions of the truth The doctrine of theological finality can never be accepted, save in a Church very ignorant of her own principles, or very indifferent to their practical application. It is not well that long years of bitter conflict should be necessary to produce the conviction, that on one very secondary point of doctrine and constitution, our theology has not yet reached completeness. On the basis of a thorough knowledge of what has been already obtained, it is the constant business of the Church, in knowledge as in practice, to reach on to more perfection. And this must be sought, not only by the private labours of individuals, but by the organised effort of the Church as a whole to increase her provision for the acquisition and the advance of sound science. That Church is not wise which grudges to spend her best wisdom, her ablest men, her richest means, on the twofold task of theological research and theological instruction.

II

ON PROPHECY

I INTRODUCTORY

GENTLEMEN,—The subject which I propose to take up
in the course of lectures which we enter upon to-day is
Old Testament prophecy. I will not trouble you with
any lengthened exposition of the plan upon which I design
to treat the subject , but it may be well to point out at
once what the main interests are by which our discussion
must be guided. In the first place, it must be our concern
to comprehend prophecy as a *fact of history*, as an element
which for many centuries was inwoven in the living
tissue of the life of the Old Testament people. In every
great crisis of Israel's history the prophets bore a part.
Their influence was always great, and often decisive
even, in shaping the external course of the history, while
no force of nearly equal importance operated on the
internal development of the people. And by this last
expression I do not wish merely to imply that prophecy
took a chief part in the development of the Old Testament
religion. That, indeed, is true, but it is not the whole
truth and not, to the historian, even the most striking
part of the truth. The remarkable thing about the
influence of the prophets on the inner life of Israel is that
they ultimately succeeded in moulding the whole national
life to a shape directly dependent on the religious ideas
of which they were the representatives. I say " ulti-

341

mately "—for the time when the national life directly
accepted the guidance of the prophetic ideas as paramount
in all its interests was not the time of Moses or of Samuel,
or even of Josiah, but the time of the great leaders of
the nation after the Captivity.   That at this period some
of the prophetic ideas had already lost their freshness
and were misunderstood by those who applied them,
does not affect the truth of our statement.   Rightly or
wrongly comprehended, the prophetic teaching furnished
from this time onwards the fountain-head from which
everything characteristic in the intellectual, moral,
spiritual, social life of the people flowed.   I must not at
present go into details on this topic.   The truth and
the importance of what I have just said will appear in
the course of these lectures.   In the meantime I simply
ask you to remember that it will be one main part of our
business during the Session to attain a proper conception
of the part which prophecy played in the history of Israel,
and to comprehend how each prophet's actions, teaching
and writings stood in a living relation to the historical,
circumstances of his own time, and exercised a living
influence, first on his own contemporaries and then upon
those who came after.   In order to do this it will be
necessary for us to follow step by step the historical
sequence of the prophets, and to interweave with our
account of the prophetic *diadoche* a more or less continuous sketch of the main epochs of Hebrew history.

When I say that our first concern will be to understand prophecy as a factor in the Old Testament history,
you must not imagine that I forget that the interest which
must dominate all our studies in this hall is not historical,
but theological.   To the Christian theologian Old Testament prophecy has more than an historical interest.
To us the prophets are not merely the leaders of the
religious life of Israel and the guides of the nation in all
its highest attainments ; they are men who bore on their
lips the word of the only true God, a word that endureth

for ever, and which is God's Word to us now as it was of old to Israel

In the view of some theologians this highest aspect of the significance of prophecy entirely overshadows all historical interest which may attach to the subject. The inspiration of the prophets appears to them not merely as the most cardinal fact which we can have before us in studying their work and writings, but as a fact so infinitely important that all human and historical aspects of the matter are vanishing quantities in comparison. The necessity for any critical enquiry into the history of prophecy, and for any attempt to trace the evolution of prophetical ideas, is held to be superseded, and even to be rendered frivolous or profane by the paramount consideration that what the prophets did and wrote they did as organs of Divine Revelation. Every endeavour to understand the prophets as men and to fit their work into the general development of the national life of Israel, with reference to the general laws of human history, is supposed to involve some measure of indifference or incredulity as respects the divine character of their mission and equipment.

This view is nowadays at least not often put forth in express terms by writers who profess to speak as scientific theologians. But it is still the view which lies at the bottom of a great part of current exegesis of the prophecies, including the whole of the pseudo-apocalyptic speculation which is still so fashionable in many circles. And on those who have too much sense for the vagaries of this school the unhistorical view of prophecy has at least a negative influence, leading them to pass by as altogether unintelligible many parts of the prophetic Scriptures which become luminous as soon as we apply to them the historical method of enquiry. That is, if we take up any chapter of the prophecies at random, the unhistorical method begins by saying . These are words of inspiration, let us try to find a lesson for us in each of them.

But perhaps the passage is such a one as the prophecy against Moab in Isaiah xv., xvi Here we have the picture of a hostile invasion sweeping over Moab The Moabites flee southward and apply for protection to the king of Judah But he remains loyal to his obligations of loyalty to the Israelites of the North, the old enemies of Moab, and refuses to trust the promises of the treacherous Moabites, whose destruction is thus rendered inevitable and the powerlessness of their false gods manifested Looked at in an unhistorical manner a prophecy like this is very puzzling unless unlimited freedom is given to an arbitrary typology only one or two minor points attract the expositor, and these have no individuality to give the prophecy special importance. The powerlessness of Moab's religion, for example, which appears to be the main lesson, is a lesson which runs through the whole Old Testament with a reiteration certainly not needed to impress upon the modern reader the vanity of polytheism.

Accordingly those who are not disposed to treat Moab as a type—in which case, by the way, the prophecy again loses all individuality and becomes one of a hundred typical expressions of the ultimate fall of the Kingdom of the World—or who are not disposed to find arbitrary references to modern events ; those, I say, who are too sober for such exegesis and who yet value prophecy only as an inspired lesson spoken directly to *us, now,* will be able to make nothing of these chapters except as a part of the evidence of prophecy, as one of many marvellous predictions confirming the reality of Revelation. And here the difficulty arises that we have no proof that the prophecy was ever fulfilled to the letter. Or, rather, we are tolerably certain that it never was so fulfilled. Such is a very simple example of the hopelessness of any study of the prophecies which ignores the necessity of basing all theological use of these parts of the Old Testament on an historical study of the meaning

of prophecy as a whole   It would, of course, be premature
to take up at this stage the historical exposition of these
chapters of Isaiah.   But it may be advantageous to
say a few words in general on the way in which we shall
be able to rise from an historical view of prophecy to considerations confirming the Divine authority of the Old
Testament revelation, and enabling us to apprehend in
a living manner the abiding significance of the prophetic
word for the New Testament dispensation.

There are two aspects of prophecy which we must
bring together, trying if possible to understand the one
through the other.   On the one hand the history of
prophecy is part of the history of Israel,—of a history,
that is, which is limited to a single nation and which
is in great measure concerned with matters of local
and temporary interest.   These limitations have left
their mark on the whole history and work of the prophets
Like all men who have left their names in the record of
human events, they were formed by circumstances   They
were the children of their country and of their age.   All
that they did and said was conditioned by their historical
surroundings.   Their inspiration itself was limited by
the law that supernatural revelation never breaks the
historical continuity of man's free agency and man's
responsibility.   They were not so raised above their fellow-
countrymen that they ceased to be Israelites, thinking
and feeling like those around them, and having their
own share of concern, and that not merely as men, but
as prophets, in all the questions of their own time, however local, temporary, and insignificant these may seem
to us.   On the other hand, these same prophets form
part of the chain of the history of Revelation, and
their words are part of that progressive series of Divine
Self-manifestations which culminated in the manifestation
of Christ and in the bringing in of a salvation which is
free from all national limitations, from all local and
temporary colouring.

The difficulty of bringing these two aspects of prophecy under a single point of view cannot be conquered by merely shutting our eyes to the lower and transitory elements in the phenomena of prophecy, and spiritualising everything that does not fit at once into the Christian scheme. For, be it observed, the difficulty about prophecy is part of a larger problem. The real difficulty lies not in any one institution of the Old Testament, but in the fact that the Christian dispensation was preceded by an Old Testament dispensation at all. Let individual limitations be spiritualised away as far as you please, it will still be true that the Old Testament dispensation as such is full of national, local, temporary interests. It will still be true that it was the history of a single nation that led up to the manifestation of Christ. Unless we are prepared to throw away the Old Testament altogether, and to say with ancient and modern Gnostics that the God of the Jews is not the God of Christians, we must face the fact that from Moses to Christ all knowledge of the true God and of His plan of Salvation was encased in local, national, temporary, earthly forms. The limitations of prophecy are the historical limitations of the whole dispensation, and from these limitations prophecy could not have been freed without ceasing to be *Old Testament* prophecy at all.

Now the limitations of a dispensation of God's grace must always be sought on the side of man, not on the side of God, who is without limitation or mutability. If an imperfect dispensation preceded Christianity, the meaning of this is that God accommodated His work of revelation and grace to the laws of limited human nature, that He unfolded His plan under the conditions of historical progress. The nexus of the successive steps in the development must be explained not with reference to Divine omnipotence, which need not have been tied to a gradual process at all; but with reference to the incapacity of man to receive spiritual truth except gradually, partially, and under forms which interpreted it in its bearings on his actual historical position and needs. We cannot understand the Old Testament dispensation, either in its own internal unity or in its unity with the New Testament, except in this way of always looking at each step in the development for a human continuity whereby the new advance in the carrying out of God's plan of Revelation and redemption fits into the general progress of history.

What is true in general must be true in the special case of prophecy which was the main agency by which God carried on His work in Israel, and led up to Christ. The limitations of prophecy in general correspond to the imperfection of the Old Covenant, which again expresses the impossibility of bringing men to understand the fulness of God's saving purpose otherwise than by a gradual training process extended through many centuries. And the particular limitations in prophecy, the local, temporary, earthly colouring of individual parts of the prophetic teaching, correspond to special features of limitation in the Old Testament history, and can be rightly appreciated only by the man who has learned to fit the whole series of the prophets into their proper historical setting. But as we learn to understand the work of the prophets in its historical connection we shall learn also to see how that work everywhere displays a Divine unity manifesting itself through the historical and variable circumstances which mould its temporary form. The progress of the Old Testament history is not a blind sequence of cause and effect, but a progress towards an end revealed in Christ. The whole Old Testament worked to prepare for Christ. And it did not work blindly. Paganism, too, was a preparation for Christ, but an unconscious preparation without any glimpse of the future for which it was the providentially appointed past. But the Old Testament development was never unconscious of its own significance. No prophet saw the fulness of the glory of Christ ; but every prophet looked in the right direction, looked toward that glory, and saw more or less clearly some of the great lines in which the Kingdom of God must move forward. That is the true significance of prophecy. It always pointed Israel and the Old Testament dispensation towards an end which in its realisation lost the idea of the nation in that of the Universal Kingdom of God, and swallowed up the Old Testament in the New. It is in this, and not in individual predictions, that the supernatural inspiration of the prophets is clearly seen. The immediate sphere of their labours might be in some petty corner of national life. Their immediate concern might be about some treaty with Egypt, some war with Edom, some matter which in its details was of the most transient importance. But in the smallest matter they held to ideas which were wide in their scope and distant in their range. They taught the people to look at everything in the light of God's work and God's purpose And that purpose was gradually made clearer and clearer to them till at length when Christ came He could look to the prophets for a declaration, unmistakable though undeveloped, of every part of His work and every characteristic of His Kingdom.

To make out clearly this most wondrous characteristic of prophecy, to show how all prophecy tends in one direction, how through all the multiplicity of historical circumstances it works ever consciously to one great end, will be the second great aim of our winter's work We shall try as we trace the prophetic succession through its work in Israel's history, to trace at the same time the marvellous way in which the prophets reached with ever-increasing clearness and fulness of view out beyond their own times and their own dispensation towards the new things of Christ and His spiritual kingdom. But these Messianic hopes we must always seek to comprehend in their connection with the circumstances and needs of the prophet's own time. No prophecy can be mechanically

divided into a part which has only historical value and a
part which is ideal truth. The highest previsions of the
prophet are inextricably intertwined with the narrowest
limitations of his historical standpoint ; and if we lose
hold of the one side we shall never be able to apprehend
the other.

These remarks are of necessity very fragmentary, and
I fear in some parts obscure. The ideas on which I have
touched will come up from time to time, and will, I hope,
be clearer when they occur in more concrete shape in connection with the actual history of prophecy. To this
history we must now turn.

I Was the Prophetic Inspiration Supernatural?

In carrying out in further detail our inquiry into the
prophetic inspiration, several courses may suggest themselves to us. In the first place, we may follow either a
purely inductive or a constructive method. The inductive method will simply take note of the result which
we have already reached—the fact that no other religion
presents phenomena strictly parallel to the self-consciousness of the prophets of Israel   It will then endeavour to
describe the phenomena of Hebrew prophecy as fully as
possible without, in the first instance, assuming that they
are necessarily supernatural   Having got the phenomena
arranged, it will then begin to ask what the phenomena
involve, and will either seek a natural explanation for
them, or, failing to find any natural explanation, will
infer with more or less confidence the reality of a special
divine power in the prophets.

If such a rigorous investigation could really be applied
in all strictness and carried through to a successful conclusion, there is no doubt that it would prove most
valuable. It may, however, be doubted whether in the
nature of things any purely religious fact falls within the
range of strict induction   The facts of religion are transcendental ; they involve the possibility and reality of

relations between God and man which rise quite above the region of phenomena, *i.e.* which cannot be defined in place and time   Let me illustrate this by a slight digression, and call your attention for a moment to certain religious facts of unquestionable reality, which are still transacted in our midst, and which yet refuse to be measured by any phenomenal standpoint. Take the great fact of *conversion*. An inductive study of religious phenomena will no doubt reach a valuable negative conclusion on this head. It will be possible to show that no mere empirical psychology has solved the question. The phenomena are of a kind which baffle the psychologist. But for this very reason the psychologist cannot prove by his inductive processes that conversion is the work of God's spirit. He cannot even discover definite empirical marks by which to recognise and identify cases of true conversion. Certain schools of religion you know have tried to do this—notably by the aid of a theory which began with Ignatius Loyola, and, passing from the Jesuits to Wesley, has formed the corner-stone of modern as distinguished from true protestant Evangelicalism.

According to this theory, conversion can be localised in time and place by certain psychical phenomena that accompany it—*e.g.* (to accept the careful analysis given by Loyola, *Ex. Spir.* Hebd ii , *ad fin* , " Of choosings "), when all doubt, or even power of doubting, is removed from the mind so that it cannot but follow the impulse to choose Christ, or when there is a clear persuasion of the divine decree for salvation, or finally, when the choice of a certain course of life as a means to salvation is made with a perfect tranquillity of mind, the soul being agitated by no contending blasts.

Such is the empirical theory of conversion ; but it always breaks down before two classes of facts : (1) the certainty that such experiences may be deceptive, and that they may be produced by merely natural means. (This experience, of course, does not puzzle Roman

Catholics, who have no doctrine of assurance apart from
use of sacraments with their *opus operatum*).   (2) Because there are truly converted men who have never
passed through such experiences — whose conversion
being, as it is, a purely transcendental transaction with
God has never been manifested in a definite time and
place.   Here, then, is an instance of a transcendental
religious reality surpassing induction—as in fact all true
cognition of God, so far as it becomes a personal thing,
and all true personal knowledge, even of our fellow-men,
is above inductive science.   The well-known scepticism
of Hume shows how no inductive philosophy can prove
the existence of *persons* and personal relations.   If
prophecy, then, is by its own profession one phase of the
personal fellowship of God with man, we must expect
that it also will be found to transcend induction.

And so, as a matter of fact, the opponents of Revelation,
whose main victories have always been gained by getting
leave to set questions in their own way, have found it to
their advantage to take up a purely inductive method
of investigating into prophecy.   They first take up the
form of prophetic inspiration, and show that dreams,
visions, ecstasies, are not necessarily supernatural occurrences   They then proceed (I follow the argument as it
is worked out by Kuenen, *Profeten*, i. p. 105 *sq.*) to ask
whether we can simply accept the testimony of the
prophets when they express to us their own conviction
of their divine inspiration.   The modern rationalism of
Kuenen does not attempt to invalidate the self-witness of
the prophets by casting any doubt upon their honesty.
But it urges that the dilemma, " sent by God or else
deceivers," is superficial, and cannot be applied to any
ancient religion.   We must, says Kuenen, take the
prophetic word itself and find some test of its supernatural
character.

The only test of an empirical character which can be
applied is then assumed to be the fulfilment of prophetic

prediction. The lofty character of the moral and religious doctrine of the prophets is not (says Kuenen) a specific mark of supernatural origin. The Old Testament literature may be proved to be loftier in point of faith and ethics than any other ancient writings, but such a difference in degree will not constitute a difference of kind. Therefore, says Kuenen, we will, with the consent of the supernatural-ists themselves, take the predictions as our touch-stone. Well, he analyses a vast mass of predictions, and shows that many of them, referring partly to Israel, partly to other nations, have not been fulfilled ; of course, since the proposed test is empirical, he means not literally fulfilled Next, he tries to show that the fulfilled predictions are not conclusive for the supernaturalistic view, while the unfulfilled ones absolutely exclude it How, then, shall we explain the fact that the prophets claim to speak the Word of Jahveh ? The explanation lies in the fact, that the Word so spoken consists of inferences from the moral character of Jahveh. The predictions flowed from religious conviction This source of the prophetic word is the characteristic of true prophecy,—*earnestness and warmth of religious and moral conviction*, that is the main point. That is what constitutes the true prophet, for that is what accounts for the courage and freedom with which he appears as the interpreter of Jahveh. The rank of each prophet is to be measured by the degree of inwardness and purity which we ascribe to his religious faith. In vain do we seek another criterion (ii 103).

I give here the mere outline of Kuenen's method. For our present purpose it is really not worth while to ask whether there are not flaws in the details of his argument, whether he has treated individual predictions fairly, and so forth If we did go into details, we should no doubt have to differ from him on many points, as we have already found him in error on so notable a point as the question of the uniqueness of the prophetic con-sciousness. But grant the justice of his method of

inquiry, and he can afford to be convicted of errors of
detail.

Allow him to start from the position that a purely
phenomenal and empirical measure is to be applied to
prophecy—that prophecy is to be measured by prediction,
and that prediction is to be tested on the letter of its
details, and the game is in his hands. But is this fair ?
What Kuenen says is, " I cannot admit that this is in a
special sense the word of God, unless you prove that it
told things, within the region of empirical verification,
which could not have been got at by human foresight."
But, according to the prophets' own account of the matter,
God's word has for its function to keep Israel in sympathy
—not with empirical facts, but with God's transcendental
plan and purpose. If it really discharged this function—
if it really enabled men to walk with God in a personal
fellowship of faith and love, and gave them so much
insight into His purposes as was needful at each moment
to cast light upon their path—if, as Isaiah puts it, the
prophets and those who hearkened to their word really
heard a word behind them saying, " This is the way, walk
ye in it," when they turned to the right hand or to the left
—then surely the prophets were right in saying that the
word was not theirs, but God's.

When the matter is put in this way, the question of
prediction and fulfilment does not cease to be important,
but it is no longer possible to treat it in the bare empirical
fashion proposed by Kuenen. On the one hand it is
perfectly conceivable that we might have the most
remarkable prediction of details verified in the most
literal way by subsequent events, and yet that in this
prediction we might receive *no* revelation of the heart and
purpose of God which should have the slightest religious
value, and therefore no real prophecy. Suppose that Dr.
Slade, when brought into the London police court, had
offered to prove his supernatural mission by telling the
price at which Russian stocks would be quoted on the day

23

when the Turkish conference broke up   The verification
of this prediction in the event would not have proved him
a true prophet.   It might prove him to be an accurate
diviner, but the thing would have no religious value.   It
would not bring God nearer to man, or in any sense
confirm to us the reality of a divine purpose and guidance
in human history.   Though every prediction in Zadkiel's
Almanac for 1877 were fulfilled to the letter, Christianity
would remain precisely where it is.   We might have
something to wonder at, but we should not have any
right to welcome a new revelation from God.   On the
other hand, it is very possible that a prophet might have
a real message from God to men, enabling men to act
under an intelligent comprehension of his guidance and
purpose, and yet that the outcome of that guidance and
purpose might take a shape not literally described beforehand by the prophet.   Why should we expect prophecy
to be a " history of future events," when we never think
of taking it as the test of the reality of the confidence
which a fellow-man reposes in us that he shall tell us
beforehand with literal precision the exact actions which
he is about to perform ?   The man would be deceiving us
if, while pretending to make us his confidants, he did not
open up to us his *heart*, the way in which he views things
and in which his action is to depend upon them ; but that
is a different matter from saying that he is to give us
beforehand an exact picture of all that he is going to do.
Of course the case of divine Revelation differs from cases
of ordinary human intercourse, inasmuch as God, unlike
man, foresees the exact turn of every event even of such
as depend on human freedom.   But then, if prophecy is
not to neutralise human freedom and destroy moral
responsibility, it is impossible for all that lies in omniscience
to be revealed to us.   *How* much of the future God is to
reveal to the prophet, and what limitations of form are
to apply to the revelation is a question which depends on
a variety of considerations which cannot be rightly

weighed until we rise above the empirical standpoint and look at the details of the question in the light of the ideal design of prophecy as the expression of a personal and confidential fellowship of God with His people. The question of the fulfilment of prophecy is not the *first* question to be taken up in dealing with prophetic inspiration, but the last. Instead of forming our ideal of prophecy from the empirical facts, let us remember that the empirical details are only intelligible in the light of the *idea* of prophecy.

In fact, this whole argument of Kuenen is closely analogous to the argument which certain men of science lately sought to apply to the subject of prayer. You remember that it was proposed to test the efficacy of prayer by a series of experiments on selected patients in an hospital. The answer to such a proposal is, of course, that the very idea of prayer excludes such experiment. Prayer in the name of Christ is the expression of that fellowship with the Father into which we enter through the redeeming work of Christ. We present our requests to God for temporal as well as spiritual blessings, because we believe that all our interests, of body as well as of soul, are of consequence to God, that He is willing to take account of them, and invites us to seek His help in them. But we have no right to determine the form which His interest and help shall take It is not because we receive literal answers to detailed petitions that we believe in the efficacy of individual petitions, but because, living in the *constant* exercise of a prayerful trust in Him, we find our whole lives ordered by His grace, and are enabled to trace His good hand upon us in every crisis of our needs. The most certain answers to prayer are often not those in which God's help comes just in the form in which we asked it, but those in which God answers the spirit of our prayer by denying the letter of it. Such answers cannot be measured and numbered by inductive science. They are addressed to the spiritual nature of the renewed man, even when they refer to his bodily and temporal needs, and they are understood only by the interpretation of His own spirit in our hearts.

The case of prophecy is quite of the same kind. The fulfilment of prophecy means that the actual history of God's redeeming work has corresponded with the spirit of prophecy—that by His revealing word God really taught His people what to look for and what to pray for. That the hopes and prayers of the Old Testament Church have in Christianity often been fulfilled in a form and in concrete details which the prophets never thought of, and could not even have conceived under the limitations of the Old Testament standpoint, is a matter of no moment if the fulfilment is spiritually adequate. But spiritual adequacy is not to be measured by an empirical analysis, in the manner of Kuenen, of all fulfilled and unfulfilled prophecy.

I cannot at this stage of our inquiries go more fully into the question of the *principle* on which prophecy is fulfilled. But it may be well to come to close quarters with Kuenen's method on one or two special features which it contains.

In the first place, I have to dispose of an objection. It will be argued that the Old Testament itself accepts Kuenen's test of the reality of supernatural prophecy. In Deut. xviii. 21 we read "If thou say in thy heart, How can we know the word which Jahveh hath not spoken? When a prophet speaks in Jahveh's name, if the thing follow not, nor come to pass, that is the word which Jahveh hath not spoken, the prophet hath spoken presumptuously, בְּזָדוֹן, Thou shalt not be afraid of him." But here you are to observe · (1) that the fulfilment of the individual prophetic word is not here taken as the matter by which the existence or non-existence of truly supernatural prophecy is to stand or fall, but as a practical test by which, the reality of true prophecy being assumed, the divine commission of an individual prophet may be

tested. Kuenen asks, How shall I know whether Jahveh
speaks to men by prophets ? The question in Deut.
is only, How shall I know the word which Jahveh hath
spoken ? Accordingly the application of the Deuteronomic test will be conditioned by a variety of considerations, derived in each individual case from the general
theory of prophecy. These will determine the measure
and nature of the fulfilment which it is fair to expect.

(2) Again, it is clear from the nature of the case that
this practical test does not cover all possible cases. It is
at best a negative test ; for in chapter xiii. 1-5 we read
that even though a prophet produces in support of his
divine commission an אות או מופת which actually comes
to pass, this shall go for nothing if his teaching is
directed to withdraw the people from Jahveh

(3) And, once more, it is clear that in many cases the
effect of the prophetic word would be wholly lost if no
heed were given to it until it had been verified in the
event. So the Deuteronomic test would stultify prophecy
altogether if it were raised to the rank of a universal rule.
It is only a subsidiary test which may be applied in cases
where the self-evidencing power of the prophetic word
is not conclusive. As a matter of fact we do not find that
it was customary for all prophets to confirm their commission by a fulfilled prediction , and strictly viewed the
passage does not require any such thing. It is purely a
negative rule, and necessarily of occasional application
merely. So we find that Jeremiah applies it in the case
of Hananiah only because the prophecy of peace given
by the latter was in its own nature suspicious. In this
case of special conflict between true and false prophecy God
did give to Jeremiah (Jer xxviii.) a special evidence that
he was the true prophet by enabling him to predict the
death of Hananiah within the year. But this was clearly
a special case which must not be extended to a general
rule. Contrast the quite different line taken by Isaiah
and Micah against the diviners, Isa. viii. 19, Micah iii 5-8,

where the appeal is to the moral evidence of true prophecy

It is proper to observe in connection with Kuenen's method that, while he regards the literal fulfilment of prediction as the proper test of the supernatural character of prophecy, he is very far from supposing that the importance and value of prophecy stands or falls by the result of this inquiry. He would have us to believe that the prophets are quite wrong in supposing that they possessed in any special sense a word from Jahveh. They were not specifically different from other seers. What they call the word of Jahveh and regard as an objective communication from Him, is simply an inference drawn from their subjective belief as to the unity, spirituality, and ethical character of God. But this does not make their work the less important. Their religious convictions were very earnest and very noble. They had reached the idea of *spiritual monotheism*, and they left that idea as a legacy to the world. Professor Kuenen is not very communicative as to the way in which they reached that idea—whether they thought it out by a process of reasoning, so that they were, in fact, a kind of philosophers, or whether they seized it by a peculiar faculty of religious intuition But be it reasoning or intuition, their reasonings and insight were juster than those of other ancient nations and formed an important step in the religious development of mankind.

Now, one is apt to suppose that if the prophets were really inspired their inspiration must display itself most clearly in the thoughts and convictions which gave to their work its world-wide importance. If the predictions are for the most part inferences which the prophets drew from their religious convictions, the true question for us to decide is, whether these religious convictions were, or were not, given to the prophets by a special divine influence. If, after all, the predictions form a small part of the prophetic writings, if they are secondary in impoitance, and if, as Kuenen, like other scholars, admits, the prophets themselves are fully alive to the fact that there is a conditional element, at least in many predictions, it is certainly curious logic to take these predictions *first*, and to settle the question *natural* or supernatural off-hand with reference to them alone, and without first ascending to the really central facts of prophecy.   Kuenen seems to feel this, for in chapter ix he makes some remarks by way of showing (1) that conditional prediction is a thing inconsistent with inspiration, and (2) that the prophetic conception of Jahveh is itself not free from error, and therefore cannot be viewed as of other than human origin   But what he says on these two vastly important questions falls far short of a full discussion, and need not long detain us.   The notion of conditional prediction is one which must be separately discussed, but for our present purpose it may be briefly stated thus   God's purpose of grace towards man is absolute and must move on to sure accomplishment.   But it is to be accomplished not mechanically upon man, but ethically in the hearts of men, by a spiritual process   Two important means used in this spiritual process are promises to the obedient, threats to the rebellious.   God gives His prophets these promises and threats to address to the people, and, of course, gives them in a form applicable to the times then present.   The promises to Israel take the form of blessings which the nation at the time needed and could appreciate, of such blessings as belonged to the Old Testament dispensation.   But the people's sins often deferred the fulfilment of these promises—deferred them, not cancelled them—for God will assuredly conduct His people to final felicity.   But, of course, as time moves on, as the church emerges from the childhood of the Old Testament to the full-grown manhood of Christianity, it would be no longer fitting to give an Old Testament fulfilment to the deferred promises.   The promise will be fulfilled, but in a better, a spiritual form.   Of course, I do not now ask how much of

the Old Testament prediction is covered by this principle
and by the allied principle—clearly recognised in Jer. xxvi.
as a thing fully understood by the Hebrews themselves—
that repentance may avert predicted judgment   But the
principle at least seems clear.   Prediction is not *mechanical*
but *ethical*, and is not meant to destroy but to direct
human freedom.   Now all that Kuenen has to say to this
is, that the theory sacrifices the *omnipotence and prescience
of God*, and that the prophets were themselves convinced
" both of Jahveh's immutability and of man's powerlessness to determine the course of the government of the
world" (E.T. p. 335 [1877])   Here we begin to see that
Dr. Kuenen's method is not so purely inductive and free
from *a priori* presuppositions as it appeared at first sight
to be.   For observe that it is an essential feature in the
theory of conditional prediction that God's purpose is
ultimately fulfilled, that His grace does in the long run
prevail over man's sin and backsliding.   So when Dr.
Kuenen ignores this point (he does not even mention
it), and says that the theory (which, be it observed, is
due to the prophets themselves) is inconsistent with the
divine perfection, and makes Him responsible for what is
really mere ebb and flow in the temper of the prophet
himself (pp. 314, 315), it is plain that his conception of
the divine purpose is pantheistic in tendency—fatalistic,
not ethical   He wishes to banish from God's dealings
with man not only all that is anthropopathic but all that
is anthropomorphic.   God's purpose must not only be
absolute in its aim, but rigidly mechanical in its execution.
It is to be wrought out in human history, but God must
not take man by the hand and adapt His language to man's
weakness as a father speaking with a child.   Individual
personal dealing of God with His people is what Kuenen
really excludes when he says that conditional promises
and threats are unworthy of divine omnipotence and
omniscience   In this he does not stand alone.   He
speaks the philosophy of his whole school   In Germany

and in Holland alike, the characteristic feature of the so-called *organic* view of the development of religion is not critical research, but pantheistic presupposition   And now a word upon his statement that "the prophets' conception of the righteousness of Jahveh deserves respect for its earnestness, but cannot be accepted as *truth* " (p. 354)   The prophets, says Kuenen, assume that in the case of individuals, or at least of nations, outward fortune is determined by moral condition.   And this, he says, is contrary to all experience.   Now, in the first place the prophets certainly teach that Divine retribution is tempered by mercy and the purpose of grace ; and, in the second place, though they have not the full New Testament doctrine of fatherly chastisement, they at least know —as comes out so clearly in the last chapter of Micah— that the judgments sent on the godly differ from those sent on the ungodly, not by a mere mechanical proportioning of the punishment to the offence but by the fact that the former have a gracious purpose and operation, so that they can be humbly accepted as consistent with God's love   Grant these two limitations to the doctrine of retribution, and it is not so plain that the doctrine is inconsistent with experience.   Or, rather, here again we come into a region that transcends mere outer experience ; we come to deal with quantities that have a spiritual meaning   The divine righteousness appears as perfect, not when it is regarded as a mechanical *lex talionis* but when each external dispensation is read as a revelation of the heart of God.   The same judgment may have a very different meaning and value to different men, or to Israel and to the heathen, and this the prophets well knew. But, thus understood and interpreted, God's righteousness *must* be the law of the Universe if there is a God at all. And it is impossible for religion to put this conviction too strongly.   The prophets do put it as strongly as possible, but to fail to do so would have been to give up faith in God.   The limitation of their standpoint, their difference

from the New Testament, is that they give body to this
faith in the forms of the Old Testament dispensation—in
earthly forms which are inadequate and which have fallen
away.   They always speak of God's righteousness as
finally manifested in the land of Canaan   And they could
not do otherwise, because God had not revealed to them
the inadequacy of the national covenant of Israel as the
sphere for the final realisation of His purpose.   But how
does this limitation affect the truth that it was from God
Himself that they derived the knowledge of His righteousness and grace which they rendered articulate by expressing it under these forms ?

It appears, then, that the arguments on which Kuenen
relies to disprove the supernatural inspiration of the
prophets are only valid against a purely mechanical
doctrine of revelation.   It is plain that the revelation
given to the prophets had limitations.   But these limitations are of a kind inseparable from the conception of a
truly *ethical* dealing of God with men   Now this we
know is the conception on which the prophets themselves
found.   We find that prophecy is represented in the Old
Testament itself as the realisation of God's personal
guiding presence to His people.   God receives the prophet
into personal confidence with Himself, dealing with him,
and with the people through him, on the analogy of
human intercourse.   The very idea of such converse
implies that in the prophetic word something of the full
splendour of God's absolute knowledge is veiled.   The
prophetic word is a limited revelation ; but to say that it
is necessarily no revelation at all is possible only upon
a priori assumptions which would be equally valid to
destroy the idea of conversion, the idea of prayer, and all
the other facts of personal religion which the Christian
Church does not receive from tradition, but realises in its
daily spiritual life.

But there is another point of view from which we may
look at Kuenen's arguments.   We find him defining the

true value of prophecy in two ways which are by no means obviously coincident. At one time he tells us that our judgment upon each prophet must rest upon " the earnestness and warmth of his religious and moral conviction, the depth and purity of his religious belief " (pp. 363, 364). On the other hand, he concludes by affirming that the permanent value of their work rests on the fact that they created ethical monotheism, and have made that belief the inalienable property of our race. On the first statement the value of the prophetic convictions appears to be in their subjective intensity ; on the second, it depends on their objective validity as convictions " which have become the inalienable property of our race." How do these two views hang together ? The mere intensity of prophetic conviction cannot be what makes it a conviction of universal validity. No convictions are intenser than those of a madman, but they are not therefore of value or fit to become the inalienable property of our race. The prophetic teaching can have value only if it is *true*. Its truth is not proved by the earnestness of the teacher. How then does Kuenen *know* that ethical monotheism is a true belief ? To this question we receive no answer except the negative one that the prophets were wrong in supposing that the truth came to them by personal communication from God Himself.

The truth is, that the school to which Kuenen belongs never seriously faces the question of the objective value of religious truth. The so-called modern school sets before it an entirely different question from that of the old theology. The old theology treated of God, His attributes, His manifestation, His dealings with men. The new school treats of religion. Its theology is a discussion of man's beliefs about God, of man's religious actions and feelings. When these have been analysed, and when their development has been traced, the modern theologian is perfectly happy. Religion has been genetically ex-

plained from its beginnings down to the present time.
Its ideas are most valuable, for they are part of the organic
development of human thought   They are the inalienable
property of the human race, just like the Pyramids or any
other great work of men's hands.   And there is no more
to be said about it, except that these ideas are sure to go
on developing in future time as they have done in the past

It is plain, I think, that no one can rest satisfied with
a view like this unless he has first accepted some form of
absolute philosophy, some pantheistic theory according
to which everything in human history is the mechanical
evolution of a hidden principle working by equally in-
flexible laws in the moral and physical spheres.   Whatever *is* is a more or less pure manifestation of the divine
The fundamental order of things is gradually clarifying
itself as it is worked out in history.   But the only thing
that is real is this progress   The individual human soul
is of as little account as a single wave in the sea.   It is
not therefore necessary that a personal religious reality
should present itself to the individual soul.   It is only
necessary that the soul be swept on in the right course of
development by a supreme religious conviction.   If we
have got the highest religious convictions current in our
time, we are, as it were, at the crest of the wave, and that
is the highest thing possible to us.

The prophets occupy this position.   A great proportion
of their convictions has continued to work on in the
subsequent development of thought, and accordingly
they are greater men than the heathen seers who contributed very little religious thought that has lived.

On this view even the ethical monotheism of the
prophets has only a relative value   It is not an absolutely
true conception, but only an approximation to the true
conception of the unity of the universe which we accept
provisionally till a better formula is found   And, of
course, the idea of personal converse with God is a pure
delusion   The highest religious life means nothing more

than sympathy with the highest accessible form of appreciation for the divine unity which underlies the progress of humanity. This appreciation—the reflection, so to speak, in the human mind of the stream of the divine progress of the universe—is all that can be meant by communion with God.

It is not my business to go into a refutation of this pantheistic theory of the universe. It is, fortunately, a theory which can be tested on other grounds than that of religion, for every argument which it directs against the true personality of God is also an argument against the true personality of man.

But I ask you to observe that every spiritual power which has stirred men's hearts, and tended to establish or to spread the spiritual monotheism of which Kuenen so freely admits the value, has been exerted by men whose convictions were directly opposed to the theory. All the prophets were filled with the conviction that they stood face to face with a personal God and in personal communion with Him. The spirit of Jahveh which filled them with might was not the immanent spirit of the universe working in their own hearts, but something distinct from themselves. And so, too, Jesus, in whom Kuenen fully acknowledges the highest of religious personalities, was never tempted to confound himself with the Father. " Not as I will, but as Thou wilt." Where can we have more clearly than in these words the distinct persuasion of personal relation to, and personal distinction from, a personal God ? Jesus, as clearly as the prophets, recognises the sharp contrast between man's thoughts and God's revelation.

"Flesh and blood hath not revealed it unto thee, but my Father which is in heaven." Here, then, is the astounding paradox of Kuenen's view. True religious ideas have been created by those who expressly reject them. The prophets advanced the truth by their intense faith in a lie. Religious creativeness has in all ages depended on faith in a relation to God which is purely imaginary. And, conversely, those who have accepted the pantheistic or organic theory of Kuenen have in the very measure of this acceptance ceased to be religiously intense and productive. If Christianity is a reality among us now its vitality is due, not to the lofty theories of advanced thinkers, but to the personal hold of a personal God which is still given to the believer by a truly supernatural work of the Spirit of Christ.

If these facts are consistent with Kuenen's theory, the whole universe is a lie and all history a delusion. If self-deception has done greater things than true philosophy truth has no meaning at all   It is absurd to say that the very feature in the religious consciousness of the prophets which gave them their courage, their power, the might to sway men's minds, is a mere accident in their belief which truer insight sweeps away as false.

In concluding these remarks, I wish to speak one word of warning against the inference which some of you may draw, that a man who holds views like Kuenen's can have no true religion at all.   The fact is, that the pantheistic theory is so unreal that no man can live consistently in it. In proportion as a man does live in it his whole personal life must be lamed   But it cannot be carried out.   Pantheists do not live as if personality were a delusion   And so men who hold a virtually pantheistic view of the place of God in the universe may, in their lives, break through their theory.   A man's speculations are often very remote from his practice.   They may be better, but they may also be worse.   You must never allow yourselves to take a man's speculative errors as the proof of an absence of personal faith, which often is nourished from very different sources and lives in spite of a blighting philosophy.

III

THE STUDY OF THE OLD TESTAMENT IN 1876

In attempting a brief sketch of what has been done for Old Testament studies in 1876, I omit some works which have already been noticed in these pages, and make no pretence to bibliographical completeness, especially as regards magazine articles and the like. Those who wish to see complete lists of publications on our subject may be referred to the fortnightly statements in the *Theologische Literaturzeitung*, and to Friederici's *Bibliotheca Orientalis* for 1876 (London Trübner & Co).

Giving the customary precedence to works of an encyclopædic character, we first take up the new edition of Herzog's great *Encyclopædia*, which began to appear last year and is to be completed within seven or eight years in 150 shilling parts. The articles bearing on the Old Testament are almost all new, and several of the best younger scholars of Germany are contributors. Thus Schürer writes on the Old Testament Apocrypha, and Baudissin displays his great erudition in the difficult field of Semitic polytheism in articles on Adrammelech and Anammelech. The minor articles are mainly by F. W. Schultz, and though carefully compiled, and better than those in the former edition, are not always quite up to the mark in fulness of information and references to relevant literature As a Bible dictionary, indeed, the *Encyclopædia*, which is properly an encyclopædia of

367

theology, does not aim at absolute completeness ; and even those who possess it may be glad to have along with it the very cheap and useful dictionary of biblical antiquities (*Handwörterbuch des biblischen Alterthums*), now appearing under the editorship of Professor Riehm, of Halle. This work, which is to be completed in one volume of 1000 pages, at the price of about 16s., is designed for educated readers in general, and makes no parade of scholarly apparatus. But every article is the work of a thoroughly competent author, who has made a special study of his department, and the lucid accuracy which is so characteristic of the editor penetrates the whole work, which promises to be the best Bible dictionary for general use, and one which scholars must not ignore.

Last year's contributions to pure philology must be rapidly passed over, as this is not the place for technical criticism. In lexicography we have to notice Ryssel's new edition of *Fuerst's Lexicon*, which contains only such improvements as were consistent with the continued use of the old stereotype plates. In Hebrew grammar there is a general feeling that what is most necessary at present is careful investigation of detached questions. Working in this direction, Dr. Giesebrecht has given us an elaborate monograph on the preposition Lamed (Halle, Lippert'sche Buchh., 112 pp.), which will be found useful in spite of the unfortunate want of an index, which in such a work is a serious inconvenience.

There have been some useful translations into English of grammatical works. The explanation of Hebrew forms by reference to a more primitive condition of the language, which throws so much light on the apparent darkness of the paradigms by which students are puzzled, was not systematically carried through any grammar accessible to the English reader till the appearance of Mr. Poole's translation of Land's *Principles of Hebrew Grammar* (Trubner, 1876). Unfortunately this work has serious defects as a manual for learners, and the student who wishes to get a clear and brief conspectus of the genesis of the Hebrew forms will probably do better to procure Mr. Curtiss's translation of Bickell's excellent *Outlines of Hebrew Grammar* (Leipzig, 1877). Both books rest mainly on the great grammar of Olshausen. The later has a very admirable table of Semitic characters by Euting, which is superior to anything of the kind previously accessible I have not seen a translation published at New York of Luzzatto's valuable Chaldee grammar.

Let us turn in the next place to works that bear on the text of the Old Testament. Among these the first place undoubtedly belongs to Strack's magnificent facsimile edition of the precious Petersburg MS. of the latter prophets, dating from A D. 916. The value of this codex lies not merely in its antiquity, though it is the oldest MS. of certain date, but still more in the fact that it is the most perfect specimen of the Babylonian system of vowel points, and exhibits more Oriental readings and more points of agreement with the Targum than any extant copy. Almost all other MSS., as is well known, have the Western vowel points, and present occidental readings in passages where the Eastern and Western schools diverge. The Petersburg codex has the Massora as well as the text For the convenience of those who wish to familiarise themselves with the very interesting system of the Babylonian punctuation, Hosea and Joel have been published separately at a low price. A second important work on the Hebrew text is Frensdorff's *Massoretisches Woerterbuch* (Hannover and Leipzig Cohen & Risch), which forms the first volume of a projected edition of the Massora Magna, on which the author has spent many years of labour. In ordinary Rabbinical Bibles the Massora appears in a very confused shape. The Massorets, or scholars, who made it their business to take care of the exact transmission of the Hebrew text, with every peculiarity of orthography and the like, wrote their notes on the margin of the Bible, but provided no

24

cross references when several passages were illustrated
by one note   Frensdorff has now arranged all the notes
in alphabetic form, adding valuable explanatory comments.

But welcome as these works are, the most serious
faults of the current Hebrew text are not to be cured by
MSS. or Massora. As this conviction spreads among
scholars, the ancient versions are becoming the subject
of renewed study.   Among last year's publications in this
field, the place of honour falls to Ceriani's magnificent
facsimile edition of the ancient Ambrosian MS. of the
Peshito, which dates from about the sixth century, and,
in the words of the editor, holds much the same place
among MSS. of the Syriac Old Testament as the
Amiatinus among copies of the Vulgate, and the Vatican
and Alexandrian MSS among those of the LXX. The
first part of this splendid work contains the Pentateuch
and part of Job   By far the most important version,
however, as a check on the Massoretic text, is the LXX.
In a pamphlet published at Moers, as the Easter programme of the Gymnasium there, Hollenberg discusses
in a very effective way the character and critical value
of the LXX of Joshua, and gains several valuable corrections of the Hebrew text.   It is important to note that
the characteristic freedom with which Hebrew scribes
made additions to the texts they copied continued to so
late a date that in the historical books the Massoretic text
contains quite large interpolations which were wanting
in the copies that lay before the Greek translators.   Thus,
in Josh. xx 3-6, which is an Elohistic passage, and
originally, as in the LXX , corresponded exactly with
Num. xxxv. 11-12, our present Hebrew has a large
insertion after Deut. iv. and xix , while in chapter xv.,
where we now find thirty-six names in a list which should
contain only twenty-nine, a hint from the LXX. enables
Hollenberg to show that part of the list was interpolated
by a copyist from the book of Nehemiah.   Facts like

these have an importance far beyond the passage which they affect. They must be kept in view by every one who wishes to understand the gradual process by which the historical books of the Old Testament came to be the complex structure which they are.

Lagarde's *Psalterium Iob Proverbia Arabice* (Gottingen, 1876) is more important for Orientalists, and for the history of the Christian East, than for text-criticism.

Among recent exegetical works none is less pretentious, while very few are so truly scholarly and calculated to be of such general use, as *The Holy Bible, with various Renderings and Readings from the best Authorities*, published by Eyre & Spottiswoode. The Old Testament is the work of Messrs. Cheyne and Driver, and the collection of various readings and interpretations is singularly accurate and complete. It is a book which should be in the hands of every Bible reader, while at the same time it will prove an invaluable help to beginners in Hebrew, and a useful book of reference to more advanced scholars, who will find it a convenient index of opinions often collected from works difficult of access.

In striking contrast to the modest work of these Oxford scholars is the flourish of trumpets with which Messrs. Jennings and Lowe introduce their treatise, *The Psalms, with Introductions and Critical Notes* (Macmillan & Co 3 vols. 1875-77) The necessary qualifications of a good commentator are unfolded in a pompous preface, claimed by implication for the authors, and illustrated by a severe *ex cathedra* criticism on Professor Perowne. The book itself does not display such exceptional scholarship as might justify this tone The writers have not been trained in the best school of Hebrew philology. Their grammatical comments lack scientific precision (as on i. 2) ; and they sometimes offer an impossible translation (as cx. 3), or adopt the caprices of P. H. Mason (as in lxxxi. 5). On the other hand, they bring to their task more rabbinical lore than is usual among recent commentators, and have the merit of candour and independence of thought along with very considerable reading. On critical questions they are moderate conservatives, not denying occasional corruptions in the text, and admitting that the titles, to which they usually adhere, are sometimes incorrect. Psalm li. is assigned to the period of the Babylonian exile, and is supposed to be a poetic conception of David's feelings Three Psalms are assigned to the Maccabæan period (xliv., lxxiv., lxxix.). The introductions contain a good deal of useful matter, together with not a little that is questionable. In adopting Aben Ezra's highly probable view that the title *Al-taschcheth* is taken from the opening words of a well-known song, Mr. Lowe might have thought of the vintage song, "Destroy it not, for a blessing is in it" (Isa lxv. 8).

Last year saw the completion of the *Speaker's Commentary on the Old Testament* in a volume (vol vi., "Ezekiel, Daniel, and the Minor Prophets") which is scarcely calculated to diminish the feelings of partial disappointment with which this work has been generally received A note at page 83 shows that among Dr. Currie's qualifications to write on Ezekiel, a knowledge of the elements of Hebrew grammar is not included. In discussing the great vision of the renewed Theocracy, the commentator does not seem to be aware of the importance which this section of the prophecies possesses for the criticism of the Pentateuchal law. He understands the vision as "portraying immediately the Church of Christ," without reference to any partial fulfilment in the restoration of the material temple. "As the Jews already knew something of the typical character of the temple services, this vision was intended to teach them more." At the same time, we are reminded that the minute details are not all in themselves symbolically important, but are requisite from the character of visionary presentation, which sets a finished picture before the eye. Manifestly, however, on this theory any lines in the picture which are new and different from the older ritual must have a special meaning. Thus, on xlv. 23, Dr Currie remarks, that instead of the graduated scale of sacrifices for the Feast of Tabernacles in Numbers, "the covenant number *seven* is preserved throughout to indicate a perfect in lieu of an imperfect covenant with God." But even such arbitrary spiritualising will not cover all the remarkable details of the case. What is the symbolism of the sentence pronounced in chapter xliv. against the Levites? Here Dr. Currie admits a historical reference; but, in direct opposition to the plain words of the text, supposes that vers. 10 *sqq.* speak only of certain apostate Levites, not of the Levites as a body, whom he supposes to have remained faithful. But what Ezekiel distinctly says is, that the Levites as a whole are to be excluded from proper priestly work, which is henceforth to be limited to the house of Zadok; and this exclusion is not based on any previous law, though it precisely corresponds with the middle books of the Pentateuch, but is set forth as a new ordinance, a punishment for the services offered by the Levites on the high places. What can we think of a commentator who does not even notice the singular problem raised by this passage, and on which Graf and other critics have built arguments which are at present agitating the whole world of Hebrew scholarship?

Mr Fuller's Daniel is a much more thorough piece of work, which incorporates a great mass of valuable material drawn, not only from books, but from MSS. communications by Assyrian scholars. Great weight is naturally laid on the testimony of Lenormant to the accuracy of the Babylonian colouring in the book, but the fullest discussion of the subject by the French scholar in his book, *La Divination et la science des présages chez les Chaldéens* (Paris, 1875), *Appendice. Les six premiers chapitres de Daniel,* seems to have appeared too late to be referred to. I may, therefore, take this opportunity of directing the reader to what is certainly the most important recent contribution to the defence of the historical character of the narrative part of the book. Lenormant thinks that an original Hebrew narrative written under the Persian empire was translated into Aramaic in the age of the Seleucids, that part of the Hebrew text was lost and replaced by this translation, which extends from ii. 4 to the end of chapter vii. We are, then, not to translate ii. 4 as saying that the Chaldeans spoke in Aramaic or Syriac. The words " in Syriack " are simply a note that we here pass to a different dialect, and should be in parenthesis This view, which has been received with some favour by Mr. Cheyne in his valuable article " Daniel " in the *Encyclopædia Britannica*, supplies a natural explanation of several difficulties which Mr. Fuller has by no means been happy in solving. The unquestionably Greek names of musical instruments in chapter iii. may be viewed as due to the translator; and the fact that the dialect of the Aramaic chapters appears to be Palestinian ceases to possess any critical importance. I must add that Lenormant frankly admits that, as the book now stands, it contains several historical blunders and other corruptions which he ascribes to ignorant correctors.[1]

It is impossible to speak in detail of the commentary by six different hands on the Minor Prophets. It is natural to compare this part of the work with the treatise of Dr. Pusey, which is likely to be very much in the hands of the same readers, and which has plainly exercised a considerable, not to say an over-great, influence on the views of the writers now before us. Professor Gandell's

[1] Another publication of 1876, which touches on the Daniel controversy, is Dean Stanley's *Jewish Church*, vol iii , presently to be noticed in another connection. The statement of the case in a note on Lect xlii. is, however, inadequate on both sides, and there are one or two positive errors (χιθδρα for χιθαρις, and the reference to the Syriac of Matt. xxiv 15).

Amos and Nahum are little more than an abridgment of Dr. Pusey. This dependence on his predecessor has lodged Mr Gandell in the curious inconsistency of dating Nahum in the time of Sennacherib, while he yet admits a reference in iii. 8 to the capture of Thebes at a much later date by Assurbanipal. Mr. Huxtable's Hosea, on the other hand, is a distinct advance on Dr. Pusey ; and though Mr Meyrick follows the Oxford professor against the best commentators in the date he assigns to Joel, and in regarding the description of the plague of locusts as a prediction, he rejects the figurative interpretation of their ravages.

Notwithstanding the extreme conservatism on critical questions which the *Speaker's Commentary* is throughout designed to advocate, Canon Drake regards the integrity of Zechariah as at least very doubtful, and in his exegesis distinctly admits that the historical groundwork of chapter xi. is to be sought in the disastrous times which preceded the fall of the kingdom of Ephraim It is very noteworthy that a conclusion of the critical school, so important as the plurality of authorship in Zechariah, and which was so long resisted as a fruit of rationalism, has at length gained almost universal acceptance, and is generally allowed to be free from danger to the faith. It may be remembered that there appeared in 1870 a commentary on Haggai, Zechariah, and Malachi, by Pfarrer Pressel, a well-known and honoured name among the evangelical clergy of Wurtemberg, which had been prepared for Lange's *Bibelwerk*, but was rejected because it did not accept the unity of Zechariah. No one apparently has been found willing to submit to the conditions imposed by the editor, for the missing part of the series has been supplied, after an interval of six years, by a commentary from the hand of Dr. Lange himself (" Die Propheten Haggai, Sacharia, Maleachi." Bielefeld, 1876). In another section of the *Bibelwerk*, which appeared last year (" Die Bücher Esra, Nehemia, und Esther," by Professor

F. W. Schultz, of Breslau), there is considerable deflection from the line of strict conservatism as represented by Keil's Introduction. In accordance with the usual opinion of recent critics, the Chronicler is recognised as the author of Esra-Nehemiah, and a rigorously historical character is not claimed for the book of Esther. As regards exegesis, this is one of the best of the Lange series.

The second part of Professor Reuss's new French translation of the Bible, with introductions and commentary, embraces the prophets (*Les Prophètes*. Par Édouard Reuss Paris, 1876. 2 vols.). The prophetic texts (in which the book of Jonah is not included) are arranged in chronological order according to the current principles of criticism, and on grounds which are briefly set forth in the introduction to each prophecy. The result is an arrangment not very different from that of Ewald, though modified in detail by the views of Hitzig and other critics, and by the characteristic sobriety of the author in matters of mere hypothesis The comments, like the introductions, may be taken as a fair account, in lucid and popular style, of the general view of the prophetic books among moderate German critics There is very little that is absolutely peculiar to the writer, and extreme and isolated opinions of previous commentators are seldom followed against the consensus of a majority of scholars. It will, of course, be understood that a veteran theologian like Professor Reuss represents rather the scholarship of the masters who are rapidly passing away than that of the newer school of rising Orientalists, whose investigations seem sometimes to be unduly neglected. No part of the book will be more interesting to readers in this country than the general introduction which sketches the history of prophecy, the leading features of the prophet's activity, the main elements of their theology, and the characteristics of their written works. The questions which arise under these heads are treated with a light but firm hand, in a very suggestive though by no means exhaustive sketch. The justification of the anthropomorphisms, and the particularism of the prophets by reference to their place in the divine preparation of mankind for the gospel, is particularly instructive. Readers who are repelled by the heavy style of German writers, and who are tempted to take the extreme position of Kuenen as typical of current criticism, may with much profit turn to the pages of Reuss, who, though in no sense allied to the conservative theology, and by no means the most orthodox of critics, gives a very different picture of prophecy from the Dutch scholar, and one much more representative I remark, in closing, that Professor Reuss seems to lay too great weight on the notion of *discipleship*, as implied in the expression, " Sons of the prophets." Though this is the current view, it is almost certainly false. Throughout the Semitic languages *son* means simply member of a college or corporation. (See G. Hoffmann's *Festschrift*, Kiel, 1873. Note 72)

English evangelical literature has, as usual, been enriched by several translations from the German. In the American series of Lange's *Bibelwerk* there have appeared vol. ii. " Exodus and Leviticus ", vol. vii. " Chronicles, Esra, Nehemiah, and Esther "; vol. xiii. " Ezekiel and Daniel." Lange's not very satisfactory commentary on Exodus is sometimes usefully corrected and supplemented by notes of Dr Mead, the translator. For Leviticus we receive not a translation of Lange, but the incorporation of a large part of his material with an independent commentary by Dr. Gardiner—a rather clumsy arrangement for the reader, whose comfort, indeed, is little consulted in this series. Professor Murphy's notes on Zockler's " Chronicles " are mainly directed to meet anything that appears a concession to the critical school. In the additional note on Ophir, p. 185, it would have been well to add a reference to Sprenger's *Alte Geographie Arabiens* (Bern, 1875), where there is an important excursus on the subject. With the translation

of Schultz's " Ezra, Nehemiah, and Esther," by Dr.
Briggs of New York, very serious fault must be found.
It is not only awkward, but sometimes positively misleading. For example, Schultz writing upon the subject
of poetical embellishment in the book of Esther says,
" If in this main passage we must recognise the influence
of transforming and embellishing fiction, it would be
inconsequent not to admit that the same influence may
possibly have place in other passages also," etc. But
the translator has · " If we were to acknowledge the
influence of . . . imagery in this chief stage of the drama,
this would still be negatived by its non-appearance in
other places." This is only one specimen, though the
most grave, of a series of changes which disguise even
when they do not, as in the passage cited, actually invert
the judgment of the German writer on the historicity of
Esther. Schrœder's commentary on Ezekiel, a very
mediocre production, is enlarged mainly by extracts from
the late Principal Fairbairn.   To Dr. Zöckler's comments
on Daniel are added a good many notes from Keil and
others, and some warm protests against the admission
that there are things in chapter xi. which must be *post
eventum*, and are therefore viewed by the commentator
as interpolations   This hypothesis of Zöckler is certainly
not plausible ; but a translator has surely no right to
insinuate that, " notwithstanding the author's disclaimer,
the insidious tincture of the prevalent rationalism of
German criticism is evident in his conclusion on this
point." Dr. Strong's own right to speak on subjects of
criticism may be measured by his assertions, that " the
Revelation of St. John, if not the apostle's, is of course
under a fictitious name " ; and that the Aramaic parts of
Daniel are " extracts taken verbatim, and as such, *from
the Babylonian State Records*."

   In Messrs. Clark's " Foreign Library " we have Keil's
Commentary on Ezekiel, translated by Rev. J. Martin,
(2 vols). and the " Theological Translation Fund " has

issued a second volume of Mr. F. Smith's translation of Ewald's *Prophets*, comprising Isaiah, Obadiah, and Micah, and carrying the reader to the end of the first volume of the original. No student of the Old Testament can afford to overlook this work of Ewald, which is not only of first-rate importance for scientific exegesis, but full of profound insight into the spirit of the prophetic writings, and so is much more useful for practical exposition than almost any other recent commentary. The translation appears to be very accurate, though Ewald's somewhat stilted style of expression looks more unnatural in the English.

Among the exegetical monographs before me, a place of honour is due to the collection of all Jewish interpreters on Isaiah liii. (Oxford : Parker. Vol. i., *Texts* ; vol. ii , *Translations*), gathered from printed books and MSS. by the well-known Orientalist, Ad. Neubauer, with translations by the editor and Mr. Driver, and an introduction by Dr. Pusey, to whose zeal and liberality the public owes so remarkable a contribution to the history of exegesis. The outcome of the laborious and bulky collection is essentially negative. No continuous thread of ancient traditional exegesis runs through these Jewish writings,—a conspicuous proof of the failure of the synagogue to reach any consistent view of the passage which with all its difficulties of detail has ever been luminous to the Church. The student who desires to practise himself in New Hebrew will find a valuable aid in the translations

The prominence given to the book of Job in university lectures in Germany has made the literature of that country unusually rich in exegetical studies on this part of the Old Testament. To these have been added *Contributions to the Criticism of Job*, by Lic. Carl Budde (*Beitrage zur Kritik des Buches Hiob*. Bonn · Marcus) ; and *Contributions to the Exposition* of the book (*Beiträge zur Erklärung d. B. Job*. Leipzig . Hinrich), by Dr. J.

Barth , besides a new and thoroughly revised edition of Professor Delitzsch's well-known *Commentary*. Dr. Barth's pamphlet comprises an essay on the date of the book, and notes on a series of difficult passages, directed in good measure against notions and conjectures of recent commentators, and for the most part worthy of consideration. It is a plausible suggestion that in xviii 7 הֹשְׁלִיו is an inverted form of הכשיל ; and the proposal to identify חבלידהם in xxxix. 3 with the Assyrian *habal* = *son* deserves attention in connection with Lagarde's explanation of xiii. 12 from the Assyrian *igabbi* = he spake. The change of guttural which Kautzsch (*T.L.Z.*, 1877, Nr. 2) views as conclusive against Dr Barth's proposal appears from Sayce's *Assyrian Grammar*, p. 106, to be no real difficulty. In what he says upon the date, our essayist is successful in indicating the precarious character of many arguments that have been adduced , but he has not always avoided what is equally precarious in discussing the many points of contact between Job and other parts of the Old Testament, though he has doubtless strengthened the already tolerably convincing proofs that the book is later than the age of Solomon, and indeed than Isaiah The chief difficulty is with the *terminus ad quem*, which is assumed without discussion to be given in the use of the book by Jeremiah But it is not impossible to argue that the author of Job has rather quoted Jeremiah (comp. Wellhausen in *T.L Z.*, 1877, 4) ; and a fresh examination of this question is the more to be desired, that Barth's essay makes it clear that the date of Job carries with it important consequences for several other parts of the Old Testament, whose age is subject of controversy. He seems, for example, to have proved that Isaiah xxxv., which many critics refer to the time of the Exile, was known to the writer of Job.

Lic. Budde defends the integrity of the book of Job in two able and interesting essays—(1) " Recent Criticism and the idea of the book ", (2) " The linguistic character

of the speeches of Elihu." The second essay is much the
most complete comparison of the language of Elihu with
that of other parts of the poem which has hitherto been
instituted ; and the results, ingeniously tabulated in a
statistical form, will certainly modify current opinion.
The author goes no further than to claim as proved that
in point of language it is perfectly possible that Elihu's
speeches are a genuine part of the book. In the first
essay the argument that the plan of the book would be
incomplete without Elihu is interwoven somewhat to the
disadvantage of the reader, with a refutation of the very
extreme theory of the original form of the book advanced
by Studer in the *Jahrbücher für prot. Theologie*, 1875.
To these German contributions is to be added the Dutch
commentary, *Het Boek Job vertaald en verklaard*, door
J. C. Matthes (Groningen : Wolters. Part i., 1876, Parts
ii and iii., 1877. To be completed in ten parts), which
is no mere revision of the author's earlier commentary,
but a new work   The exposition is lucid and scholarly,
and the survey of current views is both full and clear.

Wellhausen's contributions to the criticism of the
Pentateuch and Joshua in the *Jahrbb. für Deutsche
Theologie*, 1876 (Hft. III. and IV.), extend only to the
historical parts of these books. I cannot attempt to
explain in a few words the results of a long and complicated examination of details. The main interest lies
in the analysis of the documents which, since Hupfeld,
have been known by the names of the Jhvhist and younger
Elohist, though the epithet younger is probably a mis-
nomer. These documents, which our critic names J
and E, were as he holds fused together in a single context
JE by a third author who, in some parts (especially in the
account of the legislation at Sinai), added new matter of
his own. A much later redactor combined the work thus
produced with the document which Wellhausen calls Q or
Vierbundesbuch, which is what older critics call the book
of origins, or of the elder Elohist. Another important

point is the treatment of Exodus xxxiv. as a distinct and independent source. It is to be hoped that Wellhausen will soon add an analysis of the legal parts of the Pentateuch, as his investigation, even in its present imperfect state, points to inferences of great interest for the history of the Old Testament

In the historical studies which fall to be noticed in this survey, the period subsequent to the Exile has received most attention. The third series of Dean Stanley's *Lectures on the History of the Jewish Church* (London : Murray) extends from the captivity to the Christian era. The purpose of the volume is popular and didactic. The author makes no claim to independent research. Resting on the works of previous writers, whose labours are regarded as " exempting any later author from the duty of undertaking afresh a labour which they have accomplished once for all not to be repeated," and following in the main the guidance of Ewald, to whom an eloquent and touching tribute is paid in the preface, Dr. Stanley seeks " to disentangle the main thread of the story from unmeaning episodes, to give the most important conclusions without repeating the arguments " of larger works, and above all, " to draw out the permanent lessons " of the story. That this task has been accomplished with much literary tact and grace, and with a singular felicity of graphic detail and pictorial touches that give living colour to the narrative, is what we knew to expect from a hand that has not forgotten its cunning. Yet it cannot but be matter of regret that merits of exposition so conspicuous, applied to a period of history so thorny and tangled that skilful exposition is peculiarly helpful to the reader, were not combined with a deeper study of the available materials than seems to have lain in the plan of the author   In spite of the confidence with which Dr. Stanley accepts the guidance of his predecessors, the study hitherto devoted to this part of the history has been more prolific of controversies than of conclusions ,

and the habit of thought which has led our author habitually to elude these controversies instead of subjecting
them to critical discussion, makes no small part of the
volume more readable than instructive, and leads to
frequent sacrifices of precision and accuracy to picturesque
effect.   One is compelled to add that in not a few cases
a more thorough knowledge of recent literature and a
juster estimate of the relative value of the authorities
followed would have led to important modifications of
view, even without new personal research.   The valuable
manual of Schurer (*Lehrbuch der neutestamentlichen Zeit-
geschichte*), even without the fuller essay by the same author
in Hilgenfeld's *Zeitschrift* (1875) would, for example, have
afforded a correction of the old error, that the Alabarch
was the ruler of the Jews in Alexandria ; and the monograph of Wellhausen (*Pharisaer und Sadducaer*, 1874)
could not have failed to set the position of the Pharisees
and Sadducees in a fresh light.   That the Psalter of
Solomon is referred to the time of Antiochus Epiphanes,
and the Book of Jubilees to about B C. 100, can only be
ascribed to neglect of the many recent researches into these
compositions   In truth, it is evident from p 348 that
Dr. Stanley has not even used Roensch's indispensable
edition of the latter work.   Or once more, the exploded
opinion that the Jews gave up Hebrew for Chaldee in the
time of the captivity is reproduced without the least
reference to the existence of a different view   Such slips
in detail—and I have taken them almost at random—
diminish one's confidence in the treatment of the broader
aspects of the narrative   Into these it is impossible to
enter in the present rapid survey.   But I may ask in
passing whether the prominence given in the volume to
the Platonic doctrine of immortality as a powerful
influence on Jewish, and not merely on Hellenistic,
thought, does not rest in part on the lack of a sharp
appreciation of the distinction between the notion of
immortality and that of the resurrection.

The first part of the period covered by Dean Stanley's lectures is also taken up by the Jewish scholar, H. Graetz, in the last-published part of his *Geschichte der Juden* (vol ii. part ii. B C. 586-160. Leipzig). Like all the writings of this author the book is full of acute observation and of startling combinations, which in many cases are plainly untenable, but in others invite examination on the basis of a fuller statement of the argument than Dr. Graetz is accustomed to give. I do not venture to express any opinion as to how much of what is new in the book will bear the test of such examination. Apart from this, the volume has a real value from the great rabbinical learning of the author, who, in spite of his radical views on critical questions, and his large, though irregular, use of the results of Christian scholarship, is still essentially a rabbi in all habits of thought. A truly rabbinical whim is that which identifies Nehemiah with the messenger of the covenant in Mal. iii

An admirable historical monograph is Professor Kuenen's tract, *Over de Mannen der groote Synagoge* (Amsterdam, 1876), the argument of which may be briefly stated for those to whom the Dutch is not accessible. The men of the great synagogue are once mentioned in the Mishna, where they appear as filling the gap in Jewish oral tradition between the prophets and Antigonus of Socho. In Midrash and Gemara they are often named, and divers ordinances are ascribed to them. The later Jews went still further , and Elias Levita ascribed to Ezra and the Great Synagogue the task of closing the canon—a view which has influenced many Christian writers. The whole tradition on the subject was, however, discredited in last century by the objections raised by several Christian scholars, especially by Rau of Herborn Of late there has been a reaction, and recent writers are pretty unanimous in admitting the existence of an official body called the Great Keneseth, though there is no tolerable agreement as to its functions. Now, Pro-

fessor Kuenen points out that whatever we may think
of the *thing*, the *name* is probably late, as it is not found
in the Apocrypha, the New Testament, or Josephus.   As
Kenéseth, like συναγωγή, came to be ever more and more
confined to a meeting for worship, the inventor of the
name presumably thought of some great assembly for a
religious purpose.   The only such assembly that occurs as
suitable to the name is that described in Neh. viii.-x.
And, as a matter of fact, a number of the things related
of the great synagogue find their explanation in these
chapters, and show that such was really the original sense
of the expression to which later tradition attached so
many fables.   Of course, it follows that the whole
Talmudic idea that the great synagogue was a law-
giving body is unhistorical.   The Kenéseth, as hitherto
understood, disappears from history.   Finally, Professor
Kuenen indicates how the Talmudic ideas on this head
form an integral part of a radically false view of the
history of Israel characteristic of the whole Talmud,
which ascribes to the scribes, before the fall of the Jewish
state, the position which they actually attained only
after the dissolution of the nation.   Professor Kuenen's
argument is closely knit and convincing at every point,
and displays his critical powers at their best.

For the parts of the Biblical history prior to the
captivity there is little to record, except translations of
Assyrian texts and discussions of their bearing on biblical
problems.   New texts continue to appear in versions of
unequal merit in Messrs. Bagster's series, *Records of the
Past*.   The seventh volume (1876) contains several of
the documents most interesting to biblical students—the
annals of Sargon, the conqueror of Samaria ; the inscription of Sennacherib, in which he speaks of Hezekiah ,
and some of the legends parallel or analogous to the
narrative of Genesis, which are collected in the last great
work of the lamented George Smith, *The Chaldean Account
of Genesis* (London : Low,   1876).   Of Smith's work

25

a German translation has appeared, with valuable
" elucidations and continued researches," by the German
Assyriologist, Friederich Delitzsch (Leipzig . Hinrichs,
1876). It appears premature to attempt to estimate the
value of the Chaldean legends for the biblical student
The fragments are so mutilated and so difficult that the
translation is highly insecure. Thus in the fragment
which is supposed to give the Chaldean account of the
tower of Babel, the idea of " confusion of speech " is
introduced, as Smith himself admits, by " translating the
word *speech* with a prejudice," the word not being known
to have this meaning elsewhere. And the reference to a
tower, as we learn from a note by Delitzsch in the German
edition, is not less questionable. Again, in the so-called
story of the fall, we learn from Delitzsch that " scarcely
a line of Smith's version can claim to be correct " ; and
though the German scholar is unwilling to surrender the
belief that we really have in the passage a parallel to the
story of the fall, he rests this belief on arguments so
unsatisfactory that we must conclude with Baudissin and
v. Gutschmid that there is as yet really no evidence of
a Babylonian account of man's first sin. Or again, we
gather from Delitzsch that the grounds on which Smith
identifies the name Izdubar with Nimrod are certainly
erroneous. If so, the parallel between what is related of
the two personages is far from being so exact as to justify
the confidence with which Smith and Delitzsch alike
insist on identifying them. The most important, and
it would seem the least doubtful, parallels to biblical
narratives lie in the Chaldean accounts of the creation
and the flood, of which it must be remembered something
was already known from Damascius and the fragments
of Berossus. What is notable in the texts given by Smith
is that, in spite of the fundamental difference of religious
conception from the Bible, in spite of the fact that the
Chaldean legends are essentially polytheistic and mythological, and without ethical value, we find minute agree-

ments with Genesis in detail and expression, as well as in such broader features as were already known to us from Berossus. It is impossible, when one looks into the matter, to avoid the conviction that some of these co-incidences would not have appeared if the cuneiform texts had been translated by a person who had never seen the Bible ; and as it is just these points which are most important for a really critical examination of the subject, one cannot but wish that Assyriologists would try to free their minds more than they have hitherto done from the desire to hunt out, above all things, parallels with the Bible And when we have got a trustworthy reading of the texts, it will next be necessary to inquire much more critically than has been done by Smith into the age of these legends.   The texts come from the library of Assurbanipal (seventh century B C), but are copied from originals to which Smith ascribes an enormous age, on grounds which are anything but convincing We have no real certainty that the legends as we possess them are much older than the time of Assurbanipal ; and v. Gut-schmid has pointed out, in the series of legends which contain the Babylonian story of the flood, an apparently clear trace of Egyptian influence which cannot well be very ancient Thus, if further research confirms the singular coincidences in expression between Genesis and the inscriptions, some of which, if Smith's versions are right, can only be due to direct imitation by the writers of one or the other nation, it will still be a question on which side the priority lies ; and in discussing this question it will be necessary to remember that in literary culture and power, as well as in their religion, the Israelites were immeasurably in advance of Assyria.

When we pass to the other part of the biblical records, which are illustrated by the inscriptions, viz. the history of the kings of Israel and Judah, we find that the past year has been one of fierce and tangled controversy.   The old *quaestio vexata* of the chronology of the kings, for which the Assyrian Eponym Canon affords new data, has been afresh discussed by Oppert in a series of papers in the *Annales de Philosophie Chrétienne*, to which he gives the somewhat pretentious title, " Salomon et ses Successeurs ; solution d'un problème chronologique " (since published in a separate form by Maisonneuve et Cie, 1877). The supposed solution is not so convincing as this title would lead one to suppose. M. Oppert appears greatly to under-rate the difficulties of the problem , and he has not given due weight to the arguments of previous writers, ignoring, for example, the important paper of Wellhausen, of which an account was given in vol xxv. p 380 of this journal. Discrepancies between the Northern and Southern chronology are reconciled by hypotheses so arbitrary that they can hardly find a supporter, a second Menahem, whose reign divides Pekah's rule into two parts, and a temporary displacement of Jeroboam II., which is de-fended by a gross mistranslation of a passage of Isaiah. In discussing the Assyrian evidence, M. Oppert renews his old theory of a break of forty-seven years in the Eponym Canon to be filled up by the reign of the Chaldean Pul. Pul is the great *crux* of Assyriologists, and the difficulties which lie in the way of identifying him with Tiglathpileser, as is done by Rawlinson, Schrader, &c., have been set in a strong light, not only by Oppert, but by v. Gutschmid in a book presently to be named. But the tone of Oppert's argument, and the unpardonable brutality with which he treats George Smith, whose essay on the Eponym Canon opposes the views of the French scholar, compel one to feel that till the controversy is conducted with more modesty and appreciation of the fact that historical conclusions from the monuments are still very precarious, those who are not Assyriologists had better stand aside. As usual, part of the quarrel turns on the reading of proper names, on which score another lively controversy has been going on for some time between Schrader on one side, and Oppert, Wellhausen,

and v. Gutschmid on the other. The point here is a
supposed mention of King Azariah of Judah, for which
Schrader has completely lost his temper (*Jahrbb. fur prot.
Theol.*, 1876, II.).   Amidst all this it is not strange that
the Jena historian, A. v. Gutschmid, has raised a strong
protest against the premature introduction of Assyrio-
logical discoveries into the history of the ancient East.
His book, *Neue Beitrage zur Geschichte des alten Orients*
(Leipzig : Trubner, 1876), is essentially polemical, and
has probably overstated the case in attacking Schrader,
who is the author's main foe.   Gutschmid makes no
attempt to deny to Assyriology the character of a real
science ; but he places in a strong light the faults which
have been committed through haste to get from the new
science results immediately applicable to the Bible and
other history.   Both on this account, and from numerous
incidental contributions to questions of Bible history,
the book is of real value.   I select for notice only two
points, the remarks at p. 18 on the early currency of
Aramaic in Mesopotamia, and the interesting excursus
on the existence of the kingdom of Samaria after the fall
of Hoshea, which is one of the indisputable results of
Assyriologists, and serves to explain Isa. vii. 8, where the
sixty-five years just carry us down to Assurbanipal, who
is presumably the Osnapper of Ezra vi. 10.

Under the head of translations of historical works falls
to be noticed the English version of Ewald's valuable
Antiquities of Israel (London . Longmans).   The study
of biblical geography continues to make progress, especially through the researches of the " Palestine Exploration
Fund."   The *Quarterly Statements* for 1876 are mainly
composed of papers by Lieutenant Conder, embracing a
series of proposed identifications of Biblical and Tal-
mudical sites, together with comparisons of the survey
work with ancient Egyptian records bearing on Palestine,
and with the topography of Samaritan literature.   There
are also valuable notes on the climate and natural history

of Canaan In many cases Lieutenant Conder has provided rather materials for discussion than results to be at
once incorporated in biblical geography. This is specially
clear with regard to the identifications proposed for the
life of David (pp. 39 *seq.*), which rest in part upon questionable readings and more than questionable translations of
the Hebrew. The remarks in the paper on " Samaritan
Topography," in which " the wonderful consistency and
perfection of the topography of Judæa and Galilee contained in the book of Joshua " is contrasted with the
defective nature of what is said about the Samaritan
district, are well worthy of the attention of critics.
Lieutenant Conder would infer that this part of the book
has been mutilated ; but it is much more likely that we
have in the facts indicated a hint as to the date of the
book. A very valuable contribution to the topography
of Jerusalem is Zimmermann's *Karten und Plane zur
Topographie des alten Jerusalem* (Basel, 1876).   These
maps are based on the observations of a German architect
in Jerusalem, Hr. Conrad Schick, who for thirty years
has been collecting observations of the depth of that huge
mass of rubbish which overlies the original site of the city.
From these observations a map of the original contours
has been formed, while comparison with the present contours is facilitated by additional maps and sections. A
sheet displaying the various theoretical restorations of the
old topography, and a modest and serviceable explanatory
pamphlet, are added. In this connection I may also
mention the English translation of Socin's excellent
traveller's hand-book of Palestine, in Baedeker's series,
and the final exposure of the forged Moabitic pottery
by Kautzsch and Socin (*Die Achtheit der moabitischen
Alterthumer gepruft*, Strassburg, 1876).
    Passing on to the subject of Old Testament Theology,
we are met by the last published work of Ewald—his
posthumous essay, *Das Leben des Menschen und das Reich
Gottes* (" The Life of Man and the Kingdom of God,"

Leipzig, 1876)   This is properly the fourth volume of the author's *Theology of the Old and New Covenant*, and is not so much a biblical study as a statement of Ewald's ethical system on a biblical basis   In the hands of the latest writers on the subject, Old Testament theology is passing almost entirely into researches into the history of the religion of Israel. The method of the usual manuals (Oehler, Schultz) is to discuss first Mosaism, and then the teaching of the prophets. But so long as the date of important parts of the Pentateuch is so much disputed, this way of presenting the subject offered no security for a really genetical development of the growth of the Old Testament religion. Since Kuenen in his *Religion of Israel* delineated this development in accordance with the view that the Levitical ordinances of the Pentateuch are later than the prophetic period, friends and opponents alike have felt the necessity of renewed research into the history of the Old Testament ideas, and, instead of starting with fixed views as to the age of the different parts of the Pentateuch derived in the old way from merely literary criticism, have recognised the propriety of beginning with documents of undisputed age—mainly, that is, with the prophets—and then working backwards and forwards from such a picture of the religion of Israel as these documents afford. At the same time, the influence of the new science of comparative religion has laid upon biblical scholars the duty of examining more precisely the relation of the Hebrew faith to Semitic polytheism, and, in particular, of testing the theory so ably upheld by the Dutch school, that there is no specific difference between the development of the Old Testament religion and that of other faiths. Thus the burning questions of the moment are such as these —What is the origin and history of the spiritual monotheism of the prophets ? How does it stand related to the conception of Jehovah current among the mass ? What is the relation of Jehovah to heathen gods, and of the worship of Jehovah

in Israel to other worships ? Among works bearing on
this subject, I shall first notice in a single word Tiele's
Geschiedenis van den Godsdienst, etc. ("History of Religion
to the Sovereignty of the Universal Religions," Amsterdam, 1876.) This little manual is written from the usual
standpoint of the Leiden school, and treats the religion
of Israel simply as one branch of the Semitic religions.
There is no new research or even argument on disputed
points ; but the work will be found convenient, both as
a brief exposition of the views of an influential school,
and from the references supplied to the latest literature.

Coming now to real contributions to the history of Old
Testament religion, I have to name especially Professor
Baudissin of Strassburg's *Studien zur semitischen Religions-
geschichte* (" Studies in the History of Semitic Religion,"
Leipzig : Grünow), and Dr. E. Nestle's Haarlem prize
essay on the significance of the Hebrew proper names for
the history of religion—*Die israelitischen Eigennamen
nach ihrer religionsgeschichtlichen Bedeutung* (Haarlem,
1876). To these must be added several valuable essays—
Kuenen's paper on " Yahveh and the other gods " (*Theol.
Review*, July 1876), and Smend's essay in the *Stud. u
Krit.*, 1876, iv. " On the stage in the development of the
religion of Israel presupposed by the prophets of the eighth
century." Baudissin's volume is made up of a series of
essays, some of which have only a secondary bearing on
biblical theology. The essay on the value of Sanchuni-
athon's Phœnician history decides, with Movers, against
the opinion which has received currency through Ewald
and Renan, refusing to accept the work of Philo as the
translation of an old source, though admitting that it
contains remains of old tradition modified by the author's
euhemerism. The points in the cosmogonies of San-
chuniathon which remind us of the Old Testament—the
chaos or Βάαυ (בהו), and the πνεῦμα in the creation—are
not borrowed from the Bible, but rest on notions which
the Israelites since their origin had shared with kindred

tribes. " But while among the latter the naive notions
of a child-like age resolved themselves into the materialistic
form presented by Philo, in Israel, through the agency of
the spirit of prophecy, the notion of a physical breath of
God was transformed into that of a spiritual God " and
Creator. " This confirms what appears in all comparison
of Old Testament religion with the views of kindred
nations. The elements of a natural religion once common
to all Semitics have passed into the religion of revelation,
but in this fusion have undergone an inner purification."
While natural religion ends in self-dissolution, the Old
Testament shows us " the sway of a new principle, the
Spirit of God raising men above the mythological process,
the spirit of revelation." These sentences serve to indicate the religious standpoint of the volume. A very
learned and thorough investigation of the origin of 'Ιάω
as the name of a deity, demonstrates conclusively that
'Ιάω is a mere reproduction of the tetragrammaton, not
the name of a Canaanite or other heathen god, thus wholly
demolishing the argument maintained by Lenormant,
and in this country by Colenso, to show that the Israelites
borrowed the name Jahve from heathenism. Other
arguments for a non-Hebrew origin of the name are also
discussed and found wanting.

The essay on the symbolism of the serpent among the
Semites, especially in the Old Testament, has for its main
object to prove that it is needless to assume any influence
of Parsism, in which the serpent is connected with
Ahriman, in order to explain the story of the fall. The
character of cunning or intelligence, it is argued, is ascribed
to the serpent in the religious symbolism of all the Semites,
so far as our present knowledge extends. That knowledge, however, as appears from the examination to
which our author successively subjects the Assyrian, the
Phœnician, and the Arabian data, is very imperfect, and
a good deal that has been put forward by Movers and
others must be rejected. That the Kadmos of Greek

legend is a Phœnician serpent god seems to be one of the
best established facts bearing on the subject. It is con-
jectured that the Hebrews connected the serpent with
sorcery, and that this may have had a share in establishing
the idea of its cunning or wisdom. The etymological
arguments for such a conjecture are not very strong, and
are hardly confirmed by the suggestion that the tree of
knowledge is also connected with the well-known habit of
taking oracles from trees, more than once alluded to in
the Old Testament, and familiar to classical antiquity.
Professor Baudissin has not been able to throw any new
light on the worship of the brazen serpent abolished by
Hezekiah

In the essay on Hadad-Rimmon (Zech. xii. 11), Hitzig's
interpretation, which suggests that Hadad-Rimmon is a
name of Tammuz or Adonis, is controverted, and the old
view defended which sees in the word the name of a place
where the fall of Josiah was mourned. The argument,
in its most important part, resolves itself into an examination of the two names of deities which form the elements
of the word Hadad-Rimmon, or, as Baudissin would read,
Hadar-Rimmon. For *Rimmon*, who appears in the Bible
as a Damascene deity, our author accepts Schrader's
identification with the Assyrian Ramanu, who, according
to Schrader, is the thunder god. But as Delitzsch, in his
additions to Smith's " Genesis," appears to have refuted
Schrader's interpretation of the Assyrian name, and as
Wellhausen, in a review of Baudissin's " Studies " (*Gott.
Gel. Anz.*, 1877, St. 6), has disposed of the arguments from
Greek glosses by which our author endeavours to prove
the existence of a Syrian Raman who was also a god of
thunder, this part of the essay must be viewed as un-
successful. It appears, too, that in reading Hadar for
Hadad, Baudissin has followed a false light of the Assyrio-
logists ; for v. Gutschmid, in the work noticed above, has
brought the clearest proof that Hadad is a title of the
Syrian Baal or Sun-god, and that it is quite illegitimate

in Schrader to transform Benhadad into Benhadar, in
order to find him mentioned on the Assyrian monuments.
As Wellhausen has also made it very improbable that any
weight is to be attached to Hieronymus's evidence to the
existence of a place called Hadad-Rimmon, it remains
likely that Hitzig's interpretation is right.   Hadad is the
Sun-god.   Adonis is also the Sun-god under a special
form, which may very well be the same as the specialised
Hadad-Rimmon, though we have as yet no absolute proof
that it is so.

The part of Baudissin's book most important for
biblical theology is the very long essay on " The view
taken in the Old Testament of the gods of Heathenism "
The collection of the relevant biblical material is very
full and good, and the general argument includes interesting investigations of points of detail.   The final result is
this —Baudissin (like Kuenen in the essay named above)
thinks that the pure monotheism of Deuteronomy,
Jeremiah, and later books developed itself out of an
earlier monolatry.   But while Kuenen includes under
the name monolatry the faith of the prophets of the
eighth century B C., who use expressions that seem to
ascribe a certain reality to the heathen gods, Baudissin
more cautiously attempts a middle way, and will have it
that since the time of Hosea it was admitted that *for
Israel* the other gods were mere dead images, but that it
does not appear that the monotheistic faith implied in
this position had as yet consciously formulated the proposition that the other gods were absolute nothings even
for their own worshippers   Thus the standpoint of the
eighth century is, according to Baudissin, an *unconscious
monotheism*.   This theory certainly relieves the author of
some of the objections that may be taken against Kuenen's
more radical view.   But apart from the internal difficulty
that besets the conception of an unconscious monotheism,
Baudissin's view seems to break down before a single
expression of Hosea.   The prophet who chooses for the

restored nation the epithet " sons of the living God "
(chap. 1. 10), surely does so in the conviction that the other
nations, who in Semitic phrase are sons of *their* national
deities, have no living God.   And this is absolute and
conscious monotheism of the clearest kind.

Smend's essay, which deals with the same period, the
eighth century B.C., belongs to a different school, and is
mainly directed to prove the organic connection between
the teaching of the prophets and the earlier faith of the
nation.   It brings forward many important considerations that are apt to be overlooked in the present disposition of critics to find the whole history of Israel's
spiritual faith within the period of the prophetic literature   Whether the writer has also succeeded in showing
that there is no reason why the Levitic legislation may
not be older than Amos and Hosea is another question.
The essay takes the form of a criticism on Duhm's able
but too subtle construction of the prophetic development,
and it is thus hardly possible to reproduce its argument
here ; but, like the author's previous work, *Moses apud
Prophetas*, it gives the promise of very valuable service
in the field of biblical study.

Dr Nestle's book, confining itself to a single line of
evidence, touches many of the questions which have just
occupied our attention.   Here, too, as in Baudissin's essay,
we find a refutation of the attempts that have been
hitherto made to trace back the origin of the name Jahve
beyond the limits of Hebraism, and here, too, as in Smend's
paper, but with other arguments, recent attempts to take
away the place of Moses in the history of revelation are
combated.   After a brief history of Hebrew onomatology,
the author proposes to himself two questions—1 Which
names of God occur in proper names in the various periods
of Hebrew history ?   2. What conception of the deity
is expressed in the proper names, by the combination of
the names of God with significant words ?

The results of the discussion of the first question are

mainly these :—The proper names of the Mosaic period confirm the Pentateuchal tradition, that before Moses God was worshipped as El Shaddai, in which name (interpreted as *mighty* God) the author recognises the conception of the deity suited to a nomad tribe, which has little temptation to identify the godhead with the phenomena of nature, and, demanding of its deity guidance in wanderings and protection against foes, requires a religion that gives faith in a personal and revealing god.   In discussing the next period of Israel's religion, which is marked by the work of Moses and the name Jahve, Dr. Nestle rightly rejects the interpretations which find in Jahve the notion of him *who is*, and leans to Lagarde's view, though half inclined to prefer the interpretation advanced by the present reviewer in this journal [1]   It is then shown that, in the formation of proper names, El and Jahve came to be used indifferently, and that the use of names pointing to the worship of other gods is very rare.   The names compounded with Baal are referred to the introduction, in the time of the judges, of Canaanite ideas, and are viewed as evidence that the worship of other gods besides Jahve was not impossible even in the families of Saul and David.   The final victory over this imperfect state of religious development is traced to the age of Elijah.   It must, however, be questioned whether our author has rightly explained the use of Baal in the names to which he refers.   That Baal or Lord was a title applicable to Jahve, until the use was dropped to prevent confusion with the heathen Baalim, is a far more probable opinion, and finds in Hosea ii. a confirmation which Dr. Nestle has hardly weighed aright.   Had this opinion been adopted, the arguments which our author directs against those who practically obliterate the work of Moses from the history of revealed religion would have gained weight, and it would have been still more apparent that the polytheism, which, according to Kuenen, was held to

[1] *British and Foreign Evangelical Review*, January 1876.

by the majority of the nation as late as the Exile, was
always viewed in Israel as an irregularity, so that even
those who worshipped false gods did not venture to name
their children after them

In discussing his second question, Dr. Nestle traces in
a very interesting way the character of the pious dependence on God expressed in the proper names. Many of
these refer to the child as the gift of God to the parents,
and it is a quaint, but no doubt just observation, that
as female children were less valued, this class of names
is exclusively masculine. Other names perpetuate the
religious significance of the birth of a son into the family
in various manners. God hath helped, God hath heard,
God hath remembered, and so forth. In other names
again the religious view of national concerns is expressed
Such are many names of kings, for from Jehoshaphat the
kings of Judah always bore a name compounded with
Jahve so that Eliakim on his succession becomes Jeho-
jakim The exceptions are the godless kings, Ahaz,
Manasseh, Amon ; and we have some reason to think
that these names may have been changed, as the monuments give to Ahaz the name of Jehoahaz. Special
attention is paid to the forms that combine the Divine
name with the notion of king and father, and it is shown
how many of the expressions of Old Testament piety in
psalms, the priestly blessing, and elsewhere, are reflected
in proper names. These observations, which do not
apply only to the later names, and which are supported
by the absence of names that present a naturalistic conception of deity, make it manifest that from the earliest
times the ethical truths of revealed religion had taken a
deep hold of the mass of the Israelites. However much
may remain uncertain in the details of Dr. Nestle's investigation, this result can hardly be shaken ; and the
evidence which it bears against those who refuse to view
the corrupt nature worship of the eighth century as a
declension from an admitted standard of national religion

is of the strongest kind, though, in order to estimate its precise force, it would be necessary to examine at some length the parallelisms in point of idea between the proper names of Israel and those of other Semites That these parallelisms are in part very striking is observed by Dr. Nestle at the close of his inquiry, but the subject is not followed up. In this sketch I have mainly sought to show how much matter of general theological interest the writer has drawn from an apparently technical subject The volume also contains much scholarly research in the investigation of details, and is altogether very welcome, both as an addition to biblical literature and as a token of what we may still expect from the author.

As Goldziher's *Mythos bei den Hebraern,* and the English translations of Kuenen's and Riehm's recent books on prophecy, have been noticed in these pages in another connection, they must be excluded from our present survey

IV

THE POETRY OF THE OLD TESTAMENT [1]

THE poetical books of the Old Testament have always possessed special attractions for scholars as well as for simple readers of the Bible, and have gathered round them a copious literature in which no period of Christian theology is unrepresented   But the study of Hebrew poetry, as poetry, is a comparatively recent thing, and even in recent times the number of really important books that deal with the subject is by no means large.   It cannot indeed be supposed that there ever was a time when readers of the Old Testament were altogether insensible to the poetic genius and beauty of the Psalms and of the Prophets ; but the idea that these qualities, or indeed that any of the literary and human characteristics of Scripture demand and richly reward special study, is one which, however obvious it appears in the present day, lay quite beyond the horizon of older theologians

The purely magical conception of Scripture which prevailed in the old Catholic Church—the one-sided theory that regarded the Word of God solely as a supernatural communication of " intelligible " truths—was only consistent in laying down a canon for the study of the Bible which has nothing in common with the rules that guide

[1] From the *British Quarterly Review*, July 1877   The books mentioned at the head of the article were: Lowth's *Praelectiones* (1753), Herder's *Geist der ebräischen Poesie* (1782-83), Ewald's *Dichter des alten Bundes* (1839,[2] 1866), and E Meier's *Geschichte der poetischen Nationalliteratur der Hebräer* (1856).

us in criticising and appreciating human writings. The Reformation, with its profounder apprehension of the idea of the Word, opened a new era in biblical study. The Word of God, as conceived by Luther, is no longer the abstract imparting of intellectual truth, but the personal message of God's love in Christ, to which the saints of all ages return the equally personal answer of faith Thus the whole truths of revelation are at once brought down from the unreal world of *intelligibilia* into the sphere of true and personal human life The Word descends into history, comes near to man in his daily needs, and opens up to him the very heart of God in utterances that speak straight home to every one who is taught of the Spirit. This implies that the Word of God is given to us in the natural language of mankind, and is to be studied by the same methods of exegesis as we apply to any other ancient book. Thus in the hands of the earlier Reformers the science of biblical interpretation assumed a new aspect. The allegorical sense—that great incubus of mediæval exegesis—was cast aside, and the Bible history was laid hold of with a new and vivid interest, which bore remarkable fruit in the social and political, as well as in the purely religious development of the Protestant nations. Nor was the recognition of the genuine human character of the sacred history all that was gained. The beginnings at least of an historical interpretation of prophecy are to be found in Luther's prefaces to the German Bible. And, above all, a decisive step towards a right appreciation of the human aspects of the Old Testament poetry is taken by the great Reformer in the preface to the Psalter of 1531, where the Psalms are mainly considered, not as supernatural doctrine, but as the truly human utterance of the inmost heart of the Old Testament saints. But in this point, as in many others, the first promise of the Reformation was not fulfilled in the sequel. The spiritual insight that supplied a just point of view required to be supported by a scientific construc-

26

tion, for which means were then unattainable. The
whole realm of exegesis and criticism could not be revolutionised in a day. Methods of interpretation really
inconsistent with Protestant principles crept back in
detail. And very soon the original living conception of
God's Word began to grow stiff and cold Men's chief
interest lay in doctrinal polemic, and that interest seemed
to be best served when Scripture was viewed mainly as a
Divine body of doctrine. Even in the system of Calvin,
whose commentaries are distinguished by an attempt far
beyond his age to take a broad philosophical view of the
history of revelation, the growing tendency towards a
one-sided exaltation of what is doctrinal appears in
marked contrast to the spirit of Luther's earliest Reformation writings. And the days of the Epigoni saw the
growth of a Protestant scholasticism, which left room for
advance in the details of exegesis, but effectually checked
a just appreciation of the human characteristics of the
Bible. Theologians arose to whom the boldness of Luther
appeared audacity, and who gave up the justest results
of Calvin's exegesis as verging towards Rationalism.
The immediate perception of God's voice speaking in
Scripture had grown dull, and a generation which required
to have the divineness of the Bible proved to it by intellectual arguments had lost the firm ground which alone
could give freedom to do justice to the truly human
characters of the record of revelation. Thus one side
of the original Reformation impulse was more or less
absolutely divorced from the theology of the Church.
The desire for a more truly historical treatment of Biblical
theology expressed itself in the school of Cocceius in forms
not unsuspected by the stricter orthodoxy, and often not
free from extravagance ; while the literary and æsthetic
qualities of the Bible became an object of study to men
who shared in that revulsion against dogma which waxed
so strong towards the close of the seventeenth century.
Thus arose the breach between the theological and the

literary methods of approaching Scripture, which on both sides has been so fruitful of false science, and which cannot be healed until those who receive the Bible as the record of Divine revelation gain a faith strong enough to enable them to see that the right conception of God's Word permits, nay, demands, the freest study of the sacred record by all the methods of historical and literary criticism.

The nature and limits of the interest in the Old Testament poetry which was felt by the last champions of the period of Protestant orthodoxy, may be judged from the treatment of the subject in the learned *Introductio* of J. G. Carpzov. Of the chapter which discusses biblical poetry in general, by far the largest part is occupied with the purely formal question of the existence and nature of Hebrew metres. And it is thoroughly characteristic that the only other question that is raised is why the Divine wisdom was pleased to insert in the sacred volume several books composed in metre and tied down to rhythmic numbers. From such a state of things a reaction was inevitable ; and in the first instance, as we have said, the problem of æsthetically appreciating the Old Testament fell into the hands of men who had a keener interest in the beauty of the Hebrew poetry than in the deep religious life with which that poetry is instinct. By such hands the problem could not be solved, for in a work of art true appreciation of the form is inseparable from sympathy with the thought which the form embodies. But much was gained by the very statement of the problem. It was no small merit to make men feel that, *as poetry*, the writings of David and Isaiah are as worthy of study as the poems of Homer or of Virgil.

The idea of looking at the poetry of the Old Testament in this light was one that could not fail to grow up in many minds, almost contemporaneously, under the same historical influences. But the work which first brought the subject of Hebrew poetry, as such, distinctly before

the eyes of the world, was Lowth's *Prælectiones*. These
lectures were delivered from a chair of poetry, not of
theology, and their starting-point was the principle that
the artistic qualities of the inspired writings are not
excluded from the domain of criticism (*Præl.* ii.) [1] The
work is mainly occupied with discussion of the peculiarities,
figures, etc., of the Hebrew poetical style, and with an
investigation into the various species of Hebrew poetry.
There is not much in these inquiries that can now be read
with great pleasure or profit   The taste of the eighteenth
century was formed upon principles with which our age
has little sympathy   Lowth was far too much guided
by the analogies of Western poetry to do full justice to
the peculiarities of an Oriental literature , and as has
been already hinted, the divorce of the poetic form from
the religious contents of the Old Testament necessarily
obscured the true features of the problem. The most
lasting result of Lowth's researches lies in the doctrine of
Parallelism, and it may fairly be questioned whether
subsequent investigators have done wisely in following
him so closely on this topic. But with all its faults the
book produced, and deserved to produce, a great effect :
it struck a keynote to which the whole scholarship of
Europe gave a ready response

In almost every branch of learning and science it has
been the fatality of England to indicate fresh subjects
or strike out fresh methods of investigation, and then to
look on with apathy while foreign scholars eagerly press
forward on the newly opened path   Since the days of
Lowth our countrymen have scarcely made one contribution to the scientific criticism of Hebrew poetry, and it

---

[1] That this principle was then by no means obvious, may appear
from a single example which we select from Carpzov. Vossius had said
that the ancient Hebrew poetry was rude and unpolished. *Id*, replies
the Leipzig professor, *in Spiritum S. Biblicæ Poeseos autorem injurium
videtur, quasi fons ille sapientiæ, . . e Græcia demum lepores accersere
ac ab infidelium hominum artificio et labore veneres consectari, versuumque
expectare debuerit venustatem.*

may be doubted whether the *Prælectiones* themselves have not been more read in Germany than in England. Herder, when he gave to the world his *Geist der ebraischen Poesie*—the book which marks the next decided step in the progress of our subject—could assume that the prelections of the English bishop were familiar to all his readers.[1]

The very title of Herder's book indicates a vast advance on his predecessor. While Lowth busies himself with the *art* of Hebrew poetry, the theologian of Weimar expressly treats of its *spirit* If the former professed only to commend a choice poetry to students of polite letters (p. 22), the latter seeks to introduce his readers, through the æsthetic form, into the inmost spirit of the Old Testament His pages glow with an enthusiasm which is not the cold admiration of an indifferent critic, but the warmth of a man to whose heart the religious meaning of the Bible comes home with personal force. Thus Herder displays much more fully than Lowth the power to enter into the soul of the Old Testament writers which is essential to thorough criticism, and he recognises with wonderful keenness many of the unique features that separate the poetry of the Hebrews from that of the western nations. Lowth proposed to survey the streams of sacred poetry, without ascending to the mysterious source. Herder's great strength lies in his demonstration of the way in which the noble poetry of Israel gushes forth with natural unconstrained force from the depths of a spirit touched with divinely inspired emotion. Lowth finds in the Bible a certain mass of poetical material, and says :—" I desire to estimate the sublimity and other virtues of this literature—*i.e. its power to affect men's minds*, a power that will be proportional to its conformity to the true rules of poetic art." [2] Nay, says Herder, the true power of poetry is that it speaks from the heart and to the heart. True criticism is not the classification of poetic effects according to the principles of rhetoric, but the unfolding of

[1] Vol. 1. p. 3.   [2] *Præl.* 11. p. 19.

the living forces which moved the poet's soul.   To enjoy
a poem is to share the emotion that inspired its author.

" If the rules of art are true they flow from the nature
of the feeling with which the subject of the song is em-
braced by the poet's heart , but characteristics of the
singer, the situation, the language, always combine towards the effect.   The application of the rules then must
always be a *living* application, and so always partial ; in
brief, where they are true, who will not rather feel and
develop them afresh for himself in each song, than borrow
them from foreign models ? . . . Let the lays of the
Hebrews be examined in their primitive nature and
beauty ; let the teacher show the scholar what subject is
sung, and with what interest, what emotion dominates
the song, how it moves, into what veins of feeling it
expands, how it begins, proceeds, and ends."

Herder was deeply impressed with the conviction that
this method of looking at the Old Testament was nothing
less than the rediscovery of a lost literature, which all the
commentators had only buried deeper in the dust of ages.
Away with all practical application to modern times !
Let us see this primeval age, and in it the heart and mind
of David and his poets.[1]

The historico-psychological criticism which Herder so
warmly advocated no longer needs to be recommended in
opposition to the old method of dinning the poet's beauties
into the reader's ears , but there are still many who are but
half convinced that its application to the sacred record can
be otherwise than profane.   Yet it is obvious that he who
represents Scripture as speaking from the heart and to the
heart, has returned in a cardinal point to the genuine
Reformation conception which Protestant theology had
almost forgotten , and that the theologian who is not
prepared to assert that the Bible has no human side at all,
can exempt no element of the Psalmist's productivity
from the laws of psychology and history, unless on the
condition that in return another element shall be withdrawn from the sphere of inspiration.

[1] II. 2, ix.   Vol. ii. p. 237.

In demanding that the poetry of the Hebrews be studied according to the laws of historical psychology, Herder laid down a principle of permanent importance, but his application of the principle is marred by many defects. The plan of his work was gigantic. An introduction, which forms nearly half of all that the author actually put on paper, discusses the basis on which the Hebrew poets built—the poetic structure of the language, the primitive ideas of the race, and its earliest fortunes to the time of Moses. With Moses commences a full and elaborate history of all that influenced the poetry and poetic conceptions of Israel ; and this task is so widely conceived that, had the book been completed, almost the whole material of the Old Testament would have been worked up in its pages. So large an undertaking had for the first condition of success an accurate conception of the total historical development of Israel. That Herder was not in possession of such a conception cannot be imputed to him as a fault, for a century of further study has still left much that is obscure even in vital points of the Hebrew history. But under such circumstances the work was premature. The continuity of development which is traced has often no objective truth, and its apparent consistency means only that where it was impossible to read the poetry in the light of history, the history itself has been read by the light of poetical ideas, and the lack of precise conceptions has been concealed in a mist of genial subjectivity. In this mist the objective features of Hebrew culture, intellect, religion, melt away into indistinctness. The specific peculiarities that distinguish the religion of revelation from other primitive faiths are so little emphasised, that a product so intensely Hebrew as the Book of Job is supposed to have been the work of an Idumean poet. The whole history tends to disappear in poetry, while the objective peculiarities of the poetry itself lose their sharpness from an exaggerated endeavour to resolve everything into a purely untutored flow of natural feeling, unaided by art and uncoloured by reflection. These faults are in some measure due to the far too early date to which the criticism of the age referred many parts of the Old Testament , but it is singular that any critical prepossession should make it possible for so acute an observer to read off the simple prose of Genesis as verse, or to ignore the very high degree of conscious art that runs through so much of the poetry which Herder assigns to the remotest and most primitive antiquity.[1]

With all these defects, the labours of the poet and philosopher of Weimar made an epoch in the study of Hebrew poetry, for they vindicated for that study its proper place as an integral portion of the larger historical problem of reconstructing in its totality the life, growth, and vital activity of the Hebrew nation.   Thenceforth progress in this department of criticism was bound up with the general progress of historical research into the Old Testament development, and no great advance on Herder was possible except in connection with enlarged and more accurate views of the history of Israel as a whole.   Such views grew but slowly.   During the first decennia of our century speculation on Old Testament problems was little more than a chaos of acute but disjointed and arbitrary conjecture.   It is not therefore surprising that nearly forty years elapsed between Herder's death and the appearance of the next really important contribution to our subject ; and it was fitting that this contribution should come from the pen of the scholar who more than any other man has succeeded in gathering up the many-sided material of the Hebrew records into the oneness of a living, organic structure.   The characteristic power of Ewald is the intuition by which, without conscious induction or articulate proof, he comprehends within his gaze the whole heterogeneous data of a complicated historical or critical problem, and divines the unity in

---

[1] On this last point compare the instructive remarks of Ewald in his *Eighth Year-Book*, p. 599.

which all these fragments find their harmony. Concen-
trating this peculiar instinct on the historical monuments
of the religion of revelation, Ewald has enriched all parts
of Old Testament science with a multitude of fresh and
original views, and has everywhere struck out paths in
which even those scholars are compelled to walk who have
least sympathy with the peculiar character of his genius.
With these rare powers, Ewald it must be admitted unites
corresponding defects, which have greatly limited his
influence and often imperil the accuracy of his conclusions.
As his historical inductions are intuitive rather than
reasoned out, he lacks the power of verifying his results.
His arguments are always constructive, and he is seldom
able to acquiesce in a negative result, or to admit a doubt
as to the objective truth of a theory that satisfies his
subjective sense of harmony.   But as a constructive critic
he has no equal, and many scholars who ungenerously
depreciate his services to biblical science are themselves
doing little more than laboriously check off, and verify
or reject by the usual apparatus of historical induction,
the wealth of results, theories, and suggestions which
Ewald has lavished upon the world of science.

Since Herder's unfinished essay, only one considerable
attempt has been made to construct a comprehensive
history of Hebrew poetry.   And though the late Professor
Meier was a man of unquestionable æsthetic capacity, and
though in Germany his work has drawn forth the interest
of many who are not theologians by profession, its merits
are not such as to forbid the expression of the opinion
that even now many essential points of Hebrew history,
and many questions as to the date of the Hebrew records
remain so obscure that any such work, however interesting
and instructive, must either fall in great measure into the
shape of detached essays, or must assert the form of
historical continuity by bold guesses and large assumptions.
The character of the different epochs of Hebrew literature
is gradually growing clear to us, and some of the greatest

figures in that literature stand before us in sharply defined
outline. But much remains obscure, and, even those
results of recent criticism which seem most certain are
far from being universally admitted. While it is still
denied by influential critics that a single Psalm can safely
be ascribed to David,[1] while competent judges dispute
whether the Song of Solomon is a drama or a collection of
lyric fragments, and while the dates assigned to the Book
of Job in the critical school itself differ by many centuries,
it is obvious that if there is not much room for new
theories there is at least a call for much new proof. Such
proof must for the most part consist of an examination of
minutiæ, in which only theologians can be expected to
take much interest. Instead, therefore, of wearying our
readers by introducing them to the conflicts of detail
which at present occupy the arena of criticism, we shall
endeavour to set before them some of those results in which
all are agreed, and from which every one may find assistance towards an intelligent study even of the English
Bible.

There are two marks which characterise every real work
of fine art. The *first* of these marks is that it must embody
a *creative thought*, that it must exhibit the power of the
human spirit to seize, shape, vivify, and subdue under its
own dominion the dead matter of unformed impression
presented to the mind in the two universes of external
nature and internal feeling. And then, in addition to this
character of creativeness, a *second* mark is required to
distinguish æsthetic from scientific production. While
science values each new thought only as a fresh step
towards the intellectual comprehension of the whole

---

[1] This position was maintained by Hupfeld, mainly, one is compelled
to judge, from the general bluntness of his historic sense, which made
him partly indifferent and partly sceptical in questions of authorship
When the same thing is maintained by Kuenen, the explanation must
be sought not in indifference to the chronology of the Psalms, but
rather in the partiality of this critic for a peculiar historical (or unhistorical) theory of the religion of Israel

universe, the artist confines himself to thoughts which
possess for him a value quite independent of the inferences
that may be drawn from them for a more general body
of truth—thoughts to which he can give a self-contained
expression, without caring to use them as means to a
remoter end.   In a word, every work of art is a product
of creative thought, having its end within itself   In
science the joy of each new attainment is absorbed in the
fresh impulse to further pursuit of truth ; the search for
knowledge knows no rest till the whole universe has been
subdued.   A work of fine art points to no end beyond
itself, and urges directly to no activity save that of enjoying
to the full the satisfaction that accompanies every exertion
of completed mastery of thought over matter.

   It is obvious that the earliest efforts of human thought
could not possibly go out in the direction of scientific
construction.   The notion of an organic system of truth
advancing from generation to generation, till it grasp the
whole universe, can begin to be entertained only with the
beginning of a scientific *diadoche*, of a regular organisation
of thinkers and workers, each of whom takes up and
carries forward in fresh developments the truth received
from his predecessor or his neighbour   And this again
involves an amount of mental discipline, a power of
continuous self-denying effort, and a devotion to an
abstract aim lying far beyond the lifetime of the individual
worker, which are wholly unknown in the childhood of
society   But we are not therefore to conceive of the early
races of mankind as savages, acting only under the
pressure of material needs or the incitement of animal
instinct.   If history and psychology have a voice at all,
they declare to us that man was not developed by chance
from the lower creation, but came complete from the hands
of God Himself, with an eye to behold the harmony of
creation, a heart sensitive to emotion and sympathy, a
spirit not passive and perplexed under the myriad impressions that pour in upon it from the universe without, but

able and eager to give form and grace to these impressions by thought reproductive of the Divine idea, in which alone the beauty and order of the universe repose.

The earliest exercise of these inalienable faculties of the human spirit is childlike, but not therefore weak and childish. All primitive nations are too childlike to act except under the stimulus of imagination or emotion. Intellectual effort therefore is not calm and disciplined, but passionate and absorbing. All thought stands in immediate contact with living impressions and feelings, and so, if incapable of rising to the abstract, is prevented from sinking to the unreal   This indeed is a quality of primitive thought which we moderns are very apt to ignore or to deny.   We so uniformly speak of nature in the language of abstraction, inference, scientific theory, that we can hardly conceive that the earliest human speech offers only the direct, and therefore infallible reflection of what is felt.   If a Hebrew poet accosts the morning star as " bright-rayed son of the dawn," we are far likelier to fall into conjectures as to Semitic mythology than simply to accept the perfect image of newborn splendour floating in the lap of the early twilight.   The tendency of the modern mind which this instance exemplifies is one that must continually be guarded against in dealing with early Eastern literature, and especially in dealing with the Old Testament.   It is this misconstruction which on the one hand produces the Biblical Cosmologies, Biblical Psychologies, Mosaic Astronomies and Geologies that still perplex the unwary ; while on the other hand it has given rise to the fundamental fallacy of the negative criticism, the extraordinary delusion that the Hebrew race is indifferent to objective reality and historic truth.

To follow out these remarks would carry us too far from our present argument.   What we are now to observe is the contrast between the later habit of thought which inclines to look at everything in its logical and causal relations, and the primitive, childlike habit of thought which is completely absorbed in the one thing that is immediately before the mind.   The first kind of thought makes science, the second makes poetry.   For, as we have seen, the characteristic mark of poetry as a fine art is that it has its end within itself.   A poetic theme, therefore, is a theme in which the mind finds such interest as to have no impulse to pass away from it, such delight as to strive by every effort to attain full sympathy with its beauty, full mastery over its details.   To the primitive and childlike mind every emotion that rises above sensuality, every aspect of nature that is not directly interwoven with bodily needs, possesses these qualities and invites poetic treatment.   Each new thought is a lyric unity answering to a unity of feeling.   The thinker is of necessity a poet, whose task is not to display his idea in its relation to other thoughts, but to grasp it as it is in itself, to put upon it the impress of his own mastery, and give it enduring shape and comeliness by clothing it in articulate form.   For it is not as mere inarticulate impression or emotion that the new thing which confronts the poet with vivid concreteness and force of absorbing passion can be rightly felt and understood.   Only when bound down in fit utterance, and so made subject to the sovereignty of thought, do the subtle and many-sided phases of nature reveal themselves in their true significance and beauty.   The simplest impression of inner or outer nature bears within it something of infinitude which only the artist can grasp aright and reduce to finite expression.   Nowhere is the task of the nature-poet more pregnantly set forth than in the myth of the binding of Proteus.   The simplest manifestation of nature has countless shapes and changeful aspects, which by their glamour deceive the eyes and delude the grasp of men.   The true artist is he who, casting over Proteus the chain of artistic expression, sets forth in a single and adequate form the mobile many-sidedness of one idea, and receives as his reward a revelation of truth where other men find only illusion.

From the conception that the earliest creative thought is to be regarded as a lyrical reflection of the impressions of internal and external nature, the inference is obvious that the growth of language, so far as it rose above the crude expression of daily needs, was at first wholly shaped by poetic necessities, and urged forward by poetic motives This remark is not only true of language in general, but finds a just application to the characters that distinguish one language from another. The beginnings of prose composition, in any higher sense than that in which M. Jourdain spoke prose—in any sense therefore which can influence the subtler qualities of language—are long posterior to the differentiation of national tongues ; and, in fact, prose composition is possible only after the individuality of the language has been clearly stamped by a rich national poetry.   Thus the quality of the poetic thought of each people is imprinted on its speech, while reciprocally the psychological and artistic peculiarities of the speech permanently control the national poetry, and form perhaps the strongest influence towards the preservation of a fixed character in the nation itself.   If we desire, then, to grasp the peculiar qualities of Hebrew poetry, we cannot begin better than by following Herder in his admirable remarks on the poetical character of the language of Israel.

" Since action and delineation are of the essence of poetry, and since the *verb* is the part of speech that depicts action, or rather sets action directly before us, the language that is rich in expressive pictorial verbs is a poetical language, and is more poetical the more fully it can turn nouns to verbs   What a noun sets forth is dead, the verb sets all in motion .   . Now in Hebrew almost everything is verb—that is, everything lives and acts   . . The language is a very abyss of verbs, a sea of waves, where action rolls surging into ever new action.[1] . . . Nor does

---

[1] This acute observation receives fresh force from the exacter doctrine of the Hebrew verb forms which we owe to that scientific school

the speech lack such *nouns* and *adjectives* as it requires.
. . . It is poor in abstractions, but rich in sensuous representation, and has such a wealth of synonyms for the same
thing, because it desires always to name, and as it were to
paint the object in its full relation to all accompanying
circumstances that impress themselves on the senses.
The lion, the sword, the snake, the camel, have so many
names in Oriental (Semitic) languages because each man
originally depicted the thing as it appeared to himself,
and all these rivulets afterwards flowed into one.   Even
in the small relics of Hebrew that we possess the profusion
of sensuous epithets is very notable   More than 250
botanical names in a collection so short and so little varied
in subject as is the Old Testament.   How rich would the
language appear had we still its poetry of common life.[1]
. . . The *pronouns* stand forth in bold relief, as in all
language of the passions   The scarcity of *adjectives* is so
supplied by combinations of other words that the attribute
appears as a thing, nay, even as an active being.   With
all this, I conceive the language is as poetic as any upon
earth '' [2]

---

of Semitic grammarians of which De Sacy was the pioneer.   Our
abstract division of past, present, and future time has no existence in
the Semitic verb forms   The Semitic, but most fully the Hebrew,
distinguishes only perfect and imperfect action.   A notion that appears
in the mind of the speaker as still *growing* is put in the imperfect,
whether the objective scene of its growth is the past, the present, or the
future.   Inversely, actions conceived as complete are put in the perfect
Thus, if the Hebrew wishes to say, *I went and saw him, went*, as the
completed presupposition of the seeing, stands in the perfect , but *saw*,
which grows out of the *went*, is put in the imperfect, with only a slight
modification to show that the action is imperfect only relatively to the
went, not relatively to the speaker's present position.   Conversely, in
the sentence *I will go and see him*, the Hebrew feels that the means grow
out of the end, which, in idea, is the fixed and completed *prius*   Therefore *I will go* stands in the imperfect, but *see* in the perfect   Nothing
can show more clearly how the action and reaction of *living* ideas is the
dominating principle of the language.

[1] On this topic compare the remarks of Isaac Taylor in his *Spirit of
Hebrew Poetry*, p. 94   This ingenious treatise, though purely the work
of an amateur, and therefore quite deficient in scientific sharpness of
conception, is written in a spirit of glowing poetic sympathy, and
contains some good things   Taylor shows that the Old Testament
contains as many words about sea and water as the English language
can muster even when technicalities and colloquialisms are reckoned

[2] Vol 1. pp 15-18.

Passing to the Hebrew roots, Herder remarks how they unite picturesqueness with feeling, repose with passion, strength with softness of tone

"The northern speeches imitate the sound of nature but rudely, and as it were from without : they creak, jar, and rustle like the objects themselves. In the south the imitation of nature is more delicate. The words have passed through the finer medium of emotion, they are framed as it were in the region of the heart, and so give not coarse reproductions of sound, but images which feeling has modified by impressing upon them its softer seal. Of this union in the tones of the roots between internal feeling and external image, the Semitic languages are a model 'What!' cries the interlocutor of Herder's dialogue, 'these barbarous, gurgling, gutturals?' 'Yes,' replies Herder. 'We who live in smoke and fog speak between tongue and lip, and open our mouths but little. The Italian and the Greek again speak *ore rotundo*, and do not bite their lips together. The East draws its tones still deeper from the breast, from the heart itself, and speaks as Elihu begins.

> ' I am full of words,
> The spirit within me constrains me :
> It ferments in my breast like must corked up,
> It bursts like new bottles
> I must speak, that I may be refreshed ·
> Open my lips, and answer.'

"When these lips opened it was doubtless a living sound, image breathed forth in the stream of emotion, and this, I think, is the spirit of the Hebrew tongue." [1]

Our space precludes fuller reproduction of Herder's admirable demonstration that the Hebrew language marks out the nation that spoke it as a race through whose whole life ran a deep vein of intense but very *subjective* poetry. Let us, however, concentrate our attention on the quality

[1] Page 20   To appreciate the description of the gutturals as tones drawn from the depths of the breast, the reader must remember that the Hebrew gutturals do not, like the Scotch and German *ch*, strike the palate, but are purely breathed up from the throat like the English *h* But while our alphabet has but one such letter, the Hebrew writes four gutturals, and in pronunciation distinguished five or six

of *subjectivity*, which is the main key to the psychological criticism of the Old Testament literature.   The Hebrew language, as Herder has shown us, is fitted to express nature, not realistically, as it presents itself to the outer unsympathetic eye, nor simply sensuously idealised as in the art of Greece, but as it appears when seen through the medium of passionate human interest and transmuted in the alembic of internal feeling   The perfection of the Hebrew language as a vehicle of emotion is in truth most strikingly seen in points of grammatical structure to which Herder does not allude.   Every nicety of form and construction has for its end the expression of varying relations of feeling between the thinker and his thought. In the hands of David or Isaiah every word, every suffix, every modification of order or of tone, expresses some delicate shade of emotion hardly reproducible in another language.   Such a tongue is the fit organ of a fervid and imperious personality which refuses to be the mere interpreter of nature, and esteems nothing which cannot be brought into concrete relation to itself.   The un-impassioned, intellectual admiration of the ideal of sensuous beauty, which is the ruling principle of Greek art, is unknown to the Semite.   He values nature only in so far as it moves and affects him, or is capable of being moved and affected by him.   He has no sense therefore for that objective harmony of a beautiful scene which is independent of the varying emotions with which men may look upon it   To him nature is what he feels as he beholds it : the universe is a complex of living powers with which he enters into a fellowship of joy and woe, of love and dread, of confidence and fear ; which awe him with the utterance of infinite might, or furnish him with matter of victorious boasting if he is able to bend them to his own service.

The art which corresponds to such a view of nature is necessarily *unplastic*.   The Hebrews never attained excellence in the reproduction of natural things by the pencil

27

or in sculpture, and their poetry contains no example of
that elaborate word-painting which calls up a scene in its
objective harmony and full sensuous beauty.   It would
be wrong to conjecture as the reason of this deficiency the
want of a quick eye for outward things.   On the contrary,
the very richness of the Hebrew tongue in appropriate
names for sensible objects is sufficient proof that everything in nature that has a human interest, everything that
touches directly on the life of man, and addresses itself to
his emotions and his heart, is laid hold of with the keenest
appreciation and the subtlest sympathy.   But in truth
nature is too full of meaning, and speaks too strongly to
the heart of the Israelite, to suffer him calmly to analyse
and reproduce its individual traits.   To him the unity
and harmony of an outer scene or a train of thought is
always a unity of passion and feeling.   He does not therefore depict nature in the just balance and organic relation
of its parts, but seizes one and another isolated feature
and absorbs them into the stream of an all-transmuting
emotion.   Hence the few instances of plastic art which are
recounted in the Old Testament are all symbolic.   It is
most characteristic that we have no description of the
cherubim which would enable an artist to reconstruct
them.   The symbolic parts of which they were composed
are enumerated with care ; but we have no hint of an
attempt to give to the figure built up from these heterogeneous symbols anything of objective symmetry and
beauty   Beyond doubt no such attempt was made.[1]

The same want of plastic power characterises the delineations of Hebrew poetry.   The descriptions of Homer
or of Sophocles at once suggest pictorial treatment,

[1] If the reader desires to realise this more fully, let him turn to the
description of the heavenly procession in Canto 29 of the " Purgatorio,"
and contrast the thoroughly plastic character of the picture with the
corresponding passages of Ezekiel and of the Apocalypse   But it is
obvious that the figures of the cherubim had defeated Dante's power of
constructive imagination   He is compelled to refer his reader to
Ezekiel   " E quai li troverai nelle sue carte, Tali eran quivi."

but no pencil could reproduce the war-horse or the leviathan of Job, where the unity of the picture lies wholly in the emotion of admiration and awe into which the sensuous elements of the description are absorbed. Or for an example of a different kind take the Book of Ruth. Could a Western writer have related a story so idyllic with a harmony so poetically perfect, and yet with so complete an elimination of the plastic pictorial element ? The book is full of vivid lifelike detail. But everywhere that detail is directly subservient to the human interest of the action. There is not one touch of colouring or description that would help a painter in depicting the scene.

It must not be imagined that for this reason Hebrew poetry is remote from nature   The whole Old Testament literature is rich in small fragments of the most delicate observation embodied in a sentence, sometimes in a word , but these fragments are strung upon a thread of feeling instead of being set forth by artistic composition and grouping of parts. A typical example is the first chapter of the prophecy of Joel. Every verse sparkles with gems Each little picture, suggested rather than drawn, is in the most exquisite harmony with the feeling of the prophet. The fig tree stripped of its bark, standing white against the arid landscape ; the sackcloth-girt bride wailing for her husband ; the night watch of the supplicating priests ; the empty and ruinous garners ; the perplexed rush of the herds maddened with heat and thirst ; or the unconscious supplication in which they raise their heads to heaven with piteous lowing, are indicated with a concrete preg- nancy of language which the translator vainly strives to reproduce. But the composition is a crystallisation, not an organism, a series of boldly etched vignettes, not a single picture.

It is obvious that a poetry of this type refuses to be judged by our usual canons of criticism. We are not to ask for unity of composition where the poet himself designs only unity of feeling ; nor may we, in criticising

so subjective a poetry, condemn anything as grotesque
and inharmonious that is not disproportionate to the
dominant emotion   This remark is peculiarly applicable
to the gigantic images and metaphors of the Old Testament.   In Western poetry an image is always liable to
criticism in itself, and nothing is admitted for purposes of
illustration that would be quite fantastic as the description
of a reality.   But to the Hebrew no image is too bold to
give utterance to the emotion by which he is stirred.   It
would be absurd to class the daring figures of the Psalms
and Prophets as examples of hyperbole.   Hyperbole is the
licence that our poets take to impress their hearers more
deeply by representing objects as grander than they really
are, without absolutely distorting them from their true
form.   But when the Psalmist represents hills as skipping
and clapping hands, when Joel ascribes to his locusts the
irresistible teeth of a lion, when the Assyrian king as
pictured by Isaiah boasts that he has dried up rivers with
the soles of his feet, or when Ezekiel figures the king of
Tyre as a cherub walking within the fiery bulwarks of
the mount of God, these gigantic metaphors refuse to be
judged by the limited licence accorded to Western poets.

Thus commentators are found who gravely argue that
language so strong must have a hidden allegoric meaning,
that the Prince of Tyre, for example, is Satan.   To the
poets themselves such criticism would have seemed
ridiculous.   They were accustomed to read nature wholly
in the light of subjective emotion or spiritual truth.   The
boldness of the fancy with which they gave sensuous form
to their feelings was hampered by no habits of scientific
study of the laws of phenomena.   Regardless of external
probability they sought only a just expression for subjective experience.   What we are apt to call exaggeration
is really idealisation—the elevation of the whole scene into
a symbol of the invisible.   We have no right to call that
fantastic which truly expresses internal intuitions moulded
by the fire of a subjectivity stronger than ours.

Often the boldness of the Hebrew images lies in the combination of parts taken from several quite dissimilar figures. Mixed metaphor is not only natural, but appropriate when the world of sense offers no one phenomenon in which the fulness of the poet's emotion can be mirrored. Not only is image piled on image, but the weaker figure seems often to dissolve into one of grander force. Thus when Isaiah pictures the onset of Assyria on Judah, he hears the roar of the lion as it springs on its victim, followed by the low and awful moan which shows that the prey is secured. But presently this moan waxes more and more intense, till it passes into the grim murmur of a storm-lashed sea, while the hot breath and overshadowing terror of the lion bending over his captive are transmuted into a dark and murky storm-cloud which enwraps the land of Judah in the gloom of hopeless night.

His roar is like the lioness,
He roars like the young lions ,
And moans and clutches his prey, and bears it off and none can save.
And he moans over Judah like the moan of the sea.
When they look to the land, lo ! stifling gloom
And day grown black in lowering clouds [1]

It is not only in the absence of plastic composition and in the shape of individual images and metaphors that the poetry of the Old Testament bears the stamp of the peculiar subjectivity of the Semite. We have seen that this subjectivity dominates for the Hebrew his whole view of the universe , that all nature appears to him instinct with a life which vibrates responsive to each change in his personal feelings and spiritual relations. This way of looking at outward things makes itself felt in the matter as well as in the manner of Hebrew literature. That the poetry of such a race is certain to be rich in the expression of every human passion is too obvious to need further illustration than every Bible reader can supply for himself. But it is instructive to observe how the poets of Israel enter into human relations with impersonal things, and

[1] Isa v 29, 30.

see in them also the movings of a life not wholly incapable
of fellow feeling with man.   Herder has drawn attention
to the sympathy which Hebrew poetry always manifests
towards the brute creation [1]—a sympathy not confined
to the domestic animals, which the Israelites treated with
a consideration well brought out in the story of Balaam's
ass and in the law of Sabbatic rest, but extending to every
living thing   Nay, even inanimate objects appear as the
friends of man.   Take for example the exquisite song in
which the Hebrew women as they stand round the
fountain, waiting their turn to draw, coax forth the water
which wells up all too slowly for their impatience ·

> Spring up, O well ! (sing ye to it !)
> Well that the princes digged,
> The nobles of the people bored,
> With the sceptre and with their staves ! [2]

The simplicity of personal interest, the tenderness of
affectionate regard, with which the Hebrew maidens salute
the " living waters " that well forth, murmuring in answer
to their song, belongs to quite another sphere of fancy
from that which peopled the mountains and glades of
Hellas with the fair sisterhood,

$$αἵ τ' ἄλσεα καλὰ νέμονται$$
$$καὶ πηγὰς ποταμῶν καὶ πίσεα ποιήεντα$$

When the Greek ascribes life to the powers of nature he
gives to his personification a shapely human body as well
as a living soul, and in the same measure as his creation
gains in plastic grace it becomes less near to the daily
life of man   The nymph is no longer the fountain or the
tree, which man knows and loves, but a new being that
hides herself behind them.   But to the Semite the rippling
water is itself alive, the oaks of Bashan wail when the fire
wastes their tangled forests,[3] the cedars and cypresses of
Lebanon rejoice in mocking songs over the fall of the

---

[1] *Dial* iii. vol 1 p 66

[2] Num xxi. 17, 18   To dig with the staff, which is the symbol of
authority, means to command the well to be dug.   [3] Zech. xi 1, 2

king of Babel who so mercilessly hewed down their glory.[1]

No relation of man to nature has a stronger fascination for the Semitic mind than that of practical lordship over powers so much mightier than his own.   Every one knows how this fascination finds its expression in the wondrous Oriental tales of enslaved genii and the like.   The same thing is to be seen in the magic of Eastern nations. An Arab servant accompanying a European naturalist, would regard his master as a madman, were he not persuaded that his scientific collections are to be used in some mysterious way to enthral the powers of creation.   This tendency finds a loftier and truer, but not less characteristic, expression in the Old Testament.   If the Israelite abjured magic arts, it was not because he was indifferent to the world-sovereignty of man, but because he knew that that sovereignty is more surely rooted in the creation gift of God, which is so nobly sung in the eighth Psalm.

---

[1] Isa. xiv 8   "Living water" is the standing name in the Old Testament for spring water.   The personification of trees is constant, and it is remarkable that, while the animal fable of Aesop is not, as has sometimes been wrongly imagined, a Semitic product, we find in the Old Testament two parables of trees (Jud ix 8 *seq* , 2 Kings xiv. 9) The nearest Western analogon to this play of fancy is to be found in certain features of the Teutonic *Märchen*, which have been well explained by Heine, whose Jewish birth gave him a hereditary right to understand and delight in this subjective vein of imagination   See a passage in the *Harzreise*, where he describes an aged trembling grandmother who has sat for a quarter of a century behind the stove opposite the cupboard, till her thoughts and feelings have grown into union with all the corners of the stove and all the carvings on the cupboard   " And cupboard and stove live, for a human being has breathed into them a portion of her life."   Heine proceeds to explain how, to thoughtful, quiet folk, living a life of deep " immediate " contemplation, the inner life of inanimate objects revealed itself, and these acquired a necessary consistent character, a sweet mixture of fanciful whimsicality and true human dispositions.   Amidst all difference of detail between the imagination that shaped the *Märchen*, and that which dominates Hebrew poetry, the great point of agreement is what Heine rightly calls the " immediacy," *Unmittelbarkeit*, of both—the way in which the Teuton or the Semite stands in direct contact and personal fellowship with the life of the objects that surround him   Something of the same feeling pervades the works of a great Jewish painter, Josef Israels.

But let us choose a less familiar example of the spirit in which the Hebrew glories in the power of man's cunning and labour to subdue all nature. Such an example we shall find in Job's description of the art of mining, the Old Testament counterpart of the famous chorus of the *Antigone*:

> For there is a lode for silver · a place for gold which is fined
> Iron is brought from dust . and stones are smelted into brass.
> Man sets an end to darkness and searches out to its farthest veins .
> the stone that lies in night and gloom.
> The shaft is opened far from all sojourners   and there forgotten of human foot,
> They hang far from mortals : they flit to and fro.
> The earth—out of her groweth bread : and beneath they pierce resistless as fire.
> The place of her brightest jewels : the dust of her gold are theirs
> The path that the eagle hath not seen . the eye of the vulture hath not scanned ·
> Which the proud beasts have not trod : which the lion hath never walked.
> On the flint he layeth his hand   overturneth mountains from their roots
> Through the rock he cleaveth passages : and his eye beholds all precious things ;
> He binds up the shafts from weeping : and brings forth secret treasure to light. [1]

In lays like the Song of the Well created things appear as man's friends · in the picture that we have taken from Job they are represented as his captives and his slaves We have still to consider the more awful aspect of the powers of nature in which they present themselves as the utterances of a mysterious might, before which the strength and wisdom of man are as naught. This is the point of view from which the nature-worship of the heathen Semites appears in its proper contrast to the polytheism of Greece. In the Hellenic religion the plastic element, the sensuous ideal, predominates. " The

---

[1] Job xxviii. 1 *seq*. The allusion in the last line is to the greatest difficulty with which the miner has to contend—the breaking in of water through his shafts   The contrast with the Chorus of Sophocles (*Antig.* 362 *seq*) is instructive, but cannot be drawn out here.   I remark only the counterfoil to man's power and cunning in each case Job continues. " But where shall wisdom be found ?"   Sophocles adds : Ἄιδα μόνον φεῦξιν οὐκ ἐπάξεται.

gods that live at ease," the Olympians of Homer, are very different beings from the *El* or *Eloah*, the "mighty and dreadful one " of the Semite   The heathenism of the Canaanites and the Phœnicians is never æsthetically beautiful, but vibrates between the opposite yet allied poles of sombre horror and wildest sensuality, between the terrors of Moloch-worship and the orgies of Ashera. Always we find a religion of passionate emotion, not a worship of the outer powers and phenomena of nature in their sensuous beauty and majesty, but of those inner powers, awful because unseen, of which outer things are only the symbol.[1]

Corruptio optimi fit pessima.   The very tone of mind which makes Semitic heathenism the most hideous of false worships, enabled the Hebrew nation to grasp with unparalleled tenacity and force the spiritual idea of Jehovah   It is indeed a vain notion of Renan and other theorists that the Semitic races have a peculiar capacity for monotheism.[2]   But at least Semitic monotheism could scarcely degenerate into deism or pantheism.   Not into deism ; for to view nature as an independent and yet impersonal organism is quite impossible to a habit of thought that everywhere in nature sees life, and life bearing directly upon man   not into pantheism, for even Semitic polytheism looked on material things as symbols rather than as realities, and reverenced only the mysterious and the unseen.   To the Hebrew, force is life, and life is personality.   The one true God whom man has learned

[1] Hence the simplicity of the material objects which these nations worshipped—the sacred stone, the Ashera or sacred pole, the consecrated tree   In the English Version the characteristic features of Canaanite idolatry are disguised by more than one mistranslation   The sacred stone, *maççeba*, appears as an " image," the Ashera as a " grove "   Actual images seem to have been repulsively coarse in conception (Cf 1 Kings xv 13, Heb)

[2] This notion has been sufficiently refuted by several writers.   See especially Dillmann's tract, *Uber den Ursprung der ATlichen Religion*, p 16 *seq*   The English reader may compare a paper on Semitic monotheism in the first vol. of Mr. Max Muller's *Chips from a German Workshop*.

to know in His historical revelation is a living, loving
God, ever working and ever present to His people   Now
the whole universe is seen to be not instinct with dark
and cruel forces, but full of the spiritual harmony of a
gracious personal plan of righteousness and love.   From
such a contemplation of the world in its relation to God,
a rich religious poetry could not fail to spring.   Nature
itself in that harmony in which it is revealed to the eye
of faith is one grand poem, an embodied thought of God
set forth to be read by man, and not only to be read with
distant admiration, but to be grasped with personal
sympathy and trust.   So conceived, no part of the universe
was indifferent to the believing Israelite.   His was no
religion of asceticism, that should turn him away from the
contemplation and enjoyment of outer nature, and shut
up his spiritual life within himself.   His keen zest for the
beauties and pleasures of the outer life was only quickened,
though it was purified and solemnised by the thought that
it is God's hand that crowns the year with goodness, and
His majesty and grace that all nature proclaims.   Or
again, when nature frowns, the Hebrew, raised above
slavish fear of a malignant, destructive power, could hear
the voice of Jehovah thundering forth the declaration
that the merciful and gracious God is also the God of
judgment, whose holy justice will by no means clear the
guilty   To comprehend the full influence of the spiritual
religion on the development of the poetry of Israel, we
must remember that the idea of the universe as a natural
unity, of which our noblest nature-poetry is so full, was
entirely foreign to the Hebrew mind.   The keen observation and subtle sympathy with individual sides of natural
things which distinguishes Semitic poetry, is, as we have
already learned, altogether dissociated from the faculty
of artistic grouping and plastic composition of an organic
whole.   The only unity which the poet can realise is a
unity of feeling and purpose.   Thus a really grand and
catholic poetry of nature could be achieved by the Hebrews

only under the influence of a comprehensive and all-absorbing personal interest to which no part of nature should be alien, and which should bind up the whole universe in the oneness of a transcendental purpose. And this was an influence which only the religion of Jehovah could supply. To realise the scope of these remarks we have only to compare the Song of Solomon with the Book of Job. No Old Testament writer has a richer sensuous fancy or a truer eye for the features of nature than the poet who, nurtured amidst the northern mountains, where all that is beautiful or majestic in Canaan is gathered up, lavishes the whole wealth of his imagery in singing the love and constancy of the Shulamite. But perfect as is the poem in its kind, few Western readers can peruse it without a feeling of monotony. The infinite succession of similes, all just and even brilliant, all showing the true poet, but strung together like a necklace of pearls, only by the common theme of emotion that runs through them, at length wearies us by the very prodigality of fancy. We are perplexed by the total absence of objective grouping, the want of light and shade, which is carried so far that even the beauty of the Shulamite is praised only by the choice of a comparison for each separate feature of her person The poem is full of nature, but it is too one-sided, and strikes too exclusively only such notes as are in unison with the dominant passion, to be a great nature-poem. But while not even the noblest of merely human affections is broad enough to sustain an all-sided poetry of nature, it is otherwise with such a theme as occupies the Book of Job. To the relations of man to his Creator and Redeemer the whole universe vibrates responsive. Here there is no room for monotony, for the theme itself is infinitely varied. Nor could any pictorial grouping of images equal the sublime grandeur of the closing chapters of the book, in which all creation is marshalled in glorious wealth of disorder to do homage to the wisdom and power of the Most High Thus it is that

in the Old Testament the noblest poetry of nature and the
loftiest spiritual conceptions are linked together in an
indissoluble bond, and that universality of poetic sympathy from which nothing in nature is estranged is
realised only when creation in all its plenitude and in all
its changefulness appears as the direct expression of the
will of the ever-present King and Saviour of Israel.

We find in the Old Testament a series of Psalms in
which natural scenes are so depicted that they yield up
their spiritual meaning, and appear as witnesses to the
existence and attributes of Jehovah [1] A comparison of
these hymns with the treatment of similar themes by
Western writers is sufficiently characteristic of the Hebrew
genius. The Western poet, or even a Western prose
writer on natural theology, will not fail to begin by setting
before him the scene in its objectivity, reproducing the
natural features of his subject by pictorial description
before proceeding to draw a religious inference or lesson
But the Hebrew needs no process of inference to set
Jehovah before him as the prime mover in all he sees. He
needs no argument *a fortiori* to rise from the glory of the
creature to the supreme majesty of the Creator. The
spiritual meaning of the scene so fills his soul, so inter-
penetrates all that he beholds, that he is never able to
linger on the production of a finished picture, or to rest on
the natural scene as in itself the adequate object of poetic
contemplation His first word is praise to Jehovah, with
which his soul is overflowing, and every feature of his
description, instinct with the same emotion, looms through
a mist of religious awe, love, and fervour, and attains
harmony only in this subjective and unplastic medium.
Let the reader take up Psalm civ , and observe how no
part of nature is able to detain the poet. He hurries from
point to point, with the restless eagerness of a man who
only seeks in the objects around him food for an engrossing

[1] Among the more notable of these are Psa viii , the first part of
xix., xxix , lxv , civ

emotion. Once and again, at ver. 24, 31, this emotion
breaks out in pure song ; and at length the *point of rest*
in which every poem must end, and which could not be
found in the contemplation of nature, is reached in the
concluding strain of praise, ver. 33-35.[1]

All this is but a special application to the sphere of
religious life of the more general law that the Semitic
imagination assimilates objective phenomena only in so
far as they are held in solution by personal interest or
strong emotion. The world of nature is orderly and
beautiful only as the reflex of the world of moral and
spiritual relations. But the principle obviously works
in two directions. If the Hebrew instinctively views
nature in the light of its spiritual meaning, he as instinctively gives to every spiritual perception a symbolical and
sensuous expression. And since, as we have already seen,
the idea of natural possibility or probability does not
exist for the Semite, the expression is subject to no
condition save that of appropriateness to the thought set
forth. Thus the whole realm of visible phenomena stands
free to the poet to be dealt with as he will. The multiplicity of the universe becomes one vast chorus of living
things moving responsive to the action of the spiritual
stage, without restraint of natural law. Especially is this
the case in the description of the being and work of

---

[1] No better illustration can be found of the difference between the
Hebrew and Occidental treatment of the same ideas than is supplied by
a comparison of Buchanan's paraphrases of the nature-Psalms. A
good instance is the treatment of the sun in Ps. xix., or, to confine ourselves to Ps. civ , take the following passage, in which every variation
from the Hebrew tends to an increase of plastic pictorial delineation,
with a corresponding diminution in the directness with which the
religious emotion dominates each line of the original .

> Tum liquidi fontes imis de collibus augent
> Flumina, per virides undas volventia campos :
> Unde sitim sedent pecudes, quae pinguia tondent
> Pascua, quique feris onager saxa invia silvis
> Incolit : huc levibus quae tranant aera pennis
> Per virides passim ramos sua tecta volucres
> Concelebrant, mulcentque vagis loca sola querelis.

Jehovah. The poet's heart is full of gratitude to God : straightway sun and moon, stars and heavens, fire and hail, storm, winds, mountains, beasts and creeping things, must join in sounding forth His praise [1] David celebrates in Psalm xviii the deliverances that God has wrought for him in every crisis of his life. At once the earth shakes and trembles, the thundering voice of Jehovah rolls across the heavens, His arrowy lightnings scatter the foemen, the blast of His storm-wind lays bare the channels of the seas, and the Most High Himself, descending in smoke and flame, stretches forth His hand and rescues His servant from the waters that surge around him Or once more, when Jehovah appears to judge the earth and deliver His people, the seas roar, the rivers clap hands, the mountains exult together.[2] Or if His coming is viewed rather as a day of terror and anguish for the guilty and rebellious, then the earth reels like a drunkard, and sways like a hammock, the moon is lurid and the sun pales.[3]

It must not be supposed that this imperious subjectivity of the Hebrew, which demands that the whole universe shall blend to the conviction that burns within the poet's soul, asserts its sovereignty only in the sphere of religion. No poetry can ignore the principle of sympathy between the aspects of external nature and the changing views of the poetic observer. But there are two ways in which this principle can receive expression. The modern poet is impressed with the conviction that nature has an individuality, and a fixed character of her own She is capable of infinite sympathy, but her favour must be wooed and won by subtle appreciation of her faintest smile, by patient submission to her opposite, as well as her approving moods. Of such study of nature the Semite is wholly incapable The pathos of contrast between his own mental state and the expression of natural things, which plays so great a part in modern poetry, has for him no sweetness, or rather no existence His eyes refuse to

Ps. cxlviii   [2] *Ibid.* cxviii.   [3] Isa. xxiv.

see what his heart cannot assimilate.   The desert blossoms
with his joy, and the orchards and gardens of Carmel
wither in his despair.   The fairest things are spurned
with impatient hate, or blighted with bitter curses, if their
beauty stands in contrast to his woe.

> Ye mountains of Gilboa,
> No dew, no rain be upon you,
> Ye fields rich in oblations !
> For there the shield of the mighty lies rusting,
> The shield of Saul—not anointed with oil [1]

We have already observed that the subjective intensity
of such a poetry can appear extravagant or untruthful
only when judged by too narrow a canon of taste.   In the
nature of the case artistic truth is always more or less
partial, for the artist isolates and treats as a perfect whole
what in reality is only one factor of a larger unity of
nature or of thought.   And so, if the unity to be realised
is one of supreme emotion, it is not only legitimate, but
imperative that all opposing elements be sacrificed to the
ruling idea.   But, on the other hand, an art which proceeds
on such principles must often be obscure and unattractive
to those whose less intense subjectivity is unable to share
the resistless sweep of the poet's passion.   A Semitic
poetry of the ordinary themes of life can hardly attain to
the perfect catholicity that appeals to all minds in all
ages , for at least we of the Western races require a special
effort of cultivated literary appreciativeness to throw
ourselves into the vein of uncontrolled immediate feeling
in which the Oriental naturally moves.   But the very
characters that constitute a certain particularism of
interest in the treatment of secular themes mark out the
Hebrew poetry as the most perfect and catholic vehicle
for the æsthetic expression of religious faith.   In every
other case the artistic propriety of making all nature bend

[1] 2 Sam 1 21.   The unction by which the shield of the warrior is
kept bright is alluded to in Is xxi 5   The " fields of offerings " (A.V)
are, as Ewald rightly explains, fields so fertile that many offerings of
first-fruits are sent from them to the sanctuary.

to the personal emotion of the singer can receive only a
subjective justification   The art of the Hebrew is true
art to those who can rise to the level of his passion.   But
religious conviction is supreme where it exists at all.   And
the æsthetic necessity that all things in heaven and earth
shall bend to the Divine purpose of salvation revealed to
the poet's faith, is also the ethical necessity on which the
whole religious life depends.   That the things which are
impossible with men are possible with God is the first
axiom of a religion that shall rise with triumphant assurance over all the powers of evil and all the woes of life.
To assert with unwavering confidence the victory of
spiritual certainties over all empirical contradiction, to
vanquish earthly fears in the assurance of transcendental
fellowship with God, to lay down for all ages the pattern
of a faith which endures as seeing Him who is invisible
—such is the great work for which the poetic genius of the
Hebrews was consecrated by the providence and inspiration of the Most High.   How nobly this work was served
by that Hebrew intensity which carries one supreme
conviction with irresistible poetic fire through all things
in heaven or earth that rise up against it, may be read
alike in the personal utterances of the Psalter and in the
Messianic hopes of the prophets.   Thus it was that the
Psalmist, surrounded on all sides by the contradiction of
sinners, bowed with sickness and grief, oppressed by the
consciousness of guilt, was yet able so to cling to the
unfailing certainty of his living fellowship with a redeeming God, that danger, and sickness, and sin itself were left
behind, and he pressed forward beyond the fear of death
to the assurance of immortality at God's right hand.
Thus it was that the prophets gazing on the certainties of
Jehovah's righteousness and grace saw the creation, now
stained with sin and blasted by the strokes of Divine
indignation, transformed in new perfection and holy
loveliness, and instinct in all its parts with a sweet intelligence, so that from voice to voice of things now deemed

inanimate the prayer of man goes up to God and the answer of God descends on man :

> In that day, saith Jehovah, I will answer,
> I will answer the heavens,
> And they shall answer the earth ,
> And the earth shall answer the corn, and the wine, and the oil,
> And they shall answer Jezreel [1]

From the consideration of the characteristic *material* of feeling and fancy in which the richness of the Old Testament poetry lies, we must proceed to look at the not less characteristic *form* which the Hebrew poets impress upon their thoughts.   The most general law of poetic form is embodied in the principle of rhythm.   But while all poetry is necessarily rhythmical, rhythm is of very various kinds.   Amidst all variety of *metres*, the *rhythm* to which we Occidentals are accustomed is always more or less purely syllabic.   And of syllabic rhythm we are familiar with two types, the rhythm of accent which prevails in our northern tongues, and the rhythm of quantity (partially modified by accent) which regulates the classical poetry.   Neither type is unknown to the Semitic races. The prosody of the Arabs is based on quantity, while in Syriac, where the original distinction of long and short syllables has disappeared almost as completely as in the modern languages of Western Europe, each verse consists of a measured number of syllables, with a rise and fall of tone.   But innumerable attempts to apply to the ancient Hebrew poetry one or other of these analogies have proved vain, and scholars are now agreed that there is no syllabic rhythm in the Old Testament.   But the Hebrew poetry is not therefore unrhythmical.   The absence of metre is compensated for by a rhythm of sense.

To understand this we must go back to the first principles of æsthetic expression.   Alternate rise and fall of energy is a fundamental law of human life, which in all its forms is regulated by the necessity for repose after excite

[1] Hos. ii 21, 22.

28

ment, and by the development of new impulse to action
during the period of repose. The application of this
principle to speech, and especially to impassioned speech,
is sufficiently obvious   The wave of emotion rising in the
soul sympathetically stirs the physical system and lends
strength to the voice. In this swell of impassioned
utterance the emotion itself is momentarily exhausted,
and an interval of rest or lowered utterance supervenes
till the tide of passion again rises and produces a fresh
wave of physical utterance   Such unregulated alternation of excitement and depression does not in itself possess
any æsthetic and rhythmical character   The agony of
Philoctetes, the passion of an angry woman, the violent
weeping of a child, are all illustrations of the rise and fall
of utterance under strong emotion , yet they are the very
opposite of poetical, for they are not harmonious, but
spasmodic. Poetic expression, as we have seen, implies
indeed that the whole soul of the poet is full of some
absorbing feeling or impression, but it implies also that he
so controls and shapes his passion by utterance that he
shall appear master over his matter, not mastered by it ,
not sullenly and silently curbing his emotion, but moulding it and giving to it a harmonious completeness in which
he and others can take delight. " In the very torrent,
tempest, and (as we may say) whirlwind of his passion, he
must acquire a temperance that may give it smoothness."
And so while the poetic enthusiasm must find its expression in elevated utterance, that elevation is not allowed to
sweep on till checked by sheer exhaustion, but is regulated
by the intellect   For just as an emotion can be momentarily checked by the mere passionate effort of physical
utterance, so an effort of will concentrated on the work of
giving intelligent expression to poetic feeling produces a
similar effect. But so soon as this intelligent utterance is
reached, the emotional element again rises and calls for
new expression, and thus originates a harmonious pulsation of emotion and thought, feeling and utterance, which

is not spasmodic, but rhythmical. And as a fit of uncontrolled passion ends when physical exhaustion is
absolute, so the poetic enthusiasm gradually subsides
when the successive waves of utterance have completely
transmuted the poet's feeling into an intelligible form in
which he can rest and find his inspiration fully embodied.

Rhythm, then, in the sense in which it is an essential
quality of poetry, is the measured rise and fall of feeling
and utterance, in which the poet's effort to become fully
master of his poetic inspiration finds harmonious expression, and the external rhythm of sound is properly subordinate to the rhythmic pulsation of thought. Where
the rhythm of thought is perfect, no prosodic rules are
necessary to produce a corresponding harmony of sound,
for the words employed naturally group themselves in
balanced members, in which the undulations of the
thought are represented to the ear. But as poetry becomes more artificial there arises a tendency not to trust
wholly to the rhythm of thought, but to make the rhythm
of sound and words a special study. The balance of two
lines or metrical members is artificially marked by allitera-
tion or by rhyme ; or, again, an exact balance of time
is introduced by counting the syllables or the *moræ* of
the lines ; or, finally, a complete prosodic system carries
equilibrium of parts through all the details of the rise and
fall of the voice within each line. By these refinements
in artistic execution the external rhythm of sound has
become so independent, that we are apt to forget its
essential subordination to rhythmic flow of thought.
But it is still the latter kind of rhythm which distinguishes
the true poet from the mere versifier.

We are able from these considerations to understand
what was so great a puzzle to Lowth and other early
writers—that Hebrew poetry is truly rhythmic without
possessing any laws of metre. The whole form of a
Hebrew poem is directly dependent on the harmonious
undulation of the thought, line answering to line, not in a

mere equilibrium of sound, but in a balance or parallelism of sense   As rhythm necessarily implies the correspond- ence of at least *two* parallel parts, the ultimate unit of Hebrew poetry is a verse consisting of two members embodying two answering thoughts   And as correspond- ence of thought brings with it similarity of expression, the two members of the verse will be similar in length and possess a certain irregular harmony of accent, which can be felt though not subjected to rule, and which, having its source altogether in the intrinsic structure of the thought, can be reproduced with tolerable accuracy, even in a good prose translation.

The simplest form of Hebrew rhythm shaped on these principles is that which from the time of Lowth has been called the " synonymous parallelism " of a distich :

> There the wicked cease from troubling |
> And the weary be at rest ||
> There the prisoners are at rest together, |
> They hear not the taskmaster's voice ||
> Small and great are there the same ; |
> And the servant is free from his master. || [1]

In this simplest form the rhythm is so clearly cut that it can hardly be lost even by translators who, like those of our English Version, were not conscious of the principle involved. Effects of this kind therefore are almost always well rendered, and are quite familiar to the English reader   A more complicated figure, however, which has not always been so successfully reproduced, arises where each member of the verse becomes so long that it again falls by a *cæsura* into two subdivisions :

> How sitteth she lonely | the populous city |
> Is she become a widow | who was great among the nations |
> A princess among provinces | is become a vassal [2]

It is not, of course, necessary that the balance of parts should take the form of the repetition of similar thoughts. A relation of antithesis is equally rhythmical, and gives what Lowth calls " antithetic parallelism " :

[1] Job iii 17-19   [2] Lam. i. 1.

Mighty bowmen are cast down, |
And the stumbling gird on strength , |
The full hire themselves for bread, |
And the hungry keep holiday. ||
Yea, the barren hath born seven, |
And she that hath many sons is withered. || [1]

To the two classes of rhythm which we have hitherto exemplified the names devised by Lowth are not inappropriate ; but it is unfortunate that so narrow a word as parallelism has been so universally adopted to express all possible varieties of effect that arise under the general law, that wave after wave of feeling gives rise to wave answering wave in utterance.   Lowth's third species of parallelism, which he calls synthetic, is not parallelism at all, and very inadequately groups together a great variety of rhythmical effects which have very little in common with one another, beyond the general principle that the verse falls into two or more members, each of which represents a unity of thought, feeling, or fancy, while the transition from member to member takes place in harmonious pulsation of movement and rest   One or two examples will sufficiently illustrate the various ways in which this is realised ·

My voice———I cry unto Jehovah, |
And he hath heard me from his holy mountain ; ||
I laid me down and slept, |
I awoke, for Jehovah sustains me. || [2]

We are apt to overlook the truly rhythmic character of such passages, because to our habits of abstract thought the logical union of protasis and apodosis in a complete sentence is predominant.   But to the concrete way of thinking of the Semite, a conditional proposition consists of two distinct mental pictures, one of which flows over into the other.   Where we would say, " If he pulls down, it cannot be rebuilt," Job says, " Lo ! he pulls down, and it cannot be rebuilt " (xii. 14).   Remembering this habit of thought, we shall recognise an impressive rhythm in

[1] 1 Sam. ii. 5   [2] Ps iii

many passages which at first sight seem pure prose.
Thus—

> The Lord on thy right hand |
> Smites down kings in the day of his wrath, || [1]

is not one picture, but two distinct images, with a rapid
movement from the rest of the first to the activity of the
second.

An extremely effective example is the tristich, Ps xlv. 6,
which is entirely lost in our version .

> Thine arrows are sharp—
> People fall under thee—
> In the heart of the enemies of the king.

In the first line the warrior bends his bow, in the second his
chariot sweeps over the fallen, and then when he has
passed by it is seen that his shafts are truly planted in the
heart of the slain.

The rhythmic figures of Hebrew are not confined to the
distich and tristich. Verses occur which have four, five,
or even six members, and in these again the variety of
form got by choosing which pairs of members shall correspond is as great as the variety of rhyme possible in a
modern stanza of four or six lines   But to exemplify the
rich multiplicity of such effects would fill pages, and would
necessarily lead on to a not less intricate and much
disputed theme—the arrangement of groups of verses in
larger unities or strophes. Instead of entering on these
details, let us take simply one stanza from Ps. xlviii., which
will illustrate the majestic effect that can be produced
by the Hebrew rhythm of sense, even when recast in a very
inadequate translation .

God in her palaces | hath proved himself a stronghold
For lo the kings assembled | they sprang forth together .—
When they saw, straightway they marvelled | were panic-stricken, and
    fled ,
Tremor seized them there | pangs like a woman in travail.

---

[1] Ps. cx. 5.

With storm wind from the east | thou breakest ships of Tarshish
As we heard | so have we seen,
In the city of Jehovah of hosts | in the city of our God
God upholds her for ever [1]

Among the various *species of composition* in which the genius of Hebrew poetry finds expression, the first place is unquestionably due to the lyric. As poetry is the earliest form of literature, so the lyric is the earliest species of poetry, and must long retain its pre-eminence in a nation endued with the mental characteristics that we have found in the Hebrews. For to define lyric poetry, it is not enough to say that it is intended to be sung to the accompaniment of instrumental music In true art the music is ruled by the thought, and the lyric is sung because its contents naturally demand such an expression. It is noteworthy that in primitive times lyric recitation was accompanied not only by music but by dancing.[2] In truth, musical utterance is to ordinary language just what the dance is to that bodily action which is the natural accompaniment of all speech in nations that have not been schooled to suppress such demonstrations. Both are forms of the eager rhythmical expression which is the appropriate vehicle for absorbing personal thought Speech rises into song, and gesture becomes a dance in giving utterance to an idea which springs fresh from the fountain of the soul with a force that bends every faculty of body as well as mind to do service in setting it forth

[1] Very interesting analogies to the characteristic sense-rhythm of the Old Testament are presented by recently discovered specimens of ancient Assyrian poetry, of which English translations by Mr. Talbot appeared in the *Transactions of the Society of Biblical Archæology*, vol ii , and which have been again examined by Schrader, ' Die Hollenfahrt der Istar,' etc. (Giessen, 1874). Professor Schrader goes so far as to build on these analogies the theory that the *parallelismus membrorum* is not an original product of the Semitic races, but a form of rhythm adopted from Accadian poetry by those branches of the Semitic stem which came in contact with the early Turanian culture of Babylonia See his paper, "Semitismus und Babylonismus," in the *Jahrbb für Prot Theologie*, 1875, p 121, ff

[2] Exod. xv 20 , 1 Sam. xviii 6 , Ps cxlix. 3. Comp *Iliad*, xviii 494, 572 , *Odyssey*, i 152.

Thus Ewald seems right in contrasting the lyric as the poetry of nature with those later forms of composition in which the poet, instead of simply expressing what he sees or feels at the moment, sets before him a definite end, and enlists his fancy and poetic enthusiasm in its service. It is probable that in all nations the later forms of poetry were gradually developed from a lyrical germ, and in the poetry of Israel this process can still be distinctly traced. The Hebrew was so eminently a man of strong emotion and impulse, always deeply stirred by what was present and personal, that every interest of life was a ready source of song. The extraordinary opinion of Keil, that in Israel secular poetry was never able to thrive beside the sacred muse, finds its refutation on almost every page of the prophets and the historical books. Of the strains in which national victories were extolled or national calamity bewailed, we still possess examples in the song of Deborah,[1] in the ironical Mashal of Num. xxi. 27 *seq.*, and in the elegy of David over Saul and Jonathan.[2] The sacred record could not, of course, present us with examples of the riotous "song of the drunkard,"[3] or of the lays in which the prosperous wicked expressed their careless happiness;[4] but the darkest side of primitive life is still pictured in the savage "sword song" in which Lamech exults in the prowess of his irresistible weapon :

> Adah and Zillah, hear my voice ,
> Ye wives of Lamech, give heed to my speech
> I slay a man if he wound me,
> A young man for a stroke !
> For Cain's vengeance is sevenfold,
> But Lamech's seventy and seven [5]

The gleeful carols of the vintage,[6] and the bridal songs that celebrated the virgins of Israel,[7] have sunk into oblivion ; but the lay of the well, already quoted, still

---

[1] Judges v.   [2] 2 Sam i   [3] Ps. lxix 12.   [4] Job xxi. 11, 12

[5] The point of the conclusion lies in the contrast between Cain, the club-bearing man, and Lamech, whose family had reached the secret of forging weapons in metal

[6] Isa. xvi 10.   [7] Ps lxxviii. 63, A V. margin

preserves the memory of a graceful poetry of everyday life. Nor is the plaintive pathos of the funeral dirge forgotten, when besides the great elegy on the slain of Gilboa we can still read the simpler but not less touching words in which David mourned at the grave of Abner :

> Did Abner die a felon's death ?
> Thy hands unbound, thy feet not set in fetters.
> As falls a man before villains, thou didst fall.

An interesting but obscure indication of the varied developments of the lyric genius of the Hebrews is preserved in the titles of several of the Psalms. The longer of these titles frequently designate the melody to which the Psalm was sung by quoting two or three words of a familiar song , and our fancy is easily tempted to conjecture by such broken hints as " Hind of the morning glow," or, " Dumb dove from afar."

The first step from pure lyric to a more artificial poetry is seen in those compositions which, while exceeding the limits of a simple song, attain a larger compass, not by any intricate organisation or plan, but by the simple agglomeration of lyrical parts. The same deficiency in power to overrule the emotion of the moment, which deprives Hebrew art of plastic pictorial quality, prevents all really objective groupings of the parts of a lengthy poem   The longest of the Psalms has no plan whatever, but simply a unity of sentiment. The Book of Lamentations is a similar series of lyrical utterances all on one key , and alike in this book and in Ps. cxix. the absence of an inner principle of structure is compensated by the adoption of the purely external scheme of an alphabetic acrostic. The long historical Psalms have a less artificial structure, but in these also the unity is generally to be sought, not in any epical grouping of events, but in an underlying current of sentiment or praise which often bursts out in a periodical refrain. Of this tendency Ps. cxxxvi. is an extreme but by no means an exceptional instance.

From this kind of composition the transition is easy to properly *didactic poetry*. All deep personal feeling, such as a noble and earnest lyric expresses, stands in close relation to some universal truth. What the poet experiences in his own heart must have a validity going beyond himself ; and in particular the religious conviction that animates the Hebrew hymns has as its necessary source and counterpart a body of general religious truth. The worthless modern subjectivity which separates the religious sentiment from all persuasion of objective realities is remote from the spirit of the Old Testament , but, conversely, the general truths of the religion of Israel (except in so far as they are embodied in ritual, precept, or historic narrative) are always spoken to the heart as well as to the intellect. The Israelite never thought of framing a system of theology. His interest in religious truth was not scientific but personal. The deepest truths of the dispensation were not reasoned out scientifically, but felt as personal necessities. The doctrine of immortality, for example, to which Socrates attained by argument on the constitution of man's nature, is grasped by the Israelite in personal assurance that death itself cannot part him from God his Redeemer Truths reached by such a process—by the reasoning of the heart, not of the head —necessarily assume a poetic form, which insensibly merges into pure lyric If the hymns of the Old Testament express a personal emotion embodying and resting on a general truth, the corresponding didactic poetry expresses general truth in the tone of personal enthusiastic conviction

Of the truths so reached and set forth two things will be plain.

1. They must be sententious or aphoristic, rather than parts of a system This follows with psychological necessity from the self-containedness of personal emotion. A truth grasped by feeling stands out as a unity free from all merely rational connection. The mind of him who has

laid hold of it is ready to rest on it for its own sake.   It has come to him as the direct satisfaction of a personal need, and so it is impossible that he should value it only as a link in the chain of reasoned truth.   Such an acquisition has little to do with scientific system, but naturally assumes a poetic form, which shall set it forth as a complete thought, with a life and beauty of its own.

2. Again, such truths are sure to be practical.   They centre in human life and in real human interests.   As they were born of personal feeling, they continue to move in the personal sphere.   And being personal, they must bear directly on the practical concerns of life   The passionate subjectivity of the Hebrew has nothing in common with dreamy, unpractical sentimentalism.   The keen eye for business, the shrewdness degenerating into cunning, which is the most universally recognised characteristic of the modern Jew, is not a new feature of the nation   Exactly the same qualities appear in Jacob, whose character is as typical on this side of it as in its deep emotional and religious susceptibility.   The practical qualities which so many centuries of isolation and oppression have forced into ignoble channels appear in the Old Testament in more worthy activity.   No people has so toughly maintained national existence and prosperity in a narrow country, preserved in fertility only by unceasing industry, and exposed on all sides to the ambition of great empires.   Surely indubitable proof that the Hebrews were endowed with a strong instinct of self-preservation, with a tenacity of purpose and a power of practical insight capable of coping with the most unfavourable circumstances   It is in truth the preponderance of the emotional rather than of the rational part of the nature that makes a strong personality, able to conquer all difficulties   Intellectual acuteness is often associated with a restlessness of purpose that can attain nothing great   A really deep subjectivity is not to be stirred by slight breezes of sentiment.   It moves swiftly and fiercely, casting itself

with all fervour into the present impulse , but, just because the current at each moment flows so strong, it is not easily turned aside.   It binds circumstances to itself, and sweeps away hindrances in the whirl of its own passion   And this claim to rule over outward things that belongs to every deep impetuous personality, this assertion of man's·kingship over nature which the Old Testament so often makes, brings with it the power to command, the gift of grasping and cunningly using all that can be made subservient to the ruling purpose.   If it fail, it will do so rather by stubbornness and stiffness of neck than by infirmity of purpose.   When the nation decayed in the time of the Judges, or before the Captivity, or again before its last fall, it did so because individuality stiffened into individualism · because each man's feeling of personal worth asserted itself in refusal to acknowledge the rights of others and the supreme sovereignty of Jehovah.   It required strong family affections, national enthusiasm, and above all religious faith, to bind natures so strong and fierce ; and where these bonds were lacking, the Hebrews fell asunder into wild and reckless self-will, into a life that spurned all weaker constraint.

A race which, however little it estimated intellectual supremacy over nature, was so eager for practical sovereignty, must necessarily have a keen sense for all the precepts of practical wisdom.   A wisdom to walk by, an insight into all the secrets of human life, and of nature so far as it can be made to serve man , such was the only philosophy of the Hebrews.   Precepts of wisdom for the ruling of daily life, guided by a sense of the supreme reality of Israel's relation to Jehovah, and expressed not in scientific system, but in that sententious, often epigrammatic form in which such truth suggests itself to the tact and experience of a practical nature, and with a breath of poetic fervour that points to an origin in the heart as much as in the head—this is the peculiar wisdom of the Hebrews, the Chokma of the Old Testament.

The original germ of the Chokma is the individual proverb so familiar to us in the rich collections which make up the greater part of the Book of Proverbs.

In this kind of composition the poetic character of the thought is asserted by strict rhythmic arrangement. The proverb is almost invariably a single distich, but a distich in which the sharp antithesis of opposing members or the brilliant parallelism of moral truth and natural image gives the complete effect of symmetrical artistic finish. How perfectly, for example, is the right relation of the three generations of which a happy Hebrew family is always supposed to consist laid down in the simple distich—

> The crown of the aged are children's children.
> And the glory of children are their fathers [1]

The antithetic rhythm of the proverbs is so sharp cut that it loses little by translation, and our English Version supplies every reader with abundant material for estimating this side of the Hebrew Chokma Not quite so successful is the treatment of the proverbs which rest on a similitude between the spheres of nature and of human life. The most pointed of these similes simply give the natural image in the first member of the distich, and add the moral parallel without any such syntactical connection as the "*As . . . so is*" of the English Version. This form is peculiarly appropriate as a vehicle for the caustic humour in which the Hebrews delight

> A ring of gold in a swine's snout— [2]
> A fair woman without sense. [3]

From the simple isolated proverb the didactic poetry of the Hebrews rises in several directions to more elaborate efforts, but without showing any considerable disposition to pass from the aphoristic form to theoretical and systematic philosophy.

The brief simile is expanded into a parable like those

---

[1] Prov. xvii. 6.
[2] The nose-ring of the East corresponds to our earrings.
[3] Prov xi 22

of Jotham or of Nathan,[1] and ceases to shape itself in rhythmic form   But even the poetical Chokma in the narrower sense of the word sometimes teaches by means of a moral tale, as in the picture of the foolish young man of Prov. vii. 6, ff

In later times this kind of composition was greatly developed, and the apocryphal books of Tobit and Judith are full-blown moral romances.   Nor is it so plain as many suppose that something of the same kind is not to be found within the canonical books   That the Book of Job stands in the canon is scarcely a proof that the narrative is historical ; and many modern critics are disposed to regard the Book of Jonah as a didactic parable, written partly to enforce the truth that God regards the lives and accepts the repentance of Gentiles as well as Jews, and partly to explain that the forgiving mercy of God does not discredit the Divine commission of prophets of judgment.

In another class of compositions the sarcastic humour which we have seen to animate some of the Hebrew proverbs finds more elaborate expression.   The humour of the Old Testament is always grim and caustic, as we see in the life of Samson ; in the answer of the Danites to Micah , [2] in the parable of Jehoash , [3] or in the merciless ridicule with which the Book of Isaiah covers the idolaters.[4] Hence arises a peculiar species of mocking satire, which is so intimately connected with the proverb, that the same name (*Mashal*) covers both.   Of this Mashal the prophetic books contain several examples, of which the most powerful is the elegy on the king of Babylon in Isa. xiv. But the most ancient and peculiar of these poems is the mocking song in which the children of Israel invite the Amorites to return and fortify the demolished fastness of their king, Sihon, exalting that monarch's prowess against Moab, in order to bring into stronger light the valour of

---

[1] Judges ix , 2 Sam. xii.　　　[2] *Ibid.* xviii 22-26.
[3] 2 Kings xiv. 9.　　　[4] Isa. xli. 6, 7 , xliv. 12 *seq.*

Israel, beneath which the invincible Amorite and his stronghold had for ever fallen :

> Come into Heshbon,
> Let Sihon's city be built and made fast !
> For fire went out from Heshbon,
> Flame from the fortress of Sihon.
> It licked up the city of Moab,
> The lords of the heights of the Arnon.
> Woe unto thee, Moab ! thou art fallen, people of Chemosh.
> He [Chemosh] gave up his sons to flight, his daughters into captivity
> To the king of the Amorites, Sihon
> But *we* burned them out—fallen is Heshbon—to Dibon,
> We wasted them even to Nophah,
> With fire to Medeba [1]

Apart from the special developments of the parable and the satiric Mashal, the proverbial wisdom of Israel readily passed from individual aphorisms to larger didactic compositions, like that which occupies the first nine chapters of the Book of Proverbs We have here a long exhortation or exhortations in praise of wisdom and virtue, with no very strict plan or closely reasoned course of argument, and with characteristics both of thought and form which mark just such a relation to the single proverb as that which, in Hebrew architecture, subsists between the temple of Solomon and the simple cell.   In both cases the larger whole is formed by agglomeration of smaller parts rather than by internal development ; and the great chambers of the sanctuary, surrounded by rows of smaller cells, are an apt type of almost all the longer literary compositions of the Hebrews.   Even the late Book of Ecclesiastes does not present an essentially different construction.

The fact that no trace of *epic* poetry appears in the Hebrew literature has sometimes been explained simply from the lack of objectivity and the deficiency in the gift

---

[1] In one or two obscure or corrupt words the translation offered above follows the conjectures of Ewald   But the general sense is quite clear   Sihon had defeated Moab, but Israel overthrew Sihon   The Moabites are the sons and daughters of their god Chemosh

of organic composition which characterises the race. But
these qualities would have modified the form of the
Semitic epos, rather than have rendered such composition
altogether impossible [1] Nor is it just, with other critics,
to regard the Pentateuch as a Hebrew epic. For though
the epic poet selects a subject at least quasi-historical, his
method of treatment is the very opposite of history.
Elevating its heroes above the measure of common
humanity, and interweaving mythological with historical
characters, the epos seeks to separate the past from the
present by the widest possible gap, and so to gain an
isolated territory, in which it may freely use every creative
license   But even those critics who form a low estimate
of the accuracy of the earlier history of Israel will not deny
that the origin of the Hebrew race is told in such a way as
to emphasise the historical connection of the present with
the past   The religious pragmatism of the historical
books, so fully recognising the special providence which
gives unity to the whole story of Israel's fortunes from
the days of the Exodus, or even of the covenant with
Abraham, is directly opposed to the epical point of view.
The Israelite had no desire to isolate a part of past time,
adorning it with nobler motives and higher life than
subsequent ages could show. The God of Abraham,
Isaac, and Jacob is the everlasting God of Israel, as near
to His people now as in former days. And so more
accurate criticism has proved that the Pentateuch is not
an isolated epos, but that in composition, as well as in
subject, all the leading historical books of the Old Testament possess a certain unity, stamped upon them by

[1] It is true that not only the Hebrews, but the Arameans and Arabs
are without an epic poetry. But this kind of composition was known
at least to the Semites of Babylonia and Assyria, who perhaps derived it,
along with the mythological lore so necessary to the epic poet, from
their mysterious Turanian predecessors   The epical legend of the
descent of Istar into Hades, discovered in the library of Sardanapalus,
may be read in English in the first volume of *Records of the Past*. The
exploits of Lubara and the epic of Izdubar, discovered by the late
George Smith, are given in his *Chaldean Account of Genesis*

repeated recensions, in which the works of various authors were united into one whole.   In a word, the whole principle of the Old Testament religion, with its doctrine of the covenant of Jehovah with His people, was equally unfavourable to the rise of epic poetry, and favourable to the growth of continuous historic literature.   It seems more than probable, however, that the earliest efforts of the Hebrews to provide a literary record of past deeds took very much the form of collections of ballads and lyrics of historic reference.   The existing historical books quote at least two such collections, *The Book of the Wars of Jehovah*, and *The Book of the Upright.*[1]

In our rapid survey of the various species of Hebrew poetry we have not yet found a fit place for the Song of Solomon and the Book of Job.   The latter book no doubt is, in the largest sense of the word, a didactic poem, and competent critics are still found who can see in the former nothing but an anthology of erotic lyrics.   But it seems quite wrong to maintain that it is a mere play of subjective fancy which finds in the Song of Solomon a unity of lyric dialogue and action ;   and the critics who propose to deny, *a priori*, the capacity of the Hebrew muse for dramatic arts, must yet admit that the grand construction of the Book of Job displays an objectivity of conception and a developed artistic power which is much nearer to the genius of the dramatist than to the ordinary type of the Chokma.   The history of the Greek stage teaches us how readily the higher developments of lyric poetry lead over to the drama , and, indeed, wherever the lyric ceases to be sung by the poet alone, and is given over to be executed by a trained choir, it is inevitable that the first step towards dramatic performance shall be taken by the introduction of lyrical dialogue between two parts of the singers.   But the choral performance of trained musicians was certainly familiar to the Israelites from the time of Samuel downwards ;   and in several Psalms, especially in

[1] Num xxi 14 , Jos. x. 13 , 2 Sam. i. 18.

29

the twenty-fourth, which appears to have been sung as
the ark was led by David into Zion, it is impossible,
without undue scepticism, to ignore a peculiar adaptation
for performance by answering choirs. From the anti-
phonal psalms, or from rhetorical passages of so dramatic
a structure as the sixth chapter of Micah, there is but a
short step to such lyrical dialogue as the Song of Solomon
presents, and though this dialogue falls far short of the
complexity of the Occidental drama, it seems reasonable
to acknowledge the dramatic complexion of a poem in
which the author does not simply give scope to his own
feelings, but represents two or more characters side by
side   Nor is it likely, in an age when all lyric was composed to be sung, not read, that the same singer took the
part both of Solomon and the Shulamite   If we may not
suppose a stage with all its accessories, it is yet probable
that the victory of pure affection over the seductions of a
corrupt court and the temptations of a king was sung in
the villages of the northern kingdom by several answering
voices   Or if we hesitate to accept the attractive theory
which sees in Solomon, not the hero, but the baffled
tempter of a drama of pure pastoral love, the demand for
more unambiguous proof of the power of the Hebrew
poets to discriminate and depict in action various types of
character is simply answered by the Book of Job, in which
every interlocutor not merely upholds a distinct argument,
but does so in consistent development of a distinct personality. If we have difficulty in classing this masterpiece
of the Hebrew muse under the category of dramatic
poetry, our difficulty has its source not in the absence
of dramatic motives in the book, but in the marvellous
many-sidedness with which this quintessence of the
religious poetry of Israel combines the varied excellences
of every species of Hebrew art.   The study of the Book of
Job is the study of the whole spirit of the Old Testament,
so far as that spirit can be expressed in pure poetry without
introduction of the peculiar principles of prophecy.   The

problem of God's providence, which is the theme of the poem, is the central problem of the pre-Christian economy; and in the discussion of this grand enigma are absorbed all the treasures of wisdom and fancy, all the splendour of language and conception, that adorn the culmination of Hebrew art   It would be vain to attempt in a few lines, at the close of a paper already too long, to give even the most inadequate idea of so inexhaustible and withal so difficult a book , but our brief sketch of Hebrew poetry may fitly close when we can point to this noble and imperishable monument of the world-wide significance of the inspired genius of Israel.

V

ARABIAN STUDIES

(1880-1881)

I. Animal Tribes in the Old Testament. (July 1880)

II. A Journey in the Hejâz   (1881.)

I

ANIMAL WORSHIP AND ANIMAL TRIBES AMONG THE ARABS AND IN THE OLD TESTAMENT

THE importance of animal and plant worship for the study of primitive society has been put beyond doubt by the researches of Mr. J. F. M'Lennan, of which only the first outlines have been made public in his essay on " The Worship of Plants and Animals " in the *Fortnightly Review* for 1869, 1870. In his essay it is laid down as a working hypothesis that the ancient nations came through the Totem stage, or in other words that they came through that peculiar kind of Fetichism which has its typical representation among the aborigines of America and Australia. The totem or kobong of these peoples is an animal or plant or heavenly body appropriated as a fetich to all persons of a certain stock. These persons believe that they are descended from the totem, who is reverenced as a protector and friend, and whose name they bear. The line of descent is through the mother, who gives her totem to her children. Persons of the same totem are not allowed to marry. Where the system exists in this typical form every group necessarily contains persons of different totems. But a change in the system of kinship along with other circumstances may operate, as is seen in observed instances, to produce homogeneous groups inheriting a single totem and totem name from father to son Again the totem god of a dominant stock may come to command the worship of all the tribes in a group, the other tribal

455

gods forming subordinate deities, as in Peru. Thus little
by little the features of the original system may be
obliterated till the connection between the animal gods
and tribes bearing an animal name is no longer apparent.
In adopting as a legitimate hypothesis the opinion that the
ancient nations have passed through the totem stage,
Mr. M'Lennan is partly guided by his previous and
independent conclusion as to the universal prevalence, at
one stage of society, of exogamy and kinship through
females , but quite apart from this he has brought
evidence to prove that from the earliest times in very
many cases and in the most widely separated races
" animals were worshipped by tribes of men who were
named after them and believed to be of their breed "
This conclusion, taken along with the prevalence of the
totem system in modern savage races over a very large
part of the globe, opens up a line of inquiry of the first
importance, and suggests points of view for the study of
ancient religions which may not perhaps prove to be so
universally applicable as Mr M'Lennan's hypothesis
assumes, but which at any rate claim to be taken into
account and put to the test whenever we have to deal with
a religion that acknowledges animal gods

I am not aware that any recent writer on Semitic
religions has directed his attention to the questions
suggested by Mr. M'Lennan's speculations. There is a
controversy whether Semitic heathenism is purely astral
or whether it also includes telluric elements ; but the
latest advocate of the astral theory, Count Baudissin,
pursues his argument without any consciousness of the
important connection that subsists between plant or
animal worship and totem tribes. Nay, he puts the
animal worship of the Semites altogether aside, with the
remark that " nothing is yet known of a sacred character
being ascribed to living animals among the Semites, and
when the gods are figured in animal form or accompanied
by animals, the animal can be more or less clearly made

out to be a pictorial representation of the attributes of the celestial gods" (*Studien*, ii 146). Now it will of course be admitted that among the Semites animal gods were largely identified with astral powers. But this by no means proves that from the first the animal was a mere emblem of heavenly attributes. On the contrary the religion of Peru affords an unambiguous example of the elevation of totem gods to the skies, on the theory that "there was not any beast or bird upon the earth whose shape or image did not shine in the heavens"[1] Indeed when we look at the matter closely we find no complete proof that all Semitic animal gods were identified with planets or constellations even in the later developments of their worship What is the astral equivalent of the fly-god Beelzebub? or of Dagon, whose character as a fish-god Baudissin himself accepts as probable? Or if we turn to Arabia, what proof can be offered beyond vague analogy that the god worshipped by the Dhu-'l-kalâ', under the name and figure of an eagle (Nasr), was a form of the sun-god, or that a planetary character belonged to Yaghûth (*the helper*), whose image was that of a lion, or Ya'ûq (*the hinderer*), who was figured as a horse.[2] It would tax the ingenuity of the boldest symbolist to reduce to its astral elements the Jewish worship of all manner of creeping things and unclean beasts (Ezek. viii. 10, Deut iv. 17, 18, contrasted with ver. 19). And it is strange that Baudissin should deny that living animals had sanctity among the Semites, when he has occasion in the very same

---

[1] *Fortnightly Review*, 1870, p. 212

[2] These three appear in the Qor'ân as idols of the antediluvians, which no doubt expresses a consciousness that they are gods of the earliest antiquity Nasr is mentioned in the Talmud, Tr. 'Aboda Zara. The other two antediluvian idols Wadd and Suwâ' had the shape of a man and woman respectively. The explanation of the latter name by Osiander (*Z D M G* vii 496) rests on an appellative sense given to the word in the Qamûs which is not acknowledged in the Lexicons of Lane and Bistâny.—I have not access to Wustenfeld's genealogical tables, but learn from Osiander that in one tribe (the Qoraysh) we find as proper names "Servant of Yaghûth" and "Servant of the Lion," which presumably refer to the same cultus.

essay to speak of the sacred fish so common in Syrian sanctuaries, and of the horses of the sun among the Jews (2 Kings xxiii. 11, comp Micah i 13).

Now if the astral character of Semitic animal gods is in many cases no more than a theory, and a theory which at best is not conclusive as to the original character of these deities, it becomes a matter of great importance to ask if we can find any traces of a belief that the animal gods were progenitors of tribes which bore their name   In that case the theory that the animal forms are mere pictures of divine attributes must fall to the ground ; for a tribe would not claim to be the offspring of an attribute, but of the god himself under his proper name.

The probability that among the Semites as in other parts of the ancient world, and notably in Egypt, animal worship and animal tribes were associated in the way which Mr. M'Lennan's theory would lead us to expect, was suggested to me a considerable time ago by the examination of data in the Old Testament, which contains our earliest literary record of the forms of Semitic Polytheism. The Old Testament facts seemed to point to Arabia as the part of the Semitic field most likely to throw further light on the matter   In Aberdeen unfortunately I have no access to the Arabic texts most indispensable for complete inquiry into the subject.   But even the scanty helps which I have at hand have yielded so many relevant facts, and throw so much light on the data contained in the Bible, that I venture to put forth a provisional argument, which I hope will be found to possess sufficient consistency to justify publication, and to invite the co-operation of scholars in further research.   My results are remarkably confirmatory of Mr. M'Lennan's theory—a theory framed almost absolutely without reference to the Semitic races, but which nevertheless will be found to explain the true connection of a great number of facts which have hitherto remained unexplained and almost unobserved.   It is not often that an historical speculation receives such notable experimental verification, and in this connection I hope that the facts may receive the attention of students of early society who are not Semitic scholars.

I start from Arabia, because the facts referring to that country belong to a more primitive state of society than existed in Israel at the time when the Old Testament was written, and because in Arabia before Islam we find a condition of pure polytheism, and not as in Israel the struggle between spiritual religion and the relics of ancestral heathenism (Josh. xxiv. 2).

Moreover, the first point is to show the existence of animal tribes or families, and here it is convenient to begin with the Arabs, among whom a very great number of such tribes is found. The following examples are gathered from the *Lubbu-'l-lubâb* (Suyûṭi's dictionary of gentile names), and make no pretence to completeness.

Asad, lion; "a number of tribes." *Aws*, wolf; "a tribe of the Ançâr," or Defenders *Badan*, ibex; "a tribe (بطن) of the Kalb and others" *Tha'laba*, she-fox, "name of tribes." *Ġarâd*, locusts, "a sub-tribe of the Tamîm." *Benî Ḥamâma*, sons of the dove; "a sub-tribe of the Azd." *Thawr*, bull; "a sub-tribe of Hamdân and of 'Abd Manâh." *Ġaḥsh*, colt of an ass; "a sub-tribe of the Arabs" *Ḥida'*, kite; "a sub-tribe of Murâd." *Dhi'b*, wolf; "son of 'Amr, a sub-tribe of the Azd." *Dubey'a*, little hyæna; "son of Qays, a sub-tribe of Bekr bin Wâil, and Dubey'a bin Rabî'a bin Nizâr bin Ma'add." *Dabba*, lizard; "son of Udd bin Tâbicha bin Ilyâs bin Moḍar" (eponym of the Benî Dabba or sons of the Lizard) Also the ancestral name of families in Qoreysh and Hudheyl. *Dibâb*, lizards (pl), "son of 'Amir bin Ça'ça'a." *Dabâb*, a subdivision of the Benî Ḥârith and of the Qoreysh, is perhaps the same thing. *'Oqâb*, eagle; "a sub-tribe of Ḥaḍramaut." *'Anz*, she-goat; "son of Wâ'il, brother of Bekr" The tribe of the 'Anaza, whose eponym is represented as the uncle of Wâ'il are probably not different in origin. *Ghorâb*, raven ; " a sub-tribe of the Fazâra." *Qonfudh*, hedge-hog ; " a sub-tribe of Suleym." *Kalb*, dog , " a sub-tribe of Qodâ'a and of the Benî Leyth and of Baǵîla." *Kuleyb*, whelp ; " a sub-tribe of Tamîm and of Chozâ'a and of Nacha' " *Kılâb*, dogs (pl). Two eponyms of this name are given   The Benî Kilâb, who are Qaysites, are quite distinct from the Kalb, who are Yemenıtes *Leyth*, lion. Two eponyms of this name   The Benî Leyth have been mentioned under Kalb   *Yarbû'*, jerboa ; " a sub-tribe of the Benî Tamîm and of the Hawâzın and of the Dhubyân " *Namir*, panther ; " a sub-tribe of Rabî'a bın Nızâr, and of the Azd and of Qodâ'a " *Anmâr*, panthers ; " sub-tribes of the Arabs " Anmâr son of Nızâr is the eponym of a Ma'addıte tribe that settled ın Yemen   Anmâr ıs also a son of Saba', the eponym of the Sabaeans (Ṭabarî, i p. 225, l. 9). To the same source belong, no doubt, Numâra, " a subdivision of the Lachm and others," and Nomeyr (little panther) among the Qaysites

In these and numerous other cases the anımal name ıs undısguised.   In some cases we find a termınation *ân*, which ıs noteworthy, because the same thing occurs ın Hebrew gentılıcıa   Thus —

Ẓabyân (from ظبى gazelle), " a subdivision of the Azd ",

Wa'lân (from وعل ibex), " a subdıvısıon of Murâd " ;

Labwân (from لبوة lioness), "a subdivision of Ma'âfir."

Finally I add what seems to be the case of a mongrel. The Arabs have many fables of the Sim' (سمع), a beast begotten by the hyæna on the wolf, and so we find

Sim', "a subdivision of the Defenders (the Medînites)." Here we seem also to have the form ın ân, for Sam'ân is a subdivision of the Tamîm.   سمعى and سمعابى are a similar pair to שְׁמָעִי and שִׁמְעוֹנִי   The identity of שִׁמְעוֹן and سمع was suggested long ago by Hitzıg.

The orıgın of all these names ıs referred ın the genea-

logical system of the Arabs to an ancestor who bore the
tribal or gentile name. Thus the *Kalb* or dog-tribe
consists of the Benî Kalb—sons of Kalb (the dog), who is
in turn son of Wabra (the female rock-badger), son of
Tha'laba (the she-fox), great-great-grandson of Qoḍâ'a,
grandson of Saba', the Sheba of Scripture. A single
member of the tribe is Kalbî—a Kalbite—*Caninus*.

Such is the system. But can we assign to it historical
value ? Is the ancestral dog a real personage or a mere
personification of a dog ancestor, the eponym of a tribe
which at one time really thought, like the North American
Indians, that it was sprung of an animal stock ? That
the genealogies of the Arabs, which exhibit the relations
of the various tribes and trace them all back to Adam,
have been artificially systematised and completed by
borrowing from Hebrew and other sources, no one doubts.
The shortness of the historical memory of the Arabs has
been clearly proved by Nöldeke (*Über die Amalekiter*,
p. 25 *seq.*), who shows that in Mohammed's time they no
longer had any trustworthy traditions of great nations
who flourished after the time of Christ. That in many
cases gentile unity is ascribed to mere confederations is
shown by Sprenger in his *Geographie Arabiens*. And a
conclusive argument against the genealogical system is
that it is built on the patriarchal theory. Every nation
and every tribe must have an ancestor of the same name
from whom kinship is reckoned exclusively in the male
line. We know that this system of kinship is not primitive. According to Strabo (xvi. 4) the Arabs practised
Tibetan polyandry (the brothers having one wife in
common), of which the levirate customs alluded to in the
Qor'an (iv. 23) are a relic.[1] The succession from brother
to brother, which Strabo mentions as part of the system
of marriage and kinship, has left traces even in the Arab

[1] The connection of the levirate with polyandry of the Tibetan type
has been shown by Mr. M'Lennan, *Primitive Marriage*, chap viii
Some of the details of Strabo's account will be noticed below.

accounts of their ancestors. Such a law of marriage and succession paves the way for transition to the patriarchal system, but could not give a genealogical table of the form which to the later Arabs seemed natural and necessary. We may take it as certain, then, that in remoter times, and these not so very remote after all, gentile groups were not named from an historical ancestor.

Another very distinct proof to the same effect is afforded by tribal names which have a plural form Anmâr, Kilâb, Ḍibâb, Panthers, Dogs, Lizards are originally the names of tribes, each member of which would call himself a Panther, a Dog, a Lizard. The idea of an ancestor bearing the plural name is plainly artificial, invented in the interests of a system.

Additional light is thrown on the true meaning of these tribal names, when we compare them with others in which the name is identical with that of a deity. Here again, in default of a better source, I turn to Suyûṭî.

Shams, sun ; " a sub-tribe of the Azd. The sun was a great Arabian god " *Hilâl*, crescent moon , " a tribe of Hawâzin and of Namir." [1]   *Benî Bedr*, sons of the full moon , " a sub-tribe of Ḥaġr bin Dhû Roʻayn." *Ghanm*, " a sub-tribe of the Azd, of the Defenders, and of the Benî Asad " It is also the name of a god, Osiander, p. 500. *ʻAwf*, " son of Saʻd, a sub-tribe Qays ʻAylân " It is also the name of a god according to the ʻObâb and the Qâmûs (Lane, s.v. عوف, Osiander, p. 501)   *Nihm*, " a sub-tribe of Hamdân." *Nuhm*, " a sub-tribe of Baġîla." *Nuham*, " a sub-tribe of ʻÂmir ben Çaʻçaʻa." All these plainly belong to the god Nuhm worshipped by the Mozeyna (Bistâny, s.v. نهم).

Such tribal names as these stand on exactly the same footing with the animal names discussed above. The sons of the Moon and the sons of the Panther doubtless stood in similar relation to the beings from which they

---

[1] On the moon as a god see Osiander, *Z D.M.G* vii 466, 469, and Dimishqî in Chwolsohn's *Ssabier*, ii 404

took their respective names. There is nothing surprising
in the conception that the worshippers are sons of their
god. We find the same thing in the Old Testament.
The Moabites are called sons and daughters of Kemosh in
the old lay, Num xxi. 29, and even Malachi calls a
heathen woman the daughter of a strange god (ii. 11).
In the later stages of thought this was no doubt a metaphor. But in its origin, as we see it in these tribal names,
the idea must have been that the people were of the stock
of their god When a man called himself Shamsî, "solar,"
he meant that he really was of the stock of the sun. The
existence of such a way of speaking, and even of cases
in which a man is directly named Sun, Moon, Venus,
Canopus, or the like (Osiander, p. 466), points to another
and presumably an earlier habit of religious thought than
that which gave rise to the names 'Abd esh-Shams, 'Abd
Nuhm, " servant of the Sun," " of Nuhm," and the like.
Thus it would seem that even in the worship of the
heavenly beings a way of thinking analogous to totemism
preceded the distant and awful veneration of a remote
and inaccessible heavenly splendour which Baudissin and
others take as the type of Semitic religion.

The analogies now brought forward make it tolerably
certain that the animal names of stocks have a religious
significance. I shall now produce an instance in which
the ideas god, animal, ancestor, are all brought into
connection. The great tribe or group of tribes which bore
the name of Qaysites or Benî Qays trace their genealogy
to Qays 'Aylân son of Moḍar. Now Qays is a god
(Osiander, p 500), but what is 'Aylân ? According
to Abulfeda (*Hist. Ante-Islam.*, ed. Fleischer, p. 194, 11),
" it is said that Qays was son of 'Aylân son of Moḍar.
*Others say that 'Aylân was his horse, others that he was his
dog* Others again say that 'Aylân was the brother of
Ilyâs (and therefore son of Moḍar), and that his name
(اسم as distinct from surname) was En-nâs bin Moḍar,
and that Qays was his son." Here plainly we have

confusion among the genealogists because of an animal
link in the ancestry at the very point where the ancestor
is a god. The twofold animal interpretation of ʿAylân
must belong to two Qaysite tribes, one equine, the other
canine. Similar to this are the traditions which make the
goddess Nâila daughter of the Wolf or the Cock (Dozy,
Israelieten te Mekka, p 197), and the name Rabîʿatu-'l-
faras, " Rabîʿa of the horse," one of the four sons of Nizâr.
I imagine that many other facts of a similar kind lie
behind the genealogies in their present form. Thus
Kinda, the ancestor of the great dynasty of the Kindites,
is said to have had as his real name (not his لقب) *Thawr*,
the Bull (Abulf *H.A.-I.* p. 188; Ibn Chaldûn, Bûlâq
ed ii 257) Of the mythical character of this ancestor
of a line of seventy kings, ending in the time of the
prophet, there can be no question (Sprenger, *Geog. Ar.*
p. 225).

Now it is true that we have very little direct information connecting these facts with animal worship, and it is
also true that the greater part of the information which
we do possess about Arabic polytheism points rather to
the worship of stones, trees, and heavenly bodies. But in
estimating the significance of this circumstance we must
remember the nature of the records. It will be admitted
that no generalisation as to the true nature of Arabian
polytheism can be based on the scanty records of the
Greeks and Romans. Herodotus (iv. 7) thought that the
Arabs had but two gods, because as it appears he knew
the formula of an oath in which, as in the well-known
oath by al-Lât and al-ʿUzzâ, or by ʿAwḍ and Suʿeyr, two
deities were mentioned. If we may believe Arrian, the
Greeks under Alexander had learned nothing more.
Theophrastus (*Hist. Pl* ix. 4) and Pliny (xii. 14, 19,
Sabin, Assabin = الشمس) had heard of the sun, the great
god of the incense-bearing country, because his worship
was connected with the important traffic in incense.
Such is the character of the foreign records, and those

of the Arabs after Mohammed are little better. The
followers of Islâm were anxious to forget all but the mere
surface facts of the old religion   Even of the great gods
who had important temples of their own, and were
worshipped by wide districts, we hardly know anything
beyond a few names   Yet in the temple of Mecca alone—
the great Pantheon of the heathen Arabs—there stood
no fewer than 360 idols, and every head of a house had
his own family gods (Pococke, *Spec.* ed. White, p 112)
About these minor gods we are absolutely without
information.   Yet it is among these and not among the
great gods which had more than a mere tribal character
that we could expect to find confirmation of our present
argument   It will have been observed that the animal
names in our list generally belong to sub-tribes   That
this is precisely what is to be expected on theoretical
considerations will be shown presently. But of the
deities corresponding to such divisions there is no record.
We cannot therefore expect to hear of animal gods except
in the cases where they have gained a circle of worshippers
wider than their own stock, and have therefore laid aside
the totem character.   And in such a case a god is not
unlikely to lose his proper animal form and become a
man-god retaining, perhaps, some animal symbol or
connection as in the case of Qays 'Aylân.   In the last
period of Arab heathenism most of the great gods seem
actually to have assumed human form, and even those
which retained an animal shape, like the lion Yaghûth,
and the horse Ya'ûq, were no longer the property of a
single stock.   They had acquired a larger importance
and wars were waged for the possession of their images
(Sprenger, p. 285). This is not inconsistent with totem
origin, but at such a stage of development we can no
longer expect to find direct evidence of the more primitive
totem worship.   Yet of the few animal figures that are on
our records almost all actually appear as stock names.
Yaghûth corresponds to the Asad ; the eagle-god Nasr to

30

the 'Oqâb, or more exactly to the race of Nasr, kings of Hîra. The dove in the Ka'ba (Pococke, p. 100) answers to the Benî Ḥamâma,[1] the golden gazelles in the same temple to the Ẓabyân. But that animal worship had an extension far beyond these narrow limits is not ambiguously hinted in the Qor'ân (vi. 38), where it is taught with an obvious polemical intention that there is no manner of beast or fowl but is a people subject to God's decree and returning to Him   Conversely the doctrine of Genii in animal form is clearly the relic of an old mythology, in which, as we are told in Qor. vi. 100, the Genii were made partners with God.[2]

There is still one important point to be noticed in comparing the ancient Arabs with the races who possess the totem system.   A main characteristic of that system in its earliest forms is that totem kinship is reckoned through the mother. The connection between such a system of kinship and the practice of polyandry and exogamy has been worked out by Mr. M'Lennan. It is now to be asked whether these practices and the consequent system of kinship originally prevailed among the Arabs   We have seen that the animal names given in the tribal genealogies generally belong to sub-tribes, and that the same animal name often belongs to sub-tribes of different groups.   This is just what would come about on a system of exogamy where the totem name was transmitted through the mother.   In fact exactly the same

---

[1] The totem character of the dove among the Semites is confirmed by the fact that the Syrians would not eat it   Xen. *Anab* 1 4, 9, Lucian, *Dea Syria*, cap 14, En-Nedîm in Chwolsohn's *Ssabier*, ii 10   Compare the Hebrew name יוֹנָה.

[2] Nothing perhaps can be gathered for our argument from the sacred character acquired in certain circumstances by camels and other animals, Qor. v 102, Lane, *s.vv.* ﺳﺎﺋﺒﺔ, ﺣﺎﻡ, ﺣﻤﯿﺮ, yet from the first of these words a stock name is formed   Of sacred animals another trace is preserved (if the record can be trusted) in Arrian, vii 20   But Strabo, xvi 3, has a somewhat different account and omits the sacred animals

thing is found in North America. There is a Bear tribe among the Hurons and also among the Iroquois, and so on. That these sub-tribes were originally reckoned in the female line seems probable from the name applied to them—بطن, *batn*, that is, *venter*. The Arabic lexicographers give an explanation of the term which is plainly absurd (see Lane, *s.v.* شعب) It seems naturally to denote the offspring of one mother. But apart from this conjecture there is evidence to show that exogamy and female kinship must at one time have prevailed among the Arabs Both exogamy and polyandry are the natural outcome of an extensive practice of female infanticide.[1] But among the ancient Arabs this practice was so approved that an old proverb declares that the destruction of female children is a virtuous action. Again there is every reason to believe that the form of capture in marriage ceremonies is a relic of exogamy and marriage by actual capture Of this form the marriage ceremony of the Bedouins is one of the most familiar examples. The facts as stated by Burckhardt have already been used by Mr M'Lennan (*App.* to *Prim Mar.*). Then as to polyandry itself, the evidence of Strabo, who had excellent information as to Arabia, has been already cited. He speaks of polyandry, but in a form where kinship is not through the mother only. Though the father is unknown, the blood of the father is certain. Μοιχὸς δ' ἐστὶν ὁ ἐξ ἄλλου γένους.[2] It is clear, however, that this comparatively

---

[1] M'Lennan, *Prim Mar* chap. viii.

[2] This doctrine has curious connections Strabo says μίγνυνται δὲ καὶ μητράσι This is to be connected with Qor'ân, iv. 26, where marriage with a father's wife is forbidden, "except what is passed" He who married his father's wife was called *ḍayzan* (ضيزن), Abulf. *Hist A -I* p. 180, and the verb in the sixth form means "to demand one's father's wife, whom the pagan Arabs thought they should inherit along with the property" (Zamachsharî in the App to Golius and Freyt *s v*) This custom explains several things in the Old Testament ; the conduct of Reuben (Gen xxxv 22), the anger of Ishbosheth at Abner (2 Sam iii 7), an act which seemed to encroach on his birthright. So Absolom

artificial system is not primitive It must have been
preceded by polyandry of the cruder form which Mr.
M'Lennan names Nair polyandry, and which admits of
no kinship but through the mother. And of this there
are sufficient traces. Ammianus (xiv. 4) speaks of the
temporary marriages of the Saracens (in which, by the way,
we find the circumstance that the bride brings the tent).
Dozy (*Musulmans d'Esp*. 1. 36) cites from Al-Baçrî a case
under the Caliph Omar I., in which an old Arab gave
partnership in his wife to a younger man as hire for his
services as a shepherd. Both men swore their ignorance
that this was illegal. A curious passage from Yâḳût is
cited by Sprenger (*Geog* p. 97) with reference to the
town of Mirbât. " Die Einwohner sind Araber von der
Art der alten Araber. Sie sind gute Leute aber haben
abstossende, unvertragliche Manieren und ein starkes
Nationalgefuhl. Merkwürdig ist in ihnen die Abwesen-
heit der Eifersucht, eine Folge der Landessitte. Ihre
Frauen gehen nämlich jede Nacht ausserhalb die Stadt,
setzen sich zu fremden Mannern, unterhalten sich und
spielen mit ihnen einen grossen Theil der Nacht. Der
Ehemann, Bruder, Sohn und Neffe geht voruber, ohne
Notiz zu nehmen und unterhält sich mit einer andern."
Quite similar is the account given by Ibn Baṭûṭa, in the
fourteenth century, of the custom of Nazwa, the capital
of 'Omân. " Their women multiply corruption without
causing jealousy or offence." " Under the formal pro-

---

served himself heir to David (2 Sam. xvi 22) without exciting any
horror among the Israelites And Adonijah on asking the hand of
Abishag claimed the elder brother's inheritance (1 Kings ii 22) or at
least one part of it (vv. 15, 16) Another point in Strabo's statement
may be readily misunderstood "All are"—that is, are called—
" brothers of all." They were not brothers in our sense of the word,
and so in the anecdote that follows, the fact that the wife is called the
sister of her fifteen husbands only proves that she was of the same γένος
In other words, marriage was now endogamous. Yet marriage with a
half-sister (not uterine) occurs in the history of the Arab kings of Hîra
(Nöldeke's transl. of *Ṭabarî*, p. 133)—a well-known consequence of the
system of female kinship.

tection of the Sultan, any woman who pleases may indulge her corrupt desires, and neither her father nor her nearest relative can interfere " (vol. ii. pp. 228, 230). Thus many centuries after Mohammed the ancient polyandry was still practically kept up, at least in Southern Arabia, in a grosser form than that described by Strabo Such a custom necessarily produces a system of female kinship, and we may therefore presume that in the modern marriages between brother and sister in Mirbât, for which Knobel on Lev. xviii. 6 cites the testimony of Seetzen, the relationship was through the father as in the case cited in last footnote.   There is abundance of other evidence for the system of female kinship in occasional hints in the older Arabic histories and legends, and it is indifferent for our purpose whether the record is in each case historically accurate or not.   The queen of Sheba is the oldest evidence in point, for queens do not belong to the patriarchal system The famous queen Zabbâ is a similar case.   There are several instances in the old history where the succession is said to have gone to a sister's son (Abulf. *H.A -I.* p. 118, l. 1, p. 122, l. 6).   With this agrees the widespread practice of distinguishing princes by their mother's names (Nold. *ut supra*, p. 170)   The same usage is found in tribal names.   The Benî Chindif are expressly said to bear the name of their mother—" not mentioning their father Ilyâs " (Abulf. p 196, l. 4).   In the same way the Benî Mozeyna are named from their mother (*ib.* l. 6) ; a custom which necessarily implies that children belong to the mother , and her people were found in Zebîd as late as the time of Ibn Batûta (ii p. 167 *seq*).   The women readily consented to marry strangers, who might depart when they pleased, but the children remained with the mother, whom no inducement could draw from her native place. These facts appear sufficient to prove that Arabia did pass through a stage in which family relations and the marriage law satisfied the conditions of the totem system, and in which on that system the distribution of animal sub-tribes (*buṭûn*) among different groups, as we find it in the tribal genealogies, is perfectly natural.

At this point I must for the present close the argument as regards Arabia.   It could doubtless be greatly strengthened by a full survey of the native literature, for which I hope to find opportunity at another time   But meantime we have found unambiguous parallels to every leading feature of the totem system, and have been able to reason back to a state of matters which the purely astral theory as put by Baudissin is utterly incompetent to explain.   Of course I do not affirm that Arabic religion is merely a development of totemism—least of all in the South, where Babylonian and perhaps other foreign influences may have operated to no small extent.   Nor does totemism exhaust the religious ideas even of the typically totem nations.   The North American Indians had their Master of Life, a being who protected the totem system, and whom they identified with a lofty rock in Lake Superior (*Fort. Rev.*, 1869, p 416).   Here too the Arabic analogy is most striking · Fuls, the idol of the Tayyites, was a naked rock on Mt. Aġa' (Osiander, *ut supra*, p. 501 , comp. Dozy, p 201) [1]

I now pass on to the Biblical data.   The southern and eastern frontiers of Canaan were inhabited by tribes which had affinities both to Israel and to the Arabs   The Midianites and Amalekites were Arabs.   So were the Qenites and Rechabites notwithstanding their alliance with Israel.   And in the tribe of Judah large nomadic

---

[1] In the further development of this subject it would be desirable to keep in view the great division of the Arabs into Ma'addites and Yemenites   The same animal tribes are found in both of these divisions, but the evidence as to the law of kinship is mainly from the latter group. I may here note that according to Agatharchides (*Geog Gr Min* ed Muller, 1. 153) the totem system was also found on the other side of the Erythrean among the Troglodytes, μετὰ τῶν τέκνων τὰς γυναῖκας ἔχουσι κοινὰς πλὴν μιᾶς τῆς τυράννου (this is confirmed by Strabo, xvi 4, from Artemidorus)   Further · " They give the name of parent to no human being, but to the bull and the cow, the ram and the ewe, because from them they have their daily nourishment."

elements were incorporated, notably the Hezronites in
their two great branches of Caleb (Kalibbites) and
Jerahmeel   On this topic I simply refer to Wellhausen,
De Gentibus et Familiis Judaeis (Göttingen, 1870).   In
this district, then, we may fairly expect analogies to what
we have found in Arabia.   In fact the Kalibbites are at
once recognisable as a dog-tribe, and 'Oreb and Ze'eb, the
princes of Midian, are the Raven and the Wolf, heads, no
doubt, of tribes of the same name.   In fact Caleb (= kalib

= kalb, by the rule that بَعَل and فَعَل are interchangeable,

Lumsden, *Ar. Gr.* 348), 'Oreb, and Ze'eb are identical
with the Arabic tribal names Kalb, Ghoráb, and Dhi'b.

The most interesting case, however, is that of the
Horites (Troglodytes), the aboriginal inhabitants of Se'ir,
who were subsequently incorporated with the Edomites
(Gen. xxxvi. ; comp. Deut. ii. 12).   The tribal system
of the Horites is exhibited in the usual genealogical form,
and the names given seem to show that they were a
Semitic race   That the list in Gen. xxxvi. 20 *seq.* really
is an account of tribal or local divisions, and not a literal
genealogy, is obvious.   אַלּוּף is not a title of office
(E.V. *duke*), for the list of Edomite אַלּופִים in ver. 40 *seq*
is " according to clans and places," and includes names
that are certainly local, Elah = Elath, Mibzar (fortress)
= Bozrah.   And the Horite list also contains local names,
'Uz, 'Ebal, and perhaps others.   A large proportion,
too, of the names ends in ân or âm, equivalent to the
Hebrew termination in ôn, which in many cases seems to
be a tribal or local rather than an individual name-form.[1]
But the Horite genealogy, like the Arabic lists, is full
of animal names.   This fact has been already observed
by Dillmann, who had no theory to guide him ; and I
have only to repeat his etymologies, most of which are
indeed obvious

---

[1] On this form see Wellhausen, *ut supra*, p 37   I cannot, however,
think that he is right in making the termination a mere nunation

Shobal (שׁוֹבָל), *young lion* (diminutive from شِبْل, like

בֹּוזָל ,גוֹזָל, Ew. *Lehrb.* § 167).

Zibeon (צִבְעוֹן), *hyæna.*

'Anah (עֲנָה), *wild ass* (عَانَة).

Dishon and Dishan (דִּישׁוֹן, דִּישָׁן) a sort of *antelope,*
Deut. xiv. 5.

Thus of the " sons " of Se'ir, five have animal names
(Dishon and Dishan counting as two). Again, the sons of
Zibeon are 'Anah (עֲנָה) and Aiyah (אַיָּה) The former is
again the *Wild ass,* the latter the *Kite.* Dishon appears
again as a son of 'Anah. Of the sons of Dishan one is
the local name 'Uz ; the other is Aran (אֲרָן), that is, the
Ibex (Syr. اِرْزَيْ) 'Anah, however, claims further notice
'Anah is represented in three ways (1) as daughter of
Zibeon, verses 2 and 14, Hivite in ver. 2 being admittedly
an old error of the text for Horite , (2) as son of Se'ir and
brother of Zibeon, ver. 20 , (3) as son of Zibeon, ver. 24
These various statements show that we have here no true
genealogy, but a systematisation of tribal facts. And one
form shows that the Horite animal tribes were conceived
as introduced among the Edomites in the female line, as
we should expect to be the case. The variations in the
position of Dishon or Dishan are similarly instructive.
They show that the Antelope stock was divided over the
nation in a way that puzzled the genealogist, whose tribal
divisions take a local shape.

I cannot, of course, prove the worship of the animals
who gave names to Horite tribes. But the following point
seems worth notice. We know that one Arabic god was
worshipped in Edom, namely Koζέ, Joseph. *Arch.* xv. 7, 9,
whom Tuch and Lagarde have identified with the rainbow
god Quzaḥ I think I detect two other Arabian gods
among the names in Gen. xxxvi. At ver 14 we have a
supplementary list of descendants of 'Anah through union
with 'Esau. One is an animal, Jaalam (יַעְלָם) that is,

stripping off the terminational âm, יְעָלָה, the *Ibex* (comp. the Kenite name Jael). Another is יְעוּש, Je'ush, which is the phonetical equivalent of the Arabic lion-god Yaghûth " the protector." Again, in ver. 27, 'Akan (עֲקָן), son of Ezer, is generally identified with the " sons of Ja'akan," Deut x. 6, and I Chron. i 42 actually gives יַעֲקָן. Here again, if we reject the termination, we seem to have a form equivalent to Ya'ûq.

These Horite or Edomite names form a bridge for us to pass over to the Children of Israel, or at least to the tribe of Judah. That many Midianite and Edomite tribal names are found among the Hezronites (that is the originally nomadic inhabitants of חֲצֵרִים, nomad encampments) is a point to which Wellhausen has called attention (*ut supra*, p. 38 *seq*). I will not reproduce his list, but content myself with pointing out that some of these names are animal 'Epher, עֵפֶר, Γεφάρ = غفر, *fawn*, or *calf of the wild cow*, is Midianite, Judean, and Manassite (Gen. xxv. 4; I Chron. iv. 17; v. 24); and of the names already noticed we have in Judah Shobal and אֹרֶן which differs from Arân only in pointing. The fact that thirteen Edomite and two Midianite names appear identically or with slight variations among the Hezronites can hardly be explained except on the principles of totem kinship.

But indeed we find the same distribution of stock-names over a wide surface in the various tribes and districts of Israel itself. Here we must always bear in mind that our records are drawn from a time of comparatively high civilization and settled agricultural life. Thus we shall often have to deal with names of towns rather than of tribes or clans. But the townsmen formed a sort of clan, as is plain from the way in which towns figure in the genealogies. Thus we find 'Ophrah (עָפְרָה), *fawn*, as a town in Benjamin, a town in Manasseh, and again in the Judean genealogies (I Chron. iv. 14) as a son of

Me'ônothai (a name identical with the Arabic Me'ûnim, 2 Chron. xxvi. 7). These names are at bottom one with the 'Epher series, and also with 'Ephron (עֶפְרוֹן with the now familiar termination), which is the name of a town and mountain, and in Benjamin of the Hittite noble who gave his name to the district of Machpelah Again, from זֶמֶר, *a species of antelope* or *wild goat*, we have the Arabic race of Zimrân, Gen xxv 2, the kings of Zimri, Jer xxv. 25, a Judean name Zimri, 1 Chron. ii. 6, a Benjamite of the same name, 1 Chron. viii. 36, and a Simeonite prince, the head of a clan, Num. xxv 14 (also 1 Kings xvi. 9). From עֵגֶל, *calf*, we have 'Eglon, a king of Moab, and 'Eglon, a Judean town There is, it may be observed, an Arabic tribal name identical with this (عِجْل). Now it is generally supposed that animal names of places such as these, to which may be added Aiyalon (אַיָּלוֹן stag-town), Sha'albim (fox-town; compare the Arabic tribe Tha'laba), and so forth, are named " a cervorum vitulorum cet copia " (Gesenius). But such a theory is intrinsically unnatural. It squares very ill with the fact that the local names are constantly found also as tribal names or names of kings and other individuals ; with the association in which we find, for example, side by side, an Amorite town of foxes and another of stags (Judges 1. 35) ; and with the continuous line of connection that binds these names with the Arabic phenomena. A good instance is that of localities with a panther name. We have in the tribe of Gad, Nimrah, Beth-Nimrah or Beth-Nimrin, and near it the waters of Nimrim. Now Noldeke, *Z D M G*. xxix. p. 437, cites four places with similar panther names in the Haurân, and remarks that the numerous names of places from the root נמר probably denote the panther-like spotted or striped look of the ground. This conjecture shows the inadequacy of the usual method of explanation When we find in Arabia a Namir (Sprenger, *Geog.* p. 273) in the possession of the Beni Wâbish, a branch of the Qoḍâʻa, we at once connect the name with Namir, a sub-tribe of the Qoḍâʻa. Is it not far more probable that the same thing applies to the panther localities east of the Jordan, and that these two have their name from the panther stock which, as we have seen, turns up in so many forms in Arabia ? Perhaps we can even identify the totem deity of the name ; for Jacob of Sarûg in the text published by Martin, *Z D.M.G.* xxix. p. 110, l 52, speaks of حـنـلـعكـنة‎ " the son of panthers " as a false deity of Harran

To sum up all these scattered observations, we may say that the Arabian analogies are not merely general, but amount to the fact that the same names which appear as totem tribes in Arabia reach through Edom, Midian, and Moab into the land of Canaan. In Canaan they appear with a local distribution which at once becomes an intelligible unity if we can assume that at an early date the totem system prevailed there also   But to make this account of the names conform to the character of a legitimate hypothesis we must have reason to believe that Canaan, like Arabia, once acknowledged the system of kinship which alone can produce the necessary distribution of a totem name. Here we must distinguish between the people of Israel and the earlier inhabitants   Many of the animal names are no doubt of Canaanite origin, as we saw from Judges 1. 35. Now we have the express statement of Lev. xviii. that the Egyptians and Canaanites did form such marriages as by the Hebrew law are incestuous.[1] In Egypt this was certainly connected with the totem system. It can hardly have been otherwise in Canaan, for variations from the Hebrew law could not well follow any other principle than that of female kinship. For this we have express evidence in the case of the Phœnicians, among whom, according to Ach. Tatius cited by Selden, *De Jure Nat. et Gent.* v. 11, marriage with a sister not

---

[1] The expression גִּלָּה עֶרְוָה: means to contract a marriage, as appears from the usage witnessed to by the Arabic proverb in Freyt 1 ᴢ34

uterine was allowed. We are therefore justified in concluding that the conditions of the totem system did exist in Canaan ; and if so, the animal names and their distribution are sufficient indication that the system itself prevailed there as in Arabia In one case indeed the facts are unmistakable. The Shechemites, or at least the aristocracy of the town (Judges ix. 28), called themselves sons of Ḥămôr, the he-ass, Gen. xxxiii 19 But how was it among the Israelites ? The laws of incest, as given in Lev. xviii. xx., belong to a part of the Levitical legislation which presents considerable difficulty to critics, but at any rate they are probably later than the code of Deuteronomy, where the only prohibition of the kind is directed against marriage with one's father's wife, xxiii. 1. The precept in Deuteronomy abolishes the practice which we found subsisting in heathen Arabia, by which the son inherited his father's wife as well as his estate [1] To this offence Ezekiel xxii 11 adds two others, connection with a daughter-in-law and with a half-sister the daughter of one's father. All three forms of incest, which are put on one line with adultery and connection with a menstruous woman, were, according to the prophet, practised in Jerusalem And the history seems to show that all three were once recognised customs The taking of a father's wife was not altogether obsolete in the time of David (see above). Judah's children by Tamar became the heads of his house, being clearly (as Hupfeld long ago showed) the fruit of a legitimate extension of the levirate law. Judah indeed admits that Tamar's conduct was perfectly correct (Gen. xxxviii. 26) ; the rule is the Arab rule in Strabo, μοιχὸς ὁ ἐξ ἄλλου γένους. Finally, a marriage with a sister not uterine was contracted by Abraham, and can hardly have been forbidden in the time of David (2 Sam. xiii. 13 ; compare ver. 16 LXX.).

---

[1] In the " framework " of the Deuteronomic code we have three prohibitions father's wife (xxvii. 20), sister uterine or germane (ver 22), and wife's mother (ver 23)

The last case points to female kinship, the other two are relics of Tibetan or British polyandry. Of such polyandry we have express testimony in the eighth century B.C., Amos ii. 7.[1] The practices condemned by the higher moral sense of the prophets were, it appears, remnants of old usage. Along with these facts we find other evidences of an ancient system of kinship through women The presents by which Rebekah was purchased for Isaac went to her mother and her brother (Gen xxiv. 53) Laban claims his daughters' children as his own (Gen. xxxi. 43). The duty of blood revenge appears to lie on the kin by the mother's side (Judges viii 19) [2] Even for exogamy and marriage by capture there is a law in Deut. xxi. 10 *seq.*, and a notable case in Judges xxi The narrative in Judges seems to be tolerably recent (see Wellhausen, *Gesch* i. 246). This trait therefore is presumably the specialisation of an old custom illustrated by a narrative, as in the book of Ruth The usage itself is faintly reflected in the custom described in *Mishna Ta'anith*, cap. viii., where we learn that on a festal occasion the daughters of Jerusalem used to go out and in a dance invite the young men to choose a spouse. With such facts before us, and with the certainty that the early Hebrews had no scruple in intermarrying with the surrounding nations, it appears only natural that the totem tribes of their neighbours should reappear in Israel, as we have seen to be the case at all events in Judah.

In this connection a peculiar interest attaches to the singular history of the tribe of Simeon. Already in the blessing of Jacob Simeon is coupled with Levi as a tribe scattered in Israel There were Simeonites in the south

---

[1] Tac *Hist.* v. 5, *projectissima ad libidinem gens, alienarum concubitu abstinent ; inter se nihil illicitum* Was there historical basis for this accusation, or does Tacitus perhaps confound the Jews with their Phœnician or Arabian neighbours ?

[2] As it is well known that the law of blood revenge is often extended to the violation of women, Gen. xxxiv. and 2 Sam xiii are also cases in point

of Judah, but they do not appear there as a complete and independent local tribe, and according to Gen. xlix there must also have been branches of the tribe elsewhere. Now in the name Simeon (שִׁמְעוֹן), the ôn is a mere termination, and the gentilicium may as well be Shimei (שִׁמְעִי) as שִׁמְעֹנִי   This is clear from 1 Chron. iv 27, where Shimei is just the Judean Simeonites collectively. But there is also a family Shimei in Levi, viz. Shimei ben Gershon (Exod vi. 17). We find the same name in Reuben 1 Chron v 4, and the Benjamite Shimei who plays so important a figure in David's history was a great chieftain The connection of Simeon and Benjamin is also expressed in the genealogy which makes Jamin and Saul sons of Simeon (1 Chron. iv. 24). This dispersion of the tribe of Simeon is most easily understood on the principles of exogamy and female kinship. While the men of other stocks separated themselves out and formed a political and local unity by conquest of territory, as strong totem tribes sometimes have been known to do among the Indians (*Fort. Rev* 1869, p 413), Simeon may be supposed to have remained in the position of a divided stock, having representatives through the female line in different local groups. Hence as the old system of kinship was displaced, Simeon lost all importance and ultimately dropped from the list of tribes. In confirmation of this view we may remember that the Danites in like manner did not establish themselves as a local tribe till a comparatively late date (Judges xviii. 1 ; cf. Gen. xlix 16).[1]

I might add a number of minor confirmations to this theory by comparing proper names of different tribes or of Israel and foreign countries. For example, the Edomite or rather Horite names Bilhan and Je'ush *reappear* in Benjamin (1 Chron. vii 10) [2]   Achbor (the *Mouse*) is an

---

[1] Hitzig's identification of Simeon and Sim', which we have found as an Arabic tribe, has been noticed above.

[2] The former name is perhaps equivalent to the Arabic Bâhila (Sprenger, p 212)   May we also compare Bilhah ?

Edomite name—apparently a stock-name (Gen. xxxvi. 38),
as the jerboa and another mouse-name عَضَل (Abulf.
H.A -I. 196, 10) are among the Arabs.   The same name
occurs in Judah   But such isolated facts do not really
carry us further   What we want to complete the argument is twofold   (1) direct evidence to connect the animal
names with animal worship, and (2) proof that men with
a common animal stock-name in different tribes or nations
recognised their unity of stock.   Our most definite information as to animal worship in Israel is derived from
Ezek viii 10, 11.   There we find seventy of the elders of
Israel—that is, the heads of houses—worshipping in a
chamber which had on its walls the figures of all manner
of unclean creeping things and quadrupeds, *even all the
idols of the house of Israel.*   In some sense, then, there was
a national worship, not a foreign innovation but apparently an old superstition, on which the people had fallen
back, because, as they said, Jehovah would not attend to
them   It appears also that, though the prophet in vision
saw the seventy elders together, the actual practice was
that each elder had his own chamber of imagery (ver. 12).
We have here in short an account of gentile or family
idolatry, in which the head of each house acted as priest.
And the family images which are the object of the cult
are those of unclean reptiles and quadrupeds (רמש ובהמה
שקץ).   The last point is important.   The word שקץ is in
the Levitical law the technical term for a creature that
must not be used as food.   That such prohibitions are
associated with the totem system of animal worship is
well known   The totem is not eaten by men of its stock,
or else is eaten sacramentally on special occasions, while
conversely to eat the totem of an enemy is a laudable
exploit.   Thus in the fact that the animals worshipped
were *unclean* in the Levitical sense we gain an additional
argument that the worship was of the totem type.   And
finally, to clinch the whole matter, we find that among the

worshippers Ezekiel recognised Jaazaniah the son of
Shaphan—that is of the rock badger (E.V. coney), which
is one of the unclean quadrupeds (Deut. xiv. 7 ; Lev xi. 5),
and must therefore have been figured on the wall as his
particular stock-god and animal ancestor.   It so happens
that the totem character of the *shaphan*, or, as the Arabs
call him, the *wabr*, is certified by a quite independent piece
of testimony.   The Arabs of the Sinai peninsula to this
day refuse to eat the flesh of the *wabr*, whom they call
"man's brother," and suppose to be a human being
transformed.   Were a man to break this rule he could
never look on his father and mother again (Palmer,
Desert of the Exodus, i. p. 98).   The close connection
which we have found to exist between Arab tribes and
southern Judah, and the identity of so many of the stock-
names among the two, give this fact a direct significance.[1]

The connection between animal worship and forbidden
foods is a point which calls for special investigation
In the case of the Hebrews it is well known that no one
has yet given a satisfactory theory of the distinction
between clean and unclean animals.   But it can hardly
be doubted that there is a conscious antithesis to heathen
ceremonies in which unclean animals were sacrificed and
eaten as a religious act, as indeed is expressly affirmed
for the swine, the mouse, and the שֶׁקֶץ or unclean creatures
generally, in Isa lxvi 17 , lxv. 4 , lxvi. 3.   The mouse
has already come before us as a proper name both in Judah
and in Edom, and we have it as a stock-name in Arabia,

---

[1] There can be little doubt that the *wabr* was once an Arabic totem,
though the proverb " more contemptible than a wabr " (Fr i. p. 493)
is not respectful   Wabra (the female rock-badger) occurs in the
mythical genealogies of the Qodâ'ites (Abulf. p 182) and also as the
name of a place (Sprenger, p 39)   The people of Wabâr are in the
mythical history (Ṭabarî, i 214, Ibn Athîr ed. Bulâq, i 31) sons of
Amîm son of Lud, who dwelt in sandy Arabia and were destroyed by
God or transformed into one-legged monsters.   In spite of the *a* in the
first syllable, this seems to be the plural of *wabr* and to be a variation
of the Bedawî legend   It is curious that the Arabs call the *wabr* the
sheep of the children of Israel

while its religious importance is also indicated in 1 Sam.
vi. 4   The swine, too, occurs in the Old Testament as a
proper name, 1 Chron. xxiv. 15 , Neh. x. 21.   Whether
the heathen sacrifices of such animals were sacramental in
stocks of the same name or triumphant in hostile stocks,
I do not pretend to decide.   But the former is more likely,
because then the Mosaic prohibition would fit into the old
custom (which forbids the ordinary use of the totem as
food), while at the same time expressing protest against
the occasional sacramental use.   And in the case of the
Syrian sacred fish we know that habitual abstinence from
this kind of food did go with its use in religious ritual.[1]

Our analysis of the testimony of Ezekiel appears to
prove that superstition of the totem kind had still a hold
on the Israelites in the last years of the independence
of the kingdom of Judah.   I shall now attempt to show
that in the time of David the kinship of animal stocks was
still acknowledged between Israel and the surrounding
nations.   For this purpose I observe that David seems
to have belonged to the serpent stock.   Among his
ancestors the most prominent is Naḥshon, who bears the
serpent-name with the usual termination.   Again Abigail,
who in 1 Chron ii 16 appears as David's sister, was the
daughter of Naḥash (2 Sam. xvii. 25).   Hence it follows
either that Jesse was himself called by the stock-name
of *Serpent*, or, what is of equal force for our argument,
that the members of his stock were called children of the

---

[1] Athenaeus, lib. viii cap. 37 ; Lucian, *De Syr. Dea*, cap 14 ; Xen.
Anab. i. 4. 9, and other references in Selden, *De Diis Syris*, ii 3 , Movers,
Phoenizier, i 391.   That the Syrians would not eat pigeons has been
noticed above   On the forbidden foods of the heathen of Harran, see
En-Nedîm in Chwolsohn, ii 9 *seq*.   As I do not enlarge on Syrian animal
worship I may here cite also from the same author (Chwolsohn, p 46)
the acknowledgment in the mysteries of the Ḥarranians that dogs,
ravens, and ants are " our brothers."—Of forbidden foods among the
heathen Arabs I can say almost nothing , but some facts are certainly
to be found in the traditions of the prophet.   There were apparently
discussions about the eating of locusts and birds (Hamaker's notes on
Ps Wâkidy, p 15).

Serpent. With this it agrees that in the temple at Jerusalem a brazen serpent was worshipped up to the time of Hezekiah by burning incense before it, just as was done according to Ezekiel in the gentile worship of his day (2 Kings xviii. 4). The temple was the court chapel of David's dynasty and was not likely to contain the animal deity of another stock. David himself was beyond such worship ; but there were teraphim in his house (1 Sam. xix. 13), and many of his descendants were gross idolaters. Finally, Adonijah chose the serpent-stone as the place of his coronation (1 Kings i. 9). Now it has always been a puzzle that David was on such friendly terms with Naḥash, king of the Ammonites, who was a great enemy of Israel, and especially of Israel beyond the Jordan, with which district David from an early period cultivated friendly relations. And the curious thing is that the friendship between the two houses was not broken even by the great and bitter war that destroyed Ammonite independence, for a son of the Ammonite serpent was among the foremost to help David in his flight from Absalom (2 Sam. xvii. 27). It would seem that the true solution lies in the common serpent-stock, which was a stronger bond than all motives of national hostility. As the Ammonites were presumably less advanced in culture than Israel, it is quite possible that by their law Hanun was not of his father's stock at all.

In closing this paper I shall advert in a single word to the bearings of the subject on the great problem of the Old Testament religion. It is a favourite speculation that the Hebrews or the Semites in general have a natural capacity for spiritual religion. They are either represented as constitutionally monotheistic, or at least we are told that their worship had in it from the first, and apart from revelation, a lofty character from which spiritual ideas were easily developed. That was not the opinion of the prophets, who always deal with their nation as one peculiarly inaccessible to spiritual truths and possessing no natural merit which could form the ground of its choice as the people of Jehovah. Our investigations appear to confirm this judgment, and to show that the superstitions with which the spiritual religion had to contend were not one whit less degrading than those of the most savage nations. And indeed the second commandment, the cardinal precept of spiritual worship, is explicitly directed against the very worship of the denizens of air, earth, and water which we have been able to trace out. It does not appear that Israel was, by its own wisdom, more fit than any other nation to rise above the lowest level of heathenism.[1]

[1] The substitution of an image for the living animal god is well illustrated by the golden and silver fish used in the worship of Atergatis (Athenaeus, *l c.*), which do not affect the fact, as stated by Xenophon, that the living fish were themselves treated as divine. To the fish stock may be referred the Hebrew Ben Nun and Syriac ܠܢܘܢܐ.

II

A JOURNEY IN THE HEJÂZ

I. Introductory

JEDDAH, *February* 11, 1880.

FOR more than one reason, few Europeans see anything of the interior of the Hejâz With the exception of the holy places and their precincts, the country is not closed to travellers.   It is true that in the Hejâz foreigners in a sense exist on sufferance.   Even in Jeddah no European can hold property, and an unfriendly High Shereef and Wâly might entirely bar entrance to the upper country, or even bring back the days when the Mecca gate of Jeddah opened only to Moslems.   But for years back there has been no serious attempt at a policy of exclusion. European residents in Jeddah walk or ride without molestation in the neighbourhood of the city, and the High Shereef, the Prince of Mecca, has been always ready to grant a safeguard and escort to the few travellers who have desired to visit Hadda or Tâif.   Still, the necessity of travelling with an expensive escort, and the restrictions on free motion which such an arrangement implies, have made it a comparatively rare thing even for residents in Jeddah to enter the hilly chain that forms the eastern boundary of the maritime plain of the Tehâma.   In the nearer part of the hills there is little of interest.   To the curious traveller the upper country will repay a visit , but the journey is toilsome and costly, and hardly to be

recommended to any one who has not some knowledge of
Arabic.   There is little to attract the sportsman, and no
opening for commercial enterprise.   It is not, therefore,
surprising that even the more accessible parts of the
Hejâz have been very little visited, and very imperfectly
described.   I fancy, therefore, that some account of a
ten days' excursion to Tâif, from which I have just
returned, may prove acceptable to your readers

The town of Tâif lies nearly due east—slightly southward—of Mecca, and the three towns of Jeddah, Mecca,
and Tâif are nearly in a line   The distances are not very
great.   Mecca is reckoned to be forty miles from Jeddah,
and Tâif by the straight road is, I suppose, about the
same distance from Mecca.   But the direct road is very
difficult, ascending the great mountain of Kara by paths
impracticable except for mules and a peculiar breed of
mountain camels.   Thus the great highway from Mecca
to Tâif makes a wide sweep to the north, winding round
the Kara range, and Franks who cannot pass through
Mecca have to make a still farther deviation, so as to
keep always outside the boundaries of the Haram, or
consecrated land.   It took me four days and a half to
get to Tâif by dromedary.   I returned over the Kara
range in two days and a half, taking mules across the
mountains, and being met by the dromedaries in the
plain below.   This was hurried travelling.   The weather
had broken, and there were rumours of a war between
the 'Oteibe and the Harb, which might call for the return
of my escort to Mecca   On the other hand, our pace
going to Tâif was not rapid, the weather being not so
warm as is desirable to bring a camel to his best paces.
A fair estimate would be that Tâif can be reached by
moderately easy stages in four days by way of the Derb-
es-Seil, while the return by Kara should be spread over
three.

The Hejâz is, in theory, a province of the Turkish
Empire, and, to a certain extent, the theory is supported

by facts. There is a Wâly, or Governor-General, who
resides mainly in Mecca, or in the summer season at Tâif
Under the Wâly there are in the towns subordinate
magistrates, judges, and police of Turkish appointment.
Turkish garrisons are quartered at Jeddah, Mecca, Tâif,
Medina, Yanbo', and Rabegh. There are also armed
ports at stations along the great pilgrimage roads to
Mecca and Medina, occupied by Turkish soldiers or by
irregular Arab troops in Turkish pay. Thus far the
authority of the Turks is a reality. Moreover, the Ottoman Empire raises taxes. There is a custom-house in
Jeddah, which might yield a large revenue but for its
corrupt administration on the one hand, and the prevalence of smuggling on the other. Besides the customs,
the Sultan claims the zakâ or tithes, which, in Mohammedan law, are the legal expression of the duty of alms-
giving. But as this is a tax on agriculture and flocks,
it does not apply to the towns, and from the Bedouins
it is collected, not by Turkish officials, but through the
Emir of Mecca. The poll-tax does not apply to the Hejâz,
nor is compulsory military service exacted from the inhabitants Thus, even in theory, this province does not
feel the full weight of Turkish sovereignty. In practice
its dependence on Constantinople is still less close. Even
in the towns far less respect is paid to the commands of
the Porte than to the word of the Arabian Prince of
Mecca, the High Shereef, head of that singular aristocracy
which traces its descent to the prophet, through his
daughter Fatima, wife of the Caliph 'Aly. There are
Shereefs throughout the Mussulman world claiming and
receiving a certain respect, however poor their circumstances, but in Arabia the Shereefs are a hereditary aristocracy, to which many sovereign families, especially in
the south, claim to belong. In the Hejâz the descendants
of the Prophets are divided into Shereefs (Ashrâf) and
Seyyids (Sada). The former, I believe, are descendants
of Hasan, son of 'Aly, the latter of the younger brother,

Hosein, who fell at Karbala. But this distinction of
origin is not generally dwelt upon or even known to the
people. One of the best informed men in Jeddah insists
that the Shereefs are of the blood of Hosein, whose house
claims the birthright because Hasan resigned the Caliphate
in favour of the Ommayad dynasty. I believe this to be
a mistake, but the existence of the mistake shows that
the distinction between the stock of Hasan and Hosein
is not practically important. The real point is that the
Shereefs are the members or kinsmen of the princely
house of Mecca, while the Seyyids claim respect as descendants of the prophet, and are generally saluted by
kissing the hand, but do not form a recognised aristocracy.
The Emir of Mecca, the head of the Ashrâf, is the true
ruler of the Hejâz. He is nominated by the Porte, which
has sometimes departed from the strict laws of hereditary
succession. Indeed, the reigning Shereef Hosein is not
the head of the house according to Arabian law. He
regularly succeeded two years ago to his elder brother
Abdullah, who again followed their father, the celebrated
Mohammed Ibn 'Aun. But Ibn 'Aun was not the direct
representative of the old princes who ruled in Mecca before
the Wahhâbites overran the holy places, and was opposed
throughout his life, and for a time displaced by 'Abd el
Mutaleb, who now lives under surveillance at Constantinople, and is not without partisans in the Hejâz. But
the Porte would not venture to nominate a High Shereef
except from one of these two rival families, and as the
Arabic theory of succession lays more stress on the kin
than on the individual, the office of Emir is recognised
by the Arabs as a native and legitimate hereditary
dignity in contrast to the hated rule of the Turks, which
is viewed as little better than organised robbery. In
the desert the Turks have never been able to hold their
own. They have again and again suppressed formal
rebellions, but they have never been able to set their
mark on the country or exact from the Bedouins sub-

stantial marks of allegiance. Even the pilgrimage roads, which are specially guarded by patrols and military stations, are kept open only by payment of pensions to the adjacent tribes, and the interruption of these payments invariably leads to disorders and insecurity. Nor do the Bedouins acknowledge Turkish law and the Cadis sent from Stamboul. To travel in the Hejâz with a Turkish escort would almost mean to travel as an enemy. But the Prince of Mecca enjoys as much respect as it is in the nature of the Bedouins to pay to any authority, and an escort of his personal followers secures the traveller a good reception everywhere, except, perhaps, among some of the wildest tribes, whose ideas of obedience to any one are very little developed.

I have been forced into this somewhat long digression to explain the way in which I arranged for my journey. Instead of going to the Wâly, I addressed the Shereef through the acting British Consul (Mr. Kruyt, the Dutch Consul in Jeddah), and asked of him leave to visit Tâif, and a small escort of his household to accompany me on my journey. For several days I received no reply, and I was then advised to call on the Shereef's agent in Jeddah, who likes to have a personal share in everything that goes on, and frankly tell him my plans, which had special reference to some ancient inscriptions of which I had heard. As ʻOmar Naseef Pasha, the gentleman in question, is the most influential man in Jeddah, and also a somewhat typical personage, I think I had better give you some account of him. He is the son of a common water-carrier in town, and began life in the same business. Although very deficient in education, he is an extremely shrewd man, and his ability, combined with a total want of conscience, soon brought him forward. He pushed his way in the world, till he became agent for the late High Shereef, a post which requires address and readiness to do what is wanted, without scrupling at the means employed. In theory, the agent of the Shereef is not a

public functionary, and it is only within the last few
weeks that 'Omar Effendi has received from the Porte
the dignity of Pasha.   But in practice he is the great man
of the town, and uses his opportunities with a cynical
candour to serve his master and himself.   For example,
the Mecca post is first delivered at his house, and it is no
secret that it is his custom to open any letter containing
information he desires to be master of.   But the Wakeel
of the Shereef has at his disposal much more formidable
engines than this.   The Hejâz roads are never safe unless
it be the pleasure of the Shereef that the Bedouins be
quiet, so that the confidential agent of the Shereef has
the whole inland communications of the country practically in his hand.   It is not very long ago that an Indian
Nawab, who proposed to go up from Yanbo' to Medina
with an escort of his own people, and escape paying
bakshish, was ignominiously defeated by 'Omar Naseef
Day after day the roads were reported closed, but as soon
as the Nawab came to terms and disbursed a handsome
sum, it was discovered that the way to Medina was perfectly
safe.   A position of such influence offers many opportunities of gain to a man who does not even affect to have
scruples.   Traders think it wise to give him a share in
all manner of enterprises, especially in the lucrative
pilgrim trade.   He draws his share of profits, and forgets
to pay upon losses.   If he wants money for a speculation,
he asks a temporary loan, and keeps the money without
interest as long as is convenient for him.   Such practices
as these are the perquisites of his office, and have enabled
him to erect the finest house in Jeddah, in which he lives
in great style, surrounded by the private provisions for
sensual enjoyment, on which rather than on social enter-
tainments and open amusements the wealthy Arab loves
to spend his riches.   He has, of course, many enemies,
and his position is far from secure.   It is maintained by
constant intrigue, which makes it necessary for him to
know everything, and have his hand in everything.   It

was, therefore, a decided mistake on my part not to speak
to him at once of my proposed excursion. As soon as
he was consulted, delay was at an end, and without further
loss of time an escort was granted, and 'Omar himself
gave me every assistance   The reader must not suppose
that in describing 'Omar Effendi I am tracing an unusually
dark picture of the influential Arab.   It is men of this
type who make their way in the East, and if 'Omar were
to fall to-morrow before his rival, Moses of Bagdad, who
took his place during the short interregnum on the death
of the Emir 'Abdullah, Jeddah would certainly not have
reason to congratulate itself on the change.   That a man
without some elements of the scoundrel should hold such
a post is not to be expected for a moment.   Unprincipled
intrigue is the very life-blood of government here, and
the *morale* of the whole upper classes of Jeddah is so
thoroughly sapped that nothing short of a revolution
could put things on a sound basis.   If 'Omar Effendi
makes no pretence to honesty or morality, he is at least
a shrewd and sensible man, good-natured when his personal
interests are not at stake, and perfectly free from the
fanaticism and prejudice against infidels which has done
so much to ruin the Ottoman Empire.   The prejudices
and superstitions of Mohammedanism are much less
strong in the true Arab than in the Turk, and to men of
position Islam is generally a mere affair of society and
politics.   They care for the slave trade much more than
for the Koran.   It is in many respects convenient to en-
courage certain prejudices against the intrusive foreigner,
and the reputation of the holy places is the most profitable
stock-in-trade which the Hejâz possesses.   Every one,
therefore, is a good Mohammedan, observes the hours of
prayer with creditable regularity, adorns his conversation
with pious phrases, and abstains from drinking brandy
in too open a way.   But all this is merely on the surface,
and the conduct of a shrewd Arab like our Effendi towards
Europeans is not in the least regulated by superstitious

prejudices, but purely by a very keen sense of self-interest. Thus I found no difficulty raised against my copying ancient inscriptions in the Upper Hejâz, although in other parts—for example, in Hadramaut—such an act would give rise to great suspicion and angry feeling. There, if I recollect aright, an inscription copied by Wellsted was supposed to have enabled the English to take Aden. Here it was merely thought ridiculous that one should take an interest in half-obliterated legends which no one could read, or should care to undergo the fatigues of a journey to Tâif in the cold of winter when people were going about with chapped hands, and the vineyards and orchards showed none of their summer glory.

I am afraid that this letter is to prove very discursive, but while I am on the subject I may as well say a little more on the extreme bigotry with which the inhabitants of the Hejâz are generally credited, and of which the notorious massacre of Christians at Jeddah in 1858 is naturally regarded as sufficient evidence. In the first place, it ought to be remembered that that massacre had very little to do with religion. Its real causes were the anger of the people at threatened interference with the slave trade, jealousy of the growing competition of European traders and steamships, and alarm at recent events in India It is characteristic of Mohammedanism that all national feeling assumes a religious aspect, inasmuch as the whole polity and social forms of a Moslem country are clothed in a religious dress. But it would be a mistake to suppose that genuine religious feeling is at the bottom of everything that justifies itself by taking a religious shape. The prejudices of the Arab have their roots in a conservatism which lies deeper than his belief in Islam. It is, indeed, a great fault of the religion of the Prophet that it lends itself so readily to the prejudices of the race among whom it was first promulgated, and that it has taken under its protection so many barbarous and obsolete ideas, which even Mohammed must have

seen to have no religious worth, but which he carried
over into his system in order to facilitate the propagation
of his reformed doctrines.   Yet many of the prejudices
which seem to us most distinctively Mohammedan have
no basis in the Koran.   Even the practice of circumcision
is not a proper part of Islamism, and in some parts of
the Hejâz and of Yemen (among the Koreish, the Hodheil,
and the 'Aseer), where this ceremony takes the severer
form described by Captain Burton, all other Mohammedans
are despised and uncircumcised.   In Yemen the moustache
and shaven chin of the Turk is thought to put him in one
class with the Christian—the epithets of religious bigotry
are employed to express an antagonism which has nothing
to do with Islam.   Moslem bigotry in the proper sense
of the word, and indeed almost all earnest feeling in connection with the religion of the Prophet, belongs, as
Dozy has so forcibly pointed out, not to the Arabs, but
to the races who received the Koran from their hands.   So
within Arabia the mixed populations of the towns and
the coast, with their large element of negro blood, are
far more fanatical than the true unmixed Bedouin stems
But even in the towns the jejune, practical, and, if I may
venture to say so, constitutionally irreligious habit of the
Arabic mind maintains its ascendancy, and fanaticism
is well under the control of self-interest.   It is no secret
that the myriads of pilgrims who yearly stream to the
shrines of Mecca and Medina return disenchanted from
the supposed Holy Land, where they find the most sacred
solemnities of their religion to be thought of only as means
of pocketing an annual harvest of gold—return protesting
that true Mohammedanism is not to be found in the
Hejâz, and that the Moslem receives more justice from
Christian Powers than from his co-religionists in the
central sanctuaries of Islam   In short, the religious convictions of the Hejâz are a good deal like those of the
silversmiths of Ephesus, and owe their strength to what
can be made out of the concern.   Speaking broadly, I

have no hesitation in saying that the religion of the Hejâz is now, and probably has been from the days of Mohammed, no better than an organised hypocrisy. Hypocrisy is necessarily suspicious, and can readily assume the form of fanaticism, but it has not that strength to resist new currents of influence which belongs to genuine conviction. Of late years a great many influences have tended to break up the antipathies expressed in the massacre of 1858. It has been seen that there is no ground for jealousy of European trade and European steamers, that the Franks have opened to Arabia the doors of international commerce, while native merchants have nothing to fear from foreign competition in their own style of business. Native and European merchants work side by side in Jeddah with mutual advantage Even the pilgrim traffic is mainly conducted by co-operation between European firms and the leading Seyyids and Mohammedan notables of Jeddah. Now the whole life of an Arabian town lies in its trade. There are no *rentiers*, no landed proprietors. When the foreign merchant becomes an integral part of the commercial community he has established himself in the very heart of society, and exerts an influence on every section of the population. This influence is partly material and partly moral. The Arabs are immensely impressed by the kind of power embodied in our industries and trade, by the power of English knowledge to control the forces of nature for the service of man. " There is nothing stronger than the English except God." It is not our ships of war in the Red Sea that draw out this acknowledgment. The Arabs, at least in the uplands, are not greatly afraid of any military Power—partly from ignorance and partly from a just sense of the impossibility of a substantial conquest of the desert. It is steamers, the telegraph, the diving-bell, and things like these that raise our name, or rather the possession of these inventions in connection with the faculty of organisation on a great scale, in which the Arabs are altogether lacking   The

regular visits of such a line of steamers as the British
India are a more forcible lesson than any display of
martial strength. Respect thus obtained contains no
germs of hatred, if those whose power is admired use it
in justice, honour, and kindliness. In this respect it
cannot be said that Europeans always act up to their
responsibilities. But England, one is proud to say, has
a good name in Arabia, a far better name than some other
Christian countries. Our national reputation has been
greatly raised by the prosperity of Aden, and by the
admitted excellence of the government there. In Jeddah,
where many of the influential merchants and other inhabitants are Indian Mohammedans, the advantage of
being a British subject is thoroughly understood These,
indeed, are considerations which appeal mainly to the more
intelligent classes. The prejudices of the ignorant masses
are only to be conquered by actual experience in contact
with the foreigner, and thus every Englishman in a place
like this bears on his shoulders something of national
responsibility In Jeddah this responsibility has, on the
whole, been well discharged. The labouring man knows
the advantage of being employed by Englishmen.
Personal relations, too, are gradually formed, especially
in times of sickness, when all manner of people have
learned to come for advice and treatment to the " English
House " of Messrs. Wylde, Beyts, and Co., who formerly
held the Consulate of Great Britain, and are still the real
representatives of our country in the eyes of the people.
    Such relations break down much of the old jealousy,
especially when backed up by the really liberal spirit in
which the Government of the Shereef—far more than
that of the Turks—meets the advances of foreigners. A
little incident that took place last Christmas may not
seem important at first sight, but is really a sign of the
times. There were two English gunboats in the harbour,
and a Christmas dinner in the English house, after which
the whole company marched down in order to the quay,

preceded by the band of the *Philomel*, playing marches
and the English national air. The British Consul, who
is of recent appointment, and does not know the Arabs,
was greatly alarmed, but throughout the town there was
not one murmur of disapproval at the act which a few
years ago would certainly have produced a serious riot.
Of course there is a great deal of prejudice still to conquer,
and it is only little by little that the most unreasonable
suspicions give way. From time to time one foolish step
throws everything back, as, for example, when the English
Consul lately excited the derision of the whole community
by hoisting the Consular flag in honour of the arrival in
town of the wife of his dragoman, a woman of notoriously
spotted character. But there is no doubt that English
influence is gaining ground, and the best informed natives
themselves declare that with a wise and energetic Consul
it might soon become paramount, and engage the affections
of the whole people. In Yemen the influence emanating
from Aden is still stronger, and my native informants
tell me that if England chose to follow the ancient path
familiar to the Arabic mind, by which strong and just
States have always attracted the voluntary homage of
adjacent tribes, acting as arbitrators, and maintaining
justice in causes referred to them, all Yemen in a few years
would be English without one blow struck.

The Arabs are at this moment deeply interested in
the impending fall of the Turkish Empire, of which no
intelligent man entertains a doubt. They hate a foreign
yoke, but they know that their tribes cannot be saved
from anarchy and constant strife without the presence of
some arbitrator. The idea is certainly gaining ground
that England is the country whose protectorate would be
most acceptable and most fruitful in good results. You
must remember that I am not writing as a politician. I
express no opinion as to the duties which the course of
the next few years may lay upon us in the Red Sea. I
have simply tried to explain to you as accurately as I can

the present position of the question, and the influence
that is inevitably exercised by the extension of our commercial relations with Arabia

All this has not very much to do with my journey to
Tâif, to which I shall return in another letter, in which I
promise to be less digressive.

II. OUR COMPANY

I started for Tâif a little before noon on Wednesday,
January 28   The High Shereef, in the old spirit of
Eastern hospitality, had not only sent me a guard, but
furnished the dromedaries for our journey and made provision for my reception as his guest at Tâif.   In Arabia
the entertainment of strangers is still the duty, and in
some sense the prerogative, of princes   A young friend
from 'Oneize, in the Nejd, asked me the other day whether,
if he visited England, the Queen would receive him as
her guest   In 'Oneize, he said, the king (so they call
their ruler) would not permit a stranger to seek hospitality
with any one else.   Our cavalcade consisted of five
dromedaries.   The animal which I rode was a very handsome and well-trained beast, gaily caparisoned with
silken bridle and a mountain of gorgeous saddle trappings,
with silk tassels, and green and yellow embroideries, the
whole crowned by a crimson sheepskin laid between two
pillars of chased silver   There is no doubt a great sense
of dignity in sitting on such a throne as this, high above
the heads of the walking multitude ; but I confess that,
when I first mounted my dromedary, my chief concern
was how to keep the hinder pillar out of the small of my
back as I swayed to and fro with the undulations of the
camel's body.   A well-broken dromedary, which differs
from a common camel as a racer does from a cart horse
in breeding and fineness of points, has some paces which
are far from uncomfortable, when one has got well settled
down on a pile of soft rugs, with one leg hooked round the

front pillar of the saddle reposing on a little cushion, and
the calf of the other leg supported on the instep of the
first   But it takes a novice some time to find his seat,
and meantime every jolt, especially if the animal is walking, brings the sharp capital of the other pillar against
one's back.   I was a little uneasy, too, as to the proper
management of the Oriental dress which I had been
advised to wear, as likely to make communication less
constrained in places up the country, where Europeans
are never seen.   A long white caftan reaching to the heels,
and covered by an equally long mishlakh or cloak of fine
camel's hair, do not at first sight seem to form a good
dress to ride in.   But I found by experience that the
Eastern dress is far the most comfortable for such a
journey, both upon the camel and in camping out at night.
The only disadvantage was that it gave my native companions the opportunity to tell a great many lies about
me.   They were really a little nervous about travelling
with a Frank in out - of - the - way places, and while I
adopted the Eastern dress mainly to avoid intrusive
curiosity, they occasionally made a serious effort to pass
me off as a Mohammedan   I know that 'Abdullah Effendi,
as they chose to call me, figured in one village as a doctor
whom the Shereef had sent to inquire into the plague
which has been raging among the horses in the towns of
the Hejâz ; but as I did not appear to approve of this
fiction, I was afterwards kept in the dark as to my supposed personality.   When I say that my attendants were
nervous about travelling with a Frank, I do not of course
mean that they anticipated any danger to me while under
the protection of the Shereef   They took good care never
to let me out of their sight, and with the Emir's men
at hand, I was perfectly safe, even in a place like Zeima,
where Mr. Doughty was exposed to insult and some
hazard as a Christian, after crossing the remotest deserts
without hindrance or danger.   The Moslem who accompanies a Christian is rather nervous about his own reputa-

32

tion. I don't believe that any Arab has the slightest
personal objection to a Christian, at least if he can get a
baksheesh from him ; but something is due to public
opinion, which has decreed that to serve a Christian is
not respectable. Moreover, it is the inalienable privilege
of Moslem children to call names at an unbeliever, and
set the dogs to bark at him, and it was just as well to be
exempt from the duty of resenting such conduct. In
short, my men felt much easier in travelling with an
Effendi in semâda (head shawl), mishlakh, and caftan,
than they would have done with a *Khawâja* in coat and
trousers.

The second member of the party was Ismail, the confidential servant of my friend Mr. Wylde. Born in the
Hejâz of Egyptian parents, Ismail began life as a sad
truant, who was always running away from school from
Mecca to Jeddah, and from Jeddah to Mecca. His roving
habits clung to him as he grew up. He wandered to
Egypt, and thence in various employments to India,
the Straits, and even to China, picking up as he went a
useful knowledge of a great many Asian and African
languages Returning to Egypt, he was long in French
service, and visited Paris Since he settled in Jeddah he
has accompanied Mr. Wylde in several long and difficult
journeys through Abyssinia and the Soudan, and has
also visited London. With a very observant habit and
a tenacious memory, Ismail is a good type of the Arabic
traveller, in whom the constitutional Eastern love of ease
is crossed by a restless curiosity. With better education
and more favourable circumstances, he might have been
a modern Ibn Batûta, of whose story Ismail's traveller's
tales have often reminded me. The Arabian traveller is
quite different from ourselves. The labour of moving
from place to place is a mere nuisance to him, he has no
enjoyment in effort, and grumbles at hunger or fatigue
with all his might. You will never persuade the Oriental
that, when you get off your camel, you can have any other

wish than immediately to squat on a rug and " take your
rest (isterih)," smoking and drinking coffee. Moreover,
the Arab is little impressed by scenery. He describes
a country by the mountains, which are his landmarks,
the fountains or waterholes at which he fills his leathern
water sack, and the vegetation by the wayside. His one
enthusiasm in scenery is for orchards and gardens. A
city embowered in orchards is his ideal of a beautiful
landscape. Damascus is an image of paradise, and Tâif
the fairest scene in the Hejâz. I think it was the same
among the ancients, at least among the practical Romans.
The idea of beauty and interest in scenery was not
developed, except in connection with cultivation and
subserviency to man's uses. I suppose that all nations
have passed through a stage of the same kind, and that
the pure love of landscape, apart from associations of
utility and comfort, is a late growth. With the Arab
it is certainly a general law that his interest and curiosity
is reserved for the affairs of man, and that nature is
attractive in proportion as man has laid his hand on it.
But for anything that has human interest, the Arab's
curiosity is insatiable. He is an inexhaustible story-
teller, and never weary of listening to the most trivial
anecdote of another's adventures. Story-telling and such
books of history and travel as fall under the category of
story-telling form the one kind of literature in which
the Arabs have really excelled ; and in personal intercourse with Arabs one's chief amusement and instruction
are to be found in the same direction. I could not have
had a better attendant than Ismail for drawing out our
escort and the people with whom we met. He had seen
enough of our countrymen to enter readily into the
spirit of my inquiries, and he got the people to talk with
a freedom that would have been impossible to me by myself. Moreover, I could always get him to explain what
I did not understand, which very few Arabs have patience
to do. His own knowledge of the Bedouins was con-

siderable, and he was always ready to supplement it by
fresh inquiry.   In other respects than these Ismail was
a most useful companion, identifying himself wholly
with my interests in a way that is quite extraordinary
in an Arab   He has, indeed, taken England as his ideal,
and is much more disposed to cleave to his English master
than to his own countrymen in the Hejâz.   Up the
country, where people know little of the outer world, he
achieved an immense social success by his anecdotes of
the marvels of London, to which I listened with great
amusement from the curious effect which they produced
when translated into a form intelligible to his audience.
There was one favourite passage—a description of the
great telegraph-room at St. Martin's-le-Grand.   It was like
a scene from the *Arabian Nights*   Hundreds of maidens,
each fairer than the other, peopled this marvellous room.
Ismail moved through the enchanted scene in a sort of
transport, till at length his eyes fell on one more beautiful
than all the others—the most perfect being he had ever
seen.   Then his heart failed him, he refused to see more,
and hurried from the room.   But Ismail's observations
of Western life had gone deeper than this, and taught
him the essential superiority of our institutions, which,
without understanding their details, he knew to secure
liberty and justice.   To me, indeed, he is accustomed
to defend Arabic habits as fitter for the different conditions of the country, but at heart he is a bit of a philosopher, which in Islam is the same thing as a religious
and social free - thinker.   He separates the essence of
religion from the forms of Mohammedanism, and has no
objections to worship with Christians.   He longs, like
all thinking Moslems, for justice in the State, honesty
between man and man, and an end to the ceaseless
oppression of the poor by the rich.   To the hatred of
the Turks which all Arabs feel, he adds a hearty contempt
for the class of Arabs who now hold the reins of power
in the Hejâz.   I have almost been tempted to think him

no Oriental at all when I found that he was capable of
refusing baksheesh But this would be a superficial
judgment.   His temperament, his ambitions, his enjoy-
ments, his vanity, are thoroughly Eastern.   And I am
afraid that I shall somewhat mar his character in the
eyes of the reader when I add that, like a true Arab, he
is married, at the age of thirty, to his fifth wife—a young
beauty with a mind of her own, who tyrannises over him,
and plays the part of a severe stepmother to his son—a
young pickle who is always fishing and bird-catching
when he ought to be at school.   But it would be rude to
dwell on the secrets of his domestic life which Ismail
imparted to me in the confidence of friendship.   Let us
keep our attention for the man himself, as he sits somewhat uneasily on a very rough dromedary, above two
huge saddle bags piled with the appurtenances of our
journey.   His long sallow face peeps out from a plain
white semâda, a corner of which is brought round to
cover the chin and lower part of the face.   His dress is
a black tôb or smock frock covered by a handsome grey
'abâye, which he has borrowed from his master to cut a
good figure in travelling , and his superiority in civilisation to the ordinary Arab appears in the European shoes
and stockings that dangle over the camel's neck, instead
of the bare feet and sandals with gold-spangled straps
that are usually worn even by Arab gentlemen.

My other companions are four of the Shereef's armed
followers and a Bedouin camelman, who " eats the Emir's
bread," but is not inscribed among his regular retinue.
The leader, who is an old and favourite servant, is a very
great man in his own eyes.   By birth an Abyssinian, he
was originally, as his name shows, a slave in the family
of one of the Shereefs in the neighbourhood of 'Okâtz.
He is called the Diamond—Al Mâs, or, more specifically,
Al Mâs al kebeer, the Big Diamond, to distinguish him
from a fellow-servant of the same name.   His dark blue
head shawl, for which in the town he substitutes a hand-

some semâda of Baghdad silk, embroidered with gold
thread, shades a complexion a trifle browner than that
of the Arabs, a pair of small deep-set eyes, one of them
sightless and white, a snub nose, and short upper lip
covered with a thick black moustache. His broad
shoulders are draped in a handsome military-looking
'abâye, in stripes of white and crimson. He carries a
revolver in his belt, and a long straight sabre, with silver-
gilt hilt and scabbard, hangs in a sort of net behind his
saddle. Al Mâs has travelled with Europeans before ;
he knows that they give a good baksheesh, and he is
determined to be very civil and get as much out of me as
he can, but to make the journey as little troublesome to
himself as may be. He made himself very agreeable at
first, for he is one of those good-natured fellows who are
always pleasant when they have things their own way ;
but I soon found him to be a very bad companion to
any one who really wanted to see the country. He
was terribly bored by my searching for inscriptions,
which he declared were all the scratchings of Arab boys.
He had a theory of his own about the right way to travel
—namely, that one should get up in the morning before
sunrise, ride till breakfast time, have a comfortable meal
and a long smoke, ride on again till there is another
opportunity for food and tobacco, and finally turn in an
hour after sunset and prepare a substantial supper. He
grudged every minute of delay that he was not allowed
to spend in eating, sleeping, or smoking the great brazen
waterpipe which accompanies him even on the war-path.
As he acted as guide through an unknown country, where
halting-places necessarily depended on the presence of
water, and other points unknown to me, I was often
entirely in his hands, and he possessed in perfection the
most provoking of Oriental arts, which enables a man,
by a combination of lies and passive resistance, to get
his own way without formally disobeying orders. Moreover, Al Mâs, with all his apparent good nature, was too

selfish and overbearing to get on well with the men under
him, though they were afraid to complain of an old and
favourite servant of the princely family. With Ismail
he had an open rupture at Tâif, which threw a certain
shade over the rest of our journey. After his love for
smoking, eating, and giving himself the airs of a great
man, Al Mâs's chief characteristic was an extraordinary
talkativeness. As he has really seen a great deal of
service among the unruly Bedouins of the Hejâz, I found
his interminable stories very tolerable by night over our
camp fire. He was quite willing to be interrogated, but
his answers were always confused and useless unless they
took the shape of a narrative, when he sailed on with
great fluency and copiousness of irrelevant detail, carefully punctuating his sentences with good Moslem oaths
at the larger stops, and the words, " O, my uncle," in
the place of commas. At the close of a paragraph his
formula, whether he spoke to me or to the Arabs, was,
" Hast thou understood or not ? " His stories of personal
adventure were strongly dashed with a superstition more
African than Arabic. He was urgent that I should get
him a book of charms, and the very first story he told
me was the wonderful history of a holy man from the far
north who had spent his whole life in travelling, and
finally came to the Hajj with no possessions but a single
garment, a wallet, a sword, and a precious *Khâtme* or
copy of the Koran   The last two properties were stolen
from him at Mozdâlifa, and recovered in a marvellous
way by the directions of a dream and the help of the
Shereef and Al Mâs. In return he gave Al Mâs a wonderful talisman, or rather Hejâb—the whole Koran written
in a minute character, and enclosed in a leather case.
" Wear this," he said, " either on the arm or round your
neck, but at night hang it on a staff, and on no account
let it touch the ground." Al Mâs wore it for two years,
during which he was free from all accidents, quarrels, and
inconveniences of every sort. At length the string broke

one day while he was walking, and for fear that the treasure might fall on the ground he went on carrying it in his mouth, and when he was forced to lay it down, carefully spread his cloak under it. After a short time he returned to find it gone, without trace, and his exceptional luck gone with it. So much for Al Mâs and his superstitions, on which I need not enlarge just now, as it will be impossible for us to get to Tâif without hearing more of them.

The second in command was a pure Arab, by blood of the Qoreish, the tribe of the Prophet, and by more immediate descent a Wahhâbite. His grandfather, 'Othman, and granduncle, 'Aly, were famous leaders of their party in the days when the Wahhâbite power overran the Hejâz, and threatened to extend their Puritan empire over all Arabia. Mohsin—*the fair dealer*, a common name among the Bedouins who have no great partiality for the current religious names of Islam—is a tall muscular fellow, who wears his moustache with a military swagger, and of a cold morning appears wrapped up in a Turkish military cape. Beneath the cape is a scarlet jacket turned up with green—the favourite Arab colours. The rest of his dress is that of the Bedouin— a short tôb of rough brown cotton, a crooked dagger of Persian steel in the girdle with his pistols, a yellow semâda on the head with a mass of tassels dancing behind, his brown legs and feet bare, and a long stick with a hooked knob in his hand, with which he steers his dromedary, tapping it on the head or neck as he encourages it with a deep guttural grunt *ikh, ikhkh, ikhkhkh*. Mohsin proved a very good, manly fellow, not very talkative, but capable of being drawn out, and with a good knowledge of the country and its traditions. Wahhâbite as he was, he was extremely fond of tobacco, and we cemented our friendship over many a cigarette—a great decline from the first principles of his sect, when smoking was the second great sin after idolatry. Behind Mohsin's saddle

sits his *radeef*, or after-rider, the camelman Marzook.
It is an awkward perch, for the hind-quarters of a camel
slope away at a considerable angle, and the second rider
has to hold fast by the pommel, while his legs dangle on
either side, or more often are gathered up and twisted
together in one of the innumerable Oriental forms of
squatting. Now I understand why that pommel takes
the shape of a pillar, which, to one's first experience,
seems specially contrived to dig into the rider's back.
Without it the second rider would infallibly slide off.
And the *radeef* is an ancient and established institution
in Arabia, so much so that in the old Pagan kingdoms
the mayor of the palace, who wielded the actual power,
as in the Merovingian kingdom in France, was regularly
known by this name. Marzook is of the great 'Oteibe
tribe, from the Nejd, a true son of the desert, speaking
a far purer Arabic than even Mohsin, very fond of his
camels, whose heads he fondles and kisses as they lie
ruminating at the halting-place, but a little shy at first
towards strangers. We got very good friends soon, for
I liked his honest, weather-beaten face, with something
of a hawk-like keenness of expression in spite of the loss
of one eye, and he took very kindly to me after a discussion about the true Arabic name of a woman's camel
litter, in which I sided with him and gained the point
with a quotation from old Imrulqais. The word in
question (*ghabeet*) was known to none of the other men,
but among the 'Oteibe it is still the term for the litter
used by a Sheikh's daughter, just as it was twelve hundred
years ago. In his dress Marzook had nothing of the style
affected by the regular members of the Shereef's retinue.
A short dirty tôb bound by a girdle, and leaving his bare
legs uncovered from the knee, a coarse red head shawl,
and in cold weather, a rough brown cloak, did not distinguish him from an ordinary wanderer of the desert. But he
had adopted one innovation of the civilised cities—he wore
a pair of drawers, which the common Bedouin never does.

Our other two men were the gayest figures of the group, Hâmid and 'Abderrabbu, usually called Adrubbu, pure Africans by blood, but born in Mecca, as Mawâleed of the Shereef. It is the custom of Arabian princes to form a body of dependents from their emancipated slaves and their children. In a good house a slave seldom remains long in bondage The master frees him, finds him a wife—generally an emancipated negress— and sets him up in the world The children of such a union are called Mawâleed, and form a kind of clientship ready at any moment to serve under their master's banner, and bound to him by a strong tie of dependence. Many of these families have attained to wealth and position, but the tie is never broken, and when a Muwalled dies without natural heirs, the representative of the emancipator takes the inheritance. There are chiefs in Yemen—Sheikh Barakat was mentioned to me as one —who can call up as many as four hundred of these clients to ride with them on a foray. Such men often buy negroes and girls in large numbers simply for the purpose of liberating and marrying them, to swell the numbers of their clients. Our two negroes were very pleasant, handy fellows, with a smattering of education, and very good gentle manners. Their dress was a white tôb, with gold buttons at the throat. A white semâda, whose heavy fringes and tassels were prettily interwoven with cords of purple and blue, was secured to the head by the double twist of a great rope, called the ogal, of camel's hair, bound with gold and silver thread. Their military equipments were in pure Bedouin style. The janbeeya or crooked dirk, which is the inseparable companion of the Bedouin, and the favourite instrument of his bloody revenge, was silver hilted, and cased in a heavy silver sheath, enriched with bosses and chasing. The leather belt, in front of which the dirk is stuck, lying obliquely across the person, was gay with tassels of crimson and yellow silk On one side was a silver case, with a row of seven little powder-flasks, each holding two or three charges, behind it a silver powder-horn of quaint form, and on the other side a silver-mounted pocket for bullets. A smaller horn for the priming was hung from the shoulder by a belt enriched with silver bosses. These gorgeous accoutrements, from the hereditary armoury of the Shereef, were, however, for show rather than use. The real weapon was an American breech-loading carbine slung to the saddle, the cartridges for which were carried in a plain leather bag. The obsolete accoutrements served the purpose of a uniform, the silver dirk, when worn by any but a great man, immediately declaring its bearer a follower of the Emir A prettier uniform can hardly be conceived than these brilliant white garments, over-laid with great masses of open silver work and bright dashes of colour in the silken embroideries and tassels, in contrast to the black skins of the wearers. Hâmid, however, used to produce an effective variation by wearing a soft orange and yellow head shawl, and a very short scarlet jacket over his tôb. In virtue of these splendours and a certain experience of the world, gained by a voyage to Marseilles in the incongruous function of a stoker, he took slight precedence of Adrubbu, and filled the responsible office of cook for the company, while his comrade pounded the coffee beans and rolled cigarettes. Our fifth camel was shared between them, and they took their turns in walking or riding as radeef.

I have now introduced the reader to our whole company, and as the ceremony has been somewhat tedious, their further acquaintance must be reserved for another letter.

III. The Mecca Road

The city of Jeddah has three landward gates—the Medina gate to the north, the Yemen gate to the south, and the Mecca gate, facing the east ; but all caravans

pass through the last gate, where a tax is levied on every
camel issuing from the town.   Just outside the wall is
a sort of market-place for the Bedouin camel drivers, a
short street of shops and coffee - houses, and an open
space under the walls, where the camels lie ruminating
or munching wisps of coarse hay while their masters are
smoking, gossiping, or chaffering with the hucksters,
who sit cross-legged by the wayside, each with a tray
or basket of wares, like Alnaschar in the *Arabian Nights*
To the left is the spacious courtyard in which all Jeddah
assembles for prayer on the great annual feast, and beyond
this, to the north - east of the town, rises the cupola of
our mother Eve, the great holy place from which Jeddah
is said to take its name of " The Ancestress."   Winding
our way through the turmoil of the bazaar, we emerge
on the open desert—a long, flat expanse of sand somewhat lower than the town, which stands on a raised coral
reef.   To the right and left of our path, in the neighbourhood of the town, are one or two country houses and
several wretched hamlets of half-settled Arabs—the huts
constructed much like those on the opposite coast, of
matting and the twigs of desert bushes.   The face of the
desert is almost absolutely bare of vegetation for the
stretch of a full hour between Jeddah and the foot of
the hills   There are two trees by the roadside in the
whole of this way, and the coarse herbage on which a
few miserable sheep are trying to feed is so scanty after
the long-continued drought that it hardly gives a tinge
of colour to the grey sand.   Yet the Tehâma, as this
plain is named, is not unfertile.   Its basis is a coral
reef, in which water can always be found by sinking pits,
and the sand which covers the coral is mixed with a fine
earth forming a very good soil for cultivation.   Such a
soil is called in old Arabic *raghâm*, and a coffee-house and
police-station at the foot of the hills takes from it the
name of *Reghâme*.   From Reghâme to Jeddah, after
copious rains, the whole plain is planted with water

melons, and even with patches of the coarse millet called
dokhn. This dokhn, named from its dark or smoky
appearance, is a favourite food of the poorer classes,
and, unlike its rival, the white or red millet (dura), is
an ancient Semitic grain, being mentioned under the
same name in the Old Testament. It is interesting to
note that the names of the principal kinds of cereals,
wheat, barley, millet, lentils, are older than the differentiation of the Hebrew and Arabic languages. They are
the same in both languages, and in a form which shows
that they are not loan words. But in early times the
nomadic Arabs must have consumed far less cereal food
than the agricultural peoples of Canaan. And so the
word which in Hebrew means bread, but which radically
denotes the solid or *consistent* part of food in contrast to
the fluid water, has in Arabic the sense of flesh. Even
now the wilder Bedouin seldom tastes bread ; but in
many Arabic - speaking countries, not merely in Egypt,
as is usually stated, but equally in the Hejâz, the increased importance of cereal food has stamped its mark
on the language, and bread is called 'êsh—that is, *life.*

After Reghâme the face of the country changes Low
but rugged hills of basalt and other igneous rocks rise
before us, and the road winds between ranges of crumbling
rock in a sandy glen, without any considerable rise of
level Vegetation now increases, and the path is bordered
with the broom like *markh*, used by the Arabs for making
cordage. Before the days of flint and steel the *markh*
had another use, which is registered in the native Arabic
lexicons, but now, as far as I have been able to hear, is
remembered only in the Soudan, where Ismail, as a little
boy, saw a very old man produce fire by rubbing two
pieces of this wood together. The mountains increase
in height, and to the left opens the dreaded Robbers'
Gate, through which the northern predatory tribes are
wont to descend on the Mecca road. In something over
another hour we cross a slight eminence, and enter a

wider valley dotted with acacias of the kind called salam
This valley is infested with wolves, and we passed the
hiding-place of a hunter, a small lair built up with
branches, near which a piece of a dead camel had been
laid as a bait.   In the middle of the valley is the coffee-
house of Far'eye (the upper place), at which we stopped
to rest till the heat of the day should decline.   The
Mecca road is lined with these coffee-houses at short
intervals   The Far'eye is the third from Jeddah.   The
soldiers charged with protecting the roads have their
post beside these stations, where there is commonly a
well.   The coffee-house consists merely of a hut of straw
or branches, with a stone dais in front, shaded by a
veranda, and sometimes an open covered court.   The
furniture is a row of earthen jars for cooling water, a
hearth and apparatus for boiling coffee, hubble-bubbles,
and a few mats of plaited straw, which here are generally
circular.   A mat is spread in the shade for the traveller,
and he is served with coffee and a pipe   If any one
chooses to stay overnight, he is accommodated with firewood, and a pot in which to prepare supper   Everything else he must generally find for himself.   At Far'eye
some of our men took the opportunity to say their prayers,
which, in travelling, are put in at convenient seasons,
or more frequently omitted altogether.   Praying, like
the incessant counting of the rosary of divine names
with which the Arab fills up intervals of conversation,
is viewed as a convenient distraction when one has
nothing better to do, and in Tâif especially Al Mâs
improved his leisure by making up considerable arrears
of devotion.   In a company when talk is lagging, it is
quite common for some one to ask the time of day, and
on finding that an hour of prayer has arrived, to step out
of the circle, spread his upper garment on the floor, and
go through the prayers of such a number of rek'as.   But
when business is on hand, the prayers have to give way ,
and according to my observation, it is only the prayers

of the daybreak that are performed with precise regularity. These two are generally uttered in audible murmur, or even with a clear voice, whose cadences are not devoid of impressiveness, as the words, " God is most Great," " I testify that there is no God but God, and I testify that Mohammed is his servant and apostle," rise through the silence of the desert, and spread over the hills with the first rays of the morning light. But the more one sees of it, the less is it possible to feel any sincere respect for Moslem devotion, in which formalism and vain repetition are reduced to a system. The God of the Mohammedan is too remote from his worshipper to be addressed in the language of true prayer ; and the daily liturgy is little more than an abstract glorification of the divine qualities. Special petitions are indeed permitted though not pre-scribed, but the opening of the worshipper's heart to his Heavenly Father is not known to the faith of Islam, and help in individual need is sought rather from patron saints, or in the use of charms, among which, to be sure, the recitation of certain formulæ from the Koran has a place. There is, of course, a certain belief in the efficacy of special prayer. Some weeks ago a great procession, headed by the Wâly, went out from Jeddah in the morn-ing to pray for rain I was not fortunate enough to be able to observe this ceremony

From Far'eye the road rises through a broken country, where for the first time the granite which predominates in the upland districts is seen breaking through the basalt. In this part of the road there are two cairns by the way-side, called respectively the Zalâbâny and Kunâfâny—that is the baker of zalâbiye and the maker of kunâfe. Zalâbiye is the name of a kind of bread, fried in clarified butter, and eaten with honey. Here it is always baked in great round cakes ; in Syria it has an oblong form, and is eaten with grape syrup. Kunâfe is a favourite dish, especially in Ramadan. It is something like ver-micelli, but sweet. The legend goes that the artists who

have given their names to these cairns lived in Jeddah
and Mecca respectively. Each started to carry a burden of
his wares to the other town, and on meeting they boasted,
without adding the ordinary " If God will," that their
wares would still be hot when they reached their destina-
tion. They had scarcely parted when they were struck
dead for their impiety, and the stone heaps mark their
graves. Not far from this, beside a deserted coffee-house,
lay the scene of an adventure which befell Ismail a
fortnight before. Returning from Mecca, and travelling,
as is customary, by night, without any other attendant
than his donkey boy, he was attacked with stones by a
party of robbers. The robbers had guns, but did not
dare to use them from fear of alarming the patrol, and they
finally made off when Ismail succeeded in giving one of
them a severe blow. He was very indignant, however,
and had now brought his gun, in the hope of having a
chance of revenge. The police, inefficient as usual, had
got no trace of the robbers, and the story having got
abroad, few people cared to travel at night, except in
strong companies.

Beyond Far'eye, the first inhabited place is the negro's
coffee-house, from which the road descends into an open
plain, running down to the coast in a course a little
S. of W. We have pierced the first hilly barrier that
separates Jeddah from the interior, and join the natural
road leading up to the Nejd, along the great valley of
Wady Marr, which drains this part of the Hejâz. In
Kiepert's map you will find the valley marked as Wady
Bahra This is not a name, but merely means the Wady
in which the village of Bahra lies—a considerable hamlet,
situated at the point where the road from Jeddah, descending obliquely in a line southward of E., reaches the
axis of the valley and bends somewhat to the northward
Bahra is the half-way house between Mecca and Jeddah,
twenty miles distant from either city, and a favourite
halting-place for camel trains. Though the village is

but a group of wretched huts, with the usual coffee-house and military post, its position is one of some importance from the roads which converge upon it, the natural highway along the Wady, which is the gate of the upper country, being here intersected by the Jeddah road, through the hills on the west, and by another road across Jebel Shemeisi, which leads into Wady Magra, and so to Wady Na'aman and the high road from Mecca to Yemen.   The strategical importance of the point was at one time recognised, for close by the village, on one of the many isolated rocky eminences that stud the plain, rise the ruins of a well-built square fortress, with round corner towers—the usual type of an Arabic stronghold. Our men could tell me nothing about this castle except its name, Qasr el Gazia.   Unlike the other fortresses in the upper parts of the Wady, which were strongholds of the Wahhâbites, it appears to be of considerable age, for I have since learned that it is an object of superstitious terror to the Arabs.   It contains hidden treasures, guarded by a supernatural power which inflicts terrible punishment on those who venture to explore the secrets of the ruin.

The name of Wady Marr, or the valley of passage, is explained by the natives from the fact that this valley is the great watercourse through which the floods descending from the uplands sweep in a tremendous torrent   I fancy that the name is old, for Sprenger gives Marr-Tzahrân as the ancient name of the pilgrim station on the road from Mecca to Medina, which lies in this valley, and is now called Wady Fâtima.   The upper reaches of the Wady above Hadda are well watered with copious springs.   Below Hadda, the water is ordinarily below ground, but can be got by sinking wells, which were once numerous.   At present I think there is but one well between Bahra and Hadda used for irrigation, cultivation having gone back, as is the case in so many parts of the Hejâz.   The comparative luxuriance of the vegetation

33

shows that the water is not very far from the surface
The path is fringed with shrubs and herbaceous plants—
the rên, with its kidney-shaped, downy leaves, and yellow
and orange blossoms ; and in greater abundance the
white flowered harmel, used by the Arabs for fumi-
gating their houses. A little way off, to the right of
our path, was quite a coppice of the dark-leaved shrub
called khamt, which is plentiful in several parts of this
valley, and is burned by the natives to produce a coarse
salt, which they call black alum (*shabb aswad*), and in use
for washing. The chief seat of this manufacture is
Hodeida, in Yemen.

As we passed Bahra the sun was already sinking, and
the caravans which had been resting through the heat of
the day at Bahra or Hadda, were again in motion The
road, almost deserted between Jeddah and Bahra, was
crowded with long trains of baggage camels laden with
piece goods and grain for Mecca and the interior, and
the caravans of East Indian and Javanese pilgrims
descending to the coast. The pilgrims travel in covered
litters named *snugduf*[?], hung like a balance upon the
camel's back, so that a passenger can recline at full
length on either side, and a third, if desired, can sit
between them. Beside the camels walked the Bedouin
drivers, their heads swathed in a dirty brown cotton
wrapper, and the great dirk or janbeeya, in its brazen
sheath, projecting from the leathern belt which confines
a shirt or waist cloth of the same colour and material as
the head cloth. Travelling all night, the pilgrims would
reach Jeddah in the early morning.

An hour after sunset we reached Hadda, where
the Mecca road breaks off from the main valley, and
the fertile region of water springs begins Here there
is a fountain bursting forth under the hill-side, and
wells with gardens and a few palm trees. The village
has several hundred inhabitants, but the only tolerable
building is a large mosque, the dwellings being mainly

round huts of palm branches woven over a frame of
poles.   The pilgrims regularly halt here on their way to
and from Mecca, and the huts are let out to them at an
exorbitant figure   We, however, as the night was warm,
preferred to take up our quarters under the veranda of
the coffee-house   Our baggage was piled up on the ground
and the camels lay round it.   The veranda was laid
with mats, to which our men added a mattress and rugs
for my bed, while they formed a circle on the ground
beneath.   Al Mâs got out his favourite *sheeshe* (water-
pipe), coffee was called for, and all settled down for supper
and a long talk.   Of an evening the Arabs are excessively
garrulous, and when several parties meet at such a wayside station as Hadda the talk goes on almost all night,
the interlocutors falling out one by one as sleep over-
powers them.   New arrivals continued to come in till
long after midnight, but as the custom is to travel by
night and rest by day, the larger caravans which felt
strong enough to brave robbers only halted to drink
coffee and get the latest gossip.   The news was all about
the robber bands   We had scarcely settled down when
an almost naked muleteer came in.   His party of six
had been attacked by five men quite near the village, and
stripped of everything.   Ismail, full of his own quarrel,
seized his rifle, and was off at once to join the police of
the station, but they took the matter much more coolly,
and disappointed his hopes of revenge by insisting that
it was better to wait till morning, though the full moon
would have served them almost as well as daylight.   In
fact, there is no very strong feeling in the Hejâz against
highway robbery.   It is the duty of the Government to
keep the Bedouins quiet by allowances of money and
grain, and when the roads become very insecure, it is
generally the case, or, at least, it is generally asserted,
that these payments are in arrears.   The bandits who
infest the roads are sometimes regular outlaws—wild
men who have their retreat in the mountains.   But at

other times they are wandering parties of such powerful
tribes as the Harb and the 'Oteibe, whose depredations
are separated by a very indefinite line from the recognised
forms of Arabic warfare, and whose family connections
do not permit a weak Government to deal very severely
with them. Even the outlaws are treated with a certain
amount of consideration. It should not be difficult to
penetrate to their mountain lairs and arrest their wives
and children ; but, according to Arabic ways of thought,
this would be "a great shame," an elastic expression
which comprises every form of impropriety, from a
trifling breach of etiquette to the most serious moral
turpitude It is the law of Arabic warfare that the
women of the enemy must not be harmed, and this
privilege is extended to the robber bands, which are,
therefore, in some measure recognised as having the
status of belligerents Before we returned, the roads
had become still more insecure, and people were all
travelling through the heat of the day rather than risk
the perils of the night. The patrols along the road were
increased, and by each station the horses were standing
ready saddled for pursuit But by this time the thing
had developed into a regular Bedouin warfare. A Medina
caravan of 300 camels, under the protection of the Harb,
was attacked by the 'Oteibe, near Wady Fâtima, and
several men were killed on either side. These disturbances,
it now appeared, were connected with the severe drought
in the uplands. Finding no pasture for their flocks in
their own district of the Nejd, the 'Oteibe had scattered
far and wide in quest of grass, and a party had descended
on the lands of the Harb, on which, as old friends, they
thought themselves entitled to graze in time of need.
The Harb objected, and the attack on the caravan
followed. At the present moment a number of 'Oteibe
are lying in prison in Jeddah, but I am told by 'Omar
Naseef that as they include influential chiefs, they will
not be severely punished. They will probably be held

to ransom ; and if it appears that more of the Harb than
of the 'Oteibe fell in the fight, the latter tribe will have
to pay blood money for the balance.   Whether all the
recent robberies are the work of the 'Oteibe is not yet
known, and perhaps will never appear.   Meantime there
has been good rain in the upper country, and the dis-
persed 'Oteibe were beginning to return homewards before
I got back to Jeddah.   A good season, which may now be
looked for, will allay the turbulence of the tribes , and
whether or no, people are too well accustomed to the
insecurity of the desert to make more than a nine days'
wonder of any act of Bedouin rapine.

The state of the roads is a good measure of the weakness of the Turkish power in the Hejâz, which, practically
speaking, exists for no other public purpose than to keep
the roads to Mecca and Medina open.   Other provinces
are held for profit, and remit an annual revenue to Constantinople, after providing for the maintenance of local
government.   But the Hejâz is said to cost the Sultan
£200,000 a year more than it produces, and absorbs a
great part of the surplus revenues of Syria and Yemen
The Turks are much more devout than the Arabs, and
have a high veneration for the Holy Places, and the
Ottoman Sultans are ready to pay this price for the honour
of figuring as protectors of the Caaba and patrons of the
pilgrimage.   The money goes less for the maintenance
of troops and public officers than in payment of pensions
and innumerable allowances of grain, partly to descendants
of the Prophet and others who can in some way claim
connection with the service of Caaba, and partly to the
Bedouins who might obstruct the progress of the pilgrimage caravans.   With this vast outlay, with garrisons at
Mecca, Medina, and Jeddah, and armed forts along the
road, it might fairly be expected that the roads would be
absolutely safe   Yet the short route of forty miles
between Mecca and Jeddah is in the state which I have
described.   Even the Wâly does not pass over it without

an escort from the Shereef. And this is the great road
of the country, not merely the pilgrim route, but the
main commercial highway, over which perhaps a third
part of the imports of Jeddah (which are variously
estimated at from two to three millions sterling per
annum) is conveyed by camel transport, to the great
profit of the Bedouins themselves.

The Medina road, which is hardly less important, is
in a far more insecure state   Within the last year there
has been more than one serious collision upon it between
the Arabs and the authorities, and on one occasion a
Shereef, a near relation of the Prince of Mecca, was
seized and insulted   On this route merchants do not
venture to remit specie, but, contrary to the usual
practice of Arabian commerce, effect their payments by
bills   And the characteristic thing is, that the people
do not expect the Turks to mend matters, but hope that
the Arabs will be better kept in hand when the High
Shereef Hosein, who has been but two years in power,
has established his prestige among the Bedouins, who are
not yet disposed to pay him the same respect that was
accorded to the " iron hand " of his predecessor, Abdullah.
If the Turks fail so completely in the discharge of the one
public service which they seriously attempt, what, it
will be asked, do they really have from the Hejâz ?   The
answer is very simple   A certain number of officials
have their own private opportunities of pillage ; and as
all officers are very often changed, the great men in Constantinople who have nominations in their hands receive
a good deal of baksheesh

A man coming out here, say as Nazir of the Jeddah
custom-house, has paid a good many thousand pounds
for his post, and is perfectly aware that at any moment
some other scoundrel who has money to spend on bribes
may arrive from Constantinople with an appointment
to displace him, and turn him out of his bureau without
a moment's warning.   He is, therefore, bound to pillage

with all his might—to pillage not only enough for himself,
but enough to bribe the travelling inspector, and, if need
be, to outbid a rival at Constantinople   This system of
pillage is the one thing in which the Turks are successful,
and therefore it is not strange that, in the eyes of the
Arabs, the Turkish Government means simply an organised
robbery.

IV. Wady Fâtima

On January 29 we started from Hadda a little before
sunrise, and in a few minutes left the Mecca road on our
right, and held right up Wady Marr, passing through a
belt of *Khamt* and acacias under which were the tents
of a small encampment of the Harb Arabs.   From this
point the valley is fertile—that is, there are springs
breaking out at short intervals, each of which fertilises
a plot of garden ground, and is usually surrounded by a
palm grove   Between the plantations the valley is still
a sandy desert.   I procured a list of all the wells with
their names from the old Shereef at Wady Fâtima.   They
are thirty-three in number, the lowest being the fountain
in Hadda and the highest those of Zeima and Wady
Leimoon.   From Hadda to Zeima was a journey of two
days, as we travelled ; but we made considerable halts,
and did not keep along the valley the whole way.   So
it will be seen that for Arabia this is a district remarkably
rich in water.   Some of the springs are very strong, comparable with the famous fountains of Palestine, and
sending forth a stream sufficient to irrigate many acres of
soil.   The fountain-head is sometimes a large pond thirty
or forty feet across, and swarming with tiny fish.   Yet
I saw the springs at their weakest, for it is three years
since a flood has come down the valley.   All the springs
are private property, and most of them belong to members
of the princely house of Mecca

That water is treated as property lies in the nature of

the country, in which land without the means of irrigation
has no value, and the principle goes back to the oldest
times, as appears from the Old Testament (Genesis xxvi.,
Judges i 15). Even in Jeddah the cisterns and wells
from which the town is supplied belong to private citizens,
and the water is sold from house to house by their slaves.
Among the nomads, however, springs and wells are the
property of the tribe, not of the individual, and neighbouring tribes are allowed to drink in time of drought on
principles of mutual accommodation. In time of war, the
water and the palm groves are the possessions through
which the most vital blow can be struck at an enemy.
Thus in the ferocious struggle between Mesha, King of
Moab, and the Israelites, the order was given to stop the
wells, cut down the good trees, and mar the cultivated
patches of land with stones (2 Kings iii 19). Similar
tactics would still be used in Arabia in a desperate contest, and the destruction of palm groves has turned many
a fruitful valley into a wilderness. But in the Hejâz,
I am informed, the palms are spared except in extreme
cases—that is, the forces of the Shereef would not usually
cut down the palm groves of a rebellious tribe, but would
content themselves with driving off cattle and seizing
captives to be held to ransom. This is a modification
of the old ferocity of Semitic warfare in the same line as
the law of war in Deuteronomy.

The great abundance of spring water in the Wady
Marr, or, as it is also called, the Torrent way (Derb es
Seil) is said by the Arabs themselves to be due to subterranean currents descending from Jebel Barada, a lofty
mountain above Tâif. The upper springs are hot The
great fountain of Zeima, which issues from a cleft in the
rocky side of the mountain overhanging the village, is
about as hot water as one can comfortably put one's
hand in. I had, unfortunately, no thermometer to test
it with. It is a very sweet, pure water, extremely pleasant
to drink. and quite devoid of mineral taste. The other

upper spring in Wady Leimoon, under Jebel Mudheeq,
lay off our route, so I speak of it only from report. I
understand that some of the lower springs are also slightly
warm, particularly that of Sôla, which is but an hour
and a quarter below Zeima. But I was not told of this
till we had passed, and though I had tasted the water
I did so from a pitcher in which it had stood for some time.
I was also told that the fountain of Queen Zobeide, from
which Mecca is supplied with water, is a warm spring   It
belongs to another series of springs under Mount Kara, but
the natives make Mount Barada the ultimate source of all.
I shall describe the fountain of Zeima more fully when I
come to speak of that village, when I shall also speak of its
failure and reappearance some years ago. Meantime, I
may mention a curious well near Mecca, of which I was
told by Ismail. The water has no mineral taste, but is
valued as a cure for flatulency and indigestion, to which
it is said to give instant relief. Its water is sold in Mecca
at double the price of that from Zobeide's aqueduct, but
is chiefly drunk by women, being thought to have a
weakening effect on the other sex. We were but a little
way from Hadda when the sun rose over a sea of wild
peaks far away to the right, the mountain land of the
Qoreish, above Mecca. The Mountain of Light, famous
as the place where Mohammed first attained the conviction that he was the recipient of special revelation,
was faintly seen through the morning mists. On the
other side of the valley, above the palm groves of Rikkane,
ran the long bulwark of Jebel Dhaf. To the north were
the rocky faces of Mukasser and the Sidr, noted haunts
of robbers   All these mountains are of igneous formation,
and trap or basalt seem to be their chief components.

After three hours' journey we halted under a sand-
bank for breakfast. When their waterskins were full,
my men generally made the morning halt in a desert
spot, and even when water was at hand preferred a
draught from the skin, well cooled by evaporation, to

water drawn fresh from the spring. The first business
at every halt is to gather firewood and prepare coffee.
To do this properly an elaborate apparatus is thought
necessary—a long ladle to roast the beans, with a spoon
chained to it for stirring and turning them, a brass
mortar and pestle, and three coffee pots. When the
beans are roasted and ground, a few sharp strokes with
the pestle on the side of the mortar warn the company
that coffee will be ready immediately. The powder is
placed in one pot, the water, already boiling in the second,
is poured over it, and the liquid is allowed to simmer
gently by the fire, while two or three cloves of cardamom
and a small piece of dry ginger are pounded up and put
into the third pot. The coffee is decanted into this, and
is then ready for drinking. The small cups of thick
earthenware are produced from a canister, in which they
lie, along with the cloth used for wiping them. As there
is no saucer and no handle to the cup, it is never more
than a third filled, and every one is expected to have at
least three helpings It is a point of strict etiquette not
to fill the cup, which would be regarded as a " shame."
The Bedouins are agreed upon this, but the exact amount
which may be poured into the cup is different in different
tribes. The Benî Malik, who have other idiosyncrasies,
such as permitting their women to go unveiled, barely
cover the bottom of the cup By the time that the coffee
has been drunk, a good mass of hot embers has accumulated, and Hâmid proceeds to bake a cake of unleavened
bread, which is mixed in a metal basin and kneaded on
a skin. However large the company, there must be but
one cake (qurs or mella). The embers are scraped aside,
and the mella placed on the hot sand is covered with
them. In a few minutes it is baked, the ashes are scraped
from the hard crust, and the bread is pounded up into
rough fragments in the baking basin. Clarified butter is
poured over it from a small skin, sugar or honey is added,
and while still hot the whole is worked up with hands

into a uniform mass. This is 'Areeka [?], the favourite
travellers' food, and by no means a bad mess when skil-
fully prepared. The company sit round the basin, each
man with his right hand supported on the right knee,
while the left hand is kept aside. A small morsel is seized
with the points of the fingers, rolled into a ball and conveyed to the mouth. According to a law of politeness,
which is prescribed in the traditions of the Prophet along
with the duty of saying Bismillah and passing with the
right hand, every one must stick to his own corner of
the dish   But when one has a dainty morsel it is a polite
attention to hand it over to a neighbour. In the towns
it is a graceful act to put the morsel in your friend's
mouth ; but Marzook, as a true Bedouin, regards this
as a " shame," and will not accept what is so offered. Am
I a girl, the Bedouin argues, that I require you to feed me ?

Nothing amuses one more in the desert than the extraordinary ramifications of the notion expressed by the
word "shame" ('eyb)   We have just had two instances
of a purely conventional kind   The same expression of
condemnation is applied to the gravest moral offence, or,
on the other hand, to an error in prosody. The usage
corresponds to a peculiar development of the moral
judgment, characteristic of a state of society in which
almost unlimited personal freedom is restrained only by
the force of a public opinion based on traditional forms
and conventional prescription. The Arab knows no law
but the public opinion and usage of his people, and every
conflict with this opinion is classified as an 'eyb. But
while I have detained you with this long digression our
Arabs, who eat well but very fast, have emptied the dish
of 'Areeka. Coffee goes round once more. Al Mâs has
another pipe, and the others smoke a cigarette   The
camels are reloaded, and we move off again for Wady
Fâtima.

At Wady Fâtima the Torrent Path is crossed by the
highway from Mecca to Medina which passes behind

Jebel Sidr. There is a small village, with the ruins of a very considerable castle of the Wahhâbites. On a little eminence, commanding a fine view of the valley and the northern and western hills, is the cottage of an old Shereef who had been warned to expect us, and came out to receive us with very gracious hospitality. Rugs were brought out, and while the house was cleaned out for our reception, I sat in the shade under a wall, exchanged the usual compliments, and enjoyed the play of the sunlight on the mountain sides, which strongly recalled some of the barer hills of Skye. Beneath the house was a fine acacia, and finding me interested in the names of the different trees in the Hejâz, the old gentleman began to recount with considerable pride the great variety of species. When an Arab speaks of trees, he includes bushes which would hardly pass for trees even in Caithness. Even on this principle, the list is not a long one, but the people make the most of what they possess, and there is scarcely a plant which has not some industrial use   Of trees proper, by far the largest class are the acacias, the different species of which are not easily distinguished by a stranger, and are often confounded even in Arabic lexicons and commentaries on the poets The commonest species are the salum, the samur, the talh, and the killat   The talh is the tree of the uplands, the killat is distinguished by its hooked thorns, which inflict a smarting wound, and by its whitish bark   The samur has a dark bark, and is more gnarled than the salam, which is the prevailing tree of the lowlands, and also the most useful. It is one of the so-called khabt, or trees whose leaves are beaten off to be eaten by camels, and its wood in addition to those uses yields a brown dye. Throughout my journey I found various trees and shrubs to have a very well defined local distribution, so that my men would often identify a place by specifying what grew at it   I shall, therefore, note from time to time the various plants and their uses, as pointed out to me,

though I fear that my lack of botanical knowledge will
make these indications somewhat hazy.

The old Shereef Al Bâz (the falcon) was one of the most
patriarchal figures I have seen in Arabia. He is of the
'Abdely family—that is, of the kin of 'Abd el Muntaleb,
the rival of Ibn 'Aun. He is not one of the greater
Shereefs, but having land at Wady Fâtima, and possessing
a thorough knowledge of the Bedouins in the district, he
is much employed in local affairs by the Grand Shereef,
and is greatly respected in the neighbourhood. At the age
of sixty-five he is still hale and vigorous, with a clear
eye and erect figure. He was very plainly dressed in a
linen skull cap, and simple cotton tôb, a little soiled ;
but his white beard, which was very carefully trimmed,
gave him an air of dignity, and his manner was that of
a gentleman of position, even while he was bustling about,
serving us with his own hands, and directing the whole
hospitalities in person like a modern Abraham   These
cares occupied him so much that I could not get nearly
so much talk from him as I should have wished, for he
knew the country better than any other man I met on
my journey, and was very willing to give information.
Arab etiquette demanded that he should kill a sheep for
us, and that we should stay to dine, so after a short
interval we were invited into the house to repose while
everything was got ready. The house was a plain
cottage of stone and clay, with a clay roof. Entering
from a little courtyard, through a doorway facing
eastward, we found ourselves in a sitting-room about 20
feet long by 12 broad. The walls were whitewashed,
the ceiling of mats, laid above beams of palm wood. The
floor, and the divan which ran along two sides of the room,
were well carpeted. The other appointments were very
simple. Two large trunks, secured by padlocks, occupied
the greater part of one end wall. In the walls were
several recesses with shelves, on which some pottery
was displayed. Above the divan hung a mirror, a small

white flag, pistols, and a handsome silver-mounted belt,
with appointments similar to those of our escort. A
lantern was suspended from the roof, and in a recess
behind the door stood the water cooler and a wooden
bowl handsomely studded with silver, from which every
one drank   The room was lighted from the open doorway.   House door there was none, but a closet which
opened off the main apartment had both door and lock
This is the usual type of dwelling in the upper part of
Wady Marr, where stone houses take the place of the
mere booths found near the coast.   Though the house
stands absolutely open, the privacy of the inmates is
secured by a rigid etiquette, which forbids any one, even
a son of the house, to enter or approach the door without
the permission of the householder   I asked whether
there was no risk from robbers , but the people scouted
such an idea.   Even a robber would not venture to violate
domestic privacy.   Of course our Shereef had another
cottage for his harem, the house we were in being the
public sitting-room

The preparation of a whole sheep is a somewhat tedious
business, and while it was getting ready the hospitable
old gentleman brought me in a plate with a couple of
roast fowls, expressing his fears that I was already hungry.
He left me to eat alone, and bustled away again directly.
When I had made my meal, the dish was finished by
Ismail and Al Mâs.   By and by the servants brought
in the sheep in a great metal tray, covered with a conical
lid of plaited straw.   The sheep is always presented entire,
but several portions were set aside for us to take away.
The rest was laid upon a large dish of stewed rice.   Our
whole company sat round, along with our host, and what
was left was passed on to his servants.   This is the usual
form of a country entertainment in the Hejâz ; but the
Bedouins, if they have no rice, will dine on flesh alone,
not even using bread.   It is not customary to eat salt
with one's food, but for my sake it was called for.   Boiled

meat is the rule, but two other methods of cooking are known in the desert. One is to cut the meat in slices and broil them on hot stones, the other to improvise an oven by digging a hole, in which, when it has been raised to a glowing heat, the meat is laid and covered with stones and embers. I have seen it argued that boiling is the most ancient form of Semitic cookery, but the other methods which I have mentioned seem at least equally primitive, though from a very early date boiling seems to have been the commoner process among the Hebrews as well as the Arabs. When I am on the subject, I shall add one or two other notes about the meals of the Arabs. Beef is almost never eaten, and is thought unwholesome. Among the Bedouins the slaughter of a sheep takes place only on festival occasions, or on the arrival of a guest Ordinarily the staple of diet is milk, with dates or such cereal food as can be obtained, and the only meat eaten is game, especially the flesh of the gazelle Our men could have gone on for a long time on their diet of 'Areeka, but I was expected to give them a sheep when occasion offered, and a cauldron to boil it in could be procured. In a village there is generally at least one professional butcher who is ready to kill and cut up a sheep, receiving as his hire the head, skin, and offal. To save themselves trouble our men used to call in this functionary, but they could have done the work equally well themselves. In the towns, there is, of course, a much greater variety of food than is known in the desert, and the Bedouins, when forced by famine to betake themselves to the cities, are very loath to accommodate themselves to the strange diet. They have a peculiar contempt for vegetables, and members of a tribe who have settled down to agricultural life are stigmatised by their nomad brethren as *Khodhar*—eaters of green things I may notice two points in which our dinner at Wady Fâtima differed from the usage of the towns. The great dish was set, not on a stool, but directly on the ground, and the ewer and basin were not passed round before the meal. After eating, we stepped outside and washed. These are country manners, but even in Tâif there was no washing before meals. As for the desert, the Arab theory is that it is a perfectly clean place where it is not necessary to wash at all—or at any rate not necessary to use soap, as is always done in the towns.

After dinner and coffee we prepared to start, as the camels always go best towards evening. In ordinary cases in this district a guest can offer to his host without hesitation a sum of money, and indeed he is expected to do so, if his means permit. But as our host was a Shereef, we had to observe a more formal etiquette, and found that the proper thing was to leave four or five dollars with his son, and give a trifle to the servant who had cooked for us and filled our water skins. Europeans often complain of the mockery of hospitality which lies in the custom of paying considerably beyond its value for an entertainment at which one is nominally a guest. But when there are many passers to and fro, the exercise of gratuitous hospitality would be an intolerable burden to a man of moderate means, and as the poor must be entertained for nothing, it is not unreasonable that a European, who always passes for a rich man, should pay pretty well The present practice of the Hejâz is no doubt anomalous, and the fiction of hospitality is cumbersome both to the entertainer and the entertained. But it has its good side also, and in favourable cases the cordial welcome and assiduous attention of the host are still in the spirit of the ancient generosity of the Arab towards his guest. Our Shereef certainly did all he could for us, and when we left we carried with us a store of fowls and mutton, sufficient to provide for our wants till we reached another habitable spot. Instead of continuing our way along the main valley, our plan was to seek a shorter road through a desert mountain valley called Wady Jir'âna. We therefore struck into the great pilgrim road, and followed it in the direction of Mecca, till we were close to the mosque and shrine of Meymoon, and not very far from the pillars that mark the border of the Haram or sacred land. In passing along this road we attained a lofty point, from which there was an excellent view of the Mountain of Light and the neighbouring range, but I think that Al Mâs had planned our hours so that we should not come too near the Holy Land by full daylight, and the white cupola of Al Meymoon was only just discernible in the thickening twilight. Just as it opened before us on a turn of the road we struck off to the left and ascended a very bare but striking mountain glen, enclosed in walls of granite and floored with a beautiful white gravel. This was Wady Jir'âna, a path which none of our party had travelled before, and which would not have been our road had a Christian been allowed to set foot within the boundaries of the Haram. It soon appeared that Al Mâs was not sure of his way, and an hour and a half after sunset we came to a halt, and prepared our bivouac under the shelter of a rock.

V. Sôla Zeima and the Beheita

We had a very pleasant bivouac in Wady Jir'âna under the bright moonlight. Having eaten a tremendous meal three hours before, my men had no supper to prepare, so we drank innumerable cups of coffee and enjoyed a long chat round the fire. Al Mâs, as usual, was full of superstitions, and showed me Bedouin methods of divination. One of these is used to decide whether or not a tribe shall ride out on a foray. A circle is drawn in the sand with an arbitrary number of rays, which must not be counted, diverging from its circumference. The first and second rays are then joined by a cross stroke, so are the third and fourth, and so on. If there is an odd number of rays, one, of course, remains unconnected, and is held to symbolise an open road for war. If all the rays are

34

closed, the tribe refuses to ride out. A more complicated
test of the probability of success in anything a man has
set his heart on is to measure out three span's-lengths on
the sand. The space between must then be divided off
into finger-breadths, which is done by successive applications of the third and fourth fingers, pressing the back
of the fingers down upon the sand The row of scores
thus obtained is roughly bisected by the eye, and each
half is counted off in threes from the middle point. The
remainders give the measure of one's luck, the best result
being three at one end and two at the other. I remember
to have heard from a resident in Baghdad, that a very
similar mode of divination is practised there by counting
off in fives an arbitrarily chosen number of beads in a
rosary. This is called striking a choice (*dharab kheera*).
The Bedouins also take auguries from birds. A single
raven in one's path is a very bad token, but two are
extremely lucky. They say Akhdhareyn fa'lân zein—
" Two green (*i.e.* black) ones "—a fair omen

The Bedouins have many other superstitions about
animals, some of which it may be convenient to mention
here I inquired specially as to their usage in eating or
refusing the flesh of certain beasts The superstition as
to the flesh of the rock badger which Palmer noted in the
Peninsula of Sinai is unknown here ; but there is a
similar idea about the monkeys which frequent Mount
Kara These, it is said, were once men who came to pay
a visit to the Prophet. He set before them milk and
water, directing them to drink the former and perform
their ablutions with the latter The perverse visitors
drank the water and washed with the milk, and were
transformed into monkeys for their disobedience. As
they were once men, their flesh is not eaten This legend
is closely akin to what one reads in the fabulous history
of early Arabia about the Nasnâs and the Wabâr in the
great sandy desert Both these words are monkey names,
quite current in the present day, though not recognised by

the Lexicons. The latter is an ape, the former a monkey
with a tail The story of the Adites, who were changed
to *nasnâs* for disobeying the prophet Hud, and the tradition of the destruction of the Wabâr, whose seats were
occupied by Jinn, are therefore monkey tales of inverted
Darwinianism Except in this monkey story, I could
find no trace of the superstitious rejection of the flesh
of any animal. But some kinds of flesh have a magical
virtue attached to them. A very curious practice is to
eat the flesh of the hyæna. A man who suffers in any
member of his body seeks a cure by eating the corresponding part of a hyæna. The hyæna is also eaten in the
neighbourhood of Suez, for a friend of mine who shot one
near the wells of Moses was requested by the Bedouins
to give them a leg. A similar virtue attaches to the flesh
of the gemsbok (Wudheyhy), a rare species of antelope
found far in the interior When eaten, it draws an obstinate bullet from a wound. The man in our company who
knew most about wild animals and their supposed
qualities was Mohsin, who was acquainted with the regions
east of the Hejâz, and these, I imagine, would yield an
interesting field for the naturalist. Besides the gemsbok,
two other large antelopes are known there—the leucoryx
or reem, which is undoubtedly the unicorn of Scripture,
and a red species called *Idmy.*

 January 30.—We broke up at six, and moved up the
Wady, passing one empty well and a little patch of ground
which in better seasons had been cultivated. The morning was delightfully fresh, with a strong cool breeze from
the Eastern mountains, which continued for two days.
This wind is the saba or zephyr of the Arabic poets. It
is extremely dry, parching the lips, and chapping the
skin of the face. The Arabs, therefore, never expose
themselves to it, but swathe the mouth and lower part
of the face by bringing round a corner of the head-shawl,
and catching up the end in the ogal or fillet. In cold and
windy weather the face of a Bedouin is almost as com-

pletely concealed as that of his wife with her face veil ;
and one is tempted to ask whether the latter fashion was
adopted purely to maintain the principle of female
seclusion, or partly from reasons of comfort. The fully
developed face veil, with nothing but holes for the eyes,
is no doubt part of the Hareem principle. But it is not
used everywhere. Among the 'Oteibe, for example, the
burko' only covers the mouth and lower part of the face.
At all events, the inconvenience which we suppose to
lie in the use of the veil is very much imaginary The
heavy semâda, or the great dingy wrapper which takes
its place among the poorer classes, is equally cumbrous
at first sight. But the Arabs, like other simple peoples,
use the same dress in all seasons, and have, therefore,
chosen a covering for the head which, with a slight change
in the way of wearing it, protects from the sun in summer
and the cold in winter. After an hour's journey we
found ourselves at the opening of a real mountain pass,
rough, steep, and stony. The camels were very indignant,
and protested with loud grunts, which were renewed
more emphatically when they reached the top and found
that they were expected to go down on the other side
We had indeed lost our way northward into Wady Marr
by a long and rough bypath. The rocky road was very
trying to our dromedaries, and they gave vent to their
feelings on the subject by roaring, occasionally halting,
and generally expressing their contempt for our ignorance
of the right path. The camel always walks with his nose
in the air—to express his disgust at the human race,
which he consents to serve only under protest. Like
the true Briton—who, if there is anything in Darwinianism, is certainly of the camel stock—he does his duty
regularly and well, but can neither begin nor stop work
without a grumble He is equally unwilling to get on
his legs at starting and to kneel when asked to stop, and
the least interruption in the routine of his duties is received
with a grunt which intimates that this sort of thing is

quite intolerable, that he is a camel and not a mule, and will stand none of your confounded nonsense Having relieved his feelings he usually does what you bid him ; but he is always uncertain in his temper, and when really roused has an ugly trick of turning round and snapping at the foot of the rider, which his jaws are quite strong enough to bite through.

In the most deserted part of the road near the top of a rocky pass, we came upon a stone with a tolerably level side, on which was scored a rough·inscription, one or two names in Arabic, and a few hieroglyphics, which appeared to be imitations of the tribal marks used in branding animals, with a rough figure of the camel.   The inscription was so far interesting that it had a certain kinship to the much more ancient inscriptions of Tâif, which are executed in the same way by chipping the natural surface of a brownish stone, so that the writing appears in a lighter colour.   My men were a little surprised at the stone, and said that the Bedouins never make such scratchings now. It cannot, however, have been very old.   Beyond this pass we entered a glade full of acacia trees, and met a party of 'Oteibe taking camels to Mecca, who looked at us rather suspiciously, but fraternised with Marzook. Presently, at the wayside, we came on the shrine of a Sâlih or saint.   It was merely a circular wall of loose stones, open on the eastern side, and three or four feet high.   It was hung with rags, the offerings of devotees, and Marzook told me that the Bedouins were accustomed to sacrifice a lamb before it.   Farther down the glen we met several solitary women.   One seldom comes on a man alone in the desert, but women go everywhere alone, tending the flocks or gathering firewood.   Among the more primitive tribes the women and children have the whole charge of the flocks, with which it would be humiliating for a man to concern himself.   Among the 'Oteibe the women also help with the camels, which they ride barebacked as boldly as the men ; but this was related

to me as an exceptional thing, dependent on the habits
of a tribe in which the men care chiefly for war and pillage
To leave the flocks to the women and children is, on the
other hand, the general custom, and appears to be a very
ancient one, for it goes back to the times of Rachel,
Zipporah, and David.   I remember that this usage is
noted for the Qoreish in the history of the Prophet, who
tended the sheep, as a boy, in their mountains, and I
was, therefore, interested to find the Qoreish specially
named as a tribe in which a man would think it beneath
him to be charged with the flocks.   The men of the
Qoreish are wood-cutters—Qarrâshîn , and their name
was explained to me, with great plausibility, as coming
from this occupation

As we descended into the main valley our view was
bounded by the long level ridge of Mount Harra, which
I ought to have mentioned when we first saw it, behind
the Sidr at Wady Fâtima, bounding the northern
horizon, save where the twin cones of Jebel el Kohl
rose above it.   Harra is defined by the lexicographers
as a region composed of black rocks, looking as if they
had been burned ; and the Hejâz is said to be enclosed
between five districts of this character.   The Harra
which rises above Wady Marr answers to the description.
The millstones of Jeddah are brought from it, and consist
of a kind of black basalt, which the natives call granite
(sawwân), full of little cavities like a cinder, and of a
volcanic aspect.

After spending three hours in the mountains, we
struck the main valley near the fountain Er-Riyân, and
half an hour later halted to let the camels drink at the
pool of Embarek.   The whole plain is fertilised by these
copious springs, and the view over rich wheat fields,
gardens, and date groves, towards the great blue mountain
of Mudheeq at the head of the valley, was most striking.
The spot is the fairest and most fertile which I have seen
in Arabia, and the scene embraces every element of

landscape beauty, the towering wildness of the desolate
mountains forming an exquisite contrast to the soft
green of the irrigated plain and the darker masses of the
palm trees   Above Embarek the desert begins again
There are wells and considerable patches of land dammed
in so as to be cultivated when rain comes.   But after the
long drought the plots of garden ground were deserted,
and the houses once occupied by their cultivators falling
to ruin   Between Embarek and Jedeedah, a distance of
two and a half hours, we saw only a few girls tending
sheep, and a group of Bedouin women filling their waterskins at a well   The first part of the route was interesting,
as we had the noble mountains of Mudheeq straight
ahead.   After half an hour we turned sharply to the right,
and the scenery became monotonous   The broad torrent
bed in which we rode was cut through great banks of dust
and sand, and had little vegetation till we again neared
a region of water, when the 'Oshr (*Asclepias gigantea*),
with its broad smooth leaves, became common.   This is
the tree from which the Bedouins burn charcoal for their
coarse gunpowder   Its milky juice is in repute as a cure
for barrenness, and the pilgrims are accustomed to carry
away flasks of it.   At the fountain and palm grove of
Jedeedah the valley divides into two branches, the
northern one leading to Wady Leimoon   Following up
the southern branch, a journey of half an hour took us
to Sôla, where there is a strong spring with fields and
famous orchards, well stocked with plantains, sweet and
bitter lemons, bitter oranges (leem), apricots, and other
fruits.   The finest of these orchards belong to the Shereef,
who has begun to practise acclimatisation on a great scale,
and introduced mangoes and many other fruit-trees from
Java.   The experiment seems likely to prove successful.
At Sôla the hills change their character, and the valley is
overhung by great walls of white granite, full of enormous
amygdaloidal openings.   Under these we rode on for an
hour and a quarter, and crossing to the opposite side of

the Wady, reached the village of Zeima, where the great
highway from Mecca strikes our route.   Zeima lies
on the right or southern side of the Wady, under a
low hill crowned with a large fortress of the Wahhâbites,
now in ruins.   From the rocks under the fortress bursts
forth the hot spring which I have already mentioned.   It
issues from a natural fissure, but is conducted for a little
way in a channel artificially hewn in the rock, and then
spreads into a pool, from which it is led in a conduit
under the Mecca road to fertilise the gardens.   There was
formerly a great palm grove here, but nine years ago
the spring failed suddenly—held back, as the natives
supposed, by the power of the Jinn—and all the trees
perished save one or two.   After three years there was a
great flood, which seems to have cleared the subterranean
channels, for the water returned and now flows in a strong
stream like a small mill-rush.

Zeima was our halting-place for the night.   We got a
small hut as our quarters, and purchased a sheep for
supper.   I strolled out to examine the place, but my
escort were very nervous, and insisted on accompanying
me everywhere.   Zeima, in fact, has a very bad name.
It is occupied by a branch of the Hodheil, who farm the
gardens from the proprietor, a member of the princely
family, and are reputed very bigoted and unruly.   It
was here that Mr. Doughty was stopped and challenged
for not saying his prayers, after he had passed without
danger through some of the least-visited parts of Arabia.
Here, too, about twenty years ago—for the Arabs can
never give dates except by saying that such a thing
happened in the year of the cholera, the year of the great
flood, or the like—there was a great fight between the
Turks and the Arabs of Tâif.   The Turks, 500 in number,
defended themselves in the ruined fortress and behind the
loopholed walls of the gardens, but were ultimately forced
back towards Mecca, with the loss of their baggage and
horses, till they were joined by a reinforcement of the

Shereef's men.   I did not see any tokens of their unruli-
ness in the village, but I believe I was not known to be
a Christian.   At supper, several poor folk gathered round
our door and shared our meal, especially a privileged
deaf and dumb man, who talked very cleverly by signs
which his neighbours understood.   He was saving up
money in order to marry.   Deaf and dumb men are
often met with both in Arabia and Egypt, and I have
observed that they are always treated with great kindness.
We were joined at supper by a boy from Scinde, whose
mother is a small trader in the village.   Many Scindians
come to the Hejâz as pedlars, chiefly in iron goods.   The
father having died, his child was taken under the protection of the Hodheil, becoming, as the expression is, their
Dakheel.   Every man in the village is bound to resent
injury done to the boy as if he were his father.   Indeed,
the little fellow seemed to have been spoiled, for he was
very pert and garrulous.   He had quite forgotten his
mother tongue   The evening salutation in this village
was Allah yebayyitkum—May God give you your night-
quarters.

January 31. — Starting an hour before sunrise, we
rode up the Wady for more than five hours and then
emerged on the open upland plain of the Beheita.   From
Zeima upwards the whole country had been scourged
with severe drought.   The flocks which pasture in the
hills were perishing with hunger, and beside Zeima, and
on the road inland, lay many carcasses of sheep which had
dropped while they were being driven down the country
in search of herbage.   We passed several objects to which
legends are attached—first, a great stone by the roadside,
which is said to have been lifted by a girl, a story which
educed the information that the trial of strength by
lifting stones which Jerome describes as practised in
Palestine is still known among the Arabs.   Then on the
mountain top to our right a natural obelisk was pointed
out as a girl who had been turned into rock for casting a

stone at one of the ancient prophets.   The metamorphoses
of the Arabs have all to do with prophets, just as their
local holy places are all tombs of saints.   But the very
fact that the prophet in such legends is quite indefinite
seems to show that in the one case as in the other the
original story belongs to the period of heathenism.   By
and by Jebel Sumân (?) rises on the right, and Mohsin
has a story of a great liar who said that he was once
driving a flock down a glen here, and one sheep was so
large that it stuck between the mountains   His hearer
retorted that he had seen seven smiths making a cauldron
so large that none of them could hear his neighbour.
"For what purpose ? " " To boil your sheep "   The type
of this story is familiar, and it seems that an anecdote need
not be a solar myth to appear as the common property
of remote races   Not far from the top of the pass a rocky
slope on our left was all covered with the sickly green
stems of a shrub called the *dihn*   It is, I think, a
Euphorbia, and though sheep eat it with impunity, its
white milky juice is used as a poison for wolves   I got
this fact from the old Sheikh at Wady Fâtima, and I
have since observed that it is registered by the old lexicographers.   The formation of the ground at the top of the
Wady is very curious   The mountains on each side are
steep and rocky, and the valley is simply a river of sand.
Suddenly the river expands into a lake, the hills sweep
round to the right and left, and one enters a great plain
of sand dotted with isolated hills or broken masses of
granite, and rolling away to the north-east as far as the
eye can reach without any considerable mountain range
to break it.   In this direction, which is the line of the
Nejd road leading to 'Oneize, I am told that the ground
rises slightly for less than a day's journey as far as Rohba,
after which it again falls slowly.   In the direction of the
coast the plateau appears walled in by mountains, except
where the great Wady, from which we emerged, pierces
the barrier. Looking back from the Beheita—so the

first part of the plateau is named—our Wady appears
as a great gorge, with huge hills towering over it in the
distance. Northward, in the mountain line, another
opening was pointed out to me, where the road from
Wady Leimoon and from Medina comes in. So far as I
can learn, both the branches of Wady Marr (the Zeima
Valley and Wady Leimoon) are, so to speak, outlets of
this sandy lake, enclosing between their courses an island
of mountain The formation of the plateau is easily
understood, and follows a type constantly repeated in
the granite of the Upper Hejâz. Near the coast the
hills are trap and basalt, with an occasional patch of
granite or quartzose rock breaking through in the valleys.
But from Sôla the granite begins to preponderate, and
the plateau of the Beheita is wholly composed of dis-
integrated granite in the form of gravel The isolated
hills which rise from it are granite peaks. The rock has
the same character as at Sôla ; it is full of cavities, and
easily broken up by fierce atmospheric agencies. The
tops of the hills are entirely resolved into loose blocks
of fantastic form and great size, some rising like lofty
obelisks, others overthrown and piled in confused masses
one above the other. Disintegration has gone so far
that the accumulated debris has covered all but the
summits of the granite eruption, and the original contours
have been levelled by the spreading sand The highest
points are still hills ; the lower ones are mere piles of
detached rocks. The plains of the Upper Hejâz, through
which I passed, are all of this type—groups of granite
hill - tops, levelled and connected by the accumulation
of gravelly debris. The original aspect of such a tract,
before the hollows were filled up, can still be seen in the
region south of Mount Kara, which is simply a forest of
granitic aiguilles. As the granite contains the elements
of a fertile soil, these plains afford good pasture after rain,
and they are generally pretty thickly dotted with acacias
—*samur* and *talh*. Indeed, the finest trees I have seen in

the Hejâz, were specimens of the *talh* growing by the lowest beds by which the plateaus are intersected. Between Wady Marr and Tâif there are three such plateaus, the Beheita, 'Okâh, 'Okâtz, and the great plain called Hazm el Jemei'a, which is known as the Navel, or highest part of the Nejd. For by our Arabs this whole district, as far as Tâif, was counted to the Nejd, not to the Hejâz, and the two plateaus first mentioned are pasture grounds of the 'Oteibe, the great tribe of the western Nejd, corresponding to the ancient Hawâzin, whose lands run inland almost to 'Oneize, and whose fighting men are reckoned at 60,000. The 'Oteibe Nejd, and Hejâz, however, are very variously defined   An old gentleman of 'Oneize gave me what seems to be the most ancient definition, according to which the lower whole country, including Mecca, and running inland as far as the Beheita and 'Okâtz, is Tehâma. The Hejâz is the zone of highest elevation, Rohba, Tâif, Kara, and the great mountain land south of Tâif. The Nejd is the country beyond Rohba falling away with a gentle slope as you move inland   This seems to agree so far with the usage of the Tâif people, who, when they speak of the Hejâz road, do not mean the road to Mecca, but that into the hill country of the Benî Sofyân south of the town.

VI. From the Beheita to Tâif

My last letter closed with a general description of the Beheita, to which I have still to add some particulars. Crossing the plateau in an easterly direction we passed under the southern flank of Mount Demah, the loftiest point of the granite eruption. It appears that monkeys are found here, for Al Mâs related how he had once been compelled by tempestuous rains to bivouac for two days under the mountain, and ascending it in quest of game, saw a red-haired Jinny, which from his description was plainly a monkey. He was afraid to fire at it, but

his less scrupulous companion discharged his gun and
grazed its shoulder. On returning to Mecca, the presumptuous hunter was seized with disease in all his joints,
and died within two months—obviously of rheumatism
fever, caught by lying out in the wet. Al Mâs, however,
feels sure that the occurrence was supernatural, and
was anxious to know whether there is a specimen of a
Jinny preserved in any of the museums of Europe   I
answered him very seriously that I believed there was
not, and that it was not probable that beings who have
the power to change their form could be captured by men,
or that it would be prudent to attempt any such thing
I then told him the story of the fisherman and the pot
with Solomon's seal, from the *Arabian Nights*, which he
accepted as tolerably conclusive in favour of my argument.
This talk brought us—in about an hour·from the top of
Wady-ez-Zeima—to a depression in the plateau, where
every traveller fills his skins from water - holes in the
torrent bed.   Close by were the ruins of a small hamlet,
and some rocks with Cufic inscriptions.   The torrent is
known simply as the Seil—the Torrent *par excellence*.   It
is the point at which pilgrims descending to Mecca don
the ihram, or holy attire.   Beyond the torrent, which
is the limit of the Beheita, we diverged from the Nejd
road and again turned into the hills by a sandy pass
winding through granite walls, on which were many
Cufic inscriptions, praying for the mercy of God on such
a one, the son of such a one   Characteristically, there
were no dates, so that the writing was valueless.   This
pass is naturally the roughest bit of road on the whole
highway to Tâif, but as it is a great route, some attempt
had been made to improve it by art.   The steepest places
were paved, and at one very bad place the road was
partly built and partly cut by blasting through a thick
bed of granite and whinstone.   Works of this kind are
not undertaken at public expense, but by private individuals, and are reckoned acts of piety.   The bene-

factor in the present case was not an Arab, but an Indian.
The pass, which bears the name of Ree' ez Zelâle, is about
two hours long, and has the reputation of a haunt of
robbers.   It must always have been a very important
route, connecting the system of roads which converge
on the Beheita with Tâif and the southern Hejâz.   Its
eastern debouchment is the market-place of 'Okâtz,
which in the times before Islam was the seat of an important sanctuary and of the greatest fair of Central
Arabia   No place, therefore, could afford a fitter site for
a monument, and long before the period of the Cufic
scrawls already mentioned, a great face of brownish
granite near the middle of the pass, overhanging the road
and facing towards the north, was chosen by some ancient
king to record his name.   The centre of the rock bears
the image of the king seated, with one arm akimbo, and
the other extended, and grasping a sceptre, in a pose
which at once recalls Egyptian art.   The squaring of the
shoulders, the set of the head, the bearing of the arms and
body, and the dress, of which nothing is indicated except
a shovel-like apron, exactly resemble Egyptian drawing.
But the workmanship is altogether different, and of a
purely Arabic character.   In all the sculptured stones of
the Hejâz the natural face of the rock is left unpolished,
and the hammer-work which marks out the figures merely
breaks the surface, producing its effect mainly by the
difference of colour where the stone is chipped.   To ensure
distinctness, the stone operated on is almost always a
brownish red piece of granite, on which the inscription or
drawing stands out whitish.   One cannot take a squeeze
of such sculpture, for the natural roughness of the granite
would leave a much deeper impress than the superficial
work of the engraver.   The figure of the king is a sil-
houette, light on a dark ground, and whether from the
natural imperfection of the process, or from the injuries
of time and of the Arabs, who take the figure for a Sheitân,
the outline of the face and the details of the hands and

feet are altogether lost.   The arms, however, are drawn
with considerable vigour ; and in general one is led to
conclude that a well-skilled draughtsman was followed by
a clumsy stone-cutter   The characters which accompany
the figure are written—like all the other inscriptions of
the same class which I have seen—in vertical columns :
two columns in front of the sceptre to the right of the
stone, and a single word, probably the name of the king,
obliquely over the head.   Some of the letters are similar
to known South Semitic writing, and I hope that all may
be made out by skilled paleographists, but I am not able
to interpret them, or even guess at their origin.   There is
some tradition preserved by Arabic authors of a peculiar
writing proper to the Gorhom in Mecca, and Fâkihy in
his *History of Mecca* gives a facsimile of an inscription
distantly analogous to that of Ree' ez Zelâle, which stood
at the Maqam Ibrahim.   It is, however, to be observed
that all the inscriptions which I found were in the upper
granite country—four at Tâif, and one on the lofty
plateau of Kara.   Below Mount Kara, in the vicinity of
Mecca, there is little granite, and I saw no writing other
than Cufic, and comparatively little of that.   Except
that of Zelâle, all my inscriptions are from the country
of the Thageef.   But the Zelâle inscription is by far the
most striking, because accompanied by an attempt at
sculpture which displays a certain amount of artistic skill.
At Numoora, on Mount Kara, the inscription is associated
with the figure of a beast of prey, but the drawing is a
mere child's scrawl, and the work is in outline, whereas
in Zelâle the whole surface of the figure is hammered out
so as to be clearly visible from the road below   As the
letters at Numoora are at least as well formed and cut as
those at Zelâle, it is difficult to avoid the conclusion that the
seated figure in the latter place must have been designed
by a foreign draughtsman.   This would account for the
markedly Egyptian type of the design; but if the draughtsman was an Egyptian, working in the style of old Egyptian

art, we gain a very early date for the monument, which, on this hypothesis, can hardly be much later than the Christian era.

As the afternoon was already declining, my escort hurried me away from the monument, that we might clear the pass before dark. An hour before sunset we emerged on an opener country, and crossing a torrent bed where water is always to be found in the holes, ascended the famous plateau of 'Okâtz (the Hejâz pronunciation is 'Okâth, with a palatal " th " instead of the palatal " z " or " d " used by Syrians and Arabians , but I adopt " tz " as a conventional spelling to distinguish from the ordinary " th," which is also sounded in Hejâz and the Nejd, and not changed to " s " or " t," as is done in Jeddah, Cairo, and many parts of Syria).

'Okâtz, as I mentioned in my last letter, is a plateau of the characteristic Hejâz type, a lofty plain of gravel studded with granite bosses, the summits of hills whose bases are buried in the debris of long centuries of disintegration   In the south-east corner of the small plain, which is barely two miles across, rises a hill of loose granite rocks, crowned by an enormous pillar standing quite erect, and flanked by lower masses.   I do not think this pillar can be less than 50 or 60 feet in height, and its extraordinary aspect, standing between two lesser guards on either side, is the first thing that strikes the eye on nearing the plain.   Now, we know that the sanctuary of 'Okâtz was no temple, but consisted of rocks, round which the pilgrims made procession. The worship of remarkable rocks is a well-known feature in the religion of the ancient Arabs, and it is natural to suppose that the group selected for worship at 'Okâtz was the most striking that rose from the plain.   I could not learn that there is any tradition by which one could make quite sure of the points, and the name of the sanctuary—Al Otheydâ— was not recognised by Al Mâs, who had lived for years in the immediate vicinity , but the isolated hill suits the conditions of a sanctuary round which solemn processions circled, and the other groups of rock that stud the plain are all much less remarkable. Some of them contain individual stones hardly inferior in size. I saw one prostrate column which I estimate as quite 50 feet in length, and about 5 feet in breadth and depth. But a pillar standing erect on a lofty eminence was more likely to be made a god of. Apart from the enormous size of the blocks, the granite masses which strew the plain are noteworthy for the singular cavities they contain —bubble-like openings in which a man could hide, and which are not infrequently crossed by a twisted pillar of stone. The effect of weathering on these singular hollows is to produce most fantastic forms which might readily affect a super-stitious imagination, and add to the sanctity of the spot. I have never seen the seething and surging of a boiling fluid with all the effects of capillary attraction so perfectly rendered in stone.

Sprenger, in his book on *Arabic Geography*, has a very instructive discussion of the way in which religion and commerce went hand in hand in ancient Arabia Religion was the affair of merchants much more than of the nomads, and the sacred feasts, to which men gathered from far and wide under the security of a religious sanction, afforded the opportunity of holding great fairs without danger from the marauding tribes. 'Okâtz, which in its natural features is so well adapted to appeal to the super-stitious imagination, is also an excellent position for a great fair. It is traversed by a great highway, while another road leads off directly to the Nejd. It has on one side a great pastoral country, while on the other it is adjacent to a region of fountains and cultivated land. There are springs and orchards in the valleys, to the right of the road, almost all the way to Tâif. The fair was thus a fit meeting place for the agricultural and pastoral population. The trade was largely in leather, which was purchased for export by the capitalists of Mecca and Tâif, and carried overland to Gaza. Skins are still the chief article of export from the Hejâz, and, indeed, the only important staple of Jeddah   But in these days the trade seems to have been in manufactured leather , tanned, I suppose, with the leaves of upland trees, according to the still prevalent practice of the country.

The fair of 'Okâtz was not the affair of a day or two. It is said to have lasted twenty days, or even a month. The several tribes met to settle their old differences and commence new disputes, and business was enlivened by poetical contests, so celebrated that a verb was coined from the name of the place, meaning to contend for glory in poetical recitations.   The old poet Abu Dhueib speaks of the time—

When the booths were built on 'Okâtz, and the fair was busy, and the thousands were assembled

For such a meeting an ample supply of good water was necessary, and this was to be found in the wady which we crossed just before ascending to the plain.   The rise of Islam destroyed the ancient mart, which had essentially the character of a heathenish feast.   But the association of religion and commerce still survives in the Mecca pilgrimage, which is the lineal descendant of the old heathen spring feast   Then, as now, Minâ was the seat of a pilgrimage fair, and then, as now, a religious sanction was pleaded to protect the travellers   Even the modern distribution of grain to the Bedouins as the price of their good behaviour has its ancient analogue   There were certain families in Mecca whose charge it was to provide the Bedouins during the feast with meat and drink   The observation that for the inhabitants of Mecca the religious feasts were essentially great commercial occasions, is very instructive in connection with the present state of the pilgrimage question.   The great feast is no longer the centre of an important international commerce, though a large proportion of the pilgrims have still something to buy and sell. The development of Islam has given the pecuniary interest of Mecca another turn ; the pilgrims themselves, drawn from far lands in tens of thousands, are the great source of profit to the Hejâz ; and before the pilgrim trade the ancient traffic in skins sinks into insignificance. Almost every one in Jeddah and Mecca lives more or less off the Hajjy, and a good Hajj is spoken of in the Hejâz as a good harvest would be among us. With Mohammedanism as a religion—a monotheistic, and, in so far, a spiritual faith—the pilgrimage and the great feast have nothing to do They were retained and glorified under the new religion from the particularistic standpoint of Mecca, which is the centre not of the spiritual elements of Moslem faith, but of the superstitions by which that faith is disfigured. It is not, therefore, strange that in the Hejâz Mohammedanism appears at its worst, that religion is prostituted to the pursuit of gain, and that the holy city and its port of Jeddah are notorious for the corruption of morals and the practice of the grossest vices.

We bivouacked in 'Okâtz, under the lee of one of the great rock masses The night was bitterly cold, but the air delightfully clear and dry Starting in the morning at half - past seven, we crossed the plain, and traversed for about an hour a more broken country, with the small hamlet of Embl'. To our right lay a complicated region of hills and wadies, in which are many fountains and orchards From one of these springs, named Rayyiha, the Shereef, when resident at Tâif, has his drinking water, sending a train of camels weekly, a distance of three hours' journey, to fetch a supply. The Tâif water is itself very excellent, but that of the region of Rayyiha is esteemed the best in the Hejâz. In water, as is well known, the Arabs are great connoisseurs, and one is constantly asked, in travelling, for one's opinion of the relative sweetness of different sources. An hour from 'Okâtz the road takes a sharp rise, and presently crosses the torrent bed of Wady Nebi'at, and emerges on the lofty plateau named Hazm el Jemei'a The Hazm, which we traversed for an hour and a half in a south-easterly direction, is reckoned the highest part of the Nejd (Surrat el Nejd). It has the same general aspect as the Beheita, but is less broken with rocky knobs and bosses. In passing over it our horizon was bounded to the right by a continuous line of hills. To the left the country was open, with only isolated points or hogbacks of higher ground We crossed three torrent beds descending from the east, and clothed with fine acacia trees. Of the eastern hills the most striking was a large sugar cone which I believe is called El Qurr. It lay due east from the village of Qedeira, just beyond which we again left the Hazm. In consequence of the long drought, the Hazm, as we saw it, was very bare and desolate. It is, nevertheless, a great pasture-ground, on which five or six thousand sheep are kept. The proprietor is the Shereef, and his shepherds have the right to kill sheep or camels which trespass upon the ground. The shepherds are Bedouins living in tents, or, as they are called, houses of hair.

At Qedeira a little patch of irrigated land marks the beginning of a more fertile country. We descend into the broad bed of a wady above the considerable village of Umm el Khamt, and rest for a few moments under the shade of a row of tamarisks Besides this village the Bedouins of the district are accustomed to gather their flocks for Ramadan and celebrate the feast.

From Umm el Khamt to Tâif we rode for an hour and a half up the great Wady Elqem, so pronounced for Luqem, which descends from Mount Barad and the southern hills. In this wady there is plenty of water to be reached by sinking wells, and from the Hazm on to Tâif the desert is studded with patches of irrigated land, corn fields, orchard ground, and vineyards These patches are sunk below the natural level of the ground,

and walled in with dams of earth and stone. The water
is raised from the well by an apparatus called the Sawâny
—a plural form—two or three leathern buckets, suspended
from the same well, being always employed together.
The bucket is a skin open at the neck, and also at the
opposite end, where the aperture is the whole diameter
of the skin, and kept from closing by two cross-sticks
The skin is slung over the well by two ropes, or rather
twisted thongs of hide, attached before and behind, and
loaded with stones. The posterior thong is made to
pass over a wooden block raised considerably above the
well. The other rope passes over a roller on a lower level.
An ox is attached to both thongs, and walks up and down
an inclined plane sloping downwards from the well mouth.
As he walks up, the skin descends into the well and fills.
The driver then turns his beast. As the skin is pulled
up its weight hangs down between the mouths, and the
water cannot escape. But when it reaches the top, the
aperture dependent on the lower pulley is no longer
drawn upwards, and the skin discharges itself into a
runlet The use of this apparatus is universal in the
Tâif district. Only in one garden, the property of an
Egyptian, a water-wheel with buckets, drawn by a man
climbing up the wheel, was pointed out as a curiosity.
The usual Egyptian Saqia with toothed wheels, to be
drawn by animals, seems to be quite unknown The
Sawâny, like all other appliances of Arabian agriculture,
appear to be an ancient invention ; but in the classical
lexicons the name is referred to camels that draw water,
not to a machine. The march of the Sawâny is a proverbial figure for uninterrupted toil, as we speak of being
in the treadmill.

At Umm el Khamt and onwards to Tâif, one is struck
by a change in the appearance of the buildings. In the
Wady Marr, people live in open cottages without so
much as a door. Here the villagers' houses look like little
castles, each larger farmhouse and its courtyard being con-

structed for defence   The walls of the yard are high, the
dwelling-houses provided with loopholes, and placed so as
to serve as flanking towers. Most of the cultivated patches
have also regular towers of refuge not very strongly built
—often, indeed, mainly composed of mud—but barred
and loopholed, and provided with a barbican   I was
told that these provisions for defence extend all through
the Hejâz—that is, from Tâif upwards   The villagers
of Wady Luqem are not proprietors, but farmers, and
of the 'Oteibe tribe   In appearance they are still Bedouins,
and even in Tâif the townsmen are almost as prone to
war as the nomads   Continuing to ascend the Wady
we approached Tâif from the north. The Wady opens
into a small plain, with a background of noble mountains
dominated by the great mass of Barad in the south-west.
In the midst of the plain lies Tâif, surrounded by villages
and gardens, with the handsome summer-houses of the
grandees of Mecca.   In the foreground is the great white
palace of Shubra, the residence of the Shereef 'Aly Pasha,
encircled by the most famous orchards of the Hejâz, and
almost dwarfing the little town behind   From Shubra
a straight avenue of tamarisks leads between orchards
and wheat fields to the northern gate of Tâif.   Above
the dusky line of crumbling mud-built walls rise a few
tall houses similar in style to those of Mecca and Jeddah,
and in the upper part of the city a lofty square citadel
with round corner towers. A Turkish sentinel, his hands
and feet all chapped with frost, received us at the gate,
and directed us across a desolate-looking square to the
house which, by directions of the Shereef, had been fitted
up for my reception. But the further account of what
I saw at Tâif must be left for another letter.

VII. TÂIF

Tâif, says old Edrisi, is a small city, populous, irrigated
by sweet waters, with a salubrious climate, abounding

in crops, with ample fields especially rich in grapes, and
famed for its raisins. Most of the fruit for Mecca is brought
from it. It stands on the ridge of Mount Ghazwan,
than which no mountain of the Hejâz has a colder summit,
ice being sometimes found on it even in summer. There
are some things in this description which are not very
intelligible. I found no one in Tâif who knew the name
of Mount Ghazwan, and the city, though it lies very high,
is not placed on a mountain ridge, but in the centre of an
upland plain. It is still celebrated for its climate, its
waters, its fields, and its fruits. Its grapes are sold in
Mecca and Jeddah for six or seven months of the year ,
but the fame of its raisins seems to have been transferred
to the dates, of which it produces a unique species as
long as one's finger. Of other fruits, the most famous
is a peculiar pomegranate, weighing two pounds, with
small seeds; but all the fruits of Syria are grown—apricots,
peaches, quinces, pears, plums, plantains, the cactus fig,
and so forth   The sweet waters are less copious than of
old times, for some of the ancient springs have failed ;
but, besides many wells, there are still four fountains,
Shubra, Ja'l, El Mithna, and El Waht. The well of
Shubra is that from which the inhabitants drink. It is
conducted along the eastern wall of the town in a subterranean conduit, with two pits for drawing water, and
then flows northward to irrigate the great Shubra orchard.
El Ja'l is also to the east of the town , the other two lie
above the city, El Mithna about a mile from its gates at
a point called Ethna el Tâif, and El Waht farther up.
The fountains and wells, which never fail, secure considerable cultivation in all seasons ; but there are large tracts
of good land which can only be cultivated after rain
Two good rains are sufficient for the wheat crop, but of
late years the rain has often failed, and prices have risen
greatly. At the date of our arrival, the long-continued
drought was causing great anxiety. There had been
rain in the beginning of the Hajj—that is, in the end of

November—but since then the weather had been dry and inclement, and great anxiety was felt as to the prospects of the season   Wheat had reached almost a famine price.   The Mohtesib, or officer in charge of the market, could remember the day when the bushel (Ardebb) was sold for about 7s.—two Maria Theresa dollars.   It had gradually risen from a succession of bad seasons, and was now worth thirteen dollars   An oqqa—$2\frac{1}{4}$ lb.—of clarified butter used to be worth $2\frac{1}{2}$ piastres.   It had risen to 25 —say three shillings—but with a good season might fall to 10.   It seems to follow from these figures that the rise of prices is not so wholly dependent on bad seasons as the inhabitants suppose   The failure of the rain, which if it did not come soon could not be looked for at all, was the general theme of conversation, and when I went out to walk in the town the children in the streets kept crying, " The Christians are come to us, and the rain is sure not to come."   To our great delight the clouds gathered next day, and a thunderstorm, accompanied by showers, passed over the town   The rain was not sufficient to do much good, but the weather had broken, and abundant rains followed in a few days.   It is a curious fact that almost the same thing happened last time that a party of Europeans visited Tâif after a severe drought of three years.

I return to Edrisi's description of the climate of Tâif. It is difficult to say which of the surrounding mountains is meant when he speaks of the formation of ice in summer —probably Mount Barad, the Mountain of Hail, which is the loftiest of the surrounding peaks.   In Tâif itself ice is common in winter, and almost all the inhabitants had their hands and feet chapped with frost   The salubrity of the climate is, I imagine, overrated: the winter climate is certainly good, though cold : but in summer fever is not unknown.   The place, however, is pleasantly cool in the great heats, and is the favourite summer residence of the Hejâz   The Wâly, the Shereef, and the wealthy of Mecca always spend some months of the year in Tâif, and it is also visited from Jeddah and Medina. A large proportion of the houses belong to Mecca people or are used only as summer lodgings, and in February the town was half deserted. In Tâif, as also in Mecca and Jeddah, any one taking a house for a single week has to pay the rent of a whole year.

The natural advantages of the site leave little doubt that Tâif is a very ancient town. An absurd Arabic tradition asserts that it was supernaturally conveyed from Damascus to the Hejâz at the prayer of Abraham —a story which means nothing more than that Tâif, with its orchards, is the Damascus of the Hejâz, and a city of unknown antiquity. A still wilder etymological legend carries back the history of Tâif to the Flood, when it is said to have drifted (Taf) on the water. Perhaps a beginning of true tradition lies in the story that the walls of the city were built by a wealthy man of the Sadaf who had shed blood in Hadhramaut, and took refuge in the Wejj, as the valley of Tâif was once named. In the time of the Prophet, Tâif was the capital of the Thageef, who still hold the neighbouring mountains, and are largely represented in the town. The story of the conquest and conversion of the Tâifites is a prominent episode in the life of Mohammed, which I shall not attempt to repeat from memory ; but the point of the story lies in their reluctance to give up their tutelary goddess Al-Lat. With the leading men of Tâif this reluctance had its root in policy, not in superstition They were afraid of the common people, and we have already seen how the dominant merchant class of Mecca and Tâif made religion work hand in hand with politics and trade. This system had gained them a great influence extending to remote Bedouin tribes, so that their objection to innovation is easily conceived Of the old religion of Tâif before Islam there is still a lively tradition among the inhabitants. The highest of the three quarters of Tâif

contains two rocky eminences between which runs the
street connecting the bazaar with the western gate, or
hence called Bab el Ree'. On the northern eminence
stands the citadel ; on the southern is a great rough
block of granite, with rounded forms and many cavities,
which is traditionally named Al-Lat. The mass is now
half-buried in rubbish, from which it stands about twelve
feet high ; but it can never have been very remarkable
for size in this country of enormous boulders. The
etymology of the word Lat proposed by some Arabic
writers assumes that it was the custom to move in procession round this deity—just as was done round the
rock at 'Okâtz   If this is historically correct it confirms
the Tâif tradition   Another granite block of a white
colour, with small black grains and finer texture than is
common in the district, lies beyond the walls S W of
the great mosque, and is traditionally named " Uzza."
Uzza, according to Arabic accounts, was worshipped
under the form of a Samur tree, and her sanctuary stood
at Nakhla, remote from the Thagîf country.   One might,
therefore, be tempted to conjecture that the association
of Al-Lat and Uzza in the local tradition of Tâif is merely
borrowed from the Koran, where the two names occur
together.   But the common people of Tâif still swear
by Uzza, without thinking of the meaning of the oath.
We had a muleteer with us in crossing Mount Kara who
did so, and was very much ashamed when rallied on the
subject.   It can hardly be questioned, therefore, that
the tradition is genuine, and that the same goddess
worshipped in one place as a tree was adored in another
as a stone   Not many years ago one of the Tâif Shereefs
proposed to break up Uzza for building purposes, and
actually split the rock with a blast of gunpowder, but
the High Shereef interfered, and the fragments still lie
side by side.   A Wady under the eastern walls of Tâif,
descending from the north, and traversed for a short
distance by the Hejâz road, is traditionally associated

with the history of the Prophet.   It is called W. Majiro el
Shash because the Prophet is said to have passed though
it dragging his sash along the ground.   In this valley, a
mile above the town, are also shown the prints of his
lance—small natural holes in the rock, and on an eminence
the *Sidr*, or Spina Christi tree, under which he rested.
These relics are visited by pilgrims, who have set up many
small stones in the valley as their memorials.   A little
to the east of the Wady, in the road to the Leeya, are
the " martyrs "—the place where some of the followers
of Mohammed fell in battle against Tâif

At present the town of Tâif presents no appearance of
antiquity.   The mud-built walls date only from the time
of the Wahhâbites, who are said to have completed them
in twelve days.   It is a tradition that the town originally
stood close to the foot of Mount Sakkara, a granitic mass
covered with loose blocks, the nearest point of which now
stands about ten minutes' walk from the south - east
corner of the town.   The people of Tâif, says the tradition,
suffered much at the hands of the 'Aseer, and thought
it a precaution against surprise to move back a little
way from the mountain.   I observed no ruins to bear
out this view, but at the base of Mount Sakkara on the
south side, near the road leading to the upper fountains
and orchards, I found two considerable inscriptions in
the ancient character already mentioned.   The whole
sides of Sakkara, and, indeed, of most hills in the vicinity,
are covered with Cufic inscriptions in several styles of
writing, and some very neatly executed   There are no
dates, and the inscriptions are mainly sepulchral, or
verses of the Koran.

Tâif is divided into three quarters—the upper being
the citadel (Fog), the lower (Asfal), on the north, and on
the east the Indian quarter (Haret el Suleimaneeye).
Many of the houses are small and mean , but there is a
fair proportion of good dwellings in the same style as the
houses of Jeddah.   They are partly built of stone, but

large use is made of a sort of tenacious clay which is said to stand better than stone, and is preferred to cement (nôra) for the roofs. The Mohtesib, who acted as our host under orders from the Shereef, told us that his house had not been repaired for a hundred years. As a fair type of a small house of the better class, I may describe that which was furnished for our reception—the house of the Scingianas [?], it is called   It is a narrow building of four storeys, opening into a sort of square, near the northern gate.   Before the door is a stone platform, on which servants lounge, and which is also used as a mounting-block.   Entering through a straight narrow passage, one has in front the staircase, dark and narrow.   To the right, a small court opens off the passage, having on the street side a small office (maq'ad), and opposite to this the Divan or qâ'a, a raised platform with a lofty roof, connected with the court by an open Moorish archway. In the Divan, visits are received and business transacted. It is a characteristic feature of the Arabian house, but not quite an invariable one.   The indispensable thing is to have a room on the ground floor where visitors can be received without disturbing the privacy of the house. As the Divan is loftier than the other parts of the ground floor, the upper rooms are at various levels   The stair is a winding one in short flights, accommodated to this peculiarity.   The private rooms of the house are on the intermediate floors, and the chief sitting-room, or *mejlis*, with its appurtenances, occupies the upper storey, the kitchen being only half-a-flight of stairs off   The *mejlis* is entered through an ante-chamber called the *suffe*, which is generally slightly different in level.   In the house provided for me the *suffe* was a step lower.   It was laid with sand, and at one side was a sink with conveniences for washing   Off the other end was a small bath-room.   In the *suffe* stood a brazier with charcoal, to supply the continued demand for coffee and hot coals for the water-pipe, which goes on at all hours of the day.

Below the step which led into the *mejlis* a rough carpet
of home-spun wool and linen (*shamla*) was laid, and on
this the servants sat who were in attendance on the
gentlemen within.   Every one left his shoes in the ante-
chamber before stepping on the carpet   The *mejlis*
itself was a plain room, whitewashed, with a few shelves
and cupboards.   As the house was an empty one furnished
for the occasion, it looked barer than is usual with an
Arabian sitting-room.   But it had been very nicely
carpeted.   A line of cushions covered with bright chintz
ran round three sides of the room, and pillows for the
elbow were placed on the cushions at short intervals.
The *mejlis* has always several lattice windows, of which
one or two are oriels, and the deep seats under these were
also furnished with rugs and cushions, so that one could
curl up comfortably and smoke a pipe while looking out
on the street.   A few cane-bottomed chairs and a small
table had also been introduced   These are getting
common, and in Jeddah many of the better class always
dine seated on chairs.   In Tâif I observed that people were
still more at their ease when eating from a tray placed on
a low kursy or stool round which they could sit squatted
on their hams.   Above the *mejlis* were some store places
and a stair leading to the terrace of the roof.   The latter
is enclosed by a parapet sufficiently deep to secure semi-
privacy to persons sitting on it.   Houses built on this
plan are extremely well adapted to a tropical climate.
The sitting-room is so high above the ground that it
catches every breath of air.   In Jeddah great care is
taken to secure a through draught, and the court is so
arranged that all principal rooms shall have windows
on two or even three sides.   In Tâif this is less necessary,
and the system of architecture, but especially the absence
of window glass, which ensures that one cannot have
light without draught, is not quite suitable for the winter,
in which frosts are not infrequent.   A larger house would
differ from that I have described mainly in having two

stairs—one reserved for the Hareem, so that the *mejlis* might be freely accessible at all hours without risk of disturbing the women of the house.   In Tâif, as in Mecca and Jeddah, there is no system of drainage   The closets, which are placed inconveniently near to the doors of the chief suites of rooms, are connected with cesspools. Much is left to the absorptive power of the sandy soil, and when the cesspool becomes a serious nuisance, the custom is simply to dig a trench in the unpaved street and bury the sewage in it.   Fortunately, the water of the town is not exposed to contamination, as the conduit of Shubra flows outside the town, and skins of water are sold from house to house by negro water-carriers, who are slaves.   Such rubbish as cannot be discharged into the cesspool is generally accumulated on the housetops ; and there is a periodical clearing out, which was going on briskly at the time of my visit, in preparation for the summer season.   The Arabs of the towns are much more cleanly than the Egyptians.   Their houses are generally tidily kept, and fleas and bugs, which are such a plague in Cairo and Syria, are seldom met with.

An Arab town has three distinct aspects, and should be seen from a distance, from the streets and from the housetops   From a distance the lofty tower-like houses, irregularly grouped, and presenting the most varied skyline, always offer a picturesque appearance   There is a lack of colour, the walls and roofs being either dust-coloured or white ; but the deep shadows and strong play of sunshine on the white surfaces partly compensate for this defect   The minarets hardly add a feature to the views, for they have no architectural pretensions, and are mere slim candlesticks of stone crowned by an extinguisher   When one enters the town the first impression is of universal shapelessness—of a total absence of the sense of proportion.   The houses are like great packing-cases, set down by chance in irregular groups, intersected by narrow lanes.   There is no attempt to

give character to the wall surfaces, nothing but uniform
flat spaces of rough stonework, with string courses of
wooden beams, in the fashion which goes back to the
days of Solomon's Temple. If the house is a fine one,
the wall is stuccoed and whitewashed, and, perhaps, some
colour is introduced in the battlements, but that is all.
There are none of the admirable stone-cut mouldings of
the Egyptian Arabs, no trace of the faculty for effective
treatment of great wall spaces which appears, for example,
in the mosque of Sultan Hassan at Cairo. The upper
part of the house always looks unfinished, if not actually
ruinous, and the battlements seem to have run to seed
In the better houses of Jeddah these defects are largely
balanced by the free use of tasteful woodwork, chiefly
executed in Java teak. The doors and oriel windows are
handsomely carved, and the latter are shaded with
canopies of fantastic fretwork. A handsome sitting-
room on the top floor often has a kiosk entirely of woodwork at one or even at both ends, and the large masses
of dark teak thus introduced give relief to the insipidity
of the flat white masonwork. But I have great doubts
whether this style is original to the Arabs. The extensive
use of foreign timber which is seen in all the coast towns
becomes limited up the country, and in Tâif even the
better houses have smaller and less numerous oriels
The ordinary window is a plain lattice set flat in the wall,
which has no picturesque effect The public buildings
are even less interesting than the private houses. Tâif
has one great mosque and many small ones. But even
the great mosque of Ibn 'Abbas, beside the gate of that
name, to the south of the city, is altogether commonplace.
The type of the Arabian mosque is a courtyard with
covered piazzas, to which are added a minaret and probably a domed building covering the tomb of a saint.
This plan admits of excellent architectural effect, as is
seen in the oldest mosques of Cairo and the great mosque
of Damascus, which follow the same type. But in these

the fair pillars and arches speak of foreign influences. In Jeddah and in Tâif all is shapeless and unadorned whitewash. The piazzas are sheds and the domes mere camels' humps. After the mosque and the citadel, the chief public building of Tâif is the Bath. The use of the public bath is not common in this country. There is none in Jeddah, and that of Tâif is the recent speculation, I think, of a Turk. The inhabitants refuse to use it It is employed by visitors in summer, but the natives reckon it a " shame " to frequent a public bath Private baths, however, are numerous. The housetop view of an Arab town is always curious ; but our house being small, I did not see Tâif to advantage from this point. The terrace of his roof is the Arab's garden, and his outhouses are little chambers erected on it. In Jeddah, for example, the goats all live on the housetops In warm weather, part of the terrace, screened off with boards and mats from the gaze of neighbours in loftier dwellings, is the favourite place of the women Dinners are given on the housetop, and here the servants of adjacent houses meet to gossip In short, the roofs are a great centre of life, and their structure is as complicated as their functions. You must not think of the roof of a large house as a uniform plain. It is rather a miniature village, with half-a-dozen levels, and quite a variety of terraces and chambers and porticos, the highest parts being always reserved for the broken pottery and general rubbish of the house below There is nothing so comical as a bird's-eye view of an Arabian town.

There is one part of the town of which I have not yet spoken. I mean the bazaar. The bazaar is the centre of all public life, and the little pigeon-holes of shops, with just room for the tradesman, his son, and a customer upon the carpet, are the great centres of gossip. The bazaar of Tâif is interesting because it is crowded with Bedouins The great day is Thursday, which is the weekly market. Here you see Thageef, 'Oteibe, Qoreish,

Hodheil, and I know not how many other tribes, each distinguishable to the practised eye, not only by dress, but by the " blood " which appears in their faces.   They bring their arms with them—the inseparable janbeeya and the lance—seldom the long matchlock, which is useless in a mêlée, and fatal only when deliberately fired from an ambush.   The bazaar is stocked with sample wares, English and American cottons, the home-made *shamla* and head shawls from Baghdad, breadstuffs and rice, the dates and wild honey of .Tâif, the hard mineral salt of Jebel Marran, the coarse hot tobacco called *hummy* smoked in the water pipe, clarified butter, leather and iron wares, and weapons.

The stir is constant, for the simplest purchase may occupy an hour, and a very small number of transactions produces the appearance of immense activity.   The other streets are silent enough save for the boys and little girls playing in them.   And singularly enough it is a rule of the town that no woman or girl above eight or ten must ever be seen in the streets or precincts of the town.   'Tis no great loss to the aspect of the streets, for the out-door dress of an Arabian woman of Jeddah or Mecca —the dingy blue wrapper, the narrow cotton trousers, and the yellow Morocco stockings and slippers in which she shuffles along with an ungainly swing, so unlike the erect elastic gait of the Egyptian females—is a hideous contrast to the picturesque dress of the men, which is generally bright in colour, and always shows off to ad-vantage the well-knit forms of the young and the grave dignity of the seniors.

VIII. The Mohtesib and His Family

In my last letter I gave some description of the town of Tâif.   I must now say something of its inhabitants. The family which I can best describe is that of the Mohtesib Hosein, to whom the Shereef entrusted the charge of

36

entertaining me   Hosein is a man of five-and-fifty, with a
comfortable figure, a grey beard, an easy, good-humoured,
but somewhat selfish expression on his regular features,
and a sly look about the corners of his eyes. He was
dressed in a white caftan and orange brown jubbeh,
and under his white turban, which, as usual in Arabia,
was wound about a parti-coloured skull-cap, he wore,
as a protection from the cold, a handsome yellow semâda.
His feet were bare, except for the sandals, with their
gold embroidered straps, which he left at the door before
entering the *mejlis*, and it struck one as curious that while
the head was so carefully swathed, and the trunk protected by an under caftan of red flannel, the ankles were
left bare to the frost, and all chapped with cold. The
business of the Mohtesib is the charge of the market
It is his work to regulate the prices of articles of food,
and, if necessary, to compel merchants to throw their
stores on the market. It is not a very important office,
and Hosein is not one of the great men ot Tâif—in other
words, he is not very rich ; but his work requires a good
knowledge of the town and people and a certain local
standing which he possesses as the representative of a
good old Tâif stock of the Benî Sufyân branch of the
tribe of Thageef. Hosein owns land in the neighbourhood
—good wheat and orchard ground, with running water,
which he lets out to a farmer, receiving in return one-half
the produce in fruit and one-third of the grain crop
The farmer finds all the capital, seed, and labour—slave-
labour, of course, for there are very few free labourers
in Tâif, except for garden work requiring special skill
A skilled gardener is well paid , he may receive as much
as £1 per month, with food, clothing, and perquisites
in kind. An ordinary labourer would have food, clothing,
and four or five shillings a month. Besides his land in
the Leeya, five or six miles out of town, Hosein inherits
a good house within the city. His wife has also a small
house which is her own property, and will descend to

her children ; and as the old gentleman recently purchased
an Abyssinian slave girl—she cost him a hundred dollars—
and made her his wife according to usage when she bore
him a son, his first wife has withdrawn to her own cottage
with her daughter and two sons   There is no separation
or formal quarrel. Hosein visits his wife, but she will
not come to the house where her rival is installed. The
children naturally take their mother's side, and 'Aly, a
handsome lad of nineteen, who, with the assistance of
a slave-boy, waited on us while we were in Tâif, told
me in quite a touching way how good his mother was
and how unhappy. But the boy did not say a word
that could be construed as disrespectful to his father.
An Arab father expects of his son an almost servile
deference, which is paid cheerfully, and as a matter of
course. The son of the house, even when he is grown
up, is called on to do menial service to his father and his
father's guests, and does not feel humiliated by so doing.
'Aly was ready to wait, not only on me, but on my attendants, though they, with the exception of the conceited
Al Mâs, thought it civil to deprecate his services. Nor
would he, without the express request of his father and
myself, come and sit down in the *mejlis*, much less join
us at meals, although after the first day, during which
a stiffer etiquette was observed, every one, down to the
camel man Marzook, dined at my table. Of an evening,
when the old Mohtesib was tired, he would lie down
and call 'Aly to shampoo his feet, which was done by
gently treading on them   Salim, the eldest son, who
was twenty-three years old, was allowed a little more
independence. He went out with me into the neighbourhood, but did no menial service in the house, and came
and sat freely in the room with his father and myself.
But the old gentleman was pretty strict even with him.
Salim was very anxious to marry, and confided to me his
plans. Most fathers would certainly demand a dowry
of 100 dollars, probably also a negro slave girl, worth

60 to 70 dollars, to wait in the house. But he might have the daughter of his paternal uncle for 50 dollars, which was cheap It must be understood that the preference for marriage between cousins which exists also in Egypt has here the character of a binding custom. A father cannot refuse his daughter to his brother's son, although another suitor offer a much higher dowry, unless the cousin is of weak intellect or notoriously of bad character. The cousin, if rejected for a richer suitor, can step in even at the last moment and stop the wedding. In return for this moderate dowry, Salim's uncle would have to furnish the house of the young couple—the furniture being then the property of the wife But the old Mohtesib, who could spend 100 dollars on a concubine for himself, will not find 50 dollars for his son, and bids him go and make money, and save up enough to pay the dowry himself. In this Salim has not been very successful A year ago he had a small post as Mukharrij—that is, he had charge of the local Government transport service At present he is employed by his father, and earns nothing I was somewhat struck with the great difference in dress between father and sons. The former appeared as a substantial citizen Salim, in a coarse white tôb, an old waistcoat, and rough 'abaye, looked almost like a peasant. 'Aly served us in a white tôb, a waistcoat, and a great red handkerchief for turban. The tôb in each case was scrupulously clean, and this was the only sign that the wearers were not of the poorest class.

The Mohtesib had seen a good deal of public service. Previous to his appointment at Tâif, which was but of two years' date, he had spent seven years in Yemen with the Turkish Pasha in a post connected with the supply service. He had lost money at this work, but he was very unwilling to return to Tâif, where he had left his wife and family, and after the failure of urgent messages, Salim had gone in person to Kanfuda and fetched him

home. Hosein is said to know Turkish better than any-
one in Tâif, and is very proud of the accomplishment.
Yet he can hardly read and write, and his sons are in
the same case. It is, indeed, extraordinary how few of
the Arabs of the interior possess the elements of education
People in a very respectable position write and spell
about as well as a ploughman in Scotland, and are equally
unhappy when compelled to attempt a letter. Hosein,
who is a shrewd fellow, and full of curiosity, was anxious
to see the New Testament, and to hear how it had been
revealed   I had furnished myself with a small copy of
the excellent Beyroot version, and with some small
prints of single gospels, so I was able to gratify his wish.
I turned up the story of the Prodigal Son, but he could
not spell it out with any comfort, and I had to read it
for him. He followed it with great interest, and told me
next morning that he had it firmly in his head. He is,
indeed, somewhat of Plato's opinion that reading and
writing are of little use to a man of retentive memory,
and rather despised my intellect when he saw me always
taking notes.

I shall take this opportunity to say a word or two as
to the attitude of the Hejâz Arabs towards Christian books.
When I came here only one inhabitant of Jeddah, so far
as I am aware, possessed a copy of the Bible in Arabic.
This was Sheikh 'Aly Qâsim, a liberal-minded man who
has seen the world, and was long in the service of
Mohammed 'Ali in Egypt. He is quite aware that the
old Arabs, for whose literature he has a great love, were
much opener to foreign influences than their descendants.
He regards it as necessary to the regeneration of Arabia
that people should be willing to learn what is useful from
any source, and he finds the root of all present mischief
in fanaticism, especially the fanaticism of the Turks.
From this point of view he thinks it right to possess the
Christian Scriptures   The possession is a protest against
bigotry, but I don't think he has read very much of the

Bible. He has, indeed, the regular Arabic taste for
affected rhetoric and plays on words, to which Hareery
appears the model writer, and the simple style of the
gospels devoid of literary merit. It is the curse of Arabic
literature that form—and how artificial a form!—is
preferred to substance, and so long as this is the standard
by which books are judged, the affected rhetoric of the
Koran will secure it the preference over the Bible.

Most of the Hejâz Arabs, even of those who are fond
of books, have never seen the Bible. An Indian Mohammedan, clerk to Messrs Wylde & Co, told me that he
had long looked for an Arabic Bible, but could not find
a copy. I presented him with one, and he accepted it
very gladly In one or two other cases I first tried how
an Arabic psalter would be received It excited interest,
the Arabs all know by name the Psalms of David, which,
as one man told me, he expects to hear sung in Paradise.
But when the book was shown by its possessor to some
of the leading Mohammedans, they pronounced it bad.
It was not a genuine copy, but corrupted by the Christians
It was useless to ask the authority for this statement,
or to inquire whether the hostile judges had true copies—
the reputation of the little book was irretrievably injured.
There would be no difficulty in circulating the Scriptures
in the Hejâz, were it not that the literary authorities are
bigots, and have been taught that our Bible is blasphem-
ously corrupted from its original verity. People are quite
willing to take a book, but they are pretty sure to go and
show it to the nearest scholar, and he, either from genuine
fanaticism or simply from the native arrogance of Arabian
scholarship, is likely to condemn the Christian print. I
left a New Testament at Tâif, and gave Al Mâs another
to take to Mecca, but I greatly fear that they are not
likely to be read. These columns are not the place
to deal with this matter from a missionary point of
view; but simply in the interests of civilisation and of
that progress which is seriously retarded by the current

Moslem notion that their dry and barren literature is the most perfect that can be conceived, it is heartily to be desired that a door should be opened to the circulation of Christian literature. The good to be effected by a study of the Bible is not to be measured by the number of possible converts to Christianity   It would be an enormous advance if the reading and thinking part of the Arabs knew enough of our religion and its documents to conquer their present absurd idea that the only reason why we are not Moslems is crass and stupid ignorance of Arabic and the Koran. At present, if one shows any interest in Arabic, the people fancy that one is well on the way to be a Mohammedan   Most of them know almost nothing of their own faith except a few formulas and prayers ; but they take it for granted that the stupendous miracle of the Koran, a book which no human intellect could have produced, must convince every one who is able to read it. You testify to the unity of God—so I have often been told—what is easier than to add that Mohammed is his apostle, and secure your entrance to heaven ? For though that is not the teaching of the Prophet, all Mohammedans feel sure of heaven, and the moral obligations of their religion cost them little thought. If you reply that you are not satisfied that the Koran makes any necessary addition to the previous revelations which Mohammed himself accepted as divine, you are exhorted only to accept Islam, and then God will help you to see the perfections of his book. If you attempt to contrast the Christian laws of morality with those of Islam, the most liberal answer you can expect is that the ordinances of Islam suit the conditions of the Arabian people. And that, no doubt, is true, in the sense that Mohammed himself largely accommodated his precepts to the natural pre-judices of the Arabian mind. But, on the other hand, the Koran is largely responsible for the present slowness of the Arab to accept even the most needful reformations.

Arabian ways of thought in Mohammed's day were not
nearly so stereotyped as they have since become under
the sanction of a religion whose material successes gave
it an enormous prestige. Before Islam, Arabia was in
a state of transition. It was largely accessible to new
and foreign influences, and conservative traditions being
rather tribal than national, had not the strength which
they acquired by the religious unification of the race.
The Koran is the bulwark of all prejudices and social
backwardness in the East. I am far from saying that
no progress can be made by a Mohammedan people,
but it is indispensable to progress that a freer attitude
be taken up towards the Koran, and the best means
towards this is a better knowledge of the ethics and
religion of the Western nations.

And now to go back to Tâif. The hospitalities of
Hosein and his sons were unsparing and a little burden-
some. My host and Al Mâs between them fairly took
possession of me. I had the greatest difficulty in being
alone long enough to wash or change my clothes, and
even at night, when a bed was laid for me in the *mejlis*,
Al Mâs, and sometimes Salim, slept in the room. During
the day one or more of the family was constantly with me.
It must have been rather trying to the poor Mohtesib,
but Oriental patience, fortified by the unfailing water-
pipe, can endure much in the cause of hospitality. I,
of course, made the most of my opportunities, and collected a good deal of information about tribes' customs
and the like, of which I shall give some of the more interesting particulars in another letter. As the weather broke
the day after my arrival, I had to spend more time within
doors than I should otherwise have cared to do. But,
indeed, it required a good deal of pressure to get out into
the surrounding country. After I had seen the orchards,
which to the Arabs are the great sight of Tâif, and had
also conscientiously visited a garden in which an enter-
prising Egyptian raises European vegetables from seed

brought from France, I was held to have " done " the place, and my host's only further care was to give me plenty to eat. I had, at all events, full opportunity to make acquaintance with a characteristic local cuisine The Tâif people have three meals a day, but I struck off the midday repast, as otherwise the whole day would have been lost. For, whenever one wished to go out, the answer was, " Wait a little while, you must have something to eat first." I cannot tell you the programme of a Tâif dinner. Sweets, vegetables, and joints are mingled in an extraordinary confusion, for which it is impossible to find a law. But a few general principles were discernible. The meal should end with a dish of stewed rice, which may or may not be accompanied by sweet pastry or vermicelli. A great dinner has for its *pièce de résistance* an entire sheep stewed or baked with *samn* (clarified butter), and stuffed with rice, eggs, and almonds. On lesser occasions one eats roast fowls and a variety of stews. Several large bowls of sour milk are always on the table, and of this the natives eat a great deal. At breakfast one begins with 'Areeka, or with a sort of porridge prepared with milk and samn and made very rich. Eggs fried with vegetables are another favourite dish. Besides these, there is probably a plate of muffins soaked in honey and samn, or a bowl of samn and honey mixed, in which the bread is dipped— the butter and honey of the Old Testament The most characteristic and also the most trying dish to a stranger is called Hareesa. This is a local food eaten in the Hejâz, Yemen, and Hadhramaut, and prepared by boiling grits along with meat, and beating up the compound with a wooden spatula till it becomes a uniform paste. It is eaten with samn, sometimes with sugar, and has a very strong greasy taste. The great feature of Tâif cookery is the superabundance of *samn*. The people even drink it by the bowl. I ought perhaps to tell how it is made. The milk stands overnight, with the addition of a little sour milk as a ferment. In the morning it is skimmed, and the cream is shaken in a skin. It is then boiled for a long time, and strained several times. When well pre- pared, it will last at least a year without spoiling. The best products of Tâif are the preserved fruits in syrup. The Arabs are very fond of conserves, and various districts have their specialities   In the Nejd, for example, there is an excellent conserve of dates, in which the stones are replaced by almonds

My daily life in Tâif did not admit of much variety. I was not allowed to move out without my escort, and it was with great difficulty that I could carry my search after inscriptions more than a mile or two from the town walls. I made one expedition about three miles south, but Al Mâs was most unwilling to accompany me, sulked the whole way, and contrived to pick a quarrel with Ismail Had I not been hampered by him, I believe I could have gone far into the interior with perfect safety, for I met nothing but civility from the Bedouins abroad, who, to be sure, did not know me for a Christian. But I had no formal leave to go beyond Tâif, and could not insist on going where Al Mâs and the Mohtesib said there was danger. I, therefore, was obliged to confine myself to the vicinity of the town, where I found four inscriptions in the old character I sought for, and acquired the conviction that there is a great deal still to find   I am now certain that Al Mâs and the Mohtesib contrived to keep back from me information which they possessed, and I have since learned to my great disappointment that only three hours from Tâif there are important ruins at a place called Thimala   Had I been able to name a definite goal, I might, perhaps, have got leave to make an excursion in this direction, but I could not go to the Sheeref Fawwâz, who is the representative of the Emeer, without a definite plan. My short trip was, indeed, essentially a mere reconnaissance, in which I have at least satisfied myself that there is much to see and describe,

and that the obstacles in the way of a real exploration of
the Hejâz are not insuperable. It would probably be
necessary to settle for some time at Tâif, and hire a house,
making this the centre of exploration. It might be safer
to go when the Shereef and Wâly are themselves at Tâif—
at least, Hosein declared that then there would not be
the same danger from the Bedouins as he avers to exist
now. The Shereef, who is a liberal-minded man, like
his brother and predecessor, has no dislike to Europeans,
whom he probably prefers to the Turks But he has
sometimes to affect prejudices which he does not feel,
in deference to the tyranny of public opinion. When
the late Shereef received the captain of a French ship
of war at Tâif, he did not venture to entertain him until
after the evening prayers, lest the people should say
he was casting away religion. Certain scruples, then,
would certainly have to be respected, and certain pre-
cautions employed, but, with ordinary prudence and
tact, one might make friends everywhere, and visit almost
any part of the country It would, of course, be essential
to conform to the habits and manner of the people, for,
as the Arabic proverb says, " When you come to their
dwelling conform to their ways, or if not go and leave
them "

IX. The Arabs of the Hejâz

The town of Tâif is the farthest point at which the
Turks hold any real authority in the Hejâz. Here they
have nominally a complete official system The Wâly
visits the place in the summer, and brings his bodyguard.
There is a Turkish police, commanded by a very intelligent
officer whose acquaintance I made. There is also a
Mohafiz or governor of the town, and a Cady who is
nominated by the Turkish Cady at Mecca, and changed
with him every two years The Cady is interpreter
of the law based on the Koran and traditions. He is

paid by fees, of which one half are remitted to the superior
at Mecca. The Mohafiz is the supreme executive officer ;
but the real power lies in the hand of the Grand Shereef,
and his representative, the Shereef Fawwâz, is the strong
man of the place. Fawwâz is now an elderly man, with
a fine tall person, a keen commanding eye, and a dignified
manner. He is greatly respected and feared by the Arabs
for his severe justice. Fawwâz is a pure Arab in his
habits and ways of thought. He has never been abroad,
and is as ignorant as a child of the progress of European
ways and inventions in the East. When I called on him,
the conversation turned chiefly on railways, telegraphs,
telephones, and the like, and Ismail the Anglophile got
so eloquent on the wonders of England that the old
gentleman was perfectly confounded But he knows
the Arabs, and keeps a firm hand over them ; and as
most people would rather be judged in Arabic fashion
than by Turkish law, he is far the most important judge
in the place. His jurisdiction, however anomalous it
may appear in a district nominally Turkish, is undisputed, and includes the power of life and death. Hosein
and Al Mâs gave me a very favourable picture of the
wide jurisdiction which Fawwâz, as representative of the
Emeer, exerts even over remote tribes far away through
the Nejd. But from other and less partial sources I
gather that this picture was considerably exaggerated.
Over the settled populations of the Hejâz—the Khadhr or
agricultural Arabs—the Shereef has practically a complete
hold The Bedouins cannot altogether dispute his
authority, for they must from time to time visit the
towns to buy and sell, and thus come within the sphere
where he has effective jurisdiction. His warrant, too,
can generally be executed even in remote places when
he desires to arrest an offender. But justice among
the Arabs is properly a private matter, and parties in
a dispute may either betake themselves to self-help, or
if they appeal to a judge regard him rather in the light

of an arbitrator. In such tribes as the 'Oteibe, who live far from the towns, the ordinary appeal is to local sheikhs, their own hereditary judges, and in these Courts the reference is not to law, but to ancient precedent. Precedents, says a rhyming adage, remove uncertainties—*Al-Sawâlif tarudd el-Mohâlif* For an 'Oteibe to appeal from these judges to the Shereef would be held a "shame" Nevertheless, these tribes do in some sense acknowledge the authority of the Shereef. They pay him the tithes, for were they to refuse, he could close their markets to them; on summons they follow him to war against another tribe—drawn mainly by the prospect of booty And the Ashrâf in general, who are scattered over the country, and form a sort of tribal connection, enjoy a certain religious respect, and a much more practical security, arising from the principle that the blood-money of a Shereef is fourfold. Every Bedouin war has to be squared up by an adjustment of blood-money for the slain, so it is a serious matter to be embroiled with men each of whose heads is worth four The Shereef, then, is a real prince, with actual privileges and a palpable, though ill-defined, authority. The exact limits of his influence depend on his personal qualities, on his energy in suppressing rebels, and his skill in balancing tribe against tribe Rebellion, as far as I can gather, generally means the plundering of caravans or a raid on a neighbour's territory. In the case which occurred while I was at Tâif, and to which I have already referred, the 'Oteibe, quarrelling with the Harb, attack a caravan under the protection of the latter. In such quarrels the towns have a direct interest, and the Shereef is compelled to interfere. He recovers the booty, imposes fines and regulates the blood-money between the tribes. Another case was mentioned to me, when a body of 'Oteibe seized the Beheita. They brought down their families and camels, and while pasturing their herds in the district, plundered all travellers. Here again the Shereef interposed, broke up the force, and recovered the booty.

Of late the turbulent tribe which has made most noise in the outer world are the Harb, on the Medina road, who, under their leader, Sa'd, have of recent years so often disturbed the security of the pilgrims. But the most formidable tribe of Central Arabia is certainly the 'Oteibe, the representatives of the ancient Hawâzın Strictly speaking, the 'Oteibe are not a tribe, but a confederation of tribes, of whom I can name fourteen All these tribes acknowledge one supreme judge. They extend from the limits of Tâif and the Beheita right through the Nejd to the district of 'Oneize. They are great robbers, and much feared, but have a better character for honour and hospitality than the Harb. Their strength was estimated to me by some informants at 60,000 fighting men. But Sheikh 'Aly Qâsım, who was long employed among the tribes round Tâif as collector of tithes, assures me that 20,000 would be a fairer estimate To the south-east of the 'Oteibe are the Qahtan, a tribe nearly as strong, and hereditary enemies of the 'Oteibe All accounts agree that the Qahtan are very savage, but the practice of drinking the blood of their enemies in time of war, with which they are generally credited, is perhaps now obsolete. Mohsın, who knows the East, says that the practice still obtains in a tribe beyond the Qahtan named, if I am not mistaken, the Yâm, and he gave me a picture of the single combats of these tribesmen, in which each grasps his adversary, and plunges his dirk into his side, which formed an exact parallel to the scene at the pool of Gibeon in the war between David and Ishbosheth. The Qahtan are not subject to the Shereef, but go with the 'Aseer, and are reckoned to the race of Yemen. Not much inferior in strength to the Qahtan are the Beeshe, from whose numerous negro slaves a force of irregular horse has long been drawn for the protection of Mecca. Between

Qahtan, 'Oteibe, and Beeshe, in a fertile district of palm
trees, two days' journey in length, is a small but very
pugnacious tribe called, appropriately enough, the Sibe'
(lion's whelp). They have two towns or villages—
Ghanye and Hurme—and are constantly engaged in
war with their neighbours. Al Mâs had been more than
once in campaigns against them, for he assures me that
they are never quiet except when hungry. They ride
out to battle four or five men on one dromedary, each
brandishing several spears   These are the most important
and formidable tribes on the eastern side of the Shereef's
country   Of the tribes of the Hejâz proper, those which
I came in contact with are the Thageef, the Qoreish, and
the Hodheil. Of other tribes of the high mountain land
I heard little but the names.   I may mention in particular
the Benî Fahm, who live at no great distance from Tâif,
on beyond Thimala, and have the reputation of speaking
the best Arabic of any Hejâz tribe. To the south the
Shereef's dominions border on the powerful and warlike
country of the 'Aseer, with whom the Hejâz Arabs are
in frequent conflict.

The reader is already familiar with the division of
this part of Arabia—the Turkish province of Hejâz—
into three parts—the Tehâma or low land, the central
mountainous country or true Hejâz, and the inland
plateau or Nejd. The Nejd is a land of pure nomads.
Far inland there are settled and fertile lands, but for
many days' journey it is a country which can be inhabited
only by nomad tribes moving in their houses of hair from
place to place   The 'Oteibe in time of drought wander
far and wide. On our road home we met a band of them
within an hour's journey of Mount Arafa, travelling
homeward on the news that rain had fallen in their
own country   They had been away beyond Summar
in Yemenite territory. In the Hejâz proper, on the
other hand, the mountain plains and valleys are rich in
water, and villages with cultured land are numerous.

Tribes such as the Thageef, the Qoreish, and the Hodheil
are divided into villagers (Khadhr) in the cultivable
Wadies, and wandering mountaineers who are shepherds
and woodsmen. The Thageef occupy the mountains and
fertile valleys all round Tâif, the Leeya and the hills
beyond it, the great southern mountain of the Qurneit,
the seat of the Benî Sufyân, and the tangled region of
the Tuweriq, north-west of Tâif as far as the plateau of
Hadda on the summit of Mount Kara, where they join
the Qoreish The Qoreish and the Hodheil, who are
similar in customs and closely allied, are mainly wild
mountaineers The Qoreish are found on the plateau
of Hadda and in the mountains of Arafa—not the lowly
Mount Arafa of religious celebrity, but the wild hilly
region that rises above the valleys of Mecca and Minâ
The Hodheil lie on both sides of the Qoreish. We were
among the settled Hodheil at Sôla, and in returning
we passed through their country as we descended from
Mount Kara down Wady Na'aman They hold the upper
part of this valley, with the hills of Kabkab, which
dominate it on the right. Unlike the nomads of the
central plateau, these mountaineers fight on foot Though
they are so near the centres of civilisation, the wild
seclusion of their mountains has preserved them from
change, and the blood feuds which make exogamy
almost an impossibility have maintained among them a
distinctly marked tribal type My eye did not become
sufficiently practised to catch all the minute signs by
which a tribesman can be identified—the cut of his sandals,
the way in which the long black locks hang behind the
ear—in one tribe plaited, in another free—the length
of the dirk, and so forth. But some marks are not difficult
to grasp. The lance is one of these. That of the Qoreish
and also of the Hodheil, who are not readily to be distinguished from the Qoreish, and share their most striking
peculiarities, is a rumh or javelin of a man's height, with
a long narrow blade, inlaid with brass, and an equally

long four-sided point at the other end. The 'Oteibe use
a broad-bladed lance, with which they can cut as well as
thrust. A similar weapon used in Yemen is the shilfe.
Other tribes use a pike (ḥarb), with four-sided head.
In the Nejd the cavalry are armed with a huge spear,
tufted with ostrich feathers (qanâ), and this is the spear
borne by the Shereefs of Mecca when they ride out in
solemn religious procession. The Qoreish warrior adorns
his lance with a little tassel of silk called *kuthle*. Another
tassel of beaded work hangs on his breast. His fillet is
a leathern hoop, inlaid with mother-of-pearl. His garments are dyed with native wood, *salm* or *bashâm*, and
are either a tawny yellow or a dark reddish brown. The
features are very dark, but sharply cut, and with a keen
aquiline aspect quite unlike the mixed bloods near the
coast. The women are veiled with the burko'. Their
blue tunics, shawls, and drawers are coloured with foreign
dye. They are belted like the men, and their favourite
ornament is a golden plate hanging down on the breast.
The most extraordinary custom of the Qoreish and Hodheil in the mountains is their form of circumcision, a
fearful ordeal through which every lad must pass before
he can be married. It is performed in the presence of
the whole neighbourhood and of the bride, who would
reject her bridegroom if he uttered a single cry. The same
rite prevails among the 'Aseer, a singular circumstance,
since in other matters the 'Aseer are very unlike the
tribes of Hejâz. The most notable contrast is in the
place of the women, on which I shall make a few remarks,
though I ought to premise that this is a topic on which
it is not easy to get trustworthy information, as customs
that appear irregular or contrary to the Koran are not
willingly reported.

Arabia generally passes for a typical example of the
patriarchal system of society. The Arabs themselves
have accommodated their genealogies and early history
to this theory; and it is expressed in the laws of

inheritance and blood revenge, which do not recognise
relationship on the female side. The extreme development of this principle is naturally associated with polygamy and the inferiority of woman. But it is certain
that this system is not primitive. We have express
evidence that polyandria once prevailed in Arabia, and
traces of this practice and of female kinship are to be
found to a comparatively late date. The social system
of Islam had to fight against many remains of the earlier
polyandria Among the Bedouins, travellers of quite
recent date have observed usages which point to exogamy, marriage by capture, female kinship, and other
practices, all of which are now known, mainly through
the researches of Mr. M'Lennan, to hang together and
belong to the gradual development, of which polyandria
is one stage. So far as I can learn, usages of this kind
are not known to the Hejâz tribes. I cannot find any
trace of such a form of capture as is still practised in
the Peninsula of Sinai, and Yemenite customs, pointing distinctly to female kinship, were related to me
as a contrast to Hejâz usage. Thus, it is considered a
peculiarity of Yemen that the *Dokhla*, or consummation
of marriage, takes place in the bride's house, and that
the bridegroom stays for some nights with the bride's
people if he be inborn, but if from abroad must settle
with them In the Hejâz the dokhla takes place in the
house of the bride's family only if the bridegroom has
no house of his own. This statement agrees very well
with all that one reads in mediæval accounts. It was in
southern Arabia that relics of polyandria and female
kinship survived. And with this difference, it goes
naturally enough that, while the Hejâz women are
carefully veiled, and in Tâif the principle of female
seclusion is carried farther than in any other part of
Arabia, the women of the 'Aseer and of Hadhramaut
appear unveiled in the street, and before guests whom
they serve, though they do not eat with them. More-

over, as one passes eastward from the Hejâz into the
Nejd, one again finds a less strict law of female seclusion.
The burko' was worn by the 'Oteibe women whom I have
seen , but I believe that in many parts of this confederation only the lower part of the face is slightly disguised
by bringing round a corner of the head shawl, in the
style very common even with men.   The 'Oteibe women
ride camels like the men ; nay, even more than they.
In the Nejd, according to the account of Mohsin, the
man of the tribe who brings home a horse seized on a
foray brings it to the Sheikh's daughter and receives a
kiss.   All these traits, slight as they may seem, appear
singular to the men of the Hejâz, and indicate a certain
difference in the position of women , and they suggest
the question whether the social system of Islam is not
really the social system of the Hejâz, whether in his
social legislation Mohammed did not impress on all
Arabia a family system which properly belonged to the
central commercial cities of the country and the tribes
in their immediate vicinity.   If this is so, there is another
reason why the Arabs were so reluctant to accept Islam
till they found their profit in following its victorious
arms   Another question arises in connection with the
seclusion of women.   May it not be the case that the
origin of this seclusion lay in immediate contact with
polyandrous traditions and polyandrous neighbours,
producing a necessary reaction against the licence of
that system ?   I ought to add that one of the tribes
named to me as allowing the women to appear with
uncovered faces is the Benî Malik.   According to
Sprenger, the Qoreish are really a branch of this tribe,
which makes the divergence of their usage as to the
veiling of women somewhat singular.   The Benî Malik
are now found settled in a cultivated land on the road
inland from Tâif passing Leeya, Bissl, the salt mines
of Marran (ten hours from Tâif), Nasera, and the Benî
Sa'd.   They were once much more widely spread, and

a village of the Harb, only three miles from Jeddah, bears their name.

Of the Arabs in the Tehâma and between Mecca and Medina I have little to tell. Those in the low country near Jeddah are greatly mixed. Being slave-holders and slave-traders, they are largely tinged with negro blood. The Zobeid and the Hutêm, who are pearl fishers, use negroes to dive for them, and treat them in this avocation with great cruelty The villagers near Jeddah are little accessible to Europeans, and naturally dislike the English for their action against the slave trade. I have met on friendly terms with the people of one village only, whose Sheikh, Abdulla Wasl of the Harb, has an employment under the Shereef, in charge of the Bedouin market at the Mecca gate.

X. Arabian Customs

I had occasion in my last letter to allude to the customary law established on precedents which prevails among the Bedouins   I am now to say a little more on the subject, especially as it is connected with blood revenge and war

The Arabs, says Sheikh 'Aly Qâsim, have three great principles, which they call the three white rules   White has here a figurative sense, which is best understood from the common phrase, that a man's face becomes black when he disgraces himself by a breach of custom.

The first of these principles is, " Tent rope by tent rope." A man whose tent rope touches yours is your Jâr, your neighbour, with a claim on your protection. If you can contrive to pitch thus beside a man, you have established your claim on him.

The second rule is, sacred obligation to him who journeys with you by day and sleeps by you at night. The third imposes on a host the duty of protecting the guest who has eaten with him until he has eaten with another.

But the most important of all Arabic principles is
the law of retaliation, which has received the sanction
of religion under Islam , but as practised by the Bedouins,
is simply an affair of ancient usage. The law of retaliation goes along with the principle of self-help. If a man
strikes another, the injured person makes it his aim to
inflict in retaliation a stroke as similar as possible—eye
for eye, tooth for tooth, blood for blood. The duty of
avenging insult descends from father to son. A child
will cherish in his mind from earliest infancy the recollection of a blow inflicted on his father, and when old enough
and strong enough, will repay it. Great subtlety is
shown as to the exact balance of offence and retaliation
The most important application of the law of retaliation
is naturally in the case of slaughter. The blood of a
tribesman is the concern of the tribe. The revenge may
fall on a distant kinsman of the slayer quite innocent of
a share in the offence, and if the slaughter is compounded
by a payment of blood-money, the payment is made and
received by the tribe, not by the individual. But a
strong and proud tribe will not generally accept money
from another unless for accidental blood. The honour
of the tribe demands blood for blood, and the nearest
relations of the deceased are those whose special business
it is to exact it. The opportunity of revenge may offer
itself in the streets of a town. Even in Jeddah a Bedouin
will strike his foe with the dirk, or, if he be of the Harb,
shoot him with his pistol and flee. In Medina he will
not even flee, but boldly stand up and say, I am such a
one, son of such a one, and have killed this man in such
an affair of blood. The constant uncertainty and terror
in which a man stands who has shed blood, or otherwise
exposed himself to retaliation for a minor injury, make
it necessary that the principle should have some limitation, and a method has been devised by which an offender
can place himself under the protection of a kinsman
of the slain or injured party. He must not choose a

veiy near kinsman, who has the right to refuse and say
" Go to another for protection." Having selected a suitable person, the offender approaches him and says " *Ana
fy wajhak* "—literally, " I am in thy face." Doing
this he may touch the beard of his protector, or more
ordinarily he lays hold of the fringe of one of his garments
and ties a knot on it which is called taking '*ány* [?] with
him. A fragment of the fringe is given as a sign to the
man, who in this way becomes the *Dâkhil* of the other.
The protector then simply announces to the kin that
such a one is in his protection or " face," and all revenge
is suspended for a year and two months Before the
close of that time the offender, if he has not been able
to arrange for a peaceful solution of the difficulty, must
seek another protector. Except by a very near relation,
the protection of the '*ány* cannot be refused. It is,
however, indispensable that there should be a small
money payment, and that the refugee should make a
feast at his own expense in the house of his protector.
The customary sum demanded is seven dollars. A man
who cannot pay this loses his privilege of the '*ány*.
There is one way by which the '*ány* can be evaded Suppose that the first year of protection has almost expired,
and it is anticipated that a second protection will be
sought. A member of the injured tribe, determined
that the revenge shall not be frustrated, may now travel
away into some remote district. When the new protector is chosen and comes to announce the fact, the kin
will refuse to be answerable for the man who has left
them, though they are bound to tell him that his right of
revenge is foreclosed as soon as he reappears among them
Avoiding his own people, moving stealthily from place
to place with covered face that none may recognise him
the determined avenger of blood tracks out his victim
and slays him At once there is a tumult This man
was in our protection No, says the slayer ; I am in my
right, for the thing was never reported to me

A very curious mode of expiation called the Nagâ is
practised by those who cannot afford the 'âny. It does
not apply to murder, but only to injuries of a lesser kind.
With bare and shaven head the offender appears as a
penitent at the door of the injured person, holding a
knife in each hand, and says—

> En-nagâ naggânâ wan-nagâ naggâ-er rijâl
>   illâdhy kamâna.

That is, the nagâ purges us, yea, it purges the man
who is like us—viz. not a wicked and unrepentant
offender. Saying this, he repeatedly gashes his head
with both knives ; or, if he has not nerve enough, may
get another to do so for him. Then drawing his hands
over his bloody scalp, he wipes them on the door-post
Then the injured man must come out, cover the wounded
head with a semâda, kill a sheep, and make a feast.
The common meal ends the feud, and the offender's face
is again white. The nagâ is practised even in the towns,
in Mecca, and in Tâif. In the ceremony of entering a
man's protection I have mentioned that one form is to
lay hold of the beard. This symbolical action has many
applications   For example, if an Arab has to pass through
a hostile encampment, he will lurk at the outskirts till
he sees a little child. Calling the boy, he gives him a
small present to accompany him, lifts him on his camel,
and rides safely through the camp, the child grasping
his chin. The Bedouins have a curious way of expressing
their feelings of goodwill or reluctance by touching the
beard or the back of the neck respectively. The former
is a good sign, but if a Bedouin, in approaching you or
in answering a request, puts his hand behind his neck,
you may be sure he bears you no goodwill, however
fairly he may say *Marhabân.*

The law of blood revenge applies to the practice of
war, and certainly tends to diminish bloodshed in the
constant forays of the restless and turbulent tribes. In
Arabic warfare, a pitched battle is comparatively rare.

Al Mâs, who has seen a great deal of service, told me
that he had been present at a pitched battle only once.
This was in the great war against the 'Aseer. Generally
speaking, an Arab invasion is a mere foray. The invaders scatter, attack the villages, drive off booty, and
engage in skirmishes. The fire-arms of the Bedouins are
fit only for irregular warfare—huge matchlocks, longer
than their bearers, which can be fired with effect only
from an ambush. In this way of fighting few lives
are lost. It is more profitable to capture an enemy and
hold him to ransom. To kill more of the enemy than is
requisite to square accounts is very unwise, for when
peace is made the balance of blood must be accounted
for either in lives or money The humanest side of
Bedouin war is the respect paid to women and children,
who are never harmed , yet the women are very bold,
and are the first to stir on the men to battle. In the
campaign, and even in the heat of a fight, the women
follow their husbands or brothers, carrying water to
the combatants, urging on laggards, and striking their
cymbals over a victory

The blood revenge which tends to check fatalities in
warfare makes it more difficult to effect a lasting peace.
The Shereef in his sphere may often compel combatants
to adjust their differences and accept blood-money, but
often also scores remain open and give rise to constantly
renewed acts of violence One of the most remarkable
consequences of the standing feuds which divide so many
tribes is the restriction of exogamy, for a man will not
readily marry into a tribe if there is blood between it
and his own

I mentioned above that in Medina the blood revenge
is practised openly, and that the slayer does not need to
flee. In this city the Turkish law has even less force
than in Jeddah and Mecca, and it is generally reputed
that justice is all the better administered in consequence.
I was told a characteristic story about the Turkish

administrators there which may be repeated here   A
new Cady and Muhâfiz with their company had arrived
from Constantinople.   The great men of the town laid
their heads together and resolved that, as the Turks
came only to feed on them, it would be wise to show them
the cold shoulder, settle all disputes by arbitration
among themselves, and abstain from calling regularly,
as is the custom, on the new dignitaries.   The Turks soon
found themselves isolated   Day by day they took their
seats and expected visitors, but no one came   At length
they took counsel, and a shrewd man among their followers
said—" Make a great feast and invite all the notables of
the town, but first let me go to the bazaar and buy some
spoons to cost a dollar each."   " How absurd," they
replied, " you can have very good spoons for two or three
piastres."   " Ah, yes," was the reply, " but I want long
spoons with great handles, and I wish the guests to sit
so close that with these long spoons they cannot possibly
feed themselves."   The plan was carried out, the notables
arrived and were set down round the dinner tray.   " But
how can we reach our mouths with long ladles like
these ? "   " Oh no," replied the hosts, " you are not to
feed yourself   Do you," pointing to a man on the
other side, " feed me, and I will feed you."   The hint
was taken, cases again flowed into the Turkish court,
and in the division of the spoils the native notables
were not forgotten.

I spoke in my last letter of differences that are observ-
able in marriage customs, and generally in the place of
women, between the Hejâz and Yemen.   In travelling
between Jeddah and Suez, I obtained some additional
particulars on this head from the Wâly of Yemen, who
was my fellow-passenger   Mustafa Pasha is a very
superior type of the official Turk—a man of good education and observant habits, who has served in Syria as
well as in Yemen, and appears to have made a careful
study of the habits of the people over whom he rules

I learned from him that the Bedouins of Yemen have various traditional usages which they know to be inconsistent with Mohammedan orthodoxy, and are therefore careful to conceal from the Turks. But there is one custom among the 'Aseer which, shocking as it appears to outsiders, is openly avowed and defended from the Koran. The 'Aseer Arabs are accustomed to contract marriages of a temporary character by verbal agreement. The so-called marriage may endure but a day. It is, in fact, no more than a nominal contract to avoid the name of immorality With this it naturally goes that no weight is laid on the chastity of unmarried women. A man who contracts such a temporary marriage as I have described may already have a regular wife In that case, he visits the new wife in her own home instead of bringing her to the house where a mistress is already installed The Wâly tells me further that not only in Yemen, but among some of the tribes of the Syrian desert, the wife claims the right to leave her husband at will and take another spouse, and also that it is a recognised practice for husbands among some of the latter tribes—he specially named the 'Aneze—for husbands to make an exchange of wives. All these are obvious remains of early polyandria, and confirm the observation that the introduction of Islam was marked by great social reforms, of which we know but little, but which, in all probability, were at least as momentous as the innovations in religion which are generally regarded as forming the essence of Mohammedanism. I find, on turning up the traditions of the Prophet in Bokhary and Mowatta, that the system of temporary marriages which still lingers among the 'Aseer was well known in Mohammed's time, and abolished by him after considerable hesitation. There seems to have been a good deal of discussion on the subject even after the Prophet's death, as at one time he had conceded the practice to his followers.

Among the more savage tribes, as we now see, the reform on which Mohammed ultimately decided has never been carried through. It is, indeed, impossible to say how many relics of an earlier social system still linger in remote parts of the country. I have even been told by a Swiss resident in Baghdad, who has the reputation of a singular knowledge of that district, that marriages with a stepmother, according to the old Arabic levirate system, abolished by the Koran, have not unfrequently come under his notice.

I take this opportunity to modify a statement in my third letter. The annual deficit in the revenue of the Hejâz was estimated to me in Jeddah by an Arab official, in a position to have accurate information, at £200,000 per annum. But the Wâly of Yemen, who is more likely to give an unvarnished statement, puts the sum at fifteen million piastres, or barely £100,000, a year, two-thirds of which are defrayed from the surplus revenue of Yemen I may also add that Mustafa Pasha gives a favourable account of the Yâm, who received such a character for ferocity from Mohsin. They lie between Yemen and the 'Aseer, and though only four or five thousand strong, are formidable from their organisation and discipline, in which they much excel their neighbours. They have also a very just government At present they are at peace with the Turks, having sustained defeats, which were followed by a treaty exempting them from Turkish taxes and interference. The Bedouins, indeed, can never face the Turks in regular war ; but the latter are in like manner unable to maintain permanent control over the vanquished.

XI. Slavery and the Slave Trade in the Hejâz

I shall occupy this letter with some remarks on slavery in the Hejâz There are two points to be distinguished in speaking on this topic—the question of the slave trade and the question of slavery as an element in the constitution of Arabian society. Of slavery in the East, if it could be separated from the evils connected with the importation of negroes and Abyssinians, one might say a good deal that is favourable. From a material point of view, the slave in an Arab's house has seldom much to complain of. A domestic slave is not overworked, and in general he is well fed, and stands on wonderfully easy terms with the family. If his master has no children, he is often regarded almost as a son of the house ; and the people say that even a father will let his son hunger rather than his slave. Certainly, I have observed that an Arab father is quite as exacting towards his own children as towards his mamlooks. Moreover, the habits of the country do not attach to slavery any brand of humiliating inferiority. No one despises the slave because he is not free, and he does not feel his own position to be degrading. At Tâif, the slave boy used to sit down in the ante-room every evening and play dominoes on terms of perfect equality with 'Aly and my guards A slave in a good family is generally liberated after no very prolonged bondage, or, at any rate, upon his master's death When freed, he expects some little help to establish himself in life, for an unskilled labourer hardly is a gainer by becoming his own master. Freedmen generally continue on terms of affectionate dependence on the family they have served, and I have mentioned in a former letter how the Mawâleed, or descendants of freedmen, form a sort of *clientèle* round the houses of the great. Freedman and Mawâleed are often able to establish a good position. Many wealthy merchants in Jeddah are of such descent, and the favourite freedman of a great man is always a person of consideration. Al Mâs, for example, who was a slave, with many of the faults of a servile origin, received much more respect wherever he went than Mohsin, the pure Arab of good stock. I observed, too, that the Mawâleed who were

with me, Hâmid and 'Abderrabbu, were fond of calling
themselves slaves of the Shereef.   The title was one of
honour, not of contempt.   These conditions neutralise,
or at least modify, some of the most serious moral
objections to slavery.   The slave is not without self-
respect, and he is not without prospects of bettering
himself in life sufficient to stimulate him to exertion
and good conduct.   But, of course, there are many
exceptions to the favourable conditions I have described.
Slaves employed in field work or as boatmen—and these
form a large class—are less favourably situated.   Though
a slave is generally well treated, he is not always so, and
the means of redress which exist in theory are not always
effectual in practice.   The worst masters are the Bedouins.
I have seen a slave boy starving in the streets of Jeddah,
who had been brought into town by his Bedouin master
and deserted.   He was brought in by the police to 'omar
Naseef Pasha, and an order was given to feed him at the
charge of his master   The most notoriously cruel masters
are the pearl fishers, who keep slaves to dive for them,
and treat them with great harshness   However, apart
from the question of direct maltreatment, more serious
objections to the slave system remain behind.   The best
that can be said for the system is that, under favourable
conditions, the slave is treated very much as a child,
and that the temperament of the Arabs, habitually easy
and humane, except when fired by cupidity or revenge,
renders favourable conditions frequent.   But when one
looks upon the slave in the relations of a full-grown man,
and especially when female slavery is taken into account,
the position appears much less satisfactory.   A slave
can marry, or rather his master can make a match for
him, and cannot dissolve the tie   But as a matter of
fact, slaves seldom are married, though it is not uncommon
for a master to free his mamlook and find him a wife.
The great blot of the system lies in female slavery, with
its accompaniment of concubinage, which in the towns

is carried to a great extent, but is much less common up
the country   When the master acknowledges the infant
of a female slave, he can no longer sell her out of his
house, and it is a becoming thing in him to liberate her
and make her his wife.   But the law does not force him
to acknowledge his offspring, and cases have occurred
in Jeddah of late years where a man has exposed both
woman and child for sale.   Some of the Bedouin tribes
regularly breed slaves, but in justice it must be said that
this is not a common custom   It is needless to trace all
the social disorders, all the disturbances of family relations, which flow from this system   They have been
often pointed out, and I simply say with every emphasis
that current apologies for polygamy are inconsistent
with fact, and that in the towns, where female slavery,
concubinage, and the hareem system are fully developed,
the results on the moral and physical condition of the
people are deplorable.   Of the wastefulness of the slave
system, which necessarily encourages indolence both in
the master and his mamlook, I need not speak at large ;
but it is perhaps worth noting that persons who have
been wont to be served by slaves generally get on very
badly with hired servants.   A master and his slave
have a quarrel, but unless the latter runs off, and claims
the protection of a British gunboat, the quarrel is soon
got over, and things settle down in their old course.
But a hired servant is off at once when he has a difficulty
with his employer, and the constant changes of servants
which take place under masters who do not understand
how to manage a free servant form a chief reason why
Arabs and Egyptians are so unwilling to see the abolition
of domestic slavery.

Of the local slave trade as distinguished from contra-
band importation, I have little to say. In Jeddah,
where the eyes of European Consuls are open to what
goes on, there is no public slave mart, though there was
one some four years ago.   There are, however, various

houses in town where it is known that slaves can be
purchased, and many shopkeepers, especially those
from Hadhramaut, have a black boy sitting by them
on the mastaba of the shop, who is apparently an assistant,
but really is there to be sold. In Mecca of course, the
slave mart is much opener , and in Medina, I am told
that one often sees a boy led by the hand through the
street by one of those peripatetic auctioneers who are
always to be found in Arabian bazaars.

A great question has been raised as to the ultimate
effect on the old Arab stock of constant intermixture
with African blood, and observers who have noted this
intermixture in the Tehâma and the cities have gone so
far as to maintain that the Arabian race must ultimately
be absorbed in the inexhaustible population of Africa.
I am disposed to think that this is a false prediction.
The negro importation has gone on for so many centuries
that the limits of its influence ought to be already pretty
well defined. In the towns the blood is very mixed.
Of the natives of Jeddah comparatively few are of pure
blood. In the villages of the Tehâma, in like manner,
there are many half-castes, and the population of the
coast north and south of Jeddah has lost all claim to
rank as genuinely Arabian.   But the Qabâil or tribesmen,
the true Bedouins up the country, do not intermarry
with Africans, and their stock is still so pure that, as the
people say, the tribal blood is seen in their countenances.
Now, in spite of immigration and importation, there is
no reason to think that the population of the Hejâz is
increasing. If a town like Jeddah grows, it does so only
by foreign merchants—Syrians, Indians, and so forth—
settling for purposes of trade. I apprehend that in
Arabia, as in Egypt, the town population, apart from
immigration from the inland tribes or from abroad,
would rather diminish than increase. It can hardly be
otherwise from the unhealthy conditions in which women
live, from the careless and unhealthy way in which children

are brought up, and from the prevalence of immorality and other effects of polygamy that tend to sap the strength of a race. Now, what follows from this ? That those parts of the country where intermarriage with Africans prevails are not in a position to expand in population, and swamp the true Arabs of the uplands. Among the debased populations of the coast, and also in the blood of great families, and generally among the wealthy and luxurious, the African element is considerable, and one is startled at first sight by such a fact as that the High Shereef of Mecca is as black as a pure negro. But it is precisely the wealthy and luxurious stocks that are checked in their natural increase by unhealthy physical and moral conditions of life, while the Bedouins multiply at least fast enough to maintain their own place, and send off a certain number of emigrants to the towns to balance the negro immigration The suppression of the slave trade, whenever that is effected, must cause serious changes in the constitution of the urban populations of Arabia, and the problems of redistribution which must then arise will be of the greatest interest to students of human society. I venture to predict that one result will be the very rapid disappearance of many of the corrupt and exhausted stocks which at present hold wealth and influence in Jeddah and Mecca. On the other hand, if Arabian society has sufficient elasticity to adapt itself to new conditions the ultimate consequences cannot be otherwise than most advantageous, for without slavery polygamy, and the evils that flow from polygamy, can hardly exist. Yet the abolition of polygamy, without a change in the law of divorce, will not suffice to place family relations on a sound basis , for at present many of those who are not able to indulge in a plurality of wives—which often involves the maintenance of separate establishments—at least gratify their changing passions by divorces as frequent as those of Rome under the Empire, with fatal effects on the education of their children

I pass now to speak of the slave trade. It appears clear that the destruction of the trade would soon put an end to slavery. For, partly from frequent manumissions, which are favoured by custom and religion, partly from the small number of slave marriages, home-born slaves are few   But for this very reason, as long as slavery is a prevalent institution, the means of importing boys and girls will be sought and probably found. The Red Sea is narrow, and many parts of the coasts are very dangerous to cruisers, which can hardly thread their way through the reefs, behind which the swift native boats engaged in the trade know many convenient points at which to collect or land slaves. The British cruisers certainly inspire some terror, and occasionally, though very rarely, effect a capture ; but up to the present time, not having enjoyed the right of search in boats bearing the Turkish flag in Turkish waters, they have had to contend with difficulties which in such seas are almost insuperable. Under the new treaty it is to be hoped that the action of our cruisers will be much more efficacious, especially in checking the present system by which slaves are landed in Yemen—at Hodeida, for example, where there is no Consul to keep an eye on the trade—and sent up in small numbers by coasting boats to the Hejâz market. Still it can hardly be hoped that foreign cruisers will succeed in putting down the trade until the Egyptian and Turkish Governments are in earnest to make an end of the traffic. Are they so now ? In Egypt there has until now been one man who was in earnest—Colonel Gordon. To his efforts, much more than to any other cause or all other causes put together, must mainly be ascribed the decline which has recently taken place in the exportation of slaves from the African coast   But Colonel Gordon is no longer ruler of the Soudan, and it would be sanguine to hope for much from his native successor, though it is so far well that the coasting police is to be re-established. That Egyptian

38

officials in general are disposed to wink at the trade is beyond doubt. Even on the Nile slaves have never ceased to be sent down from the upper country, and the existence of a slave mart at Cairo is an open secret. What, then, can be looked for in the Red Sea, where every Turkish and Arabian official is interested in the maintenance of the trade ?   I believe that only last week slaves were brought over to Jeddah in the Egyptian steamer from Sawâkin.   The risk of conveyance by native *bagala* is now so appreciable that five dollars a head is the charge for carrying slaves.   The steamer takes passengers for three dollars, and the difference allows a handsome baksheesh to be paid to some Egyptian official for a passport declaring boys and girls to be passengers who are really slaves.   This is one way in which the traffic is kept up, but the *bagalas* still run. The English Consul at Jeddah gives it as his belief that no slaves have been landed at Jeddah for a good many months.   But this only means that the people do not choose that he should know what is going on , and, in fact, the affair of the *Ready* was settled in a way that has done mischief, encouraged the slave-trading Arabs, and disheartened the officers of Her Majesty's cruisers.   A boat from the *Ready* in the early part of December 1878 pursued a suspicious native vessel which, apparently from ignorance of the rights of men-of-war, refused to stop when summoned.   The British boat fired, and a slave was killed.   There was a great uproar, and the town of Jeddah was threatened by the Arabs.   Ultimately our Government arranged the matter by a payment of £550 as blood-money.   The affair was an unfortunate one, and it may have been prudent to make some payment, but certainly the sum was exorbitant ; for between Arabs and Arabs the full blood-money for a freeman does not exceed $800, or £150.   And no advantage was taken of the incident to explain that the money was paid *ex gratia*, and acquaint the natives with the unquestioned

right under international law which the *Ready's* boat
exercised in calling on the native boat to stop. As to
the matter of fact that slaves are still landed in Jeddah,
I may mention that within the last few days several
bills of sale were brought to the Dutch Consul   And it
is only the other day that the head of the Jeddah boatmen was summoned to Mecca to answer a charge of
slave-trading   Some time ago a boat belonging to this
man was seized as a slaver by the authorities of Sawâkin,
and confiscated. He asserted that it was not a slaver,
and put in before the Turkish authorities of Jeddah a
claim to have it back, and also to receive blood-money
for one of his men whom he declared to have been killed
in the affray when the boat was captured. The Qaim
Maqâm at first refused to interfere, but having received
a bribe of fifty dollars, he consented to take up the case
and put in a claim on the Egyptian authorities. Unluckily
for his client, the latter had another boat lying near
Sawâkin, and the captain and another man got drunk
in the town. The captain let out the secret that he was
engaged in the slave traffic, and the other admitted that
he was the person supposed to have been shot, for whom
blood-money was claimed. This was too much. The
Egyptians made a formal complaint to the Hejâz
authorities, who must now take the matter up. But I
fancy that it will not end very seriously for the culprit ,
indeed, if he is a clever man, he ought to be able, after
the fashion of the country, to make the affair turn to
his advantage. In this case, it will be observed that
the Turkish Governor of Jeddah is compromised. That
he received a bribe is certain. An English gentleman
of my acquaintance learned the fact from the lips of the
man who paid the money   Nor is it at all surprising
that Turkish officials should be interested, directly or
indirectly, in the slave trade. A case in point occurred
the other day at Hodeida, where the quarantine doctor
vainly reported a slave-boat, the chief of the police being

himself owner, or part owner.   The higher officials sometimes make a show of zeal.   The recently appointed
Wâly of the Hejâz, among several minor improvements
with which he thought proper to signalise his arrival,
directed one or two guard-houses to be built along the
coast to prevent slave traffic, but, as a matter of course,
no practical result has flowed from this step.   The Wâly's
zeal could not in the course of nature last more than a
month or two ; and the new functionary is now entirely
absorbed in schemes to fill his pocket, especially by mani-
pulation of the grain supplies sent from the Persian Gulf
to feed the Bedouins.   But it is no use to grumble at the
Turks.   So long as slavery is legal, the slave trade must
be winked at.   The radical cure is to abolish slavery
itself.   Meantime, it is worthy of notice that the illegal
traffic is said to be gravitating towards Hodeida, where
there is less risk of European interference, and from
which, as I have already observed, small parties of slaves
are forwarded by coasters without suspicion.

There is yet another secret in the slave traffic which
ought to stir our nation to the promptest and most decided
action.   A regular business is done by scoundrels who
kidnap little boys and girls from our Indian possessions,
and bring them to Mecca—generally under cover of
business connected with pilgrimage—where they are
sold as slaves.   Cases of this sort have repeatedly been
brought to light by boys who have escaped to Jeddah
One such discovery took place this winter (1881).   A boy
from Hyderabad escaped and reported to the Consul at
Jeddah that his sister was still in bondage.   The Consular
dragoman, a Jew, who has adopted Islam, and can therefore visit Mecca, was sent up ; but he reported that the
girl had been married and was content.   The case was
accordingly dropped, but the fact that one victim is
reported content with her fate does not make the traffic
less infamous.   The energetic and able Dutch Consul
has followed out the line of inquiry suggested by these

circumstances, and assures me that Singapore is the point through which the kidnappers work. Both Indians and Malays are kidnapped. They are brought off on various pretexts, and find themselves slaves only when they reach Mecca. Mr. Kruyt argues very justly that such doings afford a strong argument for allowing no emissary from the Hejâz to appear in English and Dutch ports without a Consular passport. It is well to respect the religious freedom of Moslems ; but it is too much to suffer this freedom to be used as a cloak for crime.

VI

REVIEWS OF BOOKS

I

WELLHAUSEN's *Geschichte Israëls*, vol. 1, from *The Academy*, May 17, 1879.

THOSE who have followed the course of Prof. Wellhausen will be prepared to recognise this important work as the fitting sequel of his earlier labours. Even when they have taken the shape of studies in textual or higher criticism all his writings have been contributions to the study of the history of Israel, and the vigour and originality of his critical analysis are mainly due to a keen perception of historical reality Hence his work is marked by a largeness of view and firmness of grasp unhappily not very common in recent German criticism. In these qualities, as well as in the essentially constructive habit of thought which appears even in his most ruthless attacks or traditional views and current speculation, Wellhausen may be called the truest living disciple of Ewald (to whose memory the volume before us is appropriately dedicated), in spite of the enormous divergence between master and scholar in their conception of the course of the Old Testament development.

This divergence turns mainly on a question which Wellhausen formulates in the first paragraph of his work —" *Is the Mosaic law the starting-point for the history of ancient Israel, or for the history of Judaism— i.e. of the sect which survived the annihilation of the nation by the Assyrians and Chaldeans ?* "

The discussion of this fundamental problem, which is

decided in favour of the second alternative, occupies the
volume now before us, filling as large a space as the author
proposes to devote in his second volume to the whole
narrative of Israel's history.   And this is not unreasonable ; for the solution of the problem in the comprehensive form in which Wellhausen presents it to his
readers involves inquiries which practically exhaust two
of the most important topics of Old Testament history.
The key to the problem of the Mosaic law lies (1) in the
history of religious observances ; (2) in the history of
the spoken or written tradition current in Israel as to
the past ages of the nation   The investigation of these
topics fills the two largest sections of the volume.   The
results are resumed, and outlying objections are met in
a third section on " Israel and Judaism," which closes
with some general considerations preparing the way for
the second volume, and indicating the bearing of our
author's historical criticism on Biblical theology.

I suppose that one must adopt the current expression,
and say that Wellhausen is a follower of the Grafian
hypothesis.   But his argument owes very little to Graf,
more to Kuenen,—whom he happily names " Graf's
Goel "—most of all to Vatke, whose book is, in Wellhausen's judgment, " the most important contribution
ever made to the history of ancient Israel," and who
appears to be almost the only scholar except Ewald who
has given our author ideas as well as information   But
Wellhausen's argument is much more telling than Vatke's,
because it rests on a thorough critical analysis of the
sources of the Pentateuch and historical books of the
Old Testament.   From this point of view the present
volume may be regarded as the historical and synthetic
complement of the analyses of the Hexateuch in the
Jahrbücher für deutsche Theologie of 1876 and 1877, and
the not less important analysis of the *prophetae priores* in
the fourth edition of Bleek's *Einleitung*

The first section of the work investigates the history

of the sanctuary, the sacrifices, the feasts, the priesthood, and the provision for the support of the clergy. Under each head an historical development is traced, beginning with observances of spontaneous and natural character, and advancing by stages corresponding to the development of the law from the Jehovistic ordinances of the Book of the Covenant through Deuteronomy to the priestly code. That this is the historical order of progress appears to be indisputable, and the main lines of evidence are not new. But Wellhausen has strengthened them by many subtle and original observations, and has greatly increased the cumulative force of the argument by showing that it is possible to work the scattered data into a consistent and intelligible historical picture more complete than anything that has been hitherto attempted. Of course such a picture must contain problematic elements. Among these must be placed what is, nevertheless, one of the most interesting things in the volume—the account of the tribe of Levi. According to our author the ancient tribe of Levi wholly disappeared during the period of the Judges under circumstances to which Gen. xlix. compared with Gen. xxxiv. supplies our only key. The later sacred tribe of Levi is an entirely new formation, which may have derived its name from the family of Moses, but cannot be regarded as connected with him by blood, inasmuch as the notion of a properly hereditary priesthood was only developed in the period of the later kings of Judah It is impossible to reproduce the whole argument, but it involves among other points the following positions (1) That Zadok had no hereditary title to priesthood—or, in other words, was not a Levite by birth ; (2) that Jonathan (Judges xvii. 7) was of Judean extraction, (3) that, according to Deut. xxxiii. 8, 9, the Levites of the northern kingdom appear as a guild based on the denial of all ties of blood, who honour Moses, not as their ancestor, but only as the founder of their profession. The first and second of these assumptions involve doubtful

questions of textual criticism   Is it certain that 2 Sam.
xv. 24 is so corrupt that no value can be put on the
association of Zadok with the Levites ?   And, on the
other hand, does not Judges xvii. 7 show marks of a later
hand in the words " of the family of Judah," which, if
taken as indicating the descent of Jonathan, are inconsistent with the statement that he was a mere *Ger* in
Bethlehem ?   The tendency to conceal the true Levitic
descent of a schismatical priest, which appears in the
Massoretic text of xviii. 30, was also at work in xvii 7
The Peshita, which has not the words ממשפהת יהודה,
effects the same end by changing " he was a Levite "
into " his name was Levi "   The exegesis proposed for
Deut. xxxiii 9 is very striking in comparison with
I Kings xii. 31 ; but Wellhausen himself indicates its
weak point when he says that it could only be in extreme
cases that a man left his wife and children to become a
priest.   A guild of priests in which the son did not, as
a rule, follow his father's profession is incredible under
the social conditions of ancient Israel, and we know that
the priesthood at Dan was hereditary in a Levitic family.

The problem of the Levites cannot be solved without
going back to the time of Moses.   Wellhausen admits it
to be possible that the priesthood was hereditary in the
descendants of Moses.   Now, the priesthood of Moses,
if it is admitted in any sense at all, must be regarded
as of national significance, and implies the existence of
some sacred ordinance or sanctuary of more than tribal
importance.   The ark answers to this condition , and,
as a matter of fact, the sanctuary of the ark has a more
than local importance in the oldest records of the history
of the Judges.   Why, then, should it be doubted that
in connection with the ark the priestly prerogative of Levi
goes back to Mosaic times?   Wellhausen objects that
there was no considerable number of priestly places open
to Levites in the time of the Judges.   But that is not
so clear.   The chief function of the priests was to give

oracles ; and oracles in such a state of society must have
been in great demand. The technical knowledge required for this function could only be propagated in a
guild which, though it might adopt outsiders like Samuel,
would for obvious motives be mainly hereditary. And of
course the best priests would be those who had their
skill by direct succession from Moses. When Micah had
a Levite to work his oracle, he was confident that Jahvé
would give a favourable response

One of the most effective arguments in the book is
directed against the peculiar theory of Noldeke that a
priestly movement for unity of the sanctuary preceded
the prophetic movement which culminated in the law of
Deuteronomy. But is not the argument unnecessarily
encumbered by the thesis that Isaiah shows no hostility
to the high places, provided they are purified of images
(Isa. xxx. 22), and that Hezekiah's abolition of the high
places is presumably unhistorical ? Can it be supposed
that in the case of the local sanctuaries there would be
any practical difference between purification and total
abolition ? Isaiah condemns the whole worship of his
contemporaries in Jerusalem and out of it ; it is all
loathsome to Jahvé. But Jerusalem has a permanent
significance in Isaiah's eyes as the local seat of God's
kingship. It is true, as Wellhausen observes, that this
distinction does not belong to the temple so much as to
the city. But Isaiah himself recognises in the clearest
way that the presence of Jahvé makes Jerusalem a seat
of worship, the hearth of God, the place of solemn and
festal assembly (iv 5 ; xxxii. 20). In these respects it
is an absolute contrast to the Bamoth whose significance
is merely superstitious and based on will-worship (i. 29 ,
xvii. 8 ; *cf.* Micah v. 13), and which in virtue of the
idols are not sanctuaries of Jahvé at all (xxxi 6, 7)
Certainly there is nothing in this teaching to cast doubt
on the record that Hezekiah, who purified the temple,
sought to put down the high places And without such

action by Hezekiah the book of Deuteronomy would be unintelligible. The task of remodelling the whole religious life of the nation to fit in with the abolition of local altars could hardly be undertaken in such detail until the problem to which Deuteronomy is addressed had emerged in a practical form.

Space forbids me to dwell on other topics in the history of *cultus*. I may direct special notice to the discussions on the use of incense, on the offering of the first-born, and on the notion of atonement, and to several excellent incidental contributions to exegesis and text criticism. But why is Wellhausen so sceptical as to the sense *obliterare* for *kapper* (Isa. xxviii. 18) ? In the Harklean Syriac *kapper* = ἐκμάσσειν, John xi. 2, xii. 3, xiii. 5. See also Syro-hex *Ep. Jer.* 13, 24 ; and Hoffman's *Bar Ali*, 5924

The second part of the volume is a critical history of the Pentateuch and historical books directed to show that the successive phases of historical tradition in Israel run parallel to the successive developments of the sacred ordinances. The latest phase is found in the Chronicles, and is thoroughly saturated with the unhistorical spirit of the priestly legislation   The main source used by the author was a Midrash (in the ordinary Jewish sense of the word) based on the canonical book of Kings. The older books are complex in structure. The final redaction is akin to Deuteronomy, is prior to the priestly law and based on the teaching of the great prophets. Behind the redaction are older elements prior to the recognition of any written Torah. Nay, as we go down to the earliest strata of the narrative, we get beyond the influence even of the prophetic ideas, and find ourselves in contact with a *naive* habit of thought such as the earliest religious ordinances of Israel presuppose. The only part of the narrative of the earlier prophets which shows any influence of the priestly law is 1 Kings vi.-viii., where interpolations and corrections can be traced.

Perhaps Wellhausen has exaggerated the extent of

these. At any rate the absence of any description of
Solomon's altar may be explained by the circumstance
that at the close of the period of the kings that altar had
disappeared. (Compare 2 Kings xvi. and xxv.) Finally,
our author comes to the Pentateuch, and addresses himself
to the proof that the narrative of the priestly code is not
such as to raise objections against the late date assigned
to the document. It will be difficult to meet his argument on this head, though Wellhausen himself does not
expect that many will join him in the view that the
priestly narrative is wholly based on the Jehovistic
story—that is, on the works of the Jehovist and the
Elohist as combined together by a later editor. From
our author's point of view the separation between the
Jehovist and the Elohist acquires a special interest He
regards the Elohist as the younger author, but does not
go into full detail on the subject.

The section on Israel and Judaism, which embraces
discussions on the language of the priestly laws, the final
redaction of the Hexateuch, the oral and written law,
the decalogue, and the idea and institution of the theocracy, must be passed over. In closing, I turn back for a
moment to suggest that the change of attitude towards
the Sabbath which Wellhausen observes in the priestly
code, where the day of rest becomes rather a sacrifice of
abstinence than a provision of humanity, may be connected with Babylonian influences. The Sabbath of
Assyria and Babylon is a day on which it is unlucky to
work—a conception entirely opposed to the original
Hebrew association of Sabbath and feast-day.

II

Histoire du Peuple d'Israel. Par ERNEST RENAN   Tome I
(Paris . Calmann Lévy   1887)

THE first volume of M Renan's new work carries down the
history of Israel to the establishment of Jerusalem as the
capital of King David.   Two more volumes are written,
though they still await the author's final touches ; these
will continue the narrative " to the epoch of Ezra, that is,
up to the definitive establishment of Judaism "   To these
volumes, for the revision of which he allows himself two
years, M. Renan hopes to add a fourth, upon the period of
the Hasmoneans ; but to this part of his plan he attaches
less importance, believing that the fourth volume will be
comparatively easy to write, and that in case of necessity
a translation of one of the many German books on the
subject would suffice to stop the gap   It is somewhat
difficult to understand how M. Renan, who is fully possessed
by the idea that the whole significance of the history of
Israel lies in the sphere of religion, comes to hold that
the period subsequent to the work of Ezra has been already
so satisfactorily elucidated that (as he puts it) " one may
almost say that there are not two ways " of writing about
it.   It would seem that he attaches little importance
to the obscure tract of two and a half centuries which
separates Ezra from the Maccabee revolt, and no doubt
as regards the political record that period is almost an
absolute blank.   But for the history of religion these
centuries are of the highest importance.   It was during
them that the religious and social life of Israel re-shaped
itself in accordance with the institutions of Ezra.   The
legal establishment of Judaism was completed by Ezra
and Nehemiah ; but the establishment of the law in the
hearts of the people was another matter.   No one who
passes from the memoirs of Nehemiah to the first book

of Maccabees can fail to perceive that in the interval
enormous changes had taken place in the type of national
life and national religion.   The problem which this observation suggests has never been thoroughly worked out ;
but materials for its solution are not lacking, and the
Psalter in particular, of which a great part must be assigned
to the latter part of the Persian period and the first generations of the Greek empire, supplies the basis for a research
not inferior in interest and importance to anything that
remains to be done for the earlier ages of the sacred history.

As regards this first volume, the author gives us fair
warning that we are to look not so much for a history as
for a half-imaginative reconstruction of the general
movement of society and religion in those dark ages that
preceded the historical period of Israel's life.   In the
history of Israel there are, we are told, no certain material
facts before David ; the sources for everything prior to his
time resolve themselves into " epical tradition."   In such
stories it is vain to ask what happened ; our business is
to picture to ourselves the various ways in which things
may have happened.   *En pareil cas toute phrase doit être
accompagnée d'un peut-être.*   Or, again : *Comme pour la
" Vie de Jésus," je réclame pour le présent volume, consacré
à des temps forts obscurs, un peu de l'indulgence qu'on a
coutume d'accorder aux voyants, et dont les voyants ont
besoin.   Même, quand j'aurais mal conjecturé sur quelques
points, je suis sûr d'avoir bien compris dans son ensemble
l'œuvre unique que le Souffle de Dieu, c'est-à-dire l'âme du
monde, a réalisée par Israel.*   These words sufficiently
characterise the difference between M Renan's method
and that of the critical historians of Germany and Holland.
It would be unfair to say that M. Renan makes no
use of the critical analysis of Hebrew texts, or that a
writer like Wellhausen is devoid of historical imagination.
But in the German school the historical imagination is
held under control, and laborious analysis and evaluation
of the sources govern the whole construction of the history.

39

In the present volume the analytical process is not only kept quite in the background, but has really very little influence on the author's conclusions The faculty of imagination, or, as M. Renan prefers to say, of divination, rules supreme, and controls the use made of critical results.

It would not be fair to pronounce a final judgment on M. Renan's work from the fragment now before us, but hitherto the auspices are far from favourable. He tells us himself that nothing in the history of Israel is explicable without the patriarchal age, and it is plain, even at this stage, that his reconstruction of the patriarchal age is altogether wrong, and must equally be wrong whether the Pentateuchal narrative is historical or legendary. On the former supposition *cadit quaestio* , it would be idle to ask whether M. Renan's view of the history can be reconciled with a literal adhesion to tradition. His position is that the patriarchs never existed, but that Genesis and the book of Job depict with a certain amount of idealisation a life which did exist in the patriarchal age Abraham is not an historical character, in truth he was borrowed by the imagination of the Hebrew nomad from the figure of an ancient king of Ur, which they had opportunities of seeing on Babylonian cylinders.[1] But the colour of the stories of Genesis is true , they represent the life of the nomadic Semites as it really was, as it still is among the Arabian Bedouins, or as it is described in the legends of the Arabs before Mohammed, especially in the " Kitāb al-Aghānī," to which M Renan makes constant references, but always—and very prudently—without descending to particulars. A generation ago it was fashionable to call Abraham an Arab sheikh · M Renan is content to say that he is the type of an Arab sheikh , but in point of fact

---

[1] By a prodigious feat of philological audacity, M Renan conjectures that Abraham means " father Orham," the letters *he* and *heth* being confounded in the most ancient Semitic But this act of prowess, which few will venture to imitate, is unhappily thrown away The Babylonian word may be read Uruk, or Amilapsi, or Urbagas, or Likbagas, or no one knows how.

it would be difficult to specify a single feature of resemblance between the patriarchal life, as described in Genesis, and the life of the modern Bedouin, which is not either superficial or part of the general difference between eastern and western society. And, on the other hand, the points of difference between the life of the patriarchs and the ordinary life of a nomad group are many and fundamental   On this question an appeal may confidently be taken to every one who either knows the modern Bedouin or has made any serious study of the " Aghānī " and other documents of Arabian life before Islam.   But, indeed, it is enough to appeal to the Bible itself.   The Hebrews knew the wild men of the desert, and the patriarchal history draws their type in the person of Ishmael.   The author who drew this figure was certainly not of M. Renan's mind as to the identity of the patriarchal and the nomadic life.   The picture of the patriarchal age is an ideal picture, but it is not idealised from the life of the Semitic nomads, whose hand was against every man and every man's hand against them.   If we accept the picture presented in Genesis literally, it displays a miraculous life.   And the miracles in the history of the patriarchs are not mere garnishing which can be stripped off and still leave the image of a real state of society.   That Abraham, Isaac, and Jacob could roam at large through Palestine without fear and without war, though they were aliens from their own kin, and had not become the protected dependants of another kin, is a standing miracle, and on this miracle everything else in the history of Genesis depends.   If the supernatural explanation is given up, the whole notion of a patriarchal age falls to the ground ; we must then assume with the Dutch and German critics that the picture in Genesis is idealised, in a way quite unhistorical, from the conditions of Hebrew life in the ninth and tenth centuries B.C., when the nomadic past of Israel already lay hid in the mists of antiquity, and we must hold that the actual condition of the Hebrews in the nomadic age was of the far ruder and wilder type to which all other evidence points. In the lives of Abraham, Isaac, and Jacob, as they are depicted in Genesis, the lack of a stable home is a mere incident dependent on the supernatural call to sojourn in a land not their own. In every other respect their life is of a type inconceivable in the true nomad, but precisely similar to that of a great householder in the time of David and his successors. They are not chiefs of tribes but heads of families, and their family life is indistinguishable from that of the earlier ages of the Hebrew kingdom, the only golden time which the prophets know   According to M. Renan's own chronology, the history of the patriarchs was set down in writing in the same age in which the prophets continually speak of the first days of the kingdom as Israel's ideal past. Are we to believe that in spite of this the ideal of the Pentateuch and the ideal of the prophets are two entirely different types of life ?

But, again, with the fall of the theory of a non-supernatural " golden age " of Semitic antiquity (*Préface*, p. 10) falls also the theory of a natural monotheistic tendency of the Semitic race, which is the corner-stone of M Renan's whole construction of the religious development of Israel. The monotheism of the patriarchs in the Book of Genesis is not natural monotheism, and it does not resemble anything which has existed in Semitic lands apart from the influence of Judaism and Christianity   It is vain to appeal to Islam or to the movements in Arabia which preceded Islam, for these are demonstrably dependent on the influence of the synagogue and the church. And everything of monotheistic tendency or of the nature of what is called monolatry which M. Renan adduces in support of his thesis from the phenomena of the older Semitic religions has it parallel among other races   To compare the Semitic tribal religions with the Pan-Hellenic religion of Homer or with the not less secondary religion of the Vedas is to beg the question. When Semitic society ceased to be purely tribal, Semitic religion showed as little tendency to monotheism as the religions of Greece or of India. It was in Israel alone, and solely through the work of the prophets, that Semitic particularism in religion grew into a universal monotheism, or even showed more tendency to grow in that direction than can be observed among other races under similar historical conditions. All this might be illustrated in detail if space permitted, but here a single example must suffice to show how boldly M. Renan bends facts to suit his hypothesis. At p. 40 he maintains that of all ancient peoples known to us the Semites were certainly the least prone to gross practices of sorcery. A very different impression is left by the Bible (*e.g.* Deut. xviii.), by the monuments of Arabian antiquity, by what we know of Harranian heathenism, and by the magical superstitions that long lingered in Christian Syria,[1] or still survive in all parts of the Semitic east. Or if monotheism is an affair of race, by what right is Babylon excluded from the induction, which all antiquity looked on as the chosen home of sorcery and magic arts? To divide Babylon from the nomadic Semites is to change the problem from one of race to one of environment.

The hypothesis of a natural monotheism, even in the attenuated form in which it appears in M. Renan's system, is simply a relic of the unhistorical deism of last century, the only form of liberal thought which appears to be easily grafted on a strict Roman Catholic education. The same influence appears in other parts of the volume, both in small matters—as when M. Renan inclines to explain the miracles of the wilderness wanderings as pious frauds, or when he sneers at David for his habit of appealing to the oracle of Jehovah—and in things of more moment, particularly in his conception of the national element in Jehovah-worship as a grievous falling away from the simplicity of patriarchal faith. One is curious to know how M. Renan will explain the work of the prophets on the view that the national character of the religion of

---

[1] See especially Lagarde, *Rel. iuris eccles ant* pp. 230 *sqq.*

Israel contributed to the development no elements of positive worth.

The limits of a notice like the present make it impossible to follow M Renan from page to page and judge every part of his construction in its relation to the whole. As regards the material facts of the early history, he is, as we have seen, disposed to reduce to very small compass all that can be certainly known for the time before David   He holds, with most recent inquirers, that the Hebrews originally issued from Arabia by the north-eastern route, and traversed as nomads the pastures bordering on the Euphrates, ascending as far as the region of Harran   Here they came in contact with Babylonian ideas, through the medium of the Aramæans of Mesopotamia, and to this early influence M. Renan ascribes the traditions embodied in the first twelve chapters of Genesis.   From Harran the nomads moved southwards into Canaan, where they found a race speaking the same language and of closely kindred stock, but of very different character, so that no fusion took place between the immigrants and the Canaanites. In the district of Hebron, however, they lived in amity with the Hittite population, whose near relatives were the Hyksos of the Egyptian delta   These " Hittites of Zoan " probably attracted to Egypt a portion of the Hebrew nomads (the tribe of Joseph), and these were afterwards joined by other bands. As regards the residence in Goshen only one thing is certain—Israel entered Egypt under a dynasty favourable to the Semites and left it under a hostile dynasty   The exodus is assigned to the period of decadence that followed the glorious reign of Ramses II., the Louis XIV. of Egypt   All the details, perhaps even the personality of Moses, are uncertain , it is not probable that the Egyptians sought to retain the Hebrews by force   The Hebrews left Egypt with their old religion changed not a little for the worse.   Egypt gave them the golden calf, the brazen serpent, the lying priestly oracle, the Levite " who was the leper of Israel ". all

mischievous things which had to be eliminated in the
future progress of religion.   Moreover, the gentle temper
of the primitive nomad was changed to harshness and
obstinacy by the yoke of oppression ; and the faith in the
special care of Jahvé for Israel, which was developed (not
without the aid of pious fraud) by the experiences of the
wilderness, strengthened national feeling at the expense of
the sublime and true idea of primitive Elohism.   " The
national idea desired a God who thought only of the
nation, and who in the interests of the nation was cruel,
unjust, an enemy of the human race."   The " adoption
of Jahvé seems to have been consummated at the Sinaitic
epoch," but what actually happened at Sinai is obscure
Sinai is a mountain of terror, whose storms were conceived
as awful theophanies   In some such storm the Israelites
believed that Jahvé appeared to them, and they left the
sacred mountain full of terror and persuaded that a very
powerful deity dwelt in its summits.   It is scarcely
probable that the theophany gave occasion to Moses to
put forth any moral precepts.   In truth the *rôle* of Moses
seems to have been " rather that of a chief like Abd-el-
Kader than of a prophet like Mahomet."

All the characteristic features in this outline of the
origins of Israel are more or less arbitrary.   There is
absolutely no evidence that the Babylonian elements in
the traditions of Genesis reached the Hebrews through
the Aramæans of Harran rather than through the Phœnicians ; it is certain that they show no sign of having been
the property of a nomadic race, and there is no probability
that they all date from the same period.   M. Renan does
not regard the first twelve chapters of Genesis as a literary
unity . on this point he accepts the analysis of modern
criticism.   But on purely subjective grounds he refuses to
believe that one of the two main documents is of the same
origin with the Levitical legislation, both forming part of
the document which is denoted by the symbol A.   He
sees that the legislation of A must be postexilic, and he

will not believe that the first chapter of Genesis is later
than the time of Hezekiah   It so happens that the unity
of the document A is the most absolutely fixed point in
criticism ; the date may still be disputed, but critics of
every school are agreed that the separation which M.
Renan desires is altogether impossible.   But this does not
affect the serene confidence with which he maintains his
own view, not bringing any new arguments (though the
thing has been often discussed before in the same form),
but merely waving the Dutch and the Germans aside with
a polite sneer as worthy people who are trammelled by
their narrow Protestant education and have not got
enlarged views of ancient history.[1]   The appeal to the
judgment of personal self-confidence as the standard of
truth is made in the most engaging manner, but the fact
remains that, on a point of capital importance for the
problems of Hebrew history, we have no better evidence
than that M Renan knows himself to be a great deal wiser
than the Germans, and that his impressions are more
valuable than their arguments.   Accordingly we may be
sure that his view about the document A will satisfy no-
body, and with its rejection all his ingenious speculations
about the Hebrews and the Hittites, and a great deal that
he has to say about Israel in the wilderness and about the
conquest of Canaan, simply fall to the ground

Not better founded is the account of the influence of
Egypt on Hebrew religion as regards the Levites and the
oracle of Jahvé.   The oracle in its oldest form is merely
the sacred lot, an institution universal among the Semites
and one of the common possessions of all early faiths.
M. Renan regards the appeal to Jahvé as a dark spot in
the record of Hebrew religion, a corruption of primitive
Elohism, and therefore he gives it a foreign origin   But
can he point to any nation in the stage of the Hebrews
under the judges which had no such way of appealing to
the decision of God ?   Finally, the conception of Moses as

[1] See his articles in the *Revue des Deux Mondes*, March 1886.

a sort of Abd-el-Kader is without all foundation in the texts and is absolutely inconsistent with Semitic analogy. It is brought in (along with an absurd idea that the warlike successes of Israel may have been due to an Egyptian contingent) to account for the military superiority of the Hebrews in their conflict with the Canaanites But the weakness of the nomadic Semites in military enterprises has never been due to want of generalship (witness the abundance of able soldiers that the first generation of Islam produced), but wholly to the want of cohesion between the tribes. And this again is due to tribal pride or vanity, which refuses to acknowledge any human authority except in a tribesman. It has been well shown by Wellhausen that according to the most ancient texts the main function of Moses was to judge between the contending interests of tribes and families by an authority not human but divine, and the same scholar has pointed out that Mohammed was largely indebted for his success to the very cause that gave authority to Moses ; his judgments did not offend family or tribal susceptibility because they were spoken in the name of Allah and therefore involved no humiliation of one kindred before another. This is the true historical use of analogy, for it compares the operation of similar causes in similar circumstances, whereas the analogy of Abd-el-Kader is not only absolutely vague, but ignores that fundamental difference between the Maghrib and the true Semitic lands which forces itself upon the notice of every student of the history of Islam.

In M. Renan's account of the conquest of Canaan and the settlement of the tribes there is little which calls for notice except a certain confusedness of treatment due to a combination of general distrust in the historical tradition with a half-hearted adherence to the document A. One detail, however, may be signalised as showing a somewhat singular misapprehension of the use of historical analogy on which our author piques himself   To illustrate the

relations of the Israelites to their Canaanite neighbours in
the cities that were not conquered, he appeals to the
relations between the Metâwila of Syria and their neighbours of other races " One must see these mixed or
rather double villages, where two populations live side by
side, hating and yet tolerating one another.   Almost all
Turkey presents the same spectacle."   But surely every
one who knows Syria is aware that this state of things
could not be maintained except under the sovereignty
of the Turkish empire   Both parties fear the pasha.
Modern Syria is a good analogy to illustrate the condition
of Palestine under the Achæmenians, but it is no analogy
for the age of the judges, when there was no external power
pressing on Hebrews and Canaanites alike.   At that time,
where Hebrews and Canaanites lived together, the relation
of the two races must have been much more similar to
the relation between Arabs and Jews in Medina before
the Hijra, and this is the conception which all the texts
bear out.

The period of the judges is treated in the volume before
us in a spirit of superficial eclecticism which is somewhat
surprising.   On M. Renan's own view that real definite
history begins with David, one is necessarily led to conclude that the preceding period lies enveloped not in absolute darkness but in a semi-historical *penumbra*.   Here,
therefore, if anywhere, exact historical criticism, the
laborious separation of primary and secondary sources,
is indispensable.   It is impossible that fable should end
and history begin quite abruptly, and equally impossible
that the transition should take place in a narrative so
visibly composite as that of the Book of Judges, without
history and legend overlapping each other in a way which
can be detected by a careful analysis of the texts   In the
story of Deborah and Barak, where a contemporary
poetical document stands side by side with a later prose
narrative, or in the story of Gideon, where two parallel
records have been carefully distinguished by modern

scholars, it seems inconceivable, on his own premisses, that
M. Renan should be able to dispense himself from the
task of critical analysis   Yet even in these cases we
find nothing but a *réchauffé* of the compound narrative,
affecting a spurious appearance of criticism by the
mechanical rejection of supernatural detail.   Even more
disappointing is the treatment of the episode of Abimelech
—perhaps the most instructive portion of the whole Book
of Judges—where M. Renan misses every point, even the
obvious one that up to this date Shechem was a purely
Canaanite city, and that the short-lived sovereignty of
Abimelech was built not on Hebrew but on Canaanite
support.[1]

The last point in M. Renan's narrative on which some
remark may here be made, is his strong prejudice against
David, in whom he can see nothing more than a clever and
successful bandit   Until recently the true founder of the
Hebrew state has been judged less as a king than as a
Psalmist, and from this point of view it was natural that
two diametrically opposite views should be taken of his
character.   The Church has consecrated him as a saint ·
the deistic reaction, unjustly but from its own standpoint
not at all unnaturally, has stigmatised him as a hypocrite.
M. Renan, who does not believe that David wrote Psalms,
or that in him the king was sunk in the liturgical dilettante
of the Book of Chronicles, ought, one imagines, to have
been able to take an independent view of a character
which, religion apart, is one of the most remarkable in
Semitic history   But his love of startling antithesis
prevails, and he sacrifices all attempt at historic justice
to a brilliant page contrasting " the brigand of Adullam
and Ziklag " with the ideal type of the Messiah, the
imaginary author of " the sentiments full of resignation

---

[1] The evidence for this fundamental point is quite independent of
certain acknowledged difficulties in the text of Judges ix , for which
various solutions have been proposed, and which the present reviewer
has attempted to remove by transposing verses 28, 29, and making them
follow on verse 22   (*Theologisch Tijdschrift*, March 1886.)

and tender melancholy contained in the most beautiful
of liturgical books." This may be literature, but it is not
history. The historian has to judge David as a king, and
to judge him from his whole career. We know that his
reign dwelt in the affectionate memory of Israel long
before the nation had become a Church and before the
renown of the warrior and judge was overshadowed by
the fame of the Psalmist. The nation was grateful for
deliverance from the Philistines, but it also remembered
that David " did justice and judgment to all his people." [1]
These are substantial titles to an honourable place in
history, against which neither the weakness of an old age
exhausted by martial toil nor the ambiguous conduct of
some parts of an adventurous youth can fairly be set.
The inner life of David as a king is revealed to us in a way
unique in ancient history, through a document evidently
dependent on the accounts of a contemporary observer,
one who read faces and noted minute details with a subtlety
which to the western reader recalls the memoirs of Saint-
Simon, but which is not uncommon among the Arabs.
This observer may have had his prejudices, but it is clear
that his passion was the study of men, and that no
prejudice would have induced him to suppress a characteristic trait   He spares none of David's weaknesses, and
yet the king appears not only a far greater man, but a
larger, better, and more generous nature than any of those
about him.   David's faults were those of his age, and the
things in him that most offend us were not those that gave
umbrage to his contemporaries.   Even his great sin in the
matter of Uriah would have been buried in oblivion but
for his repentance   Now oriental sovereignty is not the
thing to make a bad man better ; nay, even in a man
whose general aims are high and beneficent, it is eminently
calculated to produce the frame of mind which Abd-al-
Malik described as wrought in himself—" that he had
come to do good without feeling pleasure, and to do evil

---

[1] 2 Sam. viii. 18.

without feeling pain." It is fair to read David's earlier
life in the light reflected upon it by these considerations.
He passed through conditions of extraordinary difficulty
in which there was often no straight path, and in such
circumstances a certain amount of *ruse* is not only permitted but applauded by Semitic morality But throughout a seemingly tortuous course he never failed to retain
his own self-respect and the passionate devotion of all his
followers, and he emerged from trials in which an ordinary
nature would have made shipwreck to do his country
services of the first order and to take a place in which he
has no rival among Hebrew sovereigns. To condemn
him because he was ambitious would be to condemn every
great man whose career is impelled by an inward consciousness of strength : what we are to consider is that his
ambition was noble and patriotic. That he played the
traitor to Saul and to his country there is not a particle
of evidence ; that he may have hoped to succeed Saul is
possible, but this was not treason in a kingdom where there
were as yet no fixed hereditary rights. The Philistines
he certainly deceived ; but here his conduct, however
contrary to our point of honour, was not such as to trouble
the most sensitive Semitic conscience. That he had any
responsibility for the death of Abner is a pure imagination.
M. Renan wonders that he did not punish Joab, but under
the law of blood-revenge Joab was strictly within his
right. Finally, when M. Renan says that few natures
seem to have been less religious than David's, and charges
him with an absolute lack of the sentiment of justice, he
seems to use a false standard both of religion and of
justice. David's religion was not cosmopolitan ; in his
faith as in all his life he was an Israelite, bound by that
strict national feeling—and even respect for national
prejudice—which was then the basis of the whole code of
right and honour. But it is a great mistake to suppose
that the social virtues are based on cosmopolitanism,
that a religion which does not look beyond the nation

cannot be a true and powerful force in favour of right conduct   If Jahvism had not been in its origin a national religion, it could never have become a practical force ; its ethical influence within the nation was the necessary basis of its ethical influence on mankind.   M Renan seems to think that David's devotion to Jahvé was not true religion because he consulted oracles and because he was sometimes treacherous and cruel to the enemies of his country.   But this only means that a good man would not act now as David did nearly three thousand years ago   The test of individual piety is not whether a man strikes out a new code of morals in advance of his age, but whether in the fear of God he does his duty loyally and trustfully according to the standard of his times, and when he sins returns to God in true and honest repentance.   So much can safely be said of David, and it can also be said of him that in the most critical moments of his life he maintained that calm and resolute submission to the Divine will which makes the strength of a truly religious character and raises the servant of God above the fear of man.

THE END

Printed by R & R Clark, Limited, Edinburgh

[P.T.O.

NOTE

THESE four works, along with a series of important articles in the last ten volumes of the Ninth Edition of the Encyclopædia Britannica, may be said to represent nearly the whole of the literary activity of their gifted Author during the twelve years when his remarkable intellectual powers were at their greatest maturity and his scholarship at its ripest and richest.

No serious student of the religious and ecclesiastical history of English-speaking countries during the last twenty-five years can afford to neglect any one of the four; if not all equally "epoch-making," each of them at least marks a new stage in the discussion of the subject to which it relates. Nor is their interest historical merely; it cannot be said that modern thought has even yet by any means wholly absorbed or assimilated all in them that is original and destined ultimately to become the common property of those who think and know. Nor is the range of this influence still exerted by them wholly confined to English-speaking countries : two of them have been translated into German under the sponsorship of Professors Kautzsch and Rothstein, both scholars expressing themselves as at one in the desire that their educated fellow-countrymen should have easy access to the works of a writer so lucid and so vivid, so keen and candid, and at the same time so sympathetic.

The earliest in the series, **The Old Testament in the Jewish Church,** first published in 1881, had an unusually large circulation, and passed into its second edition, revised and greatly enlarged by the Author, in 1892.

The Prophets of Israel (1882) appeared in a new edition in 1895; this was enriched with an Introduction and Additional Notes by the Author's friend and fellow-worker, Professor Cheyne. Of **The Religion of the Semites,** published in 1884, the second edition, published in 1894, embodies the Author's latest corrections. The second edition of **Kinship** (1903), edited by the competent hands of Mr. Stanley Cook, incorporates notes from the Author's interleaved copy, besides being annotated by Prof. Goldziher. The work first appeared in 1885.

A. & C. BLACK, 4, 5 & 6 SOHO SQUARE, LONDON, W.

CPSIA information can be obtained
at www.ICGtesting.com
Printed in the USA
LVHW082334100622
721005LV00006B/276